Attica Intermediate Classical Greek

Attica
Intermediate Classical Greek

Readings, Review, and Exercises

Cynthia L. Claxton
University of California, Irvine

Yale UNIVERSITY PRESS

New Haven & London

Yale University Press books may be purchased in quantity for educational, business,
or promotional use. For information, please e-mail sales.press@yale.edu (U.S. office) or
sales@yaleup.co.uk (U.K. office).

Editor: Tim Shea
Publishing Assistant: Ashley E. Lago
Manuscript Editor: Susan Laity
Production Controller: Katherine Golden

Designed by James J. Johnson
Set by Tseng Information Systems, Inc.

Printed in the United States of America.

Library of Congress Cataloging-in-Publication Data

Claxton, Cynthia L.
Attica : intermediate classical Greek readings, review, and exercises / Cynthia L. Claxton.
pages. cm.
Includes selections from Xenophon, Antiphon and Euripides.
Includes bibliographical references and index.
ISBN 978-0-300-17876-0 (alk. paper)

1. Greek literature—Readers. 2. Greek language—Grammar. I. Title.
PA260.C58 2014
488.6'421—dc23
2013007841

A catalogue record for this book is available from the British Library.

This paper meets the requirements of ANSI/NISO Z39.48–1992 (Permanence of Paper).
10 9 8 7 6 5 4 3 2 1

To Mark, Rachel, and Josh

Τρέφεται δέ, ὦ Σώκρατες, ψυχὴ τίνι;
Μαθήμασιν δήπου, ἦν δ᾽ ἐγώ.

PLATO, *Protagoras* 313c

Contents

Part Two: Grammar Review   197

Part Three: Exercises   261

Appendices   293

Preface

Attica: Intermediate Classical Greek has been designed to fill a gap in the texts available for students transitioning from first-year Greek to the second year of study. Acquiring the fundamentals of Greek morphology and syntax in a single year is an arduous task for most students, and the second year is often a rocky one as they grapple with primary texts before they have fully mastered the grammar. (The fact that a summer usually intervenes between the first and second year of study exacerbates this problem.) Although this book was created as an introduction to second-year Greek, it may be used with profit any time within the second year of study. Students who are returning to Greek after a break, graduate students in need of a quick refresher, and self-learners will all find it useful.

The book helps students solidify their acquisition of classical Greek by offering guided readings and practice exercises along with a review of the grammar and syntax. Its traditional grammatical approach is based on the belief that students must have a firm mastery of the language in order to be able to read more challenging authors such as Thucydides and Demosthenes, and that reading a Greek text should be a source of pleasure and appreciation of the literary work, whether the author is Homer, Sophocles, or Thucydides.

The textbook is divided into three sections—Readings, Grammar Review, and Exercises—which may be used simultaneously or separately. The thirty-five readings, consisting of selections from Xenophon's *Hellenica,* the entire text of Antiphon's *Against the Stepmother for Poisoning* (Antiphon 1), and a brief selection from Euripides' *Electra,* offer ample material for those on the quarter or semester system. It is recommended that students begin with one of the two prose authors and turn to the Euripides selection after they have had a chance to reimmerse themselves in the process of reading prose.

Xenophon's *Hellenica* covers the period between 411 and 362 B.C.E. and details events in Greece that occurred during the final part of the Peloponnesian War (431–404 B.C.E.) as well as events of the first half of the turbulent fourth century. The selections from the *Hellenica* provide a continuous storyline that begins just after the defeat of the Athenians in the Battle of Aegospotami in 405 and continues through to the rule of the Thirty, the execution

Athens, Acropolis, three column drums in the Propylaea. Photo: Pavlos Rekas/photos.com.

of Theramenes, the battle between the Thirty and the democratic exiles at Phyle, and the reconciliation of the two sides in 403. The speeches of Critias and Theramenes, included in Readings 9 through 16, are more challenging than the narrative passages and may be omitted with little loss in the narrative action. Brief introductions are included where necessary to ease transitions between passages. By the end of these selections, students will have a good understanding of this important moment in Athenian history.

Although there is some debate about whether Antiphon's *Against the Stepmother for Poisoning* was ever delivered in court or was written solely as an academic exercise, the speech nonetheless provides an excellent introduction to the Athenian legal system. The subject matter of the case itself—the alleged poisoning of the plaintiff's father by his step-mother—offers a compelling narrative, and because of its modest length the speech can be read in its entirety during the term.

The short selection from Euripides' *Electra* has been included to give students a brief exposure to the glories of classical Greek poetry. It is a straightforward passage that should offer little difficulty, despite the challenges of reading a text with less predictable word order and more fluidity in its grammar and syntax.

What makes these readings different from those found in other beginning and inter-mediate readers is that each selection is prefaced by a section called *Focus on Reading,* which presents the passage immediately preceding the reading selection and thus helps to provide context. This passage takes the student step by step through the reading process. In the *Focus on Reading,* the complete passage is given first, and then is broken down into its individual sentences, for which vocabulary lists and detailed notes are provided. In the notes, special attention is paid to typical word-order patterns and word groupings as well as to clue words that can help students anticipate particular grammatical constructions. Following the notes, a fairly literal translation is provided. Finally, at the end of the *Focus on Reading* section, a polished translation of the entire passage is offered that will help students see how to create more fluid and idiomatic English translations. The notes to the *Focus on Reading* passages have been designed to enable students to apply the various techniques to the individual reading selections and develop their translation skills in a systematic manner. These notes, as well as those in the reading selections themselves, include references both to the review discussions within this textbook and to relevant sections in Herbert Weir Smyth's *Greek Grammar.* Students should consult these references as needed for review and to reinforce their understanding of particular grammatical concepts.

Part 2 provides a detailed review of the major grammatical constructions in Greek. Ex-planations are full and complete, with many examples for illustration. Most of the examples use simple constructions to help students grasp the essentials of the concept more quickly, though more complex constructions from the readings are also included. All the examples include both the Greek and its English translation. Instructors may choose to assign these review chapters as homework or to let students consult them when necessary. Students who already have a firm mastery of grammatical concepts will be able to go through this material quickly; others will find that the thorough discussions and accompanying examples aid their understanding.

The final section is aimed at furthering mastery of syntax and grammatical forms. It consists of ten exercise units, which may be assigned as homework in conjunction with the readings or before readings are begun, or be done by each student individually as needed. Answers to the exercises are provided on the accompanying Web page (yalebooks.com /attica). Different exercises target specific problems. All have been designed to help develop the skills necessary to read primary Greek texts and are integrated with the readings in the textbook. The vocabulary has been taken from the readings, and the sentences are simplified versions of sentences found in the readings. The first six exercises are based on the selections from Xenophon's *Hellenica*. The remaining exercises are based on Antiphon 1. A Greek to English vocabulary list is included at the end of the textbook that contains all words used in the exercises, as well as those found in the readings. Specific exercises include the following.

Form Identification: Students are drilled on various noun, verb, and adjective forms. Students must identify the case, number, and gender of nouns and adjectives and the person, number, tense, voice, and mood of verbs. Consulting the vocabulary list at the back of the book or a Greek lexicon as needed, students will practice identifying words in isolation, without their accompanying context, and thus can focus on the information contained within the word itself.

Dictionary Drill: This exercise has been designed to help students read texts more easily. Most students, when they first begin reading a text, must look up many of the words in each sentence, and this can be an intimidating and time-consuming task. It can be difficult, for example, to find the dictionary entry of a finite verb form whose stem has undergone several changes, or of a third-declension noun in the dative plural. In this exercise, students look up twenty words, either in the vocabulary list at the back of the text or in a separate lexicon. Students will thus become familiar with the techniques used to look up words, as well as with the various forms they encounter in their reading. Being able to find vocabulary easily will make reading the texts a more enjoyable experience. All the words in these drills appear in the readings.

Accent Drill: Most students have trouble mastering Greek accentuation because few beginning texts provide adequate drill practice in accents. Students need constant practice to master the rules — and their exceptions — of accentuation. The accent drills in this book offer concentrated work on accents alone. Students are asked to place the correct accent on ten words and explain the reason for their choices. The explanation is the most important element of the exercise; students need to determine whether the word is a verb, noun, or adjective and therefore whether it takes a persistent or recessive accent.

Translation Strategy Practice: This exercise has been designed to help students learn how to identify clues that will enable them to anticipate various grammatical constructions. The five sentences in this exercise are simplified versions or variations of sentences found in the readings. Students are generally asked to determine the major construction present in each sentence, identify the clue words that led to this determination, indicate the expected syntactical construction, and, finally, translate the sentence. The concentration on the process of translation forces students to think about each sentence methodically. Intermediate students have a tendency to rush through sentences without thinking about the text, trying to identify the meaning of the words first and then attempting to put those words into some sort of meaningful order, regardless of their grammatical function. When they are forced to slow down, students pay more attention to the various constructions and develop their analytical skills, both of which will facilitate the transition to reading the texts. As experience is gained, these skills will become internalized, and students will use them naturally as they read.

Translation: Students are asked to translate ten sentences that illustrate important grammatical points. Students review these constructions by translating and by parsing indicated words. The sentences are relatively simple versions of sentences found in the readings, and students should be able to work through them quickly. These sentences will help prepare students to address diverse grammatical constructions in the texts. This exercise will also further the acquisition of vocabulary.

Error Analysis: Students are given five Greek sentences with their English translations. Each translation contains at least one error and sometimes more. Students are asked to detect the error or errors, analyze why the translation is incorrect, and then write a corrected translation. The exercise is based on the types of translation errors intermediate students often make (incorrect tenses, confusion of active and passive verb forms, and so on) and will demonstrate that one error often necessitates another error to compensate for the original one. This will help students develop their analytical skills and become more meticulous in their translations.

Included at the back of the book are morphology appendices listing the most common forms of nouns, pronouns, adjectives, and verbs. Dual forms have been omitted because of their rarity, especially in Attic Greek, and because including them in a paradigm visually breaks up the paradigm, thus hindering a quick review of forms. *Attica: Intermediate Classical Greek* is a stand-alone text and should provide everything a student of intermediate Greek needs to transition to reading primary texts successfully.

Acknowledgments

The writing of this book was a long process, and many individuals deserve to be thanked for their help, suggestions, and encouragement. I would like to thank Executive Vice Chancellor Michael R. Gottfredson of the University of California, Irvine, for granting me a special research leave for the winter and spring quarters of 2006, which allowed me to start the project without the constraints that teaching responsibilities would have placed upon me. Maria Pantelia, director of the *Thesaurus Linguae Graecae,* provided much guidance and encouragement from the beginning of the project to its completion, cheerfully answered numerous questions, and helped with last-minute proofreading. Andrew Zissos, chair of the Department of Classics at the University of California, Irvine, was a thoughtful mentor whose sound advice and encouragement were more helpful than he realizes.

Hera Arsen, Susan Lape, and Deb Sandler must be thanked for reading portions of an earlier version of this textbook. I am extremely grateful to Luci Berkowitz and Leslie Collins Edwards, who read critical sections of the manuscript, and to Andromache Karanika, who took time from her already packed schedule to read the entire manuscript. The careful attention to detail of all of these readers saved me from many errors. Whatever errors remain are, of course, my own. I would also like to thank my fellow classicists who reviewed the manuscript for Yale University Press: Lillian Doherty, University of Maryland; Ralph Gallucci, University of California, Santa Barbara; Lorenzo Garcia, Jr., University of New Mexico; Mike Lippman, University of Arizona; Arti Mehta, Howard University; Helen Moritz, University of Santa Clara; and S. Douglas Olson, University of Minnesota. Each reviewer offered thoughtful suggestions that were incorporated into the final version of this text, and the result, I believe, is a clear improvement upon the original.

I extend my sincere gratitude to all the individuals at Yale University Press who contributed to the production of this book. Tim Shea, World Languages editor, skillfully and patiently guided this book to its completion and helped to demystify the whole process. Susan Laity, the manuscript editor, meticulously edited the book and pointed out many inconsistencies, and did so with grace and good humor. Ann-Marie Imbornoni, Ashley Lago,

Katherine Golden, James J. Johnson, and the freelance proofreader Roberta Klarreich also helped in the publication of this book.

This book has been written, of course, with students in mind, and I would like to thank my 2010 and 2012 Greek 100A students, who used a draft of this textbook and provided much encouragement, caught errors, and offered suggestions. Valerie Chang, Diane Cunningham, John De Soto, Jonathan Ginn, Eleni Haloftis, Kenneth Lai, Desiree Landry, Erick Lee, Jessica Leone, Christopher Locke, Alex Lopez, Talar Malakian, Emanuel Movroydis, Robin Murray, Blake Noyes, Danny Poochigian, Julia Puglisi, Matt Reiner, Melissa Sanchez, Kelsey Shaffer-Perkins, Jonathan Shoemaker, Paul Soto, Robert Stroup, and Valree Weythman all contributed to this book. Ashton Sanderson, who used the readings in an independent study, also aided the project by detecting errors and inconsistencies.

No project of this type proceeds without support from family and friends. I am grateful to Carol Carlile, Nancy Claxton, Lisa Cowles, Carol Faulkner, Sherry Miller, Janice Negron, and T. C. Wells for providing the needed pep talks. Special thanks must go to Mary Hart for her knowledgeable advice and to Janet Jaffe, who somehow always knew when to make an encouraging phone call. I am profoundly grateful to my children, Rachel and Josh, who always believed I could do this, and to my husband, Mark Ohman, whose constant encouragement got me to the end.

The texts for the readings were taken from the digital *Thesaurus Linguae Graecae.* The selections from Xenophon's *Hellenica* are from E. C. Marchant, *Xenophontis opera omnia,* vol. 1 (1900; repr. Oxford: Clarendon Press, 1968); Antiphon 1 is from L. Gernet, *Antiphon. Discours* (1923; repr. Paris: Belles Lettres, 1965), 38–46; the thirty-eight lines from Euripides' *Electra* are from J. Diggle, *Euripidis fabulae,* vol. 2 (Oxford: Clarendon, 1981), 59–113. On a few occasions, I have adopted an emendation of a difficult reading; these instances are indicated in the notes.

Abbreviations

acc.	accusative	mid.	middle voice
act.	active voice	n.	neuter
adj.	adjective	nom.	nominative
adv.	adverb	part.	participle
aor.	aorist	perf.	perfect
Att.	Attic	pers. pron.	personal pronoun
conj.	conjunction	pl.	plural
comp.	comparative	pluperf.	pluperfect
comp. adj.	comparative adjective	prep.	preposition
comp. adv.	comparative adverb	pres.	present
contr.	contraction	pron.	pronoun
dat.	dative	R	Review Discussions (of this textbook)
demon.	demonstrative		
f.	feminine	reflex. pron.	reflexive pronoun
fut.	future	rel.	relative
gen.	genitive	rel. pron.	relative pronoun
imperf.	imperfect	repr.	reprint
impers.	impersonal	S	Smyth, *Greek Grammar*
ind.	indicative	sing.	singular
indecl.	indeclinable	subjunc.	subjunctive
indecl. num.	indeclinable numeral	subst.	substantive
indef.	indefinite	sup. adj.	superlative adjective
inf.	infinitive	sup. adv.	superlative adverb
interj.	interjection	trans.	transitive
interrog.	interrogative	voc.	vocative
intrans.	intransitive	vol.	volume
m.	masculine		

PART 1

Readings

Guide to the Readings

In order for students to get the full benefit from the readings in this book, it is important that they go through all the steps laid out to facilitate understanding. Each reading consists of two sections: *Focus on Reading* and the reading selection itself. In the *Focus on Reading*, a passage is divided into its component sentences or clauses, for which vocabulary and detailed grammatical notes are provided. These notes should be read in conjunction with the passage; they highlight grammatical constructions, identify sentence clues, and offer translation strategies. In order to make it easier to find Greek words in the text when they are referenced in the notes, accents on the ultima that are grave by position appear as grave accents in the cue words as well. The notes also include references to the relevant discussion of particular grammatical constructions in the Review (R) section of this textbook as well as to H. W. Smyth's *Greek Grammar* (S). It is critical that students go through the *Focus on Reading* passage first, reading the notes carefully, though they do not need to translate the passage. A literal translation of each sentence appears following the sentence's notes, and a polished translation of the entire passage is offered at the end of the section. The full translation, which is in idiomatic English, shows how the awkwardnesses of more literal translations can be smoothed out and offers a model for the kind of translation students should aim at in their own work.

After students have gone through the entire *Focus on Reading* passage, they are ready to begin translating the reading selection. Vocabulary for these passages can be found in the list at the end of the book. Looking up vocabulary will give students practice in identifying the "dictionary form" of words, a skill that is essential for later lexicon use. Grammatical notes are provided for each reading passage, and questions about grammar and syntax are included to aid students in translating. Students should answer the questions as they translate, for they are designed to reinforce the students' acquisition of Greek grammar. Students who work through both the *Focus on Reading* passage and the reading selection carefully, paying attention to the notes, will see steady improvement in their translation skills.

Note: In the Greek texts, square brackets ([ ]) indicate a word or words that some editors suggest deleting from the text, angle brackets (< >) indicate a word or words that some editors suggest adding to the Greek text, and parentheses are used for editorial annotations. Angle brackets are also used in the notes to indicate words that must be supplied for a complete translation, and parentheses for editorial annotations.

Reading One

Xenophon, *Hellenica* 2.2.1–4

The historian and essayist Xenophon was born in about 430 B.C.E. in the Attic deme of Erchia. He died in Athens or perhaps Corinth sometime after 355. The well-educated son of an affluent family, Xenophon grew up during the Peloponnesian War, the more than twenty-year conflict between Athens and Sparta that lasted from 431 to 404. Xenophon was a prolific writer, and his fourteen books cover a wide range of topics. His most famous work is the *Anabasis,* the account of an expedition of Greek mercenary soldiers under the command of Cyrus the Younger into Persia. Xenophon himself took part in this expedition and writes from an insider's perspective. His *Hellenica,* from which the first twenty-two readings are drawn, details historical events that took place between 411 and 362. It begins at the point at which the great Greek historian Thucydides' account of the Peloponnesian War leaves off (Thucydides died before he could complete his work), and many scholars believe that Xenophon intended to finish Thucydides' masterwork. Xenophon has frequently been characterized by scholars as inferior in intellect and literary talents to Thucydides, but recent work on the *Hellenica* has been more generous in its assessment.

The first two passages in this selection are from the opening paragraphs of book 2, chapter 2. They detail the Spartan general Lysander's deeds after the defeat of the Athenians at Aegospotami in the summer of 405 B.C.E. and describe the reaction of the Athenians to the news of the defeat. Because Aegospotami was located on the Hellespont, this disaster spelled the end for Athens, as it effectively cut off the Athenians' main source of grain, which was imported from the Black Sea area and shipped through the Hellespont to Athens. The Spartans, now supported by Cyrus, the son of the Persian king Darius, were encamped at Lampsacus on the Hellespont, while the Athenians and their fleet were about two miles away, across the Hellespont at Aegospotami. On an August morning when the Athenians had gone ashore for provisions, the Spartans attacked, capturing 171 Athenian ships and overwhelming the camp. Only a few Athenian ships escaped, among them the official state trireme, the *Paralus,* which managed to return to Athens to report the news of the disaster. After a long blockade, the Athenians surrendered to the Spartans the following spring.

Focus on Reading

Read the following passage and pay close attention to word groupings, word order, and clue words.

Ἐπεὶ δὲ τὰ ἐν τῇ Λαμψάκῳ κατεστήσατο, ἔπλει ἐπὶ τὸ Βυζάντιον καὶ Καλχηδόνα.
οἱ δ' αὐτὸν ὑπεδέχοντο, τοὺς τῶν Ἀθηναίων φρουροὺς ὑποσπόνδους ἀφέντες.
οἱ δὲ προδόντες Ἀλκιβιάδῃ τὸ Βυζάντιον τότε μὲν ἔφυγον εἰς τὸν Πόντον,
ὕστερον δ' εἰς Ἀθήνας καὶ ἐγένοντο Ἀθηναῖοι. Λύσανδρος δὲ τούς τε φρουροὺς
τῶν Ἀθηναίων καὶ εἴ τινά που ἄλλον ἴδοι Ἀθηναῖον, ἀπέπεμπεν εἰς τὰς Ἀθήνας,
διδοὺς ἐκεῖσε μόνον πλέουσιν ἀσφάλειαν, ἄλλοθι δ' οὔ, εἰδὼς ὅτι ὅσῳ ἂν πλείους
συλλεγῶσιν εἰς τὸ ἄστυ καὶ τὸν Πειραιᾶ, θᾶττον τῶν ἐπιτηδείων ἔνδειαν ἔσεσθαι.
καταλιπὼν δὲ Βυζαντίου καὶ Καλχηδόνος Σθενέλαον ἁρμοστὴν Λάκωνα, αὐτὸς
ἀποπλεύσας εἰς Λάμψακον τὰς ναῦς ἐπεσκεύαζεν.

Xenophon, *Hellenica* 2.2.1–2

SENTENCE ONE

Ἐπεὶ δὲ τὰ ἐν τῇ Λαμψάκῳ κατεστήσατο, ἔπλει ἐπὶ τὸ Βυζάντιον καὶ Καλχηδόνα.

VOCABULARY

The principal parts of all verbs may be found in the vocabulary list at the back of this textbook.

ἐπεί (conj.) when, after	πλέω sail
Λάμψακος, -ου, ἡ Lampsacus	Βυζάντιον, -ου, τό Byzantium
καθίστημι settle, organize	Καλχηδών, -όνος, ἡ Chalcedon

OBSERVATIONS, STRATEGIES, AND NOTES

1. Note the temporal clause introduced by ἐπεί. Lysander, the Spartan commander, is the subject of both κατεστήσατο and ἔπλει.

2. τὰ ἐν τῇ Λαμψάκῳ: Definite articles never stand alone in Attic prose. Here the definite article τά works with the prepositional phrase ἐν τῇ Λαμψάκῳ to make a noun phrase. The phrase is literally translated as "the things in Lampsacus," but it can be rendered more freely as "the situation in Lampsacus." This use of a definite article with a prepositional phrase is very common in Greek (R2.3; S1153). Try to see these words as a unit.

3. τῇ Λαμψάκῳ: The names of most cities are feminine.

4. κατεστήσατο is the third person singular first aorist middle indicative of καθίστημι. It is common for an aorist to be translated as a pluperfect when it is used in a temporal clause (S1943). Lysander, in settling the situation in Lampsacus, established an oligarchic government there under the control of a Spartan harmost (governor).

5. Both Byzantium and Chalcedon were under Athenian control, but Lysander was able to persuade them to come over to the Spartan side.

TRANSLATION

When he (Lysander) had settled the situation in Lampsacus, he sailed to Byzantium and Chalcedon.

SENTENCE TWO

οἱ δ᾽ αὐτὸν ὑπεδέχοντο, τοὺς τῶν Ἀθηναίων φρουροὺς ὑποσπόνδους ἀφέντες.

VOCABULARY

ὑποδέχομαι   receive   ὑπόσπονδος, -ον   under a truce
φρουρός, -οῦ, ὁ   guard   ἀφίημι   release, let go

OBSERVATIONS, STRATEGIES, AND NOTES

1. This sentence is as straightforward as the first one. Note that the main clause, οἱ δ᾽ αὐτὸν ὑπεδέχοντο, is followed by a participial phrase.
2. οἱ δ᾽ denotes a switch of subject from that of the previous sentence and refers to the people of Byzantium and Chalcedon.
3. ἀφέντες: What form of ἀφίημι is this? Notice that the phi provides an indication that the simple uncompounded verb form begins with a vowel with a rough breathing. The phi has taken on the aspiration; it was originally a pi from ἀπό (the omicron has been elided). Since ἀφέντες is in the nominative case, it is modifying the implied subject of the main verb ὑπεδέχοντο.
4. As is often the case in Greek, the direct object of the participle ἀφέντες precedes it.
5. Note the attributive position of τῶν Ἀθηναίων (R2.1). Be sure to translate it with τοὺς φρουρούς, which it is modifying.

TRANSLATION

And they received him, releasing the Athenian guards under a truce.

SENTENCE THREE

οἱ δὲ προδόντες Ἀλκιβιάδῃ τὸ Βυζάντιον τότε μὲν ἔφυγον εἰς τὸν Πόντον,
ὕστερον δ᾽ εἰς Ἀθήνας καὶ ἐγένοντο Ἀθηναῖοι.

VOCABULARY

προδίδωμι betray

τότε (adv.)   at that time

φεύγω flee

Πόντος, -ου, ὁ   the Black Sea

ὕστερον (adv.)   later

εἰς (prep. + acc.)   into, to

γίγνομαι become

OBSERVATIONS, STRATEGIES, AND NOTES

1. The particle δέ marks a transition from the content of the previous sentence to the next stage of the event. This is a very common use of the particle in which δέ connects sentences and clauses that add a new detail or moment in the event without opposing what has preceded (S2836).

2. What form is προδόντες? The definite article οἱ is used with the participle προδόντες to make a substantive (R2.3); οἱ δὲ προδόντες refers to the five Byzantines who had betrayed their city to Alcibiades and the Athenians in 408 B.C.E., when the city was being besieged by the Athenians (*Hellenica* 1.3.14–21).

3. τὸ Βυζάντιον: This neuter proper noun may be either nominative or accusative (it could also be vocative). Given that οἱ προδόντες must be nominative and hence the subject, τὸ Βυζάντιον should be accusative. It is the direct object of προδόντες. What function, then, is Ἀλκιβιάδη performing?

4. τότε μὲν . . . ὕστερον δ': Note the contrast in time, which helps you to see that the sentence falls neatly into two parts.

5. εἰς Ἀθήνας: This implies a verb of motion toward. You may supply "they went" or "they arrived."

6. Ἀθηναῖοι: The Athenians awarded citizenship in return for service to Athens. Because of the strategic location of Byzantium in respect to the grain-trade routes from the Black Sea, the Byzantines' act of betrayal was highly beneficial for the Athenians.

TRANSLATION

And those who had betrayed Byzantium to Alcibiades fled at that time to the Black Sea, but later they went to Athens and became Athenians.

SENTENCE FOUR

Λύσανδρος δὲ τούς τε φρουροὺς τῶν Ἀθηναίων καὶ εἴ τινά που ἄλλον ἴδοι Ἀθηναῖον, ἀπέπεμπεν εἰς τὰς Ἀθήνας, διδοὺς ἐκεῖσε μόνον πλέουσιν ἀσφάλειαν, ἄλλοθι δ' οὔ, εἰδὼς ὅτι ὅσῳ ἂν πλείους συλλεγῶσιν εἰς τὸ ἄστυ καὶ τὸν Πειραιᾶ, θᾶττον τῶν ἐπιτηδείων ἔνδειαν ἔσεσθαι.

VOCABULARY

φρουρός, -οῦ, ὁ guard	ἄλλοθι (adv.) elsewhere, to another place
πού (adv.) anywhere, somewhere	οἶδα know
ὁράω see	ὅτι (conj.) that
ἀποπέμπω send back	ὅσῳ by how much
εἰς (prep. + acc.) into, to	πλείων, -ον (comp. adj.) more
δίδωμι give	συλλέγω assemble (meaning in passive)
ἐκεῖσε (adv.) to that place	ἄστυ, -εως, τό city
μόνον (adv.) only	θᾶττον (comp. adv.) more quickly
πλέω sail	ἐπιτήδεια, -ων, τά provisions
ἀσφάλεια, -ας, ἡ safety, safe passage	ἔνδεια, -ας, ἡ need, lack

OBSERVATIONS, STRATEGIES, AND NOTES

1. This sentence is quite complex because several different constructions are involved. Try to detect the natural breaks, using the editor's punctuation and sentence clues as aids. The first section to consider is Λύσανδρος δὲ τούς τε φρουροὺς ... εἰς τὰς Ἀθήνας.

2. Λύσανδρος and ἀπέπεμπεν are the subject and main verb of the sentence.

3. Paying attention to the τε ... καί construction is important for the correct understanding of the sentence. τε ... καί usually connects words that are being used in the same way grammatically. Remember that τε is postpositive and its sense belongs before the word it follows. Thus we see that τούς ... φρουροὺς τῶν Ἀθηναίων and εἴ τινά που ἄλλον ἴδοι Ἀθηναῖον are being connected by τε ... καί and should be performing the same grammatical function. It is easy to see that τούς ... φρουροὺς with its descriptive genitive τῶν Ἀθηναίων is a direct object of ἀπέπεμπεν; τε ... καὶ indicates that εἴ τινά που ἄλλον ἴδοι Ἀθηναῖον is also acting as a direct object.

4. εἴ τινά που ἄλλον ἴδοι Ἀθηναῖον: This is the protasis of a past general condition (R10.3; S2340) that is being used as a noun clause to stand in for a direct object. If the idea had been expressed in the form of a condition without the other details, it would have taken this form: εἰ Λύσανδρος τινά που ἄλλον ἴδοι Ἀθηναῖον, ἀπέπεμπεν εἰς τὰς Ἀθήνας. The literal translation of the protasis is "if he saw some other Athenian somewhere," but it can be translated "any other Athenian he saw elsewhere," which will make the function of the clause as a direct object clearer.

5. The next part of the sentence is διδοὺς ἐκεῖσε μόνον πλέουσιν ἀσφάλειαν, ἄλλοθι δ' οὔ. διδούς is the present active participle of δίδωμι in the nominative singular masculine, modifying the subject Λύσανδρος. Since δίδωμι is a transitive verb, ἀσφάλειαν is its direct object while πλέουσιν is the indirect object. It should be clear that πλέουσιν is the present active participial form in the dative plural rather than a third person present active indicative form (which would also be πλέουσιν) because Λύσανδρος, the subject of the sentence, is singular. Remember that contract verbs in -έω that have two syllables (like πλέω) do not contract with endings beginning in ο, ω, ου, or οι, such as -ομεν and -ουσι (S397).

6. Notice the two adverbs ἐκεῖσε and ἄλλοθι and the implied contrast between μόνον and δ'. This will help you see that these two parts go together. In Greek, words that

are used in two parts of a single sentence, clause, or phrase are rarely repeated. To do so would be considered inelegant. This part of the sentence may be translated as "giving safe passage only to those sailing there but not <to those sailing> elsewhere."

7. The last part of this sentence is εἰδὼς ὅτι ὅσῳ ἂν πλείους . . . ἔνδειαν ἔσεσθαι. εἰδὼς is the perfect participle of οἶδα, and it is important to note that any form of οἶδα may introduce an indirect statement construction. The participle εἰδώς, which is in the nominative singular masculine, is modifying the subject Λύσανδρος just as διδούς did. There is, however, an unexpected issue here. οἶδα may take the ὅτι/ὡς construction of indirect statement. This construction is usually followed by a finite verb in the indirect statement clause (R7.3), not by an infinitive, as we have here with ἔσεσθαι. This is an example of *anacoluthon,* an instance in which an author begins with one grammatical construction but ends with another, or the author blends two grammatical constructions (S3004). Xenophon began this indirect statement with a ὅτι clause, which requires a finite form for its main verb, but perhaps because of the insertion of the subordinate clause ὅσῳ . . . καὶ τὸν Πειραιᾶ, he used ἔσεσθαι instead of the expected ἔσται.

8. ὅσῳ ἂν πλείους . . . τὸν Πειραιᾶ: This subordinate clause is part of the indirect statement and has retained the original mood of its verb συλλεγῶσιν rather than switching to the corresponding tense of the optative after a secondary main verb (ἀπέπεμπεν) (R7.5). This is a comparative clause introduced by the relative adjective ὅσῳ. The comparative adverb θᾶττον completes the comparison. These clauses take the same form as conditional clauses or other conditional relative clauses (S2468, 2474, 2476). If this were expressed as a straightforward condition not in indirect statement, it would read, ἐὰν πλείους συλλεγῶσιν εἰς τὸ ἄστυ καὶ τὸν Πειραιᾶ, θᾶττον τῶν ἐπιτηδείων ἔνδεια ἔσται. Remember that πλείους is an alternate form of πλείονες and thus it is the subject of the aorist passive subjunctive συλλεγῶσιν. Note that the accent on συλλεγῶσιν distinguishes it from the present active subjunctive συλλέγωσιν. A literal translation of this part of the sentence is "knowing that by how much (ὅσῳ) more people were gathered in the city and in Piraeus, there would be a lack of supplies more quickly." This is, however, quite awkward in English, and we can translate ὅσῳ as "as." Why do you think ὅσῳ is in the dative case?

9. What type of genitive is ἐπιτηδείων?

TRANSLATION

And Lysander sent the Athenian guards and any other Athenian he saw elsewhere back to Athens, granting safe passage only to those sailing there, but not elsewhere, since he knew that as more people were gathered in the city and Piraeus there would be a need for supplies more quickly.

SENTENCE FIVE

καταλιπὼν δὲ Βυζαντίου καὶ Καλχηδόνος Σθενέλαον ἁρμοστὴν Λάκωνα, αὐτὸς ἀποπλεύσας εἰς Λάμψακον τὰς ναῦς ἐπεσκεύαζεν.

VOCABULARY

καταλείπω   leave behind
Σθενέλαος, -ου, ὁ   Sthenelaus
ἁρμοστής, -οῦ, ὁ   harmost, governor
Λάκων, -ον (gen. -ονος)   Spartan,
  Lacedaemonian

ἀποπλέω   sail away
ναῦς, νεώς, ἡ   ship
ἐπισκευάζω   repair

OBSERVATIONS, STRATEGIES, AND NOTES

1. Notice the accent on the participle καταλιπών. What tense of the participle is this?
2. The word order of Βυζαντίου καὶ Καλχηδόνος Σθενέλαον ἁρμοστὴν Λάκωνα is perhaps a bit odd. Let logic be your guide!
3. A common strategy to employ with an aorist participle plus an aorist finite verb is to translate both as finite forms and add "and." This strategy will work well with ἀποπλεύσας and ἐπεσκεύαζεν.

TRANSLATION

After he left Sthenelaus, a Spartan, as governor of Byzantium and Chalcedon, he himself sailed away to Lampsacus and repaired his ships.

POLISHED TRANSLATION

When Lysander had settled the situation in Lampsacus, he sailed to Byzantium and Chalcedon. The people there received him, releasing the Athenian guards under a truce. Those who had betrayed Byzantium to Alcibiades fled at that time to the Black Sea, but later they went to Athens and became Athenians. Lysander sent the Athenian guards and any other Athenians he saw elsewhere back to Athens, granting safe passage only to those sailing there, but not elsewhere, because he knew that, as more people were gathered in the city and Piraeus, there would be a need for supplies more quickly. After he left Sthenelaus, a Spartan, as governor of Byzantium and Chalcedon, he himself sailed away to Lampsacus and repaired his ships.

Reading Selection

The *Paralus* arrives in Athens and the defeat at Aegospotami is reported.

Ἐν δὲ ταῖς Ἀθήναις τῆς Παράλου ἀφικομένης νυκτὸς ἐλέγετο ἡ συμφορά, καὶ
οἰμωγὴ ἐκ τοῦ Πειραιῶς διὰ τῶν μακρῶν τειχῶν εἰς ἄστυ διῆκεν, ὁ ἕτερος
τῷ ἑτέρῳ παραγγέλλων· ὥστ᾿ ἐκείνης τῆς νυκτὸς οὐδεὶς ἐκοιμήθη, οὐ μόνον
τοὺς ἀπολωλότας πενθοῦντες, ἀλλὰ πολὺ μᾶλλον ἔτι αὐτοὶ ἑαυτούς, πείσεσθαι
νομίζοντες οἷα ἐποίησαν Μηλίους τε Λακεδαιμονίων ἀποίκους ὄντας,
κρατήσαντες πολιορκίᾳ, καὶ Ἱστιαιέας καὶ Σκιωναίους καὶ Τορωναίους καὶ

5

Αἰγινήτας καὶ ἄλλους πολλοὺς τῶν Ἑλλήνων. τῇ δ' ὑστεραίᾳ ἐκκλησίαν ἐποίησαν,
ἐν ᾗ ἔδοξε τούς τε λιμένας ἀποχῶσαι πλὴν ἑνὸς καὶ τὰ τείχη εὐτρεπίζειν καὶ
φυλακὰς ἐφιστάναι καὶ τἆλλα πάντα ὡς εἰς πολιορκίαν παρασκευάζειν τὴν πόλιν.
καὶ οὗτοι μὲν περὶ ταῦτα ἦσαν.   10

Xenophon, Hellenica 2.2.3–4

NOTES

1. [Lines 1–7] The first sentence is fairly straightforward despite its length. As always, read through the sentence first, before you begin to translate, and look for sentence clues that will guide your reading and comprehension.

2. [Line 1] What construction is τῆς Παράλου ἀφικομένης? Note that Πάραλος, the name of the state trireme, is feminine.

3. [Line 1] Note the time construction indicated by νυκτός. The Greeks were precise about time, which is why a genitive of time within which is used here rather than a dative of time when. The dative indicates a precise moment, whereas the genitive indicates the entire span of time within which an activity or event takes place (R3.2.4, 3.3.4). The precise moment of the arrival of the *Paralus* is not critical here, so an indication of the range of time suffices.

4. [Line 2] ἐκ τοῦ Πειραιῶς διὰ τῶν μακρῶν τειχῶν εἰς ἄστυ: Note how the wording of this information reflects the route the news of the defeat at Aegospotami would have taken as it was reported by one person to another.

5. [Lines 2–3] ὁ ἕτερος τῷ ἑτέρῳ παραγγέλλων: This is another example of an anacoluthon (S3004). Xenophon has switched subjects here. He began this part of the sentence with the subject οἰμωγὴ and its verb διῆκεν, but then moved to the nominative ὁ ἕτερος and its accompanying participle παραγγέλλων. This construction is more conversational and relaxed in tone and structure. Translate it as "one man announcing the news to another."

6. [Line 3] ὥστ' ἐκείνης τῆς νυκτὸς οὐδεὶς ἐκοιμήθη: What type of subordinate clause is this? Look at the introductory word.

7. [Line 3] ἐκείνης τῆς νυκτός: See note 3, above.

8. [Line 4] τοὺς ἀπολωλότας: The article has made this perfect participle from ἀπόλλυμι into a noun (R2.3). Why is this participle in the perfect tense? What is its grammatical function?

9. [Line 4] πενθοῦντες: Notice that Xenophon has switched from the singular οὐδείς to the plural πενθοῦντες. This is not uncommon. The agreement is with the real number or gender, and here it is obvious that more than one person is meant (S926a).

10. [Line 4] ἀλλὰ πολὺ μᾶλλον ἔτι αὐτοὶ ἑαυτούς: Supply πενθοῦντες.

11. [Lines 4–5] πείσεσθαι νομίζοντες οἷα . . . : νομίζω takes an accusative/infinitive construction in indirect statement (R7.1; S2016–22). When, however, the subject of the infinitive is the same as the subject of the main verb, it is not usually expressed or it is in the nominative case. What tense is πείσεσθαι? What verb is it from?

12. [Line 5] οἷα: This relative pronoun in the accusative plural neuter is introducing

a relative clause that is acting as the direct object of πείσεσθαι. It is also the direct object of ἐποίησαν. Its antecedent has been omitted because it would have been a demonstrative pronoun (S2509). The full expression of the idea would have been πείσεσθαι νομίζοντες <ἐκεῖνα> οἷα ἐποίησαν Μηλίους τε Λακεδαιμονίων ἀποίκους ὄντας.

13. [Line 5] τε: Pay attention to the postpositive position of τε. It belongs by sense in front of Μηλίους and is part of an extended τε . . . καί construction (τε . . . καὶ . . . καὶ . . . καὶ . . . καὶ . . . καὶ . . .), indicating that all the accusatives are being used with ἐποίησαν in the same way.

14. [Line 5] ὄντας: This is a circumstantial participle (R6.2) modifying Μηλίους. What is the function of ἀποίκους?

15. [Line 6] κρατήσαντες πολιορκίᾳ: What type of dative is this?

16. [Line 7] τῇ δ᾽ ὑστεραίᾳ: Supply ἡμέρᾳ. What type of time construction is this?

17. [Line 8] ἐν ᾗ: What is the antecedent of ᾗ?

18. [Line 8] ἔδοξε: Impersonal usage of δοκέω. When used in the third person singular, and often in the context of a meeting of the Assembly or Council, this verb literally means "seems best," but it is often translated "is decided," "is resolved," or "is decreed." The verb will take a complementary infinitive to complete its meaning. Here four infinitives—ἀποχῶσαι, εὐτρεπίζειν, ἐφιστάναι, and παρασκευάζειν—go with ἔδοξε. Notice that the direct objects of all the infinitives except παρασκευάζειν immediately precede the infinitive. The different order in the case of παρασκευάζειν is probably due to the inclusion of τἆλλα πάντα ὡς εἰς πολιορκίαν. It also provides stylistic variation and gives extra stress to τὴν πόλιν because it is placed last in the sentence, a position of emphasis.

19. [Line 9] τἆλλα πάντα: Adverbial usage. Translate it as "in all other respects." τἆλλα has undergone crasis (S62) and is the equivalent of τὰ ἄλλα.

20. [Line 9] ὡς εἰς πολιορκίαν: ὡς often indicates the thought or assertion of the subject of the sentence and expresses the subject's intention or plea. It is frequently coupled with participles or the prepositions εἰς, ἐπί, and πρός when used in this manner (S2996). Translate as "for a siege."

21. [Line 10] περὶ ταῦτα ἦσαν: Translate this idiomatic expression as "they were occupied with these matters" or something similar.

Reading Two

Xenophon, *Hellenica* 2.2.10–13

Following the passages in Reading 1, Xenophon details the activities of Lysander as he arranged affairs in the cities of Lesbos and elsewhere. After returning several cities to their original inhabitants and laying waste to the island of Salamis, Lysander anchored 150 ships outside Piraeus, the port of Athens, and blockaded it. In Reading 2, the apprehensive Athenians ponder how best to proceed during the siege.

Focus on Reading

As you read the passage, try to note words that clearly go together and break the sentence into smaller units. This strategy will help you recognize the way the words of the sentence were put together, rather than approach it as a word-by-word progression. Note that you can often keep the original word order in a good English translation.

> Οἱ δ᾽ Ἀθηναῖοι πολιορκούμενοι κατὰ γῆν καὶ κατὰ θάλατταν ἠπόρουν τί
> χρὴ ποιεῖν, οὔτε νεῶν οὔτε συμμάχων αὐτοῖς ὄντων οὔτε σίτου· ἐνόμιζον δὲ
> οὐδεμίαν εἶναι σωτηρίαν εἰ μὴ παθεῖν ἃ οὐ τιμωρούμενοι ἐποίησαν, ἀλλὰ διὰ τὴν
> ὕβριν ἠδίκουν ἀνθρώπους μικροπολίτας οὐδ᾽ ἐπὶ μιᾷ αἰτίᾳ ἑτέρᾳ ἢ ὅτι ἐκείνοις
> συνεμάχουν.
>
> Xenophon, *Hellenica* 2.2.10

PART ONE

Οἱ δ᾽ Ἀθηναῖοι πολιορκούμενοι κατὰ γῆν καὶ κατὰ θάλατταν ἠπόρουν τί χρὴ
ποιεῖν, οὔτε νεῶν οὔτε συμμάχων αὐτοῖς ὄντων οὔτε σίτου·

VOCABULARY

πολιορκέω   blockade, besiege

γῆ, γῆς, ἡ   land

θάλαττα, -ης, ἡ   sea

ἀπορέω   be at a loss about, be in doubt about

τίς, τί (interrog. pron.)   who, what

χρή   it is necessary

ποιέω   do

ναῦς, νεώς, ἡ   ship

σύμμαχος, -ου, ὁ   ally

σῖτος, -ου, ὁ   food

OBSERVATIONS, STRATEGIES, AND NOTES

1. Divide this section of the sentence into its units of meaning: [Οἱ δ᾽ Ἀθηναῖοι πολιορκούμενοι] [κατὰ γῆν καὶ κατὰ θάλατταν] [ἠπόρουν τί χρὴ ποιεῖν,] [οὔτε νεῶν οὔτε συμμάχων αὐτοῖς ὄντων οὔτε σίτου·]

2. Note that Οἱ δ᾽ Ἀθηναῖοι, a nominative plural masculine, begins the sentence. It is being modified by the circumstantial participle πολιορκούμενοι. Determine why this participle is circumstantial rather than attributive (R.6.1, 6.2).

3. The particle δ᾽ may be translated as "and." It is being used to connect successive clauses that add supplementary information that is not in contrast to what precedes it (S2836).

4. The next unit consists of the preposition κατά, which is repeated, and its two objects, γῆν and θάλατταν. This is an idiomatic expression common in military contexts meaning "by land and by sea."

5. ἠπόρουν is the main verb. It introduces the indirect question τί χρὴ ποιεῖν, which may be translated literally as "what it was necessary to do," but is better translated more idiomatically as "what they should do" or "what to do" in a polished translation. What form is ἠπόρουν?

6. Notice that the rest of this sentence contains several genitives. There are three genitive nouns, νεῶν, συμμάχων, and σίτου, each preceded by οὔτε. This repetition is an indication that the three genitive nouns are being used in the same manner. It is also important to note ὄντων, the present participle of εἰμί, which is also in the genitive case. What construction has a noun or nouns in the genitive case accompanied by a participle that is also in the genitive case (R6.5)?

7. αὐτοῖς is a dative of possession, a construction that is frequently used with forms of εἰμί (R3.3.5). This entire construction is literally translated as "neither ships nor allies nor food being to/for them," but it may be rendered more idiomatically as "since they had neither ships nor allies nor food."

TRANSLATION

And the Athenians, being besieged by land and by sea, were at a loss about what it was necessary to do, since there were neither ships nor allies nor food for them;

PART TWO

ἐνόμιζον δὲ οὐδεμίαν εἶναι σωτηρίαν εἰ μὴ παθεῖν ἃ οὐ τιμωρούμενοι ἐποίησαν,

VOCABULARY

νομίζω   think

οὐδείς, οὐδεμία, οὐδέν   not any

σωτηρία, -ας, ἡ   deliverance, salvation

εἰ μή   except

πάσχω   experience, suffer

τιμωρέω (mid.)   seek vengeance

OBSERVATIONS, STRATEGIES, AND NOTES

1. The word ἀλλά, which follows ἐποίησαν, is a strong adversative conjunction that has separated this sentence into two parts. It is reasonable to assume that each part of the sentence is likely to be grammatically complete and thus may be treated separately.

2. This sentence is a bit more complex, but it, too, may be grouped into units of meaning. Because there are subordinate constructions here, it may help to think of each unit of the first part of the sentence as leading directly to the next unit: [ἐνόμιζον δὲ οὐδεμίαν εἶναι σωτηρίαν] [εἰ μὴ παθεῖν] [ἃ οὐ τιμωρούμενοι ἐποίησαν].

3. ἐνόμιζον usually introduces an accusative/infinitive construction of indirect statement (R7.1). The accusative σωτηρίαν is the subject of the infinitive εἶναι.

4. The separation of the adjective οὐδεμίαν from σωτηρίαν, the noun it is modifying, gives the adjective extra emphasis. This is called *hyperbaton* ("transposition"), which means the separation of words that belong together (S3028). Often a verb form will be inserted in between the words to create this effect.

5. εἰ μὴ παθεῖν: Translate this as "except to experience."

6. παθεῖν: When there is a transitive verb in either a finite or an infinitive form, it is always a good idea to consider whether a direct object has been included in the sentence. Here we might ask, "Experience what?"

7. Notice that there are no nouns in the accusative case in this part of the sentence that can logically be the direct object of παθεῖν. But παθεῖν is directly followed by ἅ, a relative pronoun that is either accusative plural neuter or nominative plural neuter. In order to determine the case of the pronoun, read the rest of the relative clause to see whether there are any words that will clear up this ambiguity. Since τιμωρούμενοι can only be nominative (the vocative is not logical here), ἅ must be in the accusative case and should, as a consequence, be the direct object of ἐποίησαν, since the case of a relative pronoun is determined by its grammatical function within the relative clause (R11.1). You might wonder whether it could be the direct object of παθεῖν as well. It is very common for the antecedent of a relative pronoun to be omitted if the antecedent is a demonstrative pronoun. This is what has happened here: ἐκεῖνα or another demonstrative pronoun in the accusative neuter plural has dropped out (S2509), but it may be supplied in your translation.

8. What form is παθεῖν? Why is it in this tense?

9. οὐ τιμωρούμενοι is a nominative plural present middle participle modifying the subject of ἐποίησαν and is most logically taken concessively. Translate it as "although they were not seeking vengeance."

10. ἐποίησαν: Translate this as a pluperfect in order to put the tense of the subordinate clause into the proper time relationship with the main verb. This is permissible with aorist indicatives in relative clauses (S1943). In addition, and perhaps most important, logic also tells us that ἐποίησαν must be translated as a pluperfect for the sentence to make sense.

TRANSLATION

and they thought that there was not any deliverance except to experience <those things> that they had done although they were not seeking vengeance,

PART THREE

ἀλλὰ διὰ τὴν ὕβριν ἠδίκουν ἀνθρώπους μικροπολίτας οὐδ' ἐπὶ μιᾷ αἰτίᾳ ἑτέρᾳ ἢ ὅτι ἐκείνοις συνεμάχουν.

VOCABULARY

ὕβρις, -εως, ἡ   arrogance
ἀδικέω   injure
μικροπολίτης, -ου, ὁ   a citizen of a small town
ἐπί (prep. + dat.)   for

αἰτία, -ας, ἡ   reason, cause
ἕτερος, -α, -ον   other
ὅτι (conj.)   because
συμμαχέω   be allied with (+ dat.)

OBSERVATIONS, STRATEGIES, AND NOTES

1. This part of the sentence falls easily into logical units that are relatively straightforward to analyze: [ἀλλὰ] [διὰ τὴν ὕβριν] [ἠδίκουν ἀνθρώπους μικροπολίτας] [οὐδ' ἐπὶ μιᾷ αἰτίᾳ ἑτέρᾳ] [ἢ ὅτι ἐκείνοις συνεμάχουν].

2. διὰ τὴν ὕβριν: Always try to see prepositional phrases as units.

3. ἠδίκουν is a transitive verb and is followed by its direct object, ἀνθρώπους, which is in turn modified by the appositive μικροπολίτας. An appositive is a noun that is used to describe another noun (S916).

4. The fourth unit is introduced by a negative that is followed by the preposition ἐπί and its object, αἰτίᾳ. What words are modifying αἰτίᾳ?

5. The final unit is a causal clause introduced by ὅτι, meaning "because" (rather than its more common meaning, "that"). Like all subordinate clauses, it has its own verb, συνεμάχουν, which is accompanied by a dative.

TRANSLATION

but on account of arrogance they used to injure men of small towns not for a single other reason than because they were allied with those men (the Spartans).

POLISHED TRANSLATION

The Athenians, besieged by land and by sea, did not know what to do, since they had neither ships nor allies nor food. And they kept thinking that there was no deliverance for them except to experience what they had done when, not out of vengeance but because of their arrogance, they used to injure men of small towns for no other reason than because they were allied with the Spartans.

Reading Selection

This selection follows immediately after the passage discussed above. οἱ Ἀθηναῖοι is the subject of ἐκαρτέρουν.

δια ταῦτα τοὺς ἀτίμους ἐπιτίμους ποιήσαντες ἐκαρτέρουν, καὶ ἀποθνησκόντων
ἐν τῇ πόλει λιμῷ πολλῶν οὐ διελέγοντο περὶ διαλλαγῆς. ἐπεὶ δὲ παντελῶς ἤδη
ὁ σῖτος ἐπελελοίπει, ἔπεμψαν πρέσβεις παρ' Ἄγιν, βουλόμενοι σύμμαχοι εἶναι
Λακεδαιμονίοις ἔχοντες τὰ τείχη καὶ τὸν Πειραιᾶ, καὶ ἐπὶ τούτοις συνθήκας
ποιεῖσθαι. ὁ δὲ αὐτοὺς εἰς Λακεδαίμονα ἐκέλευεν ἰέναι· οὐ γὰρ εἶναι κύριος   5
αὐτός. ἐπεὶ δ' ἀπήγγειλαν οἱ πρέσβεις ταῦτα τοῖς Ἀθηναίοις, ἔπεμψαν αὐτοὺς
εἰς Λακεδαίμονα. οἱ δ' ἐπεὶ ἦσαν ἐν Σελλασίᾳ [πλησίον τῆς Λακωνικῆς] καὶ
ἐπύθοντο οἱ ἔφοροι αὐτῶν ἃ ἔλεγον, ὄντα οἷάπερ καὶ πρὸς Ἄγιν, αὐτόθεν αὐτοὺς
ἐκέλευον ἀπιέναι.

Xenophon, Hellenica 2.2.11–13

NOTES

1. [Line 1] δια ταῦτα τοὺς ἀτίμους ἐπιτίμους ποιήσαντες ἐκαρτέρουν: Pay attention to the word order here. Notice that the participle ποιήσαντες is preceded by its direct object, τοὺς ἀτίμους. This adjective is being used as a noun, as indicated by the definite article (R2.3).

2. [Line 1] ἐπιτίμους is a predicate accusative modifying the substantive τοὺς ἀτίμους (R3.4.4). Observe that it immediately follows τοὺς ἀτίμους and precedes ποιήσαντες. This efficient word order has a simple elegance.

3. [Lines 1–2] ἀποθνησκόντων ἐν τῇ πόλει λιμῷ πολλῶν: There are two genitives here, πολλῶν and ἀποθνησκόντων. Note that they frame the prepositional phrase ἐν τῇ πόλει and the dative λιμῷ. This means that all these words go together.

4. [Lines 1–2] What part of speech is ἀποθνησκόντων? πολλῶν is probably a substantive and should go with ἀποθνησκόντων. What construction is this?

5. [Line 2] What type of dative is λιμῷ?

6. [Line 2] ἐπεὶ δὲ: This introduces a temporal clause. What tense is ἐπελελοίπει? What does this verb form imply in respect to aspect?

7. [Lines 3–5] βουλόμενοι is a circumstantial participle (R6.2) that has two complementary infinitives (R5.3): εἶναι and ποιεῖσθαι.

8. [Line 4] ἔχοντες: Translate this as "provided they could keep" or "while still keeping."

9. [Line 4] ἐπὶ τούτοις: Translate this as "on these conditions."

10. [Line 5] ὁ δὲ: This indicates a switch of subject and refers to Agis, one of the two Spartan kings.

11. [Lines 5–6] οὐ γὰρ εἶναι κύριος αὐτός: Notice that there is no finite verb form here. There is, rather, the infinitive εἶναι and a nominative, αὐτός. This is an implied indirect statement set up by ἐκέλευεν. When you translate, you may supply "saying that" or "he said that."

12. [Line 7] οἱ δ': This indicates a switch of subject from οἱ πρέσβεις to the Athenians, implied by both τοῖς Ἀθηναίοις and αὐτούς.

13. [Line 7] [πλησίον τῆς Λακωνικῆς] is bracketed by some editors because Sellasia was actually within the borders of Laconia. It is probably an erroneous interpolation.

14. [Line 8] αὐτῶν: This goes with ἐπύθοντο, which, like ἀκούω, takes a genitive to indicate the person from whom something is heard (S1361).

15. [Line 8] ἃ ἔλεγον: The antecedent of ἅ, which would have been a demonstrative pronoun, has been omitted, as is often the case (S2509).

16. [Line 8] ὄντα οἷάπερ καὶ πρὸς Ἆγιν: The enclitic particle περ strengthens the relative pronoun οἷα. The verb of this relative clause, a verb of speaking, has been omitted because it can be supplied from context. Translate as "being the very things that they had also said to Agis."

17. [Line 9] ἐκέλευον: Remember that a verb of ordering may take an accusative/infinitive construction (R5.1).

Reading Three

Xenophon, *Hellenica* 2.2.14–18

Focus on Reading

This passage follows the selection in Reading 2 and continues the description of the situation in Athens and the Athenians' reaction to their predicament.

οἱ δὲ πρέσβεις ἐπεὶ ἧκον οἴκαδε καὶ ἀπήγγειλαν ταῦτα εἰς τὴν πόλιν, ἀθυμία
ἐνέπεσε πᾶσιν· ᾤοντο γὰρ ἀνδραποδισθήσεσθαι, καὶ ἕως ἂν πέμπωσιν ἑτέρους
πρέσβεις, πολλοὺς τῷ λιμῷ ἀπολεῖσθαι. περὶ δὲ τῶν τειχῶν τῆς καθαιρέσεως
οὐδεὶς ἐβούλετο συμβουλεύειν· Ἀρχέστρατος γὰρ εἰπὼν ἐν τῇ βουλῇ
Λακεδαιμονίοις κράτιστον εἶναι ἐφ᾽ οἷς προυκαλοῦντο εἰρήνην ποιεῖσθαι, ἐδέθη·
προυκαλοῦντο δὲ τῶν μακρῶν τειχῶν ἐπὶ δέκα σταδίους καθελεῖν ἑκατέρου·
ἐγένετο δὲ ψήφισμα μὴ ἐξεῖναι περὶ τούτων συμβουλεύειν.

Xenophon, Hellenica 2.2.14–15

SENTENCE ONE

οἱ δὲ πρέσβεις ἐπεὶ ἧκον οἴκαδε καὶ ἀπήγγειλαν ταῦτα εἰς τὴν πόλιν, ἀθυμία
ἐνέπεσε πᾶσιν· ᾤοντο γὰρ ἀνδραποδισθήσεσθαι, καὶ ἕως ἂν πέμπωσιν ἑτέρους
πρέσβεις, πολλοὺς τῷ λιμῷ ἀπολεῖσθαι.

VOCABULARY

πρέσβυς, -εως, ὁ ambassador
ἥκω return, arrive
οἴκαδε (adv.) home
ἀπαγγέλλω report back
ἀθυμία, -ας, ἡ despondency
ἐμπίπτω fall upon

οἴομαι think, suppose
ἀνδραποδίζω reduce to slavery
ἕως ἄν while
λιμός, -οῦ, ὁ famine, hunger
ἀπόλλυμι (mid.) perish utterly, die

20

OBSERVATIONS, STRATEGIES, AND NOTES

1. This sentence falls into two major parts, as is denoted by the semicolon after πᾶσιν.

2. Notice that ἐπεὶ has been placed after οἱ δὲ πρέσβεις, the subject of this temporal clause. This gives the phrase a nice stylistic variation and adds a slightly stronger emphasis to οἱ δὲ πρέσβεις. The clause is a simple temporal clause referring to a definite past act (R11.4). You may preserve the original word order in your translation. The main clause is ἀθυμία ἐνέπεσε πᾶσιν.

3. ἐνέπεσε πᾶσιν: Compound verbs often take the dative.

4. ᾤοντο γὰρ: The particle γάρ adds a critical nuance. γάρ is often used to introduce the reason or cause for the information that immediately precedes it (S2810).

5. ᾤοντο: ᾤοντο is the third person plural imperfect indicative of the deponent verb οἴομαι. Because οἴομαι is a verb of thinking, it usually introduces an accusative/infinitive construction in indirect statement (R7.1). Observe that two infinitives follow this introductory verb: ἀνδραποδισθήσεσθαι and ἀπολεῖσθαι, which are joined by καί.

6. ἀνδραποδισθήσεσθαι, ἀπολεῖσθαι: A future infinitive in an indirect statement indicates time subsequent to that of the main verb (R 7.1). ἀνδραποδισθήσεσθαι does not have a subject accusative. When the subject of the verb of thinking and the subject of the infinitive are the same, the subject of the infinitive is generally omitted, or, if it is included, it is in the nominative case (R7.1). ἀπολεῖσθαι, another infinitive, is also part of the indirect statement. Since ἀπολεῖσθαι is intransitive in the middle voice the accusative πολλοὺς is its subject.

7. ἕως ἂν πέμπωσιν ἑτέρους πρέσβεις is a subordinate clause within the indirect statement (R7.5). The subordinating temporal conjunction ἕως means "while" when followed by ἄν and the subjunctive and refers to a future act (R11.5; S2401, 2423). Although the subjunctive can be changed to an optative because ᾤοντο is in a secondary tense, the subjunctive may also be retained.

8. What type of dative is λιμῷ?

TRANSLATION

And when the ambassadors arrived home and announced these things in the city, despondency fell upon everyone, for they (the Athenians) thought that they would be enslaved and that, while they were sending other ambassadors, many would die from hunger.

SENTENCE TWO, PART ONE

περὶ δὲ τῶν τειχῶν τῆς καθαιρέσεως οὐδεὶς ἐβούλετο συμβουλεύειν· Ἀρχέστρατος γὰρ εἰπὼν ἐν τῇ βουλῇ Λακεδαιμονίοις κράτιστον εἶναι ἐφ᾽ οἷς προυκαλοῦντο εἰρήνην ποιεῖσθαι, ἐδέθη·

VOCABULARY

περί (prep. + gen.)   concerning
τεῖχος, -ους, τό   wall
καθαίρεσις, -εως, ἡ   a pulling down, a razing
βούλομαι   wish
συμβουλεύω   give advice
Ἀρχέστρατος, -ου, ὁ   Archestratus
εἶπον   said (used for aorist of λέγω)

βουλή, -ῆς, ἡ   council, Council
κράτιστος, -η, -ον   best
προκαλέω   offer, propose
εἰρήνη, -ης, ἡ   peace
ποιέω   make
δέω   bind, put in fetters, imprison

OBSERVATIONS, STRATEGIES, AND NOTES

1. Remember that verbs of wishing, like ἐβούλετο, often take complementary infinitives (R5.3).

2. περὶ δὲ τῶν τειχῶν τῆς καθαιρέσεως is a prepositional phrase governed by περί. Notice that there are two genitives that are not joined by a conjunction. Consequently, only one of these genitives is the object of περί. Logic will determine which genitive it is.

3. καθαίρεσις has a verbal notion implied in its meaning and may as a consequence take a noun in the genitive to indicate the object of that implied verbal activity. This type of genitive is called an objective genitive (R3.2.5; S1328). It is easy to see that τῶν τειχῶν is acting in this way with τῆς καθαιρέσεως. Note that objective genitives are usually in the predicate position (R2.2).

4. When translating the first part of the sentence, be sure to take δὲ into account, as it marks a contrast with the previous sentence.

5. Ἀρχέστρατος γὰρ εἰπὼν . . . ἐδέθη: The causal γάρ (S2810) indicates that this part of the sentence explains why no one wanted to talk about the destruction of the walls.

6. εἰπὼν: εἰπών is the aorist active participle in the nominative singular masculine of εἶπον, a verb which is used as the aorist of λέγω. It introduces an accusative/infinitive construction in indirect statement (R7.1), since participles take the same constructions that a finite form of that particular verb may take. The participle is followed by the infinitive expression κράτιστον εἶναι, which must be part of the indirect statement. κράτιστον εἶναι is an impersonal construction meaning "be best," and it often takes a complementary infinitive to complete its meaning (R5.3). ποιεῖσθαι, the present middle infinitive of ποιέω, is a likely possibility. Notice that εἰρήνην, an accusative, has been placed before ποιεῖσθαι. It is very common for a direct object to be placed before its verb, whether that verb is a finite form or an infinitive.

7. Λακεδαιμονίοις is a dative of association, which is especially common with words indicating hostile or friendly relationships or associations (S1523). It goes with εἰρήνην ποιεῖσθαι.

8. ἐφ' οἷς προυκαλοῦντο: As previously noted, it is common to omit the antecedent of a relative pronoun when that antecedent is a demonstrative pronoun and for the relative pronoun to be attracted into the case of the omitted antecedent (R11.3; S2509, 2522). The full expression of the idea is ἐπ' ἐκείνοις οὓς προυκαλοῦντο, and

we can translate the elliptical phrase as "on the terms that they (the Spartans) were offering."

TRANSLATION

But no one was willing to give advice concerning the destruction of the walls, for Archestratus, after saying in the Council that it was best to make peace with the Lacedaemonians on the terms that they were offering, was imprisoned;

SENTENCE TWO, PART TWO

προυκαλοῦντο δὲ τῶν μακρῶν τειχῶν ἐπὶ δέκα σταδίους καθελεῖν ἑκατέρου· ἐγένετο δὲ ψήφισμα μὴ ἐξεῖναι περὶ τούτων συμβουλεύειν.

VOCABULARY

προκαλέω	propose	ἑκάτερος, -α, -ον	each of two
μακρός, -ά, -όν	long	ψήφισμα, -ατος, τό	decree
δέκα (indecl. num.)	ten	ἔξεστι	it is possible
στάδιον, -ου, τό	stade (a unit of measurement)	συμβουλεύω	deliberate
καθαιρέω	destroy		

OBSERVATIONS, STRATEGIES, AND NOTES

1. προυκαλοῦντο δὲ: δέ marks a contrast here, and by context it is clear that this sentence is included as a parenthetical specification of the terms the Lacedaemonians were demanding from the Athenians. We will indicate this by using parentheses in the polished translation. The Lacedaemonians are the subject of προυκαλοῦντο.

2. When ἐπί is used with a measurement, no direct translation is needed.

3. σταδίους: This is the direct object of καθελεῖν. It is being modified by the indeclinable numeral δέκα. This noun is neuter in the singular, but it admits masculine forms in the plural.

4. καθελεῖν functions here as a complementary infinitive (R.5.3) with προυκαλοῦντο. What is its tense? What nuance does its tense impart?

5. τῶν μακρῶν τειχῶν: The long walls were the walls built from the city of Athens to the ports of Piraeus and Phalerum in the mid-fifth century B.C.E. to ensure access to the sea in times of siege.

6. ἑκατέρου: This refers to each of the two long walls. The order for translation is δέκα σταδίους ἑκατέρου τῶν μακρῶν τειχῶν.

7. ἐγένετο: Translate this as "was passed." ψήφισμα is the subject.

8. μὴ ἐξεῖναι περὶ τούτων συμβουλεύειν: It is not uncommon for an expression like "a decree was passed" to introduce an indirect statement. Supply "stating" and take μὴ

ἐξεῖναι as the infinitive of the indirect statement with συμβουλεύειν as the complementary infinitive.

TRANSLATION

and they (the Lacedaemonians) were proposing to destroy ten stades of each of the long walls; and a decree was passed <stating> that it was not possible to deliberate about these things.

POLISHED TRANSLATION

When the ambassadors arrived home and announced these things in the city, despondency fell upon everyone, for the Athenians thought that they would be enslaved and that many would die of hunger while they were sending other ambassadors. But no one was willing to give advice concerning the destruction of the walls, for Archestratus was imprisoned after saying in the Council that it was best to make peace with the Lacedaemonians on the terms they were offering (the Lacedaemonians were proposing to destroy ten stades of each of the long walls). A decree was passed, stating that it was not possible to deliberate about these things.

Reading Selection

Theramenes, an influential Athenian politician with oligarchic leanings who would later become one of the Thirty Tyrants (see Reading 5, below), now offers to go to the Spartan general Lysander to find out the true intentions of the Spartans. Lysander, after some delay, tells him that he does not have authority over matters of peace and war and sends Theramenes to speak to the Spartan ephors, five magistrates who were elected annually and whose power was thought to balance that of the two kings.

> τοιούτων δὲ ὄντων Θηραμένης εἶπεν ἐν ἐκκλησίᾳ ὅτι εἰ βούλονται αὐτὸν πέμψαι
> παρὰ Λύσανδρον, εἰδὼς ἥξει Λακεδαιμονίους πότερον ἐξανδραποδίσασθαι
> τὴν πόλιν βουλόμενοι ἀντέχουσι περὶ τῶν τειχῶν ἢ πίστεως ἕνεκα. πεμφθεὶς
> δὲ διέτριβε παρὰ Λυσάνδρῳ τρεῖς μῆνας καὶ πλείω, ἐπιτηρῶν ὁπότε Ἀθηναῖοι
> ἔμελλον διὰ τὸ ἐπιλελοιπέναι τὸν σῖτον ἅπαντα ὅ τι τις λέγοι ὁμολογήσειν. ἐπεὶ   5
> δὲ ἧκε τετάρτῳ μηνί, ἀπήγγειλεν ἐν ἐκκλησίᾳ ὅτι αὐτὸν Λύσανδρος τέως μὲν
> κατέχοι, εἶτα κελεύοι εἰς Λακεδαίμονα ἰέναι· οὐ γὰρ εἶναι κύριος ὧν ἐρωτῷτο
> ὑπ' αὐτοῦ, ἀλλὰ τοὺς ἐφόρους. μετὰ ταῦτα ᾑρέθη πρεσβευτὴς εἰς Λακεδαίμονα
> αὐτοκράτωρ δέκατος αὐτός. Λύσανδρος δὲ τοῖς ἐφόροις ἔπεμψεν ἀγγελοῦντα μετ'
> ἄλλων Λακεδαιμονίων Ἀριστοτέλην, φυγάδα Ἀθηναῖον ὄντα, ὅτι ἀποκρίναιτο   10
> Θηραμένει ἐκείνους κυρίους εἶναι εἰρήνης καὶ πολέμου.
>
> Xenophon, *Hellenica* 2.2.16–18

NOTES

1. [Line 1] τοιούτων δὲ ὄντων: What construction is this?
2. [Line 1] What tense is πέμψαι and why?
3. [Lines 1–2] εἰ βούλονται . . . εἰδὼς ἥξει: A mixed condition within the indirect statement set up by εἶπεν . . . ὅτι. Note that no verbs have been changed to the optative even though εἶπεν is in a secondary tense.
4. [Line 2] What form is εἰδὼς?
5. [Lines 2–3] Λακεδαιμονίους is the direct object of εἰδὼς but belongs more logically in the indirect question introduced by πότερον . . . ἤ ("whether . . . or") as the subject of ἀντέχουσι. This is called *prolepsis* ("anticipation") and refers to a situation in which the subject of the dependent clause is used as the direct object of the main verb (or participle in the principal clause, as here), in order to give greater emphasis to the subject of the dependent clause (S2182). Translate here as "<he said> that he would return when he knew whether the Lacedaemonians" (literally, "knowing the Lacedaemonians whether they").
6. [Lines 2–3] ἐξανδραποδίσασθαι τὴν πόλιν βουλόμενοι: Take the participle βουλόμενοι causally. What is the function of ἐξανδραποδίσασθαι? What is the significance of its tense?
7. [Line 3] ἕνεκα: Remember that ἕνεκα is postpositive, and as a consequence its object precedes it.
8. [Line 3] What form is πεμφθεὶς? List the principal parts of this verb.
9. [Line 4] τρεῖς μῆνας καὶ πλείω: πλείω is an alternate form of πλείονα. What type of time does the accusative express?
10. [Line 4] ἐπιτηρῶν ὁπότε: The indirect interrogative ὁπότε introduces an indirect question set up by ἐπιτηρῶν. Translate as "looking out for the time when" (literally, "looking out for when").
11. [Line 5] ἔμελλον . . . ὅ τι τις λέγοι ὁμολογήσειν: The order for translation is ἔμελλον ὁμολογήσειν ἅπαντα ὅ τι τις λέγοι διὰ τὸ ἐπιλελοιπέναι τὸν σῖτον. ἅπαντα, the direct object of ὁμολογήσειν, is amplified by ὅ τι τις λέγοι. ὅ τι τις λέγοι is a conditional relative clause (R11.2), as the indefinite relative pronoun ὅ τι indicates. It is permissible for a singular relative pronoun that has a collective force (as here) to have an antecedent in the plural (S2502c).
12. [Line 5] ἐπιλελοιπέναι: What form is this? What is its construction? What is the function of τὸν σῖτον?
13. [Line 6] τετάρτῳ μηνί: What type of time expression is this?
14. [Line 7] What is the mood of κατέχοι and κελεύοι, and why?
15. [Line 7] κελεύοι εἰς Λακεδαίμονα ἰέναι: Verbs of ordering take an accusative/infinitive construction (R5.1). The subject accusative of the infinitive ἰέναι has been omitted, but it is easily supplied by the context.
16. [Lines 7–8] οὐ γὰρ εἶναι κύριος ὧν ἐρωτῷτο ὑπ' αὐτοῦ: Supply an idea of speaking and translate as "For he said that he . . ." The subject of this part of the sentence is Lysander, as the nominative form of κύριος indicates. It is not uncommon for a verb of ordering (κελεύοι) to be followed by an implied indirect statement.

17. [Line 7] ὧν: Once again, the antecedent of a relative pronoun has been omitted because the antecedent would have been a demonstrative pronoun. Here a dual phenomenon is occurring. The antecedent of ὧν, which would have been ἐκείνων or τούτων, has been omitted. The relative pronoun, which we would expect to be in the nominative case because it is the subject of the passive form ἐρωτῷτο, has then been attracted into the case of the omitted antecedent (R11.3; S2509, 2522). The full expression would be οὐ γὰρ εἶναι κύριος ἐκείνων ἃ ἐρωτῷτο ὑπ᾽ αὐτοῦ. Remember that neuter plural subjects take singular verbs.

18. [Line 7] What is the sentence clue that indicates that ἐρωτῷτο is passive rather than middle? What mood is ἐρωτῷτο? Why?

19. [Line 8] τοὺς ἐφόρους: This is still part of the implied indirect statement. Supply εἶναι and κυρίους to complete the elliptical construction.

20. [Line 8] ἡρέθη: The subject is Theramenes. All the nominatives—πρεσβευτὴς, αὐτοκράτωρ, δέκατος αὐτός—modify the subject. Remember that αἱρέω (ἡρέθη) may mean "be selected" when used in the passive voice. What form is this?

21. [Line 9] δέκατος αὐτός: This is one way of saying that there were nine others who were also sent to Sparta.

22. [Line 9] What word is the participle ἀγγελοῦντα modifying? Remember that ὡς is not always required with a future participle when it is being used to express purpose, particularly after a verb meaning "come," "go," "send," "summon," etc. (S2065).

23. [Line 10] ἀποκρίναιτο: What form is this and why?

24. [Lines 10–11] Notice that ἀποκρίναιτο, itself part of a ὅτι indirect statement construction introduced by ἀγγελοῦντα, sets up an accusative/infinitive indirect statement (ἐκείνους κυρίους εἶναι εἰρήνης καὶ πολέμου) (R7.1, 7.3).

Reading Four

Xenophon, *Hellenica* 2.2.19–21

Focus on Reading

Theramenes and the other Athenian ambassadors are in Sellasia, a village on the frontier of Laconia about eight miles from Sparta. They have been sent to seek peace with the Spartans and to ascertain what terms the Spartans will require.

> Θηραμένης δὲ καὶ οἱ ἄλλοι πρέσβεις ἐπεὶ ἦσαν ἐν Σελλασίᾳ, ἐρωτώμενοι δὲ ἐπὶ
> τίνι λόγῳ ἥκοιεν εἶπον ὅτι αὐτοκράτορες περὶ εἰρήνης, μετὰ ταῦτα οἱ ἔφοροι
> καλεῖν ἐκέλευον αὐτούς. ἐπεὶ δ' ἧκον, ἐκκλησίαν ἐποίησαν, ἐν ᾗ ἀντέλεγον
> Κορίνθιοι καὶ Θηβαῖοι μάλιστα, πολλοὶ δὲ καὶ ἄλλοι τῶν Ἑλλήνων, μὴ σπένδεσθαι
> Ἀθηναίοις, ἀλλ' ἐξαιρεῖν.

Xenophon, Hellenica 2.2.19

SENTENCE ONE

Θηραμένης δὲ καὶ οἱ ἄλλοι πρέσβεις ἐπεὶ ἦσαν ἐν Σελλασίᾳ, ἐρωτώμενοι δὲ ἐπὶ
τίνι λόγῳ ἥκοιεν εἶπον ὅτι αὐτοκράτορες περὶ εἰρήνης, μετὰ ταῦτα οἱ ἔφοροι
καλεῖν ἐκέλευον αὐτούς.

VOCABULARY

πρέσβυς, -εως, ὁ   ambassador
ἐπεί (conj.)   when
ἐρωτάω   ask
λόγος, -ου, ὁ   reason
ἥκω   have come, arrive
εἶπον (used for aorist of λέγω)   said
αὐτοκράτωρ, -ορος, ὁ/ἡ   possessing
   full powers

περί (prep. + gen.)   concerning, about
εἰρήνη, -ης, ἡ   peace
μετά (prep. + acc.)   after
ἔφορος, -ου, ὁ   ephor
καλέω   summon
κελεύω   give orders

OBSERVATIONS, STRATEGIES, AND NOTES

1. There are several words in this sentence that are important to note: ἐρωτώμενοι, τίνι, εἶπον, and ὅτι. What constructions should you expect to find?

2. ἐπεὶ: This temporal conjunction is introducing the temporal clause ἦσαν ἐν Σελλασίᾳ. Note that the subject of ἦσαν, Θηραμένης δὲ καὶ οἱ ἄλλοι πρέσβεις, has been placed in front of ἐπεὶ. This is a nice stylistic touch: the word order gives the subject greater emphasis.

3. ἐρωτώμενοι: The circumstantial participle sets up an indirect question. Remember that indirect questions take a construction similar to the ὅτι/ὡς construction of indirect statement (R7.6; S2663, 2677). The indirect question is here introduced by the interrogative adjective τίνι, which is modifying λόγῳ. As in the ὅτι/ὡς construction, when the main verb is in a secondary tense the verb of the indirect question may switch to the corresponding tense of the optative. Since the main verb, εἶπον, is in the aorist, ἥκοιεν, the verb of the indirect question, is in the present optative and is representing the present indicative of the original direct question.

4. εἶπον ὅτι αὐτοκράτορες περὶ εἰρήνης: There is no verb after ὅτι, but because αὐτοκράτορες is in the nominative plural it is likely that a form of "be" must be supplied and that αὐτοκράτορες is acting as a predicate adjective. It is very common in Greek to omit a form of "be" if it can be supplied from logic and context. This phrase is literally translated, "they said that they were possessing full powers concerning peace," but since that is rather awkward in English, we may translate it as "they said that they had full powers concerning peace."

5. αὐτούς is the direct object of καλεῖν.

TRANSLATION

When Theramenes and the other ambassadors were in Sellasia, being asked for what reason they had come, they said that they had full powers concerning peace; after these things the ephors gave orders to summon them.

SENTENCE TWO

ἐπεὶ δ' ἧκον, ἐκκλησίαν ἐποίησαν, ἐν ᾗ ἀντέλεγον Κορίνθιοι καὶ Θηβαῖοι μάλιστα, πολλοὶ δὲ καὶ ἄλλοι τῶν Ἑλλήνων, μὴ σπένδεσθαι Ἀθηναίοις, ἀλλ' ἐξαιρεῖν.

VOCABULARY

ἥκω   arrive, have come
ἐκκλησία, -ας, ἡ   assembly
ἀντιλέγω   speak in opposition, speak against
μάλιστα (adv.)   in particular, especially

Ἕλλην, -ηνος, ὁ   a Greek
σπένδω (mid.)   make a treaty, make peace
ἐξαιρέω   demolish, destroy

OBSERVATIONS, STRATEGIES, AND NOTES

1. In this sentence, there is a brief temporal clause (ἐπεὶ δ᾽ ἧκον), a main clause (ἐκκλησίαν ἐποίησαν), a relative clause (ἐν ᾗ ἀντέλεγον Κορίνθιοι καὶ Θηβαῖοι μάλιστα, πολλοὶ δὲ καὶ ἄλλοι τῶν Ἑλλήνων) signaled by the relative pronoun ᾗ, and an infinitive clause of indirect statement (μὴ σπένδεσθαι Ἀθηναίοις, ἀλλ᾽ ἐξαιρεῖν).

2. ἐκκλησίαν ἐποίησαν: The ephors would be the ones who convened the assembly. Translate ἐποίησαν as "called."

3. Note that ἐκκλησίαν is the only possible antecedent of ᾗ, since it is the only feminine singular noun in the sentence. The subject of the relative clause is denoted by several nominatives, Κορίνθιοι, Θηβαῖοι, πολλοὶ δὲ καὶ ἄλλοι, and the accompanying verb ἀντέλεγον.

4. Omit the καί in your translation of πολλοί and ἄλλοι, because Greek often joins an adjective of quantity and an adjective of quality with a conjunction, whereas English does not. Translate as idiomatically as possible, so that your translation doesn't sound awkward in English.

5. σπένδεσθαι . . . ἐξαιρεῖν: We have a context in which speaking is occurring, as indicated by ἀντέλεγον, and thus there is an indirect statement using the accusative/infinitive construction (R7.1). Since the translation "spoke in opposition that . . ." is somewhat awkward in English, you may supply "saying" in order to make the thought clear. Translate this as "<saying> not to make peace with the Athenians but to destroy <them>."

TRANSLATION

And when they (the Athenians) arrived, they (the ephors) made an assembly, in which the Corinthians and the Thebans, in particular, and many others of the Greeks spoke in opposition, <saying> not to make peace with the Athenians but to destroy <them>.

POLISHED TRANSLATION

When Theramenes and the other ambassadors were in Sellasia, when they were asked why they had come they said that they had full powers concerning peace; the ephors then gave orders to summon them. When the Athenians arrived, the ephors called an assembly, in which the Corinthians and the Thebans in particular, as well as many other Greeks, spoke in opposition. They urged them not to make peace with the Athenians but to destroy them.

Reading Selection

In the presence of Theramenes and the other Athenian ambassadors, the Spartans continue the discussion with their allies about ending the war with Athens. The Spartans state the terms upon which they are willing to cease hostilities, and the Athenians bring this information back home.

Λακεδαιμόνιοι δὲ οὐκ ἔφασαν πόλιν Ἑλληνίδα ἀνδραποδιεῖν μέγα ἀγαθὸν
εἰργασμένην ἐν τοῖς μεγίστοις κινδύνοις γενομένοις τῇ Ἑλλάδι, ἀλλ᾽ ἐποιοῦντο
εἰρήνην ἐφ᾽ ᾧ τά τε μακρὰ τείχη καὶ τὸν Πειραιᾶ καθελόντας καὶ τὰς ναῦς πλὴν
δώδεκα παραδόντας καὶ τοὺς φυγάδας καθέντας τὸν αὐτὸν ἐχθρὸν καὶ φίλον
νομίζοντας Λακεδαιμονίοις ἕπεσθαι καὶ κατὰ γῆν καὶ κατὰ θάλατταν ὅποι ἂν   5
ἡγῶνται. Θηραμένης δὲ καὶ οἱ σὺν αὐτῷ πρέσβεις ἐπανέφερον ταῦτα εἰς τὰς
Ἀθήνας. εἰσιόντας δ᾽ αὐτοὺς ὄχλος περιεχεῖτο πολύς, φοβούμενοι μὴ ἄπρακτοι
ἥκοιεν· οὐ γὰρ ἔτι ἐνεχώρει μέλλειν διὰ τὸ πλῆθος τῶν ἀπολλυμένων τῷ λιμῷ.

Xenophon, Hellenica 2.2.20–21

NOTES

1. [Line 1] οὐκ ἔφασαν: The negative does not negate the act of speaking. οὐ φημί
   means "deny" or "say that . . . not."
2. [Line 1] Supply "they" (the Lacedaemonians) as the subject of ἀνδραποδιεῖν. In an
   accusative/infinitive construction of indirect statement, when the subject of the infinitive is the same as the verb introducing the indirect statement, it is either omitted
   or in the nominative (R7.1).
3. [Line 2] What noun is the participle εἰργασμένην modifying? What is its function?
4. [Line 3] ἐφ᾽ ᾧ: Translate as "on condition that." This idiomatic expression takes an
   infinitive or accusative/infinitive construction in what is called a proviso clause. A
   proviso clause includes a qualification, provision, or condition (S2279).
5. [Lines 3–5] Notice the nice parallel construction here in the accusative/infinitive
   construction set up by ἐφ᾽ ᾧ. The participles καθελόντας, παραδόντας, καθέντας,
   and νομίζοντας, which modify the implied subject (the Athenians) of the infinitive
   ἕπεσθαι, are all preceded by their direct objects. The subject, the Athenians, is supplied by logic and context. You may prefer to translate these circumstantial participles as finite forms parallel to ἕπεσθαι rather than as subordinate clauses in order to
   avoid awkward English.
6. [Lines 5–6] ὅποι ἂν ἡγῶνται: This is a conditional relative clause (R11.2; S2505)
   introduced by the relative adverb ὅποι. It takes the subjunctive plus ἄν in a construction similar to a present general condition.
7. [Line 8] Why is ἥκοιεν in the optative mood?
8. [Line 8] ἐνεχώρει: This is a difficult word to look up in a lexicon. Its dictionary entry
   is ἐγχωρέω (ἐν + χωρέω). This impersonal verb takes a complementary infinitive
   (R5.3). What form is it?
9. [Line 8] How is the participle ἀπολλυμένων being used?
10. [Line 8] What type of dative is τῷ λιμῷ?

Reading Five

Xenophon, *Hellenica* 2.2.22–3.2

Focus on Reading

The ambassadors report the terms of peace stipulated by the Spartans. Though there is some opposition, the Athenians decide to accept the terms.

τῇ δὲ ὑστεραίᾳ ἀπήγγελλον οἱ πρέσβεις ἐφ᾽ οἷς οἱ Λακεδαιμόνιοι ποιοῖντο
τὴν εἰρήνην· προηγόρει δὲ αὐτῶν Θηραμένης, λέγων ὡς χρὴ πείθεσθαι
Λακεδαιμονίοις καὶ τὰ τείχη περιαιρεῖν. ἀντειπόντων δέ τινων αὐτῷ, πολὺ δὲ
πλειόνων συνεπαινεσάντων, ἔδοξε δέχεσθαι τὴν εἰρήνην.

Xenophon, Hellenica 2.2.22

SENTENCE ONE

τῇ δὲ ὑστεραίᾳ ἀπήγγελλον οἱ πρέσβεις ἐφ᾽ οἷς οἱ Λακεδαιμόνιοι ποιοῖντο
τὴν εἰρήνην· προηγόρει δὲ αὐτῶν Θηραμένης, λέγων ὡς χρὴ πείθεσθαι
Λακεδαιμονίοις καὶ τὰ τείχη περιαιρεῖν.

VOCABULARY

ὑστεραῖος, -α, -ον next	προηγορέω act as a spokesman for (+ gen.)
ἀπαγγέλλω report, announce	χρή it is necessary
πρέσβυς, -εως, ὁ ambassador	πείθω (mid.) obey (+ dat.)
ποιέω make	τεῖχος, -ους, τό wall
εἰρήνη, -ης, ἡ peace	περιαιρέω take away, take down

OBSERVATIONS, STRATEGIES, AND NOTES

1. The semicolon divides this sentence into two parts. Each part may be treated as grammatically separate.

2. The first part consists of a main clause, τῇ δὲ ὑστεραίᾳ ἀπήγγελλον οἱ πρέσβεις, followed by a relative clause, ἐφ' οἷς οἱ Λακεδαιμόνιοι ποιοῖντο τὴν εἰρήνην, which has been introduced by the relative pronoun οἷς.

3. The main clause is quite straightforward. δὲ signals the next event or detail in the narration of the story. Since this is not really marking a contrast, you may translate it as "and" or omit it in your translation.

4. τῇ δὲ ὑστεραίᾳ: Supply ἡμέρᾳ. What type of time expression is this?

5. ἐφ' οἷς: The final vowel of a preposition is elided or dropped when the following word begins with a vowel. Because the relative pronoun has a rough breathing, the pi from ἐπί aspirates to phi, giving ἐφ'.

6. ἐπί (ἐφ') has many meanings, but in a context in which an agreement is being discussed, it may mean "on." You will often need to look up prepositions because their meanings are so varied.

7. Notice that there is no likely antecedent for the relative pronoun οἷς, which is dative plural masculine or neuter. Since the sentence will not make sense if οἱ πρέσβεις is taken as the antecedent of οἷς, it is possible that the antecedent has been omitted. It is clear by context that the antecedent would have been a demonstrative pronoun, but it has been omitted (S2509). Supply "these things" or "the terms."

8. ποιοῖντο: This is a third person plural present middle optative. The middle voice indicates the personal interest and benefit that the Spartans have in making peace. It is in the optative mood because the main verb, ἀπήγγελλον, "they reported," implies an indirect statement. Consequently, Xenophon has treated the relative clause as if it were part of a full indirect statement construction, in which subordinate clauses often take the optative when the main verb is in a secondary tense (R7.5).

9. What form is προηγόρει? You will need to pay close attention to the accent!

10. προηγορέω means "act as a spokesman for," and the genitive or dative case indicates for whom or for what the person is speaking. αὐτῶν, then, goes with προηγόρει and refers, by logic and context, to the ambassadors.

11. Notice that the participle λέγων is followed by ὡς, which introduces the indirect statement anticipated by λέγων. What type of participle is λέγων? (See R6 for participle review.) What noun is it modifying?

12. The indirect statement set up by λέγων ὡς is reasonably straightforward. The main verb of the indirect statement is χρὴ, an impersonal verb that takes either an infinitive or an accusative/infinitive construction. There are two infinitives, πείθεσθαι and περιαιρεῖν. πείθεσθαι may be either the present middle or passive infinitive. Because it is followed by the dative Λακεδαιμονίοις, it is more likely that it is in the middle voice because πείθω takes the dative with the middle.

TRANSLATION

And on the next day, the ambassadors reported the terms on which the Lacedaemonians were making peace; Theramenes was speaking on their behalf, saying that it was necessary to obey the Lacedaemonians and to destroy the city walls.

SENTENCE TWO

ἀντειπόντων δέ τινων αὐτῷ, πολὺ δὲ πλειόνων συνεπαινεσάντων, ἔδοξε δέχεσθαι τὴν εἰρήνην.

VOCABULARY

ἀντεῖπον (aor.)   speak against (+ dat.)   δοκεῖ   seem, seem best (impersonal)

πλείων, -ον (gen. -ονος) (comp. adj.)   more   δέχομαι   accept

συνεπαινέω   agree, consent

OBSERVATIONS, STRATEGIES, AND NOTES

1. Notice that there are a number of words in the genitive plural in this sentence, including two participles, ἀντειπόντων and συνεπαινεσάντων, as well as τινων and πλειόνων, which appear to be going with the genitive participles. When there is a genitive participle and a noun, pronoun, or adjective in the genitive that is the same gender and number as the participle, the construction is likely to be a genitive absolute (R6.5). There are actually two genitive absolutes here, ἀντειπόντων δέ τινων and πλειόνων συνεπαινεσάντων. It is important to notice the two instances of the particle δέ. The first marks a contrast with the previous sentence, while the second contrasts the second genitive absolute with the first one.

2. The aorist tense of the two participles ἀντειπόντων and συνεπαινεσάντων is important to note. Remember that the tense of a participle indicates aspect and, often, time relative to that of the main verb (R6, 6.1, 6.2).

3. Notice that πολὺ has been placed immediately preceding the comparative πλειόνων. You will recall that degree of difference is often included with a comparative form and may be indicated either by the dative or by certain adverbs, including πολύ (R3.3.8; S1513, 1514). This is translated literally as "more by much" or "much more." Since πλειόνων is plural, translate it as "many more" or "far more" for smoother English.

4. ἔδοξε: In contexts where decisions or decrees are being made, δοκέω may be used impersonally in the third person singular to mean "it seems/seemed best" or "it is/was decided." The infinitive δέχεσθαι and its direct object τὴν εἰρήνην are technically the subject of ἔδοξε, as is the case with impersonal constructions (S1984, 1985). We can, however, translate this as "it seemed best to accept the peace," rather than as "to accept the peace seemed best," which is awkward in English.

TRANSLATION

While some men spoke against him, because many more agreed, it seemed best to accept the peace.

POLISHED TRANSLATION

And on the next day the ambassadors reported the terms on which the Lacedaemonians were making peace. Theramenes spoke on their behalf, saying that it was necessary to obey the Lacedaemonians and destroy the city walls. While some men spoke against him, because many more agreed, it was decided to accept the peace.

Reading Selection

This passage describes the destruction of the walls of Athens and the apparent relief from hostilities this gave to the Athenians, though it was short-lived. Xenophon then reports about the selection of the Thirty Tyrants, whom he names individually. The Thirty, as they are often called, were politicians in Athens who were known to have pro-Spartan leanings, as they were installed with assistance from the Spartans. Some of them were extreme oligarchs, and their rule was marked by the abolition of governing bodies critical to the Athenian democracy (such as the assembly and courts), execution of their opponents, confiscation of property, limitation of citizenship, and violence. It appears that approximately fifteen hundred Athenians were executed by the Thirty. Their rule was short-lived, however, for they were overthrown by the democratic exiles led by Thrasybulus (see below, Readings 19 et seq.). Democracy was restored in September 403 B.C.E.

Several sentences from the middle of this selection have been omitted (marked by the ellipsis) because they are considered by scholars to be an interpolation by a later author.

μετὰ δὲ ταῦτα Λύσανδρός τε κατέπλει εἰς τὸν Πειραιᾶ καὶ οἱ φυγάδες κατῆσαν
καὶ τὰ τείχη κατέσκαπτον ὑπ᾽ αὐλητρίδων πολλῇ προθυμίᾳ, νομίζοντες ἐκείνην
τὴν ἡμέραν τῇ Ἑλλάδι ἄρχειν τῆς ἐλευθερίας. . . . ἔδοξε τῷ δήμῳ τριάκοντα
ἄνδρας ἑλέσθαι, οἳ τοὺς πατρίους νόμους συγγράψουσι, καθ᾽ οὓς πολιτεύσουσι.
καὶ ᾑρέθησαν οἵδε· Πολυχάρης, Κριτίας, Μηλόβιος, Ἱππόλοχος, Εὐκλείδης,   5
Ἱέρων, Μνησίλοχος, Χρέμων, Θηραμένης, Ἀρεσίας, Διοκλῆς, Φαιδρίας,
Χαιρέλεως, Ἀναίτιος, Πείσων, Σοφοκλῆς, Ἐρατοσθένης, Χαρικλῆς, Ὀνομακλῆς,
Θέογνις, Αἰσχίνης, Θεογένης, Κλεομήδης, Ἐρασίστρατος, Φείδων, Δρακοντίδης,
Εὐμάθης, Ἀριστοτέλης, Ἱππόμαχος, Μνησιθείδης.

Xenophon, Hellenica 2.2.23–3.2

NOTES

1. [Lines 1–2] Notice the construction τε . . . καί joining Λύσανδρός τε κατέπλει and οἱ φυγάδες κατῇσαν. τε . . . καί is frequently used when a third component is added (καὶ τὰ τείχη κατέσκαπτον).

2. [Line 2] The subject of κατέσκαπτον is the Athenians.

3. [Line 2] What type of dative is προθυμίᾳ?

4. [Lines 2–3] What type of construction is νομίζοντες introducing? What are the key words of this construction?

5. [Lines 2–3] νομίζοντες ἐκείνην τὴν ἡμέραν τῇ Ἑλλάδι ἄρχειν τῆς ἐλευθερίας: This line is evocative of Thucydides' *Histories* 2.12.3.

6. [Line 3] ἔδοξε τῷ δήμῳ: Translate this as "it seemed best to the people" or, more idiomatically, as "the people decided."

7. [Lines 4–5] ἑλέσθαι and ᾑρέθησαν are from the same verb. What is it? What tense is ἑλέσθαι? Why?

8. [Line 4] What form and part of speech is οἵ? Determine its antecedent and grammatical function.

9. [Line 4] What form and part of speech is οὕς? Determine its antecedent and grammatical function.

10. [Line 5] What form is ᾑρέθησαν?

Reading Six

Xenophon, *Hellenica* 2.3.11–14

Focus on Reading

After a brief account of events in Syracuse and Samos, Xenophon's narrative returns to Athens and the Thirty.

Οἱ δὲ τριάκοντα ᾑρέθησαν μὲν ἐπεὶ τάχιστα τὰ μακρὰ τείχη καὶ τὰ περὶ τὸν Πειραιᾶ καθῃρέθη· αἱρεθέντες δὲ ἐφ᾽ ᾧτε συγγράψαι νόμους, καθ᾽ οὕστινας πολιτεύσοιντο, τούτους μὲν ἀεὶ ἔμελλον συγγράφειν τε καὶ ἀποδεικνύναι, βουλὴν δὲ καὶ τὰς ἄλλας ἀρχὰς κατέστησαν ὡς ἐδόκει αὐτοῖς.

Xenophon, Hellenica 2.3.11

This selection consists of one long sentence, but to make it more manageable, it has been divided into two sections.

PART ONE

Οἱ δὲ τριάκοντα ᾑρέθησαν μὲν ἐπεὶ τάχιστα τὰ μακρὰ τείχη καὶ τὰ περὶ τὸν Πειραιᾶ καθῃρέθη·

VOCABULARY

τριάκοντα (indecl. num.)   thirty
αἱρέω (passive)   be chosen, be elected
ἐπεὶ τάχιστα   as soon as
μακρός, -ά, -όν   long

τεῖχος, -ους, τό   wall
Πειραιεύς, -έως, ὁ   Piraeus
καθαιρέω   destroy

OBSERVATIONS, STRATEGIES, AND NOTES

1. The first part of this sentence is straightforward. There is a short main clause, Οἱ δὲ τριάκοντα ᾑρέθησαν μὲν, followed by a temporal clause, ἐπεὶ τάχιστα τὰ μακρὰ τείχη καὶ τὰ περὶ τὸν Πειραιᾶ καθῃρέθη.

2. Notice that the definite article οἱ has made the indeclinable numeral τριάκοντα into a noun. Translate as "the Thirty."

3. What form is ᾑρέθησαν?

4. μὲν is answered by δὲ in the second section of the sentence.

5. τὰ περὶ τὸν Πειραιᾶ is joined to τὰ μακρὰ τείχη by καὶ, indicating that both phrases are probably being used in the same manner. Because τὰ in τὰ περὶ τὸν Πειραιᾶ is neuter plural like τείχη, we know that it is also referring to walls.

6. καθῃρέθη: This form is the third person singular aorist passive indicative of the compound verb καθαιρέω. Remember that neuter plural subjects take singular verbs; καθῃρέθη has a compound subject, τὰ μακρὰ τείχη καὶ τὰ περὶ τὸν Πειραιᾶ. The aorist tense in a temporal clause is often translated as an English pluperfect to bring out the time distinctions more clearly (S1943).

TRANSLATION

And the Thirty were elected as soon as the long walls and the walls around Piraeus had been destroyed;

PART TWO

αἱρεθέντες δὲ ἐφ᾽ ᾧτε συγγράψαι νόμους, καθ᾽ οὕστινας πολιτεύσοιντο, τούτους μὲν ἀεὶ ἔμελλον συγγράφειν τε καὶ ἀποδεικνύναι, βουλὴν δὲ καὶ τὰς ἄλλας ἀρχὰς κατέστησαν ὡς ἐδόκει αὐτοῖς.

VOCABULARY

ἐφ᾽ ᾧτε	on the condition that (+ inf.)	ἀποδείκνυμι	publish
συγγράφω	compile, draw up	βουλή, -ῆς, ἡ	Council
νόμος, -ου, ὁ	law	ἀρχή, -ῆς, ἡ	office; (pl.) magistrates
κατά (prep. + acc.)	according to	καθίστημι	establish, appoint
πολιτεύω	administer the state	δοκέω	seem best
μέλλω	put off, delay (+ pres. inf.)		

OBSERVATIONS, STRATEGIES, AND NOTES

1. Let the editor's commas help guide you through this section.

2. αἱρεθέντες δὲ: δὲ answers the μὲν following ᾑρέθησαν in the first section of the sentence. The participle may be taken temporally or concessively, but the main verb construction, ἔμελλον συγγράφειν τε καὶ ἀποδεικνύναι, makes it clear that it is better

to take the participle concessively. Translate this as "And although they had been chosen . . . ," in order to mark the contrast between what the Thirty were supposed to do and what they were actually doing. Remember that an aorist participle often indicates time prior to that of the main verb (R6.1, 6.2). You may bring this out in your translation by translating it as "had been chosen."

3. As noted previously, ἐφ᾽ ᾧτε is an idiomatic expression meaning "on condition that," and it often takes an infinitive or accusative/infinitive construction (S2279). Translate the full phrase as "but although they had been chosen on the condition that they draw up the laws." Since the subject of the infinitive is logically the Thirty and hence the same as that of the main verb, it does not need to be expressed.

4. What tense is συγγράψαι and why?

5. οὕστινας: This may be either an indirect interrogative or an indefinite relative pronoun. Since this construction is clearly not an indirect question, οὕστινας is an indefinite relative pronoun. While νόμους must be the antecedent of οὕστινας, because it is not known precisely what laws will be drawn up, the indefinite relative pronoun is used rather than the relative pronoun. The prepositional phrase is translated, "according to which."

6. πολιτεύσοιντο: The verb is a third person plural future middle optative within a relative clause of purpose, which usually takes a future indicative, although the future optative is occasionally found (S2554, 2554a). A relative clause of purpose, also known as a final relative clause, usually has an indefinite antecedent. We may translate the clause as "according to which they would administer the state."

7. ἔμελλον, κατέστησαν: These two finite verbs are the main verbs of the sentence and the construction μὲν . . . δέ helps us recognize that the two parts of the sentence are being contrasted.

8. συγγράφειν τε καὶ ἀποδεικνύναι: Note that these two infinitives go with ἔμελλον and are linked closely together by τε καί. What is the function of τούτους, βουλήν, and ἀρχὰς?

TRANSLATION

and although they had been chosen on the condition that they write up the laws according to which they would administer the state, they were always putting off drawing them up and publishing them, but they appointed the Council and the other magistrates, as it seemed best to them.

POLISHED TRANSLATION

The Thirty were elected as soon as the long walls and the walls around Piraeus had been destroyed; and although they had been chosen on the condition that they draw up the laws according to which they would administer the state, they were always putting off drawing them up and publishing them, but they appointed the Council and the other magistrates as they thought best.

Reading Selection

This passage details some of the first acts of the Thirty and follows the passage above. This is a challenging passage, but you should be able to translate it if you work carefully and methodically.

> ἔπειτα πρῶτον μὲν οὓς πάντες ᾔδεσαν ἐν τῇ δημοκρατίᾳ ἀπὸ συκοφαντίας ζῶντας
> καὶ τοῖς καλοῖς κἀγαθοῖς βαρεῖς ὄντας, συλλαμβάνοντες ὑπῆγον θανάτου· καὶ
> ἥ τε βουλὴ ἡδέως αὐτῶν κατεψηφίζετο οἵ τε ἄλλοι ὅσοι συνῄδεσαν ἑαυτοῖς μὴ
> ὄντες τοιοῦτοι, οὐδὲν ἤχθοντο. ἐπεὶ δὲ ἤρξαντο βουλεύεσθαι ὅπως ἂν ἐξείη
> αὐτοῖς τῇ πόλει χρῆσθαι ὅπως βούλοιντο, ἐκ τούτου πρῶτον μὲν πέμψαντες εἰς   5
> Λακεδαίμονα Αἰσχίνην τε καὶ Ἀριστοτέλην ἔπεισαν Λύσανδρον φρουροὺς σφίσι
> συμπρᾶξαι ἐλθεῖν, ἕως δὴ τοὺς πονηροὺς ἐκποδὼν ποιησάμενοι καταστήσαιντο
> τὴν πολιτείαν· θρέψειν δὲ αὐτοὶ ὑπισχνοῦντο. ὁ δὲ πεισθεὶς τούς τε φρουροὺς καὶ
> Καλλίβιον ἁρμοστὴν συνέπραξεν αὐτοῖς πεμφθῆναι.

Xenophon, Hellenica 2.3.12–14

NOTES

1. [Line 1] πρῶτον μὲν is contrasted with ἐπεὶ δὲ in the second sentence.
2. [Line 1] What form of οἶδα is ᾔδεσαν? What type of indirect statement construction does this verb often take?
3. [Line 1] ἀπὸ συκοφαντίας: A sycophant was someone who habitually brought legal cases against others, for monetary reasons (such as blackmail), for the financial reward that sometimes came with the successful prosecution of a case, or because a third party was behind the prosecution. The term itself had severe negative connotations, and sycophancy was considered a crime for which one could be prosecuted. In addition, if a person brought a case but dropped it shortly after the charges were brought, or the case was so lacking in merit that it did not receive one-fifth of the jurors' votes, the individual bringing the charges would be fined. Although the origins of the term are obscure, the literal meaning of συκοφάντης is "fig-denouncer."
4. [Lines 1–2] How are the participles ζῶντας and ὄντας functioning in this sentence? The verb of the relative clause provides a clue.
5. [Line 2] τοῖς καλοῖς κἀγαθοῖς: Notice the crasis in κἀγαθοῖς (= καὶ ἀγαθοῖς). The expression refers here to the oligarchic or aristocratic party.
6. [Line 2] Supply ἐκείνους as the direct object of the main verb ὑπῆγον and its accompanying participle, συλλαμβάνοντες. It is also the antecedent of οὕς. As we have seen, it is common for an antecedent to be omitted when that antecedent would have been a demonstrative pronoun (S2509). The order for translation is ἔπειτα πρῶτον μὲν συλλαμβάνοντες ὑπῆγον θανάτου <ἐκείνους> οὓς πάντες ᾔδεσαν ἐν τῇ δημοκρατίᾳ ἀπὸ συκοφαντίας ζῶντας καὶ τοῖς καλοῖς κἀγαθοῖς βαρεῖς ὄντας.
7. [Line 2] What is the aspect of συλλαμβάνοντες and ὑπῆγον? It is acceptable to translate συλλαμβάνοντες as a finite form parallel to ὑπῆγον and to insert "and." This will make a less awkward English phrase.

8. [Line 3] Remember that τε is postpositive; you should think of it as belonging in front of the word it is following. Here we have τε . . . τε (ἥ τε βουλὴ and οἵ τε ἄλλοι), which serves to connect these two clauses. The initial καὶ joins this part of the sentence with the first part.

9. [Lines 3–4] ὅσοι συνῄδεσαν ἑαυτοῖς μὴ ὄντες τοιοῦτοι: ὅσοι is a relative pronoun meaning "as many as" and its antecedent is οἵ ἄλλοι. What form is συνῄδεσαν? The verb σύνοιδα plus the dative of the reflexive pronoun (ἑαυτοῖς) is an idiomatic expression that means "be conscious that."

10. [Lines 3–4] μὴ ὄντες τοιοῦτοι: The participle ὄντες is part of a participial construction of indirect statement (R7.2) set up by συνῄδεσαν ἑαυτοῖς. There is no need to translate the reflexive pronoun ἑαυτοῖς, but be sure to add in your translation "that" after συνῄδεσαν.

11. [Line 4] οὐδὲν ἤχθοντο: At first, many Athenians approved of the appointment of the Thirty, but as their actions increased in violence, people began to realize that their true intentions were not as benign as they originally appeared.

12. [Line 4] ὅπως ἂν ἐξείη is an unusual effort clause (R12.2), with a potential optative rather than the expected future indicative (S2216).

13. [Line 5] ὅπως βούλοιντο: Translate this second ὅπως as "as." What mood is βούλοιντο and why?

14. [Line 5] ἐκ τούτου: Translate this idiomatic expression as "thereupon."

15. [Line 6] Note τε καὶ joining Αἰσχίνην and Ἀριστοτέλην, who are members of the Thirty. What is the grammatical function of these two names?

16. [Lines 6–7] ἔπεισαν Λύσανδρον φρουροὺς σφίσι συμπρᾶξαι ἐλθεῖν: This is difficult. φρουροὺς is the subject accusative of the infinitive ἐλθεῖν; φρουροὺς ἐλθεῖν acts as the object of συμπρᾶξαι. σφίσι is a dative of person that should be taken with συμπρᾶξαι. Translate the phrase as "they urged Lysander to aid them in getting a garrison" (literally, "they urged Lysander to aid them that a garrison come").

17. [Line 7] ἕως δὴ: When referring to a future event, a temporal clause introduced by ἕως takes the subjunctive plus ἄν (R11.5, no. 5; S2426). Here the optative καταστήσαιντο has replaced the subjunctive plus ἄν because ἔπεισαν implies indirect statement (S2427b). After a secondary main verb, the verb of a subordinate clause within an indirect statement may switch to the corresponding tense of the optative (R7.5). In such an instance, ἄν drops out. The use of δή is ironic since the Thirty were going after many more than just the πόνηροι.

18. [Line 8] θρέψειν: Recall that verbs of promising and threatening often take future infinitives when referring to a future event (R7.4; S1868).

19. [Lines 8–9] τούς τε φρουροὺς καὶ Καλλίβιον ἁρμοστὴν συνέπραξεν αὐτοῖς πεμφθῆναι: This construction is somewhat similar to the one discussed in note 16, above. φρουροὺς and Καλλίβιον act as the subject accusatives of the aorist passive infinitive πεμφθῆναι. These words are the objects of συνέπραξεν.

20. [Lines 8–9] The Spartans and Lysander have succeeded in establishing in Athens a government structure similar to that imposed in other defeated cities: a pro-Spartan oligarchy and a Spartan garrison with a Spartan harmost as governor, giving Lysander the potential to intervene when necessary.

Reading Seven

Xenophon, *Hellenica* 2.3.14–16

Focus on Reading

The Thirty have received the garrison sent out by Lysander and begin to enlarge their aims and to move against those whom they perceive to be opposed to their position and policies.

οἱ δ᾽ ἐπεὶ τὴν φρουρὰν ἔλαβον, τὸν μὲν Καλλίβιον ἐθεράπευον πάσῃ θεραπείᾳ, ὡς πάντα ἐπαινοίη ἃ πράττοιεν, τῶν δὲ φρουρῶν τούτου συμπέμποντος αὐτοῖς οὓς ἐβούλοντο συνελάμβανον οὐκέτι τοὺς πονηρούς τε καὶ ὀλίγου ἀξίους, ἀλλ᾽ ἤδη οὓς ἐνόμιζον ἥκιστα μὲν παρωθουμένους ἀνέχεσθαι, ἀντιπράττειν δέ τι ἐπιχειροῦντας πλείστους ἂν τοὺς συνεθέλοντας λαμβάνειν.

Xenophon, Hellenica 2.3.14

Since this selection is one long sentence, it will be divided into logical sections.

PART ONE

οἱ δ᾽ ἐπεὶ τὴν φρουρὰν ἔλαβον, τὸν μὲν Καλλίβιον ἐθεράπευον πάσῃ θεραπείᾳ, ὡς πάντα ἐπαινοίη ἃ πράττοιεν,

VOCABULARY

φρουρά, -ᾶς, ἡ   garrison
λαμβάνω   receive
Καλλίβιος, -ου, ὁ   Callibius
θεραπεύω   flatter, wheedle

θεραπεία, -ας, ἡ   flattery
ὡς (conj.)   in order that, so that
ἐπαινέω   approve
πράττω   do

41

OBSERVATIONS, STRATEGIES, AND NOTES

1. οἱ δ᾽: This indicates a switch of subject back to "the Thirty."

2. τὸν μὲν Καλλίβιον is contrasted with τῶν δὲ φρουρῶν later in the sentence.

3. What type of dative is πάσῃ θεραπείᾳ?

4. ὡς πάντα ἐπαινοίη: Xenophon sometimes uses ὡς rather than ἵνα or ὅπως to introduce a purpose clause. This usage is unique among Attic prose writers. A purpose clause takes the optative mood when the main verb is secondary (R9.1; S2193, 2196).

5. ἃ πράττοιεν: Sometimes the mood of a verb in a subordinate clause may assimilate to the mood of the verb in the clause on which the subordinate verb depends. Here πράττοιεν has assimilated to the mood of ἐπαινοίη, the verb of the purpose clause (S2183).

TRANSLATION

But they, when they received the garrison, wheedled Callibius with every flattery, so that he would approve everything that they were doing,

PART TWO

τῶν δὲ φρουρῶν τούτου συμπέμποντος αὐτοῖς οὓς ἐβούλοντο συνελάμβανον
οὐκέτι τοὺς πονηρούς τε καὶ ὀλίγου ἀξίους,

VOCABULARY

συμπέμπω	send together	πονηρός, -ά, -όν	wicked
βούλομαι	wish	ὀλίγος, -η, -ον	little
συλλαμβάνω	arrest	ἄξιος, -α, -ον	worthy of (+ gen.)
οὐκέτι (adv.)	no longer		

OBSERVATIONS, STRATEGIES, AND NOTES

1. τῶν δὲ φρουρῶν is a bit unusual, but we may understand it as a partitive genitive (R3.2.2) with an implied direct object of συμπέμποντος. The order for translation would be τούτου συμπέμποντος αὐτοῖς <ἐκείνους> τῶν φρουρῶν.

2. The construction τούτου συμπέμποντος is composed of a demonstrative pronoun and participle, both in the genitive. What construction is it?

3. αὐτοῖς: Take this with συμπέμποντος. This part may be translated, "when this one (Callibius) sent them <those> of the guards."

4. οὓς ἐβούλοντο: Notice that there is no antecedent for the relative pronoun οὓς. It would be ἐκείνους, the implied direct object of συμπέμποντος. The antecedent, a demonstrative, has dropped out (S2509). Note that the Greek is a bit ambiguous here. Some commentators take this relative clause as the object of συνελάμβανον.

5. συνελάμβανον οὐκέτι τοὺς πονηρούς τε καὶ ὀλίγου ἀξίους: This is the main clause of this section of the sentence. Note the construction τε καί linking πονηρούς and ἀξίους.

6. ὀλίγου ἀξίους: Recall that ἄξιος may take a genitive. This phrase is literally translated "worthy of a little," but you may prefer "worthless" or "of no account."

TRANSLATION

when this one sent them those of the guards whom they wanted, they were no longer arresting the wicked and worthless men,

PART THREE

ἀλλ᾽ ἤδη οὓς ἐνόμιζον ἥκιστα μὲν παρωθουμένους ἀνέχεσθαι, ἀντιπράττειν δέ τι ἐπιχειροῦντας πλείστους ἂν τοὺς συνεθέλοντας λαμβάνειν.

VOCABULARY

ἤδη (adv.)	now	ἀντιπράττω	act in opposition
νομίζω	think	ἐπιχειρέω	try, attempt
ἥκιστα (adv.)	least	πλεῖστος, -η, -ον (sup. adj.)	most
παρωθέω	push aside, reject, slight	συνεθέλων, -οντος, ὁ	supporter
ἀνέχω	be content, endure (mid.)	λαμβάνω	take

OBSERVATIONS, STRATEGIES, AND NOTES

1. You will need to supply συνελάμβανον from the previous section. The imperfect tense often indicates the beginning of an action (S1900), and that sense works well here. The antecedent of οὓς, which is the direct object of συνελάμβανον, has been omitted. Translate this as "but now they began to arrest those who they thought."

2. Recall that ἐνόμιζον takes an accusative/infinitive construction of indirect statement (R7.1). The subject accusative of the infinitive ἀνέχεσθαι is the relative pronoun οὓς.

3. Note the construction μὲν . . . δέ in ἥκιστα μὲν παρωθουμένους ἀνέχεσθαι, ἀντιπράττειν δέ τι ἐπιχειροῦντας. This is not a strong contrast but instead notes two characteristics of this new group being arrested by the Thirty.

4. παρωθουμένους ἀνέχεσθαι: Verbs of beginning, ceasing, and enduring take a supplementary participle (R6.4, no. 1; S2098). This phrase may be translated as "were least content with being pushed aside."

5. ἀντιπράττειν δέ τι . . . λαμβάνειν: This part is a bit challenging! We have a future less vivid condition within an indirect statement in which the protasis has been expressed by the participial phrase ἀντιπράττειν δέ τι ἐπιχειροῦντας. Remember that circumstantial participles may be taken conditionally. It may be helpful to consider the idea as it would have been expressed as a condition: εἰ ἀντιπράττειν τι ἐπιχειροῖεν, πλείστους ἂν τοὺς συνεθέλοντας λαμβάνοιεν, which would be translated, "if they should try to do something in opposition, they would get supporters in the great-

est number." When the condition was expressed as part of the indirect statement, a participial phrase replaced the original protasis. It took the form ἀντιπράττειν δέ τι ἐπιχειροῦντας instead of εἰ ἀντιπράττειν τι ἐπιχειροῖεν. Such a substitution for a protasis is permissible and is often used (R10.6; S2344). The apodosis, because it is the main clause of the accusative/infinitive construction of indirect statement, also underwent a change. ἂν λαμβάνοιεν, the optative plus ἄν of the apodosis of the condition, changed to ἂν λαμβάνειν, the infinitive plus ἄν required by the indirect statement. The infinitive kept the original present tense of the optative and ἄν was retained, since it is the signpost of the original optative.

6. πλείστους: Strictly speaking, this superlative adjective is in the predicate position. You may translate it as "in the greatest number" or as an attributive adjective, "most."

TRANSLATION

but now <they began to arrest> those who they thought were least content with being pushed aside and <who>, if they tried to do something in opposition, would get the most supporters.

POLISHED TRANSLATION

When they received the garrison, they wheedled Callibius with every flattery so that he would approve everything they were doing. When he sent them the guards they wanted, they no longer were arresting just the wicked and worthless men but now began to arrest those they thought were least content with being pushed aside and those who, if they tried to do something in opposition, would have the most supporters.

Reading Selection

Theramenes and Critias begin to disagree concerning the policies of the Thirty, particularly in respect to those the Thirty have decided to execute.

τῷ μὲν οὖν πρώτῳ χρόνῳ ὁ Κριτίας τῷ Θηραμένει ὁμογνώμων τε καὶ φίλος ἦν· ἐπεὶ δὲ αὐτὸς μὲν προπετὴς ἦν ἐπὶ τὸ πολλοὺς ἀποκτείνειν, ἅτε καὶ φυγὼν ὑπὸ τοῦ δήμου, ὁ δὲ Θηραμένης ἀντέκοπτε, λέγων ὅτι οὐκ εἰκὸς εἴη θανατοῦν, εἴ τις ἐτιμᾶτο ὑπὸ τοῦ δήμου, τοὺς δὲ καλοὺς κἀγαθοὺς μηδὲν κακὸν εἰργάζετο, ἐπεὶ καὶ ἐγώ, ἔφη, καὶ σὺ πολλὰ δὴ τοῦ ἀρέσκειν ἕνεκα τῇ πόλει καὶ εἴπομεν   5 καὶ ἐπράξαμεν· ὁ δέ (ἔτι γὰρ οἰκείως ἐχρῆτο τῷ Θηραμένει) ἀντέλεγεν ὅτι οὐκ ἐγχωροίη τοῖς πλεονεκτεῖν βουλομένοις μὴ οὐκ ἐκποδὼν ποιεῖσθαι τοὺς ἱκανωτάτους διακωλύειν· εἰ δέ, ὅτι τριάκοντά ἐσμεν καὶ οὐχ εἷς, ἧττόν τι οἴει τυραννίδος ταύτης τῆς ἀρχῆς χρῆναι ἐπιμελεῖσθαι, εὐήθης εἶ.

Xenophon, *Hellenica* 2.3.15–16

NOTES

1. [Line 1] τῷ . . . πρώτῳ χρόνῳ: Translate this dative of time when as "at first."

2. [Line 1] The particle οὖν is used to indicate the continuation of the narrative. It may be translated as "and so" or "thereupon" or may even be left untranslated.

3. [Line 1] Note the close linkage of ὁμογνώμων and φίλος created by the construction τε καί.

4. [Line 2] ἐπὶ τὸ πολλοὺς ἀποκτείνειν: Definite articles do not stand by themselves in Attic prose. What is the function of τό? Notice that τό and ἀποκτείνειν frame πολλοὺς. This is a clue to take πολλοὺς with ἀποκτείνειν. What is the function of πολλοὺς?

5. [Line 2] καὶ φυγὼν: Take καὶ as an adverb. What form is φυγὼν? Noting its accent will help you to identify it correctly. When φεύγω is used with ὑπό plus the genitive, it means "to be exiled by someone."

6. [Line 3] What form is εἴη and why? Take εἴη with εἰκὸς in the sense of "be reasonable."

7. [Line 4] καλοὺς κἀγαθοὺς: This is the same as καλοὺς καὶ ἀγαθούς. What is the name of this phenomenon? καλοὺς κἀγαθοὺς refers to the aristocratic class.

8. [Line 4] ἐργάζομαι takes a double accusative to mean "to do something (acc.) to someone (acc.)." What are the accusatives that go with this verb?

9. [Line 5] ἐπεὶ καὶ ἐγώ, ἔφη, καὶ σύ: Note καὶ . . . καὶ . . . here as well as at the end of the clause (καὶ εἴπομεν καὶ ἐπράξαμεν).

10. [Line 5] τοῦ ἀρέσκειν ἕνεκα: Remember that the object of the preposition ἕνεκα precedes it. What is the function of τοῦ?

11. [Line 6] ὁ δέ indicates a switch of subject back to Critias.

12. [Line 7] What mood is ἐγχωροίη and why?

13. [Line 7] τοῖς πλεονεκτεῖν βουλομένοις: Note the framing of the complementary infinitive by τοῖς and βουλομένοις. What type of participle is βουλομένοις?

14. [Line 7] μὴ οὐκ: Translate this as a single negative. Sometimes an infinitive will take μὴ οὐκ rather than μή when the verb on which it depends is itself negated. Here the infinitive ποιεῖσθαι depends on οὐκ ἐγχωροίη. The additional οὐκ is not translated and is called a "redundant" or "sympathetic" negative (S2745).

15. [Line 8] διακωλύειν: Translate this verb with τοὺς ἱκανωτάτους. An infinitive is often used with adjectives and adverbs to indicate in what respect the adjective is applicable. This is especially common with adjectives and adverbs denoting fitness or ability (S2001). This infinitive is sometimes called in commentaries an "explanatory infinitive" or "epexegetical infinitive" (R5.4).

16. [Lines 8–9] εἰ δέ . . . οἴει . . . εἶ: Note the transition to direct statement, marked by the switch to second person singular verb forms. What form is οἴει?

17. [Lines 8–9] ἧττόν τι οἴει τυραννίδος ταύτης τῆς ἀρχῆς χρῆναι ἐπιμελεῖσθαι: This is introduced by εἰ δέ. The order for translation is εἰ δὲ οἴει χρῆναι ἐπιμελεῖσθαι ταύτης τῆς ἀρχῆς ἧττόν τι τυραννίδος. χρῆναι is impersonal.

18. [Line 8] ἧττόν τι: τι is often used with comparatives; it is literally translated "less in any way," but you may translate it as "any less."

19. [Line 9] What is the function of τυραννίδος?

Reading Eight

Xenophon, *Hellenica* 2.3.17–20

Focus on Reading

Theramenes continues his opposition to Critias's extreme tactics and becomes even more vocal in his criticism. Critias and the other oligarchs decide to draw up a list of citizens who will be permitted to take part in the government. They have also decided that the list will be limited to just three thousand citizens, a decision that Theramenes considers to be a poor one.

έπεὶ δέ, ἀποθνῃσκόντων πολλῶν καὶ ἀδίκως, πολλοὶ δῆλοι ἦσαν συνιστάμενοί τε καὶ θαυμάζοντες τί ἔσοιτο ἡ πολιτεία, πάλιν ἔλεγεν ὁ Θηραμένης ὅτι εἰ μή τις κοινωνοὺς ἱκανοὺς λήψοιτο τῶν πραγμάτων, ἀδύνατον ἔσοιτο τὴν ὀλιγαρχίαν διαμένειν. ἐκ τούτου μέντοι Κριτίας καὶ οἱ ἄλλοι τριάκοντα, ἤδη φοβούμενοι καὶ οὐχ ἥκιστα τὸν Θηραμένην, μὴ συρρυείησαν πρὸς αὐτὸν οἱ πολῖται, καταλέγουσι τρισχιλίους τοὺς μεθέξοντας δὴ τῶν πραγμάτων·

Xenophon, *Hellenica* 2.3.17–18

SENTENCE ONE

έπεὶ δέ, ἀποθνῃσκόντων πολλῶν καὶ ἀδίκως, πολλοὶ δῆλοι ἦσαν συνιστάμενοί τε καὶ θαυμάζοντες τί ἔσοιτο ἡ πολιτεία, πάλιν ἔλεγεν ὁ Θηραμένης ὅτι εἰ μή τις κοινωνοὺς ἱκανοὺς λήψοιτο τῶν πραγμάτων, ἀδύνατον ἔσοιτο τὴν ὀλιγαρχίαν διαμένειν.

VOCABULARY

ἀποθνῄσκω	die, be put to death	κοινωνός, -οῦ, ὁ	partner
ἀδίκως (adv.)	unjustly	ἱκανός, -ή, -όν	sufficient
δῆλος, -η, -ον	clear, evident	λαμβάνω	take on
συνίστημι	unite, band together	πρᾶγμα, -ατος, τό (pl.)	government
θαυμάζω	wonder	ἀδύνατος, -η, -ον	impossible
πολιτεία, -ας, ἡ	constitution, state	ὀλιγαρχία, -ας, ἡ	oligarchy
πάλιν (adv.)	again	διαμένω	remain, survive

OBSERVATIONS, STRATEGIES, AND NOTES

1. ἀποθνῃσκόντων πολλῶν: What construction is this?

2. ἀποθνῃσκόντων πολλῶν is used twice. Supply it with ἀδίκως to form a second genitive absolute. Take ἀποθνῃσκόντων to mean "die" in the first genitive absolute and "be put to death" in the second to bring out the two ideas more clearly.

3. πολλοὶ δῆλοι ἦσαν συνιστάμενοί: The personal construction δῆλός εἰμι takes a construction that is technically classified as the participial construction in indirect statement (S2107), but it operates more like a supplementary participle. The literal sense of the construction is "be clearly <doing the activity indicated by the participle>." In English, however, an impersonal construction is preferred. Translate this as "It was clear that many men were banding together."

4. συνιστάμενοί τε καὶ θαυμάζοντες: Note the construction τε καί joining these two participles.

5. τί ἔσοιτο ἡ πολιτεία: What construction is this? ἔσοιτο is the third person future optative form of εἰμί. Why is this verb in the optative mood? It is interesting to note that τί rather than τίς is used for the interrogative. τίς is used to ask a question about the class or type of something, whereas τί asks a question about its nature (S1265).

6. τις: In the singular, τις is sometimes used in the collective sense. Translate it as "they."

7. λήψοιτο . . . ἔσοιτο: A condition has been expressed within the indirect statement set up by ἔλεγεν . . . ὅτι. ἔσοιτο is the verb of the apodosis and hence is also the verb of the main clause of the indirect statement. It has switched to the corresponding tense of the optative after the secondary verb ἔλεγεν (R7.3; S2599, 2615). λήψοιτο, the verb of the protasis, has also been changed to the corresponding tense of the optative because verbs of subordinate clauses within an indirect statement may also take the optative when the main verb is in a secondary tense (R7.5; S2603, 2619). What type of condition is this? The tense of the optatives provides a clue. What is the full identification of λήψοιτο?

8. τῶν πραγμάτων: Take this with κοινωνοὺς ἱκανούς. In English we would say "partners in" rather than "partners of."

9. ἀδύνατον ἔσοιτο: This is an impersonal construction that takes an accusative/infinitive construction.

TRANSLATION

But when it was clear that many people were banding together and wondering what the constitution would be, since many people were dying and were being put to death unjustly, Theramenes spoke again, <saying> that if they did not take on sufficient partners in the government, it would be impossible for the oligarchy to survive.

SENTENCE TWO

ἐκ τούτου μέντοι Κριτίας καὶ οἱ ἄλλοι τριάκοντα, ἤδη φοβούμενοι καὶ οὐχ ἥκιστα τὸν Θηραμένην, μὴ συρρυείησαν πρὸς αὐτὸν οἱ πολῖται, καταλέγουσι τρισχιλίους τοὺς μεθέξοντας δὴ τῶν πραγμάτων·

VOCABULARY

ἐκ τούτου	thereupon	πρός (prep. + acc.)	toward, to
τριάκοντα	thirty	πολίτης, -ου, ὁ	citizen
ἤδη (adv.)	already	καταλέγω	enroll
φοβέομαι	fear (mid.)	τρισχίλιοι	three thousand
ἥκιστα (adv.)	least	μετέχω	share in, take part in (+ gen.)
συρρέω	flow together, gravitate toward	δή (particle)	now, in truth, indeed

OBSERVATIONS, STRATEGIES, AND NOTES

1. μέντοι is a particle that is sometimes used to mark a transition. There is no need to translate it here.

2. ἤδη φοβούμενοι καὶ οὐχ ἥκιστα τὸν Θηραμένην: This is translated as "because they were already afraid, and not least of all of Theramenes." What type of construction does a verb of fearing take?

3. συρρυείησαν is the third person plural aorist passive optative form of συρρέω. This clause specifies why the Thirty fear Theramenes. Why is it in the optative mood? Why is it aorist?

4. Notice that the main verb of this sentence, καταλέγουσι, is in the present tense while the main verb of the previous sentence, ἔλεγεν, is in the imperfect tense. This use of the present tense is called the "annalistic present" and writers employ it to report historical events (S1884). You may translate it as a past tense.

5. τοὺς μεθέξοντας: Note the future tense of the participle. What is the function of τούς? Translate this as a relative clause: "who would take part in."

6. δὴ is ironic, since it is clear that the three thousand will not be permitted to participate in the government in any substantive manner.

TRANSLATION

Thereupon Critias and the rest of the Thirty, because they were already afraid, and not least of all of Theramenes, that the citizens might gravitate toward him, enrolled three thousand who would take part in government affairs.

POLISHED TRANSLATION

But when it was clear that many people were banding together and wondering just what the constitution would be, since many people were dying and were being put to death unjustly, Theramenes spoke again and said that if they did not take on sufficient partners in the government it would be impossible for the oligarchy to survive. Thereupon Critias and the rest of the Thirty, because they were already afraid, especially because the citizens might gravitate toward Theramenes, enrolled three thousand citizens to participate in government affairs.

Reading Selection

Theramenes bluntly criticizes Critias's decision to enroll three thousand men on the citizens list. Critias and his men decide to hold a review of those who are on the list and those who are not, so they can confiscate the weapons of anyone not on the list.

> ὁ δ' αὖ Θηραμένης καὶ πρὸς ταῦτα ἔλεγεν ὅτι ἄτοπον δοκοίη ἑαυτῷ γε εἶναι τὸ
> πρῶτον μὲν βουλομένους τοὺς βελτίστους τῶν πολιτῶν κοινωνοὺς ποιήσασθαι
> τρισχιλίους, ὥσπερ τὸν ἀριθμὸν τοῦτον ἔχοντά τινα ἀνάγκην καλοὺς καὶ ἀγαθοὺς
> εἶναι, καὶ οὔτ' ἔξω τούτων σπουδαίους οὔτ' ἐντὸς τούτων πονηροὺς οἷόν τε
> εἴη γενέσθαι· ἔπειτα δ', ἔφη, ὁρῶ ἔγωγε δύο ἡμᾶς τὰ ἐναντιώτατα πράττοντας,   5
> βιαίαν τε τὴν ἀρχὴν καὶ ἥττονα τῶν ἀρχομένων κατασκευαζομένους. ὁ μὲν ταῦτ'
> ἔλεγεν. οἱ δ' ἐξέτασιν ποιήσαντες τῶν μὲν τρισχιλίων ἐν τῇ ἀγορᾷ, τῶν δ' ἔξω
> τοῦ καταλόγου ἄλλων ἀλλαχοῦ, ἔπειτα κελεύσαντες ἀπιέναι ἀποθεμένους τὰ
> ὅπλα, ἐν ᾧ ἐκεῖνοι ἀπεληλύθεσαν πέμψαντες τοὺς φρουροὺς καὶ τῶν πολιτῶν
> τοὺς ὁμογνώμονας αὑτοῖς τὰ ὅπλα πάντων πλὴν τῶν τρισχιλίων παρείλοντο, καὶ   10
> ἀνακομίσαντες ταῦτα εἰς τὴν ἀκρόπολιν συνέθηκαν ἐν τῷ ναῷ.

Xenophon, *Hellenica* 2.3.19–20

NOTES

1. [Line 1] What mood is δοκοίη? Why?
2. [Line 1] Note the reflexive pronoun ἑαυτῷ. The particle γε emphasizes ἑαυτῷ and may indicate scorn, irony, assent, concession, and so on (S2821).
3. [Lines 1–2] Take ἄτοπον with εἶναι. This impersonal construction takes an accusative/infinitive construction. The subject accusative of the infinitive ποιήσασθαι is

implied by βουλομένους. You will need to supply "they" with this concessive circumstantial participle.

4. [Lines 1–2] τὸ πρῶτον μὲν is answered by ἔπειτα δ' in the next sentence.

5. [Line 2] Both κοινωνοὺς and ποιήσασθαι serve two functions in the sentence even though each appears only once. ποιήσασθαι is used as a complementary infinitive with βουλομένους and as the infinitive of the accusative/infinitive construction after ἄτοπον . . . εἶναι. There are two different direct objects of ποιήσασθαι: τοὺς βελτίστους and τρισχιλίους. A fuller expression is <αὐτοὺς> βουλομένους ποιήσασθαι τοὺς βελτίστους τῶν πολιτῶν κοινωνοὺς <ποιήσασθαι> τρισχιλίους <κοινωνοὺς>. What is the function of κοινωνοὺς?

6. [Lines 3–4] ὥσπερ τὸν ἀριθμὸν . . . ἀγαθοὺς εἶναι: The participle of a personal verb may be used in an accusative absolute when preceded by ὥσπερ (S2078). This is translated literally as "as if this number had some necessity to be the good and noble men," but you will want to be more flexible in your translation.

7. [Lines 4–5] Why is οἷόν τε εἴη in the optative mood? οἷόν τέ ἐστι is an idiomatic expression that means "it is possible." It may take either a complementary infinitive or an accusative/infinitive construction, as it does here.

8. [Line 5] ἔγωγε: When the particle γε is attached to certain pronouns, it makes the pronoun emphatic.

9. [Line 5] Take δύο with τὰ ἐναντιώτατα.

10. [Line 5] What is the function of the participle πράττοντας? (Hint: consider the main verb of the sentence.)

11. [Line 6] βιαίαν τε τὴν ἀρχὴν καὶ ἥττονα τῶν ἀρχομένων κατασκευαζομένους: This explains τὰ ἐναντιώτατα. What type of genitive is τῶν ἀρχομένων? Both βιαίαν and ἥττονα are being used as predicate adjectives. Note that they are linked by the construction τε . . . καί.

12. [Line 7] οἱ δ': This denotes a switch of the subject back to the Thirty. Translate it as "And they." This is a very long sentence; be sure to use the punctuation as a guide and take each part as a unit.

13. [Lines 7–8] Note the construction μὲν . . . δέ in τῶν μὲν τρισχιλίων ἐν τῇ ἀγορᾷ, τῶν δ' ἔξω τοῦ καταλόγου ἄλλων.

14. [Lines 7–8] τῶν . . . ἄλλων ἀλλαχοῦ: Different groups of those not on the list of the three thousand citizens were assembled in different locations. Supply ἐξέτασιν ποιήσαντες and note the framing of the prepositional phrase ἔξω τοῦ καταλόγου by τῶν . . . ἄλλων to make a complete unit.

15. [Lines 8–9] ἔπειτα κελεύσαντες ἀπιέναι ἀποθεμένους τὰ ὅπλα: The text is difficult here, but Dindorf's emendation, in which he substitutes ἀπιέναι ἀποθεμένους τὰ ὅπλα for ἐπὶ τὰ ὅπλα, makes sense.[1] (An emendation is a suggested correction for a difficult or incomprehensible word in a text. Often, several suggested emendations for a particular word or words will have been made by various editors over time, and different editions of a text will reflect the emendation an editor prefers.) Regardless of

---

1. See Peter Krentz, ed., *Xenophon, Hellenika II.3.11–IV.2.8* (Warminster, U.K.: Aris and Phillips, 1995), 24, 128.

which version is accepted here, the general meaning is clear: the Thirty have ordered those not on the citizens list to hand over their arms. Supply αὐτούς, referring to those not on the list, as the object of κελεύσαντες and subject of ἀπιέναι.

16. [Line 9] ἐν ᾧ ἐκεῖνοι ἀπεληλύθεσαν: This refers to those not on the citizens list. Translate ἐν ᾧ as "when."

17. [Line 9] πέμψαντες: This refers to the Thirty. What are the direct objects of this participle?

18. [Line 10] What form is παρείλοντο?

19. [Line 11] ναῷ: This refers to the Parthenon.

Reading Nine

Xenophon, *Hellenica* 2.3.21–24

Focus on Reading

The Thirty continue their violent actions against the Athenians and decide that each member of the Thirty will arrest and kill a metic. Metics were individuals from other Greek cities who were legal residents of Athens. They could not own land or vote, but they were often prosperous businessmen or intellectuals and played an important role in Athenian society. There were presumably metics in other Greek cities, but we know little about them.

Readings 9–16 contain two long speeches. Critias's speech against Theramenes begins in the reading selection in Reading 9 and Theramenes' speech in his own defense begins in Reading 13. These speeches are more difficult than the narrative portions and your instructor may prefer to skip them (you can always read them in English translation or go back to them later). The narrative picks up again in Reading 17.

> τούτων δὲ γενομένων, ὡς ἐξὸν ἤδη ποιεῖν αὐτοῖς ὅ τι βούλοιντο, πολλοὺς μὲν
> ἔχθρας ἕνεκα ἀπέκτειναν, πολλοὺς δὲ χρημάτων. ἔδοξε δ' αὐτοῖς, ὅπως ἔχοιεν
> καὶ τοῖς φρουροῖς χρήματα διδόναι, καὶ τῶν μετοίκων ἕνα ἕκαστον λαβεῖν, καὶ
> αὐτοὺς μὲν ἀποκτεῖναι, τὰ δὲ χρήματα αὐτῶν ἀποσημήνασθαι. ἐκέλευον δὲ καὶ
> τὸν Θηραμένην λαβεῖν ὅντινα βούλοιτο.
>
> Xenophon, *Hellenica* 2.3.21–22

SENTENCE ONE

τούτων δὲ γενομένων, ὡς ἐξὸν ἤδη ποιεῖν αὐτοῖς ὅ τι βούλοιντο, πολλοὺς μὲν
ἔχθρας ἕνεκα ἀπέκτειναν, πολλοὺς δὲ χρημάτων.

VOCABULARY

γίγνομαι   happen

ὡς (particle)   in the belief that (+ part.)

ἔξεστι   it is possible

ἤδη (adv.)   already

βούλομαι   wish

πολύς, πολλή, πολύ   much, many

ἔχθρα, -ας, ἡ   personal hatred

ἀποκτείνω   kill, put to death

χρῆμα, -ατος, τό (pl.)   money, wealth

OBSERVATIONS, STRATEGIES, AND NOTES

1. This sentence can be translated easily in the order in which it is written.

2. What construction is τούτων δὲ γενομένων? What tense is γενομένων? Why?

3. ὡς ἐξὸν: The participle of an impersonal verb may be used in the accusative singular neuter in an accusative absolute (R6.6; S2076). Since the participle is formed from an impersonal verb, it also takes an infinitive to complete its meaning. Remember that ἔξεστι may take either an accusative or a dative of person. Here it is taking the dative αὐτοῖς. Note that Xenophon uses ὡς before the accusative absolute to indicate the reasoning behind the Thirty's actions without implying that he accepts this reasoning (S2086, 2086d). By including the particle ὡς, Xenophon is questioning the behavior of the Thirty.

4. ὅ τι βούλοιντο: This is a conditional relative clause introduced by the indefinite relative pronoun ὅ τι. When the antecedent is unspecified or unknown, the relative clause has a conditional force and takes a form similar to a condition (R11.2; S2505b, 2506, 2560). These clauses are also called indefinite relative clauses.

5. Note the μὲν … δέ construction in πολλοὺς μὲν … πολλοὺς δέ.

6. ἀπέκτεινον: The imperfect tense often indicates the beginning of an action (S1900). You may translate ἀπέκτεινον as "they began to kill."

7. Supply ἕνεκα with χρημάτων, which is parallel to ἔχθρας.

TRANSLATION

After these things had happened, in the belief that it was now possible for them to do whatever they wished, they began to kill many on account of personal hatred <and> many <on account of> their wealth.

SENTENCE TWO

ἔδοξε δ' αὐτοῖς, ὅπως ἔχοιεν καὶ τοῖς φρουροῖς χρήματα διδόναι, καὶ τῶν μετοίκων ἕνα ἕκαστον λαβεῖν, καὶ αὐτοὺς μὲν ἀποκτεῖναι, τὰ δὲ χρήματα αὐτῶν ἀποσημήνασθαι.

VOCABULARY

ὅπως (conj.)   in order that, so that

ἔχω (+ inf.)   be able to

φρουρός, -οῦ, ὁ   guard

χρῆμα, -ατος, τό (pl.)   property, money

δίδωμι   give

μέτοικος, -ου, ὁ   metic, resident alien

εἷς, μία, ἕν   one

ἕκαστος, -η, -ον   each

λαμβάνω   take, seize, apprehend

ἀποσημαίνω (mid.)   confiscate

OBSERVATIONS, STRATEGIES, AND NOTES

1. Remember that impersonal expressions such as ἔδοξε δ' αὐτοῖς take infinitives. Here, λαβεῖν, ἀποκτεῖναι, and ἀποσημήνασθαι go with ἔδοξε. ἔδοξε δ' αὐτοῖς would be translated literally as "it seemed best to them," but you may translate it as "they decided."

2. ὅπως ἔχοιεν: A purpose clause is introduced by ἵνα, ὅπως, or ὡς (R9.1). Why is ἔχοιεν in the optative mood?

3. καὶ τοῖς φρουροῖς: καὶ is adverbial. Translate it as "too" or "as well." Recall that the Thirty had promised to pay for the garrison.

4. Take ἕνα with the partitive genitive τῶν μετοίκων. ἕκαστον refers to the members of the Thirty and is the subject accusative of the infinitives λαβεῖν, ἀποκτεῖναι, and ἀποσημήνασθαι. What is the grammatical function of ἕνα?

5. What is the tense of the infinitives λαβεῖν, ἀποκτεῖναι, and ἀποσημήνασθαι? What is the significance of this tense?

6. Xenophon has moved from the singular ἕνα to the plurals αὐτοὺς and αὐτῶν. This happens in English as well. In order for the English translation to make sense, use the singular throughout.

TRANSLATION

And it seemed best to them, in order that they would be able to give money to the garrison too, that each <member of the Thirty> take one of the metics and kill him and confiscate his money.

SENTENCE THREE

ἐκέλευον δὲ καὶ τὸν Θηραμένην λαβεῖν ὅντινα βούλοιτο.

VOCABULARY

κελεύω   order

λαμβάνω   take, seize, apprehend

ὅστις, ἥτις, ὅ τι   whoever, whatever, whichever

βούλομαι   wish

OBSERVATIONS, STRATEGIES, AND NOTES

1. Remember that verbs of ordering take an accusative/infinitive construction (R5.1).
2. What is the function of καὶ?
3. What construction is ὅντινα βούλοιτο?

TRANSLATION

And they ordered even Theramenes to seize whomever he wished.

POLISHED TRANSLATION

After these things had happened, because it was now possible for them to do whatever they wished, they began to kill many on account of personal hatred and many for their wealth. And they decided, so that they would be able to pay for the garrison as well, that each member of the Thirty should apprehend one of the metics and then kill him and confiscate his money. And they ordered even Theramenes to seize whomever he wished.

Reading Selection

Theramenes responds to the order of the Thirty, who then begin to plot against him. When the Council is convened, Critias delivers a speech against Theramenes urging his execution. While speeches are often more difficult to translate than the narrative, they are an important part of the Greek historian's methodology. They help provide a fuller picture of the event and its participants and make the account livelier. Scholars have generally assumed that historians composed these speeches themselves on the basis of speeches that were delivered orally at the time of the event. The written version of such a speech is not considered to be a verbatim record and may include points that the historian thought were appropriate even though they were not present when the speech was given orally. Often the historian included in a speech his own interpretation of an event or participants' motivations, thus creating the artifice that the interpretation is the speaker's rather than his own. In addition, in some instances it is likely that the historian composed a speech that was never given or for which he could not have had reliable evidence concerning its contents. This is particularly true for many of the speeches in the work of the Greek historian Herodotus.

ὁ δ᾽ ἀπεκρίνατο· Ἀλλ᾽ οὐ δοκεῖ μοι, ἔφη, καλὸν εἶναι φάσκοντας βελτίστους εἶναι
ἀδικώτερα τῶν συκοφαντῶν ποιεῖν. ἐκεῖνοι μὲν γὰρ παρ᾽ ὧν χρήματα λαμβάνοιεν
ζῆν εἴων, ἡμεῖς δὲ ἀποκτενοῦμεν μηδὲν ἀδικοῦντας, ἵνα χρήματα λαμβάνωμεν;
πῶς οὐ ταῦτα τῷ παντὶ ἐκείνων ἀδικώτερα; οἱ δ᾽ ἐμποδὼν νομίζοντες αὐτὸν εἶναι
τῷ ποιεῖν ὅ τι βούλοιντο, ἐπιβουλεύουσιν αὐτῷ, καὶ ἰδίᾳ πρὸς τοὺς βουλευτὰς
ἄλλος πρὸς ἄλλον διέβαλλον ὡς λυμαινόμενον τὴν πολιτείαν. καὶ παραγγείλαντες
νεανίσκοις οἳ ἐδόκουν αὐτοῖς θρασύτατοι εἶναι ξιφίδια ὑπὸ μάλης ἔχοντας
παραγενέσθαι, συνέλεξαν τὴν βουλήν. ἐπεὶ δὲ ὁ Θηραμένης παρῆν, ἀναστὰς ὁ

5

Κριτίας ἔλεξεν ὧδε. Ὦ ἄνδρες βουλευταί, εἰ μέν τις ὑμῶν νομίζει πλείους τοῦ
καιροῦ ἀποθνήσκειν, ἐννοησάτω ὅτι ὅπου πολιτεῖαι μεθίστανται πανταχοῦ   10
ταῦτα γίγνεται· πλείστους δὲ ἀνάγκη ἐνθάδε πολεμίους εἶναι τοῖς εἰς ὀλιγαρχίαν
μεθιστᾶσι διά τε τὸ πολυανθρωποτάτην τῶν Ἑλληνίδων τὴν πόλιν εἶναι καὶ διὰ τὸ
πλεῖστον χρόνον ἐν ἐλευθερίᾳ τὸν δῆμον τεθράφθαι.

Xenophon, *Hellenica* 2.3.22–24

NOTES

1. [Line 1] ὁ δ' indicates a change of subject from the previous sentence and refers to
   Theramenes. Note the capital letter in Ἀλλ', indicating a direct quotation.

2. [Line 1] οὐ δοκεῖ μοι, ἔφη, καλὸν εἶναι: There are two impersonal constructions here:
   δοκεῖ μοι and καλὸν εἶναι. Translate them as "'It does not seem to me,' he said, 'to be
   a good idea.'" καλὸν εἶναι, in turn, introduces an accusative/infinitive construction,
   with the subject accusative ἡμᾶς supplied by context to go with the infinitive ποιεῖν.
   The basic structure here is καλὸν εἶναι <ἡμᾶς> ποιεῖν ἀδικώτερα.

3. [Line 1] φάσκοντας is a circumstantial participle modifying ἡμᾶς, the supplied subject accusative of ποιεῖν. Because it is a verb of speaking, it introduces the indirect
   statement βελτίστους εἶναι. Translate φάσκοντας as "while claiming" to express the
   contrast between the Thirty's words and their actual deeds.

4. [Line 2] What is the function of τῶν συκοφαντῶν?

5. [Lines 2–3] ἐκεῖνοι refers to the sycophants. Note the explanatory γάρ as well as μὲν
   . . . δέ in ἐκεῖνοι μὲν . . . ἡμεῖς δὲ.

6. [Line 2] παρ' ὧν χρήματα λαμβάνοιεν: Since the precise identification of the victims
   of the sycophants is unknown, this relative clause has been cast as a conditional relative clause (R11.2; S2505b, 2506, 2560). As previously noted, relative clauses with
   unknown or unspecified antecedents have a conditional force and take constructions analogous to conditions. The indefinite relative pronoun is usually used in such
   an instance, but the simple relative is also permitted (S2508). Here we have εἴων, an
   imperfect indicative, in the main clause and an optative in the relative clause. This is
   analogous to a past general condition, which has εἰ plus the optative in the protasis
   and an imperfect indicative in the apodosis (R10.3; S2568). The repetitive nature of
   the activity on the part of the sycophants makes a formulation similar to a past general condition appropriate.

7. [Line 3] εἴων: This verb takes an accusative/infinitive construction, but you will
   need to supply a subject accusative to go with the infinitive ζῆν. The accusative has
   dropped out because it was a demonstrative pronoun that was also acting as the
   antecedent of ὧν (S2509). You may supply "those men" as the subject of ζῆν.

8. [Line 3] The inclusion of the personal pronoun ἡμεῖς gives particular emphasis to
   this question.

9. [Line 3] What is the tense of ἀποκτενοῦμεν? You need to supply ἐκείνους, which is
   implied by ἀδικοῦντας.

10. [Line 3] What form is λαμβάνωμεν and why?

11. [Line 4] τῷ παντὶ: Translate this as "entirely" or "altogether."

12. [Line 4] What type of genitive is ἐκείνων?

13. [Line 4] οἱ δ᾽: This indicates a change of the subject back to the rest of the Thirty.

14. [Line 4] Take ἐμποδὼν with εἶναι to mean "to be in the way" or "to be a hindrance." This idiomatic expression takes a dative to indicate what someone is hindering. What dative goes with this expression?

15. [Line 4] What type of construction is νομίζοντες introducing?

16. [Line 5] What construction is ὅ τι βούλοιντο?

17. [Line 6] ἄλλος πρὸς ἄλλον: When two different forms of ἄλλος are used together, the second part of the expression does not need to be included (S1274). So here, the literal sense is something like "one slandered <him> to one man, another slandered <him> to another man." You will need to be creative in your translation to capture the sense while still presenting the idea in clear idiomatic English. Supply αὐτόν, referring to Theramenes, as the object of διέβαλλον.

18. [Line 6] ὡς λυμαινόμενον: This refers to Theramenes. ὡς with the participle imparts a sense of alleged cause and may be translated "on the grounds that" (S2086).

19. [Line 6] What type of participle is παραγγείλαντες and what is its tense?

20. [Line 7] ξιφίδια ὑπὸ μάλης ἔχοντας: The participle of ἔχω is often used to mean "with" (S2068a). Literally, this is translated as "having daggers under their armpit(s)," but you may render it "with daggers under their armpits."

21. [Line 9] What form is πλείους? What is its function?

22. [Lines 9–10] τοῦ καιροῦ: Translate this as "than is right."

23. [Line 10] ἐννοησάτω: What form is this? It refers back to τις. The clause ὅτι ὅπου πολιτεῖαι μεθίστανται πανταχοῦ ταῦτα γίγνεται acts as an object clause with ἐννοησάτω and is itself composed of two clauses: ὅπου πολιτεῖαι μεθίστανται and πανταχοῦ ταῦτα γίγνεται.

24. [Line 11] ἀνάγκη: Supply ἐστι. This impersonal construction takes the accusative/infinitive construction: πλείστους . . . πολεμίους εἶναι.

25. [Lines 11–12] τοῖς εἰς ὀλιγαρχίαν μεθιστᾶσι: How is τοῖς functioning? What form is μεθιστᾶσι? Notice that the definite article and the participle frame the prepositional phrase εἰς ὀλιγαρχίαν. Take these words together as a unit.

26. [Lines 12–13] διά τε τὸ πολυανθρωποτάτην τῶν Ἑλληνίδων τὴν πόλιν εἶναι καὶ διὰ τὸ πλεῖστον χρόνον ἐν ἐλευθερίᾳ τὸν δῆμον τεθράφθαι: Notice the construction τε . . . καί, the repetition of διά, and that διά is followed in both instances by the definite article in the accusative singular neuter. This should lead you to suspect that parallel construction is being used here. Recalling that definite articles are not used alone in Attic prose, determine what two words should be taken with these two instances of τό. What is the appropriate grammatical label for this usage?

27. [Lines 12–13] What are the subjects of εἶναι and τεθράφθαι? What form is τεθράφθαι?

28. [Line 13] πλεῖστον χρόνον: What type of time expression is this?

Reading Ten

Xenophon, *Hellenica* 2.3.25–28

Focus on Reading

This passage is a continuation of Critias's speech about Theramenes before the Thirty and the Athenian Council.

> ἡμεῖς δὲ γνόντες μὲν τοῖς οἵοις ἡμῖν τε καὶ ὑμῖν χαλεπὴν πολιτείαν εἶναι
> δημοκρατίαν, γνόντες δὲ ὅτι Λακεδαιμονίοις τοῖς περισώσασιν ἡμᾶς ὁ μὲν δῆμος
> οὔποτ' ἂν φίλος γένοιτο, οἱ δὲ βέλτιστοι ἀεὶ ἂν πιστοὶ διατελοῖεν, διὰ ταῦτα σὺν
> τῇ Λακεδαιμονίων γνώμῃ τήνδε τὴν πολιτείαν καθίσταμεν.
>
> Xenophon, Hellenica 2.3.25

Despite its length, this sentence may be treated without division into sections.

VOCABULARY

γιγνώσκω judge, believe, know	φίλος, -η, -ον friendly
οἷος, -α, -ον of such a sort as, such as	βέλτιστος, -η, -ον (sup. adj.) best
χαλεπός, -ή, -όν difficult	πιστός, -ή, -όν faithful, loyal
πολιτεία, -ας, ἡ government	διατελέω continue
περισώζω save	γνώμη, -ης, ἡ approval
δῆμος, -ου, ὁ people	καθίστημι establish
οὔποτε (adv.) never	

OBSERVATIONS, STRATEGIES, AND NOTES

1. ἡμεῖς δὲ γνόντες μὲν . . . δημοκρατίαν: The order for translation is ἡμεῖς δὲ γνόντες μὲν δημοκρατίαν εἶναι χαλεπὴν πολιτείαν τοῖς οἵοις ἡμῖν τε καὶ ὑμῖν.

2. γνόντες μὲν . . . . γνόντες δὲ: Notice the μὲν . . . δέ construction with γνόντες. Observe that two different constructions of indirect statement are being used here with

γνόντες. When a form of γιγνώσκω is used with the accusative/infinitive construction of indirect statement, it has the sense of "judge" or "believe," whereas when used with the ὅτι/ὡς construction (S2129) it means "know." What form is γνόντες?

3. τοῖς οἵοις ἡμῖν τε καὶ ὑμῖν: οἷος is a relative pronoun and is frequently used with a nominative and a linking verb in the relative clause. Both the relative pronoun οἷος and the nominative that goes with it are often attracted into the case of the antecedent. The antecedent and the linking verb of the relative clause then drop out. In addition, it is not uncommon for the definite article to be used with the form of οἷος (S2532, 2532b). Take these datives with χαλεπὴν.

> full version: (*to those such as we and you are*)
>
> τούτοις οἷοι ἡμεῖς τε καὶ ὑμεῖς ἐσμεν
>
> | | |
>
> ~~τούτοις~~ οἷοι ἡμεῖς τε καὶ ὑμεῖς ~~ἐσμεν~~
>
> | | |
>
> succinct version: τοῖς οἵοις ἡμῖν τε καὶ ὑμῖν
>
> (*for those such as you and us*)

4. γνόντες δὲ ὅτι Λακεδαιμονίοις . . . φίλος γένοιτο: The order for translation is γνόντες δὲ ὅτι ὁ μὲν δῆμος οὔποτ᾽ γένοιτο ἂν φίλος Λακεδαιμονίοις τοῖς περισώσασιν ἡμᾶς. Remember that φίλος may take a dative.

5. Note that τοῖς indicates that the participle περισώσασιν is being used as a noun (R6.1). What tense is περισώσασιν? Why? What is the function of ἡμᾶς?

6. Notice the μὲν . . . δέ construction in ὁ μὲν δῆμος . . . οἱ δὲ βέλτιστοι. Both clauses are part of the ὅτι/ὡς construction of the indirect statement.

7. ἂν . . . γένοιτο: It is important to note the use of ἄν, for it indicates that the optative γένοιτο is a potential optative (R8.5) rather than an optative found in a ὅτι/ὡς construction of indirect statement after a secondary main verb (R7.3).

8. What form is διατελοῖεν? Why? Supply "to be" with διατελοῖεν and take πιστοὶ with it as well. In Greek, "to be" would be rendered as a participle because verbs of continuing take a supplementary participle (R6.4, no. 2; S2097). It is always possible in Greek to omit a form of the verb "to be" when it may be supplied by logic and context.

9. διὰ ταῦτα: This refers to sentiments in the indirect statement.

10. Notice that Λακεδαιμονίων is in the attributive position and thus modifies τῇ γνώμῃ.

TRANSLATION

"But we, because we believe that democracy is a difficult form of government for men such as you and us, and because we know that the people would never be friendly to the Lacedaemonians who saved us, whereas the best men would always continue to be loyal, on account of these things with the approval of the Lacedaemonians are establishing this constitution."

POLISHED TRANSLATION

"We believe that democracy is a difficult form of government for men like you and us. We also recognize that the people would never be friendly to the Lacedaemonians who saved us, whereas the aristocrats would always continue to be loyal. As a consequence, we are establishing this constitution with the approval of the Lacedaemonians."

Reading Selection

Critias continues speaking.

καὶ ἐάν τινα αἰσθανώμεθα ἐναντίον τῇ ὀλιγαρχίᾳ, ὅσον δυνάμεθα ἐκποδὼν
ποιούμεθα· πολὺ δὲ μάλιστα δοκεῖ ἡμῖν δίκαιον εἶναι, εἴ τις ἡμῶν αὐτῶν
λυμαίνεται ταύτῃ τῇ καταστάσει, δίκην αὐτὸν διδόναι. νῦν οὖν αἰσθανόμεθα
Θηραμένην τουτονὶ οἷς δύναται ἀπολλύντα ἡμᾶς τε καὶ ὑμᾶς. ὡς δὲ ταῦτα ἀληθῆ,
ἂν κατανοῆτε, εὑρήσετε οὔτε ψέγοντα οὐδένα μᾶλλον Θηραμένους τουτουὶ   5
τὰ παρόντα οὔτε ἐναντιούμενον, ὅταν τινὰ ἐκποδὼν βουλώμεθα ποιήσασθαι
τῶν δημαγωγῶν. εἰ μὲν τοίνυν ἐξ ἀρχῆς ταῦτα ἐγίγνωσκε, πολέμιος μὲν ἦν,
οὐ μέντοι πονηρός γ᾽ ἂν δικαίως ἐνομίζετο· νῦν δὲ αὐτὸς μὲν ἄρξας τῆς πρὸς
Λακεδαιμονίους πίστεως καὶ φιλίας, αὐτὸς δὲ τῆς τοῦ δήμου καταλύσεως,
μάλιστα δὲ ἐξορμήσας ὑμᾶς τοῖς πρώτοις ὑπαγομένοις εἰς ὑμᾶς δίκην ἐπιτιθέναι,   10
νῦν ἐπεὶ καὶ ὑμεῖς καὶ ἡμεῖς φανερῶς ἐχθροὶ τῷ δήμῳ γεγενήμεθα, οὐκέτ᾽ αὐτῷ
τὰ γιγνόμενα ἀρέσκει, ὅπως αὐτὸς μὲν αὖ ἐν τῷ ἀσφαλεῖ καταστῇ, ἡμεῖς δὲ δίκην
δῶμεν τῶν πεπραγμένων.

Xenophon, Hellenica 2.3.26–28

NOTES

1. [Lines 1–2] ἐάν τινα αἰσθανώμεθα . . . ἐκποδὼν ποιούμεθα: What type of condition is this?

2. [Line 1] ὅσον δυνάμεθα: Treat this separately and translate it as "as much as we can" or "so far as we can."

3. [Line 2] πολὺ δὲ μάλιστα: πολύ strengthens or emphasizes the superlative μάλιστα. Translate it as "especially" or "particularly" and take it with δίκαιον.

4. [Line 3] δίκην αὐτὸν διδόναι: Take this with the impersonal expression δίκαιον εἶναι. αὐτὸν is the subject accusative of διδόναι.

5. [Line 4] τουτονὶ is an emphatic form of τοῦτον meaning "this man here."

6. [Line 4] οἷς δύναται: Translate this as "by whatever means he can."

7. [Line 4] ἀπολλύντα: What form is this? What is its syntax?

8. [Line 4] ὡς δὲ ταῦτα ἀληθῆ: Translate ὡς as "as proof that" and supply ἐστι (S2586).

9. [Line 5] ἂν κατανοῆτε, εὑρήσετε: ἂν is another form of ἐάν. What type of condition is this?

10. [Line 5] What type of construction is εὑρήσετε introducing? What is the clue word?

11. [Line 5] Θηραμένους τουτουὶ: Another intensive form. Cf. note 5, above.

12. [Line 6] τὰ παρόντα: Translate this as "the present proceedings" or "the present undertakings." What form is παρόντα?

13. [Lines 6–7] What type of subordinate clause is ὅταν τινὰ ἐκποδὼν βουλώμεθα ποιήσασθαι τῶν δημαγωγῶν? What form is βουλώμεθα? Why?

14. [Lines 6–7] Take τινὰ with τῶν δημαγωγῶν. What type of genitive is τῶν δημαγωγῶν?

15. [Line 7] What type of condition is εἰ μὲν τοίνυν ἐξ ἀρχῆς ταῦτα ἐγίγνωσκε, πολέμιος μὲν ἦν?

16. [Line 8] οὐ μέντοι πονηρός γ᾽ ἂν δικαίως ἐνομίζετο: This clause is actually a second apodosis to εἰ μὲν τοίνυν ἐξ ἀρχῆς ταῦτα ἐγίγνωσκε, and now the condition changes type. What type of condition is it now? What is its "formula"?

17. [Lines 8–9] Note αὐτὸς μὲν . . . αὐτὸς δὲ. This is not so much a contrast as two facets of the same behavior on the part of Theramenes.

18. [Line 9] Supply ἄρξας with αὐτὸς δὲ τῆς τοῦ δήμου καταλύσεως. This phrase is in parallel construction with αὐτὸς μὲν ἄρξας τῆς πρὸς Λακεδαιμονίους πίστεως καὶ φιλίας. What form is ἄρξας? It will make most sense to render it concessively.

19. [Line 10] μάλιστα δὲ ἐξορμήσας ὑμᾶς τοῖς πρώτοις ὑπαγομένοις εἰς ὑμᾶς δίκην ἐπιτιθέναι: The order for translation is μάλιστα δὲ ἐξορμήσας ὑμᾶς ἐπιτιθέναι δίκην τοῖς πρώτοις ὑπαγομένοις εἰς ὑμᾶς. ἐπιτιθέναι δίκην means "to inflict a penalty upon" and takes a dative.

20. [Line 10] ἐξορμήσας should also be taken concessively. What form is it?

21. [Line 11] What form is γεγενήμεθα? What nuance does its tense impart?

22. [Lines 11–12] οὐκέτ᾽ αὐτῷ τὰ γιγνόμενα ἀρέσκει: Notice that this sentence began with αὐτός as the subject of the main clause but now τὰ γιγνόμενα is the subject. This is another example of anacoluthon (S3004), or grammatical inconsistency.

23. [Line 12] τὰ γιγνόμενα: Translate this as "the events" or "what is happening." What form is γιγνόμενα?

24. [Line 12] Note the μὲν . . . δέ construction in αὐτὸς μὲν . . . ἡμεῖς δὲ.

25. [Lines 12–13] What forms are καταστῇ and δῶμεν? Why?

26. [Line 13] What type of genitive is τῶν πεπραγμένων?

Reading Eleven

Xenophon, *Hellenica* 2.3.29–31

Focus on Reading

Critias continues his denunciation of Theramenes.

ὥστε οὐ μόνον ὡς ἐχθρῷ αὐτῷ προσήκει ἀλλὰ καὶ ὡς προδότῃ ὑμῶν τε καὶ
ἡμῶν διδόναι τὴν δίκην. καίτοι τοσούτῳ μὲν δεινότερον προδοσία πολέμου,
ὅσῳ χαλεπώτερον φυλάξασθαι τὸ ἀφανὲς τοῦ φανεροῦ, τοσούτῳ δ᾽ ἔχθιον, ὅσῳ
πολεμίοις μὲν ἄνθρωποι καὶ σπένδονται καὶ αὖθις πιστοὶ γίγνονται, ὃν δ᾽ ἂν
προδιδόντα λαμβάνωσι, τούτῳ οὔτε ἐσπείσατο πώποτε οὐδεὶς οὔτ᾽ ἐπίστευσε τοῦ
λοιποῦ.

Xenophon, Hellenica 2.3.29

SENTENCE ONE

ὥστε οὐ μόνον ὡς ἐχθρῷ αὐτῷ προσήκει ἀλλὰ καὶ ὡς προδότῃ ὑμῶν τε καὶ ἡμῶν
διδόναι τὴν δίκην.

VOCABULARY

ὡς (rel. adv.) as	προδότης, -ου, ὁ traitor, betrayer
ἐχθρός, -ά, -όν enemy (as subst.)	διδόναι τὴν δίκην be punished
προσήκει (impers. verb) it is fitting	

OBSERVATIONS, STRATEGIES, AND NOTES

1. ὥστε may be used at the beginning of a sentence to indicate a strong conclusion or consequence and is translated as "therefore" or "and so" (S2274a).
2. Note οὐ μόνον . . . ἀλλὰ καὶ and translate it as "not only . . . but also."

3. ὡς ἐχθρῷ ... ὡς προδότῃ: The repetition of ὡς indicates that these two datives are being used in the same manner. To what word in the sentence do these words refer?

4. προσήκει: Like many impersonal verbs, προσήκει takes a dative plus infinitive construction. The order for translation is ὥστε προσήκει αὐτῷ διδόναι τὴν δίκην οὐ μόνον ὡς ἐχθρῷ ἀλλὰ καὶ ὡς προδότῃ ὑμῶν τε καὶ ἡμῶν.

5. ὑμῶν τε καὶ ἡμῖν: Remember that τε is postpositive. τε καὶ makes a nice joining of ὑμῶν and ἡμῶν. Critias is referring to both the Thirty and the Council to which he is speaking.

TRANSLATION

"Therefore it is fitting for him to be punished not only as an enemy but also as a traitor of you and us."

SENTENCE TWO

καίτοι τοσούτῳ μὲν δεινότερον προδοσία πολέμου, ὅσῳ χαλεπώτερον φυλάξασθαι τὸ ἀφανὲς τοῦ φανεροῦ, τοσούτῳ δ᾽ ἔχθιον, ὅσῳ πολεμίοις μὲν ἄνθρωποι καὶ σπένδονται καὶ αὖθις πιστοὶ γίγνονται, ὃν δ᾽ ἂν προδιδόντα λαμβάνωσι, τούτῳ οὔτε ἐσπείσατο πώποτε οὐδεὶς οὔτ᾽ ἐπίστευσε τοῦ λοιποῦ.

VOCABULARY

καίτοι (particle)   and indeed, and further
τοσούτῳ   by so much
δεινός, -ή, -όν   terrible
προδοσία, -ας, ἡ   treason
ὅσῳ   as much as, in proportion as
χαλεπός, -ή, -όν   difficult
φυλάττω   guard against
ἀφανής, -ές   invisible
φανερός, -ά, -όν   visible

ἐχθίων, -ον   more hateful (comp. of ἐχθρός)
σπένδω   make a treaty or truce
αὖθις (adv.)   again
πιστός, -ή, -όν   trustworthy
προδίδωμι   betray, be a traitor
πώποτε (adv.)   ever
τοῦ λοιποῦ   in the future

OBSERVATIONS, STRATEGIES, AND NOTES

1. This sentence is quite difficult to put into smooth English because of the use of τοσούτῳ ... ὅσῳ ... τοσούτῳ ... ὅσῳ. We will have to be rather flexible in our polished translation as a consequence. This is a somewhat complex example of a comparative sentence (S2468) that is also using parallel construction. τοσούτῳ and ὅσῳ are datives of degree of difference (R3.3.8).

2. καίτοι τοσούτῳ μὲν δεινότερον προδοσία πολέμου: The verb is missing in this clause, and because we have two nominatives, δεινότερον and προδοσία, it is reasonable to suspect that a form of "be" has been omitted. You will need to supply ἐστι.

3. δεινότερον: This is a nominative singular neuter comparative adjective that is being used as a predicate nominative modifying προδοσία. Translate it as "a more terrible thing."

4. What type of genitive is πολέμου? The comparative δεινότερον provides the clue.

5. ὅσῳ χαλεπώτερον φυλάξασθαι τὸ ἀφανὲς τοῦ φανεροῦ: This is a similar (though not identical) construction to καίτοι τοσούτῳ μὲν δεινότερον προδοσία πολέμου. Note the lack of a finite verb. You will need to supply ἐστι; τὸ ἀφανὲς is the subject of ἐστι.

6. χαλεπώτερον: This is a nominative singular neuter comparative adjective. Translate it as "more difficult."

7. φυλάξασθαι: An infinitive is often used with an adjective to indicate the respect to which or in what way the adjective is true (R5.4; S2001). Here φυλάξασθαι is used with χαλεπώτερον.

8. τοῦ φανεροῦ: Again, a comparative provides the clue to the use of the genitive.

9. τοσούτῳ δ' ἔχθιον: You will need to supply προδοσία πολέμου and ἐστι. The construction is the same as that in note 2, above. Translate ἔχθιον as "a more hateful thing."

10. ὅσῳ πολεμίοις μὲν ἄνθρωποι: The neat parallel construction breaks down here, and a different construction is used. It is important to note the use of μὲν . . . δέ (δ') in ὅσῳ πολεμίοις μὲν ἄνθρωποι . . . ὃν δ' ἂν προδιδόντα, as two actions are being contrasted: how one might treat an enemy as compared to how one treats a traitor.

11. ὅσῳ πολεμίοις μὲν ἄνθρωποι καὶ σπένδονται καὶ αὖθις πιστοὶ γίγνονται: This clause indicates how men can become reconciled with their enemies. Note the use of καὶ . . . καί joining the two verbs σπένδονται and γίγνονται.

12. ὃν δ' ἂν προδιδόντα λαμβάνωσι: It is important to note ἂν and λαμβάνωσι, for they reveal that this is a conditional relative clause corresponding to the protasis of a present general condition (R11.2; S2567). Translate it as "whomever they catch being a traitor."

13. τούτῳ: Sometimes the antecedent of a relative pronoun is placed after, rather than before, the relative pronoun. Here, ὃν refers to τούτῳ.

14. οὔτε ἐσπείσατο . . . οὔτ' ἐπίστευσε: These verbs are gnomic aorists. A gnomic aorist expresses a general truth and is considered a primary tense (hence the subjunctive λαμβάνωσι). It is usually translated in the present tense (S1931).

TRANSLATION

"And indeed treason is a more terrible thing than war by so much, as much as the invisible is more difficult to guard against than the visible, and treason is a more hateful thing than war by so much, as much as, whereas men both make a truce with their enemies and become trustworthy again, whomever they catch being a traitor, no one ever makes a truce with this one or trusts him in the future."

POLISHED TRANSLATION

"Therefore it is fitting for him to be punished not only as an enemy but also as a traitor to you and to us. And indeed, treason is so much more a terrible thing than war, just as the invisible is more difficult to guard against than the visible. Treason is also a much more hateful thing than war because men make a truce with their enemies and become trustworthy to one another again, but if they catch someone being a traitor, no one ever makes a truce with this man or trusts him in the future."

Reading Selection

Critias furthers his criticism against Theramenes.

ἵνα δὲ εἰδῆτε ὅτι οὐ καινὰ ταῦτα οὗτος ποιεῖ, ἀλλὰ φύσει προδότης ἐστίν,
ἀναμνήσω ὑμᾶς τὰ τούτῳ πεπραγμένα. οὗτος γὰρ ἐξ ἀρχῆς μὲν τιμώμενος ὑπὸ
τοῦ δήμου κατὰ τὸν πατέρα Ἅγνωνα, προπετέστατος ἐγένετο τὴν δημοκρατίαν
μεταστῆσαι εἰς τοὺς τετρακοσίους, καὶ ἐπρώτευεν ἐν ἐκείνοις. ἐπεὶ δ' ᾔσθετο
ἀντίπαλόν τι τῇ ὀλιγαρχίᾳ συνιστάμενον, πρῶτος αὖ ἡγεμὼν τῷ δήμῳ ἐπ'   5
ἐκείνους ἐγένετο· ὅθεν δήπου καὶ κόθορνος ἐπικαλεῖται. [καὶ γὰρ ὁ κόθορνος
ἁρμόττειν μὲν τοῖς ποσὶν ἀμφοτέροις δοκεῖ, ἀποβλέπει δὲ ἀπ' ἀμφοτέρων.] δεῖ
δέ, ὦ Θηράμενες, ἄνδρα τὸν ἄξιον ζῆν οὐ προάγειν μὲν δεινὸν εἶναι εἰς πράγματα
τοὺς συνόντας, ἂν δέ τι ἀντικόπτῃ, εὐθὺς μεταβάλλεσθαι, ἀλλ' ὥσπερ ἐν νηὶ
διαπονεῖσθαι, ἕως ἂν εἰς οὖρον καταστῶσιν· εἰ δὲ μή, πῶς ἂν ἀφίκοιντό ποτε ἔνθα   10
δεῖ, εἰ ἐπειδάν τι ἀντικόψῃ, εὐθὺς εἰς τἀναντία πλέοιεν;

Xenophon, *Hellenica* 2.3.30–31

NOTES

1. [Line 1] What form is εἰδῆτε and why? It is not uncommon for a subordinate clause to be placed first in a sentence; it receives more emphasis because of this placement. The main verb is ἀναμνήσω.

2. [Line 1] οὗτος refers to Theramenes.

3. [Line 1] φύσει: Translate this as "by nature."

4. [Line 2] ἀναμιμνήσκω (fut. ἀναμνήσω) takes a double accusative construction in which both the person reminded and the topic itself are in the accusative.

5. [Line 2] τὰ τούτῳ πεπραγμένα: Note that τούτῳ is framed by πεπραγμένα and the definite article τά. This indicates that τούτῳ should be taken with πεπραγμένα. What is the function of τούτῳ?

6. [Line 3] κατὰ τὸν πατέρα Ἅγνωνα: Translate this as "like his father, Hagnon."

7. [Line 3] What form is προπετέστατος? Translate it together with the infinitive μεταστῆσαι. As we have seen, an infinitive is used with an adjective to limit the meaning of that adjective (R5.4; S2001). What tense is μεταστῆσαι and why?

8. [Line 4] εἰς τοὺς τετρακοσίους: This is a reference to the Four Hundred, the short-lived oligarchy that ruled Athens in 411 B.C.E.

9. [Lines 4–5] ἐπεὶ δ' ᾔσθετο . . . συνιστάμενον: Recall that verbs of perception often take the participial construction of indirect statement (R7.2). Be sure to insert "that" after the verb of perception for a smooth English translation.

10. [Lines 5–6] πρῶτος αὖ . . . ἐγένετο: Translate this as "he was the first to become leader again for the people." Adjectives of time, place, and order of succession are usually used as predicate adjectives. In English, we would expect an adverb (S1042).

11. [Lines 5–6] ἐπ' ἐκείνους: Another reference to the Four Hundred.

12. [Line 6] κόθορνος: A κόθορνος was a boot that could be worn on either foot.

13. [Lines 6–7] [καὶ γὰρ ὁ κόθορνος . . . ἀπ' ἀμφοτέρων]: This sentence is considered by many commentators to be a later addition that was included as an explanation of the nickname. Theramenes is the subject of ἀποβλέπει.

14. [Lines 7–9] δεῖ takes an accusative/infinitive construction. The order for translation is δεῖ δέ, ὦ Θηράμενες, ἄνδρα τὸν ἄξιον ζῆν οὐ μὲν εἶναι δεινὸν προάγειν τοὺς συνόντας εἰς πράγματα.

15. [Line 8] ἄνδρα τὸν ἄξιον ζῆν and προάγειν δεινὸν εἶναι: The infinitive ζῆν limits the adjective ἄξιον while προάγειν limits δεινὸν. See note 7, above.

16. [Lines 8–9] It is important to note the μὲν . . . δέ construction in προάγειν μὲν δεινὸν . . . ἂν δέ τι ἀντικόπτῃ.

17. [Line 9] ἂν δέ τι ἀντικόπτῃ: ἂν is an Attic form for ἐάν. What form is ἀντικόπτῃ? Why?

18. [Line 9] μεταβάλλεσθαι: This is used in a fashion similar to προάγειν with οὐ . . . δεινὸν εἶναι.

19. [Line 10] διαπονεῖσθαι: Supply δεῖ . . . ἄνδρα τὸν ἄξιον ζῆν with διαπονεῖσθαι. This construction is parallel to δεῖ . . . ἄνδρα τὸν ἄξιον ζῆν οὐ . . . δεινὸν εἶναι.

20. [Line 10] What form is καταστῶσιν and why? Note the switch to the plural, referring to the sailors on the ship.

21. [Lines 10–11] πῶς ἂν ἀφίκοιτό . . . εἰς τἀναντία πλέοιεν: This sentence is a little more complicated grammatically than it seems at first. What we have here is a future less vivid condition (R10.4) with the apodosis, πῶς ἂν ἀφίκοιτό ποτε, framed as a question and expressed first, followed by the protasis, εἰ . . . εὐθὺς εἰς τἀναντία πλέοιεν. Included within each part of the condition is an additional subordinate clause. ἔνθα δεῖ is a relative clause introduced by the relative adverb ἔνθα, and ἐπειδάν τι ἀντικόψῃ is an indefinite temporal clause. Note that ἀντικόψῃ is in the subjunctive mood and ἐπειδάν is the result of the contraction of ἐπειδή and ἄν.

22. [Line 11] εἰς τἀναντία: Translate this as "in the opposite direction."

Reading Twelve

Xenophon, *Hellenica* 2.3.32–34

Focus on Reading

Critias criticizes Theramenes for his actions after the Battle of Arginusae.

καὶ εἰσὶ μὲν δήπου πᾶσαι μεταβολαὶ πολιτειῶν θανατηφόροι, σὺ δὲ διὰ τὸ εὐμετάβολος εἶναι πλείστοις μὲν μεταίτιος εἶ ἐξ ὀλιγαρχίας ὑπὸ τοῦ δήμου ἀπολωλέναι, πλείστοις δ᾽ ἐκ δημοκρατίας ὑπὸ τῶν βελτιόνων. οὗτος δέ τοί ἐστιν ὃς καὶ ταχθεὶς ἀνελέσθαι ὑπὸ τῶν στρατηγῶν τοὺς καταδύντας Ἀθηναίων ἐν τῇ περὶ Λέσβον ναυμαχίᾳ αὐτὸς οὐκ ἀνελόμενος ὅμως τῶν στρατηγῶν κατηγορῶν ἀπέκτεινεν αὐτούς, ἵνα αὐτὸς περισωθείη.

Xenophon, Hellenica 2.3.32

SENTENCE ONE

καὶ εἰσὶ μὲν δήπου πᾶσαι μεταβολαὶ πολιτειῶν θανατηφόροι, σὺ δὲ διὰ τὸ εὐμετάβολος εἶναι πλείστοις μὲν μεταίτιος εἶ ἐξ ὀλιγαρχίας ὑπὸ τοῦ δήμου ἀπολωλέναι, πλείστοις δ᾽ ἐκ δημοκρατίας ὑπὸ τῶν βελτιόνων.

VOCABULARY

δήπου (particle)   of course
μεταβολή, -ῆς, ἡ   transition, change
πολιτεία, -ας, ἡ   constitution
θανατηφόρος, -ον   death-bringing
εὐμετάβολος, -ον   easily changeable

πλεῖστος, -η, -ον (sup. adj.)   most
μεταίτιος, -ον   accessory to (+ dat./inf.)
ἀπόλλυμι (perfect)   die, perish utterly
βελτίων, -ον (comp. adj. of ἀγαθός)   better

OBSERVATIONS, STRATEGIES, AND NOTES

1. θανατηφόροι modifies μεταβολαὶ. Why do these endings not "match"? What is the function of θανατηφόροι?

2. When confronted with a difficult clause, it may help to try to see the "skeleton," or most essential elements, of the clause first. Try to do this *not* by hunting and pecking but by allowing the sentence clues to guide you as you read along. For example, the nominative form of the second person personal pronoun σύ will lead you to expect the verb to be in the second person singular, which εἶ is. This linking verb, in turn, should lead you to expect a predicate nominative or adjective, which we find in μεταίτιος: **σὺ** δὲ διὰ τὸ εὐμετάβολος εἶναι πλείστοις μὲν **μεταίτιος εἶ** ἐξ ὀλιγαρχίας ὑπὸ τοῦ δήμου ἀπολωλέναι.

3. διὰ τὸ εὐμετάβολος εἶναι: Note that the articular infinitive τὸ εἶναι is the object of the preposition διά. The framing of εὐμετάβολος by τὸ ... εἶναι indicates that εὐμετάβολος goes with the articular infinitive and is functioning as a predicate adjective. Because εὐμετάβολος is in the nominative case, we know that it is a predicate adjective modifying σὺ, the subject of this sentence. Translate this as "on account of being easily changeable."

4. πλείστοις μὲν μεταίτιος ... πλείστοις δ' ἐκ δημοκρατίας ὑπὸ τῶν βελτιόνων: Noticing the construction μὲν ... δέ (δ'), the repetition of πλείστοις, and the prepositional phrases will help you see the parallel structure in this part of the sentence. ἐξ ὀλιγαρχίας limits πλείστοις μὲν just as ἐκ δημοκρατίας limits πλείστοις δ'. Take πλείστοις with μεταίτιος, which takes a dative of person (πλείστοις) plus an infinitive (ἀπολωλέναι). Supply ἀπολωλέναι in the second part of the sentence: πλείστοις δ' ἐκ δημοκρατίας <ἀπολωλέναι> ὑπὸ τῶν βελτιόνων. Translate πλείστοις as "a very large number."

5. What tense is ἀπολωλέναι? Why?

6. ὑπὸ τῶν βελτιόνων: βελτιόνων refers to the aristocrats or those from the oligarchic group. Translate ὑπὸ here and in the phrase ὑπὸ τοῦ δήμου as "at the hands of."

TRANSLATION

"And of course, all changes of constitutions are death-bringing, but you, on account of being easily changeable, are accessory to a very large number from the oligarchy perishing at the hands of the people and a very large number from the democracy perishing at the hands of the better men."

SENTENCE TWO

οὗτος δέ τοί ἐστιν ὃς καὶ ταχθεὶς ἀνελέσθαι ὑπὸ τῶν στρατηγῶν τοὺς καταδύντας Ἀθηναίων ἐν τῇ περὶ Λέσβον ναυμαχίᾳ αὐτὸς οὐκ ἀνελόμενος ὅμως τῶν στρατηγῶν κατηγορῶν ἀπέκτεινεν αὐτούς, ἵνα αὐτὸς περισωθείη.

VOCABULARY

τοι (particle)   surely, in truth, mark you

τάττω   appoint, order (+ inf.)

ἀναιρέω (mid.)   retrieve (bodies for burial)

στρατηγός, -οῦ, ὁ   general

καταδύω   sink down, be shipwrecked

Λέσβος, -ου, ἡ   Lesbos (an island)

ναυμαχία, -ας, ἡ   naval battle

ὅμως (conj.)   nevertheless

κατηγορέω   charge, accuse

ἀποκτείνω   bring about someone's death

περισώζω   save, save from death

OBSERVATIONS, STRATEGIES, AND NOTES

1. This sentence, with several nominative participles, is packed with many details, and we will need to be somewhat flexible in the translation in order to render it smoothly. There are several ways to translate it correctly.

2. οὗτος refers to Theramenes and is the antecedent of the relative pronoun ὅς. τοι is a postpositive enclitic particle that is used to attract the attention of the person being addressed (S2985).

3. καί may be used as an adverb to emphasize the word that follows it (S2881) and may be translated as "also" or "as well."

4. ταχθεὶς . . . ὑπὸ τῶν στρατηγῶν: The genitive of personal agent (R3.2.3) is often found with a passive verb.

5. ἀνελέσθαι is a complementary infinitive with the participle ταχθεὶς. Remember that a participle, especially one in the aorist, is often translated as a temporal clause introduced by "after." What is the full identification of ταχθεὶς? What word is it modifying?

6. τοὺς καταδύντας: δύω has an irregular second aorist. This form, a substantive (as indicated by the definite article), is the accusative plural masculine aorist active participle of καταδύω and refers to the men who had drowned after the naval battle of Arginusae, which took place in 406 B.C.E. near the island of Lesbos. The Athenians were victorious, but a storm prevented them from retrieving either the survivors or the dead from disabled ships. Theramenes and Thrasybulus were the trierarchs (commanders of the triremes). The trierarchs and the generals blamed one another for this failure, and the generals were summoned back to Athens for trial. Six of the eight generals returned home and were brought to trial as a group rather than singly, as required by Athenian law. They were condemned and executed.

7. ἐν τῇ περὶ Λέσβον ναυμαχίᾳ: Note the insertion of one prepositional phrase, περὶ Λέσβον, within another prepositional phrase, ἐν τῇ . . . ναυμαχίᾳ. As a result of this word order, περὶ Λέσβον is in the attributive position (R2.1).

8. Recall that αὐτός has a number of uses. When it is in the attributive position, it means "same," whereas when it is in the predicate position or used all by itself in the nominative, it is an intensifier, meaning "-self." It is also used as the third person personal pronoun, when it appears all by itself in cases other than the nominative. How is it being used here?

9. οὐκ ἀνελόμενος: This circumstantial participle is best translated concessively as "although." What verb is this participle from?

10. τῶν στρατηγῶν κατηγορῶν: While most verbs of accusing and charging take the genitive to indicate the charge or accusation and the accusative to indicate the person being accused, κατηγορέω has the opposite construction, using the genitive to indicate the person being charged and the accusative to denote the actual charges. This is because of the prefix κατά (S1385).

11. αὐτούς refers to τῶν στρατηγῶν.

12. ἵνα αὐτὸς περισωθείη: What type of clause is this? What form is περισωθείη? Theramenes was, presumably, trying to avoid being charged in his capacity as trierarch for not picking up the survivors and the dead after the Battle of Arginusae by deflecting the responsibility onto the generals.

TRANSLATION

"And this man, in truth, is the one who, after he was ordered by the generals to retrieve those of the Athenians who had been shipwrecked in the sea battle near Lesbos, though he himself did not retrieve <them>, nevertheless, by bringing charges against the generals, brought about their deaths, so that he himself might be saved."

POLISHED TRANSLATION

"And of course, all constitutional changes bring death, but you, on account of being so ready to change sides, have shared responsibility for a very large number of oligarchs perishing at the hands of the people and a very large number of democrats perishing at the hands of the oligarchs. And this man, in truth, is the one who, after he was ordered by the generals to retrieve the Athenians who had been shipwrecked in the sea battle near Lesbos, did not retrieve them. Nevertheless, by bringing charges against the generals, he brought about their deaths so that he himself might be saved."

Reading Selection

Critias concludes his speech against Theramenes.

ὅστις γε μὴν φανερός ἐστι τοῦ μὲν πλεονεκτεῖν ἀεὶ ἐπιμελόμενος, τοῦ δὲ καλοῦ
καὶ τῶν φίλων μηδὲν ἐντρεπόμενος, πῶς τούτου χρή ποτε φείσασθαι; πῶς δὲ
οὐ φυλάξασθαι, εἰδότας αὐτοῦ τὰς μεταβολάς, ὡς μὴ καὶ ἡμᾶς ταὐτὸ δυνασθῇ
ποιῆσαι; ἡμεῖς οὖν τοῦτον ὑπάγομεν καὶ ὡς ἐπιβουλεύοντα καὶ ὡς προδιδόντα
ἡμᾶς τε καὶ ὑμᾶς. ὡς δ' εἰκότα ποιοῦμεν, καὶ τάδ' ἐννοήσατε. καλλίστη μὲν γὰρ   5
δήπου δοκεῖ πολιτεία εἶναι ἡ Λακεδαιμονίων· εἰ δὲ ἐκείνη ἐπιχειρήσειέ τις τῶν
ἐφόρων ἀντὶ τοῦ τοῖς πλείοσι πείθεσθαι ψέγειν τε τὴν ἀρχὴν καὶ ἐναντιοῦσθαι
τοῖς πραττομένοις, οὐκ ἂν οἴεσθε αὐτὸν καὶ ὑπ' αὐτῶν τῶν ἐφόρων καὶ ὑπὸ
τῆς ἄλλης ἁπάσης πόλεως τῆς μεγίστης τιμωρίας ἀξιωθῆναι; καὶ ὑμεῖς οὖν, ἐὰν
σωφρονῆτε, οὐ τούτου ἀλλ' ὑμῶν αὐτῶν φείσεσθε, ὡς οὗτος σωθεὶς μὲν πολλοὺς   10

ἂν μέγα φρονεῖν ποιήσειε τῶν ἐναντία γιγνωσκόντων ὑμῖν, ἀπολόμενος δὲ
πάντων καὶ τῶν ἐν τῇ πόλει καὶ τῶν ἔξω ὑποτέμοι ἂν τὰς ἐλπίδας.

Xenophon, *Hellenica* 2.3.33–34

NOTES

1. [Line 1] ὅστις . . . φανερός ἐστι . . . ἐπιμελόμενος: This personal construction takes
   what is categorized as a participial construction of indirect statement (S2107), but
   the participle acts more like a supplementary participle. Although this construction
   is often translated impersonally to follow English idiom ("it is clear that . . ."), here
   it will work best to translate it personally: "whoever is obviously always taking care
   to . . ."

2. [Line 1] γε μὴν: This is a frequent combination of particles in Xenophon and may be
   translated as "however."

3. [Lines 1–2] Note the construction μὲν . . . δέ in τοῦ μὲν πλεονεκτεῖν . . . τοῦ δὲ καλοῦ
   καὶ τῶν φίλων. The genitives go with the participles ἐπιμελόμενος and ἐντρεπόμενος in
   nice parallel construction. Take τοῦ καλοῦ to mean "what is noble" or "honor."

4. [Line 1] What is the function of τοῦ in τοῦ μὲν πλεονεκτεῖν?

5. [Line 2] μηδέν, the neuter accusative form of μηδείς, is often used as an adverb, as it
   is here. Translate it here as "not at all."

6. [Lines 2–3] πῶς δὲ οὐ φυλάξασθαι: Supply χρή from the previous clause. It is rare for
   Greek to repeat a word that is used in the same manner in two parallel clauses.

7. [Line 3] εἰδότας: Supply ἡμᾶς, which also acts as the subject accusative of
   φυλάξασθαι. What type of participle is εἰδότας?

8. [Line 3] αὐτοῦ: This refers to Theramenes.

9. [Lines 3–4] ὡς μὴ καὶ ἡμᾶς ταὐτὸ δυνασθῇ ποιῆσαι: The subject of δυνασθῇ is Theramenes. Remember that negative purpose clauses may be introduced by ἵνα μή, ὅπως
   μή, and ὡς μή (R9.1). ποιῆσαι takes a double accusative, meaning "to do something
   to someone."

10. [Line 3] ταὐτὸ: Notice the coronis indicating crasis (= τὸ αὐτό). Translate it as "the
    same thing."

11. [Line 4] ὡς ἐπιβουλεύοντα καὶ ὡς προδιδόντα: ὡς with the participle indicates al-
    leged cause (S2086). Translate it as "on the grounds that . . ."

12. [Line 5] ὡς δ᾽ εἰκότα ποιοῦμεν: Sometimes a dependent clause introduced by ὡς
    (or ὅτι) is loosely attached to the main clause and has the sense "as proof that . . ."
    (S2586).

13. [Line 5] καὶ τάδ᾽ ἐννοήσατε: καί has an adverbial sense here, meaning "too," "also,"
    "as well."

14. [Lines 5–6] καλλίστη μὲν: μέν is contrasted with δέ in εἰ δὲ ἐκείνη.

15. [Line 5] What is the function of καλλίστη?

16. [Line 6] δοκεῖ πολιτεία εἶναι ἡ Λακεδαιμονίων: Notice that the definite article ἡ puts
    Λακεδαιμονίων into the attributive position (R2.1).

17. [Lines 6–8] εἰ δὲ ἐκείνη ἐπιχειρήσειέ τις τῶν ἐφόρων . . . ψέγειν τε τὴν ἀρχὴν καὶ

ἐναντιοῦσθαι τοῖς πραττομένοις: The infinitives ψέγειν and ἐναντιοῦσθαι go with ἐπιχειρήσειέ.

18. [Line 6] ἐκείνῃ: This is used here as an adverb: "there" or "in that place."

19. [Line 7] ἀντὶ τοῦ τοῖς πλείοσι πείθεσθαι: Note the articular infinitive as the object of the preposition ἀντί. Note, as well, the framing of τοῖς πλείοσι by τοῦ and πείθεσθαι. This indicates that πλείοσι should be construed with πείθεσθαι. What form is πλείοσι?

20. [Lines 7–8] ψέγειν τε τὴν ἀρχὴν καὶ ἐναντιοῦσθαι τοῖς πραττομένοις: Remember that τε is postpositive and belongs in front of the word it follows. The τε . . . καί construction closely links the two infinitives.

21. [Line 8] τοῖς πραττομένοις: Translate this substantival use of the participle as "the things being done." How do you know that the participle should be taken as a noun?

22. [Lines 8–9] οὐκ ἂν οἴεσθε αὐτὸν . . . ἀξιωθῆναι: ἄν belongs with the infinitive ἀξιωθῆναι. ἄν is frequently attached to verbs of saying and thinking, even though it belongs with the infinitive that follows (S1764).

23. [Lines 8–9] The apodosis of the condition has been expressed in the accusative/infinitive construction of indirect statement set up by οὐκ οἴεσθε. What type of condition is εἰ . . . ἐπιχειρήσειέ . . . ἄν . . . ἀξιωθῆναι? (Hint: What form would ἀξιωθῆναι have been in the original condition?)

24. [Lines 9–10] What type of condition is ἐὰν σωφρονῆτε, οὐ τούτου ἀλλ' ὑμῶν αὐτῶν φείσεσθε?

25. [Lines 10–11] Note the μὲν . . . δέ construction in σωθεὶς μὲν . . . ἀπολόμενος δέ. These participles are best taken conditionally, standing in for the protasis of the conditions implied by ἄν . . . ποιήσειε and ὑποτέμοι ἄν. It is very common for a participle to be used in place of a protasis (R10.6; S2344).

26. [Line 11] ἄν . . . ποιήσειε: This is the apodosis of what type of condition? The order for translation is ποιήσειε ἂν πολλοὺς τῶν ἐναντία γιγνωσκόντων ὑμῖν μέγα φρονεῖν.

27. [Line 11] Take ὑμῖν with ἐναντία. Note the framing of ἐναντία by τῶν and γιγνωσκόντων. This indicates that ἐναντία goes with γιγνωσκόντων. What is the function of ἐναντία?

28. [Line 12] πάντων is a genitive of possession with τὰς ἐλπίδας and is further delineated by καὶ τῶν ἐν τῇ πόλει καὶ τῶν ἔξω. Note the καὶ . . . καί construction.

29. [Line 12] τῶν ἔξω: This is a reference to the democrats in exile.

30. [Line 12] ὑποτέμοι ἄν: This is the same type of condition as ἄν . . . ποιήσειε. What is it?

Reading Thirteen

Xenophon, *Hellenica* 2.3.35–38

Focus on Reading

Theramenes responds to Critias's accusations and defends his actions.

Ὁ μὲν ταῦτ' εἰπὼν ἐκαθέζετο· Θηραμένης δὲ ἀναστὰς ἔλεξεν· Ἀλλὰ πρῶτον
μὲν μνησθήσομαι, ὦ ἄνδρες, ὃ τελευταῖον κατ' ἐμοῦ εἶπε. φησὶ γάρ με τοὺς
στρατηγοὺς ἀποκτεῖναι κατηγοροῦντα. ἐγὼ δὲ οὐκ ἦρχον δήπου τοῦ κατ' ἐκείνων
λόγου, ἀλλ' ἐκεῖνοι ἔφασαν προσταχθέν μοι ὑφ' ἑαυτῶν οὐκ ἀνελέσθαι τοὺς
δυστυχοῦντας ἐν τῇ περὶ Λέσβον ναυμαχίᾳ.

Xenophon, Hellenica 2.3.35

SENTENCE ONE

Ὁ μὲν ταῦτ' εἰπὼν ἐκαθέζετο· Θηραμένης δὲ ἀναστὰς ἔλεξεν· Ἀλλὰ πρῶτον μὲν
μνησθήσομαι, ὦ ἄνδρες, ὃ τελευταῖον κατ' ἐμοῦ εἶπε.

VOCABULARY

καθέζομαι sit down	τελευταῖος, -α, -ον last
ἀνίστημι stand up	κατά (prep. + gen.) against
μιμνήσκομαι mention	

OBSERVATIONS, STRATEGIES, AND NOTES

1. This is a very straightforward sentence. Note the construction μὲν . . . δέ in Ὁ
   μὲν . . . . Θηραμένης δὲ. Ὁ refers to Critias. Some editors capitalize the first word
   of a new paragraph, as here.

2. ταῦτ᾽ εἰπών: The direct object of a participle (or a finite verb form, for that matter) often immediately precedes it. This circumstantial participle in the aorist tense may be taken temporally: "After he said these things."

3. Note the augment in ἐκαθέζετο. This verb was apparently not treated as a compound verb! The expected form would have been καθήζετο.

4. Θηραμένης δὲ ἀναστὰς ἔλεξεν: As has been noted previously, when the main verb is in the aorist tense and is accompanied by a participle in the nominative case that is also in the aorist, it is permissible to translate both forms as finite verbs and to insert "and." Translate this as "And Theramenes stood up and said."

5. Ἀλλὰ: Note the capital letter, which marks the beginning of a direct quotation. πρῶτον μὲν is completed by ἐγὼ δὲ in sentence 3.

6. τελευταῖον: Sometimes the antecedent of a relative pronoun is placed in the relative clause itself and agrees with the relative pronoun. This is called incorporation (S2536). Here τελευταῖον, the logical object of μνησθήσομαι and the antecedent of ὅ, has been placed within the relative clause. Since τελευταῖον, as direct object of μνησθήσομαι, would have been in the accusative case, there is no change of case.

TRANSLATION

After Critias said these things, he sat down; and Theramenes stood up and said, "But I will first mention, gentlemen, the last thing that he said against me."

SENTENCE TWO

φησὶ γάρ με τοὺς στρατηγοὺς ἀποκτεῖναι κατηγοροῦντα.

VOCABULARY

φημί	assert, say	ἀποκτείνω	kill, bring about someone's death
στρατηγός, -οῦ, ὁ	general	κατηγορέω	accuse

OBSERVATIONS, STRATEGIES, AND NOTES

1. φησὶ: φημί takes the accusative/infinitive construction of indirect statement (R7.1): φησὶ . . . με . . . ἀποκτεῖναι. τοὺς στρατηγοὺς is the direct object of both the infinitive and the participle κατηγοροῦντα. When both the subject accusative of the infinitive and the accusative direct object are included, the subject frequently precedes the direct object, as here.

2. γάρ: The particle γάρ is being used here to introduce the details of what was mentioned in the previous sentence. This explanatory function can often be found with verbs of saying, showing, and the like (S2808).

3. κατηγοροῦντα: This circumstantial participle is best taken to indicate cause. Note the nice framing of τοὺς στρατηγοὺς ἀποκτεῖναι by με . . . κατηγοροῦντα to indicate that all these words form a unit.

TRANSLATION

"For he asserts that I killed the generals by accusing them."

SENTENCE THREE

ἐγὼ δὲ οὐκ ἦρχον δήπου τοῦ κατ᾽ ἐκείνων λόγου, ἀλλ᾽ ἐκεῖνοι ἔφασαν προσταχθέν μοι ὑφ᾽ ἑαυτῶν οὐκ ἀνελέσθαι τοὺς δυστυχοῦντας ἐν τῇ περὶ Λέσβον ναυμαχίᾳ.

VOCABULARY

ἄρχω begin (+ gen.)	ἀναιρέω take up, retrieve
δήπου (particle) of course	δυστυχέω be unfortunate
κατά (prep. + gen.) against	ναυμαχία, -ας, ἡ naval battle
προστάττω order	

OBSERVATIONS, STRATEGIES, AND NOTES

1. ἐγὼ δὲ: The contrast indicated by δέ is important here. Translate it as "But I."

2. τοῦ κατ᾽ ἐκείνων λόγου: Note the attributive position (R2.1) of κατ᾽ ἐκείνων (article-modifier-noun). λόγου must be rendered here as "accusation."

3. ἔφασαν . . . οὐκ ἀνελέσθαι: ἀνελέσθαι is the infinitive in the accusative/infinitive construction of indirect statement (R7.1) set up by ἔφασαν. Since there is no subject accusative of this infinitive, it must be supplied, on the basis of logic and context, from μοι: ἔφασαν . . . <με> οὐκ ἀνελέσθαι.

4. προσταχθέν μοι ὑφ᾽ ἑαυτῶν: προσταχθέν is the accusative singular neuter aorist passive participle of προστάττω and is standing in an accusative absolute. When the participle in an absolute construction is from an impersonal verb or is a passive participle used impersonally, as here, the participle will be in the accusative rather than the genitive case (R6.6; S2076B). It is best to translate this concessively. Since the literal translation is awkward ("though it had been ordered to me by them"), the phrase may be translated more idiomatically as "though I had been commanded by them" or "though they had commanded me to do so."

5. τοὺς δυστυχοῦντας: The definite article indicates that this participle is being used as a substantive (R6.1).

6. ἐν τῇ περὶ Λέσβον ναυμαχίᾳ: Note, once again, the attributive position (article-modifier-noun) of the prepositional phrase περὶ Λέσβον. This indicates that the prepositional phrase is functioning as an adjective rather than as an adverbial phrase (R2.1).

TRANSLATION

"But I did not begin, of course, the accusation against them, but those men said that though I had been commanded by them, I did not retrieve the unfortunate ones in the sea battle near Lesbos."

POLISHED TRANSLATION

After Critias said these things, he sat down, and Theramenes stood up and said, "I will first mention, gentlemen, the last thing he said against me. For he asserts that I killed the generals by accusing them. But I did not, of course, begin the accusation against them; rather, those men claimed that I did not retrieve the unfortunate men in the sea battle near Lesbos, though they had commanded me to do so."

Reading Selection

Theramenes continues his defense of his actions.

ἐγὼ δὲ ἀπολογούμενος ὡς διὰ τὸν χειμῶνα οὐδὲ πλεῖν, μὴ ὅτι ἀναιρεῖσθαι τοὺς
ἄνδρας δυνατὸν ἦν, ἔδοξα τῇ πόλει εἰκότα λέγειν, ἐκεῖνοι δ᾽ ἑαυτῶν κατηγορεῖν
ἐφαίνοντο. φάσκοντες γὰρ οἷόν τε εἶναι σῶσαι τοὺς ἄνδρας, προέμενοι
ἀπολέσθαι αὐτοὺς ἀποπλέοντες ᾤχοντο. οὐ μέντοι θαυμάζω γε τὸ Κριτίαν
†παρανενομηκέναι†· ὅτε γὰρ ταῦτα ἦν, οὐ παρὼν ἐτύγχανεν, ἀλλ᾽ ἐν Θετταλίᾳ   5
μετὰ Προμηθέως δημοκρατίαν κατεσκεύαζε καὶ τοὺς πενέστας ὥπλιζεν ἐπὶ
τοὺς δεσπότας. ὧν μὲν οὖν οὗτος ἐκεῖ ἔπραττε μηδὲν ἐνθάδε γένοιτο· τάδε γε
μέντοι ὁμολογῶ ἐγὼ τούτῳ, εἴ τις ὑμᾶς μὲν τῆς ἀρχῆς βούλεται παῦσαι, τοὺς δ᾽
ἐπιβουλεύοντας ὑμῖν ἰσχυροὺς ποιεῖ, δίκαιον εἶναι τῆς μεγίστης αὐτὸν τιμωρίας
τυγχάνειν· ὅστις μέντοι ὁ ταῦτα πράττων ἐστὶν οἶμαι ἂν ὑμᾶς κάλλιστα κρίνειν,   10
τά τε πεπραγμένα καὶ ἃ νῦν πράττει ἕκαστος ἡμῶν εἰ κατανοήσετε. οὐκοῦν μέχρι
μὲν τοῦ ὑμᾶς τε καταστῆναι εἰς τὴν βουλείαν καὶ ἀρχὰς ἀποδειχθῆναι καὶ τοὺς
ὁμολογουμένως συκοφάντας ὑπάγεσθαι πάντες ταὐτὰ ἐγιγνώσκομεν. ἐπεὶ δέ
γε οὗτοι ἤρξαντο ἄνδρας καλούς τε κἀγαθοὺς συλλαμβάνειν, ἐκ τούτου κἀγὼ
ἠρξάμην τἀναντία τούτοις γιγνώσκειν.   15

Xenophon, *Hellenica* 2.3.35–38

NOTES

1. [Line 1] ἀπολογούμενος ὡς: Remember that a participle, like a finite form of the same verb, may introduce an indirect statement. ἀπολογέομαι takes the ὅτι/ὡς construction of indirect statement (R7.3).

2. [Line 1] οὐδὲ πλεῖν, μὴ ὅτι ἀναιρεῖσθαι: μὴ ὅτι is used in the second of two equal clauses when the first clause has an expressed or implied negative (S2763). It may be translated "much less" or "to say nothing of." Note that Xenophon has chosen to

negate the complementary infinitives rather than the impersonal expression δυνατὸν ἦν on which these infinitives rely.

3. [Line 2] ἔδοξα: A personal construction is often preferred in Greek for situations where an impersonal construction is used in English (S1983).

4. [Line 3] προέμενοι is the aorist middle participle of προίημι, which may be used with an accusative/infinitive construction. Translate προέμενοι ἀπολέσθαι αὐτοὺς as "allowing them to perish." What tense of the infinitive is ἀπολέσθαι? Why?

5. [Line 4] ἀποπλέοντες ᾤχοντο: Such redundant phrases are not uncommon in Greek! You may translate this as "sailing away, they were gone" or simply, "they sailed away."

6. [Line 4] θαυμάζω γε: This is a nice use of the postpositive particle γε and adds a touch of sarcasm.

7. [Lines 4–5] τὸ Κριτίαν †παρανενομηκέναι†: The "†," an obelus, indicates that the text is corrupt and there is no easy solution to the problem. An obelus is placed in front of the word that is thought to be corrupt; if a second obelus is also used, it indicates that two or more words may be corrupt. παρανενομηκέναι, from παρανομέω, meaning "transgress the law," will clearly not work in this context. We can tell that we have an articular infinitive, as indicated by τὸ, and that the accusative Κριτίαν must be the subject of that infinitive. Some scholars accept Wolf's emendation, παρανενοηκέναι, from παρανοέω, meaning "misunderstand."[2] In that case it can be translated as "certainly I, at any rate, do not marvel at the fact that Critias misunderstood." The statement is sarcastic.

8. [Line 5] ὅτε γὰρ ταῦτα ἦν: This means "for when these things were happening" (literally, "for when these things were"). Remember that neuter plural subjects take singular verbs.

9. [Line 5] γὰρ: As is often the case, γάρ explains the previous clause.

10. [Line 5] οὐ παρὼν ἐτύγχανεν: τυγχάνω, "happen," often takes a supplementary participle (R6.4, no. 5). A good translation aid is "happen *to be doing <the action denoted by the participle>*." Here you may translate it as "he did not happen to be present."

11. [Lines 5–6] ἀλλ' ἐν Θετταλίᾳ μετὰ Προμηθέως δημοκρατίαν κατεσκεύαζε: Precisely what Critias was doing in Thessaly is uncertain, but Theramenes appears to be implying that it is Critias, not he, who changes sides back and forth.

12. [Line 7] ὧν: Supply the demonstrative τούτων as the omitted antecedent. ὧν has also been attracted into the case of the omitted antecedent (R11.3; S2509, 2531). A full expression of this sentence is τούτων ἃ μὲν οὖν οὗτος ἐκεῖ ἔπραττε μηδὲν ἐνθάδε γένοιτο. Take μηδὲν with the partitive genitive τούτων.

13. [Line 7] γένοιτο: What type of optative is this? Remember that there are two independent uses of the optative: the optative of wish and the potential optative (R8.4, 8.5). How can you determine which this one is?

14. [Line 7] τάδε γε: This is another good example of the use of γε, which often restricts the word that precedes it. There is a touch of sarcasm here. For further discussion of γε, see S2821.

---

2. See Krentz, *Xenophon*, 30.

15. [Line 8] ὁμολογέω takes an accusative to indicate what has been agreed upon. Translate τάδε as "in respect to these things." τούτῳ refers to Critias.

16. [Lines 8–9] εἴ τις ὑμᾶς μὲν . . . , τοὺς δ᾽ ἐπιβουλεύοντας . . . : ὑμᾶς is being contrasted with τοὺς ἐπιβουλεύοντας but the verbal action itself is not strongly oppositional.

17. [Lines 9–10] δίκαιον εἶναι τῆς μεγίστης αὐτὸν τιμωρίας τυγχάνειν: This is an accusative/infinitive construction of indirect statement set up by τάδε . . . ὁμολογῶ (R7.1). δίκαιον εἶναι is impersonal and it, in turn, takes an accusative/infinitive construction, αὐτὸν . . . τυγχάνειν. Remember that τυγχάνω takes a genitive object when it means "meet," "meet with," or "obtain."

18. [Line 9] τῆς μεγίστης αὐτὸν τιμωρίας: The separation of τῆς μεγίστης from its noun τιμωρίας gives the superlative adjective added emphasis. Note also the nice framing of αὐτὸν by τῆς μεγίστης and τιμωρίας.

19. [Lines 10–11] ὅστις μέντοι . . . εἰ κατανοήσετε: This is a syntactically complicated sentence with several constructions embedded within the overall framework of a future most vivid condition, in which both the protasis and the apodosis take a future indicative (R10.4; S2328). The protasis of the condition, εἰ κατανοήσετε, comes at the end of the sentence. κατανοήσετε has two objects, τά . . . πεπραγμένα and the relative clause ἃ νῦν πράττει ἕκαστος ἡμῶν, which have been joined together by a τε . . . καί construction. The demonstrative antecedent of ἃ has been omitted (S2509). You may supply "the things." The apodosis of the condition has been expressed within an accusative/infinitive construction of indirect statement set up by οἶμαι. This apodosis, ἂν ὑμᾶς κάλλιστα κρίνειν, reflects the original direct form ἂν ὑμεῖς κάλλιστα κρίνοιτε, in which a potential optative has replaced the expected future indicative. This is a permissible substitute for the future indicative (S2356), and ἂν provides the clue that the infinitive is replacing an original potential optative. There is also a relative clause introduced by the indefinite relative pronoun ὅστις, whose antecedent, τοῦτον or ἐκεῖνον, has been omitted. This omitted antecedent is the logical object of κρίνειν. Despite its complicated structure, if you consider the sentence according to its units of meaning in the order in which it has been written, it will be relatively easy to translate: [ὅστις μέντοι ὁ ταῦτα πράττων ἐστὶν] [οἶμαι ἂν ὑμᾶς κάλλιστα κρίνειν,] [τά τε πεπραγμένα καὶ ἃ νῦν πράττει ἕκαστος ἡμῶν εἰ κατανοήσετε.] Note that κάλλιστα is a superlative adverb meaning "best."

20. [Lines 11–13] οὐκοῦν **μέχρι** μὲν **τοῦ** ὑμᾶς τε **καταστῆναι** εἰς τὴν βουλείαν καὶ ἀρχὰς **ἀποδειχθῆναι** καὶ τοὺς ὁμολογουμένως συκοφάντας **ὑπάγεσθαι**: The three infinitives are being used in the same manner. Note that the subject accusative of each precedes its infinitive in a neat parallel construction. The infinitives are linked by τε . . . καὶ . . . καὶ (remember that τε is postpositive). What is the syntactical function of these infinitives? The words in boldface provide a clue.

21. [Lines 11–13] Note the construction in μέχρι μὲν . . . ἐπεὶ δέ.

22. [Lines 12–13] τοὺς ὁμολογουμένως συκοφάντας: That is, those who everyone agreed were sycophants.

23. [Line 13] ταὐτὰ: Crasis for τὰ αὐτά.

24. [Lines 13–14] ἐπεὶ δέ γε: This is a nice use of γε to emphasize or intensify Theramenes' displeasure at the increased violence of the Thirty. Translate it as "But when, at any rate, they."

25. [Line 14] καλούς τε κἀγαθοὺς: Note the crasis in κἀγαθοὺς (= καὶ ἀγαθούς) and remember that τε is postpositive. τε . . . καί indicates a close connection between the two adjectives καλούς and ἀγαθούς.

26. [Line 14] ἐκ τούτου: Translate this as "thereupon."

27. [Lines 14–15] κἀγὼ and τἀναντία: What were the original words before crasis occurred?

28. [Line 15] τούτοις: A reference to the Thirty.

Reading Fourteen

Xenophon, *Hellenica* 2.3.39–42

Focus on Reading

Theramenes continues his defense.

ᾔδειν γὰρ ὅτι ἀποθνήσκοντος μὲν Λέοντος τοῦ Σαλαμινίου, ἀνδρὸς καὶ
ὄντος καὶ δοκοῦντος ἱκανοῦ εἶναι, ἀδικοῦντος δ' οὐδὲ ἕν, οἱ ὅμοιοι τούτῳ
φοβήσοιντο, φοβούμενοι δὲ ἐναντίοι τῇδε τῇ πολιτείᾳ ἔσοιντο· ἐγίγνωσκον δὲ
ὅτι συλλαμβανομένου Νικηράτου τοῦ Νικίου, καὶ πλουσίου καὶ οὐδὲν πώποτε
δημοτικὸν οὔτε αὐτοῦ οὔτε τοῦ πατρὸς πράξαντος, οἱ τούτῳ ὅμοιοι δυσμενεῖς
ἡμῖν γενήσοιντο.

Xenophon, Hellenica 2.3.39

This long sentence has been divided into two sections.

PART ONE

ᾔδειν γὰρ ὅτι ἀποθνήσκοντος μὲν Λέοντος τοῦ Σαλαμινίου, ἀνδρὸς καὶ ὄντος
καὶ δοκοῦντος ἱκανοῦ εἶναι, ἀδικοῦντος δ' οὐδὲ ἕν, οἱ ὅμοιοι τούτῳ φοβήσοιντο,
φοβούμενοι δὲ ἐναντίοι τῇδε τῇ πολιτείᾳ ἔσοιντο·

VOCABULARY

οἶδα know	ἀδικέω injure, commit an injustice
ἀποθνήσκω be put to death	ὅμοιος, -α, -ον similar to (+ dat.)
Λέων, -οντος, ὁ Leon	φοβέω (passive and mid.) fear
Σαλαμίνιος, -α, -ον of Salamis	ἐναντίος, -α, -ον opposed to (+ dat.)
δοκέω appear, seem	πολιτεία, -ας, ἡ government
ἱκανός, -ή, -όν competent, capable	

OBSERVATIONS, STRATEGIES, AND NOTES

1. ᾔδειν: First person singular pluperfect active indicative of οἶδα. Remember that οἶδα admits both the participial and the ὅτι/ὡς constructions of indirect statement (R7.2, 7.3).

2. ἀποθνῄσκοντος μὲν Λέοντος τοῦ Σαλαμινίου: Notice that both the participle and the proper name are in the genitive. What construction is this? What is the tense of the participle and why?

3. It is helpful to note that ὄντος, δοκοῦντος, and ἀδικοῦντος all modify Λέοντος. Leon was a general whom the Thirty executed.

4. ὄντος . . . δοκοῦντος: Greeks often made the distinction between seeming and actually being. Here, Leon both seemed and actually was ἱκανός. καὶ . . . καὶ provides a nice linkage of ὄντος . . . δοκοῦντος.

5. οὐδὲ ἕν: Emphatic for οὐδέν (S349b). Translate with ἀδικοῦντος, "committing not one injustice."

6. οἱ ὅμοιοι τούτῳ: τούτῳ refers to Leon. It is permissible to translate this demonstrative pronoun as a third person personal pronoun.

7. φοβήσοιντο . . . ἔσοιντο: These are the verbs of the indirect statement. After a secondary main verb (ᾔδειν), the verbs of a ὅτι/ὡς indirect statement may switch to the corresponding tense of the optative (R7.3). This is the only use of the future optative!

TRANSLATION

"For I knew that when Leon of Salamis was being put to death, a man who both was and seemed to be capable, and <who> was committing not even one injustice, the men who were similar to him would be afraid and, since they were afraid, would be opposed to this government;"

PART TWO

ἐγίγνωσκον δὲ ὅτι συλλαμβανομένου Νικηράτου τοῦ Νικίου, καὶ πλουσίου καὶ οὐδὲν πώποτε δημοτικὸν οὔτε αὐτοῦ οὔτε τοῦ πατρὸς πράξαντος, οἱ τούτῳ ὅμοιοι δυσμενεῖς ἡμῖν γενήσοιντο.

VOCABULARY

γιγνώσκω	know	δημοτικός, -ή, -όν	for the people
συλλαμβάνω	arrest	πατήρ, -τρός, ὁ	father
Νικήρατος, -ου, ὁ	Niceratus	πράττω	do
Νικίας, -ου, ὁ	Nicias	ὅμοιος, -α, -ον	similar to (+ dat.)
πλούσιος, -α, -ον	wealthy	δυσμενής, -ές	hostile to (+ dat.)
πώποτε	ever	γίγνομαι	become

OBSERVATIONS, STRATEGIES, AND NOTES

1. As you read through this part of the sentence, notice that it is parallel in construction to the first part. Both parts of the sentence have a verb of intellectual perception introducing a ὅτι/ὡς indirect statement, a long genitive absolute expressed within the indirect statement, and the main clause of the indirect statement. Each part is placed in the same position within its own part of the sentence.

2. τοῦ Νικίου: It is very common for a Greek author to include the name of an individual's father in the genitive. Translate this as "the son of Nicias."

3. πλουσίου: Supply ὄντος with this part of the genitive absolute. As is common, a form of the verb "be" has been omitted. The καί . . . καί construction in καὶ πλουσίου καὶ οὐδὲν πώποτε . . . πράξαντος is awkward in English. It may be omitted in your translation.

4. οὔτε αὐτοῦ οὔτε τοῦ πατρὸς πράξαντος: Both Niceratus and his father act as the genitive subjects of the genitive participle πράξαντος. αὐτοῦ refers to Niceratus and is the intensive use of αὐτός. This part of the genitive absolute is literally translated "neither he himself nor his father ever did anything for the people," but you will see in the polished translation below that some flexibility is required to render it smoothly in English.

5. What tense of the participle is πράξαντος? Why?

6. οἱ τούτῳ ὅμοιοι: Note the framing of τούτῳ by the definite article οἱ and ὅμοιοι to indicate that τούτῳ, which refers to Niceratus, goes with οἱ ὅμοιοι.

7. γενήσοιντο: This future optative is the verb of the indirect statement (R7.3) and like φοβήσοιντο and ἔσοιντο above, it is replacing an original future indicative.

TRANSLATION

"and I knew that when Niceratus, the son of Nicias, was being arrested, <being> a wealthy man and he himself and his father having never done anything for the people, the men who were like him would become hostile to us."

POLISHED TRANSLATION

"For I knew that when Leon of Salamis was being put to death, a man who actually was capable as well as appearing to be so, and who had committed not even a single injustice, men who were similar to him would be afraid, and because of their fear would be opposed to this government; I also knew that when Niceratus, the son of Nicias, a wealthy man who, like his father, had never done anything for the people, was being arrested, men who were like him would become hostile to us."

Reading Selection

Theramenes delineates some of the extreme activities of the Thirty.

ἀλλὰ μὴν καὶ Ἀντιφῶντος ὑφ' ἡμῶν ἀπολλυμένου, ὃς ἐν τῷ πολέμῳ δύο τριήρεις
εὖ πλεούσας παρείχετο, ἠπιστάμην ὅτι καὶ οἱ πρόθυμοι τῇ πόλει γεγενημένοι
πάντες ὑπόπτως ἡμῖν ἕξοιεν. ἀντεῖπον δὲ καὶ ὅτε τῶν μετοίκων ἕνα ἕκαστον
λαβεῖν ἔφασαν χρῆναι· εὔδηλον γὰρ ἦν ὅτι τούτων ἀπολομένων καὶ οἱ μέτοικοι
ἅπαντες πολέμιοι τῇ πολιτείᾳ ἔσοιντο. ἀντεῖπον δὲ καὶ ὅτε τὰ ὅπλα τοῦ πλήθους   5
παρῃροῦντο, οὐ νομίζων χρῆναι ἀσθενῆ τὴν πόλιν ποιεῖν· οὐδὲ γὰρ τοὺς
Λακεδαιμονίους ἑώρων τούτου ἕνεκα βουλομένους περισῶσαι ἡμᾶς, ὅπως
ὀλίγοι γενόμενοι μηδὲν δυναίμεθ' αὐτοὺς ὠφελεῖν· ἐξῆν γὰρ αὐτοῖς, εἰ τούτου
γ' ἐδέοντο,³ καὶ μηδένα λιπεῖν ὀλίγον ἔτι χρόνον τῷ λιμῷ πιέσαντας. οὐδέ γε
τὸ φρουροὺς μισθοῦσθαι συνήρεσκέ μοι, ἐξὸν αὐτῶν τῶν πολιτῶν τοσούτους   10
προσλαμβάνειν, ἕως ῥᾳδίως ἐμέλλομεν οἱ ἄρχοντες τῶν ἀρχομένων κρατήσειν.
ἐπεί γε μὴν πολλοὺς ἑώρων ἐν τῇ πόλει τῇ ἀρχῇ τῇδε δυσμενεῖς, πολλοὺς δὲ
φυγάδας γιγνομένους, οὐκ αὖ ἐδόκει μοι οὔτε Θρασύβουλον οὔτε Ἄνυτον οὔτε
Ἀλκιβιάδην φυγαδεύειν· ᾔδειν γὰρ ὅτι οὕτω γε τὸ ἀντίπαλον ἰσχυρὸν ἔσοιτο, εἰ
τῷ μὲν πλήθει ἡγεμόνες ἱκανοὶ προσγενήσοιντο, τοῖς δ' ἡγεῖσθαι βουλομένοις   15
σύμμαχοι πολλοὶ φανήσοιντο.

Xenophon, Hellenica 2.3.40–42

NOTES

1. [Line 1] ἀλλὰ μήν is a fairly common combination of particles and means "but then" or "but surely." While it often introduces an objection, it may also merely add a new idea or detail, as here (S2786). καί is adverbial and may be translated "also" or "as well."

2. [Line 1] The first sentence is similar in structure to the previous two sentences. What type of construction is Ἀντιφῶντος ὑφ' ἡμῶν ἀπολλυμένου? What is the function of ὑφ' ἡμῶν?

3. [Line 1] ὅς: What is the function of ὅς? What is its antecedent?

4. [Lines 1–2] δύο τριήρεις εὖ πλεούσας: Note that there are no definite articles for either the noun τριήρεις or the participle πλεούσας. An attributive participle is usually used with a definite article when the participle is being used as a simple adjective (R6.1). Sometimes, however, a participle is used as an attributive adjective even without the definite article (S2049). Context and logic will help you to determine when a participle has an attributive use.

5. [Line 2] εὖ: Adverbs often precede the word they are modifying, hence the position of εὖ. This phrase is literally translated "two triremes that sail well," but you may prefer "two fast triremes," since that clearly is what is meant here.

---

3. γ' ἐδέοντο has been substituted for γε δέοιντο, following Brückner's emendation; see Krenz, *Xeno-phon*, 32.

6. [Lines 2–3] ἠπιστάμην ὅτι . . . ὑπόπτως ἡμῖν ἔξοιεν: This indirect statement construction is identical to the one seen in the previous two sentences. What tense and mood is ἔξοιεν and why? What is the first principal part of this verb?

7. [Line 2] καὶ οἱ πρόθυμοι: This is an adverbial use of καί.

8. [Lines 2–3] οἱ πρόθυμοι τῇ πόλει γεγενημένοι πάντες: These words work together as a unit. What is the force of the perfect tense of γεγενημένοι? Note that γεγενημένοι and οἱ πρόθυμοι frame τῇ πόλει to indicate that πόλει should be construed with πρόθυμοι. Noticing such framing is very helpful.

9. [Line 3] ὑπόπτως ἡμῖν ἔξοιεν: ἔχω is often used with an adverb of manner to mean "to be in a certain state" or "to be." This phrase is translated "would be suspicious toward us" or "would view us with suspicion."

10. [Line 3] καὶ ὅτε: καί is being used as an adverb.

11. [Lines 3–5] ἀντεῖπον δὲ καὶ ὅτε . . . ἀντεῖπον δὲ καὶ ὅτε: The repetition adds emphasis to what Theramenes is saying.

12. [Lines 3–4] ὅτε τῶν μετοίκων . . . χρῆναι: The order for translation is ὅτε ἔφασαν χρῆναι ἕκαστον λαβεῖν ἕνα τῶν μετοίκων. ἔφασαν introduces an accusative/infinitive construction of indirect statement (R7.1), here represented by the impersonal χρῆναι. χρῆναι, in turn, takes an accusative/infinitive construction as indicated by ἕκαστον λαβεῖν. What is the significance of the tense of λαβεῖν? What is the function of ἕνα?

13. [Line 3] τῶν μετοίκων ἕνα: What type of genitive is this?

14. [Line 4] εὔδηλον γὰρ ἦν ὅτι: Remember the explanatory force of γάρ. The impersonal εὔδηλον ἦν may take a ὅτι/ὡς construction (R7.3). What tense and mood is ἔσοιντο and why?

15. [Line 4] τούτων ἀπολομένων: What type of construction is this?

16. [Lines 4–5] καὶ οἱ μέτοικοι ἅπαντες: Is καὶ being used as an adverb or as a conjunction?

17. [Lines 5–6] τὰ ὅπλα τοῦ πλήθους παρῃροῦντο: τὰ ὅπλα is the object of the middle form παρῃροῦντο. The Thirty is its subject.

18. [Line 6] οὐ νομίζων χρῆναι ἀσθενῆ τὴν πόλιν ποιεῖν: This construction is similar to the one discussed in note 12, above. The order for translation is: νομίζων οὐ χρῆναι ποιεῖν τὴν πόλιν ἀσθενῆ. What is the function of ἀσθενῆ?

19. [Line 7] ἑώρων: Verbs of perception take the participle when the perception is physical, and either the participle or the ὅτι/ὡς construction when the perception is intellectual (R7.2; S2110). Here, the perception is probably intellectual.

20. [Lines 7–8] τούτου ἕνεκα looks forward to ὅπως ὀλίγοι . . . αὐτοὺς ὠφελεῖν.

21. [Lines 7–8] ὅπως . . . μηδὲν δυναίμεθ': What type of clause is this? What are the sentence clues? What form is δυναίμεθ'?

22. [Line 8] μηδέν is frequently used as an adverb to mean "not at all."

23. [Lines 8–9] ἐξῆν γὰρ αὐτοῖς, εἰ τούτου γ' ἐδέοντο, καὶ μηδένα λιπεῖν . . . πιέσαντας: ἐξῆν, which is in the imperfect tense, is from the impersonal verb ἔξεστι, which takes a dative of person plus an infinitive. This impersonal construction is the apodosis of a present contrary-to-fact condition (R10.5). Note that the apodosis, ἐξῆν γὰρ αὐτοῖς

καὶ μηδένα λιπεῖν ὀλίγον ἔτι χρόνον τῷ λιμῷ πιέσαντας, does not have the required ἄν. It is, however, permissible to omit ἄν in the apodosis of such a condition when its verb denotes possibility, unfulfilled obligation, or propriety (S2313). The apodosis has been split into two parts by the insertion of the protasis εἰ τούτου γ᾽ ἐδέοντο.

24. [Lines 8–9] τούτου γ᾽: Note the emphasis that γε gives to τούτου.

25. [Line 9] μηδένα . . . πιέσαντας: This is a little tricky! μηδένα is the object of λιπεῖν while πιέσαντας is its subject. πιέσαντας refers logically to αὐτοῖς (the Spartans) but has changed to the accusative since it is functioning as the subject of the infinitive. You may want to take πιέσαντας in a causal sense and translate it as "by pressing hard." How is καὶ being used?

26. [Line 9] ὀλίγον ἔτι χρόνον: What type of time expression is this? We might say, "for a little while longer." This phrase goes with πιέσαντας, as does τῷ λιμῷ. What is the function of τῷ λιμῷ?

27. [Line 10] τὸ φρουροὺς μισθοῦσθαι: What is this construction? What is its function? Notice the framing of φρουροὺς, the object of μισθοῦσθαι.

28. [Lines 10–11] ἐξὸν αὐτῶν τῶν πολιτῶν τοσούτους προσλαμβάνειν: This is another accusative absolute (R6.6; S2076). The participle will take an infinitive just as a finite form of the impersonal verb would. τοσούτους is the object of προσλαμβάνειν.

29. [Line 10] αὐτῶν τῶν πολιτῶν: Remember that determining whether αὐτός is in the attributive or predicate position will help you translate it correctly. Why is the genitive being used here?

30. [Line 12] ἑώρων: As noted, verbs of perception may take either the participial or ὅτι/ὡς construction of indirect statement (R7.2, 7.3). Here the participial construction is being used with γιγνομένους, which is used twice: πολλοὺς ἑώρων . . . δυσμενεῖς <γιγνομένους>, πολλοὺς δὲ φυγάδας γιγνομένους. Note the parallel construction.

31. [Lines 14–16] What forms are ἔσοιτο, προσγενήσοιντο, and φανήσοιντο? Why? What type of condition is being expressed here in an indirect form?

32. [Line 15] Notice the μὲν . . . δέ construction in τῷ μὲν πλήθει . . . τοῖς δ᾽ ἡγεῖσθαι βουλομένοις.

Reading Fifteen

Xenophon, *Hellenica* 2.3.43–46

Focus on Reading

Theramenes counters Critias's charges against him.

ὁ ταῦτα οὖν νουθετῶν ἐν τῷ φανερῷ πότερα εὐμενὴς ἂν δικαίως ἢ προδότης
νομίζοιτο; οὐχ οἱ ἐχθρούς, ὦ Κριτία, κωλύοντες πολλοὺς ποιεῖσθαι, οὐδ' οἱ
συμμάχους πλείστους διδάσκοντες κτᾶσθαι, οὗτοι τοὺς πολεμίους ἰσχυροὺς
ποιοῦσιν, ἀλλὰ πολὺ μᾶλλον οἱ ἀδίκως τε χρήματα ἀφαιρούμενοι καὶ τοὺς οὐδὲν
ἀδικοῦντας ἀποκτείνοντες, οὗτοί εἰσιν οἱ καὶ πολλοὺς τοὺς ἐναντίους ποιοῦντες
καὶ προδιδόντες οὐ μόνον τοὺς φίλους ἀλλὰ καὶ ἑαυτοὺς δι' αἰσχροκέρδειαν.

Xenophon, Hellenica 2.3.43

SENTENCE ONE

ὁ ταῦτα οὖν νουθετῶν ἐν τῷ φανερῷ πότερα εὐμενὴς ἂν δικαίως ἢ προδότης
νομίζοιτο;

VOCABULARY

οὖν (postpositive particle)   and so, therefore
νουθετέω   warn, advise, admonish
ἐν τῷ φανερῷ   openly
εὐμενής, -ές   well-disposed

δικαίως (adv.)   justly, rightly
προδότης, -ου, ὁ   traitor
νομίζω   consider, think

OBSERVATIONS, STRATEGIES, AND NOTES

1. Consider this sentence in terms of its units of meaning: [ὁ ταῦτα οὖν νουθετῶν] [ἐν τῷ φανερῷ] [πότερα εὐμενὴς ἂν δικαίως ἢ προδότης νομίζοιτο;]

2. ὁ ταῦτα οὖν νουθετῶν: Note that νουθετῶν is being used as a substantive (R6.1) and that its direct object, ταῦτα, is framed by the participle and the definite article.

3. πότερα . . . ἤ, meaning "whether . . . or," introduces an alternative question. It is permissible to leave out "whether" when translating.

4. It is important to pay attention to ἄν and νομίζοιτο. Since there are no other verbs or indications of subordination, we know that this must be the main verb. It must be either an optative of wish or a potential optative, which are the only independent uses of the optative (R8.4, 8.5). Since ἄν is used, we know that this is a potential optative.

5. νομίζοιτο: Always be sure to notice the voice of a verb form. Here the verb is passive. The nominatives εὐμενὴς and προδότης make this clear, since they make the most sense as a predicate adjective and a predicate nominative, respectively.

TRANSLATION

"And so would the one openly admonishing these things be rightly considered well-disposed or a traitor?"

SENTENCE TWO, PART ONE

οὐχ οἱ ἐχθρούς, ὦ Κριτία, κωλύοντες πολλοὺς ποιεῖσθαι, οὐδ᾽ οἱ συμμάχους πλείστους διδάσκοντες κτᾶσθαι, οὗτοι τοὺς πολεμίους ἰσχυροὺς ποιοῦσιν,

VOCABULARY

ἐχθρός, -οῦ, ὁ	enemy	διδάσκω	teach how (+ acc./inf.)
κωλύω	prevent	κτάομαι	get possession of
σύμμαχος, -ου, ὁ	ally	πολέμιος, -ου, ὁ	enemy
πλεῖστος, -η, -ον	most	ἰσχυρός, -ά, -όν	strong

OBSERVATIONS, STRATEGIES, AND NOTES

1. This long and challenging sentence has been divided into two sections to make it more approachable. If you note the parallel construction in the first two phrases it will be easier to translate them:

οὐχ οἱ ἐχθρούς	κωλύοντες πολλοὺς	ποιεῖσθαι,
οὐδ᾽ οἱ συμμάχους πλείστους	**διδάσκοντες**	**κτᾶσθαι,**

The definite articles indicate that the two participles are being used as nouns while the two participles in turn take infinitives. ποιεῖσθαι is in the middle voice. ἡμᾶς, the subject accusative of these infinitives, must be supplied by logic. The objects of the infinitives are the accusatives. This may be translated as "Those who prevent us from making our enemies many and those who teach us how to get possession of the most allies." The negatives are best used to negate ποιοῦσιν.

2. οὗτοι refers to οἱ κωλύοντες and οἱ διδάσκοντες.

3. ἰσχυροὺς: Note that this adjective is not in the attributive position. It is a predicate adjective.

TRANSLATION

"The men, Critias, who prevent us from making our enemies many and who teach us how to get possession of the most allies, these ones are not making our enemies strong,"

SENTENCE TWO, PART TWO

ἀλλὰ πολὺ μᾶλλον οἱ ἀδίκως τε χρήματα ἀφαιρούμενοι καὶ τοὺς οὐδὲν ἀδικοῦντας ἀποκτείνοντες, οὗτοί εἰσιν οἱ καὶ πολλοὺς τοὺς ἐναντίους ποιοῦντες καὶ προδιδόντες οὐ μόνον τοὺς φίλους ἀλλὰ καὶ ἑαυτοὺς δι᾽ αἰσχροκέρδειαν.

VOCABULARY

πολὺ μᾶλλον	much more	ἐναντίος, -α, -ον	opposed to
ἀδίκως (adv.)	unjustly	προδίδωμι	betray
χρῆμα, -ατος, τό	money, possessions (pl.)	φίλος, -ου, ὁ	friend
ἀφαιρέω	take away	αἰσχροκέρδεια, -ας, ἡ	greed
ἀδικέω	be unjust, injure		

OBSERVATIONS, STRATEGIES, AND NOTES

1. This part of the sentence is similar in construction to the first part. The two participles, ἀφαιρούμενοι and ἀποκτείνοντες, are being used as nouns, as the definite article οἱ indicates. Note that the objects of these participles immediately precede them. This is typical Greek word order.

2. οὗτοί refers to οἱ ἀφαιρούμενοι καὶ ἀποκτείνοντες. The construction is the same as in the first part of sentence 2.

3. Note that πολλοὺς is in the predicate position. It is being used as a predicate adjective, as it is in the first part of the sentence.

TRANSLATION

"but much more the men who are taking property unjustly and who are killing those who are committing no wrong, these men are the ones who are making those opposed many and who are betraying not only friends but also themselves on account of their greed."

POLISHED TRANSLATION

"And so would the man who is openly admonishing these things rightly be considered well-disposed to us or a traitor? The men, Critias, who prevent us from making our enemies many and who teach us how to get possession of the most allies are not making our enemies strong; but rather the men who are taking property unjustly and who are killing those who are committing no wrong are the ones who are making the opposition numerous and who are betraying not only their friends but also themselves on account of their greed."

Reading Selection

Theramenes continues to press his case.

εἰ δὲ μὴ ἄλλως γνωστὸν ὅτι ἀληθῆ λέγω, ὧδε ἐπισκέψασθε. πότερον οἴεσθε
Θρασύβουλον καὶ Ἄνυτον καὶ τοὺς ἄλλους φυγάδας ἃ ἐγὼ λέγω μᾶλλον ἂν
ἐνθάδε βούλεσθαι γίγνεσθαι ἢ ἃ οὗτοι πράττουσιν; ἐγὼ μὲν γὰρ οἶμαι νῦν μὲν
αὐτοὺς νομίζειν συμμάχων πάντα μεστὰ εἶναι· εἰ δὲ τὸ κράτιστον τῆς πόλεως
προσφιλῶς ἡμῖν εἶχε, χαλεπὸν ἂν ἡγεῖσθαι εἶναι καὶ τὸ ἐπιβαίνειν ποι τῆς χώρας.   5
ἃ δ' αὖ εἶπεν ὡς ἐγώ εἰμι οἷος ἀεί ποτε μεταβάλλεσθαι, κατανοήσατε καὶ ταῦτα.
τὴν μὲν γὰρ ἐπὶ τῶν τετρακοσίων πολιτείαν καὶ αὐτὸς δήπου ὁ δῆμος ἐψηφίσατο,
διδασκόμενος ὡς οἱ Λακεδαιμόνιοι πάσῃ πολιτείᾳ μᾶλλον ἂν ἢ δημοκρατίᾳ
πιστεύσειαν. ἐπεὶ δέ γε ἐκεῖνοι μὲν οὐδὲν ἀνίεσαν, οἱ δὲ ἀμφὶ Ἀριστοτέλην καὶ
Μελάνθιον καὶ Ἀρίσταρχον στρατηγοῦντες φανεροὶ ἐγένοντο ἐπὶ τῷ χώματι   10
ἔρυμα τειχίζοντες, εἰς ὃ ἐβούλοντο τοὺς πολεμίους δεξάμενοι ὑφ' αὑτοῖς καὶ τοῖς
ἑταίροις τὴν πόλιν ποιήσασθαι, εἰ ταῦτ' αἰσθόμενος ἐγὼ διεκώλυσα, τοῦτ' ἐστὶ
προδότην εἶναι τῶν φίλων;

Xenophon, *Hellenica* 2.3.44–46

NOTES

1. [Line 1] εἰ δὲ μὴ ἄλλως γνωστὸν: Supply ἐστι. Remember that a protasis is always negated by μή.

2. [Line 1] ἐπισκέψασθε: The aorist imperative is replacing the expected present indicative of the simple present condition (R10.2; S2300f). What does the tense signify?

3. [Lines 1–3] πότερον . . . ἤ: The construction introduces a question with alternative propositions. You may leave out "whether" in your translation.

4. [Line 1] οἴεσθε: This introduces an accusative/infinitive construction of indirect statement (R7.1). The infinitive is βούλεσθαι, accompanied by ἄν, which is standing for an original potential optative. ἄν must be retained in the indirect statement (S2023). Translate this as "would wish" or "would prefer." What are the subject accusatives of this infinitive?

5. [Lines 2–3] ἃ ἐγὼ λέγω μᾶλλον ἂν ἐνθάδε βούλεσθαι γίγνεσθαι: βούλεσθαι introduces another accusative/infinitive construction of indirect statement. The relative clause ἃ ἐγὼ λέγω acts as the subject accusative of the infinitive γίγνεσθαι. The ante-

cedent of ἅ has been omitted because it would have been a demonstrative pronoun. The order for translation is οἴεσθε Θρασύβουλον καὶ Ἄνυτον καὶ τοὺς ἄλλους φυγάδας ἂν βούλεσθαι <ταῦτα> ἃ ἐγὼ λέγω γίγνεσθαι ἐνθάδε μᾶλλον ἢ <ἐκεῖνα> ἃ οὗτοι πράττουσιν <γίγνεσθαι>.

6. [Line 3] ἃ οὗτοι πράττουσιν: This relative clause is also a subject of the infinitive γίγνεσθαι. οὗτοι refers to the Thirty.

7. [Lines 3–4] . . . οἶμαι . . . αὐτοὺς νομίζειν . . . πάντα . . . εἶναι: This is another double indirect statement. αὐτοὺς refers to the democrats in exile.

8. [Lines 4–5] εἰ δὲ τὸ κράτιστον . . . εἶχε, χαλεπὸν ἂν ἡγεῖσθαι: The condition is part of the accusative/infinitive indirect statement set up by οἶμαι. The protasis remains unchanged because a subordinate clause in indirect statement keeps its original form after a primary main verb (R7.5). Supply αὐτούς as the subject of the infinitive ἂν ἡγεῖσθαι. What type of condition is this? ἄν and the tense of εἶχε will help you determine the answer to this question.

9. [Line 4] τὸ κράτιστον: Translate this as "the strongest part" or "the strongest element."

10. [Line 5] ἂν ἡγεῖσθαι also sets up an accusative/infinitive construction of indirect statement (R7.1). τὸ ἐπιβαίνειν acts as the subject accusative of εἶναι, with χαλεπὸν as a predicate adjective. The order for translation is <αὐτοὺς> ἂν ἡγεῖσθαι καὶ τὸ ἐπιβαίνειν ποι τῆς χώρας εἶναι χαλεπὸν. What is the grammatical term for τὸ ἐπιβαίνειν?

11. [Line 5] καὶ τὸ ἐπιβαίνειν: Take καί as an adverb and translate it as "even."

12. [Line 5] ποι τῆς χώρας: ποι may take a partitive genitive. Translate the phrase as "anywhere in the land."

13. [Line 6] ἃ δ' αὖ εἶπεν: Occasionally a relative clause placed at the beginning of a sentence and introduced by a neuter relative pronoun in the singular or plural has the sense of "as to what" or "in respect to what." There is no specific antecedent for the relative pronoun (S2494). εἶπεν introduces an indirect statement, as is indicated by ὡς. The subject of εἶπεν is Critias.

14. [Line 6] What voice is μεταβάλλεσθαι? Why?

15. [Line 6] κατανοήσατε καὶ ταῦτα: What is the clue that indicates that καί is being used as an adverb rather than as a conjunction? What form is κατανοήσατε?

16. [Line 7] τὴν μὲν γὰρ is answered by ἐπεὶ δέ in the following sentence.

17. [Line 7] τὴν μὲν γὰρ ἐπὶ τῶν τετρακοσίων πολιτείαν: Note the framing of the prepositional phrase by the definite article τήν and its noun πολιτείαν, which puts ἐπὶ τῶν τετρακοσίων into the attributive position (R2.1). Translate ἐπὶ τῶν τετρακοσίων as "in the time of the Four Hundred" (the pro-Spartan oligarchy that took control in Athens in 411 B.C.E. and held power for just eight months).

18. [Line 7] καὶ αὐτὸς δήπου ὁ δῆμος: Remember that when αὐτός is in the predicate position, it is being used intensively to mean "-self."

19. [Line 8] διδασκόμενος ὡς: διδάσκω may take a ὅτι/ὡς construction of indirect statement (R7.3).

20. [Lines 8–9] ἄν . . . πιστεύσειαν: It is important to note ἄν and the form of πιστεύσειαν. What construction is this?

21. [Line 9] ἐκεῖνοι refers to the Lacedaemonians, who were unwilling to relax their pursuit of the war.

22. [Line 9] οὐδέν is often used as an adverb to mean "not at all."

23. [Lines 9–10] οἱ δὲ ἀμφὶ Ἀριστοτέλην καὶ Μελάνθιον καὶ Ἀρίσταρχον στρατηγοῦντες: Note the framing of the prepositional phrase and that οἱ indicates that the participle στρατηγοῦντες is being used as a noun (R2.3, 6.1). This somewhat convoluted expression refers to those who were generals along with Aristoteles, Melanthius, and Aristarchus. ἀμφὶ may be loosely translated as "along with" in order to make the thought clear. Not much is known about Aristoteles, Melanthius, and Aristarchus, but they were clearly supporters of an oligarchic structure of government for Athens.

24. [Lines 10–11] φανεροὶ ἐγένοντο . . . τειχίζοντες: φανερός with a linking verb may take a supplementary participle and be translated as "be clearly <doing the participle>" (S2107).

25. [Line 10] ἐπὶ τῷ χώματι: This is a reference to the promontory of Eetioneia, to the west of Piraeus.

26. [Line 11] εἰς ὃ ἐβούλοντο τοὺς πολεμίους δεξάμενοι: The antecedent of ὃ is ἔρυμα. The circumstantial participle δεξάμενοι is best taken to indicate the means by which the oligarchs would gain control over the city. This would literally be translated "by admitting the enemy into which," but you may translate it as "and by admitting the enemy into this fort, they wished," for less awkward-sounding English. The enemy would be the Spartans, who could then help the oligarchs in their quest to gain control in Athens.

27. [Lines 11–12] ὑφ' αὑτοῖς καὶ τοῖς ἑταίροις: Note the rough breathing on αὑτοῖς. What part of speech is this? τοῖς ἑταίροις refers to members of the oligarchic political clubs that were active in Athens at this time and in 411 B.C.E. Translate ὑφ' αὑτοῖς καὶ τοῖς ἑταίροις with τὴν πόλιν ποιήσασθαι in the sense of "to make the city subject to themselves and their companions."

28. [Line 12] What is the function of ποιήσασθαι? With what word does it go?

29. [Line 12] Notice that ταῦτ', the direct object of the participle αἰσθόμενος, immediately precedes it. This is common word order. What nuance does the tense of αἰσθόμενος impart?

30. [Line 12] διεκώλυσα: Supply τοῦτο or some similar word. Theramenes and others who favored a more moderate government of the Five Thousand over the more restricted Four Hundred managed to destroy the fort, thereby eliminating an easy means for the extreme oligarchics to allow the Spartans entry. The Four Hundred were supposed to draw up a government of the Five Thousand, which would include a wider group of political participants while still excluding those with little or no property. When the Four Hundred were deposed from power, the Five Thousand were installed. They, too, were in power for only a brief time and democracy was restored in June of 410 after the Athenians' naval victories at Cynossema and Cyzicus.

31. [Lines 12–13] τοῦτ' ἐστὶ προδότην εἶναι τῶν φίλων: This is an odd expression in its literal sense but its meaning is reasonably clear. You may translate it as "is this the action of a betrayer of friends?"

Reading Sixteen

Xenophon, *Hellenica* 2.3.47–49

Focus on Reading

Theramenes answers the charge of changing positions too easily.

ἀποκαλεῖ δὲ κόθορνόν με, ὡς ἀμφοτέροις πειρώμενον ἁρμόττειν. ὅστις δὲ
μηδετέροις ἀρέσκει, τοῦτον ᾧ πρὸς τῶν θεῶν τί ποτε καὶ καλέσαι χρή; σὺ γὰρ δὴ
ἐν μὲν τῇ δημοκρατίᾳ πάντως μισοδημότατος ἐνομίζου, ἐν δὲ τῇ ἀριστοκρατίᾳ
πάντων μισοχρηστότατος γεγένησαι.

Xenophon, Hellenica 2.3.47

SENTENCE ONE

ἀποκαλεῖ δὲ κόθορνόν με, ὡς ἀμφοτέροις πειρώμενον ἁρμόττειν.

VOCABULARY

ἀποκαλέω call	ἀμφότερος, -α, -ον both
κόθορνος, -ου, ὁ a high boot	πειράομαι try, attempt (+ inf.)
ὡς on the grounds that (+ part.)	ἁρμόττω fit, adapt (+ dat.)

OBSERVATIONS, STRATEGIES, AND NOTES

1. This is a straightforward sentence. The subject of ἀποκαλεῖ is Critias. Verbs of naming and calling take a double accusative with the sense "to name someone (acc.) something (acc.)" (R3.4.4; S1613).

2. What word does the participle πειρώμενον modify? Remember that when ὡς is used with a participle to indicate cause, it implies that the cause set forth is what the sub-

ject of the main verb or some other prominent figure in the sentence thinks, but the author does not necessarily accept its veracity (S2086, 2996).

3. ἀμφοτέροις: You will need to supply "sides" or a similar word.

TRANSLATION

"He calls me High Boot on the grounds that I attempt to adapt to both sides."

SENTENCE TWO

ὅστις δὲ μηδετέροις ἀρέσκει, τοῦτον ὦ πρὸς τῶν θεῶν τί ποτε καὶ καλέσαι χρή;

VOCABULARY

ὅστις (indef. pron.)   whoever
μηδέτερος, -α, -ον   neither of the two
ἀρέσκω   please (+ dat.)
ὦ   Oh!

πρός (prep. + gen.)   by, in the name of
καλέω   call, name
χρή   it is necessary (+ inf.)

OBSERVATIONS, STRATEGIES, AND NOTES

1. ὅστις: This introduces a conditional relative clause in the form of a simple present condition (R11.2; S2560, 2561, 2562).
2. τοῦτον is the antecedent of ὅστις, the indefinite relative pronoun.
3. ὦ πρὸς τῶν θεῶν: This exclamation is inserted to increase the drama and intensity of Theramenes' words. You may omit ὦ in your translation.
4. What part of speech is τί and what is its function?
5. ποτε may be used with an interrogative to emphasize it (S346c). It goes with τί and has the sense of "What in the world." Because this does not work well with the exclamation ὦ πρὸς τῶν θεῶν, it may be omitted in your translation.
6. The καί is adverbial and is emphasizing καλέσαι, the word that follows it (S2881), but is difficult to render into English. We would probably communicate its force by voice intonation. You may omit it in your translation.

TRANSLATION

"But whoever pleases neither of the two sides, what, in the name of the gods, is it necessary to call this man?"

SENTENCE THREE

σὺ γὰρ δὴ ἐν μὲν τῇ δημοκρατίᾳ πάντως μισοδημότατος ἐνομίζου, ἐν δὲ τῇ ἀριστοκρατίᾳ πάντων μισοχρηστότατος γεγένησαι.

VOCABULARY

δή (particle)   indeed

δημοκρατία, -ας, ἡ   democracy

πάντως (adv.)   altogether

μισόδημος, -η, -ον   hating the
common people

νομίζω   think, consider

ἀριστοκρατία, -ας, ἡ   aristocracy

μισόχρηστος, -η, -ον   hating the better people

γίγνομαι   be, become

OBSERVATIONS, STRATEGIES, AND NOTES

1. As you read through this sentence, note its parallel construction.
2. σὺ: Since the subject of a verb is always indicated by the verb ending, the nominative personal pronoun emphasizes the subject.
3. ἐν μὲν τῇ δημοκρατίᾳ . . . ἐν δὲ τῇ ἀριστοκρατίᾳ: Note the construction.
4. What degree of adjective are μισοδημότατος and μισοχρηστότατος?
5. ἐνομίζου is a somewhat difficult verb form, as is γεγένησαι. Look for the sentence clue that will help you identify the person of these two forms.
6. What tense is γεγένησαι? What nuance does this impart?

TRANSLATION

"For indeed in the democracy you were considered altogether the greatest hater of the common people, while in the aristocracy you have become the greatest of all haters of the better men."

POLISHED TRANSLATION

"He calls me High Boot on the grounds that I attempt to adapt to both sides. But whoever pleases neither group—in the name of the gods what must we call this man? For indeed in the democracy you were considered altogether the harshest hater of the common people, while in the aristocracy you have become the most ardent of all of those who despise the better men."

Reading Selection

Theramenes finishes his speech before the Thirty and the Council.

ἐγὼ δ’, ὦ Κριτία, ἐκείνοις μὲν ἀεί ποτε πολεμῶ τοῖς οὐ πρόσθεν οἰομένοις καλὴν
ἂν δημοκρατίαν εἶναι, πρὶν [ἂν] καὶ οἱ δοῦλοι καὶ οἱ δι’ ἀπορίαν δραχμῆς ἂν
ἀποδόμενοι τὴν πόλιν †δραχμῆς† μετέχοιεν, καὶ τοῖσδέ γ’ αὖ ἀεὶ ἐναντίος εἰμὶ
οἳ οὐκ οἴονται καλὴν ἂν ἐγγενέσθαι ὀλιγαρχίαν, πρὶν [ἂν] εἰς τὸ ὑπ’ ὀλίγων
τυραννεῖσθαι τὴν πόλιν καταστήσειαν. τὸ μέντοι σὺν τοῖς δυναμένοις καὶ μεθ’   5
ἵππων καὶ μετ’ ἀσπίδων ὠφελεῖν διατάττειν τὴν πολιτείαν πρόσθεν ἄριστον

ἡγούμην εἶναι καὶ νῦν οὐ μεταβάλλομαι. εἰ δ' ἔχεις εἰπεῖν, ὦ Κριτία, ὅπου ἐγὼ σὺν τοῖς δημοτικοῖς ἢ τυραννικοῖς τοὺς καλούς τε κἀγαθοὺς ἀποστερεῖν πολιτείας ἐπεχείρησα, λέγε· ἐὰν γὰρ ἐλεγχθῶ ἢ νῦν ταῦτα πράττων ἢ πρότερον πώποτε πεποιηκώς, ὁμολογῶ τὰ πάντων ἔσχατα παθὼν ἂν δικαίως ἀποθνήσκειν.   10

Xenophon, *Hellenica* 2.3.48–49

NOTES

1. [Lines 1–5] The first sentence is lengthy, but noting its nearly parallel construction will help you see its overall structure:

   ἐκείνοις μὲν ἀεί ποτε πολεμῶ
   τοῖσδέ γ' αὖ ἀεὶ ἐναντίος εἰμὶ

   τοῖς οὐ πρόσθεν οἰομένοις καλὴν ἂν δημοκρατίαν εἶναι,
   οἳ οὐκ οἴονται καλὴν ἂν ἐγγενέσθαι ὀλιγαρχίαν,

   πρὶν [ἂν] καὶ οἱ δοῦλοι καὶ οἱ δι' ἀπορίαν δραχμῆς ἂν ἀποδόμενοι τὴν πόλιν
      †δραχμῆς† μετέχοιεν,
   πρὶν [ἂν] εἰς τὸ ὑπ' ὀλίγων τυραννεῖσθαι τὴν πόλιν καταστήσειαν.

2. [Line 1] ἐκείνοις goes with τοῖς οὐ πρόσθεν οἰομένοις, despite the insertion of ἀεί ποτε πολεμῶ.

3. [Lines 1–2] τοῖς οὐ πρόσθεν οἰομένοις καλὴν ἂν δημοκρατίαν εἶναι: οἰομένοις sets up an accusative/infinitive construction of indirect statement (R7.1). ἂν goes with εἶναι and represents an original potential optative; ἂν is retained as a marker of the original potential optative (S1845, 1846, 2023). Translate this as "those who do not think that there would be a good democracy."

4. [Lines 1–2] πρόσθεν . . . πρὶν: πρόσθεν anticipates πρὶν but may be omitted in your translation (S2440).

5. [Lines 2–3] πρὶν [ἂν] . . . μετέχοιεν: Many commentators believe that the ἂν should be omitted, since a πρίν clause using the optative with ἄν is rare; this is why the word is bracketed (S2186b, 2452). The optative itself is due to assimilation to the mood of the principal clause, which would have been καλὴ ἂν δημοκρατία οὐκ εἴη if it had not been expressed within the indirect statement construction. The text is very problematic and difficult here.

6. [Lines 2–3] καὶ οἱ δοῦλοι καὶ οἱ δι' ἀπορίαν δραχμῆς ἂν ἀποδόμενοι τὴν πόλιν: Note the καὶ . . . καί construction. ἂν goes with the aorist participle ἀποδόμενοι and represents a potential optative (S1845, 1848). This participle is being used as a noun, as the definite article οἱ makes clear. What type of genitive is δραχμῆς?

7. [Line 3] †δραχμῆς†: The text here is corrupt, as the obeli indicate, and there has been an accidental repetition of δραχμῆς. Understand, instead, an idea of "of it," referring to the city or to the government, to go with μετέχοιεν. Translate the entire clause as "until both the slaves and those who would sell the city for a drachma have a share of it."

8. [Lines 3–4] τοῖσδέ . . . οἳ οὐκ οἴονται: The antecedent of οἳ is the demonstrative

τοῖσδέ. οἳ οὐκ οἴονται introduces the accusative/infinitive construction of indirect statement, καλὴν ἂν ἐγγενέσθαι ὀλιγαρχίαν. An ἄν is retained with ἐγγενέσθαι to represent an original potential optative. See note 3, above.

9. [Line 4] πρὶν [ἄν]: See note 5, above.

10. [Lines 4–5] εἰς τὸ ὑπ' ὀλίγων τυραννεῖσθαι: εἰς often indicates an idea of purpose (S1686d). Translate it as "for." Note that ὑπ' ὀλίγων is framed by τὸ and τυραννεῖσθαι. What is the function of ὑπ' ὀλίγων? What type of infinitive is τυραννεῖσθαι?

11. [Lines 5–7] τὸ μέντοι . . . μεταβάλλομαι: This is another difficult sentence. As you read through it, notice that it begins with the neuter singular form of the definite article. Remember that definite articles are not used by themselves in Attic prose, so you need to determine how it is being used. You will note that there is no neuter noun in the sentence, so it is probably being used to mark an articular infinitive (R5.2). διατάττειν is the most logical choice; πολιτείαν is its direct object. This long articular infinitive phrase, **τὸ** μέντοι σὺν τοῖς δυναμένοις καὶ μεθ' ἵππων καὶ μετ' ἀσπίδων ὠφελεῖν **διατάττειν** τὴν πολιτείαν, is the subject accusative of εἶναι, the infinitive of an accusative/infinitive construction of indirect statement set up by ἡγούμην (R7.1). What is the function of ἄριστον?

12. [Lines 5–6] σὺν τοῖς δυναμένοις καὶ μεθ' ἵππων καὶ μετ' ἀσπίδων ὠφελεῖν: δυναμένοις, meaning "be able," needs a complementary infinitive (R5.3) to complete its meaning. ὠφελεῖν provides this function, while καὶ μεθ' ἵππων καὶ μετ' ἀσπίδων specifies how or with what the aid is to be given. Theramenes is referring to citizens who have enough wealth to outfit themselves as either cavalry or hoplites, thus excluding the poorer classes.

13. [Line 7] ἔχω with the infinitive means "to be able to _____."

14. [Line 8] ἀποστερεῖν, meaning "to deprive someone of something," takes an accusative direct object and a genitive to indicate what the person is being deprived of. Which word is the genitive in this construction?

15. [Lines 9–10] What type of condition is ἐὰν γὰρ ἐλεγχθῶ . . . ὁμολογῶ . . . ? What form is ἐλεγχθῶ?

16. [Line 9] ἐλέγχω takes a supplementary participle of indirect statement (S2106). The supplementary participles are πράττων and πεποιηκώς. What case are they and why?

17. [Line 10] ὁμολογῶ introduces an accusative/infinitive construction of indirect statement (R7.1). Take ἄν with the infinitive ἀποθνήσκειν. Why is the ἄν included?

18. [Line 10] τὰ πάντων ἔσχατα is the direct object of παθών. Note its placement directly in front of the participle. τὰ πάντων ἔσχατα, "the worst things of all," refers to extreme punishment, that is, death.

Reading Seventeen

Xenophon, *Hellenica* 2.3.50–53

Focus on Reading

Critias, dismayed that the council has been influenced favorably by Theramenes' speech, takes precautions against him.

Ὡς δ' εἰπὼν ταῦτα ἐπαύσατο καὶ ἡ βουλὴ δήλη ἐγένετο εὐμενῶς ἐπιθορυβήσασα, γνοὺς ὁ Κριτίας ὅτι εἰ ἐπιτρέψοι τῇ βουλῇ διαψηφίζεσθαι περὶ αὐτοῦ, ἀναφεύξοιτο, καὶ τοῦτο οὐ βιωτὸν ἡγησάμενος, προσελθὼν καὶ διαλεχθείς τι τοῖς τριάκοντα ἐξῆλθε, καὶ ἐπιστῆναι ἐκέλευσε τοὺς τὰ ἐγχειρίδια ἔχοντας φανερῶς τῇ βουλῇ ἐπὶ τοῖς δρυφάκτοις.

Xenophon, Hellenica 2.3.50

This lengthy sentence has been divided into several sections.

PART ONE

Ὡς δ' εἰπὼν ταῦτα ἐπαύσατο καὶ ἡ βουλὴ δήλη ἐγένετο εὐμενῶς ἐπιθορυβήσασα,

VOCABULARY

ὡς (conj.)	when	γίγνομαι	become, be
εἶπον (used for aorist of λέγω)	said	εὐμενῶς (adv.)	favorably
παύω	stop	ἐπιθορυβέω	shout
δῆλος, -η, -ον	clear		

OBSERVATIONS, STRATEGIES, AND NOTES

1. ὡς has many uses and meanings; here it is used as the temporal conjunction "when." While both ἐπαύσατο and ἐγένετο are verbs in the temporal clause, the subjects of these verbs are different. By editorial convention, the first word of a paragraph in a Greek text is capitalized.

2. Noticing the placement of the accent on εἰπὼν will help you identify its form. Remember that second aorist participles are accented on the first syllable of the participial suffix rather than on the verb stem.

3. εἰπὼν ταῦτα ἐπαύσατο: Recall that παύω takes a supplementary participle (R6.4, no. 1). When παύω is in the middle voice, the participle will be in the nominative case. The subject of a middle form of παύω is stopping himself from doing the activity denoted by the participle.

4. ἡ βουλὴ δήλη ἐγένετο εὐμενῶς ἐπιθορυβήσασα: The personal construction δῆλος εἰμι or δῆλος γίγνομαι takes a supplementary participle that is categorized as an indirect statement construction (S2107). The meaning is equivalent to the impersonal expression δῆλόν ἐστι ὅτι. Here either a personal or an impersonal translation will work. You may translate this as "the Council was clearly shouting favorably" or "it was clear that the Council was shouting favorably."

TRANSLATION

But when he stopped saying these things and the Council was clearly shouting favorably,

PART TWO

γνοὺς ὁ Κριτίας ὅτι εἰ ἐπιτρέψοι τῇ βουλῇ διαψηφίζεσθαι περὶ αὑτοῦ, ἀναφεύξοιτο,

VOCABULARY

γιγνώσκω	know, recognize	διαψηφίζομαι	vote
ἐπιτρέπω	permit, allow (+ dat./inf.)	ἀναφεύγω	escape

OBSERVATIONS, STRATEGIES, AND NOTES

1. γνούς is the aorist active participle of γιγνώσκω in the nominative singular masculine. γιγνώσκω may take either the participial or the ὅτι/ὡς construction of indirect statement (R7.2, 7.3).

2. ὅτι εἰ ἐπιτρέψοι ... ἀναφεύξοιτο: ὅτι εἰ indicates that a condition is being expressed within the indirect statement. The main verb of the sentence, ἐξῆλθε, is in a secondary tense, and consequently the principal verb of the indirect statement and any subordinate verbs may switch to the corresponding tense of the optative (R7.3,

7.5; S2599, 2603, 2615, 2619). Here the future optatives ἐπιτρέψοι and ἀναφεύξοιτο are standing for original future indicatives. The condition must then be a future most vivid (R10.4), which requires a future indicative in both the protasis and the apodosis.

3. αὐτοῦ refers to Theramenes, as does the subject of ἀναφεύξοιτο.

TRANSLATION

Critias, since he knew that if he permitted the Council to vote concerning him (Theramenes), he (Theramenes) would escape,

PART THREE

καὶ τοῦτο οὐ βιωτὸν ἡγησάμενος, προσελθὼν καὶ διαλεχθείς τι τοῖς τριάκοντα ἐξῆλθε,

VOCABULARY

βιωτός, -όν   worth living, to be endured   διαλέγομαι   discuss
ἡγέομαι   think, consider   ἐξέρχομαι   go away
προσέρχομαι   come forward to speak

OBSERVATIONS, STRATEGIES, AND NOTES

1. ἡγησάμενος: This introduces a brief indirect statement, τοῦτο <εἶναι> οὐ βιωτὸν, with the infinitive εἶναι supplied.
2. What forms are προσελθὼν and διαλεχθείς? What is their function?
3. διαλέγομαι takes an accusative direct object indicating what is discussed and the dative to indicate with whom the discussion takes place. Which word is the direct object?

TRANSLATION

and since he considered that this was not to be endured, after he came forward and discussed something with the Thirty he left,

PART FOUR

καὶ ἐπιστῆναι ἐκέλευσε τοὺς τὰ ἐγχειρίδια ἔχοντας φανερῶς τῇ βουλῇ ἐπὶ τοῖς δρυφάκτοις.

VOCABULARY

ἐφίστημι (intrans.)   stand   ἔχω   have
κελεύω   order   φανερῶς (adv.)   clearly, openly
ἐγχειρίδιον, -ου, τό   dagger   δρύφακτος, –ου, ὁ   railing

OBSERVATIONS, STRATEGIES, AND NOTES

1. ἐκέλευσε: A verb of ordering takes an accusative/infinitive construction (R5.1).

2. τοὺς τὰ ἐγχειρίδια ἔχοντας: Note the framing of τὰ ἐγχειρίδια by τοὺς and the substantive participle ἔχοντας. These words work together as a unit and act as the subject accusative of the infinitive ἐπιστῆναι. Often the participial form of ἔχω is translated as "with" to make less cumbersome English. The phrase refers to the youths who were mentioned in 2.3.23.

3. φανερῶς τῇ βουλῇ: These words are translated literally as "openly to the Council," which is awkward in English. The context requires a meaning such as "in clear view of the council," so translate accordingly.

TRANSLATION

and he ordered those with daggers to stand in clear view of the Council at the railings.

POLISHED TRANSLATION

But when Theramenes stopped speaking and the Council was clearly shouting its approval, Critias knew that Theramenes would be acquitted if he permitted the Council to vote on him. Since he considered this unbearable, he went and discussed something with the Thirty and then went outside. He ordered the youths armed with daggers to stand at the railings in clear view of the Council.

Reading Selection

Critias removes Theramenes' name from the list of the Three Thousand, making it possible to condemn him without a trial. Theramenes pleads to the Council not to allow this.

πάλιν δὲ εἰσελθὼν εἶπεν· Ἐγώ, ὦ βουλή, νομίζω προστάτου ἔργον εἶναι οἵου δεῖ,
ὃς ἂν ὁρῶν τοὺς φίλους ἐξαπατωμένους μὴ ἐπιτρέπῃ. καὶ ἐγὼ οὖν τοῦτο ποιήσω.
καὶ γὰρ οἵδε οἱ ἐφεστηκότες οὔ φασιν ἡμῖν ἐπιτρέψειν, εἰ ἀνήσομεν ἄνδρα τὸν
φανερῶς τὴν ὀλιγαρχίαν λυμαινόμενον. ἔστι δὲ ἐν τοῖς καινοῖς νόμοις τῶν μὲν
ἐν τοῖς τρισχιλίοις ὄντων μηδένα ἀποθνήσκειν ἄνευ τῆς ὑμετέρας ψήφου, τῶν   5
δ' ἔξω τοῦ καταλόγου κυρίους εἶναι τοὺς τριάκοντα θανατοῦν. ἐγὼ οὖν, ἔφη,
Θηραμένην τουτονὶ ἐξαλείφω ἐκ τοῦ καταλόγου, συνδοκοῦν ἅπασιν ἡμῖν. καὶ
τοῦτον, ἔφη, ἡμεῖς θανατοῦμεν. ἀκούσας ταῦτα ὁ Θηραμένης ἀνεπήδησεν ἐπὶ
τὴν ἑστίαν καὶ εἶπεν· Ἐγὼ δ', ἔφη, ὦ ἄνδρες, ἱκετεύω τὰ πάντων ἐννομώτατα,

μὴ ἐπὶ Κριτίᾳ εἶναι ἐξαλείφειν μήτε ἐμὲ μήτε ὑμῶν ὃν ἂν βούληται, ἀλλ᾽ ὅνπερ   10
νόμον οὗτοι ἔγραψαν περὶ τῶν ἐν τῷ καταλόγῳ, κατὰ τοῦτον καὶ ὑμῖν καὶ ἐμοὶ
τὴν κρίσιν εἶναι. καὶ τοῦτο μέν, ἔφη, μὰ τοὺς θεοὺς οὐκ ἀγνοῶ, ὅτι οὐδέν μοι
ἀρκέσει ὅδε ὁ βωμός, ἀλλὰ βούλομαι καὶ τοῦτο ἐπιδεῖξαι, ὅτι οὗτοι οὐ μόνον εἰσὶ
περὶ ἀνθρώπους ἀδικώτατοι, ἀλλὰ καὶ περὶ θεοὺς ἀσεβέστατοι. ὑμῶν μέντοι,
ἔφη, ὦ ἄνδρες καλοὶ κἀγαθοί, θαυμάζω, εἰ μὴ βοηθήσετε ὑμῖν αὐτοῖς, καὶ ταῦτα   15
γιγνώσκοντες ὅτι οὐδὲν τὸ ἐμὸν ὄνομα εὐεξαλειπτότερον ἢ τὸ ὑμῶν ἑκάστου.

Xenophon, *Hellenica* 2.3.51–53

NOTES

1. [Line 1] εἰσελθὼν εἶπεν: A common way to translate an aorist participle together with an aorist finite form is to translate both as finite verbs and insert "and." This may be translated as "And he entered again and said." Another option is "And after he entered again, he said."

2. [Line 1] Ἐγώ: By convention, editors use a capital letter to denote a direct quotation.

3. [Line 1] νομίζω προστάτου ἔργον εἶναι: What type of indirect statement is νομίζω introducing?

4. [Line 1] οἵου δεῖ: This is an elliptical relative clause included within an indirect statement. The antecedent of οἵου is προστάτου, with an omitted τοιούτου ("such a sort"), a correlative that is often used with οἷος. οἵου has been attracted from the expected accusative into the case of its antecedent προστάτου <τοιούτου> (R11.3). A fuller expression of the first part of the sentence is νομίζω προστάτου <τοιούτου> ἔργον εἶναι οἷον δεῖ εἶναι. A strict literal translation of this is "I believe that it is the task of a leader of such a sort as it is necessary to be," but you may translate it as "I believe that it is the task of a leader such as is needed" or, even better, "I believe that it is the task of a proper leader."

5. [Line 2] ὃς ἂν ... μὴ ἐπιτρέπῃ: This is a conditional relative clause, as is indicated by the subjunctive ἐπιτρέπῃ with ἄν (R11.2; S2506, 2508). It is conditional (or indefinite) because the precise identification of the antecedent is unstated. Two complex constructions are mingled here; for the sake of simplicity, omit ὅς in your translation.

6. [Line 2] ὁρῶν τοὺς φίλους ἐξαπατωμένους: ὁράω, a verb of perception, may take the participial or the ὅτι/ὡς construction of indirect statement when the perception is intellectual (R7.2, 7.3; S2110, 2112). When the perception is physical, it takes the participle. In this instance, although either physical or intellectual perception is possible, it is more likely to be intellectual perception. Translate it as "when he sees that his friends are being utterly deceived."

7. [Line 3] καὶ γάρ: Translate this as "and indeed."

8. [Line 3] οἵδε οἱ ἐφεστηκότες: This is a reference to the youths with the daggers who are standing at the railing. What forms are ἐφεστηκότες and οἵδε?

9. [Lines 3–4] οὔ φασιν ... ἐπιτρέψειν, εἰ ἀνήσομεν ... : Take οὔ with ἐπιτρέψειν. This is a future most vivid condition (R10.4) expressed within an indirect statement set up

by φασιν. ἐπιτρέψειν represents the original future indicative. Its subject is the same as the subject of φασιν and thus is omitted (R7.1).

10. [Lines 3–4] ἄνδρα τὸν φανερῶς τὴν ὀλιγαρχίαν λυμαινόμενον: What type of participle is λυμαινόμενον? The definite article provides a clue. Note the framing of ὀλιγαρχίαν and the adverb φανερῶς by τὸν and λυμαινόμενον. Translate these words as a unit. What is the function of ὀλιγαρχίαν?

11. [Line 4] ἔστι δὲ ἐν τοῖς καινοῖς νόμοις: This is translated literally as "it is possible within the new laws," but you may want to be more flexible in your translation.

12. [Lines 4–6] Note the μὲν . . . δέ construction in τῶν μὲν ἐν τοῖς τρισχιλίοις ὄντων μηδένα and τῶν δ' ἔξω τοῦ καταλόγου.

13. [Lines 4–5] τῶν μὲν ἐν τοῖς τρισχιλίοις ὄντων μηδένα: Note the frame, τῶν . . . ὄντων. What type of genitive is ὄντων?

14. [Line 5] μηδένα is the subject accusative of ἀποθνῄσκειν, which is best translated here as "be killed" or "be put to death."

15. [Lines 5–6] τῶν δ' ἔξω τοῦ καταλόγου κυρίους εἶναι τοὺς τριάκοντα: The order for translation is τοὺς τριάκοντα εἶναι κυρίους τῶν ἔξω τοῦ καταλόγου.

16. [Line 6] θανατοῦν is a somewhat awkward explanatory infinitive with κυρίους, which already governs τῶν δ' ἔξω τοῦ καταλόγου. Explanatory infinitives restrict or define the meaning of an adjective (R5.4; S2001). The phrase is translated literally as "but the Thirty have authority to put to death those outside of the list of citizens," which is awkward in English. You may translate it more idiomatically as "but the Thirty have authority to put to death those not enrolled on the list of citizens."

17. [Line 7] τουτονί is an emphatic form of τοῦτον.

18. [Line 7] συνδοκοῦν is the accusative singular neuter present active participle of συνδοκέω and is being used with ἅπασιν ἡμῖν in an accusative absolute (R6.6; S2076). This is an idiomatic expression. Translate the phrase as "since we all agree" or "since all of us are in agreement."

19. [Lines 9–12] ἱκετεύω τὰ πάντων ἐννομώτατα . . . ἐξαλείφειν . . . τὴν κρίσιν εἶναι: ἐξαλείφειν and εἶναι are in apposition to ἐννομώτατα (S1987).

20. [Line 10] μὴ . . . μήτε . . . μήτε: Greek often uses a surplus of negatives. Translate μήτε . . . μήτε as "either . . . or" here.

21. [Line 10] ἐπὶ Κριτίᾳ εἶναι ἐξαλείφειν: This is an idiomatic expression meaning "to be (εἶναι) within the power of someone (ἐπί + dat.) to do something (+ inf.)." Take μὴ with εἶναι.

22. [Line 10] ὑμῶν ὃν ἂν βούληται: This conditional relative clause (R11.2) acts as the direct object of ἐξαλείφειν, along with ἐμὲ. Take ὑμῶν as a partitive genitive with the relative pronoun ὅν. Its displacement outside the relative clause gives it emphasis. What form is βούληται and why?

23. [Lines 10–12] ἀλλ' . . . τὴν κρίσιν εἶναι: The clause continues the construction set up by ἱκετεύω. The order for translation is ἀλλ' <ἱκετεύω> τὴν κρίσιν εἶναι καὶ ὑμῖν καὶ ἐμοὶ κατὰ τοῦτον νόμον ὅνπερ οὗτοι ἔγραψαν περὶ τῶν ἐν τῷ καταλόγῳ. Translate the clause as "But <I beseech you> that the judgment be . . ."

24. [Lines 10–11] ὅνπερ νόμον οὗτοι ἔγραψαν περὶ τῶν ἐν τῷ καταλόγῳ: ὅνπερ is a

strengthened form of the relative pronoun, and its antecedent, νόμον, has been incorporated into the relative clause for stylistic variation. Translate νόμον with κατὰ τοῦτον, in the sense of κατὰ τοῦτον τὸν νόμον, as indicated in note 23.

25. [Line 11] περὶ τῶν ἐν τῷ καταλόγῳ: What is the function of the definite article τῶν?

26. [Lines 12–13] καὶ τοῦτο . . . ὅτι οὐδέν μοι ἀρκέσει ὅδε ὁ βωμός: τοῦτο is amplified by ὅτι οὐδέν μοι ἀρκέσει ὅδε ὁ βωμός.

27. [Line 12] μὰ τοὺς θεούς: μά is used with the accusative of the name of a divinity or the word *god* itself to indicate the divinity by which one swears. Translate this as "by the gods" or "in the names of the gods" (S2894).

28. [Lines 13–14] οὐ μόνον . . . ἀλλὰ καί: "Not only . . . but also."

29. [Lines 15–16] καὶ ταῦτα γιγνώσκοντες: The καί is adverbial. ταῦτα is defined by ὅτι οὐδὲν . . . τὸ ὑμῶν ἑκάστου.

30. [Line 16] τὸ ὑμῶν ἑκάστου: What word must be supplied with the definite article τό?

Reading Eighteen

Xenophon, *Hellenica* 2.3.54–56

Focus on Reading

Theramenes is seized by the Thirty's henchmen.

ἐκ δὲ τούτου ἐκέλευσε μὲν ὁ τῶν τριάκοντα κῆρυξ τοὺς ἕνδεκα ἐπὶ τὸν
Θηραμένην· ἐκεῖνοι δὲ εἰσελθόντες σὺν τοῖς ὑπηρέταις, ἡγουμένου αὐτῶν
Σατύρου τοῦ θρασυτάτου τε καὶ ἀναιδεστάτου, εἶπε μὲν ὁ Κριτίας. Παραδίδομεν
ὑμῖν, ἔφη, Θηραμένην τουτονὶ κατακεκριμένον κατὰ τὸν νόμον· ὑμεῖς δὲ
λαβόντες καὶ ἀπαγαγόντες οἱ ἕνδεκα οὗ δεῖ τὰ ἐκ τούτων πράττετε.

Xenophon, Hellenica 2.3.54

This passage consists of one long sentence but has been divided into sections that may be
treated separately. Punctuation marks serve as markers of logical and grammatical breaks.

PART ONE

ἐκ δὲ τούτου ἐκέλευσε μὲν ὁ τῶν τριάκοντα κῆρυξ τοὺς ἕνδεκα ἐπὶ τὸν
Θηραμένην·

VOCABULARY

ἐκ δὲ τούτου thereupon	κῆρυξ, -υκος, ὁ herald
κελεύω order	τοὺς ἕνδεκα the Eleven

OBSERVATIONS, STRATEGIES, AND NOTES

1. Notice that the words of the sentence fall logically into their units of meaning: [ἐκ δὲ τούτου] [ἐκέλευσε μὲν] [ὁ τῶν τριάκοντα κῆρυξ] [τοὺς ἕνδεκα] [ἐπὶ τὸν Θηραμένην.]

2. ἐκέλευσε, a verb of ordering, usually takes an accusative/infinitive construction (R5.1). We see the accusative, τοὺς ἕνδεκα, a substantival use of a numeral, but notice that there is no infinitive. This probably means that the infinitive must be supplied by context.

3. Make a mental note of μὲν; ἐκεῖνοι δὲ in the next part of the sentence goes with it. This is not a situation of strong contrast and may be omitted in your translation.

4. ὁ τῶν τριάκοντα κῆρυξ: Note the attributive position of τῶν τριάκοντα.

5. τοὺς ἕνδεκα: The Eleven was the board of men that had control over condemned prisoners and imposed the death penalty.

6. ἐπὶ τὸν Θηραμένην provides a clue about what meaning is needed for the missing infinitive. Since ἐπί plus an accusative often means "to," "toward," or "against," it is likely that some idea of going or moving must be supplied. We may extend the idea a bit farther and translate it here as "to seize" since this is clearly what is required by the context.

TRANSLATION

And thereupon the herald of the Thirty ordered the Eleven <to go> against Theramenes;

Or,

And thereupon the herald of the Thirty ordered the Eleven <to seize> Theramenes;

PART TWO

ἐκεῖνοι δὲ εἰσελθόντες σὺν τοῖς ὑπηρέταις, ἡγουμένου αὐτῶν Σατύρου τοῦ θρασυτάτου τε καὶ ἀναιδεστάτου,

VOCABULARY

εἰσέρχομαι	enter	Σάτυρος, -ου, ὁ	Satyrus
ὑπηρέτης, -ου, ὁ	attendant, assistant	θρασύς, -εῖα, -ύ	bold, rash
ἡγέομαι	lead, lead the way	ἀναιδής, -ές	shameless

OBSERVATIONS, STRATEGIES, AND NOTES

1. Notice that there is no verb in this section. We will have to determine whether it is in the next part of this sentence, but for the moment, treat this section separately.

2. Group words that belong together: [ἐκεῖνοι δὲ εἰσελθόντες] [σὺν τοῖς ὑπηρέταις], [ἡγουμένου αὐτῶν Σατύρου τοῦ θρασυτάτου τε καὶ ἀναιδεστάτου,].

3. This section begins with ἐκεῖνοι, a nominative demonstrative pronoun, and εἰσελθόντες, the participle that modifies it. What type of participle is it?

4. Note the genitive participle ἡγουμένου followed by Σατύρου, a proper name in the genitive. What construction is this?

5. Take careful note of τοῦ θρασυτάτου τε καὶ ἀναιδεστάτου, which has two superlative adjectives in the attributive position, as denoted by the definite article τοῦ. These adjectives are modifying Σατύρου. Note the nice linkage provided by the τε καί construction.

6. It is tempting to take αὐτῶν with ἡγουμένου, but ἡγέομαι takes a dative, not a genitive. Remember that superlative adjectives may take partitive genitives (R3.2.2; S1315). αὐτῶν refers to the Eleven and their attendants.

TRANSLATION

and these men, after they entered with the attendants, with Satyrus, the most rash and shameless among them, leading the way,

PART THREE

εἶπε μὲν ὁ Κριτίας· Παραδίδομεν ὑμῖν, ἔφη, Θηραμένην τουτονὶ κατακεκριμένον κατὰ τὸν νόμον·

VOCABULARY

παραδίδωμι   hand over, deliver   κατά (prep. + acc.)   according to
φημί   say, speak   νόμος, -ου, ὁ   law
κατακρίνω   give a sentence against

OBSERVATIONS, STRATEGIES, AND NOTES

1. Note the natural units of meaning of this sentence: [εἶπε μὲν ὁ Κριτίας]· [Παραδίδομεν ὑμῖν], [ἔφη], [Θηραμένην τουτονὶ κατακεκριμένον] [κατὰ τὸν νόμον]·

2. Note εἶπε μὲν followed by ὑμεῖς δὲ in the next section of the sentence.

3. εἶπε μὲν ὁ Κριτίας: This consists of a finite verb plus a proper name in the nominative and thus must provide the subject and main verb of this part of the sentence. But what about ἐκεῖνοι δὲ εἰσελθόντες, the nominatives from the previous section whose verb was lacking? This is another example of anacoluthon, or grammatical inconsistency (S3004). We will have to make an adjustment in the translation of the previous section and translate it as a genitive absolute or temporal clause: "After these men entered with the attendants . . ."

4. Note that Παραδίδομεν begins with a capital letter. This is a direct quotation.

5. ὑμῖν is the indirect object of Παραδίδομεν.

6. τουτονὶ is a strengthened or emphatic form of τοῦτον.

7. Consider the form of κατακεκριμένον carefully. It is a perfect passive participle modifying Θηραμένην. The aspect of the perfect tense provides a nice nuance; it indicates a completed action with a permanent result (R4).

TRANSLATION

And Critias spoke: "We are delivering to you," he said, "this man, Theramenes, since he has been sentenced according to the law;"

PART FOUR

ὑμεῖς δὲ λαβόντες καὶ ἀπαγαγόντες οἱ ἕνδεκα οὗ δεῖ τὰ ἐκ τούτων πράττετε.

VOCABULARY

λαμβάνω	take	οὗ	where
ἀπάγω	lead away	δεῖ	it is necessary
ἕνδεκα	eleven	πράττω	do

OBSERVATIONS, STRATEGIES, AND NOTES

1. Read the sentence in terms of its units of meaning rather than word by word: [ὑμεῖς δὲ λαβόντες καὶ ἀπαγαγόντες οἱ ἕνδεκα] [οὗ δεῖ] [τὰ ἐκ τούτων] [πράττετε].

2. There is a nice framing of the sentence with ὑμεῖς at the beginning and πράττετε, a present active imperative and the verb that goes with ὑμεῖς, at the end.

3. Notice the two aorist participles λαβόντες and ἀπαγαγόντες modifying the subject ὑμεῖς. In Greek prose the writer often likes to include all details and stages of an action and frequently employs the aorist participle to do this. As we have noted previously, a common strategy for such instances is to translate the participles in the same mood and tense as the main verb and add conjunctions. Since πράττετε is in the imperative mood (which is made clear by context), you may translate the participles as imperatives. You may also translate them as temporal clauses, "After you seize . . ."

4. ὑμεῖς is modified by the appositive οἱ ἕνδεκα (S916). Translate this as "But you, the Eleven."

5. οὗ δεῖ: οὗ is a relative adverb introducing a relative clause. The antecedent, an expression like "to the place," is implied. Translate this as "where it is necessary."

6. τὰ ἐκ τούτων is an idiomatic expression. The definite article τά is used to indicate that the prepositional phrase ἐκ τούτων is being used as a noun (R2.3), and the entire expression is the direct object of πράττετε. This would literally be translated "the things from these things" but it may be translated as "what follows from this."

TRANSLATION

"and you, the Eleven, seize and take <him> where it is necessary (prison) and do what comes next (put him to death)."

POLISHED TRANSLATION

The herald of the Thirty then ordered the Eleven to seize Theramenes. These men entered with the attendants, while Satyrus, the most rash and shameless among them, was leading the way. Critias spoke: "We are delivering this man Theramenes to you," he said, "since he has been sentenced according to the law. You, the Eleven, seize him and take him to the appropriate place and do what comes next."

Reading Selection

Theramenes is dragged from the altar and put to death.

ὡς δὲ ταῦτα εἶπεν, εἷλκε μὲν ἀπὸ τοῦ βωμοῦ ὁ Σάτυρος, εἷλκον δὲ οἱ ὑπηρέται.
ὁ δὲ Θηραμένης ὥσπερ εἰκὸς καὶ θεοὺς ἐπεκαλεῖτο καὶ ἀνθρώπους καθορᾶν
τὰ γιγνόμενα. ἡ δὲ βουλὴ ἡσυχίαν εἶχεν, ὁρῶσα καὶ τοὺς ἐπὶ τοῖς δρυφάκτοις
ὁμοίους Σατύρῳ καὶ τὸ ἔμπροσθεν τοῦ βουλευτηρίου πλῆρες τῶν φρουρῶν, καὶ
οὐκ ἀγνοοῦντες ὅτι ἐγχειρίδια ἔχοντες παρῆσαν. οἱ δ' ἀπήγαγον τὸν ἄνδρα διὰ   5
τῆς ἀγορᾶς μάλα μεγάλῃ τῇ φωνῇ δηλοῦντα οἷα ἔπασχε. λέγεται δ' ἓν ῥῆμα καὶ
τοῦτο αὐτοῦ. ὡς εἶπεν ὁ Σάτυρος ὅτι οἰμώξοιτο, εἰ μὴ σιωπήσειεν, ἐπήρετο· Ἂν
δὲ σιωπῶ, οὐκ ἄρ', ἔφη, οἰμώξομαι; καὶ ἐπεί γε ἀποθνῄσκειν ἀναγκαζόμενος τὸ
κώνειον ἔπιε, τὸ λειπόμενον ἔφασαν ἀποκοτταβίσαντα εἰπεῖν αὐτόν· Κριτίᾳ τοῦτ'
ἔστω τῷ καλῷ.   10

Xenophon, *Hellenica* 2.3.55–56

NOTES

1. [Line 1] εἷλκε and εἷλκον: Theramenes is the object of both verbs. Note the repetition in εἷλκε μὲν . . . εἷλκον δὲ. This is an example of *anaphora* (S3010), the repetition, for the sake of emphasis, of a word or phrase at the beginning of successive clauses. The imperfect is used to indicate the beginning of an action (S1900). Translate the verb as "began to drag." Supply αὐτόν as the direct object of both forms.

2. [Line 2] ὥσπερ εἰκὸς: Supply ἦν for this parenthetical statement and translate this as "as was reasonable."

3. [Line 2] Note the construction καὶ θεοὺς ἐπεκαλεῖτο καὶ ἀνθρώπους.

4. [Lines 2–3] ἐπεκαλεῖτο is taking an accusative/infinitive construction here in a manner similar to a verb of ordering (R5.1).

5. [Line 3] What is the function of τὰ γιγνόμενα? What is the nuance imparted by the tense of this form?

6. [Line 3] ἡσυχίαν εἶχεν: Translate this as "kept quiet."

7. [Lines 3–4] ὁρῶσα καὶ τοὺς ἐπὶ τοῖς δρυφάκτοις ὁμοίους Σατύρῳ καὶ τὸ ἔμπροσθεν τοῦ βουλευτηρίου πλῆρες τῶν φρουρῶν: Note the καὶ . . . καί construction. ὁρῶσα is the present participle of ὁράω in the nominative singular feminine form modifying βουλή. Since ὁράω is a verb of perception, it frequently takes the participial construction of indirect statement to indicate intellectual perception (R7.2). Here the participle, which would have been a form of εἰμί, has been omitted and you will need to supply it. ὁμοίους and πλῆρες are predicate adjectives. Notice that the definite article τούς indicates that the prepositional phrase ἐπὶ τοῖς δρυφάκτοις is being used as a noun (R2.3). The definite article τό has also substantivized the adverb ἔμπροσθεν. ὁμοίους is the predicate adjective modifying τοὺς ἐπὶ τοῖς δρυφάκτοις, and πλῆρες modifies τὸ ἔμπροσθεν τοῦ βουλευτηρίου in the same manner.

8. [Line 4] What type of genitive is τῶν φρουρῶν?

9. [Line 5] What type of construction is ἀγνοοῦντες introducing? Notice that Xenophon has switched from a singular verb agreeing with ἡ βουλὴ to a plural form: ἡ δὲ βουλὴ ἡσυχίαν εἶχεν, ὁρῶσα . . . καὶ οὐκ ἀγνοοῦντες . . . The plural form refers to the individual members of the Council.

10. [Line 5] ἐγχειρίδια ἔχοντες: ἔχοντες is frequently translated as "with" in such contexts.

11. [Line 5] οἱ δ' denotes a switch of subject to Satyrus and his henchmen.

12. [Line 6] What type of dative is μεγάλῃ τῇ φωνῇ?

13. [Line 6] What is the function of δηλοῦντα? What does it modify?

14. [Line 6] οἷα ἔπασχε: This relative clause is acting as the direct object of δηλοῦντα.

15. [Lines 6–7] λέγεται δ' ἓν ῥῆμα καὶ τοῦτο αὐτοῦ: καὶ is adverbial and τοῦτο goes with ἓν ῥῆμα. Translate καὶ as "also" or "as well."

16. [Line 7] αὐτοῦ: This refers to Theramenes and is a genitive of possession.

17. [Line 7] ὅτι οἰμώξοιτο, εἰ μὴ σιωπήσειε: This is a future more vivid condition (R10.4) within an indirect statement. The apodosis is simply οἰμώξοιτο and the future optative is representing an original future indicative because the main verb, εἶπεν, is in a secondary tense (R7.3). σιωπήσειε, the verb of the protasis, also changed because of the secondary main verb (R7.5). σιωπήσῃς, the original aorist subjunctive, is represented by the aorist optative σιωπήσειε. ἐάν changed to εἰ when the subjunctive was replaced by the optative, and the person changed from second to third because of the indirect form. The original form would have been ἐὰν μὴ σιωπήσῃς, οἰμώξῃ.

18. [Lines 7–8] Ἂν δὲ σιωπῶ, οὐκ ἄρ' . . . οἰμώξομαι;: What type of condition is this? Remember that ἄν is Attic for ἐάν. Note also that it has been capitalized by the editor of the text to indicate a direct quotation.

19. [Line 9] τὸ λειπόμενον: The definite article indicates that the participle is being used as a noun (R6.1). This literally means "what remains" or "the remaining portion." The expression refers to the dregs of wine. Translate it as "dregs."

20. [Line 9] ἀποκοτταβίσαντα: This modifies αὐτόν. Cottabus was a drinking game. A player threw the remainder of his wine, the dregs, into a saucer or basin or at some other target while speaking the name of his beloved. The sound the wine dregs made

when they struck the basin was thought to portend the success or failure of the relationship.

21. [Line 9] Κριτίᾳ: The placement of Critias's name at the beginning of the sentence and separate from its modifier τῷ καλῷ gives it special emphasis. This is a sarcastic use of Critias's name in place of the beloved's. What form is ἔστω?

Reading Nineteen

Xenophon, *Hellenica* 2.4.1–6

Focus on Reading

After the death of Theramenes, the Thirty continue their violent actions.

Θηραμένης μὲν δὴ οὕτως ἀπέθανεν· οἱ δὲ τριάκοντα, ὡς ἐξὸν ἤδη αὐτοῖς
τυραννεῖν ἀδεῶς, προεῖπον μὲν τοῖς ἔξω τοῦ καταλόγου μὴ εἰσιέναι εἰς τὸ
ἄστυ, ἦγον δὲ ἐκ τῶν χωρίων, ἵν᾽ αὐτοὶ καὶ οἱ φίλοι τοὺς τούτων ἀγροὺς ἔχοιεν.
φευγόντων δὲ εἰς τὸν Πειραιᾶ καὶ ἐντεῦθεν πολλοὺς ἄγοντες ἐνέπλησαν καὶ τὰ
Μέγαρα καὶ τὰς Θήβας τῶν ὑποχωρούντων.

Xenophon, Hellenica 2.4.1

SENTENCE ONE

Θηραμένης μὲν δὴ οὕτως ἀπέθανεν· οἱ δὲ τριάκοντα, ὡς ἐξὸν ἤδη αὐτοῖς
τυραννεῖν ἀδεῶς, προεῖπον μὲν τοῖς ἔξω τοῦ καταλόγου μὴ εἰσιέναι εἰς τὸ ἄστυ,
ἦγον δὲ ἐκ τῶν χωρίων, ἵν᾽ αὐτοὶ καὶ οἱ φίλοι τοὺς τούτων ἀγροὺς ἔχοιεν.

VOCABULARY

οὕτως (adv.) in this way	προεῖπον ordered, proclaimed (+ dat./inf.)
ἀποθνήσκω die	ἔξω (prep. + gen.) outside
ὡς (conj.) since	κατάλογος, -ου, ὁ register, list
ἔξεστι be possible	εἴσειμι go into, enter
ἤδη (adv.) now	ἄστυ, -εως, τό city, town
τυραννέω rule despotically	χωρίον, -ου, τό landed property, estate
ἀδεῶς (adv.) without fear, confidently	ἀγρός, -οῦ, ὁ field

OBSERVATIONS, STRATEGIES, AND NOTES

1. Note the μέν and δέ in Θηραμένης μὲν . . . οἱ δὲ τριάκοντα.

2. ὡς ἐξὸν ἤδη αὐτοῖς τυραννεῖν ἀδεῶς: This is an accusative absolute with the impersonal verb ἔξεστι (R6.6; S2076). What is the function of τυραννεῖν?

3. ὡς ἐξὸν: What nuance does ὡς give to this accusative absolute?

4. αὐτοῖς: ἔξεστι usually takes a dative of person in Attic prose.

5. Note the construction in προεῖπον μὲν . . . ἦγον δὲ. προεῖπον is used for the aorist of προλέγω.

6. τοῖς ἔξω τοῦ καταλόγου: This is a substantival use of the prepositional phrase (R2.3). Think about these words as a unit.

7. ἦγον δὲ ἐκ τῶν χωρίων: Supply αὐτούς as the direct object of ἦγον. This clause is literally translated "they led them out of their estates," but it is clearer to translate it as "they evicted them from their estates."

8. ἵν' αὐτοὶ καὶ οἱ φίλοι τοὺς τούτων ἀγροὺς ἔχοιεν: Since ἦγον, the main verb, is in a secondary tense, the verb of a purpose clause is in the optative mood (R9.1; S2196). It is, however, always possible to retain the subjunctive mood (S2197).

9. What is the function of αὐτοί?

TRANSLATION

Theramenes, then, died in this way. But the Thirty, because it was now possible for them to rule without fear, ordered those outside the citizens list not to enter the city, and they evicted them from their estates so that they themselves and their friends might have their fields.

SENTENCE TWO

φευγόντων δὲ εἰς τὸν Πειραιᾶ καὶ ἐντεῦθεν πολλοὺς ἄγοντες ἐνέπλησαν καὶ τὰ Μέγαρα καὶ τὰς Θήβας τῶν ὑποχωρούντων.

VOCABULARY

φεύγω flee	Μέγαρα, -ων, τά Megara
ἐντεῦθεν (adv.) from that place, from there	Θῆβαι, -ῶν, αἱ Thebes
ἐμπίμπλημι fill	ὑποχωρέω withdraw, retire

OBSERVATIONS, STRATEGIES, AND NOTES

1. φευγόντων δὲ εἰς τὸν Πειραιᾶ: This genitive participle is part of a genitive absolute (R6.5). Supply αὐτῶν or τούτων to complete it since there is no noun or pronoun in the genitive to go with the participle. This missing pronoun refers to those who had been evicted by the Thirty.

2. καὶ ἐντεῦθεν: The καί is adverbial here. Translate this as "even from there" or "from there as well."

3. πολλοὺς: This is a reference to a large number of those who had been evicted from their farms.

4. Note καὶ . . . καί in καὶ τὰ Μέγαρα καὶ τὰς Θήβας.

5. ἐνέπλησαν . . . τῶν ὑποχωρούντων: Verbs meaning "fill" or "be full of" take the genitive. The genitive indicates what something is being filled with while the accusative denotes what is being filled (S1369). Notice that the definite article τῶν indicates that the participle ὑποχωρούντων is being used as a substantive (R6.1).

TRANSLATION

But when they fled to Piraeus, \<the Thirty\>, evicting many from there as well, filled both Megara and Thebes with those who were withdrawing \<from Athens\>.

POLISHED TRANSLATION

Theramenes, then, died in this way. But the Thirty, because it was now possible for them to rule without fear, proclaimed to those not on the citizens list that they could not enter the city, and they evicted them from their estates, so that they themselves and their friends might get possession of their fields. But when these men fled to Piraeus, the Thirty, evicting many from there as well, filled both Megara and Thebes with those who were leaving Athens.

Reading Selection

As the Thirty strengthen their hold on Athens and continue their violent acts against Athenian citizens and the metics, democrats flee the city. Thrasybulus, the leader of these exiles, and his men seize Phyle, a naturally defensible place on Mount Parnes near Attica's border with Boeotia, in January (403 B.C.E.). The Thirty set out against the democrats at Phyle to attempt to dislodge them.

Ἐκ δὲ τούτου Θρασύβουλος ὁρμηθεὶς ἐκ Θηβῶν ὡς σὺν ἑβδομήκοντα Φυλὴν
χωρίον καταλαμβάνει ἰσχυρόν. οἱ δὲ τριάκοντα ἐβοήθουν ἐκ τοῦ ἄστεως
σύν τε τοῖς τρισχιλίοις καὶ σὺν τοῖς ἱππεῦσι καὶ μάλ' εὐημερίας οὔσης. ἐπεὶ
δὲ ἀφίκοντο, εὐθὺς μὲν θρασυνόμενοί τινες τῶν νέων προσέβαλον πρὸς τὸ
χωρίον, καὶ ἐποίησαν μὲν οὐδέν, τραύματα δὲ λαβόντες ἀπῆλθον. βουλομένων   5
δὲ τῶν τριάκοντα ἀποτειχίζειν, ὅπως ἐκπολιορκήσειαν αὐτοὺς ἀποκλείσαντες
τὰς ἐφόδους τῶν ἐπιτηδείων, ἐπιγίγνεται τῆς νυκτὸς χιὼν παμπλήθης καὶ τῇ
ὑστεραίᾳ. οἱ δὲ νιφόμενοι ἀπῆλθον εἰς τὸ ἄστυ, μάλα συχνοὺς τῶν σκευοφόρων
ὑπὸ τῶν ἐκ Φυλῆς ἀποβαλόντες. γιγνώσκοντες δὲ ὅτι καὶ ἐκ τῶν ἀγρῶν
ληλατήσοιεν, εἰ μή τις φυλακὴ ἔσοιτο, διαπέμπουσιν εἰς τὰς ἐσχατιὰς ὅσον   10

πεντεκαίδεκα στάδια ἀπὸ Φυλῆς τούς τε Λακωνικοὺς πλὴν ὀλίγων φρουροὺς καὶ
τῶν ἱππέων δύο φυλάς. οὗτοι δὲ στρατοπεδευσάμενοι ἐν χωρίῳ λασίῳ ἐφύλαττον.
ὁ δὲ Θρασύβουλος, ἤδη συνειλεγμένων εἰς τὴν Φυλὴν περὶ ἑπτακοσίους,
λαβὼν αὐτοὺς καταβαίνει τῆς νυκτός· θέμενος δὲ τὰ ὅπλα ὅσον τρία ἢ τέτταρα
στάδια ἀπὸ τῶν φρουρῶν ἡσυχίαν εἶχεν. ἐπεὶ δὲ πρὸς ἡμέραν ἐγίγνετο, καὶ ἤδη   15
ἀνίσταντο ὅποι ἐδεῖτο ἕκαστος ἀπὸ τῶν ὅπλων, καὶ οἱ ἱπποκόμοι ψήχοντες τοὺς
ἵππους ψόφον ἐποίουν, ἐν τούτῳ ἀναλαβόντες οἱ περὶ Θρασύβουλον τὰ ὅπλα
δρόμῳ προσέπιπτον· καὶ ἔστι μὲν οὓς αὐτῶν κατέβαλον, πάντας δὲ τρεψάμενοι
ἐδίωξαν ἓξ ἢ ἑπτὰ στάδια, καὶ ἀπέκτειναν τῶν μὲν ὁπλιτῶν πλέον ἢ εἴκοσι καὶ
ἑκατόν, τῶν δὲ ἱππέων Νικόστρατόν τε τὸν καλὸν ἐπικαλούμενον, καὶ ἄλλους δὲ   20
δύο, ἔτι καταλαβόντες ἐν ταῖς εὐναῖς.

Xenophon, Hellenica 2.4.2–6

NOTES

1. [Line 1] ἐκ . . . τούτου: Translate this as "thereupon."
2. [Line 1] What form of the verb is ὁρμηθείς? In the middle and passive voices, this verb means "set out" or "start."
3. [Line 1] ὡς σὺν ἑβδομήκοντα: Supply ἀνθρώπους. When ὡς precedes a numeral it means "about."
4. [Line 2] What is the function of χωρίον . . . ἰσχυρόν?
5. [Line 2] καταλαμβάνει is an annalistic present and may be translated as a past tense (S1884).
6. [Line 3] σύν τε τοῖς τρισχιλίοις: This refers to those on the citizens list.
7. [Line 3] σὺν τοῖς ἱππεῦσι: The cavalry were supporters of the Thirty.
8. [Line 3] καὶ μάλ' εὐημερίας οὔσης: What construction is εὐημερίας οὔσης? The καί is adverbial and emphasizes μάλ' (= μάλα).
9. [Line 4] τινες τῶν νέων: What is the function of τῶν νέων?
10. [Lines 4–5] προσέβαλλον πρὸς τὸ χωρίον: Note the redundancy of πρός. This is not uncommon.
11. [Line 5] ἐποίησαν μὲν οὐδέν, τραύματα δὲ λαβόντες: Note the μὲν . . . δέ construction.
12. [Line 5] What is the form and function of οὐδέν?
13. [Lines 5–6] What are the functions of βουλομένων δὲ τῶν τριάκοντα and ἀποτειχίζειν?
14. [Lines 5–6] Note that βουλομένων δὲ τῶν τριάκοντα has introduced the purpose clause ὅπως ἐκπολιορκήσειαν αὐτοὺς (R9.1). What form is ἐκπολιορκήσειαν? It is important to note that the main verb of this sentence is ἐπιγίγνεται, a present form. Because this is another annalistic present, it is considered to be a secondary tense. Thus, the mood of ἐκπολιορκήσειαν is consistent.
15. [Line 6] What type of participle is ἀποκλείσαντες? What is its form? This participle is part of the purpose clause.

16. [Line 7] What type of time expression is τῆς νυκτός?

17. [Lines 7–8] What type of time expression is τῇ ὑστεραίᾳ?

18. [Line 8] οἱ δὲ denotes a switch of subject back to the Thirty and their supporters. What type of participle is νιφόμενοι?

19. [Line 9] ὑπὸ τῶν ἐκ Φυλῆς: A genitive of personal agent (R3.2.3) is being used with the active verb ἀποβαλόντες. Such a construction sometimes occurs when the verb has a passive notion implied by its meaning; here "losing" implies "being deprived of." It is easiest to translate the phrase as if it were a dative: "to those from Phyle." Note that the definite article τῶν works with ἐκ Φυλῆς to make a substantive phrase (R2.3). The direct object of ἀποβαλόντες is συχνούς.

20. [Lines 9–10] ἐκ τῶν ἀγρῶν λεηλατήσοιεν, εἰ μή τις φυλακὴ ἔσοιτο is part of the indirect statement set up by γιγνώσκοντες δὲ ὅτι. What type of condition is it? The subject of λεηλατήσοιεν is the men from Phyle.

21. [Line 10] διαπέμπουσιν is another annalistic present. What are the direct objects of this verb?

22. [Line 13] περὶ ἑπτακοσίους stands in for the genitive needed to complete the genitive absolute with συνειλεγμένων. What form is συνειλεγμένων?

23. [Line 14] Why is καταβαίνει in the present tense?

24. [Line 14] What type of time expression is τῆς νυκτός?

25. [Line 14] What form is θέμενος?

26. [Line 16] ἀνίσταντο: Take ἀπὸ τῶν ὅπλων with ἀνίσταντο, supplying φρουροί as the subject. What tense is ἀνίσταντο?

27. [Line 16] ὅποι ἐδεῖτο ἕκαστος: They were all performing their various duties. Translate this as "where each one needed."

28. [Line 17] ἐν τούτῳ: Translate this as "in the meantime."

29. [Line 18] What type of dative is δρόμῳ?

30. [Line 18] What is the subject of προσέπιπτον?

31. [Line 18] Note the construction of καὶ ἔστι μὲν οὓς . . . πάντας δὲ.

32. [Line 18] ἔστι μὲν οὓς αὐτῶν κατέβαλον: ἔστι οὕς is an idiomatic expression meaning "some" (S2513, 2514). αὐτῶν is a partitive genitive (R3.2.2) that goes with it.

33. [Line 19] What is the grammatical function of ἐξ ἢ ἑπτὰ στάδια?

34. [Lines 19–20] Note the μὲν . . . δέ in τῶν μὲν ὁπλιτῶν . . . τῶν δὲ ἱππέων. What type of genitive is being used here?

35. [Lines 20–21] Note the τε . . . καί in Νικόστρατόν τε τὸν καλὸν ἐπικαλούμενον, καὶ ἄλλους δὲ δύο.

Reading Twenty

Xenophon, *Hellenica* 2.4.7–10

Focus on Reading

After the battle, the Thirty recognize the need to find a refuge should the situation continue to deteriorate.

ἐπαναχωρήσαντες δὲ καὶ τροπαῖον στησάμενοι καὶ συσκευασάμενοι ὅπλα τε ὅσα ἔλαβον καὶ σκεύη ἀπῆλθον ἐπὶ Φυλῆς. οἱ δὲ ἐξ ἄστεως ἱππεῖς βοηθήσαντες τῶν μὲν πολεμίων οὐδένα ἔτι εἶδον, προσμείναντες δὲ ἕως τοὺς νεκροὺς ἀνείλοντο οἱ προσήκοντες ἀνεχώρησαν εἰς ἄστυ. ἐκ δὲ τούτου οἱ τριάκοντα, οὐκέτι νομίζοντες ἀσφαλῆ σφίσι τὰ πράγματα, ἐβουλήθησαν Ἐλευσῖνα ἐξιδιώσασθαι, ὥστε εἶναι σφίσι καταφυγήν, εἰ δεήσειε.

Xenophon, Hellenica 2.4.7–8

SENTENCE ONE

ἐπαναχωρήσαντες δὲ καὶ τροπαῖον στησάμενοι καὶ συσκευασάμενοι ὅπλα τε ὅσα ἔλαβον καὶ σκεύη ἀπῆλθον ἐπὶ Φυλῆς.

VOCABULARY

ἐπαναχωρέω retreat, return	λαμβάνω take, capture
τροπαῖον, -ου, τό trophy	σκεῦος, -ους, τό equipment
ἵστημι set up	ἀπέρχομαι go away, depart
συσκευάζω pack up	ἐπί (prep. + gen.) toward
ὅπλα, -ων, τά arms, weapons	Φύλη, -ης, ἡ Phyle
ὅσος, -η, -ον as many as, as much as	

OBSERVATIONS, STRATEGIES, AND NOTES

1. Notice the three circumstantial participles ἐπαναχωρήσαντες, στησάμενοι, and συσκευασάμενοι in the nominative case. What does the aorist tense indicate?

2. These participles and the subject of the sentence refer to Thrasybulus and his men.

3. ὅπλα τε ὅσα ἔλαβον καὶ σκεύη: Remember that τε is postpositive and belongs by sense in front of the word it follows. The τε . . . καί construction is being used here to link ὅπλα and σκεύη, the direct objects of συσκευασάμενοι.

4. ὅσα ἔλαβον: The antecedents of ὅσα, a type of relative pronoun, are ὅπλα and σκεύη. Since "as much as" or "as many as" will be awkward in English, it may be preferable to omit it in your translation. Translate ἔλαβον as "had taken" or "had seized." An aorist tense may have the force of a pluperfect in a relative clause, as well as in temporal and causal clauses (S1943).

TRANSLATION

After they returned and set up a trophy and packed up the weapons and equipment as much as they had captured, they departed toward Phyle.

Or, omitting ὅσα,

After they returned and set up a trophy and packed up the weapons and equipment they had captured, they departed toward Phyle.

SENTENCE TWO

οἱ δὲ ἐξ ἄστεως ἱππεῖς βοηθήσαντες τῶν μὲν πολεμίων οὐδένα ἔτι εἶδον, προσμείναντες δὲ ἕως τοὺς νεκροὺς ἀνείλοντο οἱ προσήκοντες ἀνεχώρησαν εἰς ἄστυ.

VOCABULARY

ἄστυ, -εως, τό city, town	προσμένω wait
ἱππεύς, -έως, ὁ horseman, cavalry	ἕως (conj.) until
βοηθέω come to aid, help	νεκρός, -οῦ, ὁ corpse, dead body
πολέμιος, -α, -ον hostile; enemy (as noun)	ἀναιρέω (mid.) take up bodies for burial
οὐδείς, οὐδεμία, οὐδέν no one, nothing	προσήκων, -οντος, ὁ relative, family member
ἔτι (adv.) still	ἀναχωρέω withdraw, return
ὁράω see	

OBSERVATIONS, STRATEGIES, AND NOTES

1. οἱ δὲ ἐξ ἄστεως ἱππεῖς: Note the framing of the prepositional phrase by the definite article and ἱππεῖς to make a single unit (R2.1).

2. τῶν μὲν πολεμίων . . . προσμείναντες δὲ: Note the μὲν . . . δέ construction.

3. εἶδον is a difficult form. It is the third person plural aorist active indicative of ὁράω. Be sure to learn the principal parts of this common verb.

4. The temporal clause ἕως τοὺς νεκροὺς ἀνείλοντο οἱ προσήκοντες has been introduced by the participle προσμείναντες. ἀνείλοντο is the aorist middle of ἀναιρέω. It may be translated as a pluperfect in a temporal clause (S1943).

TRANSLATION

And the cavalry from the city, when they came to help, saw no one of the enemy still <there>, and after they waited until the relatives had retrieved the corpses for burial, they returned to the city.

SENTENCE THREE

ἐκ δὲ τούτου οἱ τριάκοντα, οὐκέτι νομίζοντες ἀσφαλῆ σφίσι τὰ πράγματα, ἐβουλήθησαν Ἐλευσῖνα ἐξιδιώσασθαι, ὥστε εἶναι σφίσι καταφυγήν, εἰ δεήσειε.

VOCABULARY

ἐκ τούτου	thereupon	Ἐλευσίς, -ῖνος, ἡ	Eleusis
οὐκέτι (adv.)	no longer	ἐξιδιόομαι	appropriate for oneself
ἀσφαλής, -ές	safe	ὥστε (conj.)	so that
πρᾶγμα, -ατος, τό	thing; (pl.) situation, affairs	καταφυγή, -ῆς, ἡ	refuge
βούλομαι	wish	δεῖ	it is necessary

OBSERVATIONS, STRATEGIES, AND NOTES

1. νομίζοντες: When there is a verb of thinking, you should expect an accusative/infinitive construction of indirect statement (R7.1). If the infinitive is a linking verb such as εἶναι, it is very often omitted, as here.

2. σφίσι: This is the third person personal pronoun in the dative plural, used as an indirect reflexive pronoun, the only use of this pronoun in Attic prose (S325d, 1228b). An indirect reflexive pronoun is a pronoun found in a subordinate construction that refers back to the subject of the main clause (S1225). σφίσι refers to the subjects of νομίζοντες and ἐβουλήθησαν. The forms for this pronoun are listed in Appendix C.

3. ἐβουλήθησαν: Remember that deponent verbs have middle/passive forms and active meanings. For the aorist form, there are two possibilities: aorist middle or aorist passive. Deponents whose aorist forms are in the middle voice are called "middle deponents" while those that have passive forms are called "passive deponents" (S810, 811). Which one is βούλομαι?

4. ὥστε εἶναι σφίσι καταφυγήν: ὥστε is occasionally used with the accusative/infinitive construction to denote purpose or intended result (S2267). Here translate εἶναι as "would be."

5. εἰ δεήσειε: This is the protasis of a future less vivid condition (R10.4) used without its apodosis. Translate it as "if it should be necessary."

TRANSLATION

Thereupon the Thirty, since they thought that the situation was no longer safe for them, wished to appropriate Eleusis for themselves, so that there would be a refuge for them if it should be necessary.

POLISHED TRANSLATION

After they returned, set up a trophy, and packed up the weapons and equipment they had captured, they departed toward Phyle. Consequently, when the cavalry from the city came to help, they saw none of the enemy still there, and after they waited until the relatives had retrieved the dead for burial they returned to the city. Thereupon the Thirty, since they thought that the situation was no longer safe for them, wished to seize Eleusis for themselves so that they would have a refuge should it be needed.

Reading Selection

The Thirty enter Eleusis and make arrests there in order to enable them to establish their refuge in the town. Thrasybulus and his men reach Piraeus.

καὶ παραγγείλαντες τοῖς ἱππεῦσιν ἦλθον εἰς Ἐλευσῖνα Κριτίας τε καὶ οἱ ἄλλοι τῶν
τριάκοντα· ἐξέτασίν τε ποιήσαντες ἐν τοῖς ἱππεῦσι, φάσκοντες εἰδέναι βούλεσθαι
πόσοι εἶεν καὶ πόσης φυλακῆς προσδεήσοιντο, ἐκέλευον ἀπογράφεσθαι πάντας·
τὸν δὲ ἀπογραψάμενον ἀεὶ διὰ τῆς πυλίδος ἐπὶ τὴν θάλατταν ἐξιέναι. ἐπὶ δὲ τῷ
αἰγιαλῷ τοὺς μὲν ἱππέας ἔνθεν καὶ ἔνθεν κατέστησαν, τὸν δ᾽ ἐξιόντα ἀεὶ οἱ ὑπηρέται   5
συνέδουν. ἐπεὶ δὲ πάντες συνειλημμένοι ἦσαν, Λυσίμαχον τὸν ἵππαρχον ἐκέλευον
ἀναγαγόντα παραδοῦναι αὐτοὺς τοῖς ἕνδεκα. τῇ δ᾽ ὑστεραίᾳ εἰς τὸ Ὠιδεῖον
παρεκάλεσαν τοὺς ἐν τῷ καταλόγῳ ὁπλίτας καὶ τοὺς ἄλλους ἱππέας. ἀναστὰς
δὲ Κριτίας ἔλεξεν· Ἡμεῖς, ἔφη, ὦ ἄνδρες, οὐδὲν ἧττον ὑμῖν κατασκευάζομεν τὴν
πολιτείαν ἢ ἡμῖν αὐτοῖς. δεῖ οὖν ὑμᾶς, ὥσπερ καὶ τιμῶν μεθέξετε, οὕτω καὶ τῶν   10
κινδύνων μετέχειν. τῶν οὖν συνειλημμένων Ἐλευσινίων καταψηφιστέον ἐστίν,
ἵνα ταὐτὰ ἡμῖν καὶ θαρρῆτε καὶ φοβῆσθε. δείξας δέ τι χωρίον, εἰς τοῦτο ἐκέλευε
φανερὰν φέρειν τὴν ψῆφον. οἱ δὲ Λακωνικοὶ φρουροὶ ἐν τῷ ἡμίσει τοῦ Ὠιδείου
ἐξωπλισμένοι ἦσαν· ἦν δὲ ταῦτα ἀρεστὰ καὶ τῶν πολιτῶν οἷς τὸ πλεονεκτεῖν μόνον
ἔμελεν. Ἐκ δὲ τούτου λαβὼν ὁ Θρασύβουλος τοὺς ἀπὸ Φυλῆς περὶ χιλίους ἤδη   15
συνειλεγμένους, ἀφικνεῖται τῆς νυκτὸς εἰς τὸν Πειραιᾶ. οἱ δὲ τριάκοντα ἐπεὶ
ᾔσθοντο ταῦτα, εὐθὺς ἐβοήθουν σύν τε τοῖς Λακωνικοῖς καὶ σὺν τοῖς ἱππεῦσι καὶ
τοῖς ὁπλίταις· ἔπειτα ἐχώρουν κατὰ τὴν εἰς τὸν Πειραιᾶ ἁμαξιτὸν ἀναφέρουσαν.

Xenophon, *Hellenica* 2.4.8–10

NOTES

1. [Line 1] παραγγείλαντες: Usually we would find an infinitive accompanying a verb of ordering. Here it has been omitted because it may be supplied by logic. Supply "to follow." παραγγέλλω, like many compound verbs, takes a dative (S1544, 1545).

2. [Lines 1–2] Κριτίας τε καὶ οἱ ἄλλοι τῶν τριάκοντα: Note τε καὶ linking the two subjects. What is the function of τῶν τριάκοντα?

3. [Line 2] φάσκοντες εἰδέναι βούλεσθαι: φάσκω takes an accusative/infinitive construction of indirect statement. Remember that if the subject of the verb of speaking and the subject of the infinitive are the same, the subject is omitted or is in the nominative case (R7.1). Here the subject has been omitted. Supply "they."

4. [Line 2] εἰδέναι is the perfect active infinitive of οἶδα and is a complementary infinitive (R5.3) with βούλεσθαι. It also introduces the indirect questions πόσοι εἶεν and πόσης φυλακῆς προσδεήσοιντο (R7.6).

5. [Line 3] What forms are εἶεν and προσδεήσοιντο and why?

6. [Line 3] What voice is the infinitive ἀπογράφεσθαι?

7. [Line 4] τὸν δὲ ἀπογραψάμενον . . . ἐξιέναι: This continues the accusative/infinitive construction set up by ἐκέλευον, a verb of ordering (R5.1).

8. [Line 5] τοὺς μὲν ἱππέας . . . τὸν δ᾽ ἐξιόντα: Note the μὲν . . . δέ construction. What is the sentence clue that indicates that the participle ἐξιόντα is being used as a noun?

9. [Line 5] κατέστησαν: καθίστημι has both a first and a second aorist. The first aorist is transitive, while the second aorist is not. Since the first and second aorist forms are identical in the third person plural, the presence of an accusative direct object will help you determine that this is the transitive first aorist form.

10. [Line 6] συνειλημμένοι ἦσαν: This is the third person plural pluperfect passive indicative of συλλαμβάνω.

11. [Line 6] ἐκέλευον: What construction does a verb of ordering take?

12. [Line 7] ἀναγαγόντα παραδοῦναι αὐτούς: An aorist participle and an aorist infinitive within an accusative/infinitive construction may be translated in a parallel fashion as two infinitive forms joined by "and." Translate this as "to take them up and hand them over."

13. [Line 7] τῇ δ᾽ ὑστεραίᾳ: Supply ἡμέρᾳ. What type of time expression is this?

14. [Line 8] τοὺς ἐν τῷ καταλόγῳ ὁπλίτας: Take these words as a unit, as the framing indicates.

15. [Lines 8–9] ἀναστὰς: You may choose to translate this aorist participle as a finite form with ἔλεξεν. Be sure to insert "and."

16. [Line 10] What type of pronoun is ἡμῖν αὐτοῖς?

17. [Lines 10–11] καὶ τῶν κινδύνων: The καί is adverbial.

18. [Line 11] καταψηφιστέον is an impersonal verbal adjective denoting necessity (S2152). It literally means "it must be condemned," but you should translate it actively and supply "you" as the subject. καταψηφίζω takes a genitive to indicate the person being condemned. Critias is advocating that they condemn to death the Eleusinians who had been arrested so that the Thirty would have this place as a refuge.

He is making the Three Thousand partners in the Thirty's crime by forcing them to vote on the matter.

19. [Line 12] ταὐτὰ: This equals τὰ αὐτά. What is the name of this phenomenon? Translate it as "the same things."

20. [Line 12] What moods are θαρρῆτε and φοβῆσθε and why?

21. [Line 12] εἰς τοῦτο refers to τι χωρίον.

22. [Line 12] ἐκέλευε: Supply αὐτούς as the subject of the infinitive φέρειν.

23. [Line 13] Although φανερὰν is being used as a predicate adjective to modify τὴν ψῆφον, it will work best in English to translate it as an adverb. Translate it as "openly."

24. [Line 13] οἱ δὲ Λακωνικοὶ φρουροὶ: Note that Spartan guards have been placed all around the area to back up Critias's order to the Three Thousand to condemn the Eleusinians.

25. [Lines 14–15] τῶν πολιτῶν οἷς τὸ πλεονεκτεῖν μόνον ἔμελεν: Supply ἐκείνοις with τῶν πολιτῶν as the omitted antecedent of οἷς. What type of genitive is τῶν πολιτῶν?

26. [Line 14] τὸ πλεονεκτεῖν is the subject of ἔμελεν. What is the grammatical label for τὸ πλεονεκτεῖν?

27. [Line 15] Ἐκ δὲ τούτου: Translate this as "thereupon" or "then."

28. [Lines 15–16] τοὺς ἀπὸ Φυλῆς περὶ χιλίους ἤδη συνειλεγμένους: περί with a numeral means "about." περὶ χιλίους ἤδη συνειλεγμένους modifies τοὺς ἀπὸ Φυλῆς somewhat parenthetically. Translate the phrase as "the men from Phyle, about a thousand <of whom> had already gathered."

29. [Line 16] What type of time expression is τῆς νυκτὸς?

30. [Line 17] ἐβοήθουν: In a military context such as this one, βοηθέω means "go out" or "set out."

31. [Line 18] What noun does ἀναφέρουσαν modify?

Reading Twenty-One

Xenophon, *Hellenica* 2.4.18–22

Focus on Reading

Thrasybulus and the men at Phyle continue to resist the Thirty and have taken possession of Piraeus. When the Thirty realize this, they move toward the port in response. The democrats take position on the hill of Munichia. After Thrasybulus delivers words of encouragement to the men, the battle begins.

Ταῦτα δ' εἰπὼν καὶ μεταστραφεὶς πρὸς τοὺς ἐναντίους, ἡσυχίαν εἶχε· καὶ γὰρ ὁ
μάντις παρήγγελλεν αὐτοῖς μὴ πρότερον ἐπιτίθεσθαι, πρὶν [ἂν] τῶν σφετέρων
ἢ πέσοι τις ἢ τρωθείη· ἐπειδὰν μέντοι τοῦτο γένηται, ἡγησόμεθα μέν, ἐφη,
ἡμεῖς, νίκη δ' ὑμῖν ἔσται ἑπομένοις, ἐμοὶ μέντοι θάνατος, ὥς γέ μοι δοκεῖ. καὶ
οὐκ ἐψεύσατο, ἀλλ' ἐπεὶ ἀνέλαβον τὰ ὅπλα, αὐτὸς μὲν ὥσπερ ὑπὸ μοίρας τινὸς
ἀγόμενος ἐκπηδήσας πρῶτος ἐμπεσὼν τοῖς πολεμίοις ἀποθνῄσκει, καὶ τέθαπται
ἐν τῇ διαβάσει τοῦ Κηφισοῦ·

Xenophon, Hellenica 2.4.18–19

SENTENCE ONE, PART ONE

Ταῦτα δ' εἰπὼν καὶ μεταστραφεὶς πρὸς τοὺς ἐναντίους, ἡσυχίαν εἶχε·

VOCABULARY

εἶπον (used as aorist of λέγω)   said   ἐναντίοι, -ων, οἱ   adversaries, enemy
μεταστρέφω   turn   ἔχω ἡσυχίαν   keep quiet
πρός (prep. + acc.)   toward

OBSERVATIONS, STRATEGIES, AND NOTES

1. This is a very straightforward sentence with two aorist participles, εἰπών and μεταστραφείς, in the nominative case. The participles modify Thrasybulus, who is also the subject of the main verb. He has just delivered a speech to encourage his men in their fight. Notice that Ταῦτα, the direct object of εἰπών, precedes it.

2. μεταστραφείς is the nominative singular masculine aorist passive participle of μεταστρέφω. In the passive this verb means "turn about" or "turn around."

TRANSLATION

After he said these things and turned around toward the enemy, he kept quiet;

SENTENCE ONE, PART TWO

καὶ γὰρ ὁ μάντις παρήγγελλεν αὐτοῖς μὴ πρότερον ἐπιτίθεσθαι, πρὶν [ἂν] τῶν σφετέρων ἢ πέσοι τις ἢ τρωθείη·

VOCABULARY

καὶ γάρ (particle)   and in fact, and indeed
μάντις, -εως, ὁ   seer
παραγγέλλω   exhort
ἐπιτίθημι (mid.)   attack
πρίν (conj.)   until

σφέτερος, -α, -ον   their own
ἤ . . . ἤ (conj.)   either . . . or
πίπτω   fall
τιτρώσκω   wound

OBSERVATIONS, STRATEGIES, AND NOTES

1. παρήγγελλεν: Note the imperfect tense of this verb. παραγγέλλω, a verb of ordering, takes a dative of person plus the infinitive in what is essentially implied indirect discourse, since the meaning of the verb implies speaking. Since παρήγγελλεν is in a secondary tense, any accompanying subordinate verbs may switch to the corresponding tense of the optative.

2. πρότερον . . . πρὶν: πρότερον, "before," is redundant with πρὶν and may be omitted in your translation.

3. πρὶν [ἂν] . . . πέσοι . . . τρωθείη: Some editors omit ἄν because the optatives are representing an original subjunctive plus ἄν after πρίν and the ἄν should drop out. The optative has been used because of the indirect statement construction (S2449, 2452).

4. τῶν σφετέρων . . . τις: Supply "men" with τῶν σφετέρων. What type of genitive is this?

TRANSLATION

and in fact the seer was exhorting them not to attack until one of their own men either fell or was wounded;

SENTENCE ONE, PART THREE

ἐπειδὰν μέντοι τοῦτο γένηται, ἡγησόμεθα μέν, ἔφη, ἡμεῖς, νίκη δ' ὑμῖν ἔσται ἑπομένοις, ἐμοὶ μέντοι θάνατος, ὥς γέ μοι δοκεῖ.

VOCABULARY

ἐπειδάν (conj.) whenever	νίκη, -ης, ἡ victory
μέντοι (particle) yet, however, nevertheless,	ἕπομαι follow
certainly	θάνατος, -ου, ὁ death
γίγνομαι become, be	ὥς (rel. adv.) as
ἡγέομαι lead	γε (particle) at any rate, at least
φημί say	δοκέω seem, appear

OBSERVATIONS, STRATEGIES, AND NOTES

1. These are the words of the seer.
2. ἐπειδὰν μέντοι τοῦτο γένηται: This is an indefinite temporal clause which takes a construction analogous to a condition. Here we have ἐπειδὰν . . . γένηται acting as the equivalent of the protasis, followed by ἡγησόμεθα, the equivalent of the apodosis. Thus the construction is similar to a future more vivid condition with ἐάν plus the subjunctive in the protasis and the future indicative in the apodosis (R11.4; S2401).
3. ἡγησόμεθα μέν . . . νίκη δ' ὑμῖν ἔσται ἑπομένοις: Note the μέν . . . δέ construction. ἔσται has the same function as ἡγησόμεθα, while ἑπομένοις may be taken as a substitution for the protasis of the future more vivid condition (R10.4, 10.6). Translate the participle as "if you follow."
4. ἐμοὶ μέντοι θάνατος: Supply ἔσται.
5. ὥς γέ μοι δοκεῖ: The seer is foretelling his own death in battle.

TRANSLATION

"However, whenever this happens, we shall lead," he said, "and victory will be yours if you follow, yet for me there will be death, as it appears to me, at any rate."

SENTENCE TWO

καὶ οὐκ ἐψεύσατο, ἀλλ᾽ ἐπεὶ ἀνέλαβον τὰ ὅπλα, αὐτὸς μὲν ὥσπερ ὑπὸ μοίρας τινὸς ἀγόμενος ἐκπηδήσας πρῶτος ἐμπεσὼν τοῖς πολεμίοις ἀποθνῄσκει, καὶ τέθαπται ἐν τῇ διαβάσει τοῦ Κηφισοῦ·

VOCABULARY

ψεύδομαι   lie, speak falsely or in error
ἀλλά (conj.)   but
ἐπεί (conj.)   when
ἀναλαμβάνω   take up
ὥσπερ (conj.)   as if
ὑπό (prep. + gen.)   by
μοῖρα, -ας, ἡ   destiny, fate
ἄγω   lead

ἐκπηδάω   leap up
πρῶτος, -η, -ον   first
ἐμπίπτω   fall upon
ἀποθνῄσκω   die, be killed
θάπτω   bury
διάβασις, -εως, ἡ   crossing
Κηφισός, -οῦ, ὁ   Cephisus (a river)

OBSERVATIONS, STRATEGIES, AND NOTES

1. This sentence, despite its length, is straightforward.
2. Remember that αὐτός is used as an intensive pronoun meaning "-self" when it is in the nominative case. If the subject is expressed, αὐτός will be in the predicate position. If the subject is unexpressed, as here, αὐτός modifies the implied subject of the verb (S1206).
3. ὥσπερ ὑπὸ μοίρας τινὸς ἀγόμενος: Take these words together.
4. ἀποθνῄσκει is another example of an annalistic present (S1884).
5. τέθαπται: This is an excellent example of the aspect of the perfect tense, which indicates a completed action with a permanent result (R4). You may choose to translate this as "lies buried."

TRANSLATION

And he was not speaking falsely, but when they took up their weapons, he himself, as if being led by some fate, after he leapt up first and fell upon the enemy, died, and he lies buried in the crossing of the Cephisus.

POLISHED TRANSLATION

After Thrasybulus said these things and turned around toward the enemy, he kept quiet. And in fact, the seer kept exhorting them not to attack until one of their own men either fell or was wounded. "However, we shall lead, when this happens," the seer said, "and victory will be yours, if you follow, yet for me there will be death, as it appears to me, at any rate." The seer was not speaking falsely, but when they took up their weapons, he himself, as if being led by some fate, leapt up first and fell upon the enemy and then died, and he now lies buried at the ford of the Cephisus.

Reading Selection

The battle continues. Critias and other members of the Thirty are killed. While the dead are being recovered, the two sides approach each other and converse.

οἱ δ' ἄλλοι ἐνίκων καὶ κατεδίωξαν μέχρι τοῦ ὁμαλοῦ. ἀπέθανον δ' ἐνταῦθα τῶν
μὲν τριάκοντα Κριτίας τε καὶ Ἱππόμαχος, τῶν δὲ ἐν Πειραιεῖ δέκα ἀρχόντων
Χαρμίδης ὁ Γλαύκωνος, τῶν δ' ἄλλων περὶ ἑβδομήκοντα. καὶ τὰ μὲν ὅπλα
ἔλαβον, τοὺς δὲ χιτῶνας οὐδενὸς τῶν πολιτῶν ἐσκύλευσαν. ἐπεὶ δὲ τοῦτο
ἐγένετο καὶ τοὺς νεκροὺς ὑποσπόνδους ἀπεδίδοσαν, προσιόντες ἀλλήλοις   5
πολλοὶ διελέγοντο. Κλεόκριτος δὲ ὁ τῶν μυστῶν κῆρυξ, μάλ' εὔφωνος ὤν,
κατασιωπησάμενος ἔλεξεν· Ἄνδρες πολῖται, τί ἡμᾶς ἐξελαύνετε; τί ἀποκτεῖναι
βούλεσθε; ἡμεῖς γὰρ ὑμᾶς κακὸν μὲν οὐδὲν πώποτε ἐποιήσαμεν, μετεσχήκαμεν
δὲ ὑμῖν καὶ ἱερῶν τῶν σεμνοτάτων καὶ θυσιῶν καὶ ἑορτῶν τῶν καλλίστων, καὶ
συγχορευταὶ καὶ συμφοιτηταὶ γεγενήμεθα καὶ συστρατιῶται, καὶ πολλὰ μεθ' ὑμῶν   10
κεκινδυνεύκαμεν καὶ κατὰ γῆν καὶ κατὰ θάλατταν ὑπὲρ τῆς κοινῆς ἀμφοτέρων
ἡμῶν σωτηρίας τε καὶ ἐλευθερίας. πρὸς θεῶν πατρῴων καὶ μητρῴων καὶ
συγγενείας καὶ κηδεστίας καὶ ἑταιρίας, πάντων γὰρ τούτων πολλοὶ κοινωνοῦμεν
ἀλλήλοις, αἰδούμενοι καὶ θεοὺς καὶ ἀνθρώπους παύσασθε ἁμαρτάνοντες εἰς
τὴν πατρίδα, καὶ μὴ πείθεσθε τοῖς ἀνοσιωτάτοις τριάκοντα, οἳ ἰδίων κερδέων   15
ἕνεκα ὀλίγου δεῖν πλείους ἀπεκτόνασιν Ἀθηναίων ἐν ὀκτὼ μησὶν ἢ πάντες
Πελοποννήσιοι δέκα ἔτη πολεμοῦντες. ἐξὸν δ' ἡμῖν ἐν εἰρήνῃ πολιτεύεσθαι, οὗτοι
τὸν πάντων αἴσχιστόν τε καὶ χαλεπώτατον καὶ ἀνοσιώτατον καὶ ἔχθιστον καὶ
θεοῖς καὶ ἀνθρώποις πόλεμον ἡμῖν πρὸς ἀλλήλους παρέχουσιν. ἀλλ' εὖ γε μέντοι
ἐπίστασθε ὅτι καὶ τῶν νῦν ὑφ' ἡμῶν ἀποθανόντων οὐ μόνον ὑμεῖς ἀλλὰ καὶ ἡμεῖς   20
ἔστιν οὓς πολλὰ κατεδακρύσαμεν.

Xenophon, Hellenica 2.4.19–22

NOTES

1. [Line 1] The verb ἀπέθανον is not repeated with Χαρμίδης and περὶ ἑβδομήκοντα, which are also subjects of this verb. περί means "about" or "approximately" when used with a numeral.

2. [Lines 1–3] Note the μὲν . . . δέ construction in τῶν μὲν τριάκοντα, τῶν δὲ ἐν Πειραιεῖ δέκα ἀρχόντων, and τῶν δ' ἄλλων. Why is the genitive case used here?

3. [Line 2] τῶν δὲ ἐν Πειραιεῖ δέκα ἀρχόντων: Note the framing and take these words as a unit.

4. [Lines 3–4] τὰ μὲν ὅπλα . . . τοὺς δὲ χιτῶνας: Note the construction.

5. [Line 5] ὑποσπόνδους: This is technically a predicate adjective modifying νεκροὺς,

where English would use an adverb (S1043). Translate the adjective as "under a truce."

6. [Line 6] What form is ὤν? What is its function?

7. [Line 7] Note that Ἄνδρες πολῖται begins with a capital letter to indicate a direct quotation.

8. [Line 7] ἀποκτεῖναι: What is the tense of this verb? What nuance does that give to the Greek?

9. [Line 8] ἡμεῖς γὰρ ὑμᾶς: Note the stylistic juxtaposition of the two pronouns.

10. [Lines 8–10] What forms are μετεσχήκαμεν and γεγενήμεθα? Why? μετέχω, meaning "share," takes a genitive.

11. [Line 10] What is the grammatical function of συγχορευταὶ, συμφοιτηταὶ, and συστρατιῶται?

12. [Lines 11–12] ὑπὲρ τῆς κοινῆς ἀμφοτέρων ἡμῶν σωτηρίας τε καὶ ἐλευθερίας: Note that a τε καί joins the two objects of the preposition. What is the function of κοινῆς?

13. [Line 14] καὶ θεοὺς καὶ ἀνθρώπους: Notice the καὶ . . . καί construction.

14. [Line 14] ἀνθρώπους παύσασθε ἁμαρτάνοντες: παύω takes a supplementary participle. When it is in the middle voice it means "stop oneself from doing something." The participle, which will be in the nominative, will indicate the activity that is being stopped (R6.4, no. 1; S2098). What form is παύσασθε?

15. [Line 16] ὀλίγου δεῖν: This is an idiomatic expression meaning "almost." It goes with πλείους, the alternate form of πλείονας.

16. [Lines 16–17] πάντες Πελοποννήσιοι δέκα ἔτη πολεμοῦντες: Supply ἀπεκτόνασιν from the first part of the sentence. Note the fitting use of the perfect tense. What type of time expression is δέκα ἔτη?

17. [Line 17] ἐξὸν δ᾽ ἡμῖν ἐν εἰρήνῃ πολιτεύεσθαι: Impersonal verbs may take an accusative absolute (R6.6; S2076). Take this accusative absolute concessively.

18. [Lines 18–19] **τὸν** πάντων αἴσχιστόν τε καὶ χαλεπώτατον καὶ ἀνοσιώτατον καὶ ἔχθιστον καὶ θεοῖς καὶ ἀνθρώποις **πόλεμον**: Note the unusually long frame! The four superlatives are attributive adjectives and are linked together by τε καὶ . . . καὶ . . . καί. You will need to be creative in your translation in order to render all these ideas smoothly in English. καὶ θεοῖς καὶ ἀνθρώποις: Note another καὶ . . . καί construction. These datives go with ἔχθιστον.

19. [Line 18] πάντων αἴσχιστόν: What is the function of πάντων?

20. [Line 20] What form is ἐπίστασθε? What construction is it introducing?

21. [Line 20] οὐ μόνον . . . ἀλλὰ καί: "Not only . . . but also."

22. [Line 21] ἔστιν οὕς: This is an idiomatic expression (S2514). Translate it as "some" and take with the partitive genitive phrase τῶν νῦν ὑφ᾽ ἡμῶν ἀποθανόντων (R3.2.2).

23. [Line 21] πολλὰ is adverbial. Translate it as "greatly."

Reading Twenty-Two

Xenophon, *Hellenica* 2.4.39–43

Focus on Reading

After the death of Critias and the others, the Thirty are deposed by the Three Thousand and replaced by a board of ten, consisting of one man elected from each tribe. The Thirty retire to Eleusis, and the new group of ten now have governing power in Athens. Thrasybulus and his men still control Piraeus. The Thirty in Eleusis as well as their supporters in Athens send word to Sparta requesting aid. Both Lysander and Pausanias set out from Sparta with troops, and after a few skirmishes a settlement is reached between the opposing sides. The agreement allows both sides to return to their homes, with the exception of the Thirty, the Eleven, and the Ten who had ruled in Piraeus. Since these men can be prosecuted for their actions, most remain in Eleusis. Anyone left in Athens who fears remaining there is also allowed to go to Eleusis. After this agreement has been reached, Thrasybulus addresses the Athenians.

> τούτων δὲ περανθέντων Παυσανίας μὲν διῆκε τὸ στράτευμα, οἱ δ᾽ ἐκ τοῦ
> Πειραιῶς ἀνελθόντες σὺν τοῖς ὅπλοις εἰς τὴν ἀκρόπολιν ἔθυσαν τῇ Ἀθηνᾷ.
> ἐπεὶ δὲ κατέβησαν† οἱ στρατηγοί, ἔνθα δὴ ὁ Θρασύβουλος ἔλεξεν· Ὑμῖν, ἔφη,
> ὦ ἐκ τοῦ ἄστεως ἄνδρες, συμβουλεύω ἐγὼ γνῶναι ὑμᾶς αὐτούς. μάλιστα δ᾽ ἂν
> γνοίητε, εἰ ἀναλογίσαισθε ἐπὶ τίνι ὑμῖν μέγα φρονητέον ἐστίν, ὥστε ἡμῶν ἄρχειν
> ἐπιχειρεῖν.

Xenophon, Hellenica 2.4.39–40

SENTENCE ONE

τούτων δὲ περανθέντων Παυσανίας μὲν διῆκε τὸ στράτευμα, οἱ δ᾽ ἐκ τοῦ
Πειραιῶς ἀνελθόντες σὺν τοῖς ὅπλοις εἰς τὴν ἀκρόπολιν ἔθυσαν τῇ Ἀθηνᾷ.

VOCABULARY

περαίνω   accomplish, complete

Παυσανίας, -ου, ὁ   Pausanias, a Spartan king

διΐημι   dismiss

στράτευμα, -ατος, τό   army

ἀνέρχομαι   go up

σύν (prep. + dat.)   with

εἰς (prep. + acc.)   into

ἀκρόπολις, -εως, ἡ   acropolis

θύω   sacrifice

Ἀθηνᾶ, -ᾶς, ἡ   Athena

OBSERVATIONS, STRATEGIES, AND NOTES

1. τούτων δὲ περανθέντων: What construction is this? τούτων refers to the settlement between the two sides.

2. Παυσανίας μὲν . . . οἱ δ᾽ ἐκ τοῦ Πειραιῶς: Note the μὲν . . . δέ construction. In Attic Greek, the genitive of Πειραιεύς is Πειραιῶς.

3. οἱ δ᾽ ἐκ τοῦ Πειραιῶς: Treat this as a substantive unit (R2.3).

4. Noting the accent on ἀνελθόντες will help you to identify it as a second aorist participle. Often the best translation of a circumstantial participle in the aorist is as a temporal clause introduced by "after."

TRANSLATION

After these things had been completed, Pausanias dismissed the army, and the men from Piraeus, after they went up to the Acropolis with their weapons, sacrificed to Athena.

SENTENCE TWO

ἐπεὶ δὲ κατέβησαν† οἱ στρατηγοί, ἔνθα δὴ ὁ Θρασύβουλος ἔλεξεν· Ὑμῖν, ἔφη, ὦ ἐκ τοῦ ἄστεως ἄνδρες, συμβουλεύω ἐγὼ γνῶναι ὑμᾶς αὐτούς.

VOCABULARY

ἐπεί (conj.)   when

καταβαίνω   come down, descend

στρατηγός, -οῦ, ὁ   general

ἔνθα (adv.)   then

δή (particle)   indeed

λέγω   speak

φημί   speak, say

ἄστυ, -εως, τό   city

ἀνήρ, -δρός, ὁ   man, (pl.) gentlemen

συμβουλεύω   advise

γιγνώσκω   know

OBSERVATIONS, STRATEGIES, AND NOTES

1. κατέβησαν† οἱ στρατηγοί: The text is corrupt here, as the obelus indicates, and while many emendations have been proposed, there is no agreement. You may translate as is for the sake of simplicity. It is clear that Thrasybulus is speaking to the Assembly.

2. ὑμᾶς αὐτούς: This is the second person plural reflexive pronoun.

TRANSLATION

But when the generals came down, then indeed Thrasybulus spoke: "Gentlemen from the city," he said, "I advise you to know yourselves."

SENTENCE THREE

μάλιστα δ' ἂν γνοίητε, εἰ ἀναλογίσαισθε ἐπὶ τίνι ὑμῖν μέγα φρονητέον ἐστίν, ὥστε ἡμῶν ἄρχειν ἐπιχειρεῖν.

VOCABULARY

μάλιστα (sup. adv.)   most
γιγνώσκω   know
ἀναλογίζομαι   calculate, consider
ἐπί (prep. + dat.)   for

μέγα φρονητέον   one must be arrogant
ὥστε (conj.)   so that, so as
ἄρχω   rule over (+ gen.)
ἐπιχειρέω   try

OBSERVATIONS, STRATEGIES, AND NOTES

1. ἂν γνοίητε: Supply ὑμᾶς αὐτούς from the previous sentence as the direct object.

2. ἂν γνοίητε, εἰ ἀναλογίσαισθε: It is not unusual for the apodosis of a condition to be placed first for extra emphasis. What type of condition is this? What is the force of the aorist tense?

3. ἐπὶ τίνι: Translate this as "for what reason" or "why." What part of speech is τίνι?

4. φρονητέον: A verbal adjective ending in -τέος denotes necessity and is often used in an impersonal construction in combination with ἐστί, as here (S2152). The agent is expressed by the dative. This construction cannot be translated literally in a neat fashion. Translate it as "for what reason you have to be greatly arrogant."

5. ὥστε ἡμῶν ἄρχειν ἐπιχειρεῖν: Remember that ὥστε introduces a result clause (R12.1; S2249–58). Here the infinitive ἐπιχειρεῖν indicates that it is a natural result clause. What is the function of ἄρχειν?

TRANSLATION

"You would know yourselves most if you should consider for what reason you have to be so greatly arrogant as to try to rule over us."

POLISHED TRANSLATION

After the settlement had been reached, Pausanias dismissed the army, and the men from Piraeus went up to the Acropolis with their weapons and sacrificed to Athena. But when the generals came down, Thrasybulus then spoke. "Gentlemen from the city," he said, "I advise you to know yourselves. If you should consider why you have to be so arrogant as to try to rule over us, you would know yourselves very well."

Reading Selection

Thrasybulus continues his speech, and the two sides are at last reconciled. Some years later, the remnants of the Thirty try to assert themselves again, but are killed by the democrats at a conference.

πότερον δικαιότεροί ἐστε; ἀλλ' ὁ μὲν δῆμος πενέστερος ὑμῶν ὢν οὐδὲν
πώποτε ἕνεκα χρημάτων ὑμᾶς ἠδίκηκεν· ὑμεῖς δὲ πλουσιώτεροι πάντων ὄντες
πολλὰ καὶ αἰσχρὰ ἕνεκα κερδέων πεποιήκατε. ἐπεὶ δὲ δικαιοσύνης οὐδὲν
ὑμῖν προσήκει, σκέψασθε εἰ ἄρα ἐπ' ἀνδρείᾳ ὑμῖν μέγα φρονητέον. καὶ τίς
ἂν καλλίων κρίσις τούτου γένοιτο ἢ ὡς ἐπολεμήσαμεν πρὸς ἀλλήλους; ἀλλὰ   5
γνώμῃ φαίητ' ἂν προέχειν, οἳ ἔχοντες καὶ τεῖχος καὶ ὅπλα καὶ χρήματα καὶ
συμμάχους Πελοποννησίους ὑπὸ τῶν οὐδὲν τούτων ἐχόντων περιείληφθε; ἀλλ'
ἐπὶ Λακεδαιμονίοις δὴ οἴεσθε μέγα φρονητέον εἶναι; πῶς, οἵγε ὥσπερ τοὺς
δάκνοντας κύνας κλοιῷ δήσαντες παραδιδόασιν, οὕτω κἀκεῖνοι ὑμᾶς παραδόντες
τῷ ἠδικημένῳ τούτῳ δήμῳ οἴχονται ἀπιόντες; οὐ μέντοι γε ὑμᾶς, ὦ ἄνδρες, ἀξιῶ   10
ἐγὼ ὧν ὀμωμόκατε παραβῆναι οὐδέν, ἀλλὰ καὶ τοῦτο πρὸς τοῖς ἄλλοις καλοῖς
ἐπιδεῖξαι, ὅτι καὶ εὔορκοι καὶ ὅσιοί ἐστε. εἰπὼν δὲ ταῦτα καὶ ἄλλα τοιαῦτα, καὶ
ὅτι οὐδὲν δέοι ταράττεσθαι, ἀλλὰ τοῖς νόμοις τοῖς ἀρχαίοις χρῆσθαι, ἀνέστησε
τὴν ἐκκλησίαν. καὶ τότε μὲν ἀρχὰς καταστησάμενοι ἐπολιτεύοντο· ὑστέρῳ δὲ
χρόνῳ ἀκούσαντες ξένους μισθοῦσθαι τοὺς Ἐλευσῖνι, στρατευσάμενοι πανδημεὶ   15
ἐπ' αὐτοὺς τοὺς μὲν στρατηγοὺς αὐτῶν εἰς λόγους ἐλθόντας ἀπέκτειναν, τοῖς
δὲ ἄλλοις εἰσπέμψαντες τοὺς φίλους καὶ ἀναγκαίους ἔπεισαν συναλλαγῆναι. καὶ
ὀμόσαντες ὅρκους ἦ μὴν μὴ μνησικακήσειν, ἔτι καὶ νῦν ὁμοῦ τε πολιτεύονται καὶ
τοῖς ὅρκοις ἐμμένει ὁ δῆμος.

Xenophon, *Hellenica* 2.4.40–43

NOTES

1. [Line 1] πότερον introduces a question. You may omit it in your translation.
2. [Lines 1–2] ὁ μὲν δῆμος πενέστερος ὑμῶν ὤν . . . ὑμεῖς δὲ πλουσιώτεροι πάντων ὄντες:
   Note the μέν . . . δέ and the parallel construction with the two comparatives, genitives of comparison (R3.2.6), and participial forms of εἰμί.
3. [Line 2] ἕνεκα χρημάτων: It is more common for the object of ἕνεκα to precede it,
   but here and with ἕνεκα κερδέων, the genitive object follows the preposition.
4. [Line 3] πολλὰ καὶ αἰσχρὰ: In Greek an adjective of quantity and an adjective of
   quality are often joined with a conjunction. You may omit καί in your translation.
5. [Line 3] δικαιοσύνης is a partitive genitive with οὐδέν (R3.2.2).
6. [Line 4] What form is σκέψασθε?
7. [Line 4] ἐπ' ἀνδρείᾳ ὑμῖν μέγα φρονητέον: φρονητέον is a verbal adjective used impersonally to denote necessity. Translate it personally, however, as "you have to be
   arrogant because of your courage." ὑμῖν is a dative of personal agent (R3.3.6).

8. [Lines 4–5] τίς ἂν καλλίων κρίσις τούτου γένοιτο: What part of speech is τίς? How is it being used? What is the function of τούτου?

9. [Line 5] ἂν . . . γένοιτο: What type of optative construction is this?

10. [Line 6] φαίητ᾽ ἂν: φαίητ᾽ introduces an accusative/infinitive construction of indirect statement. Because the subject of the infinitive προέχειν is the same as the subject of φαίητ᾽, it is omitted (R7.1). What type of optative construction is φαίητ᾽ ἂν?

11. [Line 6] ἔχοντες is best translated concessively with "although." Note the four direct objects!

12. [Line 7] ὑπὸ τῶν οὐδὲν τούτων ἐχόντων: This prepositional phrase is a genitive of personal agent (R3.2.3) with the passive verb περιείληφθε. Note the framing of οὐδὲν τούτων by the substantive participle ἐχόντων and its definite article τῶν. If οὐδὲν is the direct object of ἐχόντων, what is the function of τούτων?

13. [Line 8] Supply ὑμῖν with μέγα φρονητέον εἶναι and translate in a similar fashion to note 7, above.

14. [Line 8] πῶς: Translate this as "how can that be?" or "how is this possible?"

15. [Line 8] οἵγε is οἵ plus γε. This imparts a notion of cause. Translate it as "since they."

16. [Line 9] παραδιδόασιν: Supply as the subject "men" or "people."

17. [Line 10] οἴχονται ἀπιόντες: This type of redundancy is common in Greek!

18. [Lines 10–11] οὐ μέντοι . . . παραβῆναι οὐδέν: The order for translation is ἐγὼ οὐ ἀξιῶ ὑμᾶς παραβῆναι οὐδὲν ὧν ὀμωμόκατε.

19. [Lines 10–11] οὐ . . . οὐδέν: One often finds double negatives in Greek. Translate οὐδέν as "any."

20. [Line 11] πρὸς τοῖς ἄλλοις καλοῖς: Translate this as "in addition to your other noble habits."

21. [Line 12] ἐπιδεῖξαι: This verb functions the same way παραβῆναι does—that is, ἀξιῶ ὑμᾶς ἐπιδεῖξαι. What is the force of the aorist tense?

22. [Line 12] ὅτι καὶ εὔορκοι καὶ ὅσιοί ἐστε defines καὶ τοῦτο, the direct object of ἐπιδεῖξαι. The καί is adverbial.

23. [Lines 12–13] Note that εἰπὼν has two direct objects and introduces the indirect statement construction ὅτι οὐδὲν δέοι ταράττεσθαι, . . . χρῆσθαι. Why is δέοι in the optative mood?

24. [Lines 14–15] Note the construction of καὶ τότε μὲν ἀρχὰς . . . ὑστέρῳ δὲ χρόνῳ.

25. [Line 15] ἀκούσαντες ξένους μισθοῦσθαι: ἀκούω may take the accusative/infinitive or the participial construction of indirect statement (R7.1, 7.2; S2144).

26. [Line 15] τοὺς Ἐλευσῖνι: The dative Ἐλευσῖνι indicates place where and is called the "locative dative." No preposition is needed with names of cities and towns (S1534). Ἐλευσῖνι and the definite article τοὺς work together as a noun phrase that is the subject of the infinitive μισθοῦσθαι. Translate this as "those in Eleusis."

27. [Lines 16–17] Note the construction of τοὺς μὲν στρατηγοὺς . . . τοῖς δὲ ἄλλοις. τοὺς μὲν στρατηγοὺς is the direct object of ἀπέκτειναν. What is the function of ἐλθόντας? Remember that second aorist participles are accented on the first syllable of the participial suffix.

28. [Line 18] ὀμόσαντες . . . μνησικακήσειν: Verbs of hoping, swearing, promising, and the like usually take future infinitives (R7.4; S1868).

29. [Line 18] ἦ μήν is used to introduce oaths. It may be omitted in your translation.

30. [Line 18] ἔτι καὶ νῦν: Translate this as "still even now."

31. [Lines 18–19] Note the τε . . . καί linking ὁμοῦ τε πολιτεύονται καὶ τοῖς ὅρκοις ἐμμένει ὁ δῆμος. Remember that τε is postpositive.

Reading Twenty-Three

Antiphon 1.1–3

Not much is known about the life of Antiphon beyond the basic details. He was born around 480 B.C.E. in the Attic deme of Rhamnus. His father, Sophilus, was from an old Athenian family. According to Thucydides (8.68), Antiphon was not a frequent participant in public affairs, generally preferring to exert his influence behind the scenes. He was noted for his cleverness, strong intellect, and consummate skills in argumentation. He stands at the beginning of the canon of the so-called Ten Attic Orators, whose members were determined by the Alexandrian scholars. (The other orators were Aeschines, Andocides, Demosthenes, Dinarchus, Hyperides, Isaeus, Isocrates, Lycurgus, and Lysias.) Although other orators were active in Athens during the fifth and fourth centuries B.C.E., the works of the Ten were the ones deemed most worthy by the Alexandrians.

Sometime around 430, Antiphon apparently became the first formal speechwriter (λογογράφος) in Athens and began to write speeches for others to deliver.[1] Of his works, six complete speeches survive. It is unknown precisely how many speeches he wrote, though fragments and titles of twenty other works are extant. Three of the surviving works were written for legal trials; the remaining works, the three Tetralogies, are considered spurious by some critics, though many now accept these as authentic. The Tetralogies are rhetorical exercises, each containing four speeches, two for the defense and two for the prosecution. Their main focus appears to have been the demonstration of different types of argument.

In 411, Antiphon apparently played a leadership role in the oligarchic coup in Athens, but rather than fleeing the city after its failure he remained to stand trial. He was convicted of treason and executed. Fragments of the speech he wrote in his defense survive, and Thucydides notes its eloquence (8.68).

Antiphon 1, *Against the Stepmother for Poisoning,* concerns a murder that occurred a number of years before the delivery of the speech. The speaker's father, whose name is not

---

1. Michael Gagarin and Douglas M. MacDowell, trans. *Antiphon and Andocides* (Austin: University of Texas Press, 1998), xi.

given, and his friend Philoneus were having dinner at Philoneus's house in Piraeus, the seaport of Athens. Philoneus's concubine, whom Philoneus was planning to set up in a brothel, served the two men their dinner. After they finished the meal, they began to drink the wine she had just poured for them to use in their libation. Immediately after drinking the wine, Philoneus died and the speaker's father became severely ill. (In his speech, the speaker describes the poisoning in vivid detail.)

Philoneus's relatives had the concubine tortured, and she revealed that the speaker's stepmother was behind the plot. The concubine claimed that the stepmother had told her that she was administering a love potion since the two women needed to regain the interest and affections of their men. The condition of the speaker's father continued to worsen, and he too died. Before his death, however, he summoned his young son, the speaker, who was apparently the son of a concubine, and enjoined the boy to bring his stepmother to justice for his murder. Since he was under age, the speaker had to wait until he was eighteen, the legal age at which a man can bring a lawsuit. The stepmother was defended by her two sons, and the case was heard before the Court of the Areopagus. Because the defendant was a female, she could not make her own decisions in a legal case and had to be represented in court by her guardian, her nearest male relative. Since her husband, the speaker's father, had died and presumably her father as well, she was represented by her sons. We do not have the speech made on behalf of the defendant, nor do we know the outcome of the case.

In this speech the prosecution bases its case largely on the fact that the defense refused to allow the stepmother's slaves to be interrogated under torture (βάσανος). The speaker claims that this denial is irrefutable evidence of the stepmother's guilt. There is no other reasonable cause, he suggests, for the refusal.

Note: In the Greek texts, square brackets ([ ]) indicate a word or words that some editors suggest deleting from the text, angle brackets (< >) indicate a word or words that some editors suggest adding to the Greek text, and parentheses are used for editorial annotations. Angle brackets are also used in the notes to indicate words that must be supplied for a complete translation, and parentheses for editorial annotations.

Focus on Reading

The opening of the speech (1.1–4) includes the typical appeal to the jury for sympathy.

Νέος μὲν καὶ ἄπειρος δικῶν ἔγωγε ἔτι, δεινῶς δὲ καὶ ἀπόρως ἔχει μοι περὶ τοῦ
πράγματος, ὦ ἄνδρες, τοῦτο μὲν εἰ ἐπισκήψαντος τοῦ πατρὸς ἐπεξελθεῖν τοῖς
αὐτοῦ φονεῦσι μὴ ἐπέξειμι, τοῦτο δὲ εἰ ἐπεξιόντι ἀναγκαίως ἔχει οἷς ἥκιστα ἐχρῆν
ἐν διαφορᾷ καταστῆναι, ἀδελφοῖς ὁμοπατρίοις καὶ μητρὶ ἀδελφῶν.

Antiphon 1.1

This long sentence has been divided into sections. Because it is a difficult sentence to translate into smooth English, we will have to be a bit loose in our translation. It is not uncommon for the opening of a speech to be challenging!

PART ONE

Νέος μὲν καὶ ἄπειρος δικῶν ἔγωγε ἔτι, δεινῶς δὲ καὶ ἀπόρως ἔχει μοι περὶ τοῦ πράγματος, ὦ ἄνδρες,

VOCABULARY

The principal parts of all verbs may be found in the vocabulary list at the back of this textbook.

νέος, -α, -ον young	ἀπόρως (adv.) helplessly, at a loss
ἄπειρος, -ον inexperienced in (+ gen.)	περί (prep. + gen.) concerning
δίκη, -ης, ἡ lawsuit	πρᾶγμα, -ατος, τό matter, situation
ἔτι (adv.) still	ἀνήρ, -δρός, ὁ man, gentleman
δεινῶς (adv.) terribly	

OBSERVATIONS, STRATEGIES, AND NOTES

1. Note the μὲν . . . δέ construction in Νέος μὲν . . . δεινῶς δὲ. The contrast is not one of strong difference; rather, two aspects of the situation the speaker finds himself in are being noted.

2. Νέος μὲν καὶ ἄπειρος: It was very common for a speaker to stress his youth and inexperience in the opening of a legal speech in order to gain the jurors' goodwill.

3. ἔγωγε: The enclitic particle γε has attached itself to the personal pronoun ἐγώ to intensify it.

4. δεινῶς δὲ καὶ ἀπόρως ἔχει μοι: ἔχω with an adverb of manner means "be in a certain state." In this sentence, ἔχει is being used impersonally with μοι and is translated literally as "it holds terribly and helplessly for me," which is awkward in English. For more polished English, translate this as "and I am terribly at a loss" or "and I am at a terrible loss." Note that the two adverbs are joined by a conjunction, whereas in English the conjunction would not be included.

TRANSLATION

I am still young and inexperienced in lawsuits, and I am at a terrible loss concerning the situation, gentlemen,

PART TWO

τοῦτο μὲν εἰ ἐπισκήψαντος τοῦ πατρὸς ἐπεξελθεῖν τοῖς αὐτοῦ φονεῦσι μὴ ἐπέξειμι,

VOCABULARY

ἐπισκήπτω enjoin, lay a strict charge upon   φονεύς, -έως, ὁ murderer
πατήρ, -τρός, ὁ father   ἐπέξειμι prosecute
ἐπεξέρχομαι prosecute (+ dat.)

OBSERVATIONS, STRATEGIES, AND NOTES

1. τοῦτο μὲν goes with τοῦτο δὲ in Part Three of this sentence. The basic sense is "on one hand . . . on the other," though it is not necessary to include this in your translation since it will be very awkward. These two clauses explain why the speaker is in such a difficult situation.

2. εἰ: This introduces an indirect question, the second part of which is introduced by the εἰ in Part Three of this sentence. εἰ . . . εἰ means "whether . . . or," but it may also be omitted in your translation. For smoother English, you may substitute "either . . . or."

3. ἐπισκήψαντος τοῦ πατρὸς ἐπεξελθεῖν τοῖς αὐτοῦ φονεῦσι: The genitive participle ἐπισκήψαντος and τοῦ πατρὸς, the noun in the genitive, combine to form a genitive absolute (R6.5). ἐπισκήπτω, "enjoin" or "lay a strict charge upon," takes either an accusative or a dative of person plus an infinitive. The infinitive ἐπεξελθεῖν is included, but the dative of person, the person receiving the order, is not. You will need to supply "me." Notice the alpha in the participle ἐπισκήψαντος: this tells you that it is an aorist participle. The tense denotes aspect and time prior to that of the main verb (R4).

4. τοῖς αὐτοῦ φονεῦσι: This goes logically with both ἐπεξελθεῖν and μὴ ἐπέξειμι as objects. Note that φονεῦσι is plural. Even though the murder charge is technically against the speaker's stepmother, he is, in effect, presenting the case as if his stepmother and his half-brothers all had a hand in the murder and its cover-up.

5. αὐτοῦ: This is the contracted form of the third person reflexive pronoun ἑαυτοῦ and refers back to τοῦ πατρὸς.

TRANSLATION

either I do not prosecute the murderers of my father, even though my father laid a strict charge upon <me>,

PART THREE

τοῦτο δὲ εἰ ἐπεξιόντι ἀναγκαίως ἔχει οἷς ἥκιστα ἐχρῆν ἐν διαφορᾷ καταστῆναι, ἀδελφοῖς ὁμοπατρίοις καὶ μητρὶ ἀδελφῶν.

VOCABULARY

ἐπέξειμι   prosecute

ἀναγκαίως (adv.)   necessarily

ἥκιστα (adv.)   least

χρή   it is necessary

διαφορά, -ᾶς, ἡ   disagreement

καθίστημι   come into a certain state, be

ἀδελφός, -οῦ, ὁ   brother

ὁμοπάτριος, -α, -ον   of the same father

μήτηρ, -τρός, ἡ   mother

OBSERVATIONS, STRATEGIES, AND NOTES

1. ἐπεξιόντι: Supply μοι. Circumstantial participles are often used conditionally, and this works well with the context (R6.2).

2. ἀναγκαίως ἔχει: The idiomatic expression may be translated "it must be." Taken with ἐπεξιόντι <μοι> . . . ἐν διαφορᾷ καταστῆναι, it would literally be translated "it must be for me, if I prosecute, to be in difficulty," but this is very awkward in English. The translation "if I do prosecute <them>, I must come into conflict" captures the sense well.

3. οἷς ἥκιστα ἐχρῆν: The antecedent of οἷς is probably, strictly speaking, ἀδελφοῖς ὁμοπατρίοις καὶ μητρὶ ἀδελφῶν, but the postponement of these words to make them the concluding note is better rhetorically. Supply ἐκείνοις as the antecedent of οἷς and translate the phrase as "with those with whom I least should." Strictly speaking, ἐχρῆν is an impersonal ("it was necessary"), but the personal translation is preferred.

TRANSLATION

or, if I do prosecute <them>, I must come into conflict with those with whom I least should, my half-brothers and their mother.

POLISHED TRANSLATION

I am still young and inexperienced in lawsuits, and I am at a terrible loss concerning the situation, gentlemen. Either I do not prosecute the murderers of my father, even though my father charged me to do so, or, if I do, I must come into conflict with those with whom I least should, my half-brothers and their mother.

Reading Selection

The speaker continues his appeal. This passage is also a bit challenging, but once the speaker has completed the opening to his speech, the Greek will become more straightforward. The opening of a speech is often difficult, for it is there that the style tends to be especially rhetorical.

ἡ γὰρ τύχη καὶ αὐτοὶ οὗτοι ἠνάγκασαν ἐμοὶ πρὸς [τούτους] αὐτοὺς τὸν ἀγῶνα καταστῆναι, οὓς εἰκὸς ἦν τῷ μὲν τεθνεῶτι τιμωροὺς γενέσθαι, τῷ δὲ ἐπεξιόντι

βοηθούς. νῦν δὲ τούτων τἀναντία γεγένηται· αὐτοὶ γὰρ οὗτοι καθεστᾶσιν
ἀντίδικοι καὶ φονῆς, ὡς καὶ ἐγὼ καὶ ἡ γραφὴ λέγει. δέομαι δ᾽ ὑμῶν, ὦ ἄνδρες,
ἐὰν ἀποδείξω ἐξ ἐπιβουλῆς καὶ προβουλῆς τὴν τούτων μητέρα φονέα οὖσαν τοῦ   5
ἡμετέρου πατρός, καὶ μὴ ἅπαξ ἀλλὰ πολλάκις ἤδη ληφθεῖσαν τὸν θάνατον τὸν
ἐκείνου ἐπ᾽ αὐτοφώρῳ μηχανωμένην, τιμωρῆσαι πρῶτον μὲν τοῖς νόμοις τοῖς
ὑμετέροις, οὓς παρὰ τῶν θεῶν καὶ τῶν προγόνων διαδεξάμενοι κατὰ τὸ αὐτὸ
ἐκείνοις περὶ τῆς καταψηφίσεως δικάζετε, δεύτερον δ᾽ ἐκείνῳ τῷ τεθνηκότι, καὶ
ἅμα ἐμοὶ μόνῳ ἀπολελειμμένῳ βοηθῆσαι.   10

Antiphon 1.2–3

NOTES

1. [Line 1] The postpositive particle γάρ is used to explain the sentiments in the previous sentence.

2. [Line 1] αὐτοὶ οὗτοι: Don't ignore the intensive use of αὐτός. When αὐτός is used
in the nominative case, it modifies either the implied subject of the verb or an expressed nominative and means "-self" or "the very." Here it is modifying οὗτοι.

3. [Lines 1–2] ἠνάγκασαν . . . τὸν ἀγῶνα καταστῆναι: ἀναγκάζω takes an accusative/
infinitive construction, with τὸν ἀγῶνα as the subject accusative of the intransitive
form καταστῆναι. Remember that second aorist forms of ἵστημι and its compounds
are intransitive.

4. [Line 1] ἐμοί: It is sometimes difficult to determine precisely how a dative is being
used. This is probably an unusual use of the dative of agent, with the passive sense of
καταστῆναι ("be established"). It is more typical to find the dative of personal agent
with the perfect passive or with a verbal adjective (R3.3.6; S1488), but it is occasionally found with other tenses (S1490).

5. [Line 1] πρὸς [τούτους] αὐτοὺς: Some editors delete τούτους because it is repetitive
with αὐτοὶ οὗτοι, but Antiphon may have liked this type of repetition. The brackets
indicate the suggested deletion. αὐτός is used intensively to mean "-self" or "the
very" when it is in the predicate position.

6. [Line 2] οὓς εἰκὸς ἦν τῷ μὲν τεθνεῶτι τιμωροὺς γενέσθαι: The imperfect indicative
of impersonal expressions of propriety (such as εἰκὸς ἦν), obligation, or necessity is
used with a complementary or dependent infinitive to indicate that the propriety is
unfulfilled (S1774). The aorist infinitive γενέσθαι indicates that the action is in the
past (S1776). Translate this as "who should have become avengers for the dead man."
The antecedent of οὓς is τούτους αὐτοὺς or just αὐτοὺς if τούτους is not retained.

7. [Line 2] Note the μὲν . . . δὲ construction in τῷ μὲν τεθνεῶτι . . . τῷ δὲ ἐπεξιόντι. What
forms are τεθνεῶτι and ἐπεξιόντι?

8. [Line 3] What form is γεγένηται?

9. [Line 3] καθεστᾶσιν is another intransitive form of καθίστημι. What form is it?

10. [Line 4] φονῆς: This is the nominative plural masculine form of φονεύς.

11. [Lines 4–8] δέομαι δ᾽ ὑμῶν . . . τιμωρῆσαι πρῶτον μὲν τοῖς νόμοις τοῖς ὑμετέροις:
The apodosis of the future more vivid condition set up by ἐὰν ἀποδείξω appears in

this sentence as part of the construction set up by δέομαι, which may take a genitive to indicate the person being asked and an infinitive to indicate what the person is being asked to do (S1991, 1992b). The original form of the apodosis would have been τιμωρήσατε πρῶτον μὲν τοῖς νόμοις τοῖς ὑμετέροις, in which τιμωρήσατε, an aorist imperative, was substituted for the expected future indicative (R10.6; S2326, 2326e). Here the infinitive τιμωρῆσαι replaces the imperative because of the construction required by δέομαι. Translate this as "I ask you first to take vengeance for your laws" or "I ask you first to take vengeance on behalf of your laws." τοῖς νόμοις τοῖς ὑμετέροις is a dative of advantage (R3.3.10; S1481).

12. [Lines 5–6] ἐὰν **ἀποδείξω** . . . **τὴν** τούτων **μητέρα** φονέα **οὖσαν** τοῦ ἡμετέρου πατρός . . . **ληφθεῖσαν**: ἀποδείκνυμι takes a participial construction of indirect statement (R7.2). The indirect statement is embedded in the protasis of a future more vivid condition (R10.4) introduced by ἐὰν ἀποδείξω.

13. [Line 5] What form is ἀποδείξω? What clue word helps you identify it?

14. [Line 5] ἐξ ἐπιβουλῆς καὶ προβουλῆς: The speaker claims that his stepmother carefully planned the murder beforehand. You may be a bit loose in your translation.

15. [Lines 6–7] ἤδη ληφθεῖσαν τὸν θάνατον τὸν ἐκείνου ἐπ᾽ αὐτοφώρῳ μηχανωμένην: Take ληφθεῖσαν with ἐπ᾽ αὐτοφώρῳ to mean "caught in the act." The participle μηχανωμένην specifies what the mother was caught doing. What form is ληφθεῖσαν? What is the function of θάνατον?

16. [Lines 6–7] Notice the formal attributive position: **τὸν** θάνατον **τὸν** ἐκείνου (article—noun—article—modifier) (R2.1).

17. [Lines 7–9] Note the construction in πρῶτον μὲν . . . δεύτερον δ᾽. Take ἐκείνῳ τῷ τεθνηκότι with τιμωρῆσαι.

18. [Lines 8–9] οὓς παρὰ τῶν θεῶν καὶ τῶν προγόνων διαδεξάμενοι κατὰ τὸ αὐτὸ ἐκείνοις περὶ τῆς καταψηφίσεως δικάζετε: The antecedent of οὓς is νόμοις and its function is as the direct object of διαδεξάμενοι. This somewhat parenthetical statement describing the laws enhances their importance.

19. [Lines 8–9] κατὰ τὸ αὐτὸ ἐκείνοις: Translate this as "in the same way as those men," a reference to the ancestors.

20. [Lines 9–10] τεθνηκότι . . . ἀπολελειμμένῳ: What nuance does the perfect tense impart?

21. [Line 10] βοηθῆσαι continues the construction with δέομαι . . . τιμωρῆσαι and is also part of the apodosis of the future more vivid condition. It is used in the same manner as τιμωρῆσαι and would have been an aorist imperative in the original form of the condition. Take the dative phrase ἐμοὶ μόνῳ ἀπολελειμμένῳ with βοηθῆσαι.

Reading Twenty-Four

Antiphon 1.4–6

Focus on Reading

The speaker concludes his opening remarks and makes a last appeal for the jurors' goodwill.

ὑμεῖς γάρ μοι ἀναγκαῖοι. οὓς γὰρ ἐχρῆν τῷ μὲν τεθνεῶτι τιμωροὺς γενέσθαι,
ἐμοὶ δὲ βοηθούς, οὗτοι τοῦ μὲν τεθνεῶτος φονῆς γεγένηνται, ἐμοὶ δ' ἀντίδικοι
καθεστᾶσι. πρὸς τίνας οὖν ἔλθῃ τις βοηθούς, ἢ ποῖ τὴν καταφυγὴν ποιήσεται
ἄλλοθι ἢ πρὸς ὑμᾶς καὶ τὸ δίκαιον;

Antiphon 1.4

SENTENCES ONE AND TWO

ὑμεῖς γάρ μοι ἀναγκαῖοι. οὓς γὰρ ἐχρῆν τῷ μὲν τεθνεῶτι τιμωροὺς γενέσθαι,
ἐμοὶ δὲ βοηθούς, οὗτοι τοῦ μὲν τεθνεῶτος φονῆς γεγένηνται, ἐμοὶ δ' ἀντίδικοι
καθεστᾶσι.

VOCABULARY

ἀναγκαῖοι, -ων, οἱ kinsfolk
χρή it is necessary
θνήσκω die
τιμωρός, -οῦ, ὁ avenger
γίγνομαι become

βοηθός, -οῦ, ὁ helper, assistant
φονεύς, -έως, ὁ murderer
ἀντίδικος, -ον, ὁ defendant, opponent
καθίστημι (perf.) become

OBSERVATIONS, STRATEGIES, AND NOTES

1. ὑμεῖς γάρ μοι ἀναγκαῖοι: Supply εἰσιν. This is a rhetorical exaggeration. The particle γάρ indicates that this is the reason the speaker has made his appeal in the previous sentence.

2. οὕς: The antecedent of the relative pronoun is οὗτοι. It is not unusual for a relative clause to precede the main clause.

3. ἐχρῆν: Like εἰκὸς ἦν in Reading 23 (see note 6 in the Reading Selection), the imperfect indicative of impersonal verbs denoting obligation, necessity, propriety, and the like, when used with an infinitive, indicates that the action was unfulfilled (S1774). The tense of the infinitive indicates whether the unfulfilled action is in the present or past. Translate οὓς γὰρ ἐχρῆν τῷ μὲν τεθνεῶτι τιμωροὺς γενέσθαι as "those who should have been avengers for the dead man."

4. Note the repeated construction in τῷ μὲν τεθνεῶτι . . . ἐμοὶ δὲ and τοῦ μὲν τεθνεῶτος . . . ἐμοὶ δ'.

5. What nuance does the perfect tense impart to the verb forms τῷ τεθνεῶτι, τοῦ τεθνεῶτος, γεγένηνται, and καθεστᾶσι?

6. ἐμοὶ δὲ βοηθούς continues the construction set up by ἐχρῆν. Translate it as "and helpers for me."

7. φονῆς is the nominative plural masculine form of φονεύς.

8. καθεστᾶσι: The perfect forms of καθίστημι have an intransitive meaning of "become."

TRANSLATION

For you are my kinsfolk. For these men, who should have become avengers for the dead man and helpers for me, are murderers of the dead man and have become my opponents.

SENTENCE THREE

πρὸς τίνας οὖν ἔλθῃ τις βοηθούς, ἢ ποῖ τὴν καταφυγὴν ποιήσεται ἄλλοθι ἢ πρὸς ὑμᾶς καὶ τὸ δίκαιον;

VOCABULARY

πρός (prep. + acc.)   to
οὖν (particle)   therefore, and so
ἔρχομαι   go, come
βοηθός, -οῦ, ὁ   assistant, helper
ποῖ (interrog.)   where, whither

καταφυγή, -ῆς, ἡ   refuge
ποιέω   make
ἄλλοθι (adv.)   elsewhere
δίκαιος, -α, -ον   just

OBSERVATIONS, STRATEGIES, AND NOTES

1. τίνας: The direct interrogative pronoun is being used as an adjective to modify βοηθούς. The insertion of οὖν ἔλθη τις between τίνας and βοηθούς is an instance of *hyperbaton,* the separation of words that belong together grammatically by the insertion of another word or words (S3028).

2. ἔλθῃ: This is a deliberative subjunctive (R8.2; S1805), and the third person is often used in contexts where the first person is clearly meant (S1805c). Your translation may reflect this.

3. ποιήσεται: The subject is τις, but it is best to keep the first person as the subject to correspond to the deliberative subjunctive. ποιήσεται is a deliberative future (S1916), which sometimes occurs with a deliberative subjunctive (S1916a).

4. ἄλλοθι ἤ: This would be literally translated as "elsewhere than," but translate it as "other than" for better English.

TRANSLATION

And so to what helpers shall I go or where shall I find refuge other than in you and in justice?

POLISHED TRANSLATION

For you are my kinsfolk. These men, who should have been avengers of the dead man and my partners, are murderers of the dead man and have become my opponents. And so to what helpers shall I go or where shall I find refuge other than in you and in justice?

Reading Selection

The speaker begins his argument, noting that his half-brothers have refused to allow the slaves to be interrogated under torture.

θαυμάζω δ' ἔγωγε καὶ τοῦ ἀδελφοῦ, ἥντινά ποτε γνώμην ἔχων ἀντίδικος
καθέστηκε πρὸς ἐμέ, καὶ εἰ νομίζει τοῦτο εὐσέβειαν εἶναι, τὸ τὴν μητέρα μὴ
προδοῦναι. ἐγὼ δ' ἡγοῦμαι πολὺ ἀνοσιώτερον εἶναι ἀφεῖναι τοῦ τεθνεῶτος τὴν
τιμωρίαν, ἄλλως τε καὶ τοῦ μὲν ἐκ προβουλῆς ἀκουσίως ἀποθανόντος, τῆς δὲ
ἑκουσίως ἐκ προνοίας ἀποκτεινάσης. καὶ οὐ τοῦτό γ' ἐρεῖ, ὡς εὖ οἶδεν ὅτι γ' οὐκ   5
ἀπέκτεινεν ἡ μήτηρ αὐτοῦ τὸν πατέρα τὸν ἡμέτερον. ἐν οἷς μὲν γὰρ αὐτῷ ἐξουσία
ἦν σαφῶς εἰδέναι, παρὰ τῆς βασάνου, οὐκ ἠθέλησεν· ἐν οἷς δ' οὐκ ἦν πυθέσθαι,
τοῦτο αὐτὸ προὐθυμήθη. καίτοι αὐτὸ τοῦτο ἐχρῆν, ὃ καὶ ἐγὼ προὐκαλούμην,
προθυμηθῆναι, ὅπως τὸ πραχθὲν ᾖ ἀληθές[, ἐπεξελθεῖν].

Antiphon 1.5–6

NOTES

1. [Lines 1–2] θαυμάζω δ' ἔγωγε καὶ τοῦ ἀδελφοῦ, ἥντινά ποτε γνώμην ἔχων ἀντίδικος καθέστηκε πρὸς ἐμέ: Sometimes the subject of a subordinate clause is positioned outside its clause and made the object of the main verb. Here, τοῦ ἀδελφοῦ is the object of θαυμάζω (which takes the genitive), but it really is the subject of the indirect question introduced by ἥντινά. This phenomenon is called *prolepsis* (S2182). Translate this part of the sentence as "I marvel at what frame of mind my brother had when he became an opponent against me." It is preferable to translate the participial phrase, ἥντινά ποτε γνώμην ἔχων, as the main idea of the indirect question while translating the main part of the indirect question, ἀντίδικος καθέστηκε πρὸς ἐμέ, as a temporal clause. ποτε has an intensifying force after an interrogative but may be left untranslated.

2. [Line 1] ἔγωγε: The γε, which emphasizes the personal pronoun ἐγώ, adds a sarcastic tone.

3. [Line 1] καὶ τοῦ ἀδελφοῦ: The καί is adverbial but may be omitted in your translation. Note that the speaker is using ἀδελφός to refer to his half-brother.

4. [Line 2] καὶ εἰ νομίζει τοῦτο εὐσέβειαν εἶναι: This is the second part of the indirect question. νομίζει introduces an accusative/infinitive construction of indirect statement (R7.1). Translate εἰ as "whether."

5. [Lines 2–3] τὸ τὴν μητέρα μὴ προδοῦναι: The articular infinitive phrase describes τοῦτο. Note the framing of τὴν μητέρα and the negative μή by the article and the infinitive to indicate that all of these words work together as a unit. Why is προδοῦναι in the aorist tense?

6. [Lines 2–3] μὴ προδοῦναι: The standard negative used with the infinitive is μή, except in an accusative/infinitive construction of indirect statement.

7. [Line 3] ἐγὼ δ' ἡγοῦμαι: The inclusion of the personal pronoun gives added emphasis. What type of construction is ἡγοῦμαι introducing?

8. [Line 3] πολὺ ἀνοσιώτερον: Degree of difference may be indicated by the dative or by an adverb (R3.3.8). Translate this as "much more impious."

9. [Line 4] ἄλλως τε καί: This is idiomatic. Translate it as "especially."

10. [Line 4] Note the construction of τοῦ μὲν ... τῆς δὲ.

11. [Lines 4–5] τοῦ μὲν ἐκ προβουλῆς ἀκουσίως ἀποθανόντος and τῆς δὲ ἑκουσίως ἐκ προνοίας ἀποκτεινάσης: These are two genitive absolutes with the genitive "subject" expressed by τοῦ μὲν and τῆς δὲ. τῆς δὲ refers to the stepmother and τοῦ μὲν refers to the speaker's father.

12. [Line 5] καὶ οὐ τοῦτό γ' ἐρεῖ: There are difficulties with the text here. The translation "and he will not say this at any rate" is not supported by the context. Cole suggests reading πῶς for καί.[2] The clause would then be translated "how will he say this," which fits with the indirect statements that follow.

13. [Lines 5–6] οὐ τοῦτό γ' ἐρεῖ ὡς εὖ οἶδεν ὅτι γ' οὐκ ἀπέκτεινεν: This is a double in-

---

2. See Michael Gagarin, ed., *Antiphon: The Speeches* (New York: Cambridge University Press, 1997), 109n6.

direct statement: ὡς εὖ οἶδεν and ὅτι γ᾽ οὐκ ἀπέκτεινεν. ὅτι γ᾽ οὐκ ἀπέκτεινεν is set up by ὡς εὖ οἶδεν, and ὡς εὖ οἶδεν ὅτι γ᾽ οὐκ ἀπέκτεινεν amplifies τοῦτό γ᾽.

14. [Lines 6–7] Note the construction of ἐν οἷς μὲν . . . ἐν οἷς δ᾽. ἐν οἷς is idiomatic and may be translated "when."

15. [Line 7] παρὰ τῆς βασάνου: The testimony of slaves was considered reliable only when extracted under torture.

16. [Line 7] οὐκ ἠθέλησεν: Translate it as "he was not willing" or "he refused."

17. [Line 7] οὐκ ἦν πυθέσθαι: ἦν is being used as an impersonal verb. Translate this as "was not possible." What is the function of πυθέσθαι?

18. [Lines 8–9] καίτοι αὐτὸ τοῦτο ἐχρῆν, ὃ καὶ ἐγὼ προὐκαλούμην, προθυμηθῆναι: Supply ἐκεῖνον or αὐτόν, referring to the speaker's half-brother, as the subject of προθυμηθῆναι. The order for translation is καίτοι ἐχρῆν <ἐκεῖνον> προθυμηθῆναι αὐτὸ τοῦτο, ὃ καὶ ἐγὼ προὐκαλούμην. αὐτὸ τοῦτο refers to subjecting the slaves to torture. The imperfect tense of ἐχρῆν indicates an unfulfilled obligation (S1774). Translate this as "he should have desired this very thing that even I had called for previously."

19. [Line 9] ὅπως τὸ πραχθὲν ᾖ ἀληθές[, ἐπεξελθεῖν]: There are problems with the text here, as the brackets indicate. The phrase would literally be translated as "so that what happened may be true to investigate." The infinitive ἐπεξελθεῖν limits the meaning of the adjective ἀληθές (R5.4; S2001). For clearer English, translate this as "so that the facts may be uncovered in an investigation" or something similar.

Reading Twenty-Five

Antiphon 1.7–9

Focus on Reading

The speaker further develops his argument concerning the implications of his half-brothers' refusal to allow the slaves to be interrogated.

μὴ γὰρ ὁμολογούντων τῶν ἀνδραπόδων οὗτός τ' εὖ εἰδὼς ἂν ἀπελογεῖτο καὶ
ἀντέσπευδε πρὸς ἐμέ, καὶ ἡ μήτηρ αὐτοῦ ἀπήλλακτο ἂν ταύτης τῆς αἰτίας. ὅπου
δὲ μὴ ἠθέλησεν ἔλεγχον ποιήσασθαι τῶν πεπραγμένων, πῶς περί γ' ὧν οὐκ
ἠθέλησε πυθέσθαι, ἐγχωρεῖ αὐτῷ περὶ τούτων εἰδέναι; [πῶς οὖν περὶ τούτων, ὦ
δικάζοντες, αὐτὸν εἰκὸς εἰδέναι, ὧν γε τὴν ἀλήθειαν οὐκ εἴληφε];

Antiphon 1.7

SENTENCE ONE

μὴ γὰρ ὁμολογούντων τῶν ἀνδραπόδων οὗτός τ' εὖ εἰδὼς ἂν ἀπελογεῖτο καὶ
ἀντέσπευδε πρὸς ἐμέ, καὶ ἡ μήτηρ αὐτοῦ ἀπήλλακτο ἂν ταύτης τῆς αἰτίας.

VOCABULARY

ὁμολογέω admit	ἀντισπεύδω oppose eagerly, contend against
ἀνδράποδον, -ου, τό slave	πρός (prep. + acc.) against
εὖ (adv.) well	ἀπαλλάττω (passive) be acquitted of (+ gen.)
οἶδα know	αἰτία, -ας, ἡ charge
ἀπολογέομαι speak in defense	

OBSERVATIONS, STRATEGIES, AND NOTES

1. μὴ γὰρ ὁμολογούντων τῶν ἀνδραπόδων: The genitive absolute is a substitution for the protasis of a present contrary-to-fact condition (R10.6; S2344). The use of μή with the participle indicates that it should be taken conditionally (S2728). Supply "anything" as the direct object of ὁμολογούντων.

2. Note the τε . . . καί construction in οὗτός τ᾽ εὖ εἰδὼς . . . καὶ ἡ μήτηρ αὐτοῦ, which links the two clauses.

3. εὖ εἰδὼς: Translate this nominative singular masculine participle of οἶδα with the adverb εὖ as "being assured," "being confident," or even "confidently."

4. ἂν ἀπελογεῖτο καὶ ἀντέσπευδε: The ἄν goes with both verbs. It is important to take it into account in order to translate them correctly. This is the apodosis of the present contrary-to-fact condition, which requires the imperfect indicative plus ἄν.

5. ἀπήλλακτο ἄν: The pluperfect indicative is used in place of the imperfect to stress the permanent result of the acquittal (S2306). This is also part of the apodosis of the present contrary-to-fact condition, as the ἄν indicates.

TRANSLATION

For if the slaves did not admit <anything>, he would speak in her defense confidently and would contend against me, and his mother would be acquitted of this accusation.

SENTENCE TWO

ὅπου δὲ μὴ ἠθέλησεν ἔλεγχον ποιήσασθαι τῶν πεπραγμένων, πῶς περί γ᾽ ὧν οὐκ ἠθέλησε πυθέσθαι, ἐγχωρεῖ αὐτῷ περὶ τούτων εἰδέναι;

VOCABULARY

ὅπου (causal adv.)	whereas, since	πῶς (interrog.)	how
ἐθέλω	wish	περί (prep. + gen.)	concerning
ἔλεγχος, -ου, ὁ	cross-examination, testing	πυνθάνομαι	inquire
ποιέω	make	ἐγχωρεῖ (impers.)	be possible (+ dat./inf.)
πράττω	do, make	οἶδα	know

OBSERVATIONS, STRATEGIES, AND NOTES

1. ὅπου introduces a causal clause, a type of subordinate clause. A causal clause takes the indicative when the cause is regarded as a fact (S2240, 2240a, 2241).

2. τῶν πεπραγμένων: The perfect passive participle of πράττω is being used as a substantive, as the definite article indicates (R6.1). It is an objective genitive with ἔλεγχον (R3.2.5; S1328, 1331). An objective genitive receives the action implied by the noun with which it is paired. Here τῶν πεπραγμένων is receiving the action of

cross-examining, as implied by ἔλεγχον. τῶν πεπραγμένων, which literally means "the things that have been done," may be translated as "what had happened" or "the facts."

3. περί γ᾽ ὧν: The antecedent of ὧν is τούτων, which follows the relative. The order for translation is πῶς ἐγχωρεῖ αὐτῷ εἰδέναι περὶ τούτων περὶ γ᾽ ὧν οὐκ ἠθέλησε πυθέσθαι;

4. εἰδέναι is the perfect active infinitive of οἶδα.

TRANSLATION

Since he did not wish to make a cross-examination of what had happened, how is it possible for him to know about these things about which he did not wish to inquire?

SENTENCE THREE

[πῶς οὖν περὶ τούτων, ὦ δικάζοντες, αὐτὸν εἰκὸς εἰδέναι, ὧν γε τὴν ἀλήθειαν οὐκ εἴληφε];

VOCABULARY

πῶς (interrog.)	how	εἰκός	reasonable, likely, probable
οὖν (particle)	and so, therefore	ἀλήθεια, -ας, ἡ	truth
δικάζω	judge, be a juror	λαμβάνω	find out, apprehend

OBSERVATIONS, STRATEGIES, AND NOTES

1. This sentence is missing from one manuscript and is bracketed by some editors because it is repetitive. However, it is not unusual for Antiphon—or any other orator, for that matter—to be repetitious when trying to make his case.

2. πῶς . . . αὐτὸν εἰκὸς εἰδέναι: Supply ἐστι with εἰκός, which takes an accusative/infinitive construction. The order for translation is οὖν, ὦ δικάζοντες, πῶς εἰκὸς <ἐστι> αὐτὸν εἰδέναι περὶ τούτων.

3. What case is δικάζοντες?

4. ὧν γε τὴν ἀλήθειαν: The antecedent of ὧν is τούτων. Translate ὧν with ἀλήθειαν as "whose truth."

5. εἴληφε: This is the third person singular perfect active indicative of λαμβάνω.

TRANSLATION

And so, jurors, how likely is it that he knows about these things whose truth he has not found out?

POLISHED TRANSLATION

For if the slaves did not admit anything, he would both speak in her defense and contend against me confidently, and his mother would be acquitted of this accusation. Since
he did not wish to conduct a cross-examination of what had happened, how is it possible
for him to know about these things concerning which he did not wish to inquire? And so,
gentlemen of the jury, how likely is it that he knows about these things whose truth he has
not found out?

Reading Selection

The speaker continues his argument about βάσανος. He notes that his stepmother had
previously been caught trying to administer what she claimed were love potions to her husband.

τί ποτε ἀπολογήσεσθαι μέλλει μοι; ἐκ μὲν γὰρ τῆς τῶν ἀνδραπόδων βασάνου
εὖ ᾔδει ὅτι οὐχ οἷόν τ' ἦν αὐτῇ σωθῆναι, ἐν δὲ τῷ μὴ βασανισθῆναι ἡγεῖτο τὴν
σωτηρίαν εἶναι· τὰ γὰρ γενόμενα ἐν τούτῳ ἀφανισθῆναι ᾠήθησαν. πῶς οὖν
εὔορκα ἀντομωμοκὼς ἔσται φάσκων εὖ εἰδέναι, ὃς οὐκ ἠθέλησε σαφῶς πυθέσθαι
ἐμοῦ ἐθέλοντος τῇ δικαιοτάτῃ βασάνῳ χρήσασθαι περὶ τούτου τοῦ πράγματος;   5
τοῦτο μὲν γὰρ ἠθέλησα μὲν τὰ τούτων ἀνδράποδα βασανίσαι, ἃ συνῄδει καὶ
πρότερον τὴν γυναῖκα ταύτην, μητέρα δὲ τούτων, τῷ πατρὶ τῷ ἡμετέρῳ θάνατον
μηχανωμένην φαρμάκοις, καὶ τὸν πατέρα εἰληφότα ἐπ' αὐτοφώρῳ, ταύτην τε οὐκ
οὖσαν ἄπαρνον, πλὴν οὐκ ἐπὶ θανάτῳ φάσκουσαν διδόναι ἀλλ' ἐπὶ φίλτροις.

Antiphon 1.8–9

NOTES

1. [Line 1] τί: The accusative singular neuter interrogative pronoun is the direct object
   of ἀπολογήσεσθαι.
2. [Line 1] ποτε is used after an interrogative for emphasis (S346c). You may omit it in
   your translation.
3. [Line 1] ἀπολογήσεσθαι μέλλει: When μέλλω takes a future infinitive, it means "intend." Translate this as "what defense does he intend to make to me?"
4. [Lines 1–2] Note the μὲν . . . δέ construction in ἐκ μὲν γὰρ . . . ἐν δὲ τῷ, as well as the
   explanatory force of γάρ. The preposition ἐκ has a causal sense here. Translate it as
   "in consequence of" or "because of."
5. [Line 2] What form is ᾔδει? What type of construction does it introduce?
6. [Line 2] σωθῆναι is a complementary infinitive (R5.3) that goes with οὐχ οἷόν τ' ἦν
   (οἷόν τέ ἐστι is an idiomatic expression meaning "it is possible"). What tense and
   voice is it?
7. [Line 2] τῷ μὴ βασανισθῆναι: The definite article indicates that the articular infini-

tive is being used in the dative case (R5.2). Infinitives are negated by μή, except when used in indirect statement. Why is the infinitive in the dative?

8. [Line 2] What type of construction is ἡγεῖτο introducing?

9. [Line 3] τὰ ... γενόμενα: The aorist participle is being used as a noun (R6.1) and would be translated literally as "the things that happened." You may translate it as "the facts."

10. [Line 3] ἐν τούτῳ: Translate this as "in this case."

11. [Line 3] ἀφανισθῆναι: The aorist passive infinitive is part of an accusative/infinitive construction of indirect statement (R7.1). Although it is rare, it is possible for an aorist infinitive to refer to the future (S1871), which is clearly what is required here by the context.

12. [Line 3] ᾠήθησαν: This is the third person plural aorist indicative of the deponent verb οἴομαι. Deponent verbs generally have either a middle or passive form in the aorist (S356c). The plural form refers to the speaker's half-brothers and presumably his stepmother as well. It is common in a legal speech for verb forms that refer to the opposing side to switch from singular to plural and vice versa. What type of construction would you expect this verb to introduce?

13. [Line 4] εὔορκα ἀντομωμοκὼς ἔσται: εὔορκα is being used adverbially and may be translated as "faithfully."

14. [Line 4] ἀντομωμοκὼς ἔσται: This is a periphrastic formation of the future perfect, consisting of the perfect participle and the future of εἰμί. The emphasis is on the permanent state. The future perfect is rare in Greek.

15. [Line 4] φάσκων εὖ εἰδέναι: φάσκων is a circumstantial participle introducing an indirect statement construction with the infinitive. Since the subject of the infinitive is the same as the subject of the main verb, it is omitted (R7.1).

16. [Line 4] ὃς οὐκ ἠθέλησε σαφῶς πυθέσθαι: What is the antecedent of ὅς?

17. [Line 5] ἐμοῦ ἐθέλοντος τῇ δικαιοτάτῃ βασάνῳ χρήσασθαι περὶ τούτου τοῦ πράγματος: This is a long genitive absolute (R6.5). Note the pronoun ἐμοῦ and the participle ἐθέλοντος. What type of word do you often find with ἐθέλω and other verbs of wishing (R5.3)?

18. [Line 5] What is the tense of χρήσασθαι and why?

19. [Line 6] τοῦτο μὲν is usually used with τοῦτο δέ in a manner similar to μὲν ... δέ, but here it is used alone. You may omit these words in your translation.

20. [Line 6] τὰ τούτων ἀνδράποδα: τούτων refers to the speaker's half-brothers and stepmother.

21. [Line 6] What is the antecedent of ἅ? What is its function?

22. [Lines 6–9] ἃ συνῄδει ... τὴν γυναῖκα ταύτην ... μηχανωμένην ... καὶ τὸν πατέρα εἰληφότα ... οὐκ οὖσαν ... φάσκουσαν: συνῄδει introduces a long participial construction of indirect statement (R7.2). Note that there are two accusative nouns, τὴν γυναῖκα and τὸν πατέρα, modified by the participles, μηχανωμένην, εἰληφότα, οὖσαν, and φάσκουσαν. Which participle modifies τὸν πατέρα?

23. [Lines 6–7] καὶ πρότερον: The καί is adverbial.

24. [Line 8] τὸν πατέρα εἰληφότα ἐπ' αὐτοφώρῳ: Supply αὐτήν as the object of εἰληφότα. λαμβάνειν ἐπ' αὐτοφώρῳ means "to catch in the act."

25. [Line 9] ἐπὶ θανάτῳ . . . ἐπὶ φίλτροις: ἐπί can include a notion of purpose. Translate it here as "for the purpose of bringing about death" and "as love charms."

26. [Line 9] φάσκουσαν διδόναι: The infinitive διδόναι is part of an accusative/infinitive construction of indirect statement set up by φάσκουσαν. The subject of the infinitive is not expressed since it is the same person as the one referred to by the participle φάσκουσαν, namely, the speaker's stepmother (R7.1).

Reading Twenty-Six

Antiphon 1.10–12

Focus on Reading

The speaker continues to discuss the importance of βάσανος.

διὰ οὖν ταῦτα ἐγὼ βάσανον τοιαύτην ἠθέλησα ποιήσασθαι περὶ αὐτῶν,
γράψας ἐν γραμματείῳ ἃ ἐπαιτιῶμαι τὴν γυναῖκα ταύτην, βασανιστάς τε
αὐτοὺς τούτους ἐκέλευον γίγνεσθαι ἐμοῦ παρόντος, ἵνα μὴ ἀναγκαζόμενοι ἃ
ἐγὼ ἐπερωτῴην λέγοιεν, ἀλλ᾽ ἐξήρκει μοι τοῖς ἐν τῷ γραμματείῳ χρῆσθαι· καὶ
αὐτό μοι τοῦτο τεκμήριον δίκαιον γενέσθαι, ὅτι ὀρθῶς καὶ δικαίως μετέρχομαι
τὸν φονέα τοῦ πατρός· εἰ δὲ ἄπαρνοι γίγνοιντο ἢ λέγοιεν μὴ ὁμολογούμενα,
<ἡ βάσανος> ἀναγκάζοι τὰ γεγονότα κατηγορεῖν· αὕτη γὰρ καὶ τοὺς τὰ ψευδῆ
παρεσκευασμένους λέγειν τἀληθῆ κατηγορεῖν ποιήσει.

Antiphon 1.10

This long sentence has been divided into sections.

PART ONE

διὰ οὖν ταῦτα ἐγὼ βάσανον τοιαύτην ἠθέλησα ποιήσασθαι περὶ αὐτῶν, γράψας
ἐν γραμματείῳ ἃ ἐπαιτιῶμαι τὴν γυναῖκα ταύτην, βασανιστάς τε αὐτοὺς τούτους
ἐκέλευον γίγνεσθαι ἐμοῦ παρόντος, ἵνα μὴ ἀναγκαζόμενοι ἃ ἐγὼ ἐπερωτῴην
λέγοιεν, ἀλλ᾽ ἐξήρκει μοι τοῖς ἐν τῷ γραμματείῳ χρῆσθαι·

VOCABULARY

διά (prep. + acc.)   on account of

οὖν (particle)   therefore, and so

ἐθέλω   be willing, wish, want

ποιέω   make

περί (prep. + gen.)   concerning

γράφω   write

γραμματεῖον, -ου, τό   tablet

ἐπαιτιάομαι   bring a charge against, accuse

γυνή, γυναικός, ἡ   woman

βασανιστής, -οῦ, ὁ   questioner, torturer

κελεύω   order, command (+ acc./inf.)

γίγνομαι   be, become

πάρειμι   be present

ἀναγκάζω   force, compel

ἐπερωτάω   ask, question

λέγω   speak

ἐξαρκέω (impers.)   it is sufficient for (+ dat.)

χράομαι   use (+ dat.)

OBSERVATIONS, STRATEGIES, AND NOTES

1. This sentence is reasonably straightforward. Use the punctuation to guide you through it.

2. What is the force of the tense of the infinitive ποιήσασθαι?

3. γράψας ἐν γραμματείῳ ἃ ἐπαιτιῶμαι τὴν γυναῖκα ταύτην: A demonstrative pronoun that is the antecedent of a relative pronoun is often omitted, as here (S2509). The literal translation of the phrase is "after I had written on the tablet <those things> that I was charging this woman" but you may translate the phrase more freely as "after I had written on the tablet the charges I was making against this woman."

4. αὐτοὺς τούτους: This is a reference to the speaker's half-brothers. You may translate it as "my half-brothers themselves."

5. ἐμοῦ παρόντος: Note the genitive pronoun and the genitive participle. What construction is this?

6. ἵνα μὴ ἀναγκαζόμενοι ἃ ἐγὼ ἐπερωτῴην λέγοιεν: The mood of the verb of a purpose clause is determined by the tense of the main verb of the sentence. Here there are two main verbs, ἠθέλησα and ἐκέλευον, which are both secondary verbs. Consequently, the optative is used in the purpose clause (R9.1). The slaves are the subject of λέγοιεν. μὴ negates λέγοιεν.

7. ἀναγκαζόμενοι: The circumstantial participle would literally be translated as "being forced," but it may be translated more freely as "under compulsion." It refers to the individual slaves who are being tortured. Note that the masculine plural form is used even though ἀνδράποδα, the word for "slaves," is neuter plural. This is not uncommon when the noun itself is not used.

8. ἃ ἐγὼ ἐπερωτῴην: The demonstrative pronoun antecedent has again been omitted. See note 3, above. ἐπερωτῴην is in the optative because the verb has been assimilated into the same mood used in the purpose clause (S2183).

9. ἐξήρκει: ἐξαρκέω may be used in the third person singular as an impersonal verb meaning "be sufficient for" or "be enough for."

10. τοῖς ἐν τῷ γραμματείῳ: This refers to the questions the speaker had recorded on the tablet. Translate it as "the questions I had written on the tablet."

TRANSLATION

Therefore, on account of these things, I wanted to conduct this inquiry under torture concerning these events, after I had written on the tablet the charges I was making against this woman, and I ordered my half-brothers themselves to be the questioners, while I was present, so that the slaves would not answer under compulsion the things that I was asking, but it was sufficient for me to use the questions I had written on the tablet;

PART TWO

καὶ αὐτό μοι τοῦτο τεκμήριον δίκαιον γενέσθαι, ὅτι ὀρθῶς καὶ δικαίως μετέρχομαι τὸν φονέα τοῦ πατρός·

VOCABULARY

τεκμήριον, -ου, τό proof, evidence	ὀρθῶς (adv.) correctly, rightly
δίκαιος, -α, -ον just, right	δικαίως (adv.) justly
γίγνομαι be, become	μετέρχομαι pursue
ὅτι (conj.) that	φονεύς, -έως, ὁ murderer

OBSERVATIONS, STRATEGIES, AND NOTES

1. αὐτό refers to the speaker's willingness to use written questions.
2. μοι: The dative of reference is a noun or pronoun that indicates the person in whose opinion a statement is accurate (R3.3.12; S1496). Translate this as "in my opinion."
3. τοῦτο: The demonstrative τοῦτο goes with αὐτό. You may translate it as "this in itself."
4. δίκαιον: Supply ἐστι. The order for translation is μοι δίκαιον <ἐστι> αὐτό τοῦτο γενέσθαι τεκμήριον.

TRANSLATION

and in my opinion, it is just that this in itself is proof that I am pursuing the murderer of my father correctly and justly;

PART THREE

εἰ δὲ ἄπαρνοι γίγνοιντο ἢ λέγοιεν μὴ ὁμολογούμενα, <ἡ βάσανος> ἀναγκάζοι τὰ γεγονότα κατηγορεῖν·

VOCABULARY

ἄπαρνος, -ον denying utterly	ἀναγκάζω: force, compel
ἤ (conj.) or	κατηγορέω make an accusation; declare
ὁμολογέω agree	

OBSERVATIONS, STRATEGIES, AND NOTES

1. εἰ δὲ ἄπαρνοι γίγνοιντο . . . <ἡ βάσανος> ἀναγκάζοι: This is a somewhat problematic future less vivid condition. It is clear from the context and from αὕτη in part four of the sentence that βάσανος must be supplied as the subject of ἀναγκάζοι, as αὕτη in the next part of this sentence clearly must refer to βάσανος. In addition, ἄν has been omitted from the apodosis. Michael Gagarin notes that it is not uncommon for Antiphon to omit ἄν in such an instance.[3]

2. ἄπαρνοι γίγνοιντο: Translate this as "should deny." The slaves are the subject of γίγνοιντο.

3. What is the function of μὴ ὁμολογούμενα? μή is used instead of οὐ to negate the substantive ὁμολογούμενα because of the indefinite nature of what the slaves may say (S2734).

4. ἀναγκάζοι: Supply αὐτούς as the direct object of ἀναγκάζοι and the subject accusative of the infinitive κατηγορεῖν.

5. τὰ γεγονότα: Translate this as "what had happened" or "the facts." What form is γεγονότα?

6. κατηγορεῖν usually means "to charge" or "to make an accusation," but it also permits the meaning "to declare."

TRANSLATION

but if the slaves should deny <it> or should say things not in agreement, the inquiry under torture would compel <them> to declare what had happened;

PART FOUR

αὕτη γὰρ καὶ τοὺς τὰ ψευδῆ παρεσκευασμένους λέγειν τἀληθῆ κατηγορεῖν ποιήσει.

VOCABULARY

ψευδής, -ές	false	ἀληθής, -ές	true
παρασκευάζω	prepare	κατηγορέω	charge, declare

OBSERVATIONS, STRATEGIES, AND NOTES

1. καὶ τοὺς τὰ ψευδῆ παρεσκευασμένους λέγειν: The καί is adverbial. Translate it as "even." Note the framing of τὰ ψευδῆ by the definite article and participle to indicate that τὰ ψευδῆ should be taken with the participle and its complementary infinitive λέγειν as the direct object. Note that the infinitive stands outside the frame.

2. τἀληθῆ: This form is the result of crasis (= τὰ ἀληθῆ) and functions as the direct object of κατηγορεῖν.

---

3. Gagarin, *Antiphon*, 112n10.

TRANSLATION

for this will make even those prepared to say false things declare the truth.

POLISHED TRANSLATION

Therefore, because of these things, I wanted to conduct this inquiry under torture concerning these events, once I had written on the tablet the charges I was making against this woman. I ordered my half-brothers themselves to be the questioners while I was present so that the slaves would not answer under compulsion the things that I personally was asking. It was sufficient for me to use the questions I had written on the tablet. And in my opinion, it is right that this in itself is proof that I am pursuing the murderer of my father correctly and justly. But if the slaves should deny it or should say things that are inconsistent, the inquiry under torture would compel them to declare what had happened. For this will make even those prepared to say false things declare the truth.

Reading Selection

The speaker suggests what his opponents would think if they had offered to have the slaves interrogated and he had turned them down.

καίτοι εὖ οἶδά γ', εἰ οὗτοι πρὸς ἐμὲ ἐλθόντες, ἐπειδὴ τάχιστα αὐτοῖς ἀπηγγέλθη
ὅτι ἐπεξίοιμι τοῦ πατρὸς τὸν φονέα, ἠθέλησαν τὰ ἀνδράποδα ἃ ἦν αὐτοῖς
παραδοῦναι, ἐγὼ δὲ μὴ ἠθέλησα παραλαβεῖν, αὐτὰ ἂν ταῦτα μέγιστα τεκμήρια
παρείχοντο ὡς οὐκ ἔνοχοί εἰσι τῷ φόνῳ. νῦν δ', ἐγὼ γάρ εἰμι τοῦτο μὲν ὁ θέλων
αὐτὸς βασανιστὴς γενέσθαι, τοῦτο δὲ τούτους αὐτοὺς κελεύων βασανίσαι ἀντ'   5
ἐμοῦ, ἐμοὶ δή που εἰκὸς ταὐτὰ ταῦτα τεκμήρια εἶναι ὡς εἰσὶν ἔνοχοι τῷ φόνῳ. [εἰ
γὰρ τούτων θελόντων διδόναι εἰς βάσανον ἐγὼ μὴ ἐδεξάμην, τούτοις ἂν ἦν ταῦτα
τεκμήρια. τὸ αὐτὸ οὖν τοῦτο καὶ ἐμοὶ γενέσθω, εἴπερ ἐμοῦ θέλοντος ἔλεγχον
λαβεῖν τοῦ πράγματος αὐτοὶ μὴ ἠθέλησαν δοῦναι.] δεινὸν δ' ἔμοιγε δοκεῖ εἶναι,
εἰ ὑμᾶς μὲν ζητοῦσι <παρ>αιτεῖσθαι ὅπως αὐτῶν μὴ καταψηφίσησθε, αὐτοὶ δὲ   10
σφίσιν αὐτοῖς οὐκ ἠξίωσαν δικασταὶ γενέσθαι δόντες βασανίσαι τὰ αὐτῶν
ἀνδράποδα.

Antiphon 1.11–12

NOTES

1. [Lines 1–4] εἰ οὗτοι πρὸς ἐμὲ ἐλθόντες ... ἠθέλησαν ... ἐγὼ δὲ μὴ ἠθέλησα ... ἂν ... παρείχοντο: This is a mixed contrary-to-fact condition (R10.5, 10.6) using the protasis of a past contrary-to-fact condition (εἰ + aorist indicative) and the apodosis of a present contrary-to-fact condition (imperfect indicative + ἄν). Mixed contrary-to-fact conditions are not uncommon.

2. [Line 1] ἐλθόντες: It is preferable to insert καί and translate the circumstantial parti-

ciple as a finite form with ἠθέλησαν. Translate it as "if these men had come to me . . . and had wished."

3. [Line 1] ἐπειδὴ τάχιστα: Translate this as "as soon as."

4. [Line 1] ἀπηγγέλθη: This verb introduces a ὅτι/ὡς construction of indirect statement (R7.3).

5. [Line 2] What form is ἐπεξίοιμι and why?

6. [Line 2] ἃ ἦν αὐτοῖς: In Greek, details that to our sensibilities are obvious and irrelevant are frequently included. αὐτοῖς is a dative of possession (R3.3.5). Translate it as "which they had" or simply, "their slaves."

7. [Line 3] What form is παραδοῦναι and why?

8. [Line 3] ἐγὼ δὲ μὴ ἠθέλησα παραλαβεῖν: It is important to include δέ in your translation. μή is used as the negative because this is still part of the protasis of the mixed contrary-to-fact condition.

9. [Lines 3–4] αὐτὰ ἂν ταῦτα μέγιστα τεκμήρια παρείχοντο: The direct object of παρείχοντο is αὐτὰ ταῦτα, "these things themselves," while μέγιστα τεκμήρια is the predicate accusative (R3.4.4; S1613). Translate this as "they would offer these things themselves as the greatest proofs." The subject of παρείχοντο is the speaker's half-brothers. This is the apodosis of the mixed contrary-to-fact condition.

10. [Line 4] ὡς οὐκ ἔνοχοί εἰσι τῷ φόνῳ: The subordinate clause explains τεκμήρια.

11. [Lines 4–5] εἰμι . . . ὁ θέλων αὐτός: Translate this as "I myself am the one who wishes."

12. [Lines 4–5] Note τοῦτο μὲν . . . τοῦτο δὲ, which is used just like μὲν . . . δέ.

13. [Line 6] ἐμοὶ δή που εἰκὸς . . . τῷ φόνῳ: Supply ἐστι and translate it with εἰκός, which may take an accusative/infinitive construction. The order for translation is εἰκός <ἐστι> δή που ταὐτὰ ταῦτα εἶναι τεκμήρια ἐμοὶ ὡς εἰσὶν ἔνοχοι τῷ φόνῳ. ταὐτὰ has undergone crasis (= τὰ αὐτά).

14. [Line 6] δή που: This expression may be printed as one word (δήπου) or two. While it has several meanings, here an appropriate choice is "doubtless" or "I should hope" (S2850).

15. [Lines 6–9] [εἰ γὰρ τούτων . . . ἠθέλησαν δοῦναι]: Some commentators bracket these two sentences on the grounds that they are repetitive. Gagarin suggests that Antiphon is merely emphasizing one of the more important points of his argument.[4]

16. [Lines 6–8] εἰ . . . ἐγὼ μὴ ἐδεξάμην . . . ἂν ἦν ταῦτα τεκμήρια: This is another mixed contrary-to-fact condition. See note 1, above.

17. [Line 7] τούτων θελόντων διδόναι εἰς βάσανον: Supply τὰ ἀνδράποδα as the direct object of διδόναι. What construction is τούτων θελόντων?

18. [Line 8] τὸ αὐτὸ οὖν τοῦτο καὶ ἐμοὶ γενέσθω: Translate τὸ αὐτὸ τοῦτο as "this same thing" and take the καί as an adverb. What form is γενέσθω?

19. [Lines 8–9] τὸ αὐτὸ . . . γενέσθω, εἴπερ . . . αὐτοὶ μὴ ἠθέλησαν δοῦναι: This is another mixed condition, with the apodosis of a simple present condition, in which an im-

---

4. Gagarin, *Antiphon*, 113n12.

perative has been substituted for the expected present indicative. The protasis is that of a simple past condition. See R10.2; S2298, 2300 f.

20. [Lines 8–9] ἐμοῦ θέλοντος ἔλεγχον λαβεῖν τοῦ πράγματος: What construction is ἐμοῦ θέλοντος? What is the function of λαβεῖν?

21. [Line 9] Note the use of γε in ἔμοιγε. Translate the word as "to me, at any rate."

22. [Line 10] Note the construction of εἰ ὑμᾶς μὲν ζητοῦσι . . . αὐτοὶ δὲ.

23. [Line 10] <παρ>αιτεῖσθαι: Some editors emend αἰτεῖσθαι to παραιτεῖσθαι because "beseech" fits the context better than "ask."

24. [Line 10] ὅπως αὐτῶν μὴ καταψηφίσησθε: What type of clause is this?

25. [Line 10] αὐτῶν: Some verbs of condemning, such as καταψηφίζω, take the genitive to indicate the person being condemned.

26. [Line 11] δόντες: Take this circumstantial participle with τὰ αὐτῶν ἀνδράποδα as its direct object. Translate δόντες as "by handing over." What is the function of αὐτῶν?

27. [Line 11] βασανίσαι: Though the usage is somewhat rare, it is possible to use the infinitive to express purpose, especially with verbs of giving (S2009). Translate this as "in order to interrogate them" or, more loosely, "for interrogation."

Reading Twenty-Seven

Antiphon 1.13–16

Focus on Reading

The speaker concludes his argument concerning the importance of βάσανος.

περὶ μὲν οὖν τούτων οὐκ ἄδηλον ὅτι αὐτοὶ ἔφευγον τῶν πραχθέντων τὴν
σαφήνειαν πυθέσθαι· ᾔδεσαν γὰρ οἰκεῖον σφίσι τὸ κακὸν ἀναφανησόμενον,
ὥστε σιωπώμενον καὶ ἀβασάνιστον αὐτὸ ἐᾶσαι ἐβουλήθησαν. ἀλλ᾽ οὐχ ὑμεῖς
γε, ὦ ἄνδρες, ἔγωγ᾽ εὖ οἶδα, ἀλλὰ σαφὲς ποιήσετε. ταῦτα μὲν οὖν μέχρι τούτου·
περὶ δὲ τῶν γενομένων πειράσομαι ὑμῖν διηγήσασθαι τὴν ἀλήθειαν· δίκη δὲ
κυβερνήσειεν.

Antiphon 1.13

SENTENCE ONE

περὶ μὲν οὖν τούτων οὐκ ἄδηλον ὅτι αὐτοὶ ἔφευγον τῶν πραχθέντων τὴν
σαφήνειαν πυθέσθαι· ᾔδεσαν γὰρ οἰκεῖον σφίσι τὸ κακὸν ἀναφανησόμενον, ὥστε
σιωπώμενον καὶ ἀβασάνιστον αὐτὸ ἐᾶσαι ἐβουλήθησαν.

VOCABULARY

ἄδηλος, -ον uncertain, unclear
ὅτι (conj.) that
φεύγω shrink from doing, avoid
   doing (+ inf.)
πράττω do
σαφήνεια, -ας, ἡ plain truth
πυνθάνομαι learn
οἰκεῖος, -α, -ον belonging to one's own
   house, residing in one's own home

κακός, -ή, -όν evil, bad
ἀναφαίνω show forth, bring to light
ὥστε (conj.) so that (introduces a result
   clause)
σιωπάω (passive) be kept secret
ἀβασάνιστος, -ον unexamined
ἐάω allow
βούλομαι wish

160

OBSERVATIONS, STRATEGIES, AND NOTES

1. οὐκ ἄδηλον: Supply ἐστι. In Greek, a double negative is frequently used to express an affirmative for an emphatic effect. This rhetorical figure is called *litotes* (S3032).

2. ἔφευγον . . . πυθέσθαι: φεύγω takes an object infinitive to indicate what is being avoided (S1993). The imperfect tense often indicates that an action has been attempted. This is known as the conative imperfect (S1895) and fits the context well here. Translate this as "they themselves were trying to avoid learning."

3. τῶν πραχθέντων: A participle is being used as a substantive when it has a definite article and is not modifying a noun (R6.1). Translate it as "the things that had been done" or "the events." What is the full identification of πραχθέντων?

4. ᾔδεσαν: This is the third person plural pluperfect active indicative of οἶδα. As a verb of perception, οἶδα may take a participial construction of indirect statement (R7.2; S2106). The participle ἀναφανησόμενον is a future passive participle of ἀναφαίνω and is modifying τὸ κακὸν. What is the function of οἰκεῖον?

5. ὥστε σιωπώμενον καὶ ἀβασάνιστον αὐτὸ ἐᾶσαι ἐβουλήθησαν: ὥστε introduces a result clause (R12.1; S2249). Is this an actual or natural result clause? What is the function of ἐᾶσαι?

6. σιωπώμενον καὶ ἀβασάνιστον: Supply εἶναι.

TRANSLATION

And so concerning these things, it is clear that they themselves were trying to avoid learning the plain truth about the events. For they knew that the evil would be shown to be residing in their own home, so they desired to allow it to be kept silent and unexamined.

SENTENCE TWO

ἀλλ᾽ οὐχ ὑμεῖς γε, ὦ ἄνδρες, ἔγωγ᾽ εὖ οἶδα, ἀλλὰ σαφὲς ποιήσετε.

VOCABULARY

ἀλλά (conj.)	but	εὖ (adv.)	well
γε (particle)	at any rate, at least	σαφής, -ές	clear

OBSERVATIONS, STRATEGIES, AND NOTES

1. ἀλλ᾽ οὐχ ὑμεῖς γε: Supply ἐάσετε τοῦτο, implied from the previous sentence. Translate it as "But you, at least, will not allow this."

2. Note the use of the particle γε in ὑμεῖς γε and ἔγωγ᾽.

TRANSLATION

But you, at least, will not <allow this>, gentlemen, I know well; you will, rather, make <it> clear.

SENTENCE THREE

ταῦτα μὲν οὖν μέχρι τούτου· περὶ δὲ τῶν γενομένων πειράσομαι ὑμῖν διηγήσασθαι τὴν ἀλήθειαν· δίκη δὲ κυβερνήσειεν.

VOCABULARY

οὖν (postpositive particle)   and so, therefore

μέχρι (prep. + gen.)   even to, as far as

γίγνομαι   be, become

πειράω   attempt, try

διηγέομαι   set out in detail

ἀλήθεια, -ας, ἡ   truth

δίκη, -ης, ἡ   justice

κυβερνάω   act as a helmsman, guide

OBSERVATIONS, STRATEGIES, AND NOTES

1. ταῦτα μὲν οὖν μέχρι τούτου: This is idiomatic. Translate it as "Enough of this."
2. περὶ δὲ τῶν γενομένων: Translate τῶν γενομένων as "the things that happened" or "what happened."
3. κυβερνήσειεν: An independent optative will be either an optative of wish or a potential optative. If you remember that a potential optative requires ἄν, whereas the optative of wish does not, you will easily be able to distinguish them (R8.4, 8.5; S1814).

TRANSLATION

Enough of this; I will try to set out in detail for you the truth about what happened; may justice be my helmsman.

POLISHED TRANSLATION

And so concerning these things, it is clear that they themselves were trying to avoid learning the plain truth about the events. For they knew that the evil would be shown to be residing in their own home, so they wished to allow it to be kept silent and unexamined. But you will not allow this, gentlemen, I am certain. You will, rather, make everything clear. Enough of this. I will try to set out in detail for you the truth about what happened. May justice guide me.

Reading Selection

The speaker begins the narration of the events of the murders by setting the stage.

ὑπερῷόν τι ἦν τῆς ἡμετέρας οἰκίας, ὃ εἶχε Φιλόνεως ὁπότ᾽ ἐν ἄστει διατρίβοι,
ἀνὴρ καλός τε καὶ ἀγαθὸς καὶ φίλος τῷ ἡμετέρῳ πατρί· καὶ ἦν αὐτῷ παλλακή, ἣν
ὁ Φιλόνεως ἐπὶ πορνεῖον ἔμελλε καταστῆσαι. ταύτην οὖν [πυθομένη] ἡ μήτηρ
τοῦ ἀδελφοῦ ἐποιήσατο φίλην. αἰσθομένη δ᾽ ὅτι ἀδικεῖσθαι ἔμελλεν ὑπὸ τοῦ
Φιλόνεω, μεταπέμπεται, καὶ ἐπειδὴ ἦλθεν, ἔλεξεν αὐτῇ ὅτι καὶ αὐτὴ ἀδικοῖτο ὑπὸ   5
τοῦ πατρὸς τοῦ ἡμετέρου· εἰ οὖν ἐθέλοι πείθεσθαι, ἔφη ἱκανὴ εἶναι ἐκείνη τε τὸν
Φιλόνεων φίλον ποιῆσαι καὶ αὐτὴ τὸν ἐμὸν πατέρα, εἶναι φάσκουσα αὑτῆς μὲν
τοῦτο εὕρημα, ἐκείνης δ᾽ ὑπηρέτημα. ἠρώτα οὖν αὐτὴν εἰ ἐθελήσοι διακονῆσαί οἱ,
καὶ ἡ ὑπέσχετο τάχιστα, ὡς οἶμαι. μετὰ ταῦτα ἔτυχε τῷ Φιλόνεῳ ἐν Πειραιεῖ ὄντα
ἱερὰ Διὶ Κτησίῳ, ὁ δὲ πατὴρ ὁ ἐμὸς εἰς Νάξον πλεῖν ἔμελλεν.   10

Antiphon 1.14–16

NOTES

1. [Line 1] τῆς ἡμετέρας οἰκίας: Translate this possessive genitive as "in our house" for smoother English.

2. [Line 1] What is the antecedent of the relative pronoun ὅ? What is its function within the relative clause?

3. [Line 1] Φιλόνεως: This proper name is from the Attic declension (S237). This form is in the nominative case.

4. [Line 1] ὁπότ᾽ ἐν ἄστει διατρίβοι: Indefinite temporal clauses (R11.4) are considered to have a conditional force and take constructions similar to conditions. This particular indefinite temporal clause, when taken together with the main clause, ὑπερῷόν τι ἦν τῆς ἡμετέρας οἰκίας, has a structure similar to a past general condition (R10.3).

5. [Line 2] καὶ ἦν αὐτῷ παλλακή: What is the function of αὐτῷ?

6. [Line 3] ἐπὶ πορνεῖον: Translate this as "in a brothel."

7. [Line 3] ἔμελλε καταστῆσαι: μέλλω very occasionally takes the aorist infinitive when it means "intend" or "be about to." When μέλλω is used in this sense, the future infinitive is the most common choice (S1959).

8. [Line 3] [πυθομένη]: Some editors bracket πυθομένη because it is repetitive with αἰσθομένη, but both participles work well in their respective sentences.

9. [Line 4] ἀδικεῖσθαι ἔμελλεν: μέλλω may also take the present infinitive when it means "intend" or "be about to" (S1959a).

10. [Lines 4–5] τοῦ Φιλόνεω: The definite article helps you determine the case of this proper noun of the Attic declension. See note 3, above.

11. [Line 5] μεταπέμπεται: The use of the present tense in what is clearly a past context may be categorized as either a historical present (S1883) or an annalistic present (S1884). The two are closely related, and it is often difficult to distinguish between them. The historical present is usually used to increase the dramatic effect of the nar-

ration of a past event and presents the event as if it were occurring at the same moment it is being reported. The annalistic present records historical events and details. Both may be used with past tense verbs in the rest of the sentence or larger context. Here, μεταπέμπεται is a historical present.

12. [Line 5] ὅτι καὶ αὐτὴ ἀδικοῖτο: αὐτὴ refers to the stepmother. καὶ is an adverb and may be translated as "as well" or "too." What mood is ἀδικοῖτο and why?

13. [Line 6] εἰ οὖν ἐθέλοι πείθεσθαι: This is part of the indirect statement set up by ἔφη, which follows this protasis. This is a simple present condition inserted into the indirect statement. Why is ἐθέλοι in the optative?

14. [Line 6] ἔφη: This verb takes an accusative/infinitive construction of indirect statement (R7.1). Note that the subject of the infinitive εἶναι is the same as the subject of ἔφη, as is indicated by the nominative form of ἱκανή.

15. [Line 7] φίλον is used with both τὸν Φιλόνεων and τὸν ἐμὸν πατέρα as a predicate accusative (R3.4.4).

16. [Line 7] φάσκουσα: What type of indirect statement does φάσκω introduce?

17. [Lines 7–8] Note the construction of αὐτῆς μὲν . . . ἐκείνης δ'. The genitives of possession are in the predicate of the sentence (R3.2.1).

18. [Line 8] εἰ ἐθελήσοι: Indirect questions take a construction similar to the ὅτι/ὡς construction of indirect statement, in which the verb of the indirect question may change to the corresponding tense of the optative when the main verb is secondary (R7.6; S2677). Verbs of wishing are sometimes expressed in the future tense in Greek in instances where they would be in the present in English (S1913).

19. [Line 8] οἱ: This is the third person personal pronoun in the dative singular (enclitic form). It is rare in Attic prose (Appendix C; S325). It refers to the stepmother and should be taken with διακονῆσαί, which takes a dative.

20. [Line 9] καὶ ἥ: This indicates a switch of subject to Philoneus's mistress. ἥ is the nominative singular feminine form of the demonstrative pronoun ὅς, ἥ, ὅ ("this"), which is used frequently in Homeric Greek. In later Greek it is used in the nominative with καί at the beginning of a clause or sentence as a personal pronoun (S1113). Translate this as "And she."

21. [Lines 9–10] ἔτυχε τῷ Φιλόνεῳ ἐν Πειραιεῖ ὄντα ἱερὰ Διὶ Κτησίῳ: ἱερὰ is the subject of ἔτυχε. Remember that neuter plural subjects take singular verbs. ὄντα is the supplementary participle with ἔτυχε (R6.4, no. 5). The clause would literally be translated "sacred rites to Zeus Ctesias in Piraeus happened to be for Philoneus," but you may translate it more freely as "Philoneus happened to have sacred rites <to perform> in Piraeus to Zeus Ctesias." Zeus Ctesias was a god of the household, and Philoneus had to perform these rituals at his home.[5]

---

5. See Gagarin, *Antiphon,* 115n16.

Reading Twenty-Eight

Antiphon 1.16–18

Focus on Reading

The speaker notes that Philoneus decided to entertain the speaker's father.

κάλλιστον οὖν ἐδόκει εἶναι τῷ Φιλόνεῳ τῆς αὐτῆς ὁδοῦ ἅμα μὲν προπέμψαι εἰς τὸν Πειραιέα τὸν πατέρα τὸν ἐμὸν φίλον ὄντα ἑαυτῷ, ἅμα δὲ θύσαντα τὰ ἱερὰ ἑστιᾶσαι ἐκεῖνον. ἡ οὖν παλλακὴ τοῦ Φιλόνεω ἠκολούθει τῆς θυσίας ἕνεκεν.

Antiphon 1.16

SENTENCE ONE

κάλλιστον οὖν ἐδόκει εἶναι τῷ Φιλόνεῳ τῆς αὐτῆς ὁδοῦ ἅμα μὲν προπέμψαι εἰς τὸν Πειραιέα τὸν πατέρα τὸν ἐμὸν φίλον ὄντα ἑαυτῷ, ἅμα δὲ θύσαντα τὰ ἱερὰ ἑστιᾶσαι ἐκεῖνον.

VOCABULARY

οὖν (postpositive particle)   therefore, and so
δοκέω   seem, appear (+ dat./inf.)
Φιλόνεως, -εω, ὁ   Philoneus
ὁδός, -οῦ, ἡ   journey, road
ἅμα (adv.)   at the same time

προπέμπω   escort, send off
φίλος, -ου, ὁ   friend
θύω   sacrifice
ἱερά, -ῶν, τά   sacred rites, sacrifices
ἑστιάω   entertain

OBSERVATIONS, STRATEGIES, AND NOTES

1. κάλλιστον: This is the superlative of καλός. Translate it as "an excellent idea" or "a superb idea."

2. ἐδόκει: This verb is used impersonally with the dative τῷ Φιλόνεῳ, the infinitive εἶναι, and κάλλιστον. προπέμψαι goes with κάλλιστον ... εἶναι.

3. τῆς αὐτῆς ὁδοῦ: The genitive may be used to indicate the place within which an action occurs (S1448), but translate this as "on the same journey" for more idiomatic English.

4. Note ἅμα μὲν ... ἅμα δὲ. There is no contrast here really. Antiphon is just noting two different parts of Philoneus's decision. It will work best to omit the μὲν and to translate the δὲ as "and." ἅμα may be omitted as well.

5. τὸν πατέρα τὸν ἐμὸν: Note the formal attributive position (R2.1) of the modifier ἐμόν.

6. φίλον ὄντα ἑαυτῷ: Translate this simply as "his friend."

7. θύσαντα τὰ ἱερά: The participle θύσαντα may be either the accusative singular masculine or the accusative (or nominative) plural neuter form. Here it is the accusative singular and is the subject accusative of the infinitive ἑστιᾶσαι. It refers to Philoneus. The accusative plural neuter τὰ ἱερά is the direct object of θύσαντα.

8. ἑστιᾶσαι ἐκεῖνον: Philoneus's house is in Piraeus.

TRANSLATION

And so it seemed to Philoneus to be an excellent idea to escort my father, his friend, on the same journey to Piraeus and, after he completed the sacrifices, to entertain him.

SENTENCE TWO

ἡ οὖν παλλακὴ τοῦ Φιλόνεω ἠκολούθει τῆς θυσίας ἕνεκεν.

VOCABULARY

παλλακή, -ῆς, ἡ   mistress, concubine   ἕνεκεν (prep. + gen.)   on account of,
ἀκολουθέω   follow   because of
θυσία, -ας, ἡ   sacrifice

OBSERVATIONS, STRATEGIES, AND NOTES

1. What form is ἠκολούθει?

2. ἕνεκεν is a postpositive preposition. This means that it follows its object. Its more common form is ἕνεκα.

TRANSLATION

Philoneus's mistress followed on account of the sacrifice.

POLISHED TRANSLATION

And so it seemed to Philoneus to be an excellent idea to escort my father, his friend, on the same journey to Piraeus and to entertain him after he had completed the sacrifices. Philoneus's mistress followed because of the sacrifice.

Reading Selection

The speaker continues his narration of the events.

καὶ ἐπειδὴ ἦσαν ἐν τῷ Πειραιεῖ, οἷον εἰκός, ἔθυεν. καὶ ἐπειδὴ αὐτῷ ἐτέθυτο
τὰ ἱερά, ἐντεῦθεν ἐβουλεύετο ἡ ἄνθρωπος ὅπως ἂν αὐτοῖς τὸ φάρμακον δοίη,
πότερα πρὸ δείπνου ἢ ἀπὸ δείπνου. ἔδοξεν οὖν αὐτῇ βουλευομένῃ βέλτιον
εἶναι μετὰ δεῖπνον δοῦναι, τῆς Κλυταιμνήστρας ταύτης [τούτου μητρὸς] ταῖς
ὑποθήκαις ἅμα διακονοῦσαν. καὶ τὰ μὲν ἄλλα μακρότερος ἂν εἴη λόγος περὶ τοῦ   5
δείπνου ἐμοί τε διηγήσασθαι ὑμῖν τ' ἀκοῦσαι· ἀλλὰ πειράσομαι τὰ λοιπὰ ὡς ἐν
βραχυτάτοις ὑμῖν διηγήσασθαι, ὡς γεγένηται ἡ δόσις τοῦ φαρμάκου. ἐπειδὴ γὰρ
ἐδεδειπνήκεσαν, οἷον εἰκός, ὁ μὲν θύων Διὶ Κτησίῳ κἀκεῖνον ὑποδεχόμενος, ὁ δ'
ἐκπλεῖν τε μέλλων καὶ παρ' ἀνδρὶ ἑταίρῳ αὐτοῦ δειπνῶν, σπονδάς τε ἐποιοῦντο
καὶ λιβανωτὸν ὑπὲρ αὐτῶν ἐπετίθεσαν.   10

Antiphon 1.17–18

NOTES

1. [Line 1] οἷον εἰκός: This is a parenthetical statement. Supply ἦν and translate it as "as was fitting."

2. [Line 1] ἔθυεν: The subject is Philoneus.

3. [Lines 1–2] αὐτῷ ἐτέθυτο τὰ ἱερά: The subject of ἐτέθυτο is τὰ ἱερά since neuter plural subjects take singular verbs. What form is ἐτέθυτο? What is the function of αὐτῷ?

4. [Line 2] ἐβουλεύετο: The imperfect is often used to indicate the beginning of an action (S1900). Translate it as "began to plan."

5. [Line 2] ἡ ἄνθρωπος: This word is often applied pejoratively to those of lower social status, especially slaves. Translate it as something like "this woman here." While the exact status of Philoneus's concubine is unknown, it is possible that she was a slave.[6]

6. [Line 2] ὅπως ἂν αὐτοῖς τὸ φάρμακον δοίη: This is a clause of effort introduced by ἐβουλεύετο. While it is more common for the verb of an effort clause to be a future

---

6. See Gagarin, *Antiphon*, 116n17.

indicative (R12.2; S2211), a potential optative is sometimes found (S2216). Translate it as "how she might give the drug to them."

7. [Line 3] πότερα πρὸ δείπνου ἢ ἀπὸ δείπνου: Supply ἄν . . . δοίη from the effort clause and translate it as "whether she should give it." This amplifies the effort clause.

8. [Line 4] What tense is δοῦναι and why?

9. [Line 4] τῆς Κλυταιμνήστρας: The speaker is characterizing his stepmother by comparing her to Clytemnestra, who killed her husband, Agamemnon, upon his return from the Trojan War. She murdered him to exact vengeance for his sacrifice of their daughter Iphigenia and also because she was having an affair with Aegisthus, his cousin.

10. [Line 4] [τούτου μητρὸς]: Some editors delete these words on the grounds that they are repetitive. Antiphon, however, likes to remind his readers of familial relationships and of the violation of those relationships.

11. [Lines 4–5] ταῖς ὑποθήκαις ἅμα διακονοῦσαν: διακονοῦσαν refers back to the concubine in αὐτῇ βουλευομένῃ. The accusative, rather than the dative, is used because διακονοῦσαν is the subject accusative of the infinitive δοῦναι. Translate διακονοῦσαν as "following" in order to fit the context. The order for translation is ἅμα διακονοῦσαν ταῖς ὑποθήκαις τῆς Κλυταιμνήστρας ταύτης [τούτου μητρὸς]. What type of genitive is Κλυταιμνήστρας?

12. [Line 5] καὶ τὰ μὲν ἄλλα: Translate this as "and as for the rest."

13. [Line 5] ἂν εἴη λόγος: What type of optative is this?

14. [Line 6] ἐμοί τε διηγήσασθαι ὑμῖν τ' ἀκοῦσαι: Note τε . . . τε and the parallel word order. The infinitives are explanatory infinitives and specify in what respect the adjective μακρότερος is relevant (R5.4; S2001).

15. [Lines 6–7] ὡς ἐν βραχυτάτοις: Supply λόγοις. ὡς with a superlative means "as _____ as possible." Translate this as "in as few words as possible" or "as briefly as possible."

16. [Line 7] ὡς γεγένηται ἡ δόσις τοῦ φαρμάκου: Translate ὡς as "how." What form is γεγένηται?

17. [Line 8] What form is ἐδεδειπνήκεσαν?

18. [Line 8] οἷον εἰκός: Supply ἦν.

19. [Lines 8–9] ὁ μὲν θύων Διὶ Κτησίῳ . . . αὐτοῦ δειπνῶν: In order to highlight the outrageousness of the deed, Antiphon reminds us that Philoneus was fulfilling religious obligations and acting as a gracious host to his dear friend, who was about to depart on a trip.

20. [Lines 8–9] ὁ δ' ἐκπλεῖν τε μέλλων καὶ παρ' ἀνδρὶ ἑταίρῳ αὐτοῦ δειπνῶν: Note the τε . . . καί construction linking the two participial phrases. Remember that τε is postpositive.

21. [Lines 9–10] σπονδάς τε ἐποιοῦντο καὶ λιβανωτὸν ὑπὲρ αὐτῶν ἐπετίθεσαν: Note the construction joining the two verbs. Frankincense was added to libations on certain occasions.

22. [Line 10] ὑπὲρ αὐτῶν: They were presumably making a libation for a safe journey for Philoneus's friend.

Reading Twenty-Nine

Antiphon 1.19–22

Focus on Reading

The speaker vividly describes the administration of the poison.

ἡ δὲ παλλακὴ τοῦ Φιλόνεω τὴν σπονδὴν ἅμα ἐγχέουσα ἐκείνοις εὐχομένοις ἃ οὐκ ἔμελλε τελεῖσθαι, ὦ ἄνδρες, ἐνέχει τὸ φάρμακον. καὶ ἅμα οἰομένη δεξιὸν ποιεῖν πλέον δίδωσι τῷ Φιλόνεῳ, ἴσως <ὡς>, εἰ δοίη πλέον, μᾶλλον φιλησομένη ὑπὸ τοῦ Φιλόνεω· οὔπω γὰρ ᾔδει ὑπὸ τῆς μητρυιᾶς τῆς ἐμῆς ἐξαπατωμένη, πρὶν ἐν τῷ κακῷ ἤδη ἦν· τῷ δὲ πατρὶ τῷ ἡμετέρῳ ἔλασσον ἐνέχει.

Antiphon 1.19

SENTENCE ONE

ἡ δὲ παλλακὴ τοῦ Φιλόνεω τὴν σπονδὴν ἅμα ἐγχέουσα ἐκείνοις εὐχομένοις ἃ οὐκ ἔμελλε τελεῖσθαι, ὦ ἄνδρες, ἐνέχει τὸ φάρμακον.

VOCABULARY

παλλακή, -ῆς, ἡ mistress	εὔχομαι pray, pray for
σπονδή, -ῆς, ἡ libation	μέλλω be about to, going to be (+ inf.)
ἅμα (adv.) at the same time	τελέω accomplish
ἐγχέω pour in, pour, pour wine in	φάρμακον, -ου, τό drug

OBSERVATIONS, STRATEGIES, AND NOTES

1. τὴν σπονδὴν ἅμα ἐγχέουσα: The mistress was pouring the wine for the men to use in the libation. Translate this as "pouring wine for the libation."
2. εὐχομένοις ἃ οὐκ ἔμελλε τελεῖσθαι: This detail adds a dramatic touch to the narrative.

169

The antecedent of the relative pronoun ἅ has been omitted, as frequently happens when the antecedent would have been a demonstrative pronoun (S2509). τελεῖσθαι is the future infinitive with ἔμελλε.

3. What form is ἐνέχει?

TRANSLATION

But at the same time Philoneus's mistress was pouring wine for the libation for those men as they were praying for things that were not going to be accomplished, gentlemen, she poured in the drug.

SENTENCE TWO

καὶ ἅμα οἰομένη δεξιὸν ποιεῖν πλέον δίδωσι τῷ Φιλόνεῳ, ἴσως <ὡς>, εἰ δοίη πλέον, μᾶλλον φιλησομένη ὑπὸ τοῦ Φιλόνεω· οὔπω γὰρ ᾔδει ὑπὸ τῆς μητρυιᾶς τῆς ἐμῆς ἐξαπατωμένη, πρὶν ἐν τῷ κακῷ ἤδη ἦν· τῷ δὲ πατρὶ τῷ ἡμετέρῳ ἔλασσον ἐνέχει.

VOCABULARY

ἅμα (adv.) at the same time	ὑπό (prep. + gen.) by
οἴομαι think	οὔπω (adv.) not yet
δεξιός, -ά, -όν clever	μητρυιά, -ᾶς, ἡ stepmother
πλέων, -ον (gen. -ονος) more	ἐξαπατάω deceive thoroughly
δίδωμι give	πρίν (conj.) until
ἴσως (adv.) perhaps	κακός, -ή, -όν evil
ὡς (particle) on the grounds that, because (+ part.)	ἤδη (adv.) already
	ἡμέτερος, -α, -ον our
μᾶλλον (adv.) more	ἐλάσσων, -ον (gen. -ονος) less
φιλέω love	ἐγχέω pour in

OBSERVATIONS, STRATEGIES, AND NOTES

1. οἰομένη δεξιὸν ποιεῖν πλέον δίδωσι τῷ Φιλόνεῳ: Note that οἰομένη is nominative singular feminine. It is modifying the implied subject of δίδωσι and sets up an indirect statement. Since οἰομένη is a verb of thinking, it takes an accusative/infinitive construction of indirect statement. The subject of the infinitive is the same as the subject of the main verb, so it is not expressed (R7.1). What is the function of the adjective δεξιόν?

2. Notice that δίδωσι is in the present tense. This is another example of a historical present (S1883).

3. ἴσως <ὡς> . . . φιλησομένη ὑπὸ τοῦ Φιλόνεω: This continues the indirect statement set up by οἰομένη, though now a participle is used. The participle represents the future indicative of the apodosis of a future more vivid condition; the prota-

sis is εἰ δοίη πλέον. Some editors add ὡς to qualify the statement as an alleged cause (S2086).

4. εἰ δοίη πλέον: Both historical and annalistic presents are usually considered secondary tenses. Consequently, the verb of the subordinate clause in the indirect statement is in the optative. The original mood would have been the subjunctive, as required for the protasis of a future more vivid condition. ἐάν has been changed to εἰ, as is appropriate for the use of the optative (R7.5).

5. φιλησομένη: Some verbs use the future middle in a passive sense (S808). Note that ὑπὸ τοῦ Φιλόνεω, a genitive of personal agent (R3.2.3), helps you to see that φιλησομένη has a passive meaning.

6. ᾔδει . . . ἐξαπατωμένη: ᾔδει is the third person singular pluperfect active indicative of οἶδα, which sets up a participial construction of indirect statement (R7.2).

7. πρὶν ἐν τῷ κακῷ ἤδη ἦν: πρίν with the indicative means "until" (R11.5, no. 2). This would literally be translated, "until she was already in the evil," but we may translate it more freely as "until she was already caught up in the evil act."

TRANSLATION

And at the same time, because she was thinking that she was doing a clever thing, she gave more to Philoneus, <thinking> perhaps that if she gave more, she would be loved more by Philoneus, for she did not yet know that she was being thoroughly deceived by my stepmother until she was already <caught up> in the evil <act>, and she poured in less for my father.

POLISHED TRANSLATION

But as Philoneus's mistress was pouring the wine for the libation for those men while they were praying for things that were not going to be accomplished, gentlemen, she poured in the drug. And at the same time, because she was thinking that she was doing a clever thing, she gave more to Philoneus. Perhaps she thought that if she gave Philoneus more, she would be loved more by him, for she did not know that she was being thoroughly deceived by my stepmother until she was already caught up in the evil act. She poured in less for my father.

Reading Selection

The speaker concludes his narration of the events and asks the jurors to avenge his father's death.

καὶ ἐκεῖνοι ἐπειδὴ ἀπέσπεισαν, τὸν ἑαυτῶν φονέα μεταχειριζόμενοι ἐκπίνουσιν
ὑστάτην πόσιν. ὁ μὲν οὖν Φιλόνεως εὐθέως παραχρῆμα ἀποθνήσκει, ὁ δὲ πατὴρ
ὁ ἡμέτερος εἰς νόσον ἐμπίπτει, ἐξ ἧς καὶ ἀπώλετο εἰκοσταῖος. ἀνθ' ὧν ἡ μὲν
διακονήσασα καὶ χειρουργήσασα ἔχει τὰ ἐπίχειρα ὧν ἀξία ἦν, οὐδὲν αἰτία οὖσα —
τῷ γὰρ δημοκοίνῳ τροχισθεῖσα παρεδόθη —, ἡ δ' αἰτία τε ἤδη καὶ ἐνθυμηθεῖσα   5
ἕξει, ἐὰν ὑμεῖς τε καὶ οἱ θεοὶ θέλωσιν. σκέψασθε οὖν ὅσῳ δικαιότερα ὑμῶν

δεήσομαι ἐγὼ ἢ ὁ ἀδελφός. ἐγὼ μέν γε τῷ τεθνεῶτι ὑμᾶς κελεύω καὶ τῷ ἠδικημένῳ
τὸν ἀΐδιον χρόνον τιμωροὺς γενέσθαι· οὗτος δὲ τοῦ μὲν τεθνεῶτος πέρι οὐδὲν
ὑμᾶς αἰτήσεται, ὃς ἄξιος καὶ ἐλέου καὶ βοηθείας καὶ τιμωρίας παρ' ὑμῶν τυχεῖν,
ἀθέως καὶ ἀκλεῶς πρὸ τῆς εἱμαρμένης ὑφ' ὧν ἥκιστα ἐχρῆν τὸν βίον ἐκλιπών, ὑπὲρ   10
δὲ τῆς ἀποκτεινάσης δεήσεται ἀθέμιτα καὶ ἀνόσια καὶ ἀτέλεστα καὶ ἀνήκουστα καὶ
θεοῖς καὶ ὑμῖν, δεόμενος ὑμῶν . . . ἃ αὐτὴ ἑαυτὴν οὐκ ἔπεισε μὴ κακοτεχνῆσαι.

Antiphon 1.20–22

NOTES

1. [Line 1] ἐκεῖνοι: The subject of a subordinate clause is sometimes positioned in front
   of the subordinating conjunction in order to emphasize it.

2. [Line 1] τὸν ἑαυτῶν φονέα μεταχειριζόμενοι: Note that the direct object of the participle immediately precedes it. This is a typical word placement. φονέα refers to the
   poisoned drink. This is quite a dramatic presentation of the evil deed!

3. [Line 1] ἑαυτῶν: A genitive is often used with nouns that have a verbal notion implied by their meaning. The genitive acts as the object of the verbal notion and is
   called an objective genitive (R3.2.5).

4. [Lines 1–3] ἐκπίνουσιν, ἀποθνῄσκει, ἐμπίπτει: The historical presents are used for increased vividness (S1883).

5. [Line 2] What construction is used in ὁ μὲν οὖν Φιλόνεως . . . ὁ δὲ πατὴρ?

6. [Line 2] εὐθέως παραχρῆμα: Redundancy, formally called *pleonasm*, also increases
   the vividness and drama of the presentation (S3042a).

7. [Line 3] ἐξ ἧς καὶ ἀπώλετο εἰκοσταῖος: Take the καί as an adverb. What is the antecedent of ἧς? Note that εἰκοσταῖος, meaning "on the twentieth day," is technically an
   adjective, though it is adverbial in meaning.

8. [Line 3] ἀνθ' ὧν: ὧν refers to all the events of the poisoning. Translate this as "in return for these deeds."

9. [Lines 3–5] Note the construction of ἡ μὲν διακονήσασα . . . ἡ δ' αἰτία. ἡ μὲν refers
   to Philoneus's mistress while ἡ δ' refers to the speaker's stepmother. Be sure to note
   that αἰτία is an adjective here, not a noun.

10. [Line 4] οὐδὲν αἰτία οὖσα: Translate οὖσα, a circumstantial participle, concessively:
    "although she was not at all responsible <for them>." οὐδέν is being used as an ad-
    verb to mean "not at all."

11. [Lines 5–6] ἡ δ' αἰτία τε ἤδη καὶ ἐνθυμηθεῖσα ἕξει, ἐὰν ὑμεῖς τε καὶ οἱ θεοὶ θέλωσιν:
    Supply τὰ ἐπίχειρα as the direct object of ἕξει. The apodosis precedes the protasis for
    extra emphasis. What type of condition is this?

12. [Line 5] Note the τε . . . καί construction linking the two modifiers αἰτία and
    ἐνθυμηθεῖσα. αἰτία is again the adjective, not the noun. What form is ἐνθυμηθεῖσα?

13. [Line 6] What form is σκέψασθε?

14. [Line 6] ὅσῳ δικαιότερα: ὅσῳ is a dative of degree of difference with the comparative
    δικαιότερα (R3.3.8). Translate this as "consider how much more just <the plea> I am
    asking you is than my brother's."

15. [Line 7] δεήσομαι: The future tense is sometimes used in place of the present to indicate what is happening or what is possible at the very moment of speaking (S1915). Translate δεήσομαι in the present tense to conform to English idiom.

16. [Lines 7–8] Note the μὲν ... δέ construction in ἐγὼ μέν ... οὗτος δὲ. γε gives added emphasis.

17. [Lines 7–8] κελεύω: This verb takes an accusative of person plus the infinitive (R5.1). The order for translation is κελεύω ὑμᾶς γενέσθαι τιμωροὺς τῷ τεθνεῶτι καὶ τῷ ἠδικημένῳ τὸν ἀΐδιον χρόνον. τῷ τεθνεῶτι and τῷ ἠδικημένῳ both refer to the speaker's father and are datives of interest (S1474) or datives of advantage (R3.3.10; S1481). These two datives are closely related. Why is γενέσθαι in the aorist?

18. [Line 8] What type of time expression is τὸν ἀΐδιον χρόνον?

19. [Line 8] οὗτος refers to the speaker's half-brother.

20. [Lines 8–11] Note the construction of τοῦ μὲν τεθνεῶτος πέρι ... ὑπὲρ δὲ τῆς ἀποκτεινάσης, contrasting the speaker's dead father and his murderous stepmother.

21. [Line 8] τοῦ μὲν τεθνεῶτος: What form is τεθνεῶτος? What is the force of its tense?

22. [Line 8] πέρι: When an object precedes its preposition, by convention the accent shifts to the penult. The object of πέρι is τοῦ τεθνεῶτος.

23. [Line 9] αἰτήσεται: οὐδὲν is the object of αἰτήσεται.

24. [Line 9] ἄξιος: Supply ἐστι and take it with τυχεῖν, which limits ἄξιος and is an explanatory infinitive (R5.4; S2001). Since τυχεῖν takes a genitive, translate ἐλέου, βοηθείας, and τιμωρίας with it.

25. [Line 10] ὑφ' ὧν ἥκιστα ἐχρῆν: The antecedent of ὧν has been omitted because it would have been a demonstrative pronoun (S2509). The relative pronoun has been attracted into the case of the omitted antecedent (R11.3; S2522). The full expression would have been ὑπ' ἐκείνων οὓς ἥκιστα ἐχρῆν. This is an elliptical expression which should be translated as "by those who least should have killed him" or "by those who should have been the last to kill him."

26. [Line 10] τὸν βίον ἐκλιπών: The phrase is here used euphemistically for "killed," hence the genitive of personal agent, ὑφ' ὧν.

27. [Line 11] ἀθέμιτα καὶ ἀνόσια καὶ ἀτέλεστα καὶ ἀνήκουστα: The alpha at the beginning of each of these adjectives is called an alpha privative. It negates the word to which it is attached (S885.1).

28. [Lines 11–12] καὶ θεοῖς καὶ ὑμῖν: The dative of personal agent is used with verbal adjectives such as ἀτέλεστα and ἀνήκουστα (R3.3.6; S1488).

29. [Line 12] δεόμενος ὑμῶν ... ἃ αὐτὴ ἑαυτὴν οὐκ ἔπεισε μὴ κακοτεχνῆσαι: The ellipsis indicates that there is a lacuna, or gap, in the text. Some editors prefer Thalheim's suggested emendation μὴ τιμωρῆσαι,[7] which would result in the translation "asking you not to punish the base acts she did not persuade herself not to do." This works well enough in the context.

30. [Line 12] κακοτεχνῆσαι: The verb means "act basely," but it will work best in English if some of the meaning is transferred to the relative pronoun ἃ, which was translated as "base acts" in note 29, above.

---

7. See Gagarin, *Antiphon*, 118–19n22.

Reading Thirty

Antiphon 1.22–25

Focus on Reading

The speaker continues his appeal to the jurors.

ὑμεῖς δ᾽ οὐ τῶν ἀποκτεινάντων ἐστὲ βοηθοί, ἀλλὰ τῶν ἐκ προνοίας ἀποθνησκόντων, καὶ ταῦτα ὑφ᾽ ὧν ἥκιστα αὐτοὺς ἐχρῆν ἀποθνήσκειν. ἤδη οὖν ἐν ὑμῖν ἐστι τοῦτ᾽ ὀρθῶς διαγνῶναι, ὃ καὶ ποιήσατε.

Antiphon 1.22

SENTENCE ONE

ὑμεῖς δ᾽ οὐ τῶν ἀποκτεινάντων ἐστὲ βοηθοί, ἀλλὰ τῶν ἐκ προνοίας ἀποθνησκόντων, καὶ ταῦτα ὑφ᾽ ὧν ἥκιστα αὐτοὺς ἐχρῆν ἀποθνήσκειν.

VOCABULARY

ἀποκτείνω kill	ἀποθνήσκω be killed
βοηθός, -οῦ, ὁ assistant, helper	ὑπό (prep. + gen.) by
ἀλλά (conj.) but	ἥκιστα (adv.) least
ἐκ (prep. + gen.) out of	χρή it is necessary (+ acc./inf.)
προνοία, -ας, ἡ forethought	

OBSERVATIONS, STRATEGIES, AND NOTES

1. τῶν ἀποκτεινάντων: The participle is being used as a substantive, as the definite article indicates (R6.1). Translate it as an objective genitive with βοηθοί. Remember that an objective genitive indicates the object of the verbal notion implied by certain nouns (R3.2.5; S1328).

2. ἐστὲ is the second person plural present indicative of εἰμί. Note that the imperative form is ἔστε, which is not an enclitic, and that μή rather than οὐ is the negative used with an imperative.

3. καὶ ταῦτα: This adds a circumstance in addition to what has just been stated. Translate it as "and in addition" or "what is more."

4. ὑφ' ὧν: The antecedent of the relative pronoun ὧν has been omitted because it would have been a demonstrative pronoun (S2509).

5. ὑφ' ὧν ἥκιστα αὐτοὺς ἐχρῆν ἀποθνῄσκειν: The imperfect indicative of impersonal expressions such as ἐχρῆν may be used with an infinitive to indicate an unfulfilled obligation. The present infinitive denotes an unfulfilled obligation in present time (S1774, 1775). Translate this as "by those <by> whom they should least be killed." It is an unfulfilled obligation because the speaker's father and Philoneus were actually killed.

TRANSLATION

And you are not assistants of the killers but of those who were killed with forethought, and what is more, <they were killed> by those <by> whom they should least be killed.

SENTENCE TWO

ἤδη οὖν ἐν ὑμῖν ἐστὶ τοῦτ' ὀρθῶς διαγνῶναι, ὃ καὶ ποιήσατε.

VOCABULARY

ἤδη (adv.) now		ὀρθῶς (adv.)	rightly, justly
οὖν (postpositive particle) therefore		διαγιγνώσκω	give judgment, decide

OBSERVATIONS, STRATEGIES, AND NOTES

1. ἐν ὑμῖν ἐστί is an idiomatic expression that takes an infinitive. Translate it as "it is in your power."

2. The antecedent of the relative pronoun ὃ is τοῦτ'. A literal translation will not work here. Translate this as "and so do it!"

3. What form is ποιήσατε?

TRANSLATION

Therefore it is now in your power to decide this justly, and so do it!

POLISHED TRANSLATION

You are not assistants of the killers. You are, rather, defenders of those who were killed with forethought, and, what is more, killed by those by whom least of all they should be killed. Therefore it is now in your power to decide this justly—and so do it!

Reading Selection

The speaker contrasts his actions with those of his brothers.

δεήσεται δ᾽ ὑμῶν οὗτος μὲν ὑπὲρ μητρὸς τῆς αὐτοῦ ζώσης, τῆς ἐκεῖνον
διαχρησαμένης ἐπιβούλως τε καὶ ἀθέως, ὅπως δίκην μὴ δῷ, ἂν ὑμᾶς πείθῃ, ὧν
ἠδίκηκε· ἐγὼ δ᾽ ὑμᾶς ὑπὲρ πατρὸς τοὐμοῦ τεθνεῶτος αἰτοῦμαι, ὅπως παντὶ
τρόπῳ δῷ. ὑμεῖς δέ, ὅπως διδῶσι δίκην οἱ ἀδικοῦντες, τούτου γε ἕνεκα καὶ
δικασταὶ ἐγένεσθε καὶ ἐκλήθητε. καὶ ἐγὼ μὲν ἐπεξέρχομαι [λέγων], ἵνα δῷ   5
δίκην ὧν ἠδίκηκε καὶ τιμωρήσω τῷ τε πατρὶ τῷ ἡμετέρῳ καὶ τοῖς νόμοις τοῖς
ὑμετέροις· ταύτῃ καὶ ἄξιόν μοι βοηθῆσαι ὑμᾶς ἅπαντας, εἰ ἀληθῆ λέγω· οὗτος δὲ
τἀναντία, ὅπως ἡ τοὺς νόμους παριδοῦσα μὴ δῷ δίκην ὧν ἠδίκηκε, ταύτῃ βοηθὸς
καθέστηκε. καίτοι πότερον δικαιότερον τὸν ἐκ προνοίας ἀποκτείναντα δοῦναι
δίκην ἢ μή; καὶ πότερον δεῖ οἰκτεῖραι μᾶλλον τὸν τεθνεῶτα ἢ τὴν ἀποκτείνασαν;   10
ἐγὼ μὲν οἶμαι τὸν τεθνεῶτα· καὶ γὰρ <ἂν> δικαιότερον καὶ ὁσιώτερον καὶ πρὸς
θεῶν καὶ πρὸς ἀνθρώπων γίγνοιτο ὑμῖν.

Antiphon 1.23–25

NOTES

1. [Lines 1–3] Note the μὲν . . . δέ construction in οὗτος μὲν . . . ἐγὼ δ᾽.
2. [Line 1] ὑπὲρ μητρὸς τῆς αὐτοῦ ζώσης: The definite article τῆς indicates that ζώσης is being used as an attributive participle to modify μητρός (R2.1, 6.1). This is also the case with τῆς ἐκεῖνον διαχρησαμένης. Notice that both the possessive genitive αὐτοῦ and the direct object ἐκεῖνον are framed by the definite article and the participle. A word that is dependent on the participle may be placed between the article and the participle (S1166).
3. [Line 2] δῷ: What form is δῷ and why? What is the significance of its tense?
4. [Line 2] ἂν ὑμᾶς πείθῃ: This is a protasis of a future more vivid condition, but the apodosis is unexpressed since the protasis is just a parenthetical statement, as the commas indicate. Remember that ἂν is another form of ἐάν (S2283).
5. [Lines 2–3] ὧν ἠδίκηκε: Take the relative clause with δίκην. The antecedent of ὧν has been omitted and the relative pronoun has been attracted into the case of the omitted antecedent (R11.3; S2509, 2522). A full expression would have been ὅπως μὴ δῷ δίκην τούτων ἃ ἠδίκηκε. Note the hyperbaton (S3028) in the insertion of ἂν ὑμᾶς πείθῃ between δῷ and ὧν.
6. [Line 3] What form is ἠδίκηκε? What nuance does it impart?

7. [Line 3] τοὐμοῦ is an instance of crasis (= τοῦ ἐμοῦ) (S62).

8. [Line 3] What type of participle is τεθνεῶτος? What is its form?

9. [Lines 3–4] ὅπως παντὶ τρόπῳ δῷ: The subject of δῷ is the stepmother. Translate παντὶ τρόπῳ as "fully" or "in every way." What type of clause is this?

10. [Line 4] ὑμεῖς: The inclusion of the nominative form of the pronoun gives extra emphasis to the subject.

11. [Line 4] ὅπως διδῶσι δίκην οἱ ἀδικοῦντες: This refers to τούτου γε ἕνεκα, which immediately follows it. This placement gives the clause prominence. What form is διδῶσι and why?

12. [Lines 4–5] Note καὶ ... καὶ in καὶ δικασταὶ ἐγένεσθε καὶ ἐκλήθητε.

13. [Line 5] What form is ἐκλήθητε?

14. [Line 5] [λέγων]: Some editors delete this word because of its redundancy.

15. [Line 6] ὧν ἠδίκηκε: See note 5, above.

16. [Line 6] What form is τιμωρήσω and why?

17. [Lines 6–7] τῷ τε πατρὶ τῷ ἡμετέρῳ καὶ τοῖς νόμοις τοῖς ὑμετέροις: Note the τε ... καί construction. Take the datives with τιμωρήσω. τιμωρέω takes a dative to indicate the person (or thing) that is being avenged.

18. [Line 7] Translate ταύτῃ as "thus."

19. [Line 7] ἄξιόν: Supply ἐστι. The impersonal construction takes an accusative/infinitive construction.

20. [Line 7] μοι βοηθῆσαι: Many verbs of helping take a dative to indicate the person being helped (R3.3.13, no. 1).

21. [Line 8] τἀναντία: This is an instance of crasis (= τὰ ἐναντία) and is used adverbially. Translate it as "in contrast" or "in an opposite fashion."

22. [Line 8] ἡ τοὺς νόμους παριδοῦσα: Notice the framing of νόμους by the definite article and the participle. All these words go together. What is the function of νόμους?

23. [Line 8] What form is παριδοῦσα?

24. [Lines 8–9] ταύτῃ βοηθὸς καθέστηκε belongs with οὗτος δὲ τἀναντία. The purpose clause has been inserted between the subject and predicate of the main clause for stylistic variation and emphasis.

25. [Line 8] ταύτῃ: This refers to the stepmother.

26. [Line 9] καθέστηκε: What form is this?

27. [Lines 9–10] πότερον ... ἤ ("whether ... or") is used to indicate a question with two alternatives. You may omit "whether" in your translation.

28. [Line 11] ἐγὼ μὲν οἶμαι τὸν τεθνεῶτα: This is an elliptical indirect statement set up by οἶμαι. You may supply δεῖν οἰκτεῖραι μᾶλλον, which is implied by the question.

29. [Lines 11–12] καὶ γὰρ <ἂν> δικαιότερον καὶ ὁσιώτερον ... γίγνοιτο: Most editors add ἄν since it is required for a potential optative. δικαιότερον καὶ ὁσιώτερον refers to the necessity of pitying the murdered man.

30. [Lines 11–12] καὶ πρὸς θεῶν καὶ πρὸς ἀνθρώπων: Note the καὶ ... καί construction.

Reading Thirty-One

Antiphon 1.25–28

Focus on Reading

The speaker reminds the jurors of the premeditated actions of his stepmother.

ἤδη οὖν ἐγὼ ἀξιῶ, ὥσπερ κἀκεῖνον ἀνελεημόνως καὶ ἀνοικτίστως αὕτη ἀπώλεσεν,
οὕτω καὶ αὐτὴν ταύτην ἀπολέσθαι ὑπό τε ὑμῶν καὶ τοῦ δικαίου. ἡ μὲν ἑκουσίως
καὶ βουλεύσασα ἀπέκτεινεν, ὁ δ᾽ ἀκουσίως καὶ βιαίως ἀπέθανε.

Antiphon 1.25–26

SENTENCE ONE

ἤδη οὖν ἐγὼ ἀξιῶ, ὥσπερ κἀκεῖνον ἀνελεημόνως καὶ ἀνοικτίστως αὕτη ἀπώλεσεν,
οὕτω καὶ αὐτὴν ταύτην ἀπολέσθαι ὑπό τε ὑμῶν καὶ τοῦ δικαίου.

VOCABULARY

ἤδη (adv.)   now
οὖν (postpositive particle)   so, and so, therefore
ἀξιόω   think worthy (+ acc./inf.)
ὥσπερ   just as

ἀνελεημόνως (adv.)   without mercy
ἀνοικτίστως (adv.)   without pity
ἀπόλλυμι (act.)   destroy; (mid.) perish
οὕτω (adv.)   thus, in this way

OBSERVATIONS, STRATEGIES, AND NOTES

1. ἀξιῶ: ἀξιόω may take an accusative/infinitive construction in the sense of "think <someone> worthy <to do something>." Translate the phrase as "I think that this woman herself is worthy to be put to death."
2. κἀκεῖνον: This is another example of crasis (= καὶ ἐκεῖνον).

3. What part of speech is αὕτη?

4. ἀπώλεσεν, ἀπολέσθαι: ἀπόλλυμι means "destroy" in the active voice and "perish" in the middle voice. Translate ἀπολέσθαι more loosely as "be put to death" so that ὑπό τε ὑμῶν καὶ τοῦ δικαίου, two genitives of personal agent (R3.2.3), will work well in English.

5. καὶ αὐτὴν ταύτην: αὐτός may be used in the predicate position as an intensifier, even without a definite article. The καί is adverbial.

6. ὑπό τε ὑμῶν καὶ τοῦ δικαίου: Note the τε . . . καί construction.

7. τοῦ δικαίου: This adjective is being used as a substantive in the neuter singular. Translate it as "by justice."

TRANSLATION

And so now, just as this woman destroyed that man without mercy and without pity, I think that she herself is also worthy to be put to death by you and by justice.

SENTENCE TWO

ἡ μὲν ἑκουσίως καὶ βουλεύσασα ἀπέκτεινεν, ὁ δ' ἀκουσίως καὶ βιαίως ἀπέθανε.

VOCABULARY

ἑκουσίως (adv.)   voluntarily, willingly   ἀκουσίως (adv.)   unvoluntarily, unwillingly
βουλεύω   plan   βιαίως (adv.)   by force, by violence
ἀποκτείνω   kill   ἀποθνήσκω   die

OBSERVATIONS, STRATEGIES, AND NOTES

1. Note the construction of ἡ μὲν . . . ὁ δ'.

2. βουλεύσασα: The circumstantial participle would literally be translated as "after she planned" or "having planned," but you may translate it as "with deliberation" or "in a premeditated manner."

3. What form is ἀπέθανε?

TRANSLATION

She killed <him> voluntarily and with premeditation, while he died unwillingly and by force.

POLISHED TRANSLATION

And so now, just as this woman destroyed my father without mercy and pity, I think that she herself is also worthy to be put to death by you and by justice. She killed him of her own accord in a premeditated manner, while he died unwillingly, by force.

Reading Selection

The speaker continues his appeal, reminding the jurors of his father's innocence and his stepmother's outrageous and impious actions.

πῶς γὰρ οὐ βιαίως ἀπέθανεν, ὦ ἄνδρες, ὅς γ' ἐκπλεῖν ἔμελλεν ἐκ τῆς γῆς τῆσδε,
παρά τε ἀνδρὶ φίλῳ αὐτοῦ εἱστιᾶτο; ἡ δὲ πέμψασα τὸ φάρμακον καὶ κελεύσασα
ἐκείνῳ δοῦναι πιεῖν ἀπέκτεινεν ἡμῶν τὸν πατέρα, πῶς οὖν ταύτην ἐλεεῖν ἄξιόν
ἐστιν ἢ αἰδοῦς τυγχάνειν παρ' ὑμῶν ἢ ἄλλου του, ἥτις αὐτὴ οὐκ ἠξίωσεν ἐλεῆσαι
τὸν ἑαυτῆς ἄνδρα, ἀλλ' ἀνοσίως καὶ αἰσχρῶς ἀπώλεσεν; οὕτω δέ τοι καὶ ἐλεεῖν   5
ἐπὶ τοῖς ἀκουσίοις παθήμασι μᾶλλον προσήκει ἢ τοῖς ἑκουσίοις καὶ ἐκ προνοίας
ἀδικήμασι καὶ ἁμαρτήμασι. καὶ ὥσπερ ἐκεῖνον αὕτη οὔτε θεοὺς οὔθ' ἥρωας οὔτ'
ἀνθρώπους αἰσχυνθεῖσα οὐδὲ δείσασ' ἀπώλεσεν, οὕτω καὶ αὐτὴ ὑφ' ὑμῶν καὶ
τοῦ δικαίου ἀπολομένη, καὶ μὴ τυχοῦσα μήτ' αἰδοῦς μήτ' ἐλέου μήτ' αἰσχύνης
μηδεμιᾶς παρ' ὑμῶν, τῆς δικαιοτάτης ἂν τύχοι τιμωρίας. θαυμάζω δὲ ἔγωγε τῆς   10
τόλμης τοῦ ἀδελφοῦ καὶ τῆς διανοίας, τὸ διομόσασθαι ὑπὲρ τῆς μητρὸς εὖ εἰδέναι
μὴ πεποιηκυῖαν ταῦτα. πῶς γὰρ ἄν τις εὖ εἰδείη οἷς μὴ παρεγένετο αὐτός;

Antiphon 1.26–28

NOTES

1. [Line 2] παρά τε ἀνδρὶ φίλῳ αὐτοῦ: παρά with the dative is like Latin *apud* or French *chez* and means "at the house of." What is the function of αὐτοῦ?

2. [Line 2] ἡ δὲ: The definite article has a demonstrative sense when used with the particles μέν, δέ, γε, and τοι and the conjunction καί. With δέ, it often marks a change of subject from that of the previous main verb. Translate it here as "but she" (S1106, 1112).

3. [Line 2] πέμψασα and κελεύσασα are best taken as attributive participles, for which the article is not always required (S2049). Antiphon is reminding his audience of each step in the premeditated murder.

4. [Lines 2–3] κελεύσασα ἐκείνῳ δοῦναι: Supply αὐτήν, referring to Philoneus's mistress, as the subject of δοῦναι. τὸ φάρμακον is the direct object of δοῦναι.

5. [Line 3] πιεῖν: What tense is the infinitive? The accent is a clue! An infinitive may be used to indicate purpose with verbs of giving (S2008, 2009).

6. [Line 3] ταύτην: This is both the direct object of ἐλεεῖν and the subject of τυγχάνειν. Remember that τυγχάνω takes the genitive. ἄξιόν ἐστιν sets up the accusative/infinitive construction.

7. [Line 4] του: This is the alternate form of τινος (τις, τι), the indefinite pronoun. See Appendix C for the paradigm.

8. [Line 4] ἐλεῆσαι: What form is this?

9. [Lines 5–7] ἐλεεῖν ἐπὶ τοῖς ἀκουσίοις παθήμασι μᾶλλον προσήκει ἢ τοῖς ἑκουσίοις καὶ ἐκ προνοίας ἀδικήμασι καὶ ἁμαρτήμασι: Supply τινα as the direct object of ἐλεεῖν. Translate ἐπί as "for" and take it with τοῖς ἀκουσίοις παθήμασι, τοῖς ἑκουσίοις, and ἀδικήμασι καὶ ἁμαρτήμασι.

10. [Lines 6–7] ἐκ προνοίας ἀδικήμασι: Translate this as "premeditated injuries."

11. [Line 7] What is the difference between αὕτη and αὐτή?

12. [Lines 7–8] οὔτε θεοὺς οὔθ' ἥρωας οὔτ' ἀνθρώπους: These are the direct objects of both αἰσχυνθεῖσα and δείσασ'.

13. [Line 8] αἰσχυνθεῖσα: What form is this? Here the verb means "feel shame before someone."

14. [Line 9] ἀπολομένη, μὴ τυχοῦσα: These circumstantial participles may be taken conditionally.

15. [Line 10] ἂν τύχοι: What construction is this? What is the form of τύχοι?

16. [Line 11] τὸ διομόσασθαι: The articular infinitive further defines τῆς τόλμης τοῦ ἀδελφοῦ καὶ τῆς διανοίας. Translate it as "that he solemnly swore." This infinitive introduces an accusative/infinitive construction of indirect statement. The subject of the infinitive εἰδέναι is omitted because it is the same as the subject of διομόσασθαι (R7.1).

17. [Lines 11–12] εὖ εἰδέναι μὴ πεποιηκυῖαν ταῦτα: εἰδέναι, which is itself a part of an indirect statement, sets up another indirect statement. Remember that οἶδα often takes the participial construction of indirect statement (R7.2).

18. [Line 12] ἄν τις εὖ εἰδείη: What construction is this?

19. [Line 12] οἷς: The antecedent of the relative pronoun has been omitted since it would have been a demonstrative pronoun (S2509). οἷς is dative plural neuter. The full expression would be πῶς γὰρ ἄν τις εὖ εἰδείη <ἐκεῖνα> οἷς μὴ παρεγένετο αὐτός, or something similar.

Reading Thirty-Two

Antiphon 1.28–31

Focus on Reading

The speaker continues to focus on his stepmother's secretive behavior and his half-brothers' willingness to believe in her innocence.

οὐ γὰρ δή που μαρτύρων γ᾽ ἐναντίον οἱ ἐπιβουλεύοντες τοὺς θανάτους τοῖς πέλας μηχανῶνταί τε καὶ παρασκευάζουσιν, ἀλλ᾽ ὡς μάλιστα δύνανται λαθραιότατα καὶ ὡς ἀνθρώπων μηδένα εἰδέναι·

Antiphon 1.28

VOCABULARY

δή που (indef. adv.) doubtless, of course
μάρτυς, -υρος, ὁ witness
ἐναντίον (prep. + gen.) in the presence of
ἐπιβουλεύω plot, plot against
θάνατος, -ου, ὁ death
πέλας (adv.) near, nearby

μηχανάομαι devise, scheme, plot
παρασκευάζω prepare
μάλιστα (sup. adv.) most
δύναμαι be able
λαθραῖος, -ον secret

OBSERVATIONS, STRATEGIES, AND NOTES

1. δή που may be printed as one word or two.
2. ἐναντίον: The object of the preposition ἐναντίον is μαρτύρων, which precedes it.
3. τοὺς θανάτους: English idiom requires that this be translated in the singular.
4. τοῖς πέλας: The definite article indicates that the adverb is being used as a noun (R2.3). This is a common phrase used to mean "neighbors."
5. Note the construction that links the two verbs in μηχανῶνταί τε καὶ παρασκευάζουσιν. Remember that τε is postpositive.

182

6. ἀλλ' ὡς μάλιστα . . . εἰδέναι: Supply "they plot" or a similar idea implied by the previous part of the sentence.

7. ὡς μάλιστα δύνανται λαθραιότατα: Translate this as "as secretly as they can."

8. καὶ ὡς . . . εἰδέναι: In English we would probably omit the conjunction καί, but Greek authors sometimes use conjunctions in this manner.

9. ὡς ἀνθρώπων μηδένα εἰδέναι: While it is more common for a result clause to be introduced by ὥστε (R12.1), ὡς is also used (S2250). Is this a natural or actual result clause?

10. ἀνθρώπων μηδένα: μηδένα is the subject accusative of the infinitive and ἀνθρώπων is a partitive genitive (R3.2.2).

11. εἰδέναι: This is the perfect active infinitive of οἶδα.

TRANSLATION

For indeed those plotting death for their neighbors do not scheme and prepare in the presence of witnesses but <plot> as secretly as they are able and so that no one knows.

POLISHED TRANSLATION

For indeed those plotting death for their neighbors do not scheme and prepare in the presence of witnesses but make their plans as secretly as possible so that no one knows.

Reading Selection

The speaker concludes his remarks, noting that the gods below have a stake in these events.

οἱ δὲ ἐπιβουλευόμενοι οὐδὲν ἴσασι, πρίν γ' ἤδη ἐν αὐτῷ ὦσι τῷ κακῷ καὶ
γιγνώσκωσι τὸν ὄλεθρον ἐν ᾧ εἰσί. τότε δέ, ἐὰν μὲν δύνωνται καὶ φθάνωσι
πρὶν ἀποθανεῖν, καὶ φίλους καὶ ἀναγκαίους τοὺς σφετέρους <αὐτῶν> καλοῦσι
καὶ μαρτύρονται, καὶ λέγουσιν αὐτοῖς ὑφ' ὧν ἀπόλλυνται, καὶ ἐπισκήπτουσι
τιμωρῆσαι σφίσιν αὐτοῖς ἠδικημένοις· ἃ κἀμοὶ παιδὶ ὄντι ὁ πατήρ, τὴν ἀθλίαν   5
καὶ τελευταίαν νόσον νοσῶν, ἐπέσκηπτεν· ἐὰν δὲ τούτων ἁμαρτάνωσι, γράμματα
γράφουσι, καὶ οἰκέτας τοὺς σφετέρους αὐτῶν ἐπικαλοῦνται μάρτυρας, καὶ
δηλοῦσιν ὑφ' ὧν ἀπόλλυνται. κἀκεῖνος ἐμοὶ νέῳ ἔτι ὄντι ταῦτα ἐδήλωσε
καὶ ἐπέστειλεν, ὦ ἄνδρες, οὐ τοῖς ἑαυτοῦ δούλοις. ἐμοὶ μὲν οὖν διήγηται καὶ
βεβοήθηται τῷ τεθνεῶτι καὶ τῷ νόμῳ. ἐν ὑμῖν δ' ἐστὶ σκοπεῖν τὰ λοιπὰ πρὸς ὑμᾶς   10
αὐτοὺς καὶ δικάζειν τὰ δίκαια. οἶμαι δὲ καὶ θεοῖς τοῖς κάτω μέλειν οἳ ἠδίκηνται.

Antiphon 1.29–31

NOTES

1. [Line 1] ἴσασι: What form is this? What is the first principal part of ἴσασι?

2. [Line 1] πρίν γ᾽ ἤδη ἐν αὐτῷ ὦσι τῷ κακῷ: After a negative main clause, πρίν plus a subjunctive refers to a future or repeated act (R11.5, no. 3). It is unusual for ἄν to be omitted in a πρίν clause with the subjunctive, but it does occasionally happen in Attic prose (S2444b). The hyperbaton (S3028)—here the insertion of ὦσι in the middle of the prepositional phrase ἐν αὐτῷ τῷ κακῷ—adds emphasis because of the unexpected word order. Remember that αὐτός, when used in the predicate position, is an intensifier meaning "-self."

3. [Line 2] ἐν ᾧ εἰσί: The relative clause seems unnecessary to us, but such obvious details are often included in Greek. You might translate this as "in which they now find themselves." The antecedent of ᾧ is ὄλεθρον.

4. [Lines 2–6] Note the construction of ἐὰν μὲν δύνωνται . . . ἐὰν δὲ τούτων ἁμαρτάνωσι.

5. [Lines 2–4] ἐὰν μὲν δύνωνται καὶ φθάνωσι . . . καλοῦσι καὶ μαρτύρονται: What type of condition is this?

6. [Lines 2–3] φθάνωσι πρὶν ἀποθανεῖν: Supply "the situation" or "the state they are in" as the direct object of φθάνωσι.

7. [Line 3] πρὶν ἀποθανεῖν: After an affirmative main clause, πρίν with an infinitive is translated as "before" (R11.5, no. 1). Why is the infinitive ἀποθανεῖν in the aorist tense?

8. [Line 3] σφετέρους <αὐτῶν>: Many editors insert αὐτῶν for the third person plural reflexive form (S1202.2b) to indicate possession.

9. [Line 4] ὑφ᾽ ὧν ἀπόλλυνται: The antecedent of the relative pronoun ὧν has been omitted (S2509). It would have been ἐκείνους or τούτους. Translate this as "by whom they are being destroyed" or "by whom they are being murdered."

10. [Line 5] σφίσιν αὐτοῖς ἠδικημένοις: σφίσιν αὐτοῖς is the third person reflexive pronoun (S329). What type of participle is ἠδικημένοις? What is the force of its tense?

11. [Line 5] The relative pronoun ἃ refers to the contents of the previous sentence. You may translate it simply as "this."

12. [Line 5] κἀμοὶ: This is an instance of crasis (= καὶ ἐμοί); the καί is adverbial.

13. [Line 5] παιδὶ ὄντι: Take this participial phrase concessively.

14. [Lines 6–8] ἐὰν δὲ τούτων ἁμαρτάνωσι, . . . δηλοῦσιν: What type of condition is this?

15. [Line 6] τούτων ἁμαρτάνωσι: τούτων refers to the family and friends mentioned above.

16. [Line 7] οἰκέτας . . . ἐπικαλοῦνται μάρτυρας: Verbs of naming, calling, and the like take a double accusative construction (R3.4.4).

17. [Line 7] σφετέρους αὐτῶν: See note 8, above.

18. [Line 8] ὑφ᾽ ὧν ἀπόλλυνται: See note 9, above.

19. [Line 8] κἀκεῖνος: This is another example of crasis (= καὶ ἐκεῖνος).

20. [Line 8] ἐμοὶ νέῳ ἔτι ὄντι: Compare this to κἀμοὶ παιδὶ ὄντι above, note 13.

21. [Lines 8–9] ἐμοὶ νέῳ ἔτι ὄντι . . . οὐ τοῖς ἑαυτοῦ δούλοις: The speaker is emphasizing

his filial duty: his father had commanded him, his son, and not the household slaves to see to it that the murderers were punished.

22. [Lines 9–10] ἐμοὶ μὲν οὖν διήγηται καὶ βεβοήθηται: The dative of the personal pronoun is the dative of personal agent with the perfect passive verbs (R3.3.6). Translate these verbs in the active voice, however, for more idiomatic English.

23. [Line 10] βεβοήθηται τῷ τεθνεῶτι καὶ τῷ νόμῳ: Verbs of helping often take datives as objects (R3.3.13, no. 1)

24. [Line 10] ἐν ὑμῖν δ' ἐστὶ: This is another instance of the idiomatic expression "be in someone's power." Translate it as "it is in your power."

25. [Lines 10–11] πρὸς ὑμᾶς αὐτοὺς: Translate this as "for yourselves."

26. [Line 11] καὶ θεοῖς τοῖς κάτω: The definite article puts the adverb κάτω into the attributive position (R2.1). Translate the phrase as "even to the gods below."

27. [Line 11] μέλειν: The infinitive is part of an accusative/infinitive construction of indirect statement set up by οἶμαι (R7.1).

28. [Line 11] οἳ ἠδίκηνται: The antecedent of οἳ would have been the demonstrative pronoun ἐκείνους or something similar and has consequently been omitted (S2509). <ἐκείνους> οἳ ἠδίκηνται is the subject of the infinitive μέλειν.

29. [Line 11] ἠδίκηνται: What form is this? What nuance does its tense impart?

Reading Thirty-Three

Euripides, *Electra* 300–310

Euripides was born in the Attic deme of Phyla sometime around 484 B.C.E. and died in 406 in Macedonia, having left Athens in the final years of the Peloponnesian War. The youngest of the three best-known Athenian playwrights, he was apparently the least successful in the tragic competitions: though he wrote at least ninety plays, he won only five prizes. Eighteen plays are extant, including the *Cyclops,* a satyr play. (The *Rhesus* is now thought by many scholars to be the work of another tragedian.) Euripides was known for his creative treatment of myth, his formal innovations, his skeptical attitude toward the gods, the extreme nature of his characters' personalities, and the intensity of their suffering. Although his plays may not have enjoyed much competitive success during his lifetime, they were immensely popular after his death and were performed widely throughout the Greek world.

The *Electra* was written sometime between 420 and 410. Taking its subject from the saga of the House of Atreus, the play opens after Clytemnestra and her lover, Aegisthus, have killed Agamemnon, Clytemnestra's husband and the king of Argos, who had just returned from the Trojan War. Electra, the daughter of Agamemnon and Clytemnestra, has been married off to a lowly farmer to prevent her from producing a noble son who might then seek vengeance for the murder of Agamemnon. Though she bears no ill will toward her peasant husband, Electra does blame her mother and resents the living conditions she has been forced to accept. Without Electra's knowledge, Orestes and his friend Pylades return to Argos to punish Clytemnestra and Aegisthus for the murder. In this brief selection from the play, Electra bemoans her situation to a stranger who has come to her house, unaware that the stranger is her brother. Once his identity is revealed to her, the two will plot how to exact a fitting revenge.

Reading tragedy presents unique challenges to a student of Greek. Because tragedies were written in meter, the word order is less predictable than in prose works. Adjectives may not be placed near the nouns they modify, although they may be; poetic forms and unusual vocabulary frequently appear; and there is much greater flexibility in syntax. Yet reading tragedy and other works of Greek poetry can be immensely satisfying, even as it illustrates how difficult it is to capture in translation the full richness of a text.

Note: In the Greek texts, square brackets ([ ]) indicate a word or words that some editors suggest deleting from the text, angle brackets (< >) indicate a word or words that some editors suggest adding to the Greek text, and parentheses are used for editorial annotations. Angle brackets are also used in the notes to indicate words that must be supplied for a complete translation, and parentheses for editorial annotations.

Focus on Reading

λέγοιμ' ἄν, εἰ χρή — χρὴ δὲ πρὸς φίλον λέγειν —
τύχας βαρείας τὰς ἐμὰς κἀμοῦ πατρός.

Euripides, Electra 300–301

VOCABULARY

The principal parts of all verbs may be found in the vocabulary list at the back of this textbook.

λέγω　speak, relate	τύχη, -ης, ἡ　misfortune
χρή　it is necessary (+ inf.)	βαρύς, -εῖα, -ύ　heavy, oppressive, grievous
πρός (prep. + acc.)　to	ἐμός, -ή, -όν　my, mine
φίλος, -ου, ὁ　friend	πατήρ, -τρός, ὁ　father

OBSERVATIONS, STRATEGIES, AND NOTES

1. This is a straightforward sentence, but be sure to note the mood of λέγοιμ' and the particle ἄν. The potential optative is used to indicate a future possibility, propriety, or likelihood (R8.5; S1824). While the more common translations are "would," "might," or "should," sometimes "will" is the most appropriate choice for the context.

2. Since λέγοιμ' is a transitive verb, it may take a direct object if it is not followed by an indirect statement construction. Notice that the direct object is in the second line. What is it?

3. χρὴ δὲ πρὸς φίλον λέγειν: The dashes mark this clause off as a parenthetical statement that interrupts the main thought. This is relatively common in tragedy as it follows more natural speech patterns.

4. τὰς ἐμάς: Note the formal attributive position of the possessive adjective ἐμάς (R2.1).

5. κἀμοῦ: This is the result of crasis (= καὶ ἐμοῦ). This genitive is to be taken with τύχας βαρείας.

TRANSLATION

I will relate, if it is necessary—and it is necessary to speak to a friend—
my heavy misfortunes and <those> of my father.

POLISHED TRANSLATION

I will relate, if I must—and I must speak to a friend—
my own grievous misfortunes as well as my father's.

Reading Selection

ἐπεὶ δὲ κινεῖς μῦθον, ἱκετεύω, ξένε,
ἄγγελλ᾽ Ὀρέστῃ τἀμὰ καὶ κείνου κακά,
πρῶτον μὲν οἵοις ἐν πέπλοις αὐλίζομαι,
πίνῳ θ᾽ ὅσῳ βέβριθ᾽, ὑπὸ στέγαισί τε   305
οἵαισι ναίω βασιλικῶν ἐκ δωμάτων,
αὐτὴ μὲν ἐκμοχθοῦσα κερκίσιν πέπλους,
ἢ γυμνὸν ἔξω σῶμα κἀστερήσομαι,
αὐτὴ δὲ πηγὰς ποταμίους φορουμένη,
ἀνέορτος ἱερῶν καὶ χορῶν τητωμένη.   310

Euripides, *Electra* 302–10

NOTES

1. [Line 303] ἄγγελλ᾽: The final epsilon has been elided. What form is ἄγγελλε?
2. [Line 303] τἀμὰ καὶ κείνου κακά: τἀμά has undergone crasis; the full form of the phrase is τὰ ἐμὰ καὶ κείνου κακά. Note that both ἐμὰ and κείνου are in the attributive position (R2.1).
3. [Line 303] κείνου is a poetic form for ἐκείνου.
4. [Line 304] οἵοις ἐν πέπλοις: Note that οἵοις has been placed outside the prepositional phrase ἐν πέπλοις, even though it is modifying πέπλοις. This is a common type of word order in poetry.
5. [Line 304] οἵοις: This introduces an indirect exclamation (S2685, 2686) and should be taken as an amplification of τἀμὰ καὶ κείνου κακά. ὅσῳ in line 305 and οἵαισι in line 306 are also used in this manner.
6. [Line 305] πίνῳ θ᾽ ὅσῳ: Remember that τε will drop the epsilon when followed by a word that begins with a vowel. Because of the rough breathing in the following word, ὅσῳ, the tau takes on the aspiration and becomes a theta. τε, as always, is postpositive. Notice the slightly displaced word order of πίνῳ ὅσῳ; we would expect ὅσῳ πίνῳ in prose.
7. [Lines 305–6] ὑπὸ στέγαισί τε / οἵαισι: The τε belongs by sense in front of ὑπό. Notice that οἵαισι follows στέγαισι, rather than preceding it.

8. [Line 306] οἵαισι: This is the dative plural feminine of οἷος. The ending -αισι is often found in poetry (S215).

9. [Line 306] βασιλικῶν ἐκ δωμάτων: The adjective has again been placed outside the prepositional phrase. Translate ἐκ as "far from."

10. [Lines 307–9] Note αὐτὴ μὲν . . . αὐτὴ δὲ. The intensive use of αὐτή increases the pathos of Electra's complaint about her living situation.

11. [Line 307] What type of dative is κερκίσιν?

12. [Line 308] γυμνὸν ἔξω σῶμα: Note the position of the adjective γυμνόν.

13. [Line 308] What form is ἔξω? What is its first principal part?

14. [Line 308] κἀστερήσομαι: Notice the coronis designating crasis. This is the equivalent of καὶ ἐστερήσομαι.

15. [Lines 309, 310] φορουμένη, τητωμένη: These participles may be translated as finite verbs, if you prefer.

Reading Thirty-Four

Euripides, *Electra* 311–25

Focus on Reading

ἀναίνομαι γυναῖκας οὖσα παρθένος,
ἀναίνομαι δὲ Κάστορ᾽, ᾧ πρὶν ἐς θεοὺς
ἐλθεῖν ἔμ᾽ ἐμνήστευον, οὖσαν ἐγγενῆ.

Euripides, Electra 311–13

VOCABULARY

ἀναίνομαι   renounce, disown
γυνή, -αικός, ἡ   woman
παρθένος, -ου, ἡ   maid, virgin
Κάστωρ, -ορος, ὁ   Castor
πρίν (conj.)   before

ἐς (εἰς) (prep. + acc.)   into, to
θεός, -οῦ, ὁ   god
ἔρχομαι   go, come
μνηστεύω   promise in marriage
ἐγγενής, -ές   related, kindred

OBSERVATIONS, STRATEGIES, AND NOTES

1. οὖσα is the nominative singular feminine present participle of εἰμί. Take παρθένος with this circumstantial participle, which is indicating cause.

2. Κάστορ᾽: Castor and his twin brother, Polydeuces, were the brothers of Helen and Clytemnestra. Leda was the mother of all four children, and Zeus was the father of Helen and Polydeuces while Tyndareus was the father of Castor and Clytemnestra.

3. πρὶν ἐς θεοὺς / ἐλθεῖν: This temporal clause with πρίν (R11.5, no. 1) is inserted in the middle of the relative clause ᾧ ἔμ᾽ ἐμνήστευον, οὖσαν ἐγγενῆ. Remember that πρίν means "before" after an affirmative main clause and takes an accusative/infinitive construction. Κάστορ᾽ (Κάστορα) is the antecedent of the relative pronoun ᾧ and the subject accusative of ἐλθεῖν.

4. ἔμ' has lost its final epsilon through elision.

5. οὖσαν ἐγγενῆ: This modifies ἔμ'. What form is ἐγγενῆ?

TRANSLATION

I renounce women since I am a maiden
and I renounce Castor, to whom, before he went
to the gods, they promised me in marriage since I was related.

POLISHED TRANSLATION

Since I am a virgin, I shun married women,
and I avoid Castor, to whom, before he went to live among the gods,
they promised me in marriage, since I was his kin.

Reading Selection

μήτηρ δ' ἐμὴ Φρυγίοισιν ἐν σκυλεύμασιν
θρόνῳ κάθηται, πρὸς δ' ἕδραισιν Ἀσίδες   315
δμωαὶ στατίζουσ', ἃς ἔπερσ' ἐμὸς πατήρ,
Ἰδαῖα φάρη χρυσέαις ἐζευγμέναι
πόρπαισιν. αἷμα δ' ἔτι πατρὸς κατὰ στέγας
μέλαν σέσηπεν, ὃς δ' ἐκεῖνον ἔκτανεν,
ἐς ταὐτὰ βαίνων ἅρματ' ἐκφοιτᾷ πατρί,   320
καὶ σκῆπτρ' ἐν οἷς Ἕλλησιν ἐστρατηλάτει
μιαιφόνοισι χερσὶ γαυροῦται λαβών.
Ἀγαμέμνονος δὲ τύμβος ἠτιμασμένος
οὔπω χοάς ποτ' οὐδὲ κλῶνα μυρσίνης
ἔλαβε, πυρὰ δὲ χέρσος ἀγλαϊσμάτων.   325

Euripides, *Electra* 314–25

NOTES

1. [Lines 314–18] The first sentence is quite straightforward. Use the marks of punctuation as a guide to help you through it.

2. [Line 314] Φρυγίοισιν ἐν σκυλεύμασιν: Note that the modifier has once again been placed outside the prepositional phrase. Learn to see such word groupings as a unit.

3. [Line 315] θρόνῳ: The dative is used in poetry with even greater flexibility than in prose. In poetry the dative is often used without a preposition to indicate place (S1531). We would probably find ἐν θρόνῳ in prose.

4. [Lines 315–19] πρὸς δ'. . . αἷμα δ'. . . ὃς δ': δέ is often used to link successive sen-

tences and clauses that provide new details that are not in contrast to previously mentioned information (S2836).

5. [Line 316] What is the antecedent of ἅς? What is its grammatical function?

6. [Lines 317–18] Ἰδαῖα φάρη χρυσέαις ἐζευγμέναι / πόρπαισιν: It is common in poetry to postpone descriptive details since the inflected nature of Greek will make clear what word the participle or adjective is modifying. This participial phrase modifies δμωαὶ in line 316. How are φάρη and πόρπαισιν being used grammatically? What form is ἐζευγμέναι?

7. [Lines 318–19] αἷμα δ᾽ ἔτι πατρὸς κατὰ στέγας / μέλαν σέσηπεν: Note the framing of ἔτι πατρὸς κατὰ στέγας by αἷμα and its adjective μέλαν.

8. [Line 318] κατὰ στέγας: Translate this as "throughout the house."

9. [Line 319] σέσηπεν: The perfect form σέσηπεν is used as a present tense of σήπομαι. ἔτι adds a nice touch as it highlights the length of the time since the murder of Agamemnon and the continuous sacrilegious behavior on the part of Clytemnestra and Aegisthus. Translate this as "still lies rotten" or "is rotten still."

10. [Line 319] ὃς δ᾽ ἐκεῖνον ἔκτανεν: As we have seen in prose, it is common for the antecedent of a relative pronoun to be omitted when that antecedent would have been a demonstrative pronoun (S2509). Supply καὶ οὗτος or ὅδε, which refers to Aegisthus, and translate it as "and this man who." ἐκεῖνον refers to Agamemnon.

11. [Line 319] ἔκτανεν: This is a second aorist form of κτείνω, which is usually found in poetry. In prose, the verb usually appears in its compound form, ἀποκτείνω.

12. [Line 320] ἐς ταὐτὰ βαίνων ἅρματ᾽ ἐκφοιτᾷ πατρί: The order for translation is βαίνων ἐς ταὐτὰ ἅρματ᾽ πατρὶ ἐκφοιτᾷ. ταὐτά has undergone crasis and is the equivalent of τὰ αὐτά. Remember that when a form of αὐτός is used in the attributive position, it means "same" (S328). The dative is used with αὐτός to limit its meaning (S1500). The phrase without βαίνων would literally be translated as "into the same chariot as my father," but with βαίνων you may translate it as "mounting my father's chariot."

13. [Lines 321–22] καὶ σκῆπτρ᾽ ἐν οἷς Ἕλλησιν ἐστρατηλάτει / μιαιφόνοισι χερσὶ γαυροῦται λαβών: Verbs of emotion may take a supplementary participle to indicate the cause of the emotion (R6.4, no. 3; S2100). λαβών is the supplementary participle with the verb of emotion γαυροῦται, while σκῆπτρ᾽ is the direct object of λαβών. Translate this as "he prides himself in taking the scepter in his blood-stained hands." σκῆπτρ᾽, though technically plural, is best translated as a singular. Supply ἐν with μιαιφόνοισι χερσί.

14. [Line 321] ἐν οἷς Ἕλλησιν ἐστρατηλάτει: The subject of ἐστρατηλάτει is Agamemnon. ἐν is used to indicate instrument here (S1687c). Translate it as "with which."

15. [Line 323] What form is ἠτιμασμένος? What is the significance of its tense?

16. [Line 325] χέρσος: Notice that χέρσος is a two-ending adjective and is modifying πυρά. You will need to supply ἐστι.

Reading Thirty-Five

Euripides, *Electra* 326–38

Focus on Reading

μέθῃ δὲ βρεχθεὶς τῆς ἐμῆς μητρὸς πόσις
ὁ κλεινός, ὡς λέγουσιν, ἐνθρῴσκει τάφῳ
πέτροις τε λεύει μνῆμα λάϊνον πατρός,
καὶ τοῦτο τολμᾷ τοὔπος εἰς ἡμᾶς λέγειν·

Euripides, Electra 326–29

VOCABULARY

μέθη, -ης, ἡ   strong drink
βρέχω   wet, soak
πόσις, -ιος, ὁ   husband
κλεινός, -ή, -όν   famous, illustrious
ὡς (rel. adv.)   as
ἐνθρῴσκω   leap on (+ dat.)
τάφος, -ου, ὁ   tomb, grave

πέτρος, -ου, ὁ   rock, stone
λεύω   pelt, throw stones at
μνῆμα, -ατος, τό   memorial, monument
λάϊνος, -η, -ον   of stone
τολμάω   dare
ἔπος, -ους, τό   word
εἰς (prep. + acc.)   before

OBSERVATIONS, STRATEGIES, AND NOTES

1. Notice the circumstantial participle βρεχθείς. What form is it? What noun is it modifying?

2. ὁ κλεινός: Electra is obviously being sarcastic in describing Aegisthus this way.

3. τάφῳ: This goes with ἐνθρῴσκει.

4. πέτροις τε λεύει: Remember that τε is postpositive and belongs by sense in front of πέτροις. What type of dative is πέτροις?

194

5. τοὖπος is a contraction of τὸ ἔπος following the rules of crasis. Note that τοῦτο modifies τοὖπος, despite the insertion of the verb τολμᾷ.

6. What type of infinitive is λέγειν?

TRANSLATION

The husband of my mother, soaked with wine,
the famous one, as they say, leaps on the tomb
and pelts the stone memorial of my father with rocks,
and dares to say this word to us;

POLISHED TRANSLATION

The illustrious husband of my mother, besotted with wine,
leaps upon my father's tomb, they say,
and pelts his marble memorial with rocks,
and dares to say this to us;

Reading Selection

Ποῦ παῖς Ὀρέστης; ἆρά σοι τύμβῳ καλῶς   330
παρὼν ἀμύνει; —ταῦτ᾽ ἀπὼν ὑβρίζεται.
ἀλλ᾽, ὦ ξέν᾽, ἱκετεύω σ᾽, ἀπάγγειλον τάδε.
πολλοὶ δ᾽ ἐπιστέλλουσιν, ἑρμηνεὺς δ᾽ ἐγώ,
αἱ χεῖρες ἡ γλῶσσ᾽ ἡ ταλαίπωρός τε φρήν,
κάρα τ᾽ ἐμὸν ξυρῆκες, ὅ τ᾽ ἐκεῖνον τεκών.   335
αἰσχρὸν γάρ, εἰ πατὴρ μὲν ἐξεῖλεν Φρύγας,
ὁ δ᾽ ἄνδρ᾽ ἕν᾽ εἷς ὢν οὐ δυνήσεται κτανεῖν,
νέος πεφυκὼς κἀξ ἀμείνονος πατρός.

Euripides, *Electra* 330–38

NOTES

1. [Line 331] Both παρὼν and ἀπὼν refer to Orestes.
2. [Line 331] ταῦτ᾽ ἀπὼν ὑβρίζεται: ταῦτα is being used as an adverb. Translate it as "in this respect," or "in this way."
3. [Line 332] σ᾽: The final epsilon has been elided.
4. [Line 332] What form is ἀπάγγειλον?
5. [Line 333] πολλοὶ δ᾽ ἐπιστέλλουσιν: This is elliptical. Translate it as "many are enjoining him to come home."
6. [Line 333] ἑρμηνεὺς δ᾽ ἐγώ: Supply εἰμι. What is the grammatical function of ἑρμηνεὺς?

7. [Lines 334–35] χεῖρες, γλῶσσ', φρήν, κάρα, and ὅ τ' ἐκεῖνον τεκών are all in apposition to πολλοί.

8. [Line 335] ὅ τ' ἐκεῖνον τεκών: This is a reference to Agamemnon. Remember that τε is postpositive.

9. [Line 336] αἰσχρὸν γάρ: Supply ἐστι.

10. [Lines 336–37] εἰ πατὴρ μὲν . . . ὁ δ': ὁ δ' refers to Orestes. Take εἷς ὤν with it. What are the function and form of ὤν?

11. [Line 337] ἄνδρ' ἕν': The final alpha has been elided. What is the function of these words?

12. [Line 337] What form is κτανεῖν? What does its tense imply?

13. [Line 338] What is the function of πεφυκώς? What form is it?

14. [Line 338] κἀξ: This is an instance of crasis (= καὶ ἐξ).

PART 2

Grammar Review

Contents

Review One

Accents

In the Grammar Review, square brackets ([]) are used for editorial additions and parentheses for annotations *except* in the examples from the Readings, where angle brackets (< >) indicate a word or words that some editors suggest adding to the Greek text and parentheses are used for editorial annotations.

1.1 Terminology

There are three accents in ancient Greek: acute (´), grave (`), and circumflex (ˆ). Specific rules of accentuation dictate how each will be used. The following technical terms are essential for understanding discussions of accentuation:

ultima: the final syllable of a word [ἄνθρω**πος**]
penult: the syllable immediately preceding the last syllable of the word [ἄν**θρω**πος]
antepenult: the syllable immediately preceding the penult [**ἄν**θρωπος]

Greek accents may fall *only* on one of these three syllables, regardless of the length of the word.

Other useful accentuation terms include:

oxytone: a word with an acute accent on its ultima [ἐπιστολή, καλούς]
paroxytone: a word with an acute accent on its penult [γνώμη, προδότην]
proparoxytone: a word with an acute accent on its antepenult [ἄνθρωπος, ἐπαίδευε]
perispomenon: a word with a circumflex on its ultima [γῆ, θεῶν]
properispomenon: a word with a circumflex on its penult [δῶρον, εἷλον]

1.2 Quantity

Greek accentuation depends on the quantity, or length, of the ultima — that is, whether the ultima is long or short — and on the quantity of the vowel on which the accent falls. A circumflex, for example, may fall only on a long vowel or diphthong.

A syllable is long by nature if it contains a long vowel or diphthong and short if it contains a short vowel. Etas and omegas are always long; epsilons and omicrons are always short. Alphas, iotas, and upsilons may be either long or short depending on the word or on the length of these vowels in an inflectional ending. A formal lexicon will often indicate the length of vowels within a word; a morphological chart will usually indicate the length of a vowel in an inflectional ending. If there is no macron (long mark) above an alpha, iota, or upsilon, the vowel is short. Diphthongs (αι, αυ, ει, ευ, ηυ, οι, ου, υι) and improper diphthongs (ᾳ, ῃ, ῳ) are always long, with the exception of final αι and οι. *When a word ends in either -αι or -οι, the ultima is considered short for the purposes of accentuation.*

N.B.: This rule does not hold for the optative mood or for the word οἴκοι.

1.3 General Rules for the Use of the Three Accents

1.3.1 ACUTE

1. The acute accent may be used on long vowels, short vowels, and diphthongs.

2. The acute accent may fall on any one of the last three syllables of a word (antepenult, penult, or ultima).

3. The acute accent may fall on the antepenult *only* if the ultima is short.

Examples: ἄνθρωπος, θηρίον, ἐπιστολή

1.3.2 GRAVE

1. The grave accent may fall on long vowels, short vowels, and diphthongs.

2. The grave accent may fall *only* on the ultima of a word.

3. If a word is naturally accented with an acute on the ultima, the acute changes to a grave when the word is followed by another word without an intervening mark of punctuation, unless the word that follows is an enclitic. In such cases, the acute accent does not change to a grave.

Examples: ἐπιστολὴ καλή, οἱ αἰσχροὶ λόγοι, ἐπιστολή τις

1.3.3 CIRCUMFLEX

1. The circumflex may fall *only* on a long vowel or diphthong.

2. The circumflex may fall on either the penult or the ultima.

3. When a long penult is followed by a short ultima *and* the penult is supposed to receive the accent, that accent *must* be a circumflex.

Examples: δῶρον, τιμῶν, ἰατρῷ

1.4 Accentuation of Verbs

The accent of finite (i.e., conjugated) verb forms is *recessive*. This means that the accent will fall as far away from the ultima as it can. Remember that the accent may fall only as far back as the antepenult.

1.4.1 VERB FORMS WITH THREE OR MORE SYLLABLES

1. If the ultima is short, the antepenult receives an acute accent.

Examples: παύομεν, πείθετε, ἀναγράφουσι

2. If the ultima is long, the penult receives an acute accent.
Examples: παιδεύω, καταλαμβάνεις, κελεύει

1.4.2 VERB FORMS WITH TWO SYLLABLES

1. If the ultima is short and the penult is long, the penult receives a circumflex.
Examples: ἦγε, ἦδες, λῦε
2. If the ultima and the penult are both short, the penult takes an acute accent.
Examples: ἄγε, ἔχες, πέμπε
3. If the ultima is long, the penult receives an acute accent regardless of its quantity.
Examples: ἄγω, ἔχεις, ἀκούει

1.4.3 COMPOUND VERBS

1. The accent on a compound verb may not precede an augment or reduplication.
Examples: ἀπῆγε, ἀπῆχα, ἄπαγε
2. The accent on a compound verb may not precede the final syllable of the prepositional prefix or be placed on the first of two prepositional prefixes.
Examples: παράδος, ἐπίδος, συνέκδος

1.5 Accentuation of Nouns and Adjectives

The accentuation of nouns and adjectives is *persistent:* that is, the accent stays on the
vowel or diphthong on which it falls in the nominative singular form, unless the quantity of
the ultima changes.

1. If the quantity of the ultima does not change, then the accent remains in the position it has in the nominative.
Examples: ἄνθρωπος, ἄνθρωπον, ἄνθρωποι
2. If the ultima changes from short to long, and the accent in the nominative singular
is an acute on the antepenult, the acute accent shifts one syllable to the penult.
Examples: ἀνθρώπῳ, ἀνθρώπων, ἀνθρώποις
3. If the penult is accented in the nominative singular with a circumflex and the quantity of the ultima becomes long through an inflectional change, the circumflex changes to an
acute. If the accent was originally an acute, there is no change in the type of accent.
Examples: δῶρον, δώρου, λόγος, λόγου
4. A first- or second-declension noun or adjective with an acute accent on the ultima
in the nominative singular (an oxytone) takes a circumflex in both the singular and plural
genitive and dative cases.
Examples: ἀγαθός, ἀγαθοῦ, ἀρχή, ἀρχαῖς
5. All first-declension nouns take a circumflex on the ultima of the genitive plural, regardless of where the accent falls in the nominative singular.
Examples: ἐπιστολή, ἐπιστολῶν, βοήθεια, βοηθειῶν

1.6 Accentuation of Infinitives

Because infinitives are classified as verbal nouns, their accents are persistent. The accent for the infinitive of each tense falls on a certain specified syllable. Since infinitives do not conjugate, there will be no change in accent.

Example: λείπειν, λιπεῖν, λελοιπέναι, λειφθῆναι

1.7 Accentuation of Enclitics

An enclitic is a word that is closely connected with the word that precedes it. Whether it is accented will depend upon the number of syllables in the preceding word and where the accent of that word falls. Often an enclitic will lose its accent entirely.

1. A monosyllabic enclitic is generally not accented, except in circumstances described in no. 6, below.

Examples: τέκνον τι, ῥήτωρ τις

2. A disyllabic enclitic is usually not accented. However, when it is preceded by a word with an acute accent on the penult (a paroxytone), the enclitic receives an accent on its ultima. If this enclitic is followed by another word with no intervening marks of punctuation, the acute accent changes to a grave.

Examples: δώρων τινῶν, δώροις τισί, οἱ λίθοι εἰσὶ λευκοί

3. When a word with an acute accent on its ultima (an oxytone) is followed by an enclitic, the acute accent does not change to a grave.

Examples: καλοί τινες, ἀγαθοί εἰσιν οἱ ἄνθρωποι

4. When a word with a circumflex on its ultima is followed by an enclitic, the circumflex remains.

Examples: ὁδῶν τινων, ἀγαθοῖς τισι

5. When a word with an acute accent on its antepenult or a circumflex on its penult is followed by an enclitic, an extra acute accent is added to the ultima of that word.

Examples: οἱ ἄνθρωποί εἰσιν ἀγαθοί, δῶρά τινα

6. When two or more enclitics are used one after the other, the final enclitic is not accented. The preceding enclitics take acute accents. This applies to both monosyllabic and disyllabic enclitics. Disyllabic enclitics take an acute accent on the ultima in such instances.

Examples: ὅτε τινές τι εἴποιεν, ὅταν τίς τινα γράφῃ

7. When a proclitic precedes an enclitic, the proclitic takes an acute accent while the enclitic remains unaccented. Proclitics include the nominative forms of the definite article (ὁ, ἡ, οἱ, αἱ), the prepositions εἰς (ἐς), ἐκ (ἐξ), and ἐν, and εἰ, ὡς, οὐ (οὐκ, οὐχ); they are closely connected with the words that follow them, and they generally do not take an accent except when they precede an enclitic. It is important to note that οὐ will take an acute when it is the final word in a sentence.

Examples: εἴ τις γράφοι, οἱ λίθοι οὔκ εἰσι λευκοί

Review Two

Attributive and Predicate Position; Substantives

The definite article has functions in Greek that extend beyond the article's meaning. Its presence can indicate that an adjective is being used attributively rather than as a predicate or that a noun is the subject of a linking verb, rather than a predicate nominative. The definite article may also specify the case of an articular infinitive and can turn adjectives, adverbs, participles, and even prepositional phrases into nouns.

2.1 Attributive Position of a Modifier

The definite article is used to indicate that an adjective or other modifier, such as a prepositional phrase or adverb, is being used attributively to describe a noun. When a modifier is in the attributive position, the definite article will usually precede it. There are three common word orders.

article — **adjective/modifier** — noun	ὁ **δίκαιος** ἄνθρωπος
	τὰ **ἐν τῇ ἀγορᾷ** τέκνα
	ὁ **ἐκ τῆς χώρας** φεύγων κλώψ
article — noun — article — **adjective/modifier**	ὁ ἄνθρωπος ὁ **δίκαιος**
	τὰ τέκνα τὰ **ἐν τῇ ἀγορᾷ**
	ὁ κλώψ ὁ **ἐκ τῆς χώρας** φεύγων
noun — article — **adjective/modifier**	ἄνθρωπος ὁ **δίκαιος**
	τέκνα τὰ **ἐν τῇ ἀγορᾷ**
	κλώψ ὁ **ἐκ τῆς χώρας** φεύγων

In each possible order, the article directly precedes the adjective or modifying phrase, and thus the modifier is in the attributive position. All the Greek phrases may be translated in precisely the same way: "the just man" for the first phrase, "the children in the marketplace" for the second, and "the thief fleeing out of the land" or "the thief who is fleeing out of the land" for the last phrase. The difference in word order, however, imparts a slight difference in emphasis. The second order is more formal and less commonly found than the first. The noun rather than the adjective receives greater emphasis in the second example; the adjective has been added as a qualifier or delimiter. It gives here the sense of "the man, the just one" or "the children, the ones in the marketplace," though it does not need to be translated in this manner. In the third order, the modifier has been added as an explanatory afterthought. This is the least common order, and the noun itself does not need or require the definite article. Note that any words that go with the modifier, such as the prepositional phrase ἐκ τῆς χώρας that modifies φεύγων in the third example, are not taken into consideration when determining whether a modifier is in the attributive position. The definite article ὁ is still considered to be preceding φεύγων despite the inclusion of ἐκ τῆς χώρας.

2.2 Predicate Position of a Modifier

If an adjective or other modifier is positioned outside of the article-noun pairing and does not have an article directly preceding it, the modifier is in the predicate position. Often an adjective in the predicate position is used in combination with the noun it is modifying to make a sentence. A linking verb may be present in this case, but the linking verb "be" is frequently omitted and supplied by context. Examples of other linking verbs in English include forms of the verbs "seem," "appear," and "become."

ὁ ἄνθρωπος **ἀγαθός.**   The man is noble.
οἱ παῖδές εἰσιν **ἐν τῇ ἀγορᾷ.**   The children are in the marketplace.

2.3 Substantive Use of an Adjective or Other Modifier

Substantive is a synonym for *noun,* but it is also used to refer to any phrase or other word that functions as a noun within a particular sentence. In Greek, an adjective or other modifier together with its definite article is frequently used in place of a noun. The inflectional system makes the gender of the modifier clear and thus allows it to stand for "man," "woman," or "thing," depending on its gender; the words ἄνθρωπος, γυνή, and χρῆμα are not needed. Although it is not incorrect to include such words, it is more common and more stylistically sophisticated to omit them.

ὁ δίκαιος = ὁ δίκαιος ἄνθρωπος = the just man
ἡ δικαία = ἡ δικαία γυνή = the just woman
τὸ δίκαιον = τὸ δίκαιον χρῆμα = the just thing

οἱ ἐν τῇ ἀγορᾷ = οἱ ἐν τῇ ἀγορᾷ ἄνθρωποι = the men in the marketplace
αἱ ἐν τῇ ἀγορᾷ = αἱ ἐν τῇ ἀγορᾷ γυναῖκες = the women in the marketplace
τὰ ἐν τῇ ἀγορᾷ = τὰ ἐν τῇ ἀγορᾷ χρήματα = the things in the marketplace

Substantives may be found in any case, singular or plural.

Review Three

Use of Cases

3.1 Nominative

3.1.1 SUBJECT OF A VERB

The nominative case indicates the subject of a finite verb. A singular subject takes a singular verb while a plural subject takes a plural verb, with one exception: *neuter plural subjects take singular verbs.* There is no requirement in Greek that a sentence always contain a nominative since the subject of the verb is also implied by the verb ending.

ὁ **διδάσκαλος** γράφει.   The teacher is writing.
γράφει.   He/She is writing.
τὰ τέκνα γράφει.   The children are writing.

3.1.2 PREDICATE NOMINATIVE

A predicate nominative is a noun in the nominative case that is used with a linking verb, either expressed or implied (forms of "be," in particular, are frequently omitted in Greek), to describe the subject of the sentence. A predicate nominative appears in the predicate position without the definite article to differentiate it from the subject of the sentence.

ὁ ἄνθρωπος **διδάσκαλος**.   The man is a teacher.
θησαυρὸς ὁ βίος ἐστίν.   Life is a treasure.
οἱ νόμοι **δῶρα** τῶν θεῶν.   The laws are gifts of the gods.

3.1.3 PREDICATE ADJECTIVE

An adjective that is positioned outside the article-noun pairing and used in combination with a linking verb, either expressed or implied, is a predicate adjective. This adjective is never directly preceded by a definite article. Both the subject of the sentence and the predicate adjective are in the nominative case. The predicate adjective also agrees with the subject in number and gender.

ὁ ἄνθρωπος **δίκαιος**.   The man is just.
καλὸς ὁ διδάσκαλός ἐστιν.   Noble is the teacher. (Or, The teacher is noble.)
τὰ τέκνα **ἄξια**.   The children are worthy.

3.2 Genitive

3.2.1 GENITIVE OF POSSESSION

The genitive of possession indicates ownership, possession, or belonging. The genitive of possession is usually in the attributive position.

ὁ **τοῦ μαθητοῦ** ἵππος   the horse of the student/the student's horse

Personal pronouns may also be used as genitives of possession, but they usually appear in the predicate position. For the third person, the genitive of αὐτός is more common than the third-person personal pronouns, which are rare in Attic prose.

μὴ βλάπτετε τοὺς ἵππους **ἡμῶν**.   Don't keep harming our horses.
τοῖς φίλοις **αὐτῶν** πιστεύομεν.   We have confidence in their friends.

Other genitives of possession may also appear in the predicate position, often with a form of "be."

ἡ σκηνή ἐστι **τοῦ δεσπότου**.
The tent belongs to the master. (Literally, The tent is of the master.)

Possession may also be indicated by the dative; see 3.3.5.

3.2.2 PARTITIVE GENITIVE/GENITIVE OF THE WHOLE

After words denoting or implying a part of something, the genitive is used to indicate the whole or the entirety from which the part has been taken. The partitive genitive is placed directly before or after the noun denoting the part, outside the article-noun pairing. It is only rarely found in the attributive position.

οἱ ἄδικοι **τῶν Ἀθηναίων**	the unjust among the Athenians
δέκα **τῶν τέκνων**	ten of the children

The following phrases have similar meanings, but those using the partitive genitive are more specific about the group being characterized.

οἱ ἄδικοι τῶν Ἀθηναίων	the unjust among the Athenians
οἱ ἄδικοι Ἀθηναῖοι	the unjust Athenians
δέκα τῶν τέκνων	ten of the children
δέκα τέκνα	ten children

The partitive genitive is often used with comparatives and superlatives:

ὁ φοβερώτερος **τῶν ἀδελφῶν**	the more timid of the (two) brothers
ὁ φοβερώτατος **τῶν ἀδελφῶν**	the most timid of the (three or more) brothers

3.2.3 GENITIVE OF PERSONAL AGENT

The agent of a passive verb is indicated by the preposition ὑπό plus the genitive.

τὸ βιβλίον **ὑπὸ τοῦ ποιητοῦ** γράφεται.   The book is being written by the poet.

3.2.4 GENITIVE OF TIME WITHIN WHICH

The genitive case is used without a preposition to indicate the time within which an event or action occurs.

οἱ ἐν τῇ ἐκκλησίᾳ γράψουσι δέκα **ἡμερῶν** τάσδε τὰς σπονδάς.
The men in the assembly will propose this truce within ten days.

3.2.5 SUBJECTIVE AND OBJECTIVE GENITIVE

Certain nouns have a verbal notion inherent in their meanings. These are nouns like "hope," "fear," "love," "desire," and so on. In Greek, such nouns are often used in conjunction with another noun in the genitive. This genitive may be either a subjective or an objective genitive, depending on the context of the sentence and general logic.

A subjective genitive indicates the doer of the verbal notion that is implied by the noun; an objective genitive indicates the object or recipient of that verbal activity. The subjective genitive is often in the attributive position; the objective genitive is generally in the predicate position. The translation of a phrase with a subjective genitive may be identical to that of a phrase with an objective genitive, though often a subjective genitive is translated as a possessive. Sometimes an objective genitive may be translated as "for" rather than "of."

> ὁ **ἐκείνου** φόβος ἐστὶ κακός.
> The fear of that man is cowardly. (Literal translation.)
> That man's fear is cowardly. (Subjective genitive; the man has the fear.)

> ὁ φόβος **ἐκείνου** ἐστὶ κακός.
> Fear of that man is cowardly. (Objective genitive; the man is the object of somebody else's fear.)

3.2.6 GENITIVE OF COMPARISON

The genitive case can be used to indicate a comparison. The word in the genitive indicates the second member of the comparison. The genitive of comparison may be placed just before or immediately after the comparative.

> ἐκείνη ἡ δέσποινα σοφωτέρα **ταύτης** ἐστίν.
> That mistress is wiser than this one.

For comparison with ἤ, see Review 13.

3.2.7 GENITIVE OF PRICE AND VALUE

The genitive can indicate the price or value of something. In such cases, no preposition is needed to indicate "for" or "of." This genitive is used in particular with verbs meaning "buy," "sell," "cost," "value," and "exchange."

> ὁ στρατιώτης δέκα **δραχμῶν** ἐπώλησε τὸν ἵππον.
> The soldier sold the horse for ten drachmas.

> ἤμειψε τὸν ἵππον **τοῦ βοός**.
> He exchanged the horse for the ox.

3.2.8 GENITIVE OF SEPARATION

The genitive of separation is used with verbs meaning "cease," "restrain," "remove," "release," "fail," "differ," and the like, and indicates the person or thing from which someone or something has been separated or distinguished. Transitive verbs from this group may also take a direct object.

οὐ παύσομεν αὐτὸν **ἐκείνης τῆς μάχης**.   We will not keep him from that battle.
λύσατέ με **τούτων τῶν ἔργων**.   Release me from these tasks.

Verbs of needing, wanting, lacking, emptying, and so on also take the genitive of separation.

οἱ κακοὶ **τῆς ἀληθείας** οὐ δέονται.   Evil men have no need of the truth.

3.3 Dative

3.3.1 INDIRECT OBJECT

The indirect object indicates the person or thing for whom the action of the verb is done or the indirect recipient of that action. The indirect object will be in the dative case, and no preposition is used.

ἐκείνῳ **τῷ τέκνῳ** ὁ διδάσκαλος γράφει τὴν ἐπιστολήν.
The teacher writes the letter to that child.
The teacher writes that child the letter.

3.3.2 INSTRUMENTAL DATIVE/DATIVE OF MEANS

The instrumental dative, or dative of means, indicates the instrument or means by which the action of the verb is carried out. It is generally used without a preposition, although it is sometimes found with the prepositions ὑπό, σύν, or ἐν, especially in poetry. The instrumental dative is frequently translated into English by the preposition "with."

τοῖς λίθοις ὁ ἄνθρωπος βάλλει τοὺς ἵππους.
The man strikes the horses with the stones.

3.3.3 DATIVE OF CAUSE

Related to the instrumental dative is the dative of cause, which is used to indicate the cause or reason the activity of the verb took place. It is used without a preposition and its translation will vary according to logic, context of the sentence, and English idiom.

ἐκεῖνο τὸ τέκνον **νόσῳ** ἀπέθανεν.   That child died of disease.
ἀγνοίᾳ ὁ μαθητὴς ἐποίησε τάδε.   The student did these things because of ignorance.

3.3.4 DATIVE OF TIME WHEN

The precise moment at which an event occurs is indicated by the dative case, usually without a preposition, though sometimes the preposition ἐν is used.

οἱ ἐν τῇ ἐκκλησίᾳ **δεκάτῃ ἡμέρᾳ** γράψουσι τάσδε τὰς σπονδάς.
The men in the assembly will propose this truce on the tenth day.

3.3.5 DATIVE OF POSSESSION

The dative case is often used in conjunction with a form of εἰμί ("be"), γίγνομαι ("become," "be"), or another, similar verb to indicate the possessor of an object. The object being possessed, which may be either a concrete thing or an abstract idea, is in the nominative case and is the subject of the form of "be." A literal translation of this construction is often awkward in English, but it is important to understand how the construction works in order to translate it into more idiomatic English. For the following examples, compare the literal translations with the preferred translations.

ἀσπίδες **τοῖς στρατιώταις** εἰσίν.
Shields are to/for the soldiers. (Literal translation.)
The soldiers have shields. (Preferred translation.)

καὶ **τοῖς ναύταις** φόβος τῆς θαλάττης ἐστίν.
Fear of the sea is even to/for the sailors. (Literal translation.)
Even the sailors have fear of the sea. (Preferred translation.)

To translate this construction into fluid English, it is best to translate the dative of possession (the actual possessor) as the subject of the sentence. Then translate the verb as a verb of possession such as "have" and translate the subject of the original sentence (what is possessed) as the direct object of the verb of possession, as in the examples above.

The dative of possession highlights the object or idea that is possessed, whereas the genitive of possession (3.2.1) gives more emphasis to the possessor or owner of the object or idea.

3.3.6 DATIVE OF PERSONAL AGENT

The dative case is used with passive verbs in the perfect system and with verbal adjectives ending in -τός and -τέος to indicate the doer of the action indicated by these constructions. No preposition is used.

τάδε **ἡμῖν** πέπρακται ἵνα τὴν πόλιν σώσωμεν.
These things have been done by us so that we may save the city.

οἱ ἐν τῇ χώρᾳ κακοὶ **ἡμῖν** εἰσιν φοβητέοι.
The evil men in the countryside must be feared by us.
We must fear the evil men in the countryside.

Only passive verbs in the perfect system take the dative of agent. The genitive of personal agent (3.2.3) is used with all other tenses.

3.3.7 DATIVE OF MANNER

The dative of manner indicates how the activity of the verb is carried out or the circumstances under which the activity of the verb occurs. No preposition is used. This construction is also called the dative of accompanying circumstances and is sometimes translated into English by an adverb.

οἱ κλέπται ἐκ τῆς ἀγορᾶς **δρόμῳ** σπεύδουσιν.
The thieves hasten out of the marketplace at a run.

οἱ πολῖται **σιγῇ** ἦλθον εἰς τὴν ἐκκλησίαν.
The citizens came into the assembly silently.

3.3.8 DATIVE OF DEGREE OF DIFFERENCE

To indicate how or the degree to which one thing differs from another, the dative of degree of difference is used. No preposition is used. Certain adverbs expressing ideas such as "much," "not at all," and "a little" may also be used in this way. Usually these are adverbs formed from adjectives like πολύς and ὀλίγος.

ἐκεῖνος ὁ ποιητής ἐστι **πολλῷ** αἰτιώτερος τῶν σπονδῶν ἢ οἱ στρατηγοί.
That poet is much more responsible for the truce than the generals [are].
(Literally, "more responsible by much.")

ἡ τοῦ ποιητοῦ θυγάτηρ δέκα **ἡμέραις** ὕστερον ἀπέθανεν.
The poet's daughter died ten days later. (Literally, "later by ten days.")

ὁ κακὸς **πολὺ** ἀφιλώτερος τοῦ ποιητοῦ ἐστιν.
The cowardly man is much more unfriendly than the poet.

3.3.9 DATIVE OF RESPECT

With verbs and adjectives expressing a state of being, quality, or characteristic, the dative is often used to make the description more specific. Unlike the accusative of respect (3.4.5), when the dative is used in this manner it does not simply limit the extent to which the descriptor is true; it adds an instrumental nuance.

ἐκεῖνο τὸ τέκνον σοφὸν **ψυχῇ** ἐστιν.
That child is wise in spirit. (Literally, "by means of his spirit.")

3.3.10 DATIVE OF ADVANTAGE OR DISADVANTAGE

The dative case may be used to indicate for whose advantage or disadvantage the activity of the verb is carried out.

ἥδε ἡ ἡμέρα **τοῖς πολεμίοις** μεγάλων κακῶν ἄρξει.
This day will be the beginning of great misfortunes for the enemy.

3.3.11 DATIVE OF MILITARY ACCOMPANIMENT

The dative of military accompaniment is used in descriptions of various types of military movements and maneuvers. It denotes the troops, ships, and other military units that are accompanying a leader. It is generally used without a preposition but may also be used with σύν.

Δωριεὺς ὁ Διαγόρου εἰς Ἑλλήσποντον εἰσέπλει δέκα **ναυσίν.**
Dorieus, the son of Diagoras, was sailing into the Hellespont with ten ships.

3.3.12 DATIVE OF REFERENCE

A pronoun or noun in the dative case indicates the individual or group in whose opinion the statement being made is accurate.

τοῦτο τὸ τεκμήριόν ἐστί **μοι** ἀληθές.
In my opinion, this evidence is true.

3.3.13 VERBS AND ADJECTIVES THAT TAKE THE DATIVE

Certain verbs and adjectives that are related to these verbs take the dative for their object. The dictionary listing of these words usually indicates this.

Such verbs and adjectives can be categorized according to their meanings, listed below.

1. Verbs and related adjectives meaning "benefit," "help," "injure," "please," "displease," "be friendly," "be hostile," "be angry," "blame," "threaten," or "envy."
    ἐκεῖνος ὁ διδάσκαλος ἀεὶ **βοηθεῖ τοῖς μαθηταῖς.**
    That teacher always helps the students.

    ὁ βασιλεὺς **ἐχθρὸς** τῷ ἀγαθῷ **ποιητῇ** ἦν.
    The king was hostile to the good poet.
    N.B.: A few verbs of injuring and helping, such as βλάπτω, take the accusative.
2. Verbs and related adjectives meaning "meet," "approach," or "yield."
    μὴ **πελάσητε** τοῖς **θηρίοις.**
    Don't go near the wild beasts.

3. Verbs and related adjectives meaning "to be like," "to be unlike," "befit," or variants of these ideas.

ἡ τοῦ στρατιώτου ἀσπὶς **ὁμοία ἐμῇ** ἐστιν.
The soldier's shield is similar to mine.

4. Verbs and related adjectives meaning "obey," "serve," "pardon," or "trust."

δουλεύει ἐκείνῳ τῷ κακῷ **βασιλεῖ.**
He serves (or, is a slave to) that wicked king.

ἐκεῖνος τῷ **βασιλεῖ δούλειος** ἦν.
That man was servile to the king.

3.4 Accusative

3.4.1 DIRECT OBJECT

The accusative indicates the direct object of a transitive verb. The direct object directly receives the action of the verb.

ὁ διδάσκαλος **τὸ βιβλίον** γράφει.   The teacher is writing the book.

3.4.2 ACCUSATIVE OF DURATION OF TIME

The accusative case is used without a preposition to indicate the duration of an event.

οἱ ἐν τῇ ἐκκλησίᾳ δέκα **ἡμέρας** ἔγραφον τάσδε τὰς σπονδάς.
The men in the assembly kept proposing this truce for ten days.

3.4.3 ACCUSATIVE OF EXTENT OF SPACE

The accusative case used without a preposition can also indicate the extent of space or the area covered by a verb of motion.

οἱ στρατιῶται τοὺς τοῦ στρατηγοῦ ἵππους δέκα **στάδια** ἦγον.
The soldiers were leading the general's horses for ten stades.

3.4.4 DOUBLE ACCUSATIVES WITH VERBS OF NAMING, APPOINTING, AND THE LIKE

Verbs of naming, appointing, electing, choosing, making, calling, considering, and so on take two accusatives: one indicates the direct object (who or what is receiving the action of the verb), the other, a predicate accusative, specifies what the direct object has been named, elected, called, and so on. One way to distinguish the two is that a definite article is often used with the direct object, but it is not used with a predicate accusative. When the direct object is a pronoun, no definite article is used.

οἱ ἐν τῇ ἐκκλησίᾳ **τὸν ποιητὴν στρατηγὸν** αἱροῦνται.
The men in the assembly choose the poet [to be] general.

ἀεὶ ἐνομίζομεν **αὐτὴν ἡμετέραν** δέσποιναν.
We always considered her our mistress.

3.4.5 ACCUSATIVE OF RESPECT

With verbs and adjectives expressing a state of being, quality, or characteristic, the accusative is often used to make the description more specific.

ἐκεῖνοι οἱ στρατιῶται ἀγαθοὶ **μάχην**.
Those soldiers are brave in battle. (Literally, "brave in respect to battle.")

σοφώτεροι **ἔργα** γιγνόμεθα.
We are becoming wiser in our actions. (Literally, "wiser in respect to our actions.")

3.5 Vocative

The vocative is used for the direct address of a person or thing or in exclamations. It is frequently used with the particle ὦ.

ὦ διδάσκαλε, τί βιβλίον γράφεις;   Teacher, what book are you writing?

Review Four

Aspect

The aspect of a verb indicates whether the action is in progress, habitual, or repeated (present stem forms); a simple occurrence (aorist stem forms); or a completed event that has a permanent or lasting result (perfect stem forms). In the indicative mood, the tense of the verb indicates the aspect of the action as well as the time the action took place. In all other moods, the tense indicates aspect but not time. For the participle and the infinitive, the tense indicates aspect and often time relative to that of the main verb (see 6.1, 7.1). The aspect of verbs formed from the future stem may indicate either action in progress or simple occurrence. The present indicative may also indicate simple occurrence rather than habitual or repeated action or action in progress; it will always indicate present time. Sometimes the aspect of a verb is not reflected in its translation. Consider how aspect influences the reader's understanding of the genitive absolute in the following sentences.

τοῦ πολεμίου στρατιώτου **ἀποθνήσκοντος** οἱ πολῖται ἔφυγον.
While the enemy soldier was dying, the citizens fled.
Because the enemy soldier was dying, the citizens fled.
(Present participle indicates action in progress.)

τοῦ πολεμίου στρατιώτου **ἀποθανόντος** οἱ πολῖται ἔφυγον.
After the enemy soldier had died/died, the citizens fled.
Because the enemy soldier had died/died, the citizens fled.
(Aorist participle indicates simple occurrence of action.)

τοῦ πολεμίου στρατιώτου **ἀποτεθνηκότος** οἱ πολῖται ἔφυγον.
Because the enemy soldier was dead, the citizens fled.
(Perfect participle indicates completed action with permanent result.)

Example from Readings

διὰ ταῦτα τοὺς ἀτίμους ἐπιτίμους **ποιήσαντες ἐκαρτέρουν**, καὶ **ἀποθνῃσκόντων**
ἐν τῇ πόλει λιμῷ πολλῶν οὐ **διελέγοντο** περὶ διαλλαγῆς.

On account of these things, after they made the disenfranchised enfranchised, they
kept holding out, and though many in the city were dying from hunger, they were not
talking about reconciliation.   Xenophon, *Hellenica* 2.2.11

Review Five
Uses of the Infinitive

An infinitive is a verbal noun, and as such it has characteristics of both verbs and nouns. It
shows aspect and voice (and occasionally time), but it does not indicate person or number. In addition, it can take a direct or an indirect object or be modified by an adverb. Like
nouns, it may be used as the subject of a verb under certain circumstances, and it may also
act as the object of a verb or even the object of a preposition. The most common uses of the
infinitive are discussed below.

5.1 Accusative/Infinitive with Verbs of Ordering, Persuading, and Commanding

An accusative/infinitive construction is used with a verb of ordering, persuading, or
commanding to specify the person receiving the order (accusative) and the activity this person is supposed to do (infinitive).

Verb	Object
I persuade	X
I persuade	[the teacher]
I persuade	[the teacher *to write* the letters]

In this example, the entire phrase "the teacher to write the letters" is acting as the object of
"persuade" in the same way as "the teacher" or "X." To express this idea in Greek, an accusa-

tive/infinitive construction is used. (In some grammars, this use of the infinitive is called an "object infinitive.") The subject of the infinitive is nearly always in the accusative, although certain verbs of ordering may take a dative. The infinitive may in turn take a direct object, also in the accusative case. Logic, context, and word order will help you distinguish between the subject and the direct object of the infinitive: often the subject accusative is placed before the accusative direct object. Here is the example translated into Greek.

Verb	Object
πείθω	[X]
πείθω	[τὸν διδάσκαλον]
πείθω	[τὸν διδάσκαλον γράφειν τὰς ἐπιστολάς]

As with most other infinitives, the tense of the infinitive indicates aspect but not time. The present infinitive indicates repeated or continuous action or action in progress, while the aorist infinitive indicates that the action is a single, discrete event.

Example from Readings

καὶ **ἐπιστῆναι ἐκέλευσε τοὺς** τὰ ἐγχειρίδια **ἔχοντας** φανερῶς τῇ βουλῇ ἐπὶ τοῖς δρυφάκτοις.

And he ordered those with daggers to stand in clear view of the Council at the railings.   Xenophon, *Hellenica* 2.3.50

5.2 Articular Infinitive

When an infinitive is used as a noun, it is often accompanied by the definite article, which indicates the case in which the infinitive is being used. In Greek, unlike Latin, there is no separate form for a gerund (a verbal noun); the articular infinitive is used instead. The article is always neuter and singular and will always be found when the infinitive is being used in the genitive or dative case. It may be omitted when the infinitive is being used in the nominative or in some uses of the accusative case, since its grammatical function is usually unambiguous in these cases. Because the infinitive is a verbal noun, the tense of the articular infinitive indicates aspect (and never time), and the infinitive may be modified by adverbs or prepositional phrases, or it may take a subject (in the accusative case), a direct object, or an indirect object. μή, rather than οὐ, is used to negate an articular infinitive.

5.2.1 NOMINATIVE USE

The primary use of the infinitive in the nominative case is as the subject of a finite verb. The article is often omitted in such instances.

τὸ ἀδικεῖν ἐστι κακόν.   To commit an injustice is evil.

5.2.2 GENITIVE USE

The articular infinitive in the genitive case may be used in any construction that normally requires the genitive. It is especially common as the object of prepositions that take the genitive.

ἀντὶ **τοῦ φυγεῖν** ἐκεῖνοι οἱ στρατιῶται ὡς κράτιστα ἐμάχοντο.
Instead of fleeing, those soldiers were fighting as bravely as possible.

5.2.3 DATIVE USE

As with the genitive, the articular infinitive in the dative case may be used in most dative constructions, including means and instrument, manner, cause, and as the object of a preposition that takes the dative case.

τῷ ἀεὶ **φυλάττειν** τὴν πόλιν ἐσώσαμεν.
By always keeping watch, we saved the city.

5.2.4 ACCUSATIVE USE

As noted above, a definite article is not required for an articular infinitive in the accusative case, but when it is used the syntax is easier to determine. The articular infinitive in the accusative case may be used as a direct object, as the object of a preposition, as the subject of an infinitive within an indirect statement construction, or in any other use that is appropriate for the accusative.

οἱ πολῖται νομίζουσι **τὸ** ἐν τῇ μάχῃ **μένειν** ἀγαθὸν εἶναι.
The citizens think that remaining in battle is noble.

The examples for the dative and accusative uses demonstrate a typical feature of the articular infinitive. The word or words that go with this infinitive—for example, an adverb, a prepositional phrase, the accusative subject—will often be positioned between the article and the infinitive.

Example from Readings

σὺ δὲ διὰ **τὸ** εὐμετάβολος **εἶναι** πλείστοις μὲν μεταίτιος εἶ ἐξ ὀλιγαρχίας ὑπὸ τοῦ δήμου ἀπολωλέναι, πλείστοις δ᾽ ἐκ δημοκρατίας ὑπὸ τῶν βελτιόνων.

But you, on account of being easily changeable, are accessory to a very large number from the oligarchy perishing at the hands of the people and a very large number from the democracy perishing at the hands of the better men.   Xenophon, *Hellenica* 2.3.32

5.3 Complementary Infinitive

Certain verbs, especially those that indicate notions of will, desire, intention, and ability, often need an infinitive to complete their meaning. In many instances, these infinitives act as the object of the verb (in some grammar books, these infinitives are also called "object infinitives"). The tense of the infinitive denotes aspect only.

σπεύδω **ποιεῖν** εἰρήνην.
I am eager to make peace.

Example from Readings

... **βουλόμενοι** σύμμαχοι **εἶναι** Λακεδαιμονίοις ἔχοντες τὰ τείχη καὶ τὸν Πειραιᾶ, καὶ ἐπὶ τούτοις συνθήκας **ποιεῖσθαι.**

... wishing to be allies with the Lacedaemonians while <still> holding the walls and Piraeus, and to make a treaty upon these terms.   Xenophon, *Hellenica* 2.2.11

5.4 Explanatory Infinitives with Adjectives and Adverbs

Both adjectives and adverbs may have their meanings limited by an infinitive. This construction is particularly common with adjectives and adverbs denoting ideas of fitness, ability, and capacity but may be used with other adjectives and adverbs as well. This infinitive is often called an explanatory or epexegetical infinitive and it works similarly to an accusative of respect: the infinitive will indicate in what way the adjective or adverb is true. If context permits, it is acceptable to translate the infinitive using the "-ing" form of the verb.

ἐκεῖνός ἐστιν ἀξιώτατος **ἄρχειν.**	That man is most worthy to rule.
ἐκεῖνος ἦν δεινὸς **λέγειν.**	That man was clever in speaking.

Example from Readings

ὁ δέ ... ἀντέλεγεν ὅτι οὐκ ἐγχωροίη τοῖς πλεονεκτεῖν βουλομένοις μὴ οὐκ ἐκποδὼν ποιεῖσθαι τοὺς **ἱκανωτάτους διακωλύειν·**

And he ... countered that it was not possible for those wishing to gain the upper hand not to put out of the way those most able to hinder <them>.   Xenophon, *Hellenica* 2.3.16

Review Six

Uses of the Participle

A participle is an adjective that is formed from the stem of a verb and exhibits characteristics of both parts of speech.

Like a verb, a participle's form indicates both tense and voice. Its tense always indicates aspect; in most contexts, it also indicates time relative to that of the main verb. A participle may take a direct object or an indirect object and may also be modified by adverbs and prepositional phrases. It may also introduce indirect statement constructions, purpose clauses, and the like. Unlike finite or conjugated verb forms, however, the form of the participle does not indicate person.

Because it is an adjective, it is inflected, and when modifying a noun it must agree with that noun in case, number, and gender. There are participles in the present, future, aorist, and perfect tenses. The participle may be used to express complex stages of action in an elegant yet efficient way as well as to provide additional information that is important in respect to content but not essential grammatically. It also offers an alternative to various subordinate clauses and other grammatical constructions. The most common uses are reviewed below.

6.1 Attributive Participle

When the participle is used attributively, it acts as an adjective and modifies a noun. In its basic sense, the attributive participle communicates the verbal action as a characteristic of the noun. It is generally used with the definite article in the attributive position, although it is sometimes found without the article. Like all adjectives, the attributive participle agrees in case, number, and gender with the noun it is modifying. The tense of the participle denotes aspect (see Review 4). The tense may also indicate time relative to that of the main verb; this will be determined by context and logic. The present participle indicates time contemporaneous to that of the main verb, the aorist participle time prior to that of the main verb, the future participle time subsequent to that of the main verb, and the perfect participle time and action immediately preceding that of the main verb that has a permanent result that is contemporary with that of the main verb. Sometimes such distinctions are important to the meaning of the text; at other times, they are not critical. Context and logic will help determine when it is necessary to bring out such distinctions in translation. It should be noted that it is common (and acceptable) to translate an attributive participle as a relative clause (which is fundamentally adjectival in nature), as in the second example below.

ἡ **μέλπουσα** κόρη τέρπει τὸν πατέρα καὶ τὴν μητέρα.
The singing girl delights her father and mother.

ὁ πολίτης **ὁ** τὸν κλέπτην **διώκων** εἰς τὸ ἱερὸν ἦλθεν.
The citizen, the one pursuing the thief, came into the temple.
The citizen who was pursuing the thief came into the temple.

Example from Readings

> δεήσεται δ᾿ ὑμῶν οὗτος μὲν ὑπὲρ μητρὸς **τῆς** αὑτοῦ **ζώσης, τῆς** ἐκεῖνον
> **διαχρησαμένης** ἐπιβούλως τε καὶ ἀθέως, ὅπως δίκην μὴ δῷ, ἂν ὑμᾶς πείθῃ, ὧν
> ἠδίκηκε·

And this one will appeal to you on behalf of his mother, who is still alive and who destroyed that man treacherously and impiously, so that she may not be punished, if he persuades you, for the injustices she has committed.   Antiphon 1.23

The attributive participle may also be used as a substantive, like any other adjective. In such instances, the article and the participle are used together without a specified noun being modified by the participle. A relative clause or a noun derived from the verbal action of the participle will often be used to translate the substantive. In addition, the participles of certain verbs are used as substantives with particular meanings within specific genres. For example, ὁ διώκων, which literally means "the pursuing one" or "the pursuer," usually means "the prosecutor" in a legal context. These specialized meanings are listed in most lexicons.

> ὁ ἐν τῷ ἀγῶνι **νικῶν** ὑπὸ τῶν πολιτῶν ἐτιμάζετο.
> The victor in the contest was being honored by the citizens.
> The one who was victorious in the contest was being honored by the citizens.

> ἡ **θύουσα** εἰς τὸ ἱερὸν ἦλθεν.
> The woman who was making sacrifices came into the sacred place.
> The sacrificing woman came into the sacred place.

Example from Readings

> οἱ δὲ **προδόντες** Ἀλκιβιάδῃ τὸ Βυζάντιον τότε μὲν ἔφυγον εἰς τὸν Πόντον,
> ὕστερον δ᾿ εἰς Ἀθήνας καὶ ἐγένοντο Ἀθηναῖοι.

And those who had betrayed Byzantium to Alcibiades fled at that time to the Black Sea, but later they went to Athens and became Athenians.   Xenophon, *Hellenica* 2.2.1

6.2 Circumstantial Participle

The most common use of the participle in Greek is as a circumstantial participle, which allows the greatest flexibility in translating. It is used to indicate the circumstances under which the action of the verb occurred. These include notions of time, cause, manner, concession, means, and condition. A circumstantial participle is most often translated as a subordinate clause introduced by a subordinating conjunction such as "when," "after," "since," "because," or "although" that communicates these types of relationships. It is thus essentially adverbial in nature and may be used in conjunction with a verb. A circumstantial participle is not grammatically necessary to a sentence or clause, but it supplies additional (and often important) information. As with an attributive participle, its tense indicates aspect as well as time relative to that of the main verb. The circumstantial participle is *never* used with the definite article. As with all participles, the circumstantial participle must agree with the noun it is modifying in case, number, and gender; like the attributive participle, it may modify any noun in a sentence.

Since a circumstantial participle may convey a wide range of information, from questions of time to notions about a concession or condition, it may be translated in a variety of ways, depending on logic, context, and individual interpretation of the text. It is possible for several translations of a single participle to be correct, as indicated in the examples below.

ἐκεῖνος τάδε **ἀγγέλλων** τὴν ἀλήθειαν ἔκρυψεν.
That man, while reporting these things, hid the truth. (Time.)
That man, as he was reporting these things, hid the truth. (Time.)
That man, by reporting these things, hid the truth. (Means.)
That man, because he was reporting these things, hid the truth. (Cause.)

ἐν τῷ ἀγῶνι νικᾶν **βουλόμενος** γυμνάζομαι πάσῃ ἡμέρᾳ.
When I wish to be victorious in the contest, I exercise every day. (Time.)
Because I wish to be victorious in the contest, I exercise every day. (Cause.)

Sometimes particular words are used in conjunction with circumstantial participles that indicate how the participle should be understood. The most common of these clue words are listed here.

ἄτε	(causal adverb) inasmuch as, because (implies that the writer is presenting the cause as a fact)
καίπερ	(concessive adverb) although
μή	(negative) not (When μή is used with a participle it usually gives a negative conditional force to the participle and is translated "if . . . not.")
ὡς	(causal adverb) on the grounds that, because (ὡς usually implies that the writer does not vouch for the accuracy of the stated cause.)

ἄτε τῶν κακῶν ἔργων αἴτιος **ὢν** ὁ νεανίας ἐκ τῆς ἀγορᾶς ἔφυγεν.
Because he was responsible for the wicked deeds, the youth fled from the marketplace.

ἐκεῖνος **καίπερ δουλεύων** πολλάκις ἐβοήθει τοῖς πολίταις.
That man, although he was a slave, was often aiding the citizens.

τάδε ταχέως **μὴ ἀγγέλλων** τὸν στρατηγὸν οὐ σώσεις.
If you do not report these things quickly, you will not save the general.

Example from Readings

Παυσανίας μὲν διῆκε τὸ στράτευμα, οἱ δ᾽ ἐκ τοῦ Πειραιῶς **ἀνελθόντες** σὺν τοῖς
ὅπλοις εἰς τὴν ἀκρόπολιν ἔθυσαν τῇ Ἀθηνᾷ.

Pausanias dismissed the army, and the men from Piraeus, after they went up to the
Acropolis with their weapons, sacrificed to Athena.   Xenophon, *Hellenica* 2.4.39

6.3 Future Participle Used to Express Purpose

The future participle is often used to express purpose, especially with verbs of motion.
ὡς may be used with the future participle in this construction, but is not required. When it
is used, ὡς precedes the future participle. Any words that go with the participle, such as an
indirect or a direct object, may be placed between ὡς and the participle.

εἰς τὴν πόλιν ἤλθομεν **ὡς** σῖτον **ὠνησόμενοι**.
We came into the city in order to buy food.
We came into the city to buy food.

ὡς τοὺς ὁμήρους **σώσοντες** οἱ πολῖται κήρυκά τινα πρὸς τὸν τῶν πολεμίων στρατηγὸν
ἔπεμψαν.
The citizens sent a messenger to the enemy's general in order to save the hostages.
The citizens sent a messenger to the enemy's general to save the hostages.

Example from Readings

Λύσανδρος δὲ τοῖς ἐφόροις ἔπεμψεν **ἀγγελοῦντα** μετ᾽ ἄλλων Λακεδαιμονίων
Ἀριστοτέλην, φυγάδα Ἀθηναῖον ὄντα, ὅτι ἀποκρίναιτο Θηραμένει ἐκείνους
κυρίους εἶναι εἰρήνης καὶ πολέμου.

And Lysander sent Aristoteles, an Athenian exile, with other Lacedaemonians to the
ephors to announce that he had responded to Theramenes that they had authority over
peace and war.   Xenophon, *Hellenica* 2.2.18

6.4 Supplementary Participle

A supplementary participle is used in conjunction with certain verbs to specify in what
respect the action of the verb takes place. Because it is a verbal adjective, the supplementary
participle, like all participles, will modify a noun. In the supplementary usage, it will modify
either the subject or the direct object. The subject may be expressed by a nominative or implied by the verb form. The direct object is expressed by the accusative case. The dictionary
entry of a verb will indicate whether it takes a supplementary participle. The tense of the
supplementary participle will indicate aspect but not time relative to that of the main verb.
Below is a list of certain types of verbs that take a supplementary participle.

1. Verbs meaning "cease," "stop," "begin," "endure," "put up with," "grow weary," and the like.

ἄρχωμεν ἐπαινοῦντες τοὺς ἐν τῷ ἀγῶνι νικῶντας.
Let us begin praising the victors in the contest.

ἔπαυσά σε **μέλποντα.**
I stopped you from singing.

οἱ νεανίαι οὐκ **ἐπαύσαντο** περὶ τοῦ διδασκάλου κακῶς **λέγοντες.**
The young men did not stop talking inappropriately about the teacher.

κάμνουσιν ἐν τοῖς ἀγροῖς πάσῃ ἡμέρᾳ **πονοῦντες.**
They are growing weary of working in the fields each day.

Example from Readings

αἰδούμενοι καὶ θεοὺς καὶ ἀνθρώπους **παύσασθε ἁμαρτάνοντες** εἰς τὴν πατρίδα,
καὶ μὴ πείθεσθε τοῖς ἀνοσιωτάτοις τριάκοντα.

Respecting both gods and men, stop doing wrong to your country, and do not obey the most impious Thirty.
                                                      Xenophon, *Hellenica* 2.4.21

2. Verbs meaning "continue," "keep on," "be continuously," and so on.
   οἱ παῖδες τὰ γράμματα **μανθάνοντες διαμένουσιν.**
   The children continue learning the alphabet.

   ἐκεῖνοι οἱ στρατιῶται ὡς ἄριστα **μαχόμενοι διάγουσιν.**
   Those soldiers keep on fighting as bravely as possible.

3. Verbs of emotion.
   νέα **ποιοῦντες χαίρομεν.**
   We take delight in doing new things.

   οὐκ **αἰσχύνομαι** βοηθείας **δεόμενος.**
   I am not ashamed of needing help.

4. Verbs meaning "to do well" or "to do ill," "be inferior," "surpass," "overcome," and so on. The supplementary participle specifies in what way or manner the verb is true.
   οἱ στρατιῶται **ἠδίκουν** τὰ τέκνα τε καὶ τὰς γυναῖκας **βλάπτοντες.**
   The soldiers were wrong in harming the women and children.

   εὖ ἐποίησας τὴν δέσποιναν ἀπὸ τοῦ θηρίου **σώσας.**
   You did well in saving the mistress from the wild beast.

5. τυγχάνω ("happen"), λανθάνω ("escape the notice of"), and φθάνω ("anticipate"). The use of the supplementary participle with these three verbs is less straightforward than with the verbs listed previously. With these verbs, the supplementary participle will agree with the subject of the main verb. Study the following examples:

τυγχάνω ("happen")

ἐκεῖνοι οἱ μαθηταὶ τὰ γράμματα **μανθάνοντες** τήμερον **τυγχάνουσιν.**
Those students happen to be learning the alphabet today.
Those students are just now learning the alphabet today.

ὁ γεωργὸς **πονῶν ἔτυχεν** ἐν τῷ ἀγρῷ.
The farmer happened to be working in the field.
The farmer was just now working in the field.

Translation aid: happen to be doing [*the action denoted by the participle*]; be just
now doing [*the action denoted by the participle*]. The tense of the participle indicates
aspect, and an aorist participle usually indicates time coinciding with that of the
main verb. However, when τυγχάνω is in the present or imperfect and the participle
is in the aorist, the action denoted by the participle is usually prior to that of the
main verb:

ὁ γεωργὸς **πονήσας ἐτύγχανεν** ἐν ἐκείνῳ τῷ ἀγρῷ.
The farmer happened to have worked in that field.

Example from Readings

ὅτε γὰρ ταῦτα ἦν, οὐ **παρὼν ἐτύγχανεν**, ἀλλ᾽ ἐν Θετταλίᾳ μετὰ Προμηθέως
δημοκρατίαν κατεσκεύαζε καὶ τοὺς πενέστας ὥπλιζεν ἐπὶ τοὺς δεσπότας.

For when these things were happening, he (Critias) did not happen to be present,
but he was establishing democracy in Thessaly with Prometheus and was arming the poor
against their masters.   Xenophon, *Hellenica* 2.3.36

λανθάνω ("escape the notice of")

οἱ πολέμιοι εἰς τὴν πόλιν **ἐλθόντες ἔλαθον.**
The enemy came into the city without being noticed.
(Literally, The enemy escaped notice, having come into the city.)

οἱ νεανίαι τοὺς φύλακας **ἔλαθον** τὸν θησαυρὸν **κλέψαντες.**
The young men stole the treasure without the guards knowing it.
The young men stole the treasure without being seen by the guards.
(Literally, The young men, having stolen the treasure, escaped the notice of the
guards.)

Translation aid: Take the verbal idea of the supplementary participle and translate
it as the main verb, using the same tense for its translation as the tense of the finite
form of λανθάνω. Then add a phrase such as *without being noticed, without being seen,
without [direct object] knowing it,* or *with [direct object] unaware.* If there is no direct

object for the finite form of λανθάνω, use *without being noticed* or *without being seen*. If there is a direct object use *without [direct object] knowing it,* or *with [direct object] unaware.* The direct object of λανθάνω will be the "subject" of this phrase. A finite form of λανθάνω in the aorist will usually be accompanied by a supplementary participle in the aorist; a present form of λανθάνω will usually have a supplementary participle in the present tense.

φθάνω ("anticipate")

οἱ στρατιῶται εἰς τὴν πόλιν **ἐλθόντες** τοὺς πολεμίους **ἔφθασαν**.
The soldiers came into the city ahead of the enemy.
(Literally, The soldiers, having come into the city, anticipated the enemy.)

ὁ νεανίας **ἔφθασε** τὴν περὶ τῆς σχολῆς ἀλήθειαν **ἀγγείλας**.
The young man reported the truth about the school first.
(Literally, The young man, having reported the truth about the school, anticipated.)

Translation aid: The verbal idea of the supplementary participle should be translated as a finite verb in the same tense as the tense of φθάνω. If φθάνω has a direct object, add a prepositional phrase in English, *ahead of [direct object]* or *before [direct object]*. Use the direct object of φθάνω as the object of the prepositional phrase. If there is no direct object, add the word "first" to capture the idea of φθάνω, as is done in the second sentence above. Usually an aorist form of φθάνω will be used with a supplementary participle in the aorist. A present form of φθάνω will most often have a supplementary participle in the present tense.

6.5 Genitive Absolute

The genitive absolute is one of the most common and most elegant uses of the circumstantial participle. In its usual form, a genitive absolute consists of a noun or pronoun in the genitive case and a participle that modifies that noun. The noun of the genitive absolute cannot refer to another noun in the sentence; it is completely unconnected grammatically with any other part of the sentence. (This is why the construction is called "absolute": the word comes from the Latin *absolvere*, "to free" or "to loosen," so a genitive absolute is separate from, or "freed from," the rest of the sentence.) Like other circumstantial participles, the genitive absolute expresses attendant circumstances, especially denoting cause, concession, time, and condition. As with all participles, the participle in a genitive absolute can take a direct object, an indirect object, a prepositional phrase, or another construction. Often these accompanying words will be placed in between the genitive noun and the genitive participle. The tense of the participle indicates aspect (4) and, most often, time relative to that of the main verb (see 6.1). Logic and context will help in translating the genitive absolute. It is usually preferable to avoid a literal translation because this sounds awkward in English. Translate a genitive absolute by using a subordinate clause introduced by an appropriate subordinating conjunction such as "when," "because," "after," or "although." In the examples below, a literal translation is given first, followed by one or more possible translations using a subordinate clause. The genitive absolute has been set in brackets.

Genitive Absolute	Main Clause
[noun, participle]	subject, direct object, main verb
[τῆς θυγατρὸς τοῖς θεοῖς θυούσης]	ὁ βασιλεὺς πάντας τοὺς ἀγαθοὺς ἐκάλεσεν.

[The daughter sacrificing to the gods,] the king summoned all the brave men. (Literal translation.)
[While his daughter was sacrificing to the gods,] the king summoned all the brave men.
[When his daughter was sacrificing to the gods,] the king summoned all the brave men.

Genitive Absolute	Main Clause
[participle, pronoun]	subject, prepositional phrase, main verb
[ἀγγελθέντων τούτων]	οἱ στρατιῶται εἰς τὴν ἀγορὰν ἦλθον.

[These things having been announced], the soldiers came into the marketplace. (Literal translation.)
[After these things had been/were announced], the soldiers came into the marketplace.
[Because these things had been/were announced], the soldiers came into the marketplace.

Example from Readings

ἀντειπόντων δέ **τινων** αὐτῷ, πολὺ δὲ **πλειόνων συνεπαινεσάντων**, ἔδοξε δέχεσθαι τὴν εἰρήνην.

While some men spoke against him, because many more agreed, it seemed best to accept the peace.   Xenophon, *Hellenica* 2.2.22

6.6 Accusative Absolute

Impersonal verbs such as δεῖ and ἔξεστι may be used in an accusative absolute. This construction is similar to a genitive absolute except that the participle, formed from an impersonal verb or expression, is in the accusative neuter singular (sometimes plural). The subject of the impersonal expression is usually an infinitive, which may be expressed or implied. There is no noun or pronoun in the accusative that is being modified by the participle. Passive participles that are being used impersonally may also be found in an accusative absolute construction. Like the genitive absolute, the accusative absolute is not grammatically connected to the rest of the sentence and is considered a type of circumstantial participle. It is best translated as a subordinate clause appropriate to the context of the sentence. In the examples below, the accusative absolute has been set in brackets.

[τοὺς ὁμήρους σῶσαι **ἔξον**] τάξωμεν τοὺς στρατιώτας.
[To save the hostages being possible], let us equip the soldiers. (Literal translation.)
[Because it is possible to save the hostages], let us equip the soldiers.

[τὴν πόλιν ἀπολιπεῖν **δέον**] πάντες οἱ πολῖται μένειν ἐθέλουσιν.
[To abandon the city being necessary], all the citizens wish to remain. (Literal translation.)
[Although it is necessary to abandon the city], all the citizens wish to remain.

Example from Readings

οἱ δὲ τριάκοντα, ὡς **ἐξὸν** ἤδη αὐτοῖς τυραννεῖν ἀδεῶς, προεῖπον μὲν τοῖς ἔξω τοῦ καταλόγου μὴ εἰσιέναι εἰς τὸ ἄστυ.

But the Thirty, because it was now possible for them to rule without fear, ordered those outside the citizens list not to enter the city.   Xenophon, *Hellenica* 2.4.1

Review Seven
Indirect Statement and Indirect Questions

When a statement is presented within a sentence as the words, thoughts, or perceptions of the subject of a verb of saying, thinking, or perceiving rather than as a direct independent sentence, the grammatical construction is called indirect statement or indirect discourse. In Greek, there are three possible ways to express indirect statement: the accusative/infinitive construction, the ὅτι/ὡς construction, and the participial construction. Which construction is used depends on the introductory verb of speaking, thinking, or perceiving. A lexicon or grammar will indicate the construction that a particular verb takes. An indirect question is a question that has been embedded into a sentence and expressed in an indirect form. It takes a construction similar to the ὅτι/ὡς construction of indirect statement.

7.1 Accusative/Infinitive Construction of
Indirect Statement

Certain verbs of saying and thinking take the accusative/infinitive construction of indirect statement. After a verb of saying or thinking, the verb of the direct statement changes to an infinitive in the same tense and voice as the original verb. For example, a present active indicative becomes a present active infinitive; an aorist passive indicative is changed to an aorist passive infinitive. An imperfect indicative is represented by a present infinitive, and a pluperfect indicative by a perfect infinitive, because there are no corresponding infinitives for these tenses.

The subject of the direct statement then becomes the subject of the infinitive. Since the accusative is generally used for the subject of an infinitive, the subject of the direct statement changes from the nominative to the accusative case. Any adjectives or participles modifying the subject also change to the accusative. If, however, the subject of the verb of saying or thinking is the same as the subject of the indirect statement, the subject of the infinitive either is omitted or, if it is included for emphasis, is also in the nominative, and any adjectives or participles modifying the subject are in the nominative as well. The other words in the direct statement, such as direct and indirect objects or prepositional phrases, remain unchanged. Note that in this particular construction of indirect statement, there is no word in the Greek for "that"; it must be supplied in translation.

In most constructions in which the infinitive is used, the tense of the infinitive generally indicates only aspect. It has no time significance. In indirect statement, however, the tense of the infinitive indicates both aspect and time relative to that of the main verb: a present infinitive indicates time contemporaneous to that of the main verb, the aorist infinitive indicates time prior to that of the main verb, and the future infinitive indicates time subsequent to that of the main verb. The perfect infinitive, like all perfect tense verb forms, indicates a permanent result and the time is simultaneous with or prior to (often immediately so) that of the main verb, depending on logic and the context of the sentence. These time relationships are true regardless of the tense of the main verb.

Direct Statement: ὁ ποιητὴς [nom.] τὸ βιβλίον γράφει [pres. act. ind.]. The poet is writing the book.
Indirect Statement: **νομίζει τὸν ποιητὴν** [acc.] τὸ βιβλίον **γράφειν** [pres. act. inf.]. He thinks that the poet is writing the book.

Direct Statement: ὁ ποιητὴς [nom.] τὸ βιβλίον γράψει [fut. act. ind.]. The poet will write the book.
Indirect Statement: **νομίζει τὸν ποιητὴν** [acc.] τὸ βιβλίον **γράψειν** [fut. act. inf.]. He thinks that the poet will write the book.

Direct Statement: ὁ ποιητὴς [nom.] τὸ βιβλίον ἔγραψεν [aor. act. ind.]. The poet wrote the book.
Indirect Statement: **νομίζει τὸν ποιητὴν** [acc.] τὸ βιβλίον **γράψαι** [aor. act. inf.]. He thinks that the poet wrote the book.

Direct Statement: ὁ ποιητὴς [nom.] τὸ βιβλίον γράφει [pres. act. ind.]. The poet is writing the book.
Indirect Statement: **ἐνόμισε τὸν ποιητὴν** [acc.] τὸ βιβλίον **γράφειν** [pres. act. inf.]. He thought that the poet was writing the book.

Direct Statement: ὁ ποιητὴς [nom.] τὸ βιβλίον γράψει [fut. act. ind.]. The poet will write the book.
Indirect Statement: **ἐνόμισε τὸν ποιητὴν** [acc.] τὸ βιβλίον **γράψειν** [fut. act. inf.]. He thought that the poet would write the book.

Direct Statement: ὁ ποιητὴς [nom.] τὸ βιβλίον ἔγραψεν [aor. act. ind.]. The poet wrote the book.

Indirect Statement: ἐνόμισε τὸν ποιητὴν [acc.] τὸ βιβλίον γράψαι [aor. act. inf.]. He thought that the poet had written the book.

Direct Statement: τὸ βιβλίον γράψει [fut. act. ind.]. He will write the book.
Indirect Statement: ἐνόμισε τὸ βιβλίον γράψειν [fut. act. inf.]. He thought that he would write the book.

Direct Statement: αὐτὸς [nom.] τὸ βιβλίον γράψει [fut. act. ind.]. He himself will write the book.
Indirect Statement: ἐνόμισε τὸ βιβλίον αὐτὸς [nom.] γράψειν [fut. act. inf.]. He thought that he himself would write the book.

The most common verbs of speaking and thinking that take the accusative/infinitive construction of indirect statement are listed below. Some of these verbs admit the other constructions of indirect statement as well. Verbs of promising, hoping, and swearing usually take the future infinitive since they inherently refer to the future (see 7.4).

Verbs of speaking: ἀμφισβητέω ("dispute"), ἀπαρνέομαι ("deny"), ὄμνυμι ("swear"), ὁμολογέω ("confess"), ὑπισχνέομαι ("promise"), φάσκω ("say," "speak"), φημί ("say," "speak").

Verbs of thinking: δοκέω ("think"), εἰκάζω ("guess"), ἐλπίζω ("hope"), ἡγέομαι ("think"), νομίζω ("think"), οἶμαι, οἴομαι ("think"), πιστεύω ("trust," "feel confident"), ὑπολαμβάνω ("suppose"), ὑποπτεύω ("suspect").

Example from Readings

φησὶ γάρ με τοὺς στρατηγοὺς ἀποκτεῖναι κατηγοροῦντα.

For he asserts that I killed the generals by accusing them.   Xenophon, *Hellenica* 2.3.35

7.2 Participial Construction of Indirect Statement

A supplementary participle may also be used with verbs of knowing and showing, as well as verbs of perception, to express indirect statement. This construction is similar to the accusative/infinitive construction, but a participle rather than an infinitive is used to represent the verb of the direct statement. When the subject of the main verb and the subject of the indirect statement are not the same, the subject of the indirect statement is in the accusative, as is the participle, which is technically modifying that subject. If the subject of the main verb and the subject of the indirect statement are the same, the participle is in the nominative case.

The participle takes the same tense and voice as the finite verb in the direct statement and must always be formed from the same stem as the original verb: a present participle replaces both a present and imperfect indicative, and a perfect participle replaces a perfect and pluperfect indicative. If an adverb is present, it will indicate whether the original verb was an imperfect or pluperfect indicative. As with the infinitive in indirect statement, the tense of the participle shows aspect as well as time relative to that of the main verb. A present participle indicates time contemporaneous to that of the main verb, an aorist participle time prior, and a future participle time subsequent. Verbs that take this construction express ideas of knowing, being ignorant of, learning, remembering, forgetting, showing, appearing, proving, acknowledging, and announcing. Verbs of perception include ideas of seeing, hearing, perceiving, and learning by inquiry, and such verbs may also take the participial construction of indirect statement when they denote intellectual rather than physical perception. Many of the verbs of knowing, showing, and perceiving also take the ὅτι/ὡς construction of indirect statement. Just as with the accusative/infinitive construction, the word "that" must be inserted in English translations.

Direct Statement: οἱ κακοὶ [nom.] φεύγουσιν [pres. act. ind.] εἰς τὴν πόλιν. The evil men are fleeing into the city.
Indirect Statement: **ἀγγέλλει** τοὺς **κακοὺς** [acc. pl. m.] **φεύγοντας** [acc. pl. m. pres. act. part.] εἰς τὴν πόλιν. He reports that the evil men are fleeing into the city.

Direct Statement: οἱ κακοὶ [nom.] ἔφυγον [aor. act. ind.] εἰς τὴν πόλιν. The evil men fled into the city.
Indirect Statement: **ἀγγέλλει τοὺς κακοὺς** [acc. pl. m.] **φυγόντας** [acc. pl. m. aor. act. part.] εἰς τὴν πόλιν. He reports that the evil men fled into the city.

Direct Statement: οἱ κακοὶ [nom.] φεύξονται [fut. mid. ind.] εἰς τὴν πόλιν. The evil men will flee into the city.
Indirect Statement: **ἀγγέλλει τοὺς κακοὺς** [acc. pl. m.] **φευξομένους** [acc. pl. m. fut. mid. part.] εἰς τὴν πόλιν. He reports that the evil men will flee into the city.

Direct Statement: οἱ κακοὶ [nom.] φεύγουσιν [pres. act. ind.] εἰς τὴν πόλιν. The evil men are fleeing into the city.
Indirect Statement: **ἔμαθε τοὺς κακοὺς** [acc. pl. m.] **φεύγοντας** [acc. pl. m. pres. act. part.) εἰς τὴν πόλιν. He learned that the evil men were fleeing into the city.

Direct Statement: οἱ κακοὶ [nom.] ἔφυγον [aor. act. ind.] εἰς τὴν πόλιν. The evil men fled into the city.
Indirect Statement: **ἔμαθε τοὺς κακοὺς** [acc. pl. m.] **φυγόντας** [acc. pl. m. aor. act. part.] εἰς τὴν πόλιν. He learned that the evil men had fled into the city.

Direct Statement: οἱ κακοὶ [nom.] φεύξονται [fut. mid. ind.] εἰς τὴν πόλιν. The evil men will flee into the city.
Indirect Statement: **ἔμαθε τοὺς κακοὺς** [acc. pl. m.] **φευξομένους** [acc. pl. m. fut. mid. part.] εἰς τὴν πόλιν. He learned that the evil men would flee into the city.

Direct Statement: τότε φεύξομαι εἰς τὴν πόλιν. I will flee into the city at that time.
Indirect Statement: **οἶδα** τότε **φευξόμενος** [nom. sing. m. fut. mid. part.] εἰς τὴν πόλιν. I know that I will flee into the city at that time.

Compare the following examples with ἀκούω, a verb of sense perception:

ἀκούω τοῦ διδασκάλου λέγοντος. I hear the teacher talking. (Physical perception; ἀκούω + gen. of person.)

ἀκούω τὸν διδάσκαλον ἀεὶ **λέγοντα** περὶ τοῦ πολέμου. I hear that the teacher is always talking about the war. (Intellectual perception; ἀκούω + acc. and supplementary participle.)

The most common verbs that take the participial construction of indirect statement are listed below. Some of these verbs may take other constructions as well.

Verbs of knowing and showing: ἀγγέλλω ("announce"), ἀγνοέω ("not know"), ἀποφαίνω ("show"), γιγνώσκω ("learn," "know"), δείκνυμι ("show"), δηλόω ("make clear," "declare"), ἐλέγχω ("prove"), ἐπιλανθάνομαι ("forget"), ἐπίσταμαι ("know"), οἶδα ("know"), φαίνω ("reveal").

Verbs of perception: αἰσθάνομαι ("perceive"), ἀκούω ("hear"), ὁράω ("see"), πυνθάνομαι ("learn by inquiry").

Example from Readings

οὔπω γὰρ **ᾔδει** ὑπὸ τῆς μητρυιᾶς τῆς ἐμῆς **ἐξαπατωμένη,** πρὶν ἐν τῷ κακῷ ἤδη ἦν·

For she did not yet know that she was being thoroughly deceived by my stepmother until she was already <caught up> in the evil <act>.   Antiphon 1.19

7.3 ὅτι/ὡς Construction of Indirect Statement

In this construction, a verb of speaking is followed by a subordinate clause introduced by either ὅτι or ὡς ("that"). The words or thoughts being reported indirectly are contained in the subordinate clause. If the main verb is categorized as primary, the verb in the subordinate clause remains unchanged. However, if the main verb is in a secondary tense, the verb of the subordinate clause may change to the corresponding tense of the optative. Primary tenses refer to present or future time and include the present, future, and perfect tenses of the indicative. Independent uses of the subjunctive and optative, as well as the imperative, are categorized as primary tenses since they look toward the future. Secondary tenses refer to past time and include the imperfect, aorist, and pluperfect tenses of the indicative. While the original mood is sometimes retained after a secondary main verb, usually the verb of the indirect statement is in the optative.

It is rare to find an original imperfect indicative or pluperfect indicative that has changed to the optative after a secondary main verb. An imperfect indicative, since it is built on the present stem, would change to the present optative, making it difficult to determine whether that present optative was originally a present indicative, indicating time contemporaneous with that of the main verb, or an imperfect indicative, indicating time prior to that of the main verb. The original imperfect indicative is thus most often retained. The same is true of the pluperfect indicative, which, since it is formed from the perfect stem, would switch to a perfect optative that itself could be standing in for either an original perfect or pluperfect indicative. As with the imperfect indicative, the pluperfect indicative is usually retained. In addition, an original indicative plus ἄν from a contrary-to-fact condition or an original optative plus ἄν from a potential optative are similarly retained.

> *Direct Statement:* ὁ παῖς κλέπτει [pres. ind.] τὰ βιβλία. The child is stealing the books.
> *Indirect Statement:* **εἶπεν ὅτι** ὁ παῖς **κλέπτοι** [pres. opt.] τὰ βιβλία. He said that the child was stealing the books.

Since εἶπεν, an aorist, is secondary, the verb of the indirect statement changes to the corresponding tense of the optative. The present indicative changes to the present optative.

> *Direct Statement:* ὁ παῖς κλέπτει [pres. ind.] τὰ βιβλία. The child is stealing the books.
> *Indirect Statement:* **λέγει** [primary tense] **ὅτι** ὁ παῖς **κλέπτει** [pres. ind.] τὰ βιβλία. He says that the child is stealing the books.

> *Direct Statement:* ὁ παῖς κλέψει [fut. ind.] τὰ βιβλία. The child will steal the books.
> *Indirect Statement:* **λέγει** [primary tense] **ὅτι** ὁ παῖς **κλέψει** [fut. ind.] τὰ βιβλία. He says that the child will steal the books.

> *Direct Statement:* ὁ παῖς ἔκλεψε [aor. ind.] τὰ βιβλία. The child stole the books.
> *Indirect Statement:* **λέγει** [primary tense] **ὅτι** ὁ παῖς **ἔκλεψε** [aor. ind.] τὰ βιβλία. He says that the child stole the books.

> *Direct Statement:* ὁ παῖς κλέψει [fut. ind.] τὰ βιβλία. The child will steal the books.
> *Indirect Statement:* **εἶπεν** [secondary tense] **ὅτι** ὁ παῖς **κλέψοι** [fut. opt.] τὰ βιβλία. He said that the child would steal the books. (Switch to optative.)

> *Direct Statement:* ὁ παῖς ἔκλεψε [aor. ind.] τὰ βιβλία. The child stole the books.
> *Indirect Statement:* **εἶπεν** [secondary tense] **ὅτι** ὁ παῖς **κλέψειε** [aor. opt.] τὰ βιβλία. He said that the child had stolen the books. (Switch to optative.)

> *Direct Statement:* ὁ παῖς ἔκλεπτε [imperf. ind.] τὰ βιβλία. The child was stealing the books.
> *Indirect Statement:* **εἶπεν** [secondary tense] **ὅτι** ὁ παῖς **ἔκλεπτε** [imperf. ind.] τὰ βιβλία. He said that the child was stealing the books. (Imperfect indicative retained.)

> *Direct Statement:* ὁ παῖς κλέψειεν [aor. opt.] ἄν τὰ βιβλία. The child might steal the books.
> *Indirect Statement:* **εἶπεν** [secondary tense] **ὅτι** ὁ παῖς **κλέψειεν** [aor. opt.] ἄν τὰ βιβλία. He said that the child might steal the books. (Potential optative.)

Verbs that may take the ὅτι/ὡς construction of indirect statement are listed below. Compound forms of these verbs may also take this construction. Some of these verbs take other constructions of indirect statement as well.

Verbs of speaking: ἀποκρίνομαι ("answer"), εἶπον ("said"), λέγω ("say," "speak"), φράζω ("point out"), φωνέω ("speak")

Other verbs: ἀγγέλλω ("report"), γιγνώσκω ("know"), γράφω ("write"), θαυμάζω ("wonder"), οἶδα ("know")

Example from Readings

ᾔδειν γὰρ **ὅτι** ἀποθνῄσκοντος μὲν Λέοντος τοῦ Σαλαμινίου, ἀνδρὸς καὶ ὄντος καὶ δοκοῦντος ἱκανοῦ εἶναι, ἀδικοῦντος δ' οὐδὲ ἕν, οἱ ὅμοιοι τούτῳ **φοβήσοιντο**, φοβούμενοι δὲ ἐναντίοι τῇδε τῇ πολιτείᾳ **ἔσοιντο**· (Original indicative forms φοβήσονται and ἔσονται changed to optatives after secondary main verb.)

For I knew that when Leon of Salamis was being put to death, a man who both was and seemed to be capable, and <who> was committing not even one injustice, the men who were similar to him would be afraid and, since they were afraid, would be opposed to this government.   Xenophon, *Hellenica* 2.3.39

7.4 Future Infinitive with Verbs of Hoping, Threatening, and the Like

Verbs denoting ideas of hoping, threatening, promising, expecting, and swearing regularly take a future infinitive when referring to a future event. This is considered a type of indirect statement, and if the subject of the infinitive is different from that of the main verb, it will be in the accusative. If the subject of the infinitive is the same as that of the main verb, it will either be omitted or, in cases of emphasis, be in the nominative.

ἐλπίζω ὑμᾶς τὰ τέκνα εὖ **διδάξειν**.
I hope that you will teach the children well.

ἀπειλοῦσιν ἐλᾶν τοὺς ἵππους εἰς τὴν θάλατταν.
They are threatening to drive the horses into the sea.

Example from Readings

καὶ **ὀμόσαντες** ὅρκους ἦ μὴν μὴ **μνησικακήσειν**, ἔτι καὶ νῦν ὁμοῦ τε πολιτεύονται καὶ τοῖς ὅρκοις ἐμμένει ὁ δῆμος.

And after they swore oaths that they would not recall past injuries, still even now they live together as citizens and the people abide by their oaths.   Xenophon, *Hellenica* 2.4.43

It is also possible for these verbs to take an aorist or, less commonly, a present infinitive. In such instances, the infinitive is an object infinitive. That is to say, the infinitive is viewed as the object of the verb of hoping or threatening in the sense of "he is threatening [to do the action]" rather than being seen as part of an indirect statement. In both instances, however, the subject of the infinitive, if different from that of the main verb, is in the accusative. There is a nuanced difference in meaning between the two constructions insofar as they indicate a difference in the way the author views the action. However, in terms of their general sense, the constructions do not differ dramatically.

7.5 Subordinate Clauses in Indirect Statement

When a complex sentence with one or more subordinate clauses is also part of an indirect statement, the verb of the principal clause takes one of the constructions of indirect statement and thus changes to the infinitive or to a participle, or is in a finite form after ὅτι or ὡς. When the main verb of the complex sentence is in a primary tense, the verb of any subordinate clause(s) will keep its original mood and tense. However, if the main verb is in a secondary tense, the verb of the subordinate clause, if it is in the present, future, or perfect indicative or any tense of the subjunctive, may switch to the corresponding tense of the optative. Subjunctives with ἐάν or ἄν drop the ἐάν or ἄν if they change to the optative. If the verb of the subordinate clause is in the imperfect, aorist, or pluperfect indicative or any tense of the optative, it does not change. In this instance, if the verb of the original subordinate clause was accompanied by ἄν, the ἄν is retained.

Direct Statement
ἐὰν οἱ παῖδες **μανθάνωσι** τὰ γράμματα, εὐδαίμων **ἔσται** ὁ διδάσκαλος. (Future more vivid.)
If the children learn the alphabet, the teacher will be happy.

Condition Expressed Within Indirect Statement
1. ἡ μήτηρ **λέγει ὅτι ἐὰν** οἱ παῖδες **μανθάνωσι** τὰ γράμματα, εὐδαίμων **ἔσται** ὁ διδάσκαλος.
The mother says that if the children learn the alphabet, the teacher will be happy.

Because the main verb of speaking is in a primary tense, there is no change in the subordinate clause or in the main clause of the ὅτι/ὡς construction of indirect statement. The original future more vivid condition thus has the same form it had in the direct statement.

2. ἡ μήτηρ **εἶπεν ὅτι εἰ** οἱ παῖδες **μανθάνοιεν** τὰ γράμματα, εὐδαίμων **ἔσοιτο** ὁ διδάσκαλος.
The mother said that if the children learned the alphabet, the teacher would be happy.

εἶπεν, a secondary main verb of speaking, permits the verb of both the subordinate clause and the main clause of the indirect statement to switch to the corresponding tense of the optative. μανθάνωσι, which is in the present subjunctive in the protasis of the original future more vivid condition, changes to μανθάνοιεν (present optative) in the indirect statement. ἔσται, the main verb of the apodosis, changes from the future indicative to ἔσοιτο (future optative). ἐάν is replaced by εἰ, since the optative is being used instead of the original subjunctive. The original subjunctive could also be retained.

3. ἡ μήτηρ **ἔφη** εὐδαίμονα **ἔσεσθαι** τὸν διδάσκαλον **εἰ** οἱ παῖδες **μανθάνοιεν** τὰ γράμματα.
The mother said that the teacher would be happy if the children learned the alphabet.

ἔφη takes the accusative/infinitive construction of indirect statement, and thus the main verb of the indirect statement is the future infinitive (ἔσεσθαι) with its subject in the accusative (τὸν διδάσκαλον). The verb of the subordinate clause has switched to the corresponding tense of the optative (from μανθάνωσι to μανθάνοιεν) since ἔφη is in a secondary tense. As in sentence 2, ἐάν has been replaced by εἰ.

4. ἡ μήτηρ **ἤγγειλε** τὸν διδάσκαλον **ἐσόμενον** εὐδαίμονα **εἰ** οἱ παῖδες **μανθάνοιεν** τὰ γράμματα.
The mother announced that the teacher would be happy if the children learned the alphabet.

Since ἀγγέλλω may take the participial construction of indirect statement, ἔσται, the main verb from the original direct statement, has changed to ἐσόμενον, the accusative masculine singular of the future participle, with its "subject," τὸν διδάσκαλον, also in the accusative. ἤγγειλε, as a secondary verb, permits the verb of the subordinate clause to change to the corresponding tense of the optative (from μανθάνωσι to μανθάνοιεν) and ἐάν to change to εἰ.

Example from Readings

πάλιν **ἔλεγεν** ὁ Θηραμένης ὅτι **εἰ** μή τις κοινωνοὺς ἱκανοὺς **λήψοιτο** τῶν πραγμάτων, ἀδύνατον **ἔσοιτο** τὴν ὀλιγαρχίαν διαμένειν. (Future most vivid condition in indirect statement.)

Theramenes spoke again, <saying> that if they did not take on sufficient partners in the government, it would be impossible for the oligarchy to survive.

Xenophon, *Hellenica* 2.3.17

7.6 Indirect Questions

The construction used for indirect questions is similar to the ὅτι/ὡς construction of indirect statement. The main difference is that instead of ὅτι or ὡς there is an interrogative pronoun, adjective, or adverb. The verb of the main sentence may be a verb of asking as well as a verb of knowing, perceiving, learning, wondering, or the like. The critical element is the interrogative, which is the marker of an indirect question. As with indirect statement, if the main verb is primary the tense and mood of the verb in the indirect question are the same as they are in the direct question. If the main verb is secondary, the mood of the verb in the indirect question may switch to the corresponding tense of the optative. Imperfect and pluperfect indicatives are generally retained after a secondary main verb. The indirect question must be introduced by an interrogative word, which may be the same as words used to introduce direct questions (e.g., τίς, τί) or by an indirect interrogative such as ὅστις, ὅ τι, ὅπου, or ὅποτε. If the original direct question contained ἄν — in a potential optative, for example — it will be retained.

> *Direct Question:* τίς τόδε ἐποίησεν; Who did this?
> *Indirect Questions:* **ἐρωτῶ ὅστις** τόδε **ἐποίησεν**. I am asking who did this.
> **ἠρώτησεν ὅστις** τόδε **ποιήσειεν**. He asked who had done this.

> *Direct Question:* ποῖ οἱ νεανίαι ἔφυγον; Where did the young men flee?
> *Indirect Questions:* **θαυμάζομεν ὅποι** οἱ νεανίαι **ἔφυγον**. We are wondering where the young men fled.
> **ἠρωτήσαμεν ὅποι** οἱ νεανίαι **φύγοιεν**. We asked where the young men had fled.

Example from Readings

> Θηραμένης δὲ καὶ οἱ ἄλλοι πρέσβεις ἐπεὶ ἦσαν ἐν Σελλασίᾳ, **ἐρωτώμενοι** δὲ ἐπὶ **τίνι** λόγῳ **ἥκοιεν** εἶπον ὅτι αὐτοκράτορες περὶ εἰρήνης, μετὰ ταῦτα οἱ ἔφοροι καλεῖν ἐκέλευον αὐτούς.

When Theramenes and the other ambassadors were in Sellasia, being asked for what reason they had come, they said that they had full powers concerning peace; after these things the ephors gave orders to summon them.   Xenophon, *Hellenica* 2.2.19

Review Eight

Independent Uses of the Subjunctive and Optative

The subjunctive and optative are used in both independent and dependent constructions. An independent subjunctive or optative is the main verb of the sentence. There are three main constructions that use the independent subjunctive: the hortatory subjunctive, the deliberative subjunctive, and the prohibitive subjunctive. Two constructions use the optative: the optative of wish and the potential optative. Before translating a subjunctive or an optative, it is important to determine whether it has a dependent or an independent use.

8.1 Hortatory Subjunctive

The hortatory subjunctive expresses a request, proposal, or exhortation and is used in either the present or aorist tense. The tense always denotes aspect; it never indicates time since the subjunctive by its nature looks toward the future. It is always in the first person and usually plural, though it is occasionally found in the singular. It is negated by μή, the standard negative used with the subjunctive. The common translation of the plural is "let us [perform the action]," and of the singular, "let me [perform the action]."

ἀεὶ **πιστεύωμεν** τοῖς ἐν τῇ ἐκκλησίᾳ καλοῖς.
Let us always rely on the noble men in the assembly.

ὡς τάχιστα εἰς τὴν ἀγορὰν **ἔλθωμεν**.
Let us go into the marketplace as quickly as possible.

8.2 Deliberative Subjunctive

When a speaker asks himself or herself what to do or say, or what is going to happen, the subjunctive is used. This is known as the deliberative subjunctive and is often found in drama or in dialogues and speeches, particularly to express anxiety, confusion, or bewilderment. It has a notion of propriety or expediency embedded within it. The deliberative subjunctive is generally used in the first person and may be singular or plural. The third person is occasionally used to represent the first person (S1805c), as in the example from Antiphon 1, below. The present or aorist tense may be used, again expressing aspect rather than time. The deliberative subjunctive is negated by μή. You can distinguish it from the hortatory subjunctive by context and by the fact that it is a question rather than a statement.

πιστεύωμεν τοῖς ἐν τῇ ἐκκλησίᾳ ἀγαθοῖς;
Shall we rely on the noble men in the assembly?

ποῖ **ἔλθω**;
Where shall I go?

Example from Readings

πρὸς τίνας οὖν **ἔλθῃ** τις βοηθούς, ἢ ποῖ τὴν καταφυγὴν ποιήσεται ἄλλοθι ἢ πρὸς ὑμᾶς καὶ τὸ δίκαιον;

And so to what helpers shall I go or where shall I find refuge other than in you and in justice?
                                                                                    Antiphon 1.4

8.3 Prohibitive Subjunctive

The prohibitive subjunctive expresses a prohibition. It is always used with μή. This construction is found in the second and third persons, both singular and plural. The aorist tense is virtually always used and will express the simple occurrence of the action. To express a prohibition in which the action is repeated or in progress, the present imperative with μή is used.

μὴ **ποιήσητε** ἐκεῖνα τὰ κακὰ ἔργα.
Don't do those evil deeds [at this time or in this situation]. (Prohibitive subjunctive.)

μὴ **ποιεῖτε** ἐκεῖνα τὰ κακὰ ἔργα.
Don't keep doing those evil deeds. (Present imperative.)

8.4 Optative of Wish

The optative of wish is used to indicate a wish that refers to the future. The words εἰ γάρ and εἴθε are frequently used with the optative of wish and serve as clue words for this construction. They may be translated as "would that" or "if only." If the wish is negative, μή is used rather than οὐ. The tense of the optative indicates aspect.

ὁ ποιητὴς ἐν τῷ ἀγῶνι **νικῴη**.
May the poet be victorious in the contest!

εἴθε οἱ παῖδες τὰ γράμματα **μανθάνοιεν**.
If only the children would keep learning the alphabet.

Example from Readings

ὧν μὲν οὖν οὗτος ἐκεῖ ἔπραττε μηδὲν ἐνθάδε **γένοιτο**.

And so may nothing of the things that this man was doing there happen here.

Xenophon, *Hellenica* 2.3.37

8.5 Potential Optative

The potential optative indicates a probability, potentiality, likelihood, or possibility. These notions are expressed as the opinion of the speaker or writer. It is always accompanied by the particle ἄν, which serves as a marker of this independent use of the optative. The ἄν is often placed just after the verb, but it may also appear elsewhere in the sentence. It may not, however, begin a sentence or clause. The use of ἄν makes it possible to distinguish this construction from an optative of wish that does not include εἰ γάρ or εἴθε. If the potential optative is negative, οὐ rather than μή is used, another aid to distinguishing between the two constructions. The potential optative is often translated by "may," "might," "would," or "should."

ἐκεῖνος ὁ ἔνδοξος ποιητὴς ἐν τῷ ἀγῶνι **νικῴη ἄν**.
That reputable poet should be victorious in the contest.

οὗτοι οἱ παῖδες καὶ τὰ γράμματα οὐ **μανθάνοιεν ἄν**.
These children might not learn even the alphabet.

Example from Readings

ὁ ταῦτα οὖν νουθετῶν ἐν τῷ φανερῷ πότερα εὐμενὴς **ἄν** δικαίως ἢ προδότης **νομίζοιτο**;

And so would the one openly admonishing these things be rightly considered well-disposed or a traitor?
Xenophon, Hellenica 2.3.43

Review Nine

Dependent Uses of the Subjunctive and Optative

Two of the most common subordinate uses of the subjunctive and optative are in purpose and fear clauses. Whether the main verb is categorized as primary or secondary will determine which mood is used. Primary tenses look toward the present or future and include the present, future, perfect, and future perfect indicative. Any tense of the subjunctive, imperative, or optative is also classified as a primary tense when it is the main verb because these moods look toward the future by their very nature. The tense in these moods denotes aspect only, whether they are being used independently or dependently. Secondary verbs, which look back to past time, include the imperfect, aorist, and pluperfect indicative. If the verb of the main clause is primary, a subjunctive will be used in the subordinate clause. If the verb of the main clause is secondary, an optative will most often be used, though a subjunctive is sometimes found after a secondary main verb to make the communication more vivid.

9.1 Purpose Clauses

A purpose clause, also called a final clause, indicates the purpose for which the action of the main verb was done. It is introduced by the subordinating conjunctions ἵνα, ὅπως, or ὡς, or, if the clause is negative, by ἵνα μή, ὅπως μή, ὡς μή, or simply μή. These conjunctions are generally translated as "in order that" or "so that," or "in order that . . . not" or "so that . . . not." When the main verb is in a primary tense, the verb of the purpose clause will be in the subjunctive. When the main verb is in a secondary tense, the verb of the purpose clause is usually in the optative. Occasionally, the subjunctive is used in place of the optative. The Greeks considered this to be a more vivid form of presentation and sometimes used the subjunctive to increase the drama or tension of a situation. The tense of either the subjunctive or optative in a purpose clause will indicate aspect.

Main Clause	Purpose Clause
Present Indicative	Subjunctive
οἱ στρατιῶται τὰ μακρὰ τείχη **φυλάττουσιν**	**ἵνα** τὴν πόλιν **σώζωσιν**.
The soldiers are guarding the long walls	so that they may save the city.
The soldiers are guarding the long walls	in order to save the city.
The soldiers are guarding the long walls	to save the city.
Aorist Indicative	Optative
οἱ πολῖται **εἵλοντο** ἐκεῖνον τὸν ῥήτορα στρατηγὸν	**ὅπως** τοὺς πολεμίους **νικήσειαν**.
The citizens chose that speaker as general	so that they might conquer the enemy.
The citizens chose that speaker as general	in order to conquer the enemy.
The citizens chose that speaker as general	to conquer the enemy.
Present Subjunctive (Hortatory)	Subjunctive
πέμπωμεν πάντας τοὺς παῖδας εἰς τὴν σχολὴν	**ἵνα μανθάνωσι** γράφειν.
Let us send all the children to school	so that they may learn to write.
Let us send all the children to school	in order that they may learn to write.
Let us send all the children to school	to learn to write.

Example from Readings

ἔδοξε δ᾽ αὐτοῖς, **ὅπως ἔχοιεν** καὶ τοῖς φρουροῖς χρήματα διδόναι, καὶ τῶν μετοίκων ἕνα ἕκαστον λαβεῖν, καὶ αὐτοὺς μὲν ἀποκτεῖναι, τὰ δὲ χρήματα αὐτῶν ἀποσημήνασθαι.

And it seemed best to them, in order that they would be able to give money to the garrison too, that each <member of the Thirty> take one of the metics and kill him and confiscate his money.   Xenophon, *Hellenica* 2.3.21

9.2 Fear Clauses

A fear clause indicates a fear that something may or may not happen in the future. It is a type of object clause—that is, it acts as a noun clause, specifically as the direct object of the verb of fearing. Fear clauses are introduced by μή if the verb of the fear clause is positive and μὴ οὐ if it is negative. μή is usually translated as "that" or "lest," μὴ οὐ as "that . . . not" or "lest . . . not." If the main verb is primary, the verb of the fear clause will be in the subjunctive. If the main verb is secondary, the verb of the fear clause will usually be in the optative, but the subjunctive may be used to present the fear more vividly. As always, the tense of the subjunctive or optative indicates aspect. The main verb will be a verb of fearing, such as φοβέομαι or δέδοικα, or an expression of fear (φόβος ἐστί, φοβερόν ἐστι, φοβερός εἰμι, etc.).

Main Clause	Fear Clause
Present Indicative	Subjunctive
φοβοῦμαι	**μὴ** ὁ παῖς εἰς τὸ ὕδωρ **πέσῃ**.
I fear	lest the child fall into the water.
I fear	that the child may fall into the water.

Imperfect Indicative	Optative
οἱ Ἀθηναῖοι **ἐφοβοῦντο**	**μὴ** ὁ στρατηγὸς ἐν τῇ μάχῃ **οὐ νικήσειεν**.
The Athenians feared	that the general might not be victorious in the battle.

Aorist Subjunctive (Prohibitive)	Subjunctive
μὴ φοβήσησθε	**μὴ** ἐκεῖνοι οἱ κακοὶ ὑμᾶς **βλάπτωσιν**.
Don't be afraid	that those evil men may harm you.

Example from Readings

εἰσιόντας δ᾽ αὐτοὺς ὄχλος περιεχεῖτο πολύς, **φοβούμενοι μὴ** ἄπρακτοι **ἥκοιεν**.

And a large crowd poured around them as they were entering, fearing that they had arrived without success.
Xenophon, Hellenica, 2.2.21

9.3 Fear Clauses with the Indicative

A fear clause that refers to a present or past fear that is actually occurring or has occurred will take the indicative rather than the subjunctive or optative. The clause is introduced by μή or μὴ οὐ and the main verb will be a verb of fearing or an expression of fear.

Main Clause	Fear Clause
Present Indicative	Present Indicative
φοβοῦμαι	**μὴ** ὁ παῖς εἰς τὸ ὕδωρ **πίπτει**.
I fear	that the child is falling into the water.

Present Indicative	Aorist Indicative
φοβοῦμαι	**μὴ** ὁ παῖς εἰς τὸ ὕδωρ **ἔπεσεν**.
I fear	that the child fell into the water.

Review Ten

Conditions

10.1 Types of Conditions

A conditional sentence is composed of two clauses: the protasis and the apodosis. The protasis is the if-clause. It is introduced by ἐάν or εἰ and states a condition (something which may or may not happen). ἐάν is a contraction of εἰ and ἄν, and three forms of the word are found: ἐάν, the most common form in Attic prose; ἤν (εἰ + ἄν), an earlier form found in Thucydides and in tragedy; and ἄν (ἤ + ἄν; ἤ is another form of εἰ), a later form (S2283a). The apodosis is the main clause of the sentence and contains the result that will occur if the activity in the protasis takes place. In Greek, the mood of the verbs of both the protasis and the apodosis depends on the type of condition. Conditions are categorized according to time (past, present, or future), the likelihood of fulfillment, and whether the condition refers to a particular or a general situation. Grammars vary somewhat in the precise terminology used; in this text, we will use the terms most commonly found.

The types of conditions may be classified as follows:
Simple Conditions
General Conditions
Future Conditions
Contrary-to-Fact Conditions

In all conditions, the protasis is negated by μή and the apodosis by οὐ. However, if the apodosis is in a construction that requires μή as its negative (see 10.2, 10.6), it will be negated by μή.

10.2 Simple Conditions

Simple conditions refer to specific events in the present or past and do not indicate anything about the likelihood of the event's actual occurrence. These are the most straightforward of the Greek conditions and are translated literally. They are sometimes called particular conditions or simple particular conditions.

	Protasis	Apodosis
Simple Present	εἰ + pres. or perf. ind.	pres. or perf. ind.

εἰ ἡ τοῦ βασιλέως θυγάτηρ **νικᾷ** ἐν τούτῳ τῷ ἀγῶνι, αὐτὴν **τιμῶμεν**.
If the king's daughter is victorious in this contest, we honor her.

	Protasis	Apodosis
Simple Past	εἰ + any past ind.	past ind.
	(imperf., aor., pluperf.)	(imperf., aor., pluperf.)

εἰ ἡ τοῦ βασιλέως θυγάτηρ **ἐνίκησεν** ἐν τούτῳ τῷ ἀγῶνι, αὐτὴν **ἐτιμῶμεν**.
If the king's daughter was victorious in this contest, we were honoring her.

εἰ ἡ τοῦ βασιλέως θυγάτηρ ἐν τῷ ἀγῶνι **ἐνίκησεν**, αὐτὴν **ἐτιμήσαμεν**.
If the king's daughter was victorious in the contest, we honored her.

The apodosis of a simple condition generally has an indicative, but an imperative, an optative of wish, a potential optative, a prohibitive subjunctive, or another appropriate expression may be substituted. In those cases, the apodosis is negated by either μή or οὐ, depending on the construction.

εἰ ἡ τοῦ βασιλέως θυγάτηρ ἐν τούτῳ τῷ ἀγῶνι **νικᾷ**, οἱ πολῖται αὐτὴν **τιμώντων**.
If the king's daughter is victorious in this contest, let the citizens honor her.

Example from Readings

Ὦ ἄνδρες βουλευταί, **εἰ** μέν τις ὑμῶν **νομίζει** πλείους τοῦ καιροῦ ἀποθνῄσκειν, **ἐννοησάτω** ὅτι ὅπου πολιτεῖαι μεθίστανται πανταχοῦ ταῦτα γίγνεται. (Simple present condition with imperative substituted in apodosis.)

Members of the Council, if one of you thinks that more are being killed than is right, let him consider that these things happen everywhere when constitutions are being changed.

Xenophon, *Hellenica* 2.3.24

10.3 General Conditions

General conditions refer indefinitely to habitual, customary, repeated, or general events. In addition, they often state a general truth. The act or event that is presupposed may occur at some unspecified time in the present or past. The protasis of a present general condition is introduced by ἐάν, ἤν, or ἄν, the protasis of a past general condition by εἰ. The tense of the subjunctive or optative indicates aspect.

	Protasis	Apodosis
Present General	ἐάν + subjunc.	pres. ind.

ἐὰν ἡ κόρη **νικᾷ** ἐν τῷ ἀγῶνι, αὐτὴν **τιμῶμεν**.
If the girl is (ever) victorious in the contest, we honor her.

	Protasis	Apodosis
Past General	εἰ + opt.	imperf. ind.

εἰ ἡ κόρη **νικήσειεν** ἐν τῷ ἀγῶνι, αὐτὴν **ἐτιμῶμεν**.
If the girl was (ever) victorious in the contest, we were honoring her.
If the girl was (ever) victorious in the contest, we honored her.

Example from Readings

ἐὰν γὰρ **ἐλεγχθῶ** ἢ νῦν ταῦτα πράττων ἢ πρότερον πώποτε πεποιηκώς, **ὁμολογῶ** τὰ πάντων ἔσχατα παθὼν ἂν δικαίως ἀποθνήσκειν. (Present general condition with an accusative/infinitive construction of indirect statement set up by ὁμολογῶ.)

For if I am ever shown either to be doing these things now or to have ever done them previously, I agree that I would be put to death justly by suffering the most extreme penalty.

Xenophon, *Hellenica* 2.3.49

10.4 Future Conditions

Future conditions refer to events that may or may not happen in the future. There are three forms, and which form a future condition takes depends on how likely the speaker believes its fulfillment to be. Future conditions may refer to particular situations or to general ones. The three types of future conditions are future most vivid, future more vivid, and future less vivid. As in all conditions, the tense of a subjunctive or optative denotes aspect. The future most vivid condition is the least common; it is found predominantly in drama and is sometimes called the emotional future condition or minatory-monitory condition as it expresses strong emotion and often includes a threat or warning. The likelihood of fulfillment of a future more vivid condition is considered strong whereas in the future less vivid condition the proposition and its conclusion are less distinct, more hypothetical, and therefore less likely to occur. This condition is often called a should-would condition because it is best translated with those words.

	Protasis	Apodosis
Future Most Vivid	εἰ + fut. ind.	fut. ind.

εἰ ἡ κόρη μὴ **νικήσει** ἐν τῷ ἀγῶνι, παρὰ αὐτῆς δίκην **ληψόμεθα**.
If the girl is not victorious in the contest, we will punish her.

	Protasis	Apodosis
Future More Vivid	ἐάν + subjunc.	fut. ind.

ἐὰν ἡ κόρη **νικᾷ** ἐν τῷ ἀγῶνι, αὐτὴν **τιμήσομεν**.
If the girl is victorious in the contest, we will honor her.

	Protasis	Apodosis
Future Less Vivid	εἰ + opt.	opt. + ἄν

εἰ ἡ κόρη **νικῴη** ἐν τῷ ἀγῶνι, αὐτὴν **τιμῷμεν** ἄν.
If the girl should be victorious in the contest, we would honor her.

Note that in the future most vivid, the future indicative in the protasis is translated in English as a present in accordance with English idiom.

Example from Readings

πῶς **ἂν ἀφίκοιντό** ποτε ἔνθα δεῖ, **εἰ** . . . εὐθὺς εἰς τἀναντία **πλέοιεν**; (Future less vivid condition, with the apodosis framed as a direct question.)

How would they ever reach where it is necessary <to go> if they should immediately sail in the opposite direction? Xenophon, *Hellenica* 2.3.31

10.5 Contrary-to-Fact Conditions

Sometimes a condition refers to the supposition stated in the protasis in such a way that it implies that the supposition is or was not true. The apodosis then indicates what would have happened if the protasis had been true. This type of condition is usually called a contrary-to-fact condition. (In some grammar books it is called an unreal condition.) In Greek, contrary-to-fact conditions use the indicative mood in both the protasis and apodosis. In the apodosis, ἄν is included as a marker of the unreality of the situation. A present contrary-to-fact condition, which takes the imperfect indicative in both clauses, refers to either an event or a situation in present time or, occasionally, to an act in progress or repeated in past time. A past contrary-to-fact takes the aorist indicative in both clauses and refers to the simple occurrence (actually, the nonoccurrence!) of the event in the past. The following formulas are used in translation:

Present Contrary-to-Fact: were (verb) + would (verb)
Past Contrary-to-Fact: had (verb) + would have (verb)

	Protasis	Apodosis
Present Contrary-to-Fact	εἰ + imperf. ind.	imperf. ind. + ἄν

εἰ ἡ κόρη **ἐνίκα** ἐν τῷ ἀγῶνι, αὐτὴν **ἐτιμῶμεν ἄν**.
If the girl were victorious in the contest [but she isn't], we would be honoring her.

Past Contrary-to-Fact	εἰ + aor. ind.	aor. ind. + ἄν

εἰ ἡ κόρη **ἐνίκησεν** ἐν τῷ ἀγῶνι, αὐτὴν **ἐτιμήσαμεν ἄν**.
If the girl had been victorious in the contest [but she wasn't], we would have honored her.

Example from Readings

εἰ μὲν τοίνυν ἐξ ἀρχῆς ταῦτα **ἐγίγνωσκε**, πολέμιος μὲν ἦν, οὐ μέντοι πονηρός γ᾽
ἄν δικαίως **ἐνομίζετο**. (Present contrary-to-fact condition.)

If he (Theramenes) were thinking these things from the beginning, he was an
enemy, but he would not rightly be considered base.   Xenophon, *Hellenica* 2.3.27

10.6 Mixed Conditions and Substitutions

Sometimes the protasis of one type of condition is used with the apodosis of another.
This is called a mixed condition, and often the best strategy for translating such conditions
is to treat each clause as if it were part of a non-mixed form of the condition. It is especially
common to find a mixed contrary-to-fact condition in which the protasis of a past contrary-
to-fact is combined with the apodosis of a present contrary-to-fact condition.

Mixed Contrary-to-Fact: **εἰ** ἡ κόρη **ἐνίκησεν** ἐν τῷ ἀγῶνι, αὐτὴν νῦν **ἐτιμῶμεν ἄν**.
If the girl had been victorious in the contest, we would now honor her.

It is also common to find substitutions for the apodosis of certain conditions using the
indicative. As noted of simple conditions (10.2), it is possible to substitute an imperative,
an optative of wish, a potential optative, a hortatory subjunctive, a prohibitive subjunctive,
or another appropriate expression for the indicative of the apodosis. These substitutions can
also be made for the future indicative of the apodosis of a future most vivid or future more
vivid condition.

Substitution in Apodosis
ἐὰν ἡ κόρη **νικᾷ** ἐν τῷ ἀγῶνι, αὐτὴν **τιμᾶτε**.
If the girl is victorious in the contest, honor her.

ἐὰν ἡ κόρη μὴ **νικᾷ** ἐν τῷ ἀγῶνι, αὐτὴν μὴ **τιμήσατε**.
If the girl is not victorious in the contest, do not honor her.

Substitutions are also possible in the protasis. A circumstantial participle with the εἰ or ἐάν omitted may be used in place of the protasis. This is particularly common when a circumstantial participle has been negated by μή. Conditional participles are negated by μή rather than οὐ (see 6.2), and so in such an instance the conditional force of the participle is explicit. If the participle is positive, whether it should be taken conditionally is determined from context. A genitive absolute may also be used as a substitute for the protasis in a similar fashion.

Substitution in Protasis

ἡ κόρη **μὴ νικῶσα** ἐν τῷ ἀγῶνι οὐ **τιμηθήσεται**.
If the girl is not victorious in the contest, she will not be honored.

τῆς κόρης ἐν τῷ ἀγῶνι **νικώσης** ἡ μήτηρ τε καὶ ὁ πατὴρ εὐδαίμονες **ἔσονται**.
If the girl is victorious in the contest, her mother and father will be happy.

Example from Readings

μὴ γὰρ **ὁμολογούντων τῶν ἀνδραπόδων** οὗτός τ᾽ εὖ εἰδὼς **ἂν ἀπελογεῖτο** καὶ **ἀντέσπευδε** πρὸς ἐμέ. (Present contrary-to-fact condition with genitive absolute standing for protasis.)

For if the slaves did not admit <anything>, he would speak in her defense confidently and would contend against me.   Antiphon 1.7

Review Eleven
Relative and Temporal Clauses

A relative clause is a subordinate clause introduced by a relative pronoun. The relative pronoun refers to a word in another part of a sentence that is its antecedent, and the relative clause acts adjectivally by giving additional information about the antecedent. The antecedent is often found in the main clause of the sentence, but it may also be in another subordinate clause. In English, the relative pronouns are "who," "whom," "whose," "which," and "that."

A temporal clause is another kind of subordinate clause. It is introduced by a temporal conjunction such as "when," "after," or "while" and is adverbial in function.

11.1 Relative Clauses

In Greek the form of the relative pronoun is determined by two things: its antecedent and its function within the relative clause. The relative pronoun will take its gender and number from its antecedent since that is what it is referring to. The case of the relative pronoun, however, is determined by its grammatical function within the clause. If the relative pronoun is acting as the subject of the relative clause, it will be in the nominative; if it is the direct object, it will be in the accusative; if it is the object of a preposition, it will take the case required by the preposition, and so on.

The relative clause (bracketed in the following examples) is often found between the subject and verb of the main clause:

main subject	[relative clause]		main verb
ὁ διδάσκαλος	[ὃς τὰ τοῦ δεσπότου τέκνα παιδεύει]	εἰς τὴν χώραν	πέμπεται.

The relative pronoun is ὅς, which is masculine and singular. Its antecedent must also be masculine and singular, and in this sentence there is only one possibility: ὁ διδάσκαλος. ὅς is in the nominative case, which indicates that it is the subject of the relative clause. This sentence is translated, "The teacher who is educating the master's children is being sent into the countryside."

The entire main clause often precedes the relative clause:

main subject and verb	[relative clause]
ἐδίωκον τοὺς κακοὺς	[οἳ τοὺς τοῦ στρατηγοῦ ἵππους ἔβλαψαν].

οἳ is the relative pronoun and its antecedent must be masculine and plural since οἳ is masculine and plural. There are two possibilities: τοὺς κακούς, a masculine plural substantive (adjective being used as a noun), or the implied subject of the main verb ἐδίωκον, which may be either third person plural or first person singular. Word order and logic dictate that τοὺς κακούς is the more reasonable choice because a relative pronoun is usually positioned immediately after or closely after its antecedent. οἳ is in the nominative, unlike its antecedent, because it is the subject of the relative clause. The sentence makes the most logical sense translated as "They were pursuing the evil men who harmed the general's horses." It is also possible that the main verb is in the first person, and if so the sentence would be translated as "I was pursuing the evil men who harmed the general's horses." Context will help you determine whether the verb is third person plural or first person singular.

Here the relative pronoun is in an oblique case (a case other than the nominative or vocative):

main subject	[relative clause]		main verb
ὁ κριτὴς	[οὗ τέκνα τὰ βιβλία ἐν τῇ ἀγορᾷ ἔκλεψε]	κακός	ἐστιν.

The relative pronoun, οὗ, is singular and either masculine or neuter. The only possible choice for its antecedent is κριτής, the only noun in the main clause. Since it is masculine, οὗ is also masculine. It is in the genitive and therefore is functioning within the relative clause as some sort of genitive construction. Since the following word is τέκνα, it is a genitive of possession. This sentence would be translated, "The judge whose children stole the books in the marketplace is wicked." When the relative pronoun is in the genitive and is not being used as the object of a preposition, it is frequently translated as "whose."

The relative pronoun can also be the object of a preposition:

main subject	[relative clause]	main verb
ἡ χώρα	[εἰς **ἣν** τοὺς τῶν ἵππων κλέπτας διώκομεν] οὐκ εὔξενός	ἐστιν.

The relative pronoun ἥν must refer to an antecedent that is feminine and singular: χώρα. ἥν is in the accusative because it is the object of the preposition εἰς, which takes the accusative. The sentence may be translated, "The land into which we are pursuing the thieves of the horses is not hospitable."

These examples illustrate the importance of distinguishing between the main clause and the relative clause. Words that belong to the relative clause must be translated with the relative clause, and not with the main clause. Sometimes the same word is used in both the main clause and the relative clause; in those instances, the word will appear in only one of these clauses since words that are used more than once in a sentence are not usually repeated in Greek; the reader's sense of logic and context are needed to supply the missing word in the second usage. Often it is the verb that is being used in both clauses, as in this example:

main subject and verb	[relative clause]
ἀλλὰ ἐγὼ πιστεύσω τοῖς αὐτοῖς κριταῖς	[**οἷς** καὶ σύ].

Since all subordinate clauses must have their own verbs, either a form of "be" must be supplied in the relative clause, if contextually appropriate, or the verb from the main clause must be repeated in the relative clause. There is no predicate nominative or adjective in the relative clause, which makes it unlikely that the missing verb is a form of εἰμί. Therefore the same verb is probably being used in both the main clause and the relative clause. The person of the verb will not be the same since the subject of the main clause is ἐγώ while the subject of the relative clause is σύ. The sentence may be translated as "But I shall trust the same judges whom you also [trust]."

Example from Readings

ἐπεὶ δ' ἧκον, **ἐκκλησίαν** ἐποίησαν, ἐν ᾗ ἀντέλεγον Κορίνθιοι καὶ Θηβαῖοι μάλιστα, πολλοὶ δὲ καὶ ἄλλοι τῶν Ἑλλήνων, μὴ σπένδεσθαι Ἀθηναίοις, ἀλλ' ἐξαιρεῖν.

And when they (the Athenians) arrived, they (the ephors) made an assembly, in which the Corinthians and the Thebans, in particular, and many others of the Greeks spoke in opposition, <saying> not to make peace with the Athenians but to destroy <them>.

Xenophon, *Hellenica* 2.2.19

11.2 Conditional Relative Clauses

A conditional relative clause is a relative clause which has either an indefinite or an unspecified (implied) antecedent and thus is considered to have a conditional force. A conditional relative clause and its main clause take the same form as the corresponding condition. The only difference is that the protasis of the condition is replaced by a conditional relative clause introduced by the indefinite relative pronoun ὅστις, ἥτις, ὅ τι ("whoever," "whatever," "whichever") or an indefinite relative adverb such as ὅπου or ὅποι ("wherever," "whithersoever"), rather than by ἐάν or εἰ. The standard relative pronoun ὅς, ἥ, ὅ is also used to introduce a conditional relative clause. The critical feature of a conditional relative clause is that the antecedent is unknown or indefinite. If the protasis would have been introduced by ἐάν, then ἄν will be used in the conditional relative clause in conjunction with the relative pronoun or adverb. The negative of a conditional relative clause is μή, as it is for a negative protasis of a condition. These clauses are also called indefinite relative clauses.

> **ὅστις** ἐν τῷ ἀγῶνι **ἐνίκησεν** ὑπὸ τῶν πολιτῶν **ἐπῃνέθη**.
> Whoever was victorious in the contest was commended by the citizens.

This sentence has an aorist indicative (ἐνίκησεν) in the conditional relative clause (ὅστις ἐν τῷ ἀγῶνι ἐνίκησεν) and an aorist indicative (ἐπῃνέθη) in the main clause (ὑπὸ τῶν πολιτῶν ἐπῃνέθη). It is thus analogous to a simple past condition, which takes a past indicative (imperfect, aorist, or pluperfect) in both the protasis and the apodosis.

> **ὅστις ἄν** ἐν τῷ ἀγῶνι **νικᾷ** ὑπὸ τῶν πολιτῶν **ἐπαινεθήσεται**.
> Whoever is victorious in the contest will be commended by the citizens.

Since ἐάν, the subordinating conjunction used to introduce the protasis of future more vivid and present general conditions, has been replaced here by ἄν and an indefinite pronoun (ὅστις), this must be a conditional relative clause. The subjunctive νικᾷ in conjunction with ἐπαινεθήσεται, the future indicative of the main clause, indicates that the construction is analogous to a future more vivid condition, which takes a subjunctive in the protasis and a future indicative (or equivalent) in the apodosis.

> **ὅστις** ἐν τῷ ἀγῶνι **νικῴη** ὑπὸ τῶν πολιτῶν **ἐπαινοῖτο** ἄν.
> Whoever should be victorious in the contest would be commended by the citizens.

Both verbs, νικῴη and ἐπαινοῖτο, are in the optative. The inclusion of ἄν with the main verb ἐπαινοῖτο makes it clear that this sentence is analogous to a future less vivid or should-would condition in which both the verb of the protasis and the verb of the apodosis are in the optative. In the apodosis of a future less vivid condition, ἄν must accompany the optative, as it does here in the main clause of this sentence.

In the examples above, there was no specified antecedent of the indefinite relative pronoun. This is a common occurrence in this construction. It is also possible for the indefinite relative pronoun to have an expressed antecedent that is indefinite because its precise nature and identity are unknown:

ὠνησόμεθα βιβλία **ἅτινα** ἂν οὗτος ὁ ποιητὴς **γράφῃ**.
We will buy whatever books this poet writes.
(Literal translation: We will buy books, whatever ones this poet writes.)

In this sentence, both the indefinite relative pronoun ἅτινα and ἂν lead the reader to expect the verb of the clause to be the subjunctive γράφῃ. The precise nature of the books—the number, the type, the subject matter, and so on—is unknown and thus indefinite. Since the main verb, ὠνησόμεθα, is in the future indicative, this sentence is similar to a future more vivid condition and is translated accordingly.

As noted earlier, the regular relative pronoun may also be used in conditional relative clauses. Compare the following version with the sentence above.

ὠνησόμεθα βιβλία **ἃ** ἂν οὗτος ὁ ποιητὴς **γράφῃ**.
We will buy whatever books this poet writes.
(Literal translation: We will buy books, whatever ones this poet writes.)

The ἂν and the subjunctive γράφῃ indicate that this clause is still a conditional relative clause and that it should be translated in precisely the same way as the clause using the indefinite relative pronoun. Contrast the sentence below, which uses the regular relative pronoun, with the previous sentence.

ὠνησόμεθα **τὰ** βιβλία **ἃ** οὗτος ὁ ποιητὴς **γράφει**.
We will buy the books that this poet is writing.

Here the indicative verb γράφει, the relative pronoun ἃ, and the definite article τά make it clear that specific books are being indicated. Consequently, this relative clause is not a conditional relative clause.

Example from Readings

ὅστις δὲ μηδετέροις **ἀρέσκει**, τοῦτον ᾧ πρὸς τῶν θεῶν τί ποτε καὶ καλέσαι **χρή**;
(Structure similar to a simple present condition.)

But whoever pleases neither of the two sides, what, in the name of the gods, is it necessary to call this man?   Xenophon, *Hellenica* 2.3.47

11.3 Attraction

When a relative pronoun changes from its proper case into the case of its antecedent, it is called attraction: the relative pronoun has been attracted into the case of its antecedent. Attraction occurs most often when the relative pronoun changes from the accusative into the genitive or dative.

> ἐκεῖνος ὁ ποιητὴς οὐκ ἔστιν ἄξιος τῆς τιμῆς **ἧς** ἡ πόλις αὐτῷ δίδωσιν.
> That poet is not worthy of the honor that the city is giving to him.

The genitive singular feminine form of the relative pronoun, ἧς, has been used instead of the expected accusative form ἥν. Since τιμῆς, the antecedent of the relative pronoun, is in the genitive case, attraction has occurred.

> ὁ ἐμὸς ἀδελφὸς ὅμοιος εἶδός ἐστιν ἐκείνῳ **ᾧ** χθὲς εἴδομεν.
> My brother is similar in appearance to that man whom we saw yesterday.

The antecedent of the relative pronoun ᾧ is ἐκείνῳ, which is in the dative case. Since the relative pronoun is acting as the direct object, it should be in the accusative. However, ᾧ has been attracted into the dative.

When the antecedent of a relative pronoun is a demonstrative pronoun, the antecedent is frequently omitted and the relative pronoun is attracted into the case of the omitted antecedent:

> ἐκεῖνος ὁ ποιητὴς οὐκ ἔστιν ἄξιος **ὧν** ἡ πόλις αὐτῷ δίδωσιν.
> That poet is not worthy of those things which the city is giving to him.

The relative pronoun ὧν has been attracted into the case of its omitted antecedent τούτων. A fuller expression of this sentence and one without attraction is:

> ἐκεῖνος ὁ ποιητὴς οὐκ ἔστιν ἄξιος **τούτων ἃ** ἡ πόλις αὐτῷ δίδωσιν.

This sentence would be translated the same way as the one above; although it is not grammatically incorrect, it would be considered less polished stylistically.

11.4 Definite and Indefinite Temporal Clauses

A temporal clause is a subordinate clause that is introduced by a specific temporal conjunction or relative adverb that has time as its focus. Words like "when," "after," "until," and "as often as" are examples of such words in English. In Greek, a temporal clause may be either definite or indefinite. If the clause refers to a definite event as a fact and that event occurred in the present or past, the verb of the temporal clause will be in the indicative mood. Following are some examples of simple temporal clauses.

ἐπεὶ οἱ στρατιῶται **ἔσωσαν** τὴν πόλιν, οἱ πολῖται εἰς τὴν ἀγορὰν ἦλθον.
After the soldiers had saved/saved the city, the citizens came into the marketplace.

ὅτε ὁ γέρων **ἀπέθνῃσκεν**, ὁ ἰατρὸς ἐπείρασε σῶσαι αὐτόν.
When the old man was dying, the physician tried to save him.

When a temporal clause refers to the future or to an indefinite time in the present, future, or past, it will take a construction analogous to one of the conditional clauses, just as conditional relative clauses do (see 11.2). If the subjunctive is used in the temporal clause, ἄν will be included with the subjunctive. Very often ἄν will be combined with the subordinating conjunction or relative adverb to produce a compound word:

ὅτε + ἄν → ὅταν
ὁπότε + ἄν → ὁπόταν
ἐπειδή + ἄν → ἐπειδάν
ἐπεί + ἄν → ἐπάν

When ἄν is not combined with the subordinating conjunction, it will follow the conjunction directly and may be separated from it only by postpositive particles and conjunctions such as μέν, δέ, γάρ, and the like.

1. Temporal clauses referring to indefinite time in the present or past or to repeated or customary action in the present or past will take a construction analogous to a present or past general condition.
   ὅταν ἐκεῖνος ὁ καλὸς γέρων **ἔλθῃ** εἰς τὴν ἀγοράν, αὐτὸν **ἐπαινοῦμεν**.
   Whenever that noble old man comes into the marketplace, we commend him.

   ὅτε ἐκεῖνος ὁ καλὸς γέρων **ἔλθοι** εἰς τὴν ἀγοράν, αὐτὸν **ἐπῃνοῦμεν**.
   Whenever that noble old man came into the marketplace, we commended him.

2. Since the future is inherently unknown, temporal clauses referring to the future are indefinite by nature. These clauses take constructions analogous to the future conditions, especially future more vivid and future less vivid.
   ὅταν ἐκεῖνος ὁ καλὸς γέρων **ἔλθῃ** εἰς τὴν ἀγοράν, αὐτὸν **ἐπαινέσομεν**.
   Whenever that noble old man comes into the marketplace, we will commend him.

   ὅτε ἐκεῖνος ὁ καλὸς γέρων **ἔλθοι** εἰς τὴν ἀγοράν, αὐτὸν **ἐπαινοῖμεν ἄν**.
   Whenever that noble old man should come into the marketplace, we would commend him.

Example from Readings

Definite Temporal Clause
   ἐπεὶ δ᾽ **ἀπήγγειλαν** οἱ πρέσβεις ταῦτα τοῖς Ἀθηναίοις, **ἔπεμψαν** αὐτοὺς εἰς Λακεδαίμονα.

But when the ambassadors announced these things to the Athenians, they sent them to Sparta. *Xenophon, Hellenica* 2.2.12

Indefinite Temporal Clause

ἐπειδὰν μέντοι τοῦτο **γένηται**, **ἡγησόμεθα** μέν, ἔφη, ἡμεῖς, νίκη δ᾽ ὑμῖν **ἔσται** ἑπομένοις, ἐμοὶ μέντοι θάνατος. (Indefinite temporal clause with a construction similar to a future more vivid condition.)

"However, whenever this happens, we shall lead," he said, "and victory will be yours if you follow, yet for me there will be death." *Xenophon, Hellenica* 2.4.18

11.5 Temporal Clauses with πρίν, μέχρι, and ἕως

Three temporal conjunctions that specify time, πρίν, μέχρι, and ἕως, take particular constructions. πρίν may mean "before" or "until," depending on whether the main verb is positive or negative. If the main verb is positive, πρίν means "before" and the temporal clause takes an accusative/infinitive construction. If the subject of the main verb and the subject of the temporal clause are the same, the subject of the temporal clause is generally unexpressed; if it is used for emphasis, it will be in the nominative. The tense of the infinitive indicates aspect; the aorist infinitive appears most often. If the main verb has been negated, πρίν is translated as "until" and the verb of the temporal clause is in the indicative if definite time is being indicated or in the subjunctive or optative if the time is indefinite. μέχρι and ἕως mean "while," "so long as," or "until" and take an indicative when referring to a definite past act, and the subjunctive or optative when that act either is repeated or will occur in the future.

1. Affirmative main clause + πρίν ("before") + accusative/infinitive construction:
οἱ μαθηταὶ ἐλθεῖν ἕτοιμοι **ἦσαν πρὶν** τὸν διδάσκαλον τὸ μάθημα **τελέσαι**.
The students were ready to go before the teacher finished the lesson.

ὁ γέρων **ἀπέθανε πρὶν** τὴν ἀλήθειαν τὴν περὶ τοῦ προδότου **ἀγγεῖλαι**.
The old man died before he reported the truth about the traitor.

2. Negative main clause + πρίν ("until") + past indicative (usually aorist) to indicate a definite past act:
οἱ μαθηταὶ ἐκείνῃ τῇ ἡμέρᾳ ἐλθεῖν ἕτοιμοι **οὐκ ἦσαν πρὶν** ὁ διδάσκαλος τὸ μάθημα **ἐτέλεσεν**.
On that day, the students were not ready to go until the teacher finished the lesson.

ὁ γέρων **οὐκ ἀπέθανε πρὶν** τὴν ἀλήθειαν τὴν περὶ τοῦ προδότου **ἤγγειλεν**.
The old man did not die until he reported the truth about the traitor.

3. Negative main clause + πρίν ("until") + subjunctive with ἄν to indicate a future or repeated act:
οἱ μαθηταὶ ἐλθεῖν ἕτοιμοι **οὔποτέ εἰσι πρὶν ἂν** ὁ διδάσκαλος **τελῇ** τὸ μάθημα.
The students are never ready to go until the teacher finishes the lesson.

οἱ μαθηταὶ ἐλθεῖν ἕτοιμοι **οὐκ ἔσονται πρὶν ἂν** ὁ διδάσκαλος **τελῇ** τὸ μάθημα.
The students will not be ready to go until the teacher finishes the lesson.

The subjunctive is used after a main verb in a primary tense when the main verb refers to a future act or event or to repeated action. The temporal clause takes a form analogous to the protasis of a present general or a future more vivid condition.

4. Affirmative/negative main clause + ἕως or μέχρι + indicative to indicate a definite act in the present or past:

οἱ μαθηταὶ οἴκαδε ἐλθεῖν ἕτοιμοι **οὐκ εἰσιν ἕως** ἐκεῖνος ὁ φιλόσοφος **λέγει**.
The students are not ready to go home while that philosopher is speaking.

οἱ Λακεδαιμόνιοι στρατιῶται **ἐγυμνάζοντο μέχρι** ἡ μάχη **ἦρξεν**.
The Lacedaemonian soldiers were exercising until the battle began.

οἱ κλέπται ἐν τῇ σκηνῇ **ἔμενον ἕως** ὁ διδάσκαλος **παρῆν**.
The thieves were staying in the tent so long as the teacher was present.

The temporal conjunctions ἕως and μέχρι have the meaning "while," "so long as," or "until," depending on the context.

5. Affirmative/negative main clause + ἕως or μέχρι + subjunctive + ἄν to indicate a future act or repeated action:

οἱ κλέπται ἐν τῇ σκηνῇ **μενοῦσιν ἕως ἂν** ὁ διδάσκαλος **μὴ παρῇ**.
The thieves will stay in the tent so long as the teacher is not present.

οἱ Λακεδαιμόνιοι στρατιῶται ἀεὶ **γυμνάζονται μέχρι ἂν** ἡ μάχη **ἄρξῃ**.
The Lacedaemonian soldiers always exercise until the battle begins.

οἱ μαθηταὶ οὐκ **ἀκούσονται ἕως ἂν** ἐκεῖνος ὁ αἰσχρὸς **λέγῃ**.
The students will not listen while that wretched man is speaking.

Like πρίν with the subjunctive, this construction is analogous to the protasis of a future more vivid or present general condition. If the temporal clause is negative, it is negated by μή.

Example from Readings

οἱ δὲ ἐξ ἄστεως ἱππεῖς βοηθήσαντες τῶν μὲν πολεμίων οὐδένα ἔτι εἶδον, προσμείναντες δὲ **ἕως** τοὺς νεκροὺς **ἀνείλοντο** οἱ προσήκοντες **ἀνεχώρησαν** εἰς ἄστυ.

And the cavalry from the city, when they came to help, saw no one of the enemy still <there>, and after they waited until the relatives had retrieved the corpses for burial, they returned to the city.
                                                            Xenophon, *Hellenica* 2.4.7

Review Twelve

Result Clauses and Clauses of Effort

12.1 Result Clauses

A result clause, also known as a consecutive clause, indicates the result or consequence of the activity of the main clause. A result clause is almost always introduced by ὥστε, and its verb will be either in the indicative or an infinitive, depending on the type of result clause. There are two types of result clauses. An actual result clause indicates that the result actually occurred. Its verb will be in the indicative, and if it is negative, οὐ will be used. In a natural result clause, the result is expressed as the intended, expected, or reasonable consequence of the action of the main clause. The focus is on the result as a natural consequence, not on whether it actually happened. However, while a natural result clause does not indicate whether the result *did* happen, it *may* have happened. Whether it did is implied by context.

The verb of a natural result clause will be the infinitive, and the subject of that infinitive will be in the accusative if it is not also the subject of the main verb. The tense of the infinitive will denote aspect but not time and is usually present or aorist. As with all accusative/infinitive constructions, if the subjects of the main verb and the infinitive of the result clause are the same, the subject of the result clause will be in the nominative, if emphatic, or will be omitted. The infinitive of a natural result clause is negated by μή. It is common to find in the main clause such clue words as οὕτω and οὕτως ("so," "thus"), τοιοῦτος ("such"), and τοσοῦτος ("so great"), which help set up the result clause. ὥστε should be translated as "that," "so that," or "so as," depending on the type of result clause and what will work best in English.

The difference between the two types of result clauses is nuanced and will often operate at the subtext level. There will not necessarily be any difference in translation.

> ὁ κριτὴς **οὕτω** δίκαιός ἐστιν **ὥστε** οἱ μαθηταὶ τούτῳ ἀεὶ **πιστεύουσιν**. (Actual result.)
> The judge is so just that the students always have faith in him.
> ὁ κριτὴς **οὕτω** δίκαιός ἐστιν **ὥστε τοὺς μαθητὰς** τούτῳ ἀεὶ **πιστεύειν**. (Natural result.)
> The judge is so just that the students always have faith in him.

> ἐκεῖνος ὁ ποιητὴς τοιοῦτός ἐστιν **ὥστε** βιβλία ἀεὶ **γράφει**. (Actual result.)
> That poet is of such a sort that he is always writing books.
> ἐκεῖνος ὁ ποιητὴς τοιοῦτός ἐστιν **ὥστε** βιβλία ἀεὶ **γράφειν**. (Natural result.)
> That poet is of such a sort that he is always writing books.
> That poet is of such a sort so as to be always writing books.

Example from Readings

> ᾔδεσαν γὰρ οἰκεῖον σφίσι τὸ κακὸν ἀναφανησόμενον, **ὥστε** σιωπώμενον καὶ ἀβασάνιστον αὐτὸ ἐᾶσαι **ἐβουλήθησαν**. (Actual result.)

For they knew that the evil would be shown to be residing in their own home, so they desired to allow it to be kept silent and unexamined.   Antiphon 1.13

12.2 Clauses of Effort

A clause of effort is another type of object clause. Effort clauses are introduced by ὅπως, and the verb of the effort clause will be in the future indicative regardless of whether the main verb is a secondary or primary tense. Occasionally, the future optative is found in place of the future indicative. ὅπως should be translated as either "how" or "that," depending on the sentence. Effort clauses are negated by μή. The main verb is generally a verb indicating effort, striving, or caring. The clause itself will indicate the specific goal of the effort of the main verb. It answers, in a sense, the questions "what?" or "what is receiving the effort?" and the sentence is not grammatically complete without the effort clause (hence its categorization as an object clause). Verbs of effort that are used in this construction include πράττω ("bring about," "accomplish"), μηχανάομαι ("contrive," "devise"), παρασκευάζω ("prepare"), ἐπιμελέομαι ("take care"), σκοπέω ("see to it"), ὁράω ("see to it"), and other similar verbs.

οἱ στρατιῶται πράττουσιν **ὅπως** τὴν πόλιν **σώσουσιν**.
The soldiers are bringing it about that they will save the city.

οἱ προδόται ἐμηχανῶντο **ὅπως** τὴν πόλιν **καταλύσουσιν**.
The traitors were contriving to destroy the city.

σκόπει **ὅπως** φρόνιμος καὶ σοφὸς ἀεὶ **ἔσῃ**.
See to it that you will always be prudent and wise.

Sometimes there is no main clause with a verb of effort and the effort clause is used by itself idiomatically to denote a warning or urgent exhortation. This construction may be used as an alternative to a prohibitive subjunctive, an imperative, or a hortatory subjunctive.

ὅπως μὴ κακοὶ ἐν τῇ μάχῃ **γενήσεσθε**.
Don't be cowardly in battle!
[See to it that] you are not cowardly in battle.

The line between a purpose clause and an effort clause may sometimes be a fine one, but it will be helpful to note that a purpose clause is adverbial in nature while the effort clause, as an object clause, is a noun clause. It is easier to see the difference in the Greek, however, since the two are grammatically distinct: a purpose clause takes the subjunctive or optative and an effort clause takes the future indicative. The purpose clause answers the question "why?" and the effort clause answers the question "what?"

τάδε πράττομεν ὅπως ἐλεύθεροι τῆς τυραννίδος ὦμεν. (Purpose.)
We are doing these things so that we may be free from tyranny.

πράττομεν ὅπως ἐλεύθεροι τῆς τυραννίδος ἐσόμεθα. (Effort.)
We are bringing it about that we will be free from tyranny.

Review Thirteen
Comparison with ἤ

In addition to the use of the genitive of comparison (3.2.6), the conjunction ἤ ("than") may be used with the comparative of an adjective or adverb to indicate the comparison of two things. The things being compared are usually in the same case. (They will always be in the same case when governed by the same verb.)

ἐκείνη ἡ δέσποινα σοφωτέρα **ἤ** ἥδε ἐστίν.
That mistress is wiser than this one.

When another construction in the sentence takes a genitive, ἤ is preferred over the genitive of comparison in order to avoid confusion and the use of too many genitives:

οὗτος ὁ νεανίας ἀξιώτερος τιμῆς ἤ ὁ ποιητής ἐστιν
rather than
οὗτος ὁ νεανίας ἀξιώτερος τιμῆς τοῦ ποιητοῦ ἐστιν.
This youth is more worthy of honor than the poet.

PART 3

Exercises

Exercise One

I. Form Identification

Identify the following forms. List all possibilities.

1. φρουρούς
2. ἀπέπεμπεν
3. ἔφυγον
4. εἶναι
5. προδόντες
6. ἀσφάλειαν
7. παραγγέλλων
8. ὄντας
9. ἀποχῶσαι
10. συνεμάχουν
11. ἀποθνησκόντων
12. πόλει
13. ἐπελελοίπει
14. τείχη
15. ἰέναι
16. ἔσεσθαι
17. ὕβριν
18. αἰτίᾳ
19. ἦσαν
20. συλλέγωσι

II. Dictionary Drill

List the dictionary entry and meaning of each of the following words. You may use a standard lexicon or the vocabulary list at the back of this textbook.

1. ἴδοι
2. ἐγένοντο
3. κατεστήσατο
4. ἀφικομένης
5. νυκτός
6. ἔδοξε
7. ἠπόρουν
8. παθεῖν
9. ἠδίκουν
10. ἔπεμψαν
11. πείσεσθαι
12. ἐπεσκεύαζε
13. διελέγοντο
14. καταλιπών
15. πρέσβεις
16. ἀπήγγειλαν
17. ἐπύθοντο
18. οὐδεμίαν
19. ἐποίησαν
20. πολιορκούμενοι

Athens, Acropolis, the Temple of Athena Nike. Photo: M. D. Ohman.

III. Accent Drill

Place the correct accents on the following words and justify your choices.

1. καταλιποντος
2. Ἀθηναιοι
3. ἐφυγομεν
4. των
5. ἐνδειων
6. ἁρμοστου

7. ἐπεσκευαζον
8. ποιειν
9. θαλατται
10. σιτου
11. ποιησαντες
12. πεμψεται

IV. Translation Strategy Practice

For each of the following sentences, first read the entire sentence, looking for translation clues. Then translate the sentence. Pay particular attention to the participles and determine how each participle is being used. (See R6 for a review of participles.)

1. οἱ τριάκοντα πέμψαντες εἰς Λακεδαίμονα Αἰσχίνην τε καὶ Ἀριστοτέλην ἔπεισαν Λύσανδρον φρουροὺς σφίσι δοῦναι.
2. Λύσανδρος τοὺς φρουροὺς τῶν Ἀθηναίων ἀπέπεμπεν εἰς τὰς Ἀθήνας, διδοὺς ἐκεῖσε μόνον τοῖς πλέουσιν ἀσφάλειαν, ἄλλοθι δ'οὔ.
3. οἱ τριάκοντα ἀνακομίσαντες τὰ τῶν ἔξω τοῦ καταλόγου ὅπλα συνέθηκαν ἐν τῷ ναῷ.
4. ἀποθνησκόντων ἐν τῇ πόλει λιμῷ πολλῶν οἱ Ἀθηναῖοι οὐ διελέγοντο περὶ διαλλαγῆς.
5. οἱ τριάκοντα νῦν συνελάμβανον ἐκείνους οἳ ἥκιστα παρωθούμενοι ἀνείχοντο.

V. Translation

Translate the following sentences into clear and grammatical English. Identify the form and explain the syntax of each of the boldfaced words.

1. περὶ τῆς τῶν τειχῶν καθαιρέσεως οὐδεὶς τῶν **Ἀθηναίων** ἐβούλετο συμβουλεύειν.
2. ἐπεὶ ὁ Λύσανδρος **τὰ** ἐν τῇ Λαμψάκῳ κατεστήσατο, ἔπλει ἐπὶ τὸ Βυζάντιον καὶ Καλχηδόνα.
3. εἰ Λύσανδρος **ἴδοι** τινά που ἄλλον Ἀθηναῖον, ἀπέπεμπεν εἰς τὰς Ἀθήνας.
4. οἱ τριάκοντα πολλοὺς μὲν **ἔχθρας** ἕνεκα ἀπέκτειναν, πολλοὺς δὲ χρημάτων.
5. ὅταν Λύσανδρος **ἴδῃ** τινά που ἄλλον Ἀθηναῖον, ἀποπέμψει εἰς τὰς Ἀθήνας.
6. τειχῶν κατασκαφέντων οἱ Ἀθηναῖοι ἐνόμιζον ἐκείνην τὴν **ἡμέραν** τῇ Ἑλλάδι ἄρχειν τῆς ἐλευθερίας.
7. οἱ τριάκοντα κατέστησαν τὰς ἄλλας **ἀρχὰς** ὡς ἐδόκει αὐτοῖς.
8. πάντες ᾔδεσάν τινας ἐν τῇ δημοκρατίᾳ ἀπὸ συκοφαντίας **ζῶντας**.
9. τῶν μακρῶν τειχῶν καθαιρεθέντων οἱ τριάκοντα ᾑρέθησαν ἵνα τοὺς νόμους **συγγράψειαν**.
10. ὁ Θηραμένης ἀντέκοπτε λέγων ὅτι οὐκ εἰκὸς **εἴη** θανατοῦν τοσούτους.

VI. Error Analysis

Each of the English translations of the Greek sentences contains a translation error. Detect the error (or errors), determine what is incorrect, and write a correct translation.

1. οἱ τριάκοντα ἀπέκτεινον ἐκείνους μηδὲν ἀδικοῦντας ἵνα χρήματα λαμβάνοιεν.
   The Thirty were killing those men although they are doing no wrong so that they may take their money.

2. εἰ γὰρ τοῖς Λακεδαιμονίοις οἱ Ἀθηναῖοι μήποτε φίλοι γένοιντο.
   For if the Athenians never become friends to the Lacedaemonians.

3. εἰ μὴ οὗτοι κοινωνοὺς ἱκανοὺς λαμβάνοιεν, ἀδύνατον ἂν εἴη τὴν ὀλιγαρχίαν διαμένειν.
   If these men do not take on sufficient partners, it would be impossible for the oligarchy to survive.

4. ὁ Ἆγις εἶπεν ὅτι αὐτὸς τοὺς Ἀθηναίους εἰς Λακεδαίμονα κελεύοι ἰέναι.
   Agis said that he himself would order the Athenians to go to Lacedaemon.

5. ἐὰν Λύσανδρος ἴδῃ τινά που ἄλλον Ἀθηναῖον, ἀποπέμψει εἰς τὰς Ἀθήνας.
   If Lysander should see some other Athenian somewhere, he would send him back to Athens.

Exercise Two

I. Form Identification

Identify the following forms. List all possibilities.

1. ἐνέπεσε
2. πέμπωσιν
3. ἦσαν
4. ἀνδραποδιεῖν
5. παραδόντας
6. ἐπιλελοιπέναι
7. λέγοι
8. καθελόντας
9. ἐδέθη
10. κατέπλει

11. συνεπαινεσάντων
12. ὄντων
13. πολιτεύσουσι
14. ἡρέθησαν
15. ἥκοιεν
16. ᾤοντο
17. πέμψαι
18. ἀνδραποδισθήσεσθαι
19. ὤν
20. ἀπολεῖσθαι

II. Dictionary Drill

List the dictionary entry and meaning of each of the following words. You may use a standard lexicon or the vocabulary list at the back of this textbook.

1. ἐπιτηρῶν
2. ὁμολογήσειν
3. προυκαλοῦντο
4. φυγάδα
5. ἐπανέφερον
6. ἡγῶνται
7. τινων
8. προηγόρει
9. ᾑρέθη
10. κατέστησαν

11. καθελεῖν
12. εἰργασμένην
13. ἐνεχώρει
14. ἐρωτῷτο
15. ἑλέσθαι
16. κατέσκαπτον
17. ὑπῆγον
18. συνῄδεσαν
19. ἐξεῖναι
20. συμπρᾶξαι

III. Accent Drill

Place the correct accents on the following words and justify your choices.

1. καλοις
2. ελθειν
3. θανατου
4. συνεπραξε
5. νομοι
6. συγγραψουσι

7. προθυμιων
8. της
9. εδοξε
10. πολιτευσοιντο
11. ταυτα
12. θανατοι

IV. Translation Strategy Practice

Each of the following sentences contains a genitive absolute (R6.5). Underline the noun and participle that constitute the genitive absolute. Then translate the sentence.

1. οἱ Λακεδαιμόνιοι καὶ οἱ ἄλλοι Πελοποννήσιοι ἐξῆσαν πανδημεὶ παραγγείλαντος τοῦ ἑτέρου Λακεδαιμονίων βασιλέως Παυσανίου.

2. Δωριεὺς ὁ Διαγόρου ἐκ Ῥόδου εἰς Ἑλλήσποντον εἰσέπλει ἀρχομένου χειμῶνος τέτταρσι καὶ δέκα ναυσίν.

3. οἱ τριάκοντα ᾑρέθησαν τῶν μακρῶν τειχῶν καθαιρεθέντων.

4. τειχῶν κατασκαφέντων οἱ Ἀθηναῖοι εἶπον ὅτι ἐκείνη ἡ ἡμέρα τῇ Ἑλλάδι ἄρχοι τῆς ἐλευθερίας.

5. πολλῶν ἀδίκως ἀποθνησκόντων πάντες ἐθαύμαζον τί ἔσοιτο ἡ πολιτεία.

V. Translation

Translate the following sentences into clear and grammatical English. Identify the form and explain the syntax of each of the boldfaced words.

1. οἱ τριάκοντα τοῖς καλοῖς βαρεῖς **ὄντας** ἐκείνους συλλαμβάνοντες ὑπῆγον θανάτου.

2. ὁρῶ ἔγωγε ἡμᾶς δύο τὰ ἐναντιώτατα **πράττοντας**.

3. οἱ τριάκοντα ἐξέτασιν ἐποίησαν τῶν μὲν **τρισχιλίων** ἐν τῇ ἀγορᾷ, τῶν δ' ἔξω τοῦ καταλόγου ἄλλων ἀλλαχοῦ.

4. νῦν οὖν αἰσθανόμεθα Θηραμένην **ἀπόλλυντα** ἡμᾶς τε καὶ ὑμᾶς.

5. ἐὰν **κατανοῆτε**, εὑρήσετε οὐδένα ψέγοντα μᾶλλον **Θηραμένους**.

6. ἐν δὲ ταῖς Ἀθήναις τῆς Παράλου **ἀφικομένης** ἐλέγετο ἡ συμφορὰ ὥστε ἐκείνης τῆς νυκτὸς οὐδεὶς **ἐκοιμήθη**.

7. Λύσανδρος δ' ἐκ τοῦ Ἑλλησπόντου **ναυσὶ** διακοσίαις ἀφικόμενος εἰς Λέσβον κατεσκευάζετο τάς τε ἄλλας πόλεις καὶ Μυτιλήνην.

8. Ἐτεόνικος τὰ ἐπὶ Θρᾴκης χωρία πρὸς **Λακεδαιμονίους** μετέστησεν.

9. οἱ Ἀθηναῖοι διὰ τὴν ὕβριν ἠδίκουν ἀνθρώπους **μικροπολίτας** οὐδ' ἐπὶ μιᾷ αἰτίᾳ ἑτέρᾳ ἢ ὅτι τοῖς Λακεδαιμονίοις συνεμάχουν.

10. ἐπεὶ οἱ τῶν Ἀθηναίων πρέσβεις ἧκον οἴκαδε καὶ ἀπήγγειλαν **ταῦτα** εἰς τὴν πόλιν, ἀθυμία ἐνέπεσε πᾶσιν.

VI. Error Analysis

Each of the English translations of the Greek sentences contains a translation error. Detect the error (or errors), determine what is incorrect, and write a correct translation.

1. οἱ Ἀθηναῖοι ἐφοβοῦντο μὴ Θηραμένης καὶ οἱ σὺν αὐτῷ πρέσβεις ἄπρακτοι ἥκοιεν.
   The Athenians fear that Theramenes and the ambassador with him might return without success.

2. φάσκοντες βέλτιστοι εἶναι οἱ τριάκοντα ἀδικώτερα τῶν συκοφαντῶν ἐποίουν.
   While claiming that they were the best men, the Thirty were doing more unjust things of the sycophants.

3. πάντες ἐνόμιζόν τινας ἐν τῇ δημοκρατίᾳ ἀπὸ συκοφαντίας ζῆν.
   Everyone thought some men in the democracy to live from sycophancy.

4. Κόνων ταῖς ἐννέα ναυσὶ φεύγων ἔγνω τῶν Ἀθηναίων πράγματα διεφθαρμένα.
   As he was fleeing with nine ships, Conon knew the destroyed affairs of the Athenians.

5. ἐπεὶ Θηραμένης καὶ οἱ ἄλλοι πρέσβεις ἦσαν ἐν Σελλασίᾳ, ἠρωτήθησαν ἐπὶ τίνι λόγῳ ἥκοιεν.
   When Theramenes and the other ambassadors were in Sellasia, they asked for what reason they had come.

Exercise Three

I. Form Identification

Identify the following forms. List all possibilities.

1. πεισθείς
2. ἐπαινοίη
3. ἦν
4. φυγών
5. ἔλεγε
6. ἐξέτασιν
7. παρωθουμένους
8. γενομένων
9. ἐξόν
10. εἶ
11. παραγενέσθαι
12. οὕς
13. μεθίστανται
14. πολιτῶν
15. ἄρξας
16. ἐτιμᾶτο
17. συρρυείησαν
18. περισώσασι
19. πεμφθῆναι
20. θέσθαι

II. Dictionary Drill

List the dictionary entry and meaning of each of the following words. You may use a standard lexicon or the vocabulary list at the back of this textbook.

1. ἤχθοντο
2. λήψοιτο
3. ἀπεληλύθεσαν
4. εἴων
5. συνιστάμενοι
6. γνόντες
7. ἐξορμήσας
8. ἀποκτενοῦμεν
9. ἀσφαλεῖ
10. ἀποσημήνασθαι
11. ἀντέκοπτε
12. λαβεῖν
13. μεθέξοντας
14. καταστάσει
15. γεγενήμεθα
16. βουλευτάς
17. τετράφθαι
18. παραγγείλαντες
19. ἀναστάς
20. παρείλοντο

III. Accent Drill

Place the correct accents on the following words and justify your choices.

1. δυναμεθα
2. λυμαινεται
3. γνωμη
4. χρηματων
5. πονηροις
6. δημου

7. φυγειν
8. δημον
9. ἀπεκρινατο
10. πολιτειαι
11. της
12. ἐκεινοι

IV. Translation Strategy Practice

Each of the following sentences includes an indirect statement (R7). For each sentence, determine the type of indirect statement being used. Then translate the sentence.

1. ὁ Κριτίας φησὶ τὸν Θηραμένην τοὺς στρατηγοὺς ἀποκτεῖναι κατηγοροῦντα.
2. ὁ Θηραμένης εἶπεν ὅτι οἱ τριάκοντα δύο τὰ ἐναντιώτατα πράττοιεν.
3. οἱ Ἀθηναῖοι ᾔδεσαν πολλοὺς ἐν τῇ πόλει λιμῷ ἀπολουμένους.
4. ὁ Θηραμένης ἔλεγεν ὅτι οὐκ εἰκὸς εἴη θανατοῦν τινα ὃς μὲν ἐτιμᾶτο ὑπὸ τοῦ δήμου, τοὺς δὲ καλοὺς κἀγαθοὺς μηδὲν κακὸν εἰργάζετο.
5. οἱ Ἀθηναῖοι ᾤοντο ἀνδραποδισθήσεσθαι ὑπὸ τῶν Λακεδαιμονίων.

V. Translation

Translate the following sentences into clear and grammatical English. Identify the form and explain the syntax of each of the boldfaced words.

1. τοῖς Λακεδαιμονίοις οἱ Ἀθηναῖοι οὔποτε ἂν φίλοι **γένοιντο**.
2. εἰ ἐκεῖνος ἐξ ἀρχῆς ταῦτα ἐγίγνωσκεν, οὐ μέντοι πονηρός γ᾽ ἂν δικαίως **ἐνομίζετο**.
3. ἐὰν σωφρονῆτε, τούτου τοῦ κακοῦ οὐ **φείσεσθε**.
4. Λύσανδρος εἰς τὰ ἐπὶ Θρᾴκης χωρία ἔπεμψε δέκα τριήρεις **ἔχοντα** Ἐτεόνικον.
5. ὁ Λύσανδρος δῃώσας Σαλαμῖνα ὡρμίσατο πρὸς τὸν Πειραιᾶ **ναυσὶ** πεντήκοντα καὶ ἑκατόν.
6. οἱ Ἀθηναῖοι ἔπεμψαν πρέσβεις παρ᾽ Ἆγιν, **βουλόμενοι** σύμμαχοι εἶναι τοῖς Λακεδαιμονίοις ἔχοντες τὰ τείχη καὶ τὸν Πειραιᾶ.
7. ὁ Ἆγις τοὺς **Ἀθηναίους** εἰς Λακεδαίμονα ἐκέλευεν ἰέναι.
8. οἱ Ἀθηναῖοι εἶπον ὅτι αὐτοὶ **ἀνδραποδισθήσοιντο** ὑπὸ τῶν Λακεδαιμονίων.
9. οἱ τῶν Ἀθηναίων πολλοὶ ἐν τῇ πόλει λιμῷ **ἀπόλοιντο** ἄν.
10. ἐπεὶ Ἀρχέστρατος ἔφη ἐν τῇ βουλῇ κράτιστον **εἶναι** εἰρήνην ποιεῖσθαι, ἐδέθη.

VI. Error Analysis

Each of the English translations of the Greek sentences contains a translation error. Detect the error (or errors), determine what is incorrect, and write a correct translation.

1. εἰ Λύσανδρος ἴδοι τινά που ἄλλον Ἀθηναῖον, ἀποπέμψειεν ἂν εἰς τὰς Ἀθήνας.
   If Lysander saw some other Athenian somewhere, he sent him back to Athens.

2. οὐ πολλαῖς ἡμέραις ὕστερον ἦλθεν ἐξ Ἀθηνῶν Θυμοχάρης ἔχων ναῦς ὀλίγας.
   Thymochares came from Athens in many days with a few ships.

3. τειχῶν κατασκαφέντων οἱ Ἀθηναῖοι ᾔδεσαν ἐκείνην τὴν ἡμέραν τῇ Ἑλλάδι ἄρχουσαν τῆς ἐλευθερίας.
   After the walls had been torn down, the Athenians knew that that day would be the beginning of freedom for Greece.

4. οἱ Λακεδαιμόνιοι προυκαλοῦντο τῶν μακρῶν τειχῶν δέκα σταδίους καθελεῖν.
   The Lacedaemonians will propose to tear down ten stades of the long walls.

5. τοῖς Ἀθηναίοις ἔδοξε παρασκευάζειν τὴν πόλιν ὡς εἰς πολιορκίαν.
   The Athenians prepared the city for a siege.

Exercise Four

I. Form Identification

Identify the following forms. List all possibilities.

1. γνόντες
2. αἰσθανώμεθα
3. εὑρήσετε
4. εἰδότας
5. ἐσπείσατο
6. δυνασθῇ
7. κατηγορῶν
8. φυλάξασθαι
9. σωφρωνῆτε
10. πεπραγμένα

11. ἀναμνήσω
12. εἰπών
13. ἀποδειχθῆναι
14. σωθείς
15. εἰδῆτε
16. γένοιτο
17. ἐννοήσατε
18. βουλώμεθα
19. ὑποτέμοι
20. προδίδοντα

II. Dictionary Drill

List the dictionary entry and meaning of each of the following words. You may use a standard lexicon or the vocabulary list at the back of this textbook.

1. εἰσιόντας
2. ἀνελέσθαι
3. ᾔσθετο
4. ἀφανές
5. ἀπολόμενος
6. ἀξιωθῆναι
7. δυστυχοῦντας
8. σῶσαι
9. ᾤχοντο
10. ἔφασαν

11. ἀπολωλέναι
12. φείσασθαι
13. συνόντας
14. ἐλπίδας
15. χειμῶνα
16. κατεσκεύαζε
17. μεταστῆσαι
18. συκοφάντας
19. ἠρξάμην
20. ὥπλιζε

III. Accent Drill

Place the correct accents on the following words and justify your choices.

1. παυσαι
2. ὁμολογω
3. ἐκεινοι
4. ἀρχας
5. στρατηγους
6. ὑπαγεσθαι
7. ἐγιγνωσκομεν
8. ἀπολογουμενος
9. κατανοησετε
10. τουτου
11. εἰναι
12. ἀρχης

IV. Translation Strategy Practice

Each of the following sentences expresses a condition (R10). Determine what type of condition each sentence expresses before translating it.

1. ἐὰν πολλοὶ συλλεγῶσιν εἰς τὴν πόλιν καὶ τὸν Πειραιᾶ, θᾶττον τῶν ἐπιτηδείων ἔνδεια ἔσται.
2. εἰ πολλοὶ τότε συνελέγοντο εἰς τὴν πόλιν καὶ τὸν Πειραιᾶ, θᾶττον τῶν ἐπιτηδείων ἔνδεια ἦν.
3. εἰ πολλοὶ συλλεγεῖεν εἰς τὴν πόλιν καὶ τὸν Πειραιᾶ, θᾶττον τῶν ἐπιτηδείων ἔνδεια εἴη ἄν.
4. εἰ πολλοὶ συνελέγοντο εἰς τὴν πόλιν καὶ τὸν Πειραιᾶ, θᾶττον τῶν ἐπιτηδείων ἔνδεια ἦν ἄν.
5. εἰ πολλοὶ συνελέχθησαν εἰς τὴν πόλιν καὶ τὸν Πειραιᾶ, θᾶττον τῶν ἐπιτηδείων ἔνδεια ἐγένετο ἄν.

V. Translation

Translate the following sentences into clear and grammatical English. Identify the form and explain the syntax of each of the boldfaced words.

1. εἰ σωφρονοῖτε, τούτου τοῦ κακοῦ οὐ **φείσαισθε** ἄν.
2. οἱ Ἀθηναῖοι εἶπον ὅτι **τινὲς** ἐν τῇ δημοκρατίᾳ ἀπὸ συκοφαντίας ζῷεν.
3. **εἰσιόντας** εἰς τὴν πόλιν πρέσβεις ὄχλος περιεχεῖτο πολύς.
4. ὁ Θηραμένης ἐνόμιζε τοὺς τριάκοντα δύο τὰ ἐναντιώτατα **πράττειν**, βιαίαν τε τὴν ἀρχὴν καὶ ἥττονα τῶν ἀρχομένων κατασκευαζομένους.
5. τοῖς Λακεδαιμονίοις, ὦ Ἀθηναῖοι, φίλοι **γιγνώμεθα**;
6. ἐάν τινα **αἰσθανώμεθα** ἐναντίον τῇ ὀλιγαρχίᾳ, ἐκποδὼν ποιούμεθα.
7. εἰ κατανοοῖτε, **εὕροιτε** ἄν οὐδένα ψέγοντα μᾶλλον Θηραμένους.
8. τῇ ὑστεραίᾳ ἡμέρᾳ οἱ Ἀθηναῖοι ἐκκλησίαν ἐποίησαν, ἐν ᾗ ἔδοξε τούς τε λιμένας **ἀποχῶσαι** πλὴν ἑνὸς καὶ τὰ τείχη εὐτρεπίζειν.
9. καὶ ἐγὼ καὶ σὺ πολλὰ τοῦ **ἀρέσκειν** ἕνεκα τῇ πόλει εἴπομεν καὶ ἐπράξαμεν.
10. τοῖς Λακεδαιμονίοις, ὦ Ἀθηναῖοι, φίλοι **γιγνώμεθα**.

VI. Error Analysis

Each of the English translations of the Greek sentences contains a translation error. Detect the error (or errors), determine what is incorrect, and write a correct translation.

1. ἐὰν Λύσανδρος ἴδῃ τινά που ἄλλον Ἀθηναῖον, ἀποπέμψει εἰς τὰς Ἀθήνας.

   If Lysander sees some other Athenians somewhere, he sends them back to Athens.

2. οἱ τριάκοντα ἤρξαντο βουλεύεσθαι ὅπως ἔσται αὐτοῖς τῇ πόλει χρῆσθαι.

   The Thirty began to plan how to use the city.

3. ἔξεστι ποιεῖν τοῖς τριάκοντα ὅ τι βούλωνται.

   It was possible for the Thirty to do whatever they wish.

4. ὁ Κριτίας ἐνόμιζεν εἰκὸς εἶναι θανατοῦν τοσούτους.

   Critias was thinking to be reasonable to put to death so many people.

5. ἐκεῖνοι τὸν Καλλίβιον θεραπεύουσι πάσῃ θεραπείᾳ ἵνα πάντα ἐπαινῇ.

   Those men were flattering Callibius with every flattery so that he might agree to everything.

Exercise Five

I. Form Identification

Identify the following forms. List all possibilities.

1. ἐκαθέζετο
2. ὄντος
3. ἑώρων
4. γενήσοιντο
5. λιπεῖν
6. δεξάμενοι
7. ᾔδειν
8. ἐνομίζου
9. πέσοι
10. ἀνέλαβον
11. πολιτείᾳ
12. πιστεύσειαν
13. καλέσαι
14. εἶναι
15. ἀποδόμενοι
16. μετέχοιεν
17. ὤν
18. ἐπισκέψασθε
19. ἀνίεσαν
20. γεγένησαι

II. Dictionary Drill

List the dictionary entry and meaning of each of the following words. You may use a standard lexicon or the vocabulary list at the back of this textbook.

1. μνησθήσομαι
2. προσταχθέν
3. δυσμενεῖς
4. παρῃροῦντο
5. πενέστας
6. διεκώλυσα
7. καταστήσειαν
8. ἡγούμην
9. ἀφαιρούμενοι
10. ἀνεπήδησε
11. πράξαντος
12. ἠπιστάμην
13. κρατήσειν
14. χώματι
15. ἐπεχείρησα
16. πιέσαντες
17. ἐψηφίσατο
18. κτᾶσθαι
19. παθών
20. διαλεχθείς

III. Accent Drill

Place the correct accents on the following words and justify your choices.

1. προσελθων
2. νομιζω
3. καινοις
4. θανατουμεν
5. θεων
6. περι
7. εγραψαν
8. βωμου
9. εξηλθε
10. ἀνησομεν
11. τοις
12. οὑτοι

IV. Translation Strategy Practice

Each of the following sentences contains a purpose or fear clause (R9.1, 9.2). Before translating each sentence, underline the main verb, the subordinating conjunction that introduces the fear or purpose clause, and the subjunctive or optative in this clause. Remember that a primary main verb will be followed by a subjunctive in the subordinate clause, while an optative is usually found in the subordinate clause when the main verb is secondary. Then translate the sentence.

1. τῶν μακρῶν τειχῶν καθαιρεθέντων οἱ τριάκοντα αἱρεθήσονται ἵνα τοὺς νόμους συγγράψωσιν.
2. οἱ Ἀθηναῖοι φοβοῦνται μὴ Θηραμένης καὶ οἱ σὺν αὐτῷ πρέσβεις ἄπρακτοι ἥκωσιν.
3. οἱ τριάκοντα τοὺς μὲν μετοίκους ἀπέκτειναν καὶ τὰ δὲ χρήματα αὐτῶν ἀπεσημήναντο ὅπως ἔχοιεν τοῖς φρουροῖς χρήματα.
4. ἡμεῖς δὲ ἀποκτενοῦμεν ἐκείνους μηδὲν ἀδικοῦντας ἵνα χρήματα λάβωμεν;
5. ὁ Κριτίας τε καὶ οἱ ἄλλοι τριακόντα ἐφοβοῦντο μὴ συρρυείησαν πρὸς Θηραμένην οἱ πολῖται.

V. Translation

Translate the following sentences into clear and grammatical English. Identify the form and explain the syntax of each of the boldfaced words.

1. εἰ μὴ οὗτοι κοινωνοὺς ἱκανοὺς λήψονται, ἀδύνατον **ἔσται** τὴν ὀλιγαρχίαν διαμένειν.
2. τούτων **γενομένων** ἐξῆν ποιεῖν ἐκείνοις ὅ τι **βούλοιντο**.
3. μὴ **γένησθε**, ὦ Ἀθηναῖοι, φίλοι τοῖς Λακεδαιμονίοις.
4. ἐάν τινα **αἰσθανώμεθα** ἐναντίον τῇ ὀλιγαρχίᾳ, ἐκποδὼν ποιησόμεθα.
5. εἰ ἐκεῖνος ἐξ ἀρχῆς ταῦτα ἔγνω, πονηρός γ᾽ ἂν δικαίως **ἐνομίσθη**.
6. ἵνα δὲ **εἰδῆτε** ὅτι οὐ καινὰ ταῦτα οὗτος ποιεῖ, ἀναμνήσω ὑμᾶς τὰ τούτῳ πεπραγμένα.
7. εἰ οὗτος ὁ κακὸς ἀπόλοιτο, **ὑποτέμοι** ἂν τὰς ἐλπίδας τὰς πάντων τῶν προδοτῶν.
8. οἱ Ἀθηναῖοι ᾤοντο πολλοὺς ἐν τῇ πόλει λιμῷ **ἀπολεῖσθαι**.
9. εἰ οὗτος **σωθείη**, πολλὰ κακὰ πρὸς τὴν πόλιν ποιήσειεν ἄν.
10. Θηραμένης πεμφθεὶς διέτριβε παρὰ Λυσάνδρῳ τρεῖς **μῆνας**.

VI. Error Analysis

Each of the English translations of the Greek sentences contains a translation error. Detect the error (or errors), determine what is incorrect, and write a correct translation.

1. ὅταν Λύσανδρος ἴδῃ τινά που ἄλλον Ἀθηναῖον, ἀποπέμψει εἰς τὰς Ἀθήνας.
   Whenever Lysander should see some other Athenian somewhere, he would send him back to Athens.

2. ἔλεγεν ὁ Θηραμένης ὅτι εἰ μὴ κοινωνοὺς ἱκανοὺς λαμβάνοιεν τῶν πραγμάτων, ἀδύνατον ἔσοιτο τὴν ὀλιγαρχίαν διαμένειν.
   Theramenes said that if sufficient partners in the government were not taken, it would be impossible for the oligarchy to survive.

3. ἐκεῖνοι τὸν Καλλίβιον ἐθεράπευον ἵνα πάντα ἐπαινοίη.
   Those men were flattering Callibius so that all things might be approved.

4. εἰ οὗτος ἐσώθη, πολλὰ κακὰ πρὸς τὴν πόλιν ἐποίησεν ἄν.
   If that man is saved, he will commit many wrongs against the city.

5. εἰ γὰρ οἱ τῶν Ἀθηναίων πολλοὶ ἐν τῇ πόλει λιμῷ μὴ ἀπόλοιντο.
   Many of the Athenians in the city might not die from hunger.

Exercise Six

I. Form Identification

Identify the following forms. List all possibilities.

1. εἰσελθόντες
2. ἄστεως
3. κατακεκριμένον
4. ἀφίκοντο
5. κεκινδυνεύκαμεν
6. ἀπήγαγον
7. λεηλατήσοιεν
8. παραγγείλαντες
9. ἀνίσταντο
10. καθορᾶν

11. εἶεν
12. ἐβοήθουν
13. συνειλημμένων
14. παρῆσαν
15. πέσοι
16. ἐπιδεῖξαι
17. στησάμενοι
18. λαβόντες
19. ὀμόσαντες
20. ἔστω

II. Dictionary Drill

List the dictionary entry and meaning of each of the following words. You may use a standard lexicon or the vocabulary list at the back of this textbook.

1. ἀπαγαγόντες
2. ἐνέπλησαν
3. ἀποβαλόντες
4. ἀνεχώρησαν
5. ἐξωπλισμένοι
6. συσκευασάμενοι
7. συνειλεγμένων
8. ἀπέθανον
9. σιωπήσειε
10. παραδόντες

11. εἷλκε
12. ὁρμηθείς
13. προσέπιπτον
14. ἔπιε
15. μεταστραφείς
16. ὑπηρέται
17. τρεψάμενοι
18. ἀπῆλθον
19. κατέβησαν
20. ἐξιόντα

III. Accent Drill

Place the correct accents on the following words and justify your choices.

1. μισθουσθαι
2. ηδικηκε
3. θεους
4. ανθρωποις
5. θυσιων
6. ελεξε

7. χιτωνας
8. θεαις
9. γενηται
10. επεισαν
11. δοκει
12. παραδιδοασιν

IV. Translation Strategy Practice

Each of the following sentences contains an indefinite relative or temporal clause (R11.1, 11.2, 11.4). Be sure to bring out this distinction in your translation.

1. ὅταν ἄνθρωποι κοινωνοὺς ἱκανοὺς μὴ λαμβάνωσιν, ἀδύνατόν ἐστι τὴν δημοκρατίαν διαμένειν.
2. Θηραμένης ἐπετήρει ὁπότε Ἀθηναῖοι ἔμελλον διὰ τὸ ἐπιλελοιπέναι τὸν σῖτον ἅπαντα ἅτινά τις λέγοι ὁμολογήσειν.
3. οἱ τριάκοντα τὸν Καλλίβιον ἐθεράπευον πάσῃ θεραπείᾳ ἵνα πάντα ἐπαινοίη ἃ πράττοιεν.
4. ὅταν Λύσανδρος ἴδῃ τινά που ἄλλον Ἀθηναῖον, ἀποπέμπει εἰς τὰς Ἀθήνας.
5. ἐπειδάν τινα αἰσθανώμεθα ἐναντίον τῇ ὀλιγαρχίᾳ, ἐκποδὼν ποιησόμεθα.

V. Translation

Translate the following sentences into clear and grammatical English. Identify the form and explain the syntax of each of the boldfaced words.

1. εἰ οἱ τριάκοντά τινα αἰσθάνοιντο ἐναντίον τῇ ὀλιγαρχίᾳ, ἐκποδὼν **ποιοῖντο** ἄν.
2. οἱ Λακεδαιμόνιοι οὐκ ἔφασαν πόλιν Ἑλληνίδα **ἀνδραποδιεῖν** μέγα ἀγαθὸν **εἰργαμένην** ἐν τοῖς μεγίστοις κινδύνοις γενομένοις τῇ Ἑλλάδι.
3. ὁ Κριτίας προπετὴς ἦν ἐπὶ τὸ πολλοὺς **ἀποκτείνειν** ἅτε φυγὼν ὑπὸ τοῦ δήμου.
4. ὁ Κριτίας ἀντέλεγεν ὅτι οὐκ ἐγχωροίη τοῖς πλεονεκτεῖν βουλομένοις μὴ οὐκ ἐκποδὼν ποιεῖσθαι τοὺς ἱκανωτάτους **διακωλύειν**.
5. εἰ μὴ οἱ τριάκοντα κοινωνοὺς ἱκανοὺς λαμβάνοιεν τῶν πραγμάτων, ἀδύνατον **εἴη** ἂν τὴν ὀλιγαρχίαν διαμένειν.
6. εἰ ἐσωφρονήσατε, τούτου τοῦ κακοῦ οὐκ **ἐφείσασθε** ἄν.
7. ὁ Κριτίας καὶ ὁ Θηραμένης πολλὰ τοῦ **ἀρέσκειν** ἕνεκα τῇ πόλει καὶ εἶπον καὶ ἔπραξαν.
8. οἱ τριάκοντα ἐκέλευον τὸν Θηραμένην λαβεῖν **ὅντινα** τῶν μετοίκων βούλοιτο.
9. ἐξῆν ποιεῖν τοῖς τριάκοντα ὅ τι **βούλοιντο**.
10. οἱ συκοφάνται ἐκείνους παρ' ὧν χρήματα **λαμβάνοιεν** ζῆν εἴων.

VI. Error Analysis

Each of the English translations of the Greek sentences contains a translation error. Detect the error (or errors), determine what is incorrect, and write a correct translation.

1. ἐὰν οὗτος σωθῇ, πολλὰ κακὰ πρὸς τὴν πόλιν ποιήσει.
   If this man saves, he will do many evil things against the city.

2. εἰ Λύσανδρος εἶδε τινά που ἄλλον Ἀθηναῖον, ἀπέπεμψεν ἂν εἰς τὰς Ἀθήνας.
   If Lysander saw some other Athenian somewhere, he sent him back to Athens.

3. οἱ Ἀθηναῖοι εἶπον ὅτι πολλοὶ ἐν τῇ πόλει λιμῷ ἀποθανοῖντο.
   The Athenians said that many people in the city had died of hunger.

4. ἐκεῖνοι ἀνακομίσαντες τὰ ὅπλα τῶν πάντων πλὴν τῶν τρισχιλίων εἰς τὴν ἀκρόπολιν συνέθηκαν ἐν τῷ ναῷ.
   Those men, after they carried the weapons of everyone except the three thousand into the Acropolis, were deposited in the temple.

5. οἱ τριάκοντα διέβαλλον τὸν Θηραμένην ὡς λυμαινόμενον τὴν πολιτείαν.
   The Thirty were slandering Theramenes on the grounds that he had ruined the government.

Exercise Seven

I. Form Identification

Identify the following forms. List all possibilities.

1. πράγματος
2. φονεῦσι
3. γενέσθαι
4. προθυμηθῆναι
5. ἦν
6. ὁμολογούντων
7. πατρός
8. ἥντινα
9. καταψηφίσεως
10. ἠνάγκασαν
11. φονέα
12. ἀποκτεινάσης
13. ἐχρῆν
14. εἰδέναι
15. ἐπισκήψαντος
16. εἰδώς
17. ποιήσασθαι
18. γεγένηται
19. μητέρα
20. οὖσαν

II. Dictionary Drill

List the dictionary entry and meaning of each of the following words. You may use a standard lexicon or the vocabulary list at the back of this textbook.

1. ἐπεξελθεῖν
2. καταστῆναι
3. καθεστᾶσιν
4. ληφθεῖσαν
5. τεθνεῶτι
6. πυθέσθαι
7. προδοῦναι
8. ἠθέλησαν
9. πεπραγμένων
10. ἀπήλλακτο
11. ἐπιδείξω
12. ἐπεξιόντι
13. ἀφεῖναι
14. ἀποθανόντος
15. τιμωρῆσαι
16. προύθυμήθη
17. καθέστηκε
18. ἀπολελειμμένῳ
19. ἔλθῃ
20. ἐγχωρεῖ

III. Accent Drill

Place the correct accents on the following words and justify your choices.

1. βοηθησαι
2. ἀδελφου
3. γνωμων
4. νομιζει
5. ἐκεινοις
6. διαφορα

7. ἀπεκτεινε
8. βουλης
9. ἀδελφους
10. μητρι
11. τουτο
12. ἡγουμαι

IV. Translation Strategy Practice

Each of the following sentences contains a relative clause (R11.1). Determine the antecedent of the relative pronoun and the function of the relative pronoun within its clause, then translate the sentence.

1. ἦν τῷ Φιλόνεῳ παλλακὴ ἣν ἐπὶ πορνεῖον ἔμελλε καταστῆσαι.
2. ὑπερῷόν τι ἦν τῆς ἡμετέρας οἰκίας ὃ εἶχε ὁ Φιλόνεως ὁπότ᾽ ἐν ἄστει διατρίβοι.
3. ὁ Φιλόνεως τε καὶ ὁ πατὴρ ὁ ἐμὸς ηὔχοντο ταῦτα ἃ οὐκ ἔμελλε τελεῖσθαι.
4. ὁ πατὴρ ὁ ἡμέτερος εἰς νόσον ἐνέπεσεν ἐξ ἧς ἀπώλετο εἰκοσταῖος.
5. ὁ ἐμὸς ἀδελφὸς περὶ τοῦ τεθνεῶτος οὐδὲν ὑμᾶς αἰτήσεται, ὃς ἄξιός ἐστι καὶ ἐλέου καὶ βοηθείας παρ᾽ ὑμῶν τυχεῖν.

V. Translation

Translate the following sentences into clear and grammatical English. Identify the form and explain the syntax of each of the boldfaced words.

1. ὁ Φιλόνεως ἦν ἀνὴρ καλός τε κἀγαθὸς καὶ **φίλος** τῷ ἡμετέρῳ πατρί.
2. ἡ μήτηρ τοῦ ἀδελφοῦ ἐποιήσατο τὴν τοῦ Φιλόνεω παλλακὴν **φίλην**.
3. ἔγωγε τῷ **τεθνεῶτι** ὑμᾶς κελεύω τὸν ἀΐδιον **χρόνον** τιμωροὺς γενέσθαι.
4. ἐκεῖνος ὁ κακὸς ὑπὲρ τῆς **ἀποκτεινάσης** δεήσεται ἀθέμιτα καὶ ἀνόσια.
5. δικασταὶ ἐγένεσθε ὅπως **διδοῖεν** δίκην οἱ ἀδικοῦντες.
6. εἴθε ἐκείνη ἡ κακὴ τῆς δικαιοτάτης τιμωρίας **τύχοι**.
7. πειράσομαι ὡς ἐν βραχυτάτοις λόγοις ὑμῖν **διηγήσασθαι** ὅπως γεγένηται ἡ δόσις τοῦ φαρμάκου.
8. ἡ μήτηρ τοῦ ἀδελφοῦ ᾔσθετο ὅτι ἡ τοῦ Φιλόνεω παλλακὴ ἀδικεῖσθαι ἔμελλεν ὑπὸ **ἐκείνου**.
9. ἐβουλεύετο τάδε ἡ παλλακὴ ὅπως αὐτοῖς τὸ φάρμακον **δοίη**.
10. ἔδοξεν οὖν τῇ παλλακῇ βουλευομένῃ βέλτιον εἶναι μετὰ δεῖπνον δοῦναι **φάρμακον**.

VI. Error Analysis

Each of the English translations of the Greek sentences contains a translation error. Detect the error (or errors), determine what is incorrect, and write a correct translation.

1. μακρότερος ἂν εἴη λόγος περὶ τούτου τοῦ πράγματος ἐμοὶ διηγήσασθαι.
   The account about this matter is rather long for me to relate.

2. ἐπειδὴ ὁ Φιλόνεως καὶ ὁ πατὴρ ὁ ἐμὸς ἐδεδειπνήκεσαν, σπονδάς τ᾽ ἐποιοῦντο καὶ λιβανωτὸν ὑπὲρ αὐτῶν ἐπετίθεσαν.
   When Philoneus and my father dined, they were making libations and putting frankincense over them.

3. ἐὰν ἡ παλλακὴ δῷ πλέον τοῦ φαρμάκου τῷ Φιλόνεῳ, αὐτὴ μᾶλλον φιλήσεται ὑπὸ αὐτοῦ.
   If the concubine gave more of the drug to Philoneus, she herself loved him more.

4. τάχιστα ἐκείνοις ἀπηγγέλθη ὅτι ἐπεξίοιμι τοῦ πατρὸς τὸν φονέα.
   It was announced to those men very quickly that I had prosecuted the murderer of my father.

5. ἐκεῖνος ὁ κακὸς ἐνόμιζεν οἷόν τ᾽ εἶναι αὐτῇ σωθῆναι.
   That evil man thought that it is possible to save her.

Exercise Eight

I. Form Identification

Identify the following forms. List all possibilities.

1. ἀπολογήσεσθαι
2. μηχανωμένην
3. ᾠήθησαν
4. ἡγεῖτο
5. οὖσαν
6. ἐλθόντες
7. χρήσασθαι
8. ἀναφανησόμενον
9. ἐᾶσαι
10. γίγνοιντο
11. κατηγορεῖν
12. ᾔδει
13. γράψας
14. ἀπηγγέλθη
15. κυβερνήσειε
16. πυθέσθαι
17. λέγοιεν
18. καταψηφίσησθε
19. πραχθέντων
20. γενέσθω

II. Dictionary Drill

List the dictionary entry and meaning of each of the following words. You may use a standard lexicon or the vocabulary list at the back of this textbook.

1. γυναῖκα
2. ἠθέλησα
3. διδόναι
4. ἀντομωμοκώς
5. ἐδεξάμην
6. ἀφανισθῆναι
7. διηγήσασθαι
8. ζητοῦσιν
9. τεκμήρια
10. δόντες
11. βασανισθῆναι
12. φάσκουσαν
13. εἰληφότα
14. βασανιστάς
15. δοῦναι
16. ἠξίωσαν
17. ἐβουλήθησαν
18. ἐξῆρκει
19. ἔφευγον
20. αἰτεῖσθαι

III. Accent Drill

Place the correct accents on the following words and justify your choices.

1. τουτοις
2. ἐγω
3. κακῳ
4. ποιησετε
5. μετερχομαι
6. λαβειν

7. ἀναγκαζοι
8. ἐθελοντων
9. βασανῳ
10. πατρι
11. ἀληθειαν
12. ἐκελευον

IV. Translation Strategy Practice

Each of the following sentences contains the same future more vivid condition, but in four of the sentences a substitution has been made for the future indicative, which is most often found in the apodosis of this condition (R10.6). Identify the type of substitution that has been made, then translate the sentence.

1. ἐὰν ἐπιδείξω τὴν τούτων μητέρα φονέα οὖσαν τοῦ ἡμετέρου πατρός, τιμωρησόμεθα τοῖς νόμοις τοῖς ἡμετέροις καὶ ἐκείνῳ τῷ τεθνηκότι.
2. ἐὰν ἐπιδείξω τὴν τούτων μητέρα φονέα οὖσαν τοῦ ἡμετέρου πατρός, τιμωρήσασθε τοῖς νόμοις τοῖς ὑμετέροις καὶ ἐκείνῳ τῷ τεθνηκότι.
3. ἐὰν ἐπιδείξω τὴν τούτων μητέρα φονέα οὖσαν τοῦ ἡμετέρου πατρός, τιμωρησώμεθα τοῖς νόμοις τοῖς ἡμετέροις καὶ ἐκείνῳ τῷ τεθνηκότι.
4. ἐὰν ἐπιδείξω τὴν τούτων μητέρα φονέα οὖσαν τοῦ ἡμετέρου πατρός, τιμωρησαίμεθα ἂν τοῖς νόμοις τοῖς ἡμετέροις καὶ ἐκείνῳ τῷ τεθνηκότι.
5. εἰ γὰρ τιμωρησαίμεθα τοῖς νόμοις τοῖς ἡμετέροις καὶ ἐκείνῳ τῷ τεθνηκότι, ἐὰν ἐπιδείξω τὴν τούτων μητέρα φονέα οὖσαν τοῦ ἡμετέρου πατρός.

V. Translation

Translate the following sentences into clear and grammatical English. Identify the form and explain the syntax of each of the boldfaced words.

1. πῶς γὰρ ἄν τις εὖ **εἰδείη** τάδε;
2. ἡ μήτηρ αὐτοῦ **ἀπαλλαχθείη** ἂν τῆς αἰτίας.
3. εἰ ἤθελον τὰ ἀνδράποδα παραδοῦναι, αὐτὰ ἂν ταῦτα μέγιστα τεκμήρια **παρείχοντο** ὡς οὐκ ἔνοχοί εἰσι τῷ φόνῳ.
4. ἐμοῦ **θέλοντος** ἔλεγχον λαβεῖν τοῦ πράγματος αὐτοὶ οὐκ ἠθέλησαν δοῦναι.
5. ᾔδεσαν οἰκεῖον τὸ κακὸν **ἀναφανησόμενον** ὥστε σιωπώμενον καὶ ἀβασάνιστον αὐτὸ ἐᾶσαι **ἐβουλήθησαν**.
6. περὶ τῶν γενομένων πειράσομαι ὑμῖν **διηγήσασθαι** τὴν ἀλήθειαν.
7. ἡ μήτηρ τοῦ ἀδελφοῦ ᾔσθετο τὴν τοῦ Φιλόνεω παλλακὴν **ἀδικουμένην** ὑπὸ αὐτοῦ.
8. μετὰ δεῖπνον ἡ παλλακὴ ἐβούλετο αὐτοῖς τὸ φάρμακον **δοῦναι**.

9. ἡ παλλακὴ ἡ τοῦ Φιλόνεω τὴν σπονδὴν ἅμα **ἐγχέουσα** ἐκείνοις εὐχομένοις ἐνέχει τὸ φάρμακον.
10. ὁ πατὴρ ὁ ἐμὸς τὴν ἀθλίαν καὶ τελευταίαν νόσον **νοσῶν** ἀπέθανεν.

VI. Error Analysis

Each of the English translations of the Greek sentences contains a translation error. Detect the error (or errors), determine what is incorrect, and write a correct translation.

1. δίκη δὲ κυβερνήσειεν ἐκεῖνον.
   Justice should guide that man.
2. ἡ παλλακὴ ἐνόμιζεν εἰ δοίη πλέον τοῦ φαρμάκου τῷ Φιλόνεῳ, μᾶλλον φιλήσεσθαι ὑπὸ τοῦ Φιλόνεω.
   The concubine thinks that if she gives more of the drug to Philoneus, she will love him more.
3. ὑμεῖς δ᾽ οὐ τῶν ἀποκτεινάντων ἐστὲ βοηθοί, ἀλλὰ τῶν ἐκ προνοίας ἀποθνῃσκόντων.
   Don't you be helpers of the killers, but rather be helpers of those who are being deliberately killed.
4. ἐκείνη ἡ κακὴ τῆς δικαιοτάτης τιμωρίας ἂν τύχοι.
   That woman met the most just vengeance.
5. εἰ ἐθέλοιεν τὰ ἀνδράποδα παραδοῦναι, αὐτὰ ἂν ταῦτα μέγιστα τεκμήρια παρέχοιντο ὡς οὐκ ἔνοχοί εἰσι τῷ φόνῳ.
   If they wished to hand over their slaves, they offered these things themselves as the greatest proofs that they were not complicit in the murder.

Exercise Nine

I. Form Identification

Identify the following forms. List all possibilities.

1. διατρίβοι
2. αἰσθομένη
3. πείθεσθαι
4. ἤν
5. διακονῆσαι
6. εἴη
7. πειράσομαι
8. ἐδεδειπνήκεσαν
9. ὑποθήκαις
10. μεταπέμπεται

11. ἀδικοῖτο
12. ἠρώτα
13. θύων
14. ἐπετίθεσαν
15. φιλησομένη
16. δοίη
17. ἐκπίνουσι
18. ἐβουλεύετο
19. ἦν
20. ἐνέχει

II. Dictionary Drill

List the dictionary entry and meaning of each of the following words. You may use a standard lexicon or the vocabulary list at the back of this textbook.

1. πλεῖν
2. ἐτέθυτο
3. ὑπέσχετο
4. ἔλεξε
5. ἐθελήσει
6. ἀπέσπεισαν
7. παρεδόθη
8. εὐχομένοις
9. ἕξει
10. ἐνθυμηθεῖσα

11. ἔτυχε
12. δοῦναι
13. ἀπώλετο
14. ἐγχέουσα
15. ἡμετέρας
16. ᾔδει
17. θύσαντα
18. ἔμελλε
19. ἔφη
20. σκέψασθε

III. Accent Drill

Place the correct accents on the following words and justify your choices.

1. ἐθυε
2. ἀνδρι
3. παλλακη
4. ἱερα
5. διακονησασα
6. ὁδου

7. ἱκανων
8. ἀνθρωπους
9. ἠκολουθει
10. ἐμης
11. γεγενηται
12. δειπνου

IV. Translation Strategy Practice

Determine what type of condition (R10) is contained in each of the following sentences, then translate the sentence. Underline the clue words.

1. εἰ τὰ ἀνδράποδα μὴ ὡμολόγει ταῦτα, οὗτος ἂν ἀπελογεῖτο καὶ ἀντέσπευδε πρὸς ἐμέ.
2. εἰ τὰ ἀνδράποδα μὴ ὁμολογοίη ταῦτα, οὗτος ἂν ἀπολογοῖτο καὶ ἀντισπεύδοι πρὸς ἐμέ.
3. ἐὰν τὰ ἀνδράποδα μὴ ὁμολογῇ ταῦτα, οὗτος ἀπολογεῖται καὶ ἀντισπεύδει πρὸς ἐμέ.
4. ἐὰν τὰ ἀνδράποδα μὴ ὁμολογῇ ταῦτα, οὗτος ἀπολογήσεται καὶ ἀντισπεύσει πρὸς ἐμέ.
5. εἰ τὰ ἀνδράποδα μὴ ὡμολόγησε ταῦτα, οὗτος ἂν ἀπελογήσατο καὶ ἀντέσπευσε πρὸς ἐμέ.

V. Translation

Translate the following sentences into clear and grammatical English. Identify the form and explain the syntax of each of the boldfaced words.

1. ὁ ἐμὸς ἀδελφὸς εἶπεν ὅτι τὸ τὴν μητέρα μὴ προδοῦναι **εἴη** εὐσέβεια.
2. εἴθε ἡ μήτηρ αὐτοῦ μὴ **ἀπαλλαχθείη** τῆς αἰτίας.
3. ἐὰν **ἐθέλωσι** τὰ ἀνδράποδα παραδοῦναι, αὐτὰ ταῦτα μέγιστα τεκμήρια παρέχονται ὡς οὐκ ἔνοχοί εἰσι τῷ φόνῳ.
4. εἰ ἐκείνη ἡ κακὴ μὴ τύχοι αἰδοῦς ἢ ἐλέου ἢ αἰσχύνης παρ' ὑμῶν, τῆς δικαιοτάτης τιμωρίας ἂν **τύχοι**.
5. θαυμάζω ἔγωγε τῆς τόλμης τοῦ **ἀδελφοῦ**.
6. οὐ μαρτύρων ἐναντίον οἱ **ἐπιβουλεύοντες** τοὺς θανάτους τοῖς πέλας μηχανῶνται τε καὶ παρασκευάζουσιν.
7. εἰ ἐπιδείξαιμι τὴν τούτων μητέρα φονέα οὖσαν τοῦ ἡμετέρου πατρός, **τιμωρήσαισθε** ἂν τοῖς νόμοις τοῖς ὑμετέροις καὶ ἐκείνῳ τῷ τεθνηκότι.
8. οἱ δ' ἐπιβουλευόμενοι οὐδὲν ἴσασιν, πρίν γ' ἤδη **ὦσιν** ἂν ἐν αὐτῷ τῷ κακῷ.
9. ὁ ἀδελφὸς ὁ ἐμὸς δεήσεται ὑμῶν ὑπὲρ τῆς μητρὸς τῆς ἐκείνον **διαχρησαμένης** ἀβούλως τε καὶ ἀθέως ὅπως δίκην μὴ δῷ.
10. ἐκείνον αὕτη οὔτε θεοὺς οὔθ' ἥρωας οὔτε ἀνθρώπους **αἰσχυνθεῖσα** οὐδὲ δείσασ' ἀπώλεσεν.

VI. Error Analysis

Each of the English translations of the Greek sentences contains a translation error. Detect the error (or errors), determine what is incorrect, and write a correct translation.

1. εἰ γὰρ ἡ ἀλήθεια καὶ ἡ δίκη κυβερνήσειαν ἐκεῖνον.

   Truth and justice guided that man.

2. καὶ ἔγωγε ἐπεξέρχομαι αὐτῇ ὅπως τιμωρήσω τῷ τε πατρὶ τῷ ἡμετέρῳ καὶ τοῖς νόμοις τοῖς ἡμετέροις.

   And I, at any rate, prosecuted her so that I might avenge our father and our laws.

3. ἐκείνη αὐτὴ οὐκ ἠξίωσεν ἐλεῆσαι τὸν ἑαυτῆς ἄνδρα, ἀλλ᾽ ἀνοσίως καὶ αἰσχρῶς ἀπώλεσεν.

   That woman herself did not pity her own husband, but he was impiously and disgracefully destroyed.

4. εἰ ἡ παλλακὴ δοίη πλέον τοῦ φαρμάκου τῷ Φιλόνεῳ, αὐτὴ μᾶλλον φιλοῖτο ἂν ὑπὸ αὐτοῦ.

   If the concubine gave more of the drug to Philoneus, she herself was loved more by him.

5. ἐμοὶ παιδὶ ὄντι ὁ πατὴρ ταῦτα ἐδήλωσε καὶ ἐπέστειλεν.

   Being a child, I revealed and enjoined these things to my father.

Exercise Ten

I. Form Identification

Identify the following forms. List all possibilities.

1. δεήσομαι
2. ἀποκτεινάσης
3. κακοτεχνῆσαι
4. εἱστιᾶτο
5. διομόσασθαι
6. ἀποθνῄσκειν
7. αἰσχυνθεῖσα
8. διαχρησαμένης
9. γιγνώσκωσι
10. ἠδίκηκε

11. ζώσης
12. ἴσασι
13. ποιήσατε
14. πέμψασα
15. τεθνεῶτι
16. ἀπώλεσε
17. παθήμασι
18. γράμματα
19. βεβοήθηται
20. ἁμαρτάνωσι

II. Dictionary Drill

List the dictionary entry and meaning of each of the following words. You may use a standard lexicon or the vocabulary list at the back of this textbook.

1. εἱμαρμένης
2. ἐκλιπών
3. ἀπολομένη
4. ἠδίκηνται
5. δηλοῦσι
6. ἐκλήθητε
7. δούλοις
8. τυχοῦσα
9. καθέστηκε
10. ἐλεεῖν

11. ἁμαρτήμασι
12. διαγνῶναι
13. ἐπέσκηπτε
14. παριδοῦσα
15. εἰδέναι
16. πείθῃ
17. ἐλέου
18. αἰτοῦμαι
19. φθάνωσι
20. ἠξίωσε

III. Accent Drill

Place the correct accents on the following words and justify your choices.

1. ὑμεις
2. θανατου
3. ἀπεκτεινε
4. δυνωνται
5. ὀλεθροι
6. τιμωριας

7. ἐπι
8. ὀλεθρους
9. ἀνδρα
10. θαυμαζομεν
11. γιγνοιτο
12. παιδι

IV. Translation Strategy Practice

Each of the following sentences includes an indirect statement construction (R7). By noting the clue words, determine what type of construction is being used, then translate the sentence.

1. ὁ ἐμὸς ἀδελφὸς νομίζει τὸ τὴν μητέρα μὴ προδοῦναι εἶναι εὐσέβειαν.
2. ἡ μήτηρ τοῦ ἀδελφοῦ ἐνόμιζε τὴν τοῦ Φιλόνεω παλλακὴν ἀδικεῖσθαι ὑπὸ αὐτοῦ.
3. ἡ παλλακὴ οὐκ ᾔδει ὑπὸ τῆς μητρυιᾶς τῆς ἐμῆς ἐξαπατωμένη.
4. ἐκεῖνος ὁ κακὸς εὖ ᾔδει ὅτι οὐχ οἷόν τ᾽ ἦν αὐτῇ σωθῆναι.
5. ὁ ἐμὸς ἀδελφὸς εἶπεν ὅτι τὸ τὴν μητέρα μὴ προδοῦναι εἴη ἂν εὐσέβεια.

V. Translation

Translate the following sentences into clear and grammatical English. Identify the form and explain the syntax of each of the boldfaced words.

1. ἐκείνη ἡ κακὴ **αὐτὴ** τὸν ἐμὸν πατέρα ἀνελεημόνως τε καὶ ἀνοικτίστως ἀπώλεσεν.
2. ἐγὼ ἀξιῶ τὴν ἐμὴν μητρυιὰν τὴν κακὴν ἀπολέσθαι ὑφ᾽ **ὑμῶν** καὶ τοῦ δικαίου.
3. εἰ ἐπέδειξα τὴν τούτων μητέρα φονέα οὖσαν τοῦ ἡμετέρου πατρός, **ἐτιμωρήσασθε** ἂν τοῖς νόμοις τοῖς ὑμετέροις καὶ ἐκείνῳ τῷ τεθνηκότι.
4. ἔγωγε ἐπεξέρχομαι αὐτῇ ὅπως δῷ δίκην **ὧν** ἠδίκηκεν.
5. δεῖ οἰκτεῖραι μᾶλλον τὸν **τεθνεῶτα** ἢ τὴν ἀποκτείνασαν.
6. ἐὰν ἐκείνη ἡ κακὴ μὴ τύχῃ αἰδοῦς ἢ ἐλέου ἢ αἰσχύνης παρ᾽ ὑμῶν, τῆς δικαιοτάτης τιμωρίας **τεύξεται**.
7. πῶς ἐλεεῖν ἄξιον **εἴη** ἂν ἐκείνην τὴν κακὴν **ἢ** τὸν πατέρα τὸν ἐμὸν ἀπέκτεινεν;
8. ἐὰν **δύνωνται**, οἱ ἐπιβουλευόμενοι λέγουσι τοῖς φίλοις τὰ ὀνόματα ἐκείνων ὑφ᾽ ὧν ἀπόλλυνται.
9. ἐὰν **ἐθέλωσι** τὰ ἀνδράποδα παραδοῦναι, αὐτὰ ταῦτα μέγιστα τεκμήρια παρέξονται ὡς οὐκ ἔνοχοί εἰσι τῷ φόνῳ.
10. ὁ ἐμὸς ἀδελφὸς διώμοσεν αὐτὸς εὖ **εἰδέναι** τὴν μητέρα μὴ **πεποιηκυῖαν** ταῦτα.

VI. Error Analysis

Each of the English translations of the Greek sentences contains a translation error. Detect the error (or errors), determine what is incorrect, and write a correct translation.

1. ἡ παλλακὴ εἶχε τὰ ἐπίχειρα ὧν ἀξία ἦν.

   The concubine received the punishments which were worthy.

2. δίκη δὲ κυβερνήσειεν ἂν ἐκεῖνον.

   Justice guided that man.

3. ἡ μητρυιὰ ἡ ἐμὴ ἐκέλευσεν ὑπὸ τῆς παλλακῆς δόσθαι τῷ ἐμῷ πατρὶ τὸ φάρμακον.

   My stepmother ordered the concubine to give the drug to my father.

4. ἡ παλλακὴ εἶπεν ὅτι εἰ δοίη πλέον τοῦ φαρμάκου τῷ Φιλόνεῳ, μᾶλλον φιλήσοιτο ὑπὸ αὐτοῦ.

   The concubine said that if more of the drug was given to Philoneus, she would be loved more by him.

5. εἰ ὁ ἀδελφὸς ὁ ἐμὸς ὑμᾶς πείσειεν, ἡ μητρυιὰ δίκην οὐ δοίη ἄν.

   If my brother persuaded you, my stepmother was not punished.

Appendices

Contents

Appendix A: **Nouns**

First Declension

		Fem.(-**η**, -**ης**)	Fem. (-**ᾱ**, -**ᾱς**)	Fem. (-**ᾰ**, -**ης**)	Fem. (-**ᾰ**, -**ᾱς**)
Sing.	Nom.	σκηνή	χώρᾱ	δέσποινα	ἀλήθεια
	Gen.	σκηνῆς	χώρᾱς	δεσποίνης	ἀληθείᾱς
	Dat.	σκηνῇ	χώρᾳ	δεσποίνῃ	ἀληθείᾳ
	Acc.	σκηνήν	χώρᾱν	δέσποιναν	ἀλήθειαν
	Voc.	σκηνή	χώρᾱ	δέσποινα	ἀλήθεια
Pl.	Nom.	σκηναί	χῶραι	δέσποιναι	ἀλήθειαι
	Gen.	σκηνῶν	χωρῶν	δεσποινῶν	ἀληθειῶν
	Dat.	σκηναῖς	χώραις	δεσποίναις	ἀληθείαις
	Acc.	σκηνάς	χώρᾱς	δεσποίνᾱς	ἀληθείᾱς
	Voc.	σκηναί	χῶραι	δέσποιναι	ἀλήθειαι

		Masc. (-**ης**, -**ου**)	Masc. (-**ᾱς**, -**ου**)
Sing.	Nom.	μαθητής	νεανίᾱς
	Gen.	μαθητοῦ	νεανίου
	Dat.	μαθητῇ	νεανίᾳ
	Acc.	μαθητήν	νεανίᾱν
	Voc.	μαθητά	νεανίᾱ
Pl.	Nom.	μαθηταί	νεανίαι
	Gen.	μαθητῶν	νεανιῶν
	Dat.	μαθηταῖς	νεανίαις
	Acc.	μαθητάς	νεανίᾱς
	Voc.	μαθηταί	νεανίαι

Cape Sounion, the Temple of Poseidon. Photo: M. D. Ohman.

Second Declension

		Masc.	Masc.	Fem.	Neut.
Sing.	Nom.	διδάσκαλος	θησαυρός	νῆσος	δῶρον
	Gen.	διδασκάλου	θησαυροῦ	νήσου	δώρου
	Dat.	διδασκάλῳ	θησαυρῷ	νήσῳ	δώρῳ
	Acc.	διδάσκαλον	θησαυρόν	νῆσον	δῶρον
	Voc.	διδάσκαλε	θησαυρέ	νῆσε	δῶρον
Pl.	Nom.	διδάσκαλοι	θησαυροί	νῆσοι	δῶρα
	Gen.	διδασκάλων	θησαυρῶν	νήσων	δώρων
	Dat.	διδασκάλοις	θησαυροῖς	νήσοις	δώροις
	Acc.	διδασκάλους	θησαυρούς	νήσους	δῶρα
	Voc.	διδάσκαλοι	θησαυροί	νῆσοι	δῶρα

Third Declension

Stems Ending in a Consonant

		Masc.	Masc.	Masc.	Masc.
Sing.	Nom.	ῥήτωρ	δαίμων	γέρων	κλώψ
	Gen.	ῥήτορος	δαίμονος	γέροντος	κλωπός
	Dat.	ῥήτορι	δαίμονι	γέροντι	κλωπί
	Acc.	ῥήτορα	δαίμονα	γέροντα	κλῶπα
	Voc.	ῥῆτορ	δαῖμον	γέρον	κλώψ
Pl.	Nom.	ῥήτορες	δαίμονες	γέροντες	κλῶπες
	Gen.	ῥητόρων	δαιμόνων	γερόντων	κλωπῶν
	Dat.	ῥήτορσι(ν)	δαίμοσι(ν)	γέρουσι(ν)	κλωψί(ν)
	Acc.	ῥήτορας	δαίμονας	γέροντας	κλῶπας
	Voc.	ῥήτορες	δαίμονες	γέροντες	κλῶπες

		Masc.	Fem.	Fem.	Neut.
Sing.	Nom.	φύλαξ	ἀσπίς	χάρις	ὄνομα
	Gen.	φύλακος	ἀσπίδος	χάριτος	ὀνόματος
	Dat.	φύλακι	ἀσπίδι	χάριτι	ὀνόματι
	Acc.	φύλακα	ἀσπίδα	χάριν	ὄνομα
	Voc.	φύλαξ	ἀσπί	χάρι	ὄνομα
Pl.	Nom.	φύλακες	ἀσπίδες	χάριτες	ὀνόματα
	Gen.	φυλάκων	ἀσπίδων	χαρίτων	ὀνομάτων
	Dat.	φύλαξι(ν)	ἀσπίσι(ν)	χάρισι(ν)	ὀνόμασι(ν)
	Acc.	φύλακας	ἀσπίδας	χάριτας	ὀνόματα
	Voc.	φύλακες	ἀσπίδες	χάριτες	ὀνόματα

Stems Ending in a Sigma

		Fem.	Neut.
Sing.	Nom.	τριήρης	γένος
	Gen.	τριήρους	γένους
	Dat.	τριήρει	γένει
	Acc.	τριήρη	γένος
	Voc.	τριῆρες	γένος
Pl.	Nom.	τριήρεις	γένη
	Gen.	τριήρων	γενῶν
	Dat.	τριήρεσι(ν)	γένεσι(ν)
	Acc.	τριήρεις	γένη
	Voc.	τριήρεις	γένη

Stems Ending in a Vowel (-ευ, -ι, -αυ, -υ)

		Masc.	Fem.	Fem.	Neut.
Sing.	Nom.	βασιλεύς	πόλις	ναῦς	ἄστυ
	Gen.	βασιλέως	πόλεως	νεώς	ἄστεως
	Dat.	βασιλεῖ	πόλει	νηΐ	ἄστει
	Acc.	βασιλέα	πόλιν	ναῦν	ἄστυ
	Voc.	βασιλεῦ	πόλι	ναῦ	ἄστυ
Pl.	Nom.	βασιλῆς/-εῖς	πόλεις	νῆες	ἄστη
	Gen.	βασιλέων	πόλεων	νεῶν	ἄστεων
	Dat.	βασιλεῦσι(ν)	πόλεσι(ν)	ναυσί(ν)	ἄστεσι(ν)
	Acc.	βασιλέας	πόλεις	ναῦς	ἄστη
	Voc.	βασιλῆς/-εῖς	πόλεις	νῆες	ἄστη

Irregular Stems in -ερ and -ρ

		Masc.	Masc.	Fem.
Sing.	Nom.	πατήρ	ἀνήρ	μήτηρ
	Gen.	πατρός	ἀνδρός	μητρός
	Dat.	πατρί	ἀνδρί	μητρί
	Acc.	πατέρα	ἄνδρα	μητέρα
	Voc.	πάτερ	ἄνερ	μῆτερ
Pl.	Nom.	πατέρες	ἄνδρες	μητέρες
	Gen.	πατέρων	ἀνδρῶν	μητέρων
	Dat.	πατράσι(ν)	ἀνδράσι(ν)	μητράσι(ν)
	Acc.	πατέρας	ἄνδρας	μητέρας
	Voc.	πατέρες	ἄνδρες	μητέρες

Appendix B: **Adjectives**

First and Second Declension

With Three Endings
-ος, -η, -ον

		Masc.	Fem.	Neut.
Sing.	Nom.	καλός	καλή	καλόν
	Gen.	καλοῦ	καλῆς	καλοῦ
	Dat.	καλῷ	καλῇ	καλῷ
	Acc.	καλόν	καλήν	καλόν
	Voc.	καλέ	καλή	καλόν
Pl.	Nom.	καλοί	καλαί	καλά
	Gen.	καλῶν	καλῶν	καλῶν
	Dat.	καλοῖς	καλαῖς	καλοῖς
	Acc.	καλούς	καλάς	καλά
	Voc.	καλοί	καλαί	καλά

-ος, -ᾱ, -ον

		Masc.	Fem.	Neut.
Sing.	Nom.	δίκαιος	δικαίᾱ	δίκαιον
	Gen.	δικαίου	δικαίᾱς	δικαίου
	Dat.	δικαίῳ	δικαίᾳ	δικαίῳ
	Acc.	δίκαιον	δικαίᾱν	δίκαιον
	Voc.	δίκαιε	δικαίᾱ	δίκαιον
Pl.	Nom.	δίκαιοι	δίκαιαι	δίκαια
	Gen.	δικαίων	δικαίων	δικαίων
	Dat.	δικαίοις	δικαίαις	δικαίοις
	Acc.	δικαίους	δικαίᾱς	δίκαια
	Voc.	δίκαιοι	δίκαιαι	δίκαια

With Two Endings
-ος, -ον

		Masc./Fem.	Neut.
Sing.	Nom.	εὔξενος	εὔξενον
	Gen.	εὐξένου	εὐξένου
	Dat.	εὐξένῳ	εὐξένῳ
	Acc.	εὔξενον	εὔξενον
	Voc.	εὔξενε	εὔξενον
Pl.	Nom.	εὔξενοι	εὔξενα
	Gen.	εὐξένων	εὐξένων
	Dat.	εὐξένοις	εὐξένοις
	Acc.	εὐξένους	εὔξενα
	Voc.	εὔξενοι	εὔξενα

Contracted

		Masc.	Fem.	Neut.
Sing.	Nom.	χρυσοῦς	χρυσῆ	χρυσοῦν
	Gen.	χρυσοῦ	χρυσῆς	χρυσοῦ
	Dat.	χρυσῷ	χρυσῇ	χρυσῷ
	Acc.	χρυσοῦν	χρυσῆν	χρυσοῦν
	Voc.	χρυσοῦς	χρυσῆ	χρυσοῦν
Pl.	Nom.	χρυσοῖ	χρυσαῖ	χρυσᾶ
	Gen.	χρυσῶν	χρυσῶν	χρυσῶν
	Dat.	χρυσοῖς	χρυσαῖς	χρυσοῖς
	Acc.	χρυσοῦς	χρυσᾶς	χρυσᾶ
	Voc.	χρυσοῖ	χρυσαῖ	χρυσᾶ

Third Declension

With Two Endings
-ων, -ον

		Masc./Fem.	Neut.
Sing.	Nom.	σώφρων	σῶφρον
	Gen.	σώφρονος	σώφρονος
	Dat.	σώφρονι	σώφρονι
	Acc.	σώφρονα	σῶφρον
	Voc.	σῶφρον	σῶφρον
Pl.	Nom.	σώφρονες	σώφρονα
	Gen.	σωφρόνων	σωφρόνων
	Dat.	σώφροσι(ν)	σώφροσι(ν)
	Acc.	σώφρονας	σώφρονα
	Voc.	σώφρονες	σώφρονα

-ης, -ες

		Masc./Fem.	Neut.
Sing.	Nom.	ἀληθής	ἀληθές
	Gen.	ἀληθοῦς	ἀληθοῦς
	Dat.	ἀληθεῖ	ἀληθεῖ
	Acc.	ἀληθῆ	ἀληθές
	Voc.	ἀληθές	ἀληθές
Pl.	Nom.	ἀληθεῖς	ἀληθῆ
	Gen.	ἀληθῶν	ἀληθῶν
	Dat.	ἀληθέσι(ν)	ἀληθέσι(ν)
	Acc.	ἀληθεῖς	ἀληθῆ
	Voc.	ἀληθεῖς	ἀληθῆ

Mixed Declension

-ύς, -εῖα, -ύ

		Masc.	Fem.	Neut.
Sing.	Nom.	βαρύς	βαρεῖα	βαρύ
	Gen.	βαρέος	βαρείας	βαρέος
	Dat.	βαρεῖ	βαρείᾳ	βαρεῖ
	Acc.	βαρύν	βαρεῖαν	βαρύ
	Voc.	βαρύ	βαρεῖα	βαρύ
Pl.	Nom.	βαρεῖς	βαρεῖαι	βαρέα
	Gen.	βαρέων	βαρειῶν	βαρέων
	Dat.	βαρέσι(ν)	βαρείαις	βαρέσι(ν)
	Acc.	βαρεῖς	βαρείᾱς	βαρέα
	Voc.	βαρεῖς	βαρεῖαι	βαρέα

πᾶς, πᾶσα, πᾶν

		Masc.	Fem.	Neut.
Sing.	Nom.	πᾶς	πᾶσα	πᾶν
	Gen.	παντός	πάσης	παντός
	Dat.	παντί	πάσῃ	παντί
	Acc.	πάντα	πᾶσαν	πᾶν
	Voc.	πᾶς	πᾶσα	πᾶν
Pl.	Nom.	πάντες	πᾶσαι	πάντα
	Gen.	πάντων	πασῶν	πάντων
	Dat.	πᾶσι(ν)	πάσαις	πᾶσι(ν)
	Acc.	πάντας	πάσᾱς	πάντα
	Voc.	πάντες	πᾶσαι	πάντα

Irregular

μέγας, μεγάλη, μέγα

		Masc.	Fem.	Neut.
Sing.	Nom.	μέγας	μεγάλη	μέγα
	Gen.	μεγάλου	μεγάλης	μεγάλου
	Dat.	μεγάλῳ	μεγάλῃ	μεγάλῳ
	Acc.	μέγαν	μεγάλην	μέγα
	Voc.	μεγάλε/μέγας	μεγάλη	μέγα
Pl.	Nom.	μεγάλοι	μεγάλαι	μεγάλα
	Gen.	μεγάλων	μεγάλων	μεγάλων
	Dat.	μεγάλοις	μεγάλαις	μεγάλοις
	Acc.	μεγάλους	μεγάλᾱς	μεγάλα
	Voc.	μεγάλοι	μεγάλαι	μεγάλα

πολύς, πολλή, πολύ

		Masc.	Fem.	Neut.
Sing.	Nom.	πολύς	πολλή	πολύ
	Gen.	πολλοῦ	πολλῆς	πολλοῦ
	Dat.	πολλῷ	πολλῇ	πολλῷ
	Acc.	πολύν	πολλήν	πολύ
	Voc.	—	—	—
Pl.	Nom.	πολλοί	πολλαί	πολλά
	Gen.	πολλῶν	πολλῶν	πολλῶν
	Dat.	πολλοῖς	πολλαῖς	πολλοῖς
	Acc.	πολλούς	πολλάς	πολλά
	Voc.	πολλοί	πολλαί	πολλά

Comparative Adjectives Ending in -ων, -ον

		Masc./Fem.	Neut.
Sing.	Nom.	κακίων	κάκιον
	Gen.	κακίονος	κακίονος
	Dat.	κακίονι	κακίονι
	Acc.	κακίονα/κακίω	κάκιον
	Voc.	κάκιον	κάκιον
Pl.	Nom.	κακίονες/κακίους	κακίονα/κακίω
	Gen.	κακιόνων	κακιόνων
	Dat.	κακίοσι(ν)	κακίοσι(ν)
	Acc.	κακίονας/κακίους	κακίονα/κακίω
	Voc.	κακίονες/κακίους	κακίονα/κακίω

Appendix C: **Definite Article and Pronouns**

Definite Article

		Masc.	Fem.	Neut.
Sing.	Nom.	ὁ	ἡ	τό
	Gen.	τοῦ	τῆς	τοῦ
	Dat.	τῷ	τῇ	τῷ
	Acc.	τόν	τήν	τό
Pl.	Nom.	οἱ	αἱ	τά
	Gen.	τῶν	τῶν	τῶν
	Dat.	τοῖς	ταῖς	τοῖς
	Acc.	τούς	τάς	τά

Personal Pronouns

		First Person	Second Person	Third Person[1]
Sing.	Nom.	ἐγώ	σύ	—
	Gen.	ἐμοῦ/μου	σοῦ/σου	οὗ
	Dat.	ἐμοί/μοι	σοί/σοι	οἷ
	Acc.	ἐμέ/με	σέ/σε	ἕ
Pl.	Nom.	ἡμεῖς	ὑμεῖς	σφεῖς
	Gen.	ἡμῶν	ὑμῶν	σφῶν
	Dat.	ἡμῖν	ὑμῖν	σφίσι
	Acc.	ἡμᾶς	ὑμᾶς	σφᾶς

---

1. The third person personal pronoun is not used in Attic prose, except as an indirect reflexive pronoun. For the third person personal pronoun, αὐτός is used in all cases except the nominative. The demonstrative pronouns ἐκεῖνος and οὗτος may also be used as third person personal pronouns.

Reflexive Pronouns

		First Person		Second Person	
		Masc.	Fem.	Masc.	Fem.
Sing.	Nom.	——	——	——	——
	Gen.	ἐμαυτοῦ	ἐμαυτῆς	σεαυτοῦ/σαυτοῦ	σεαυτῆς/σαυτῆς
	Dat.	ἐμαυτῷ	ἐμαυτῇ	σεαυτῷ/σαυτῷ	σεαυτῇ/σαυτῇ
	Acc.	ἐμαυτόν	ἐμαυτήν	σεαυτόν/σαυτόν	σεαυτήν/σαυτήν
Pl.	Nom.	——	——	——	——
	Gen.	ἡμῶν αὐτῶν	ἡμῶν αὐτῶν	ὑμῶν αὐτῶν	ὑμῶν αὐτῶν
	Dat.	ἡμῖν αὐτοῖς	ἡμῖν αὐταῖς	ὑμῖν αὐτοῖς	ὑμῖν αὐταῖς
	Acc.	ἡμᾶς αὐτούς	ἡμᾶς αὐτάς	ὑμᾶς αὐτούς	ὑμᾶς αὐτάς

		Third Person		
		Masc.	Fem.	Neut.
Sing.	Nom.	——	——	——
	Gen.	ἑαυτοῦ/αὑτοῦ	ἑαυτῆς/αὑτῆς	ἑαυτοῦ/αὑτοῦ
	Dat.	ἑαυτῷ/αὑτῷ	ἑαυτῇ/αὑτῇ	ἑαυτῷ/αὑτῷ
	Acc.	ἑαυτόν/αὑτόν	ἑαυτήν/αὑτήν	ἑαυτό/αὑτό
Pl.	Nom.	——	——	——
	Gen.	ἑαυτῶν/αὑτῶν	ἑαυτῶν/αὑτῶν	ἑαυτῶν/αὑτῶν
	Dat.	ἑαυτοῖς/αὑτοῖς	ἑαυταῖς/αὑταῖς	ἑαυτοῖς/αὑτοῖς
	Acc.	ἑαυτούς/αὑτούς	ἑαυτάς/αὑτάς	ἑαυτά/αὑτά

Relative Pronoun

		Masc.	Fem.	Neut.
Sing.	Nom.	ὅς	ἥ	ὅ
	Gen.	οὗ	ἧς	οὗ
	Dat.	ᾧ	ᾗ	ᾧ
	Acc.	ὅν	ἥν	ὅ
Pl.	Nom.	οἵ	αἵ	ἅ
	Gen.	ὧν	ὧν	ὧν
	Dat.	οἷς	αἷς	οἷς
	Acc.	οὕς	ἅς	ἅ

Indefinite Relative Pronoun and Indirect Interrogative Pronoun/Adjective

		Masc.	Fem.	Neut.
Sing.	Nom.	ὅστις	ἥτις	ὅ τι
	Gen.	οὗτινος/ὅτου	ἧστινος	οὗτινος/ὅτου
	Dat.	ᾧτινι/ὅτῳ	ᾗτινι	ᾧτινι/ὅτῳ
	Acc.	ὅντινα	ἥντινα	ὅ τι

Pl.		Masc.	Fem.	Neut.
	Nom.	οἵτινες	αἵτινες	ἅτινα/ἅττα
	Gen.	ὧντινων/ὅτων	ὧντινων	ὧντινων/ὅτων
	Dat.	οἷστισι(ν)/ὅτοις	αἷστισι(ν)	οἷστισι(ν)/ὅτοις
	Acc.	οὕστινας	ἅστινας	ἅτινα/ἅττα

Interrogative Pronoun/Adjective

		Masc./Fem.	Neut.
Sing.	Nom.	τίς	τί
	Gen.	τίνος/τοῦ	τίνος/τοῦ
	Dat.	τίνι/τῷ	τίνι/τῷ
	Acc.	τίνα	τί
Pl.	Nom.	τίνες	τίνα
	Gen.	τίνων	τίνων
	Dat.	τίσι(ν)	τίσι(ν)
	Acc.	τίνας	τίνα

Indefinite Pronoun/Adjective

		Masc./Fem.	Neut.
Sing.	Nom.	τις	τι
	Gen.	τινός/του	τινός/του
	Dat.	τινί/τῳ	τινί/τῳ
	Acc.	τινά	τι
Pl.	Nom.	τινές	τινά/ἄττα
	Gen.	τινῶν	τινῶν
	Dat.	τισί(ν)	τισί(ν)
	Acc.	τινάς	τινά/ἄττα

Demonstrative Pronouns/Adjectives

οὗτος, αὕτη, τοῦτο

		Masc.	Fem.	Neut.
Sing.	Nom.	οὗτος	αὕτη	τοῦτο
	Gen.	τούτου	ταύτης	τούτου
	Dat.	τούτῳ	ταύτῃ	τούτῳ
	Acc.	τοῦτον	ταύτην	τοῦτο
Pl.	Nom.	οὗτοι	αὗται	ταῦτα
	Gen.	τούτων	τούτων	τούτων
	Dat.	τούτοις	ταύταις	τούτοις
	Acc.	τούτους	ταύτᾱς	ταῦτα

ὅδε, ἥδε, τόδε

		Masc.	Fem.	Neut.
Sing.	Nom.	ὅδε	ἥδε	τόδε
	Gen.	τοῦδε	τῆσδε	τοῦδε
	Dat.	τῷδε	τῇδε	τῷδε
	Acc.	τόνδε	τήνδε	τόδε
Pl.	Nom.	οἵδε	αἵδε	τάδε
	Gen.	τῶνδε	τῶνδε	τῶνδε
	Dat.	τοῖσδε	ταῖσδε	τοῖσδε
	Acc.	τούσδε	τάσδε	τάδε

ἐκεῖνος, ἐκείνη, ἐκεῖνο

		Masc.	Fem.	Neut.
Sing.	Nom.	ἐκεῖνος	ἐκείνη	ἐκεῖνο
	Gen.	ἐκείνου	ἐκείνης	ἐκείνου
	Dat.	ἐκείνῳ	ἐκείνῃ	ἐκείνῳ
	Acc.	ἐκεῖνον	ἐκείνην	ἐκεῖνο
Pl.	Nom.	ἐκεῖνοι	ἐκεῖναι	ἐκεῖνα
	Gen.	ἐκείνων	ἐκείνων	ἐκείνων
	Dat.	ἐκείνοις	ἐκείναις	ἐκείνοις
	Acc.	ἐκείνους	ἐκείνᾱς	ἐκεῖνα

Appendix D: Ω-Verbs

Present System

παύω, παύσω, ἔπαυσα, πέπαυκα, πέπαυμαι, ἐπαύθην

Active Voice

		Present Indicative	Imperfect Indicative	Present Subjunctive
Sing.	1st	παύω	ἔπαυον	παύω
	2nd	παύεις	ἔπαυες	παύῃς
	3rd	παύει	ἔπαυε(ν)	παύῃ
Pl.	1st	παύομεν	ἐπαύομεν	παύωμεν
	2nd	παύετε	ἐπαύετε	παύητε
	3rd	παύουσι(ν)	ἔπαυον	παύωσι(ν)

		Present Optative	Present Imperative
Sing.	1st	παύοιμι	—
	2nd	παύοις	παῦε
	3rd	παύοι	παυέτω
Pl.	1st	παύοιμεν	—
	2nd	παύοιτε	παύετε
	3rd	παύοιεν	παυόντων

Present Infinitive: παύειν
Present Participle: παύων, παύουσα, παῦον

Middle/Passive Voice

		Present Indicative	Imperfect Indicative	Present Subjunctive
Sing.	1st	παύομαι	ἐπαυόμην	παύωμαι
	2nd	παύῃ/παύει	ἐπαύου	παύῃ
	3rd	παύεται	ἐπαύετο	παύηται

Pl.	1st	παυόμεθα	ἐπαυόμεθα	παυώμεθα
	2nd	παύεσθε	ἐπαύεσθε	παύησθε
	3rd	παύονται	ἐπαύοντο	παύωνται

		Present Optative	Present Imperative
Sing.	1st	παυοίμην	—
	2nd	παύοιο	παύου
	3rd	παύοιτο	παυέσθω

Pl.	1st	παυοίμεθα	—
	2nd	παύοισθε	παύεσθε
	3rd	παύοιντο	παυέσθων

Present Infinitive: παύεσθαι
Present Participle: παυόμενος, παυομένη, παυόμενον

Future System
παύω, παύσω, ἔπαυσα, πέπαυκα, πέπαυμαι, ἐπαύθην

Active Voice

		Future Indicative	Future Optative
Sing.	1st	παύσω	παύσοιμι
	2nd	παύσεις	παύσοις
	3rd	παύσει	παύσοι

Pl.	1st	παύσομεν	παύσοιμεν
	2nd	παύσετε	παύσοιτε
	3rd	παύσουσι(ν)	παύσοιεν

Future Infinitive: παύσειν
Future Participle: παύσων, παύσουσα, παῦσον

Middle Voice

		Future Indicative	Future Optative
Sing.	1st	παύσομαι	παυσοίμην
	2nd	παύσῃ/παύσει	παύσοιο
	3rd	παύσεται	παύσοιτο

Pl.	1st	παυσόμεθα	παυσοίμεθα
	2nd	παύσεσθε	παύσοισθε
	3rd	παύσονται	παύσοιντο

Future Infinitive: παύσεσθαι
Future Participle: παυσόμενος, παυσομένη, παυσόμενον

Passive Voice

		Future Indicative	Future Optative
Sing.	1st	παυθήσομαι	παυθησοίμην
	2nd	παυθήσῃ/παυθήσει	παυθήσοιο
	3rd	παυθήσεται	παυθήσοιτο

Pl.	1st	παυθησόμεθα	παυθησοίμεθα
	2nd	παυθήσεσθε	παυθήσοισθε
	3rd	παυθήσονται	παυθήσοιντο

Future Infinitive: παυθήσεσθαι
Future Participle: παυθησόμενος, παυθησομένη, παυθησόμενον

First Aorist System
παύω, παύσω, ἔπαυσα, πέπαυκα, πέπαυμαι, ἐπαύθην

Active Voice

		Aorist Indicative	Aorist Subjunctive	Aorist Optative
Sing.	1st	ἔπαυσα	παύσω	παύσαιμι
	2nd	ἔπαυσας	παύσῃς	παύσαις/παύσειας
	3rd	ἔπαυσε(ν)	παύσῃ	παύσαι/παύσειε(ν)
Pl.	1st	ἐπαύσαμεν	παύσωμεν	παύσαιμεν
	2nd	ἐπαύσατε	παύσητε	παύσαιτε
	3rd	ἔπαυσαν	παύσωσι(ν)	παύσαιεν/παύσειαν

		Aorist Imperative
Sing.	2nd	παῦσον
	3rd	παυσάτω
Pl.	2nd	παύσατε
	3rd	παυσάντων

Aorist Infinitive: παῦσαι
Aorist Participle: παύσᾱς, παύσασα, παῦσαν

Middle Voice

		Aorist Indicative	Aorist Subjunctive	Aorist Optative
Sing.	1st	ἐπαυσάμην	παύσωμαι	παυσαίμην
	2nd	ἐπαύσω	παύσῃ	παύσαιο
	3rd	ἐπαύσατο	παύσηται	παύσαιτο
Pl.	1st	ἐπαυσάμεθα	παυσώμεθα	παυσαίμεθα
	2nd	ἐπαύσασθε	παύσησθε	παύσαισθε
	3rd	ἐπαύσαντο	παύσωνται	παύσαιντο

		Aorist Imperative
Sing.	2nd	παῦσαι
	3rd	παυσάσθω
Pl.	2nd	παύσασθε
	3rd	παυσάσθων

Aorist Infinitive: παύσασθαι
Aorist Participle: παυσάμενος, παυσαμένη, παυσάμενον

Passive Voice

		Aorist Indicative	Aorist Subjunctive	Aorist Optative
Sing.	1st	ἐπαύθην	παυθῶ	παυθείην
	2nd	ἐπαύθης	παυθῇς	παυθείης
	3rd	ἐπαύθη	παυθῇ	παυθείη
Pl.	1st	ἐπαύθημεν	παυθῶμεν	παυθείημεν/παυθεῖμεν
	2nd	ἐπαύθητε	παυθῆτε	παυθείητε/παυθεῖτε
	3rd	ἐπαύθησαν	παυθῶσι(ν)	παυθείησαν/παυθεῖεν

		Aorist Imperative
Sing.	2nd	παύθητι
	3rd	παυθήτω
Pl.	2nd	παύθητε
	3rd	παυθέντων

Aorist Infinitive: παυθῆναι

Aorist Participle: παυθείς, παυθεῖσα, παυθέν

Perfect System

παύω, παύσω, ἔπαυσα, πέπαυκα, πέπαυμαι, ἐπαύθην

Active Voice

		Perfect Indicative	Pluperfect Indicative	Perfect Subjunctive[2]
Sing.	1st	πέπαυκα	ἐπεπαύκη	πεπαυκὼς (-υῖα) ὦ
	2nd	πέπαυκας	ἐπεπαύκης	πεπαυκὼς (-υῖα) ᾖς
	3rd	πέπαυκε(ν)	ἐπεπαύκει(ν)	πεπαυκὼς (-υῖα, -ὸς) ᾖ
Pl.	1st	πεπαύκαμεν	ἐπεπαύκεμεν	πεπαυκότες (-υῖαι) ὦμεν
	2nd	πεπαύκατε	ἐπεπαύκετε	πεπαυκότες (-υῖαι) ἦτε
	3rd	πεπαύκασι(ν)	ἐπεπαύκεσαν	πεπαυκότες (-υῖαι) ὦσι
				(neuter pl. πεπαυκότα ᾖ)

		Perfect Optative[3]	Perfect Imperative[4]
Sing.	1st	πεπαυκὼς (-υῖα) εἴην	—
	2nd	πεπαυκὼς (-υῖα) εἴης	πεπαυκὼς (-υῖα) ἴσθι
	3rd	πεπαυκὼς (-υῖα, -ὸς) εἴη	πεπαυκὼς (-υῖα, -ὸς) ἔστω
Pl.	1st	πεπαυκότες (-υῖαι) εἴημεν/εἶμεν	—
	2nd	πεπαυκότες (-υῖαι) εἴητε/εἶτε	πεπαυκότες (-υῖαι) ἔστε
	3rd	πεπαυκότες (-υῖαι) εἴησαν/εἶεν	πεπαυκότες (-υῖαι) ἔστων
		(neuter pl. πεπαυκότα εἴη)	(neuter pl. πεπαυκότα ἔστω)

Perfect Infinitive: πεπαυκέναι

Perfect Participle: πεπαυκώς, πεπαυκυῖα, πεπαυκός

---

2. Rare perfect active subjunctive forms include the simple forms πεπαύκω, πεπαύκῃς, etc. (S383).

3. Rare perfect active optative forms include the simple forms πεπαύκοιμι, πεπαύκοις, etc. (S383).

4. Rare perfect active imperative forms include the simple forms πέπαυκε, πεπαυκέτω, etc. (S383).

Middle/Passive Voice

		Perfect Indicative	Pluperfect Indicative	Perfect Subjunctive
Sing.	1st	πέπαυμαι	ἐπεπαύμην	πεπαυμένος (-η) ὦ
	2nd	πέπαυσαι	ἐπέπαυσο	πεπαυμένος (-η) ᾖς
	3rd	πέπαυται	ἐπέπαυτο	πεπαυμένος (-η, -ον) ᾖ
Pl.	1st	πεπαύμεθα	ἐπεπαύμεθα	πεπαυμένοι (-αι) ὦμεν
	2nd	πέπαυσθε	ἐπέπαυσθε	πεπαυμένοι (-αι) ἦτε
	3rd	πέπαυνται	ἐπέπαυντο	πεπαυμένοι (-αι) ὦσι
				(neuter pl. πεπαυμένα ᾖ)

		Perfect Imperative	Perfect Optative
Sing.	1st	—	πεπαυμένος (-η) εἴην
	2nd	πέπαυσο	πεπαυμένος (-η) εἴης
	3rd	πεπαύσθω	πεπαυμένος (-η, -ον) εἴη
Pl.	1st	—	πεπαυμένοι (-αι) εἴημεν/εἶμεν
	2nd	πέπαυσθε	πεπαυμένοι (-αι) εἴητε/εἶτε
	3rd	πεπαύσθων	πεπαυμένοι (-αι) εἴησαν/εἶεν
			(neuter pl. πεπαυμένα εἴη)

Perfect Infinitive: πεπαῦσθαι
Perfect Participle: πεπαυμένος, πεπαυμένη, πεπαυμένον

Labial-Stem Verbs
γράφω (γραφ-)

		Perfect Indicative	Pluperfect Indicative	Perfect Subjunctive
Sing.	1st	γέγραμμαι	ἐγεγράμμην	γεγραμμένος (-η) ὦ
	2nd	γέγραψαι	ἐγέγραψο	γεγραμμένος (-η) ᾖς
	3rd	γέγραπται	ἐγέγραπτο	γεγραμμένος (-η, -ον) ᾖ
Pl.	1st	γεγράμμεθα	ἐγεγράμμεθα	γεγραμμένοι (-αι) ὦμεν
	2nd	γέγραφθε	ἐγέγραφθε	γεγραμμένοι (-αι) ἦτε
	3rd	γεγραμμένοι (-αι) εἰσί (neuter pl. γεγραμμένα ἐστί)	γεγραμμένοι (-αι) ἦσαν (neuter pl. γεγραμμένα ἦν)	γεγραμμένοι (-αι) ὦσι (neuter pl. γεγραμμένα ᾖ)

		Perfect Imperative	Perfect Optative
Sing.	1st	—	γεγραμμένος (-η) εἴην
	2nd	γέγραψο	γεγραμμένος (-η) εἴης
	3rd	γεγράφθω	γεγραμμένος (-η, -ον) εἴη
Pl.	1st	—	γεγραμμένοι (-αι) εἴημεν/εἶμεν
	2nd	γέγραφθε	γεγραμμένοι (-αι) εἴητε/εἶτε
	3rd	γεγράφθων	γεγραμμένοι (-αι) εἴησαν/εἶεν
			(neuter pl. γεγραμμένα εἴη)

Perfect Infinitive: γεγράφθαι
Perfect Participle: γεγραμμένος, γεγραμμένη, γεγραμμένον

Palatal-Stem Verbs
διώκω (διωκ-)

		Perfect Indicative	Pluperfect Indicative	Perfect Subjunctive
Sing.	1st	δεδίωγμαι	ἐδεδιώγμην	δεδιωγμένος (-η) ὦ
	2nd	δεδίωξαι	ἐδεδίωξο	δεδιωγμένος (-η) ᾖς
	3rd	δεδίωκται	ἐδεδίωκτο	δεδιωγμένος (-η, -ον) ᾖ
Pl.	1st	διδιώγμεθα	ἐδεδιώγμεθα	δεδιωγμένοι (-αι) ὦμεν
	2nd	δεδίωχθε	ἐδεδίωχθε	δεδιωγμένοι (-αι) ἦτε
	3rd	δεδιωγμένοι (-αι) εἰσί	δεδιωγμένοι (-αι) ἦσαν	δεδιωγμένοι (-αι) ὦσι
		(neuter pl. δεδιωγμένα ἐστί)	(neuter pl. δεδιωγμένα ἦν)	(neuter pl. δεδιωγμένα ᾖ)

		Perfect Imperative	Perfect Optative
Sing.	1st	—	δεδιωγμένος (-η) εἴην
	2nd	δεδίωξο	δεδιωγμένος (-η) εἴης
	3rd	δεδιώχθω	δεδιωγμένος (-η, -ον) εἴη
Pl.	1st	—	δεδιωγμένοι (-αι) εἴημεν/εἶμεν
	2nd	δεδίωχθε	δεδιωγμένοι (-αι) εἴητε/εἶτε
	3rd	δεδιώχθων	δεδιωγμένοι (-αι) εἴησαν/εἶεν
			(neuter pl. δεδιωγμένα εἴη)

Perfect Infinitive: δεδιῶχθαι
Perfect Participle: δεδιωγμένος, δεδιωγμένη, δεδιωγμένον

Dental-Stem Verbs
πείθω (πειθ-)

		Perfect Indicative	Pluperfect Indicative	Perfect Subjunctive
Sing.	1st	πέπεισμαι	ἐπεπείσμην	πεπεισμένος (-η) ὦ
	2nd	πέπεισαι	ἐπέπεισο	πεπεισμένος (-η) ᾖς
	3rd	πέπεισται	ἐπέπειστο	πεπεισμένος (-η, -ον) ᾖ
Pl.	1st	πεπείσμεθα	ἐπεπείσμεθα	πεπεισμένοι (-αι) ὦμεν
	2nd	πέπεισθε	ἐπέπεισθε	πεπεισμένοι (-αι) ἦτε
	3rd	πεπεισμένοι (-αι) εἰσί	πεπεισμένοι (-αι) ἦσαν	πεπεισμένοι (-αι) ὦσι
		(neuter pl. πεπεισμένα ἐστί)	(neuter pl. πεπεισμένα ἦν)	(neuter pl. πεπεισμένα ᾖ)

		Perfect Imperative	Perfect Optative
Sing.	1st	—	πεπεισμένος (-η) εἴην
	2nd	πέπεισο	πεπεισμένος (-η) εἴης
	3rd	πεπείσθω	πεπεισμένος (-η, -ον) εἴη
Pl.	1st	—	πεπεισμένοι (-αι) εἴημεν/εἶμεν
	2nd	πέπεισθε	πεπεισμένοι (-αι) εἴητε/εἶτε
	3rd	πεπείσθων	πεπεισμένοι (-αι) εἴησαν/εἶεν
			(neuter pl. πεπεισμένα εἴη)

Perfect Infinitive: πεπεῖσθαι
Perfect Participle: πεπεισμένος, πεπεισμένη, πεπεισμένον

Liquid-Stem Verbs
ἀγγέλλω (ἀγγελ-)

		Perfect Indicative	Pluperfect Indicative	Perfect Subjunctive
Sing.	1st	ἤγγελμαι	ἠγγέλμην	ἠγγελμένος (-η) ὦ
	2nd	ἤγγελσαι	ἤγγελσο	ἠγγελμένος (-η) ᾖς
	3rd	ἤγγελται	ἤγγελτο	ἠγγελμένος (-η, -ον) ᾖ
Pl.	1st	ἠγγέλμεθα	ἠγγέλμεθα	ἠγγελμένοι (-αι) ὦμεν
	2nd	ἤγγελθε	ἤγγελθε	ἠγγελμένοι (-αι) ἦτε
	3rd	ἠγγελμένοι (-αι) εἰσί (neuter pl. ἠγγελμένα ἐστί)	ἠγγελμένοι (-αι) ἦσαν (neuter pl. ἠγγελμένα ἦν)	ἠγγελμένοι (-αι) ὦσι (neuter pl. ἠγγελμένα ᾖ)

		Perfect Imperative	Perfect Optative
Sing.	1st	—	ἠγγελμένος (-η) εἴην
	2nd	ἤγγελσο	ἠγγελμένος (-η) εἴης
	3rd	ἠγγέλθω	ἠγγελμένος (-η, -ον) εἴη
Pl.	1st	—	ἠγγελμένοι (-αι) εἴημεν/εἶμεν
	2nd	ἤγγελθε	ἠγγελμένοι (-αι) εἴητε/εἶτε
	3rd	ἠγγέλθων	ἠγγελμένοι (-αι) εἴησαν/εἶεν (neuter pl. ἠγγελμένα εἴη)

Perfect Infinitive: ἠγγέλθαι
Perfect Participle: ἠγγελμένος, ἠγγελμένη, ἠγγελμένον

Second Aorist System
λείπω, λείψω, ἔλιπον, λέλοιπα, λέλειμμαι, ἐλείφθην

		Active Voice		
		Aorist Indicative	Aorist Subjunctive	Aorist Optative
Sing.	1st	ἔλιπον	λίπω	λίποιμι
	2nd	ἔλιπες	λίπῃς	λίποις
	3rd	ἔλιπε(ν)	λίπῃ	λίποι
Pl.	1st	ἐλίπομεν	λίπωμεν	λίποιμεν
	2nd	ἐλίπετε	λίπητε	λίποιτε
	3rd	ἔλιπον	λίπωσι(ν)	λίποιεν

		Aorist Imperative
Sing.	2nd	λίπε
	3rd	λιπέτω
Pl.	2nd	λίπετε
	3rd	λιπόντων

Aorist Infinitive: λιπεῖν
Aorist Participle: λιπών, λιποῦσα, λιπόν

Middle Voice

		Aorist Indicative	Aorist Subjunctive	Aorist Optative
Sing.	1st	ἐλιπόμην	λίπωμαι	λιποίμην
	2nd	ἐλίπου	λίπῃ	λίποιο
	3rd	ἐλίπετο	λίπηται	λίποιτο
Pl.	1st	ἐλιπόμεθα	λιπώμεθα	λιποίμεθα
	2nd	ἐλίπεσθε	λίπησθε	λίποισθε
	3rd	ἐλίποντο	λίπωνται	λίποιντο

		Aorist Imperative
Sing.	2nd	λιποῦ
	3rd	λιπέσθω
Pl.	2nd	λίπεσθε
	3rd	λιπέσθων

Aorist Infinitive: λιπέσθαι
Aorist Participle: λιπόμενος, λιπομένη, λιπόμενον

-άω Contract Verbs

Present System
τιμάω, τιμήσω, ἐτίμησα, τετίμηκα, τετίμημαι, ἐτιμήθην

Active Voice

		Present Indicative	Imperfect Indicative	Present Subjunctive
Sing.	1st	τιμῶ	ἐτίμων	τιμῶ
	2nd	τιμᾷς	ἐτίμας	τιμᾷς
	3rd	τιμᾷ	ἐτίμα	τιμᾷ
Pl.	1st	τιμῶμεν	ἐτιμῶμεν	τιμῶμεν
	2nd	τιμᾶτε	ἐτιμᾶτε	τιμᾶτε
	3rd	τιμῶσι(ν)	ἐτίμων	τιμῶσι(ν)

		Present Optative	Present Imperative
Sing.	1st	τιμῴην/(τιμῷμι)[5]	——
	2nd	τιμῴης/(τιμῷς)	τίμα
	3rd	τιμῴη/(τιμῷ)	τιμάτω
Pl.	1st	(τιμῴημεν)/τιμῷμεν	——
	2nd	(τιμῴητε)/τιμῷτε	τιμᾶτε
	3rd	(τιμῴησαν)/τιμῷεν	τιμώντων

Present Infinitive: τιμᾶν
Present Participle: τιμῶν, τιμῶσα, τιμῶν

---

5. Forms in parentheses are less common.

Middle/Passive Voice

		Present Indicative	Imperfect Indicative	Present Subjunctive
Sing.	1st	τιμῶμαι	ἐτιμώμην	τιμῶμαι
	2nd	τιμᾷ	ἐτιμῶ	τιμᾷ
	3rd	τιμᾶται	ἐτιμᾶτο	τιμᾶται
Pl.	1st	τιμώμεθα	ἐτιμώμεθα	τιμώμεθα
	2nd	τιμᾶσθε	ἐτιμᾶσθε	τιμᾶσθε
	3rd	τιμῶνται	ἐτιμῶντο	τιμῶνται

		Present Optative	Present Imperative
Sing.	1st	τιμῴμην	——
	2nd	τιμῷο	τιμῶ
	3rd	τιμῷτο	τιμάσθω
Pl.	1st	τιμῴμεθα	——
	2nd	τιμῷσθε	τιμᾶσθε
	3rd	τιμῷντο	τιμάσθων

Present Infinitive: τιμᾶσθαι
Present Participle: τιμώμενος, τιμωμένη, τιμώμενον

-έω Contract Verbs

Present System
φιλέω, φιλήσω, ἐφίλησα, πεφίληκα, πεφίλημαι, ἐφιλήθην

Active Voice

		Present Indicative	Imperfect Indicative	Present Subjunctive
Sing.	1st	φιλῶ	ἐφίλουν	φιλῶ
	2nd	φιλεῖς	ἐφίλεις	φιλῇς
	3rd	φιλεῖ	ἐφίλει	φιλῇ
Pl.	1st	φιλοῦμεν	ἐφιλοῦμεν	φιλῶμεν
	2nd	φιλεῖτε	ἐφιλεῖτε	φιλῆτε
	3rd	φιλοῦσι(ν)	ἐφίλουν	φιλῶσι(ν)

		Present Optative	Present Imperative
Sing.	1st	φιλοίην/(φιλοῖμι)[6]	——
	2nd	φιλοίης/(φιλοῖς)	φίλει
	3rd	φιλοίη/(φιλοῖ)	φιλείτω
Pl.	1st	(φιλοίημεν)/φιλοῖμεν	——
	2nd	(φιλοίητε)/φιλοῖτε	φιλεῖτε
	3rd	(φιλοίησαν)/φιλοῖεν	φιλούντων

Present Infinitive: φιλεῖν
Present Participle: φιλῶν, φιλοῦσα, φιλοῦν

---

6. Forms in parentheses are less common.

Middle/Passive Voice

		Present Indicative	Imperfect Indicative	Present Subjunctive
Sing.	1st	φιλοῦμαι	ἐφιλούμην	φιλῶμαι
	2nd	φιλῇ/φιλεῖ	ἐφιλοῦ	φιλῇ
	3rd	φιλεῖται	ἐφιλεῖτο	φιλῆται
Pl.	1st	φιλούμεθα	ἐφιλούμεθα	φιλώμεθα
	2nd	φιλεῖσθε	ἐφιλεῖσθε	φιλῆσθε
	3rd	φιλοῦντο	ἐφιλοῦντο	φιλῶνται

		Present Optative	Present Imperative
Sing.	1st	φιλοίμην	——
	2nd	φιλοῖο	φιλοῦ
	3rd	φιλοῖτο	φιλείσθω
Pl.	1st	φιλοίμεθα	——
	2nd	φιλοῖσθε	φιλεῖσθε
	3rd	φιλοίντο	φιλείσθων

Present Infinitive: φιλεῖσθαι
Present Participle: φιλούμενος, φιλουμένη, φιλούμενον

-όω Contract Verbs

Present System
δηλόω, δηλώσω, ἐδήλωσα, δεδήλωκα, δεδήλωμαι, ἐδηλώθην

Active Voice

		Present Indicative	Imperfect Indicative	Present Subjunctive
Sing.	1st	δηλῶ	ἐδήλουν	δηλῶ
	2nd	δηλοῖς	ἐδήλους	δηλοῖς
	3rd	δηλοῖ	ἐδήλου	δηλοῖ
Pl.	1st	δηλοῦμεν	ἐδηλοῦμεν	δηλῶμεν
	2nd	δηλοῦτε	ἐδηλοῦτε	δηλῶτε
	3rd	δηλοῦσι(ν)	ἐδήλουν	δηλῶσι(ν)

		Present Optative	Present Imperative
Sing.	1st	δηλοίην/(δηλοῖμι)[7]	——
	2nd	δηλοίης/(δηλοῖς)	δήλου
	3rd	δηλοίη/(δηλοῖ)	δηλούτω
Pl.	1st	(δηλοίημεν)/δηλοῖμεν	——
	2nd	(δηλοίητε)/δηλοῖτε	δηλοῦτε
	3rd	(δηλοίησαν)/δηλοῖεν	δηλούντων

Present Infinitive: δηλοῦν
Present Participle: δηλῶν, δηλοῦσα, δηλοῦν

---

7. Forms in parentheses are less common.

Middle/Passive Voice

		Present Indicative	Imperfect Indicative	Present Subjunctive
Sing.	1st	δηλοῦμαι	ἐδηλούμην	δηλῶμαι
	2nd	δηλοῖ	ἐδηλοῦ	δηλοῖ
	3rd	δηλοῦται	ἐδηλοῦτο	δηλῶται
Pl.	1st	δηλούμεθα	ἐδηλούμεθα	δηλώμεθα
	2nd	δηλοῦσθε	ἐδηλοῦσθε	δηλῶσθε
	3rd	δηλοῦνται	ἐδηλοῦντο	δηλῶνται

		Present Optative	Present Imperative
Sing.	1st	δηλοίμην	——
	2nd	δηλοῖο	δηλοῦ
	3rd	δηλοῖτο	δηλούσθω
Pl.	1st	δηλοίμεθα	——
	2nd	δηλοῖσθε	δηλοῦσθε
	3rd	δηλοῖντο	δηλούσθων

Present Infinitive: δηλοῦσθαι
Present Participle: δηλούμενος, δηλουμένη, δηλούμενον

Appendix E: MI-Verbs

δίδωμι, δώσω, ἔδωκα, δέδωκα, δέδομαι, ἐδόθην

Present System
Active Voice

		Present Indicative	Imperfect Indicative	Present Subjunctive
Sing.	1st	δίδωμι	ἐδίδουν	διδῶ
	2nd	δίδως	ἐδίδους	διδῷς
	3rd	δίδωσι(ν)	ἐδίδου	διδῷ
Pl.	1st	δίδομεν	ἐδίδομεν	διδῶμεν
	2nd	δίδοτε	ἐδίδοτε	διδῶτε
	3rd	διδόᾱσι(ν)	ἐδίδοσαν	διδῶσι(ν)

		Present Optative	Present Imperative
Sing.	1st	διδοίην	—
	2nd	διδοίης	δίδου
	3rd	διδοίη	διδότω
Pl.	1st	διδοίημεν/διδοῖμεν	—
	2nd	διδοίητε/διδοῖτε	δίδοτε
	3rd	διδοίησαν/διδοῖεν	διδόντων

Present Infinitive: διδόναι
Present Participle: διδούς, διδοῦσα, διδόν

Middle/Passive Voice

		Present Indicative	Imperfect Indicative	Present Subjunctive
Sing.	1st	δίδομαι	ἐδιδόμην	διδῶμαι
	2nd	δίδοσαι	ἐδίδοσο	διδῷ
	3rd	δίδοται	ἐδίδοτο	διδῶται

Pl.	1st	διδόμεθα	ἐδιδόμεθα	διδώμεθα
	2nd	δίδοσθε	ἐδίδοσθε	διδῶσθε
	3rd	δίδονται	ἐδίδοντο	διδῶνται

		Present Optative	Present Imperative
Sing.	1st	διδοίμην	—
	2nd	διδοῖο	δίδοσο
	3rd	διδοῖτο	διδόσθω

Pl.	1st	διδοίμεθα	—
	2nd	διδοῖσθε	δίδοσθε
	3rd	διδοῖντο	διδόσθων

Present Infinitive: δίδοσθαι
Present Participle: διδόμενος, διδομένη, διδόμενον

Aorist System
Active Voice

		Aorist Indicative	Aorist Subjunctive	Aorist Optative
Sing.	1st	ἔδωκα	δῶ	δοίην
	2nd	ἔδωκας	δῷς	δοίης
	3rd	ἔδωκε(ν)	δῷ	δοίη

Pl.	1st	ἔδομεν	δῶμεν	δοίημεν/δοῖμεν
	2nd	ἔδοτε	δῶτε	δοίητε/δοῖτε
	3rd	ἔδοσαν	δῶσι(ν)	δοίησαν/δοῖεν

		Aorist Imperative
Sing.	2nd	δός
	3rd	δότω

Pl.	2nd	δότε
	3rd	δόντων

Aorist Infinitive: δοῦναι
Aorist Participle: δούς, δοῦσα, δόν

Middle Voice

		Aorist Indicative	Aorist Subjunctive	Aorist Optative
Sing.	1st	ἐδόμην	δῶμαι	δοίμην
	2nd	ἔδου	δῷ	δοῖο
	3rd	ἔδοτο	δῶται	δοῖτο

Pl.	1st	ἐδόμεθα	δώμεθα	δοίμεθα
	2nd	ἔδοσθε	δῶσθε	δοῖσθε
	3rd	ἔδοντο	δῶνται	δοῖντο

Sing.   2nd   Aorist Imperative
δοῦ
3rd   δόσθω

Pl.   2nd   δόσθε
3rd   δόσθων

Aorist Infinitive: δόσθαι
Aorist Participle: δόμενος, δομένη, δόμενον

τίθημι, θήσω, ἔθηκα, τέθηκα, τέθειμαι, ἐτέθην

Present System
Active Voice

		Present Indicative	Imperfect Indicative	Present Subjunctive
Sing.	1st	τίθημι	ἐτίθην	τιθῶ
	2nd	τίθης	ἐτίθεις	τιθῇς
	3rd	τίθησι(ν)	ἐτίθει	τιθῇ
Pl.	1st	τίθεμεν	ἐτίθεμεν	τιθῶμεν
	2nd	τίθετε	ἐτίθετε	τιθῆτε
	3rd	τιθέᾱσι(ν)	ἐτίθεσαν	τιθῶσι(ν)

		Present Optative	Present Imperative
Sing.	1st	τιθείην	—
	2nd	τιθείης	τίθει
	3rd	τιθείη	τιθέτω
Pl.	1st	τιθείημεν/τιθεῖμεν	—
	2nd	τιθείητε/τιθεῖτε	τίθετε
	3rd	τιθείησαν/τιθεῖεν	τιθέντων

Present Infinitive: τιθέναι
Present Participle: τιθείς, τιθεῖσα, τιθέν

Middle/Passive Voice

		Present Indicative	Imperfect Indicative	Present Subjunctive
Sing.	1st	τίθεμαι	ἐτιθέμην	τιθῶμαι
	2nd	τίθεσαι	ἐτίθεσο	τιθῇ
	3rd	τίθεται	ἐτίθετο	τιθῆται
Pl.	1st	τιθέμεθα	ἐτιθέμεθα	τιθώμεθα
	2nd	τίθεσθε	ἐτίθεσθε	τιθῆσθε
	3rd	τίθενται	ἐτίθεντο	τιθῶνται

		Present Optative	Present Imperative
Sing.	1st	τιθείμην	—
	2nd	τιθεῖο	τίθεσο
	3rd	τιθεῖτο	τιθέσθω

Pl.	1st	τιθείμεθα	—
	2nd	τιθεῖσθε	τίθεσθε
	3rd	τιθεῖντο	τιθέσθων

Present Infinitive: τίθεσθαι
Present Participle: τιθέμενος, τιθεμένη, τιθέμενον

Aorist System
Active Voice

		Aorist Indicative	Aorist Subjunctive	Aorist Optative
Sing.	1st	ἔθηκα	θῶ	θείην
	2nd	ἔθηκας	θῇς	θείης
	3rd	ἔθηκε(ν)	θῇ	θείη
Pl.	1st	ἔθεμεν	θῶμεν	θείημεν/θεῖμεν
	2nd	ἔθετε	θῆτε	θείητε/θεῖτε
	3rd	ἔθεσαν	θῶσι(ν)	θείησαν/θεῖεν

		Aorist Imperative
Sing.	2nd	θές
	3rd	θέτω
Pl.	2nd	θέτε
	3rd	θέντων

Aorist Infinitive: θεῖναι
Aorist Participle: θείς, θεῖσα, θέν

Middle Voice

		Aorist Indicative	Aorist Subjunctive	Aorist Optative
Sing.	1st	ἐθέμην	θῶμαι	θείμην
	2nd	ἔθου	θῇ	θεῖο
	3rd	ἔθετο	θῆται	θεῖτο
Pl.	1st	ἐθέμεθα	θώμεθα	θείμεθα
	2nd	ἔθεσθε	θῆσθε	θεῖσθε
	3rd	ἔθεντο	θῶνται	θεῖντο

		Aorist Imperative
Sing.	2nd	θοῦ
	3rd	θέσθω
Pl.	2nd	θέσθε
	3rd	θέσθων

Aorist Infinitive: θέσθαι
Aorist Participle: θέμενος, θεμένη, θέμενον

ἵστημι, στήσω, ἔστησα/ἔστην, ἔστηκα, ἔσταμαι, ἐστάθην

Present System
Active Voice

		Present Indicative	Imperfect Indicative	Present Subjunctive
Sing.	1st	ἵστημι	ἵστην(ῑ)	ἱστῶ
	2nd	ἵστης	ἵστης	ἱστῇς
	3rd	ἵστησι(ν)	ἵστη	ἱστῇ
Pl.	1st	ἵσταμεν	ἵσταμεν	ἱστῶμεν
	2nd	ἵστατε	ἵστατε	ἱστῆτε
	3rd	ἱστᾶσι(ν)	ἵστασαν	ἱστῶσι(ν)

		Present Optative	Present Imperative
Sing.	1st	ἱσταίην	—
	2nd	ἱσταίης	ἵστη
	3rd	ἱσταίη	ἱστάτω
Pl.	1st	ἱσταίημεν/ἱσταῖμεν	—
	2nd	ἱσταίητε/ἱσταῖτε	ἵστατε
	3rd	ἱσταίησαν/ἱσταῖεν	ἱστάντων

Present Infinitive: ἱστάναι
Present Participle: ἱστάς, ἱστᾶσα, ἱστάν

Middle/Passive Voice

		Present Indicative	Imperfect Indicative	Present Subjunctive
Sing.	1st	ἵσταμαι	ἱστάμην(ῑ)	ἱστῶμαι
	2nd	ἵστασαι	ἵστασο	ἱστῇ
	3rd	ἵσταται	ἵστατο	ἱστῆται
Pl.	1st	ἱστάμεθα	ἱστάμεθα	ἱστώμεθα
	2nd	ἵστασθε	ἵστασθε	ἱστῆσθε
	3rd	ἵstanται	ἵσταντο	ἱστῶνται

		Present Optative	Present Imperative
Sing.	1st	ἱσταίμην	—
	2nd	ἱσταῖο	ἵστασο
	3rd	ἱσταῖτο	ἱστάσθω
Pl.	1st	ἱσταίμεθα	—
	2nd	ἱσταῖσθε	ἵστασθε
	3rd	ἱσταῖντο	ἱστάσθων

Present Infinitive: ἵστασθαι
Present Participle: ἱστάμενος, ἱσταμένη, ἱστάμενον

Aorist System
Active Voice

		Aorist Indicative[8]	Aorist Subjunctive	Aorist Optative
Sing.	1st	ἔστην	στῶ	σταίην
	2nd	ἔστης	στῇς	σταίης
	3rd	ἔστη	στῇ	σταίη
Pl.	1st	ἔστημεν	στῶμεν	σταίημεν/σταῖμεν
	2nd	ἔστητε	στῆτε	σταίητε/σταῖτε
	3rd	ἔστησαν	στῶσι(ν)	σταίησαν/σταῖεν

		Aorist Imperative
Sing.	2nd	στῆθι
	3rd	στήτω
Pl.	2nd	στῆτε
	3rd	στάντων

Aorist Infinitive: στῆναι
Aorist Participle: στάς, στᾶσα, στάν

---

8. This verb also has the first aorist form ἔστησα. The first aorist is transitive in meaning while the second aorist is intransitive. Only second aorist forms are listed in this appendix because the first aorist forms are regular.

Perfect System
Active Voice

		Perfect Indicative	Pluperfect Indicative	Perfect Subjunctive
Sing.	1st	ἔστηκα	εἱστήκη	ἑστῶ
	2nd	ἔστηκας	εἱστήκης	ἑστῇς
	3rd	ἔστηκε(ν)	εἱστήκει	ἑστῇ
Pl.	1st	ἔσταμεν	ἔσταμεν	ἑστῶμεν
	2nd	ἔστατε	ἔστατε	ἑστῆτε
	3rd	ἑστᾶσι(ν)	ἔστασαν	ἑστῶσι(ν)

		Perfect Optative	Perfect Imperative
Sing.	1st	ἑσταίην	—
	2nd	ἑσταίης	ἔσταθι
	3rd	ἑσταίη	ἑστάτω
Pl.	1st	ἑσταίημεν/ἑσταῖμεν	—
	2nd	ἑσταίητε/ἑσταῖτε	ἔστατε
	3rd	ἑσταίησαν/ἑσταῖεν	ἑστάντων

Perfect Infinitive: ἑστάναι
Perfect Participle: ἑστώς, ἑστῶσα, ἑστός

ἵημι,[9] ἥσω, ἧκα, εἷκα, εἷμαι, εἵθην

Present System
Active Voice

		Present Indicative	Imperfect Indicative	Present Subjunctive
Sing.	1st	ἵημι	ἵην	ἱῶ
	2nd	ἵης/ἱεῖς	ἵεις	ἱῇς
	3rd	ἵησι	ἵει	ἱῇ
Pl.	1st	ἵεμεν	ἵεμεν	ἱῶμεν
	2nd	ἵετε	ἵετε	ἱῆτε
	3rd	ἱᾶσι(ν)	ἵεσαν	ἱῶσι(ν)

		Present Optative	Present Imperative
Sing.	1st	ἱείην	—
	2nd	ἱείης	ἵει
	3rd	ἱείη	ἱέτω
Pl.	1st	ἱείημεν/ἱεῖμεν	—
	2nd	ἱείητε/ἱεῖτε	ἵετε
	3rd	ἱείησαν/ἱεῖεν	ἱέντων

Present Infinitive: ἱέναι
Present Participle: ἱείς, ἱεῖσα, ἱέν

Middle/Passive Voice

		Present Indicative	Imperfect Indicative	Present Subjunctive
Sing.	1st	ἵεμαι	ἱέμην	ἱῶμαι
	2nd	ἵεσαι	ἵεσο	ἱῇ
	3rd	ἵεται	ἵετο	ἱῆται
Pl.	1st	ἱέμεθα	ἱέμεθα	ἱώμεθα
	2nd	ἵεσθε	ἵεσθε	ἱῆσθε
	3rd	ἵενται	ἵεντο	ἱῶνται

		Present Optative	Present Imperative
Sing.	1st	ἱείμην	—
	2nd	ἱεῖο	ἵεσο
	3rd	ἱεῖτο	ἱέσθω
Pl.	1st	ἱείμεθα	—
	2nd	ἱεῖσθε	ἵεσθε
	3rd	ἱεῖντο	ἱέσθων

Present Infinitive: ἵεσθαι
Present Participle: ἱέμενος, ἱεμένη, ἱέμενον

---

9. Initial iota is long in all forms in the present system.

Aorist System
Active Voice

		Aorist Indicative	Aorist Subjunctive	Aorist Optative
Sing.	1st	ἧκα	-ὦ[10]	-εἵην
	2nd	ἧκας	-ῇς	-εἵης
	3rd	ἧκε(ν)	-ῇ	-εἵη
Pl.	1st	-εἷμεν	-ὦμεν	-εἵημεν/-εἷμεν
	2nd	-εἷτε	-ῆτε	-εἵητε/-εἷτε
	3rd	-εἷσαν	-ὦσι(ν)	-εἵησαν/-εἷεν

		Aorist Imperative
Sing.	2nd	-ἕς
	3rd	-ἕτω
Pl.	2nd	-ἕτε
	3rd	-ἕντων

Aorist Infinitive: -εἷναι
Aorist Participle: -εἵς, -εἷσα, -ἕν

---

10. Forms preceded by a hyphen usually occur in compounds.

Middle Voice

		Aorist Indicative	Aorist Subjunctive	Aorist Optative
Sing.	1st	-εἵμην[11]	-ὦμαι	-εἵμην
	2nd	-εἷσο	-ῇ	-εἷο
	3rd	-εἷτο	-ῆται	-εἷτο
Pl.	1st	-εἵμεθα	-ὥμεθα	-εἵμεθα
	2nd	-εἷσθε	-ῆσθε	-εἷσθε
	3rd	-εἷντο	-ὦνται	-εἷντο

		Aorist Imperative
Sing.	2nd	-οὗ
	3rd	-ἕσθω
Pl.	2nd	-ἕσθε
	3rd	-ἕσθων

Aorist Infinitive: -ἕσθαι
Aorist Participle: -ἕμενος, -ἑμένη, -ἕμενον

---

11. Forms preceded by a hyphen usually occur in compounds.

δείκνυμι, δείξω, ἔδειξα, δέδειχα, δέδειγμαι, ἐδείχθην

Present System
Active Voice

		Present Indicative	Imperfect Indicative	Present Subjunctive
Sing.	1st	δείκνῡμι	ἐδείκνῡν	δεικνύω
	2nd	δείκνῡς	ἐδείκνῡς	δεικνύῃς
	3rd	δείκνῡσι(ν)	ἐδείκνῡ	δεικνύῃ
Pl.	1st	δείκνυμεν	ἐδείκνυμεν	δεικνύωμεν
	2nd	δείκνυτε	ἐδείκνυτε	δεικνύητε
	3rd	δεικνύᾱσι(ν)	ἐδείκνυσαν	δεικνύωσι(ν)

		Present Optative	Present Imperative
Sing.	1st	δεικνύοιμι	—
	2nd	δεικνύοις	δείκνῡ
	3rd	δεικνύοι	δεικνύτω
Pl.	1st	δεικνύοιμεν	—
	2nd	δεικνύοιτε	δείκνυτε
	3rd	δεικνύοιεν	δεικνύντων

Present Infinitive: δεικνύναι
Present Participle: δεικνύς, δεικνῦσα, δεικνύν

Middle/Passive Voice

		Present Indicative	Imperfect Indicative	Present Subjunctive
Sing.	1st	δείκνυμαι	ἐδεικνύμην	δεικνύωμαι
	2nd	δείκνυσαι	ἐδείκνυσο	δεικνύῃ
	3rd	δείκνυται	ἐδείκνυτο	δεικνύηται
Pl.	1st	δεικνύμεθα	ἐδεικνύμεθα	δεικνυώμεθα
	2nd	δείκνυσθε	ἐδείκνυσθε	δεικνύησθε
	3rd	δείκνυνται	ἐδείκνυντο	δεικνύωνται

		Present Optative	Present Imperative
Sing.	1st	δεικνυοίμην	—
	2nd	δεικνύοιο	δείκνυσο
	3rd	δεικνύοιτο	δεικνύσθω
Pl.	1st	δεικνυοίμεθα	—
	2nd	δεικνύοισθε	δείκνυσθε
	3rd	δεικνύοιντο	δεικνύσθων

Present Infinitive: δείκνυσθαι
Present Participle: δεικνύμενος, δεικνυμένη, δεικνύμενον

Appendix F: Irregular Verbs

εἰμί, ἔσομαι, ——, ——, ——, —— (be)

Present System

		Present Indicative	Imperfect Indicative	Present Subjunctive
Sing.	1st	εἰμί	ἦ/ἦν	ὦ
	2nd	εἶ	ἦσθα	ἦς
	3rd	ἐστί(ν)	ἦν	ἦ
Pl.	1st	ἐσμέν	ἦμεν	ὦμεν
	2nd	ἐστέ	ἦτε/ἦστε	ἦτε
	3rd	εἰσί(ν)	ἦσαν	ὦσι(ν)

		Present Optative	Present Imperative
Sing.	1st	εἴην	—
	2nd	εἴης	ἴσθι
	3rd	εἴη	ἔστω
Pl.	1st	εἴημεν/εἶμεν	—
	2nd	εἴητε/εἶτε	ἔστε
	3rd	εἴησαν/εἶεν	ἔστων

Present Infinitive: εἶναι
Present Participle: ὤν, οὖσα, ὄν

Future System

		Future Indicative	Future Optative
Sing.	1st	ἔσομαι	ἐσοίμην
	2nd	ἔσῃ/ἔσει	ἔσοιο
	3rd	ἔσται	ἔσοιτο

Pl.	1st	ἐσόμεθα	ἐσοίμεθα
	2nd	ἔσεσθε	ἔσοισθε
	3rd	ἔσονται	ἔσοιντο

Future Infinitive: ἔσεσθαι
Future Participle: ἐσόμενος, ἐσομένη, ἐσόμενον

φημί, φήσω, ἔφησα, ——, ——, ——

Present System

		Present Indicative	Imperfect Indicative	Present Subjunctive
Sing.	1st	φημί	ἔφην	φῶ
	2nd	φής	ἔφησθα/ἔφης	φῇς
	3rd	φησί(ν)	ἔφη	φῇ
Pl.	1st	φαμέν	ἔφαμεν	φῶμεν
	2nd	φατέ	ἔφατε	φῆτε
	3rd	φασί(ν)	ἔφασαν	φῶσι(ν)

		Present Optative	Present Imperative
Sing.	1st	φαίην	—
	2nd	φαίης	φαθί/φάθι
	3rd	φαίη	φάτω
Pl.	1st	φαίημεν/φαῖμεν	—
	2nd	φαίητε	φάτε
	3rd	φαίησαν/φαῖεν	φάντων

Present Infinitive: φάναι
Present Participle: (prose) φάσκων (from φάσκω), φάσκουσα, φάσκον; (poetry) φάς, φᾶσα, φάν

εἶμι, ——, ——, ——, ——, —— (go)

Present System

		Present Indicative	Imperfect Indicative	Present Subjunctive
Sing.	1st	εἶμι	ᾖα/ᾔειν	ἴω
	2nd	εἶ	ᾔεισθα/ᾔεις	ἴῃς
	3rd	εἶσι(ν)	ᾔειν/ᾔει	ἴῃ
Pl.	1st	ἴμεν	ᾖμεν	ἴωμεν
	2nd	ἴτε	ᾖτε	ἴητε
	3rd	ἴᾱσι(ν)	ᾖσαν/ᾔεσαν	ἴωσι(ν)

		Present Optative	Present Imperative
Sing.	1st	ἴοιμι/ἰοίην	——
	2nd	ἴοις	ἴθι
	3rd	ἴοι	ἴτω

Pl.	1st	ἴοιμεν	——
	2nd	ἴοιτε	ἴτε
	3rd	ἴοιεν	ἰόντων

Present Infinitive: ἰέναι
Present Participle: ἰών, ἰοῦσα, ἰόν

οἶδα, εἴσομαι, ——, ——, ——, ——

Perfect System[12]

		Perfect Indicative	Pluperfect Indicative	Perfect Subjunctive
Sing.	1st	οἶδα	ᾔδη/ᾔδειν	εἰδῶ
	2nd	οἶσθα	ᾔδησθα/ᾔδεις	εἰδῇς
	3rd	οἶδε(ν)	ᾔδει(ν)	εἰδῇ
Pl.	1st	ἴσμεν	ᾔδεμεν/ᾖσμεν	εἰδῶμεν
	2nd	ἴστε	ᾔδετε/ᾖστε	εἰδῆτε
	3rd	ἴσᾱσι(ν)	ᾔδεσαν/ᾖσαν	εἰδῶσι(ν)

		Perfect Optative	Perfect Imperative
Sing.	1st	εἰδείην	——
	2nd	εἰδείης	ἴσθι
	3rd	εἰδείη	ἴστω
Pl.	1st	εἰδείημεν/εἰδεῖμεν	——
	2nd	εἰδείητε/εἰδεῖτε	ἴστε
	3rd	εἰδείησαν/εἰδεῖεν	ἴστων

Perfect Infinitive: εἰδέναι
Perfect Participle: εἰδώς, εἰδυῖα, εἰδός

---

12. οἶδα is perfect in form but has a present meaning.

Appendix G: **Participles**

Ω-Verbs

παύω, παύσω, ἔπαυσα, πέπαυκα, πέπαυμαι, ἐπαύθην

Present Active

		Masc.	Fem.	Neut.
Sing.	Nom.	παύων	παύουσα	παῦον
	Gen.	παύοντος	παυούσης	παύοντος
	Dat.	παύοντι	παυούσῃ	παύοντι
	Acc.	παύοντα	παύουσαν	παῦον
	Voc.	παύων	παύουσα	παῦον
Pl.	Nom.	παύοντες	παύουσαι	παύοντα
	Gen.	παυόντων	παυουσῶν	παυόντων
	Dat.	παύουσι(ν)	παυούσαις	παύουσι(ν)
	Acc.	παύοντας	παυούσᾱς	παύοντα
	Voc.	παύοντες	παύουσαι	παύοντα

Present Middle/Passive

		Masc.	Fem.	Neut.
Sing.	Nom.	παυόμενος	παυομένη	παυόμενον
	Gen.	παυομένου	παυομένης	παυομένου
	Dat.	παυομένῳ	παυομένῃ	παυομένῳ
	Acc.	παυόμενον	παυομένην	παυόμενον
	Voc.	παυόμενε	παυομένη	παυόμενον
Pl.	Nom.	παυόμενοι	παυόμεναι	παυόμενα
	Gen.	παυομένων	παυομένων	παυομένων
	Dat.	παυομένοις	παυομέναις	παυομένοις
	Acc.	παυομένους	παυομένᾱς	παυόμενα
	Voc.	παυόμενοι	παυόμεναι	παυόμενα

Future Active

		Masc.	Fem.	Neut.
Sing.	Nom.	παύσων	παύσουσα	παῦσον
	Gen.	παύσοντος	παυσούσης	παύσοντος
	Dat.	παύσοντι	παυσούσῃ	παύσοντι
	Acc.	παύσοντα	παύσουσαν	παῦσον
	Voc.	παύσων	παύσουσα	παῦσον
Pl.	Nom.	παύσοντες	παύσουσαι	παύσοντα
	Gen.	παυσόντων	παυσουσῶν	παυσόντων
	Dat.	παύσουσι(ν)	παυσούσαις	παύσουσι(ν)
	Acc.	παύσοντας	παυσούσᾱς	παύσοντα
	Voc.	παύσοντες	παύσουσαι	παύσοντα

Future Middle

		Masc.	Fem.	Neut.
Sing.	Nom.	παυσόμενος	παυσομένη	παυσόμενον
	Gen.	παυσομένου	παυσομένης	παυσομένου
	Dat.	παυσομένῳ	παυσομένῃ	παυσομένῳ
	Acc.	παυσόμενον	παυσομένην	παυσόμενον
	Voc.	παυσόμενε	παυσομένη	παυσόμενον
Pl.	Nom.	παυσόμενοι	παυσόμεναι	παυσόμενα
	Gen.	παυσομένων	παυσομένων	παυσομένων
	Dat.	παυσομένοις	παυσομέναις	παυσομένοις
	Acc.	παυσομένους	παυσομένᾱς	παυσόμενα
	Voc.	παυσόμενοι	παυσόμεναι	παυσόμενα

Future Passive

		Masc.	Fem.	Neut.
Sing.	Nom.	παυθησόμενος	παυθησομένη	παυθησόμενον
	Gen.	παυθησομένου	παυθησομένης	παυθησομένου
	Dat.	παυθησομένῳ	παυθησομένῃ	παυθησομένῳ
	Acc.	παυθησόμενον	παυθησομένην	παυθησόμενον
	Voc.	παυθησόμενε	παυθησομένη	παυθησόμενον
Pl.	Nom.	παυθησόμενοι	παυθησόμεναι	παυθησόμενα
	Gen.	παυθησομένων	παυθησομένων	παυθησομένων
	Dat.	παυθησομένοις	παυθησομέναις	παυθησομένοις
	Acc.	παυθησομένους	παυθησομένᾱς	παυθησόμενα
	Voc.	παυθησόμενοι	παυθησόμεναι	παυθησόμενα

First Aorist Active

		Masc.	Fem.	Neut.
Sing.	Nom.	παύσᾱς	παύσασα	παῦσαν
	Gen.	παύσαντος	παυσάσης	παύσαντος
	Dat.	παύσαντι	παυσάσῃ	παύσαντι
	Acc.	παύσαντα	παύσασαν	παῦσαν
	Voc.	παύσᾱς	παύσασα	παῦσαν

Pl.	Nom.	παύσαντες	παύσασαι	παύσαντα
	Gen.	παυσάντων	παυσασῶν	παυσάντων
	Dat.	παύσασι(ν)	παυσάσαις	παύσασι(ν)
	Acc.	παύσαντας	παυσάσᾱς	παύσαντα
	Voc.	παύσαντες	παύσασαι	παύσαντα

First Aorist Middle

		Masc.	Fem.	Neut.
Sing.	Nom.	παυσάμενος	παυσαμένη	παυσάμενον
	Gen.	παυσαμένου	παυσαμένης	παυσαμένου
	Dat.	παυσαμένῳ	παυσαμένῃ	παυσαμένῳ
	Acc.	παυσάμενον	παυσαμένην	παυσάμενον
	Voc.	παυσάμενε	παυσαμένη	παυσάμενον

Pl.	Nom.	παυσάμενοι	παυσάμεναι	παυσάμενα
	Gen.	παυσαμένων	παυσαμένων	παυσαμένων
	Dat.	παυσαμένοις	παυσαμέναις	παυσαμένοις
	Acc.	παυσαμένους	παυσαμένᾱς	παυσάμενα
	Voc.	παυσάμενοι	παυσάμεναι	παυσάμενα

Aorist Passive

		Masc.	Fem.	Neut.
Sing.	Nom.	παυθείς	παυθεῖσα	παυθέν
	Gen.	παυθέντος	παυθείσης	παυθέντος
	Dat.	παυθέντι	παυθείσῃ	παυθέντι
	Acc.	παυθέντα	παυθεῖσαν	παυθέν
	Voc.	παυθείς	παυθεῖσα	παυθέν

Pl.	Nom.	παυθέντες	παυθεῖσαι	παυθέντα
	Gen.	παυθέντων	παυθεισῶν	παυθέντων
	Dat.	παυθεῖσι(ν)	παυθείσαις	παυθεῖσι(ν)
	Acc.	παυθέντας	παυθείσᾱς	παυθέντα
	Voc.	παυθέντες	παυθεῖσαι	παυθέντα

Perfect Active

		Masc.	Fem.	Neut.
Sing.	Nom.	πεπαυκώς	πεπαυκυῖα	πεπαυκός
	Gen.	πεπαυκότος	πεπαυκυίᾱς	πεπαυκότος
	Dat.	πεπαυκότι	πεπαυκυίᾳ	πεπαυκότι
	Acc.	πεπαυκότα	πεπαυκυῖαν	πεπαυκός
	Voc.	πεπαυκώς	πεπαυκυῖα	πεπαυκός

Pl.	Nom.	πεπαυκότες	πεπαυκυῖαι	πεπαυκότα
	Gen.	πεπαυκότων	πεπαυκυιῶν	πεπαυκότων
	Dat.	πεπαυκόσι(ν)	πεπαυκυίαις	πεπαυκόσι(ν)
	Acc.	πεπαυκότας	πεπαυκυίᾱς	πεπαυκότα
	Voc.	πεπαυκότες	πεπαυκυῖαι	πεπαυκότα

Perfect Middle/Passive

		Masc.	Fem.	Neut.
Sing.	Nom.	πεπαυμένος	πεπαυμένη	πεπαυμένον
	Gen.	πεπαυμένου	πεπαυμένης	πεπαυμένου
	Dat.	πεπαυμένῳ	πεπαυμένη	πεπαυμένῳ
	Acc.	πεπαυμένον	πεπαυμένην	πεπαυμένον
	Voc.	πεπαυμένε	πεπαυμένη	πεπαυμένον
Pl.	Nom.	πεπαυμένοι	πεπαυμέναι	πεπαυμένα
	Gen.	πεπαυμένων	πεπαυμένων	πεπαυμένων
	Dat.	πεπαυμένοις	πεπαυμέναις	πεπαυμένοις
	Acc.	πεπαυμένους	πεπαυμένᾱς	πεπαυμένα
	Voc.	πεπαυμένοι	πεπαυμέναι	πεπαυμένα

λείπω, λείψω, ἔλιπον, λέλοιπα, λέλειμμαι, ἐλείφθην

Second Aorist Active

		Masc.	Fem.	Neut.
Sing.	Nom.	λιπών	λιποῦσα	λιπόν
	Gen.	λιπόντος	λιπούσης	λιπόντος
	Dat.	λιπόντι	λιπούση	λιπόντι
	Acc.	λιπόντα	λιποῦσαν	λιπόν
	Voc.	λιπών	λιποῦσα	λιπόν
Pl.	Nom.	λιπόντες	λιποῦσαι	λιπόντα
	Gen.	λιπόντων	λιπουσῶν	λιπόντων
	Dat.	λιποῦσι(ν)	λιπούσαις	λιποῦσι(ν)
	Acc.	λιπόντας	λιπούσᾱς	λιπόντα
	Voc.	λιπόντες	λιποῦσαι	λιπόντα

Second Aorist Middle

		Masc.	Fem.	Neut.
Sing.	Nom.	λιπόμενος	λιπομένη	λιπόμενον
	Gen.	λιπομένου	λιπομένης	λιπομένου
	Dat.	λιπομένῳ	λιπομένη	λιπομένῳ
	Acc.	λιπόμενον	λιπομένην	λιπόμενον
	Voc.	λιπόμενε	λιπομένη	λιπόμενον
Pl.	Nom.	λιπόμενοι	λιπόμεναι	λιπόμενα
	Gen.	λιπομένων	λιπομένων	λιπομένων
	Dat.	λιπομένοις	λιπομέναις	λιπομένοις
	Acc.	λιπομένους	λιπομένᾱς	λιπόμενα
	Voc.	λιπόμενοι	λιπόμεναι	λιπόμενα

-άω Contract Verbs
τιμάω, τιμήσω, ἐτίμησα, τετίμηκα, τετίμημαι, ἐτιμήθην

Present Active

		Masc.	Fem.	Neut.
Sing.	Nom.	τιμῶν	τιμῶσα	τιμῶν
	Gen.	τιμῶντος	τιμώσης	τιμῶντος
	Dat.	τιμῶντι	τιμώσῃ	τιμῶντι
	Acc.	τιμῶντα	τιμῶσαν	τιμῶν
	Voc.	τιμῶν	τιμῶσα	τιμῶν
Pl.	Nom.	τιμῶντες	τιμῶσαι	τιμῶντα
	Gen.	τιμῶντων	τιμωσῶν	τιμῶντων
	Dat.	τιμῶσι(ν)	τιμώσαις	τιμῶσι(ν)
	Acc.	τιμῶντας	τιμώσᾱς	τιμῶντα
	Voc.	τιμῶντες	τιμῶσαι	τιμῶντα

Present Middle/Passive

		Masc.	Fem.	Neut.
Sing.	Nom.	τιμώμενος	τιμωμένη	τιμώμενον
	Gen.	τιμωμένου	τιμωμένης	τιμωμένου
	Dat.	τιμωμένῳ	τιμωμένῃ	τιμωμένῳ
	Acc.	τιμώμενον	τιμωμένην	τιμώμενον
	Voc.	τιμώμενε	τιμωμένη	τιμώμενον
Pl.	Nom.	τιμώμενοι	τιμώμεναι	τιμώμενα
	Gen.	τιμωμένων	τιμωμένων	τιμωμένων
	Dat.	τιμωμένοις	τιμωμέναις	τιμωμένοις
	Acc.	τιμωμένους	τιμωμένᾱς	τιμώμενα
	Voc.	τιμώμενοι	τιμώμεναι	τιμώμενα

-έω Contract Verbs
φιλέω, φιλήσω, ἐφίλησα, πεφίληκα, πεφίλημαι, ἐφιλήθην

Present Active

		Masc.	Fem.	Neut.
Sing.	Nom.	φιλῶν	φιλοῦσα	φιλοῦν
	Gen.	φιλοῦντος	φιλούσης	φιλοῦντος
	Dat.	φιλοῦντι	φιλούσῃ	φιλοῦντι
	Acc.	φιλοῦντα	φιλοῦσαν	φιλοῦν
	Voc.	φιλῶν	φιλοῦσα	φιλοῦν
Pl.	Nom.	φιλοῦντες	φιλοῦσαι	φιλοῦντα
	Gen.	φιλούντων	φιλουσῶν	φιλούντων
	Dat.	φιλοῦσι(ν)	φιλούσαις	φιλοῦσι(ν)
	Acc.	φιλοῦντας	φιλούσᾱς	φιλοῦντα
	Voc.	φιλοῦντες	φιλοῦσαι	φιλοῦντα

Present Middle/Passive

		Masc.	Fem.	Neut.
Sing.	Nom.	φιλούμενος	φιλουμένη	φιλούμενον
	Gen.	φιλουμένου	φιλουμένης	φιλουμένου
	Dat.	φιλουμένῳ	φιλουμένη	φιλουμένῳ
	Acc.	φιλούμενον	φιλουμένην	φιλούμενον
	Voc.	φιλούμενε	φιλουμένη	φιλούμενον
Pl.	Nom.	φιλούμενοι	φιλούμεναι	φιλούμενα
	Gen.	φιλουμένων	φιλουμένων	φιλουμένων
	Dat.	φιλουμένοις	φιλουμέναις	φιλουμένοις
	Acc.	φιλουμένους	φιλουμένᾱς	φιλούμενα
	Voc.	φιλούμενοι	φιλούμεναι	φιλούμενα

-όω Contract Verbs
δηλόω, δηλώσω, ἐδήλωσα, δεδήλωκα, δεδήλωμαι, ἐδηλώθην

Present Active

		Masc.	Fem.	Neut.
Sing.	Nom.	δηλῶν	δηλοῦσα	δηλοῦν
	Gen.	δηλοῦντος	δηλούσης	δηλοῦντος
	Dat.	δηλοῦντι	δηλούσῃ	δηλοῦντι
	Acc.	δηλοῦντα	δηλοῦσαν	δηλοῦν
	Voc.	δηλῶν	δηλοῦσα	δηλοῦν
Pl.	Nom.	δηλοῦντες	δηλοῦσαι	δηλοῦντα
	Gen.	δηλούντων	δηλουσῶν	δηλούντων
	Dat.	δηλοῦσι(ν)	δηλούσαις	δηλοῦσι(ν)
	Acc.	δηλοῦντας	δηλούσᾱς	δηλοῦντα
	Voc.	δηλοῦντες	δηλοῦσαι	δηλοῦντα

Present Middle/Passive

		Masc.	Fem.	Neut.
Sing.	Nom.	δηλούμενος	δηλουμένη	δηλούμενον
	Gen.	δηλουμένου	δηλουμένης	δηλουμένου
	Dat.	δηλουμένῳ	δηλουμένη	δηλουμένῳ
	Acc.	δηλούμενον	δηλουμένην	δηλούμενον
	Voc.	δηλούμενε	δηλουμένη	δηλούμενον
Pl.	Nom.	δηλούμενοι	δηλούμεναι	δηλούμενα
	Gen.	δηλουμένων	δηλουμένων	δηλουμένων
	Dat.	δηλουμένοις	δηλουμέναις	δηλουμένοις
	Acc.	δηλουμένους	δηλουμένᾱς	δηλούμενα
	Voc.	δηλούμενοι	δηλούμεναι	δηλούμενα

MI-Verbs[13]

δίδωμι, δώσω, ἔδωκα, δέδωκα, δέδομαι, ἐδόθην

Present Active

		Masc.	Fem.	Neut.
Sing.	Nom.	διδούς	διδοῦσα	διδόν
	Gen.	διδόντος	διδούσης	διδόντος
	Dat.	διδόντι	διδούσῃ	διδόντι
	Acc.	διδόντα	διδοῦσαν	διδόν
	Voc.	διδούς	διδοῦσα	διδόν
Pl.	Nom.	διδόντες	διδοῦσαι	διδόντα
	Gen.	διδόντων	διδουσῶν	διδόντων
	Dat.	διδοῦσι(ν)	διδούσαις	διδοῦσι(ν)
	Acc.	διδόντας	διδούσᾱς	διδόντα
	Voc.	διδόντες	διδοῦσαι	διδόντα

Aorist Active

		Masc.	Fem.	Neut.
Sing.	Nom.	δούς	δοῦσα	δόν
	Gen.	δόντος	δούσης	δόντος
	Dat.	δόντι	δούσῃ	δόντι
	Acc.	δόντα	δοῦσαν	δόν
	Voc.	δούς	δοῦσα	δόν
Pl.	Nom.	δόντες	δοῦσαι	δόντα
	Gen.	δόντων	δουσῶν	δόντων
	Dat.	δοῦσι(ν)	δούσαις	δοῦσι(ν)
	Acc.	δόντας	δούσᾱς	δόντα
	Voc.	δόντες	δοῦσαι	δόντα

τίθημι, θήσω, ἔθηκα, τέθηκα, τέθειμαι, ἐτέθην

Present Active

		Masc.	Fem.	Neut.
Sing.	Nom.	τιθείς	τιθεῖσα	τιθέν
	Gen.	τιθέντος	τιθείσης	τιθέντος
	Dat.	τιθέντι	τιθείσῃ	τιθέντι
	Acc.	τιθέντα	τιθεῖσαν	τιθέν
	Voc.	τιθείς	τιθεῖσα	τιθέν

---

13. The participles of **μι**-verbs that do not present any difficulty in declension, such as the present middle/passive participle or the aorist middle participle, are not listed in this appendix. The nominative forms of these participles are listed in Appendix E.

Pl.	Nom.	τιθέντες	τιθεῖσαι	τιθέντα
	Gen.	τιθέντων	τιθεισῶν	τιθέντων
	Dat.	τιθεῖσι(ν)	τιθείσαις	τιθεῖσι(ν)
	Acc.	τιθέντας	τιθείσᾱς	τιθέντα
	Voc.	τιθέντες	τιθεῖσαι	τιθέντα

Aorist Active

		Masc.	Fem.	Neut.
Sing.	Nom.	θείς	θεῖσα	θέν
	Gen.	θέντος	θείσης	θέντος
	Dat.	θέντι	θείσῃ	θέντι
	Acc.	θέντα	θεῖσαν	θέν
	Voc.	θείς	θεῖσα	θέν
Pl.	Nom.	θέντες	θεῖσαι	θέντα
	Gen.	θέντων	θεισῶν	θέντων
	Dat.	θεῖσι(ν)	θείσαις	θεῖσι(ν)
	Acc.	θέντας	θείσᾱς	θέντα
	Voc.	θέντες	θεῖσαι	θέντα

ἵστημι, στήσω, ἔστησα/ἔστην, ἕστηκα, ἕσταμαι, ἐστάθην

Present Active

		Masc.	Fem.	Neut.
Sing.	Nom.	ἱστάς	ἱστᾶσα	ἱστάν
	Gen.	ἱστάντος	ἱστάσης	ἱστάντος
	Dat.	ἱστάντι	ἱστάσῃ	ἱστάντι
	Acc.	ἱστάντα	ἱστᾶσαν	ἱστάν
	Voc.	ἱστάς	ἱστᾶσα	ἱστάν
Pl.	Nom.	ἱστάντες	ἱστᾶσαι	ἱστάντα
	Gen.	ἱστάντων	ἱστασῶν	ἱστάντων
	Dat.	ἱστᾶσι(ν)	ἱστάσαις	ἱστᾶσι(ν)
	Acc.	ἱστάντας	ἱστάσᾱς	ἱστάντα
	Voc.	ἱστάντες	ἱστᾶσαι	ἱστάντα

Aorist Active

		Masc.	Fem.	Neut.
Sing.	Nom.	στάς	στᾶσα	στάν
	Gen.	στάντος	στάσης	στάντος
	Dat.	στάντι	στάσῃ	στάντι
	Acc.	στάντα	στᾶσαν	στάν
	Voc.	στάς	στᾶσα	στάν
Pl.	Nom.	στάντες	στᾶσαι	στάντα
	Gen.	στάντων	στασῶν	στάντων
	Dat.	στᾶσι(ν)	στάσαις	στᾶσι(ν)
	Acc.	στάντας	στάσᾱς	στάντα
	Voc.	στάντες	στᾶσαι	στάντα

ἵημι, ἥσω, ἧκα, εἷκα, εἷμαι, εἵθην

Present Active

		Masc.	Fem.	Neut.
Sing.	Nom.	ἱείς	ἱεῖσα	ἱέν
	Gen.	ἱέντος	ἱείσης	ἱέντος
	Dat.	ἱέντι	ἱείσῃ	ἱέντι
	Acc.	ἱέντα	ἱεῖσαν	ἱέν
	Voc.	ἱείς	ἱεῖσα	ἱέν
Pl.	Nom.	ἱέντες	ἱεῖσαι	ἱέντα
	Gen.	ἱέντων	ἱεισῶν	ἱέντων
	Dat.	ἱεῖσι(ν)	ἱείσαις	ἱεῖσι(ν)
	Acc.	ἱέντας	ἱείσᾱς	ἱέντα
	Voc.	ἱέντες	ἱεῖσαι	ἱέντα

Aorist Active

		Masc.	Fem.	Neut.
Sing.	Nom.	-εἵς[14]	-εἷσα	-ἕν
	Gen.	-ἕντος	-είσης	-ἕντος
	Dat.	-ἕντι	-είσῃ	-ἕντι
	Acc.	-ἕντα	-εἷσαν	-ἕν
	Voc.	-εἵς	-εἷσα	-ἕν
Pl.	Nom.	-ἕντες	-εἷσαι	-ἕντα
	Gen.	-ἕντων	-εισῶν	-ἕντων
	Dat.	-εἷσι(ν)	-είσαις	-εἷσι(ν)
	Acc.	-ἕντας	-είσᾱς	-ἕντα
	Voc.	-ἕντες	-εἷσαι	-ἕντα

---

14. Forms preceded by a hyphen usually occur in compounds.

δείκνυμι, δείξω, ἔδειξα, δέδειχα, δέδειγμαι, ἐδείχθην

Present Active

		Masc.	Fem.	Neut.
Sing.	Nom.	δεικνύς	δεικνῦσα	δεικνύν
	Gen.	δεικνύντος	δεικνύσης	δεικνύντος
	Dat.	δεικνύντι	δεικνύσῃ	δεικνύντι
	Acc.	δεικνύντα	δεικνῦσαν	δεικνύν
	Voc.	δεικνύς	δεικνῦσα	δεικνύν
Pl.	Nom.	δεικνύντες	δεικνῦσαι	δεικνύντα
	Gen.	δεικνύντων	δεικνυσῶν	δεικνύντων
	Dat.	δεικνῦσι(ν)	δεικνύσαις	δεικνῦσι(ν)
	Acc.	δεικνύντας	δεικνύσᾱς	δεικνύντα
	Voc.	δεικνύντες	δεικνῦσαι	δεικνύντα

Irregular Verbs

εἰμί, ἔσομαι, ——, ——, ——, —— (be)

Present

		Masc.	Fem.	Neut.
Sing.	Nom.	ὤν	οὖσα	ὄν
	Gen.	ὄντος	οὔσης	ὄντος
	Dat.	ὄντι	οὔσῃ	ὄντι
	Acc.	ὄντα	οὖσαν	ὄν
	Voc.	ὤν	οὖσα	ὄν
Pl.	Nom.	ὄντες	οὖσαι	ὄντα
	Gen.	ὄντων	οὐσῶν	ὄντων
	Dat.	οὖσι(ν)	οὔσαις	οὖσι(ν)
	Acc.	ὄντας	οὔσᾱς	ὄντα
	Voc.	ὄντες	οὖσαι	ὄντα

εἶμι, ——, ——, ——, ——, —— (go)

Present

		Masc.	Fem.	Neut.
Sing.	Nom.	ἰών	ἰοῦσα	ἰόν
	Gen.	ἰόντος	ἰούσης	ἰόντος
	Dat.	ἰόντι	ἰούσῃ	ἰόντι
	Acc.	ἰόντα	ἰοῦσαν	ἰόν
	Voc.	ἰών	ἰοῦσα	ἰόν
Pl.	Nom.	ἰόντες	ἰοῦσαι	ἰόντα
	Gen.	ἰόντων	ἰουσῶν	ἰόντων
	Dat.	ἰοῦσι(ν)	ἰούσαις	ἰοῦσι(ν)
	Acc.	ἰόντας	ἰούσᾱς	ἰόντα
	Voc.	ἰόντες	ἰοῦσαι	ἰόντα

οἶδα, εἴσομαι, ——, ——, ——, ——

Perfect[15]

		Masc.	Fem.	Neut.
Sing.	Nom.	εἰδώς	εἰδυῖα	εἰδός
	Gen.	εἰδότος	εἰδυίᾱς	εἰδότος
	Dat.	εἰδότι	εἰδυίᾳ	εἰδότι
	Acc.	εἰδότα	εἰδυῖαν	εἰδός
	Voc.	εἰδώς	εἰδυῖα	εἰδός
Pl.	Nom.	εἰδότες	εἰδυῖαι	εἰδότα
	Gen.	εἰδότων	εἰδυιῶν	εἰδότων
	Dat.	εἰδόσι(ν)	εἰδυίαις	εἰδόσι(ν)
	Acc.	εἰδότας	εἰδυίᾱς	εἰδότα
	Voc.	εἰδότες	εἰδυῖαι	εἰδότα

---

15. οἶδα is perfect in form but has a present meaning.

Greek to English Vocabulary

The following vocabulary list includes most of the words that appear in the readings and exercises. Long final alphas on first-declension nouns and adjectives have been marked with a macron as an aid in the accentuation exercises. The principal parts of all verbs have been included. A hyphen before a principal part indicates that it is usually found in a compound form. A dash indicates that a form is not extant in Attic prose. Note that this does not necessarily mean that the form never existed; it just does not appear in the works that have survived.

ἀβασάνιστος, -ον unexamined; not examined by torture, untortured

ἀβούλως (adv.) inconsiderately

ἀγαθός, -ή, -όν good

Ἀγαμέμνων, -ονος, ὁ Agamemnon

ἀγγέλλω, ἀγγελῶ, ἤγγειλα, ἤγγελκα, ἤγγελμαι, ἠγγέλθην announce, proclaim

Ἄγις, -εως, ὁ Agis (a Spartan king)

ἀγλάϊσμα, -ατος, τό ornament, honor

ἀγνοέω, ἀγνοήσω, ἠγνόησα, ἠγνόηκα, ἠγνόημαι, ἠγνοήθην not know, be ignorant

Ἄγνων, -ωνος, ὁ Hagnon (the adoptive father of Theramenes)

ἀγορά, -ᾶς, ἡ marketplace

ἄγω, ἄξω, ἤγαγον, ἦχα, ἦγμαι, ἤχθην lead

ἀγών, -ῶνος, ὁ trial, contest

ἀδελφός, -οῦ, ὁ brother

ἀδικέω, ἀδικήσω, ἠδίκησα, ἠδίκηκα, ἠδίκημαι, ἠδικήθην be unjust; injure, do wrong

ἀδίκημα, -ατος, τό wrong, injury

ἄδικος, -ον unjust

ἀδύνατος, -ον unable; impossible

ἀεί (adv.) always

ἀθέμιτος, -ον lawless

ἀθέως (adv.) impiously

Ἀθῆναι, -ῶν, αἱ Athens

Ἀθηναῖος, -ᾱ, -ον Athenian

ἄθλιος, -ᾱ, -ον (or -ος, -ον) wretched, miserable

ἀθῡμίᾱ, -ᾱς, ἡ despondency

αἰγιαλός, -οῦ, ὁ seashore, beach

Αἰγινήτης, -ου, ὁ Aeginetan, an inhabitant of the island of Aegina

αἰδέομαι, αἰδέσομαι, ᾐδεσάμην, ——, ᾔδεσμαι, ᾐδέσθην respect; feel shame

ἀΐδιος, -ον eternal, everlasting

αἰδώς, -οῦς, ἡ shame; respect, regard

αἷμα, -ατος, τό blood

αἱρέω, αἱρήσω, εἷλον, ᾕρηκα, ᾕρημαι, ᾑρέθην take, seize; (mid.) elect, select; (pass.) be chosen

αἰσθάνομαι, αἰσθήσομαι, ᾐσθόμην, ——, ᾔσθημαι, —— perceive, learn

Αἰσχίνης, -ου, ὁ Aeschines (a member of the Thirty)

αἴσχιστος, -η, -ον (sup. adj. of **αἰσχρός**) most disgraceful

αἰσχρός, -ά, -όν disgraceful

αἰσχρῶς (adv.) disgracefully

αἰσχύνη, -ης, ἡ shame, disgrace

αἰσχύνω, αἰσχυνῶ, ᾔσχυνα, ——, ——, ᾐσχύνθην disgrace, shame; (pass.) feel ashamed, feel shame before

αἰτέω, αἰτήσω, ᾔτησα, ᾔτηκα, ᾔτημαι, ᾐτήθην ask, demand

αἰτίᾱ, -ᾱς, ἡ reason, cause; blame, charge, accusation

αἴτιος, -ᾱ, -ον blameworthy, responsible for (+ gen.)

ἀκλεῶς (adv.) ingloriously

ἀκολουθέω, ἀκολουθήσω, ἠκολούθησα, ἠκολούθηκα, ——, —— follow, go after, go with

ἀκούσιος, -ον against one's will, involuntary

ἀκουσίως (adv.) involuntarily

ἀκούω, ἀκούσομαι, ἤκουσα, ἀκήκοα, ——, ἠκούσθην hear

ἀκρόπολις, -εως, ἡ Acropolis (of Athens), citadel

ἀλήθεια, -ᾱς, ἡ truth

ἀληθής, -ές true

ἀλλά (ἀλλ') (conj.) but

ἀλλαχοῦ (adv.) elsewhere

ἀλλήλων, -οις/-αις, -ους/-ᾱς (reciprocal pron.) of one another, of each other

ἄλλοθι (adv.) elsewhere

ἄλλος, -η, -ον other, another

ἄλλως (adv.) otherwise

ἅμα (adv.) at the same time

ἁμάξιτος, -ον (as subst., with or without **ὁδός**) wagon road

ἁμαρτάνω, ἁμαρτήσομαι, ἥμαρτον, ἡμάρτηκα, ἡμάρτημαι, ἡμαρτήθην err, make a mistake; be deprived of, lack (+ gen.)

ἁμάρτημα, -ατος, τό failure, fault

ἀμείνων, -ον (gen. **–ονος**) (comp. adj. of **ἀγαθός**) better

ἀμύνω, ἀμυνῶ, ἤμυνα, ——, ——, —— defend, assist, aid (+ dat.)

ἀμφί (prep. + acc.) around

ἀμφότερος, -ᾱ, -ον both

ἄν Attic for **ἐάν**; marker of optative mood

ἀναγκάζω, ἀναγκάσω, ἠνάγκασα, ἠνάγκακα, ἠνάγκασμαι, ἠναγκάσθην force, compel

ἀναγκαῖοι, -ων, οἱ kinsmen, relatives

ἀνάγκη, -ης, ἡ necessity, constraint, force

ἀνάγω, ἀνάξω, ἀνήγαγον, ——, ἀνῆγμαι, ἀνήχθην take up

ἀναίνομαι, ——, ἀνηνάμην, ——, ——, —— renounce, disown, reject

ἀναιρέω, ἀναιρήσω, ἀνεῖλον, ἀνῄρηκα, ἀνῄρημαι, ἀνῃρέθην (mid.) retrieve bodies for burial

ἀνακομίζω, ——, ἀνεκόμισα, ——, ἀνακεκόμισμαι, ἀνεκομίσθην carry up

ἀναλαμβάνω, ἀναλήψομαι, ἀνέλαβον, ἀνείληφα, ἀνείλημμαι, —— take up

ἀναλογίζομαι, ἀναλογιοῦμαι, ἀνελογισάμην, ——, ——, —— calculate, consider

ἀναμιμνήσκω, ἀναμνήσω, ἀνέμνησα, ——, ἀναμέμνημαι, ἀνεμνήσθην remind one of something (+ double acc.)

ἀναπηδάω, ἀναπηδήσομαι, ἀνεπήδησα, ——, ——, —— leap up

ἀναφαίνω, ἀναφανῶ, ἀνέφηνα, ἀναπέφηνα, ἀναπέφασμαι, ἀνεφάνην bring to light, show, show forth

ἀναφέρω, ἀνοίσω, ἀνήνεγκα, ἀνενήνοχα, ἀνενήνεγμαι, ἀνηνέχθην lead up

ἀναφεύγω, ἀναφεύξομαι, ἀνέφυγον, ——, ——, —— escape

ἀναχωρέω, ἀναχωρήσω, ἀνεχώρησα, ἀνακεχώρηκα, ——, —— withdraw; return

ἀνδραποδίζω, ἀνδραποδιῶ, ἠνδραπόδισα, ——, ἠνδραπόδισμαι, ἠνδραποδίσθην enslave

ἀνδράποδον, -ου, τό slave

ἀνδρείᾱ, -ᾱς, ἡ courage

ἀνελεημόνως (adv.) without mercy

ἀνέορτος, -ον without a share in (+ gen.)

ἀνέρχομαι, ——, ἀνῆλθον, ἀνελήλυθα, ——, —— go up

ἄνευ (prep. + gen.) without

ἀνέχω, ἀνέξω, ἀνέσχον, ——, ——, ——
(mid.) put up with, endure

ἀνήκουστος, -ον not to be granted, not to be
heard

ἀνήρ, -δρός, ὁ man

ἄνθρωπος, -ου, ὁ/ἡ human being, man,
woman (may be used contemptuously)

ἀνίημι, ἀνήσω, ἀνῆκα, ἀνεῖκα, ἀνεῖμαι,
ἀνείθην let go, give way, relax

ἀνίστημι, ἀναστήσω, ἀνέστησα/ἀνέστην,
ἀνέστηκα, ——, ἀνεστάθην (trans.)
break up; (intrans.) stand up, rise up
to go

ἀνοικτίστως (adv.) pitilessly

ἀνόσιος, -ον unholy, profane, impious

ἀνοσίως (adv.) impiously

ἀντεῖπον (used for the aorist of ἀντιλέγω)
spoke against (+ dat.)

ἀντέχω, ἀνθέξω, ἀντέσχον, ——, ——, ——
hold out

ἀντί (prep. + gen.) instead of, in return for

ἀντίδικος, -ου, ὁ defendant; opponent

ἀντικόπτω, ἀντικόψω, ἀντέκοψα, ——, ——,
—— resist, oppose, stand in the way

ἀντιλέγω, ἀντιλέξω, ἀντέλεξα, ——, ——,
—— speak against, answer (ἀντερῶ and
ἀντεῖπον are more commonly used for
the future and aorist)

ἀντίπαλον, -ου, τό opposition, rival party

ἀντίπαλος, -ον rivaling, opposing

ἀντιπράττω, ἀντιπράξω, ἀντέπραξα, ——,
——, —— act in opposition

ἀντισπεύδω, ——, ——, ——, ——, ——
oppose eagerly, contend against

ἀντόμνυμι, ——, ἀντώμοσα, ἀντομώμοκα,
——, —— swear in turn

Ἄνυτος, -ου, ὁ Anytos (a leader of the exiles
at Phyle)

ἄξιος, -ᾱ, -ον worthy, worthy of (+ gen.)

ἀξιόω, ἀξιώσω, ἠξίωσα, ἠξίωκα, ἠξίωμαι,
ἠξιώθην think worthy; think worthy of
(+ gen.); think (someone) worthy (to do
something) (+ acc./inf.)

ἀπαγγέλλω, ἀπαγγελῶ, ἀπήγγειλα,

ἀπήγγελκα, ἀπήγγελμαι, ἀπηγγέλθην
report, announce, report back

ἀπάγω, ἀπάξω, ἀπήγαγον, ——, ἀπῆγμαι,
ἀπήχθην lead away

ἀπαλλάττω, ἀπαλλάξω, ἀπήλλαξα, ἀπήλλαχα,
ἀπήλλαγμαι, ἀπηλλάχθην/ἀπηλλάγην
set free, release, deliver; (pass.) be
acquitted of

ἅπαξ (adv.) once

ἄπαρνος, -ον denying utterly

ἅπας, ἅπασα, ἅπαν all

ἄπειμι (εἶμι), ——, ——, ——, ——, —— go
away, depart

ἄπειμι (εἰμί), ἀπέσομαι, ——, ——, ——,
—— be away

ἀπέρχομαι, ——, ἀπῆλθον, ἀπελήλυθα, ——,
—— go away

ἀπό (prep. + gen.) after, from

ἀποβάλλω, ἀποβαλῶ, ἀπέβαλον, ἀποβέβληκα,
——, —— lose

ἀποβλέπω, ἀποβλέψω, ἀπέβλεψα, ——, ——,
—— look away, look

ἀπογράφω, ἀπογράψω, ἀπέγραψα,
ἀπογέγραφα, ἀπογέγραμμαι, ἀπεγράφην
register

ἀποδείκνυμι, ἀποδείξω, ἀπέδειξα, ἀποδέδειχα,
ἀποδέδειγμαι, ἀπεδείχθην point out,
show; appoint, assign

ἀποδίδωμι, ἀποδώσω, ἀπέδωκα, ἀποδέδωκα,
ἀποδέδομαι, ἀπεδόθην give back; (mid.)
sell

ἀποθνήσκω, ἀποθανοῦμαι, ἀπέθανον, ——,
——, —— die; be killed; be put to death

ἄποικος, -ου, ὁ colonist

ἀποκαλέω, ἀποκαλῶ, ἀπεκάλεσα, ——, ——,
—— call

ἀποκλείω/ἀποκλήω, ἀποκλείσω/
ἀποκλήσω, ἀπέκλεισα/ἀπέκλησα,
——, ἀποκέκλειμαι/ἀποκέκλημαι,
ἀπεκλείσθην/ἀπεκλήσθην shut off

ἀποκοτταβίζω, ——, ἀπεκοττάβισα, ——,
——, —— dash out the last drops of
wine (as is done in the game cottabus)

ἀποκρίνω, ἀποκρινῶ, ἀπέκρινα, ——,
ἀποκέκριμαι, ἀπεκρίθην separate,
choose; (mid.) answer, reply

ἀποκτείνω, ἀποκτενῶ, ἀπέκτεινα, ἀπέκτονα, ——, —— kill; condemn to death

ἀπολείπω, ἀπολείψω, ἀπέλιπον, ἀπολέλοιπα, ἀπολέλειμμαι, ἀπελείφθην leave behind

ἀπόλλυμι, ἀπολῶ, ἀπώλεσα/ἀπωλόμην, ἀπολώλεκα/ἀπόλωλα, ——, —— destroy, kill; (mid.; perf. act.) perish

ἀπολογέομαι, ἀπολογήσομαι, ἀπελογησάμην, ——, ἀπολελόγημαι, ἀπελογήθην defend oneself, speak in defense, make a defense

ἀποπέμπω, ἀποπέμψω, ἀπέπεμψα, ——, ——, ἀπεπέμφθην send away

ἀποπλέω, ἀποπλεύσομαι/ἀποπλευσοῦμαι, ἀπέπλευσα, ——, ——, —— sail away

ἀπορέω, ἀπορήσω, ἠπόρησα, ἠπόρηκα, ἠπόρημαι, ἠπορήθην be at a loss; be in doubt about

ἀπορίᾱ, -ᾶς, ἡ poverty, difficulty

ἀποσημαίνω, ——, ἀπεσήμηνα, ——, ——, —— confiscate (mid.)

ἀποσπένδω, ——, ἀπέσπεισα, ——, ——, —— pour out wine (for an offering)

ἀποστερέω, ἀποστερήσω/ἀποστεροῦμαι, ἀπεστέρησα, ἀπεστέρηκα, ἀπεστέρημαι, ἀπεστερήθην deprive

ἀποτειχίζω, ἀποτειχιῶ, ἀπετείχισα, ——, ἀποτετείχισμαι, ἀπετειχίσθην blockade

ἀποτίθημι, ἀποθήσω, ἀπέθηκα, ——, ——, ἀπετέθην lay aside, put off, defer

ἀποχώννυμι, ——, ἀπέχωσα, ——, ——, —— bank up

ἄπρακτος, -ον without success

ἄρα (postpositive particle) therefore, then

ἆρα (interrog. particle) denotes a question to which a negative answer is expected

ἀρέσκω, ἀρέσω, ἤρεσα, ——, ——, —— please (+ dat.)

ἀρεστός, -ή, -όν acceptable, pleasing (+ dat.)

ἀριθμός, -οῦ, ὁ number

Ἀρίσταρχος, -ου, ὁ Aristarchus (Athenian general)

ἄριστος, -η, -ον (sup. adj. of ἀγαθός) best

Ἀριστοτέλης, -ου, ὁ Aristoteles (Athenian general)

ἀρκέω, ἀρκέσω, ἤρκεσα, ——, ——, —— defend, assist

ἅρμα, -ατος, τό chariot

ἁρμοστής, -οῦ, ὁ governor, harmost

ἁρμόττω, ἁρμόσω, ἥρμοσα, ——, ἥρμοσμαι, ἡρμόσθην fit

ἀρχαῖος, -ᾱ, -ον ancient, old

ἀρχή, -ῆς, ἡ beginning; rule, power, government, office; (pl.) magistrates

ἄρχω, ἄρξω, ἦρξα, ἦρχα, ἦργμαι, ἤρχθην begin (+ gen., inf., or part.), make a beginning of (+ gen.), be the beginning of (+ gen.); rule, rule over (+ gen.)

ἄρχων, -οντος, ὁ ruler, leader, archon

ἀσεβέστατος, -η, -ον most unholy

ἀσεβής, -ές unholy, impious

ἀσθενής, -ές weak

Ἀσίς, -ίδος Asian, Asiatic

ἀσπίς, -ίδος, ἡ shield

ἄστυ, -εως, τό city

ἀσφάλεια, -ᾱς, ἡ safety, security

ἀσφαλής, -ές safe; ἐν ἀσφαλεῖ in safety

ἅτε (particle) because, inasmuch as (used with a participle)

ἀτέλεστος, -ον not deserving of accomplishment; unaccomplished

ἀτιμάζω, ἀτιμάσω, ἠτίμασα, ἠτίμακα, ἠτίμασμαι, ἠτιμάσθην dishonor; hold in no honor

ἄτιμος, -ον deprived of the privileges of a citizen, disenfranchised

ἄτοπος, -ον strange, odd

αὖ (adv.) again, moreover

αὐλητρίς, -ίδος, ἡ flute girl

αὐλίζομαι, ——, ηὐλισάμην, ——, ——, ηὐλίσθην live, take up one's abode

αὐτόθεν (adv.) at once

αὐτοκράτωρ (gen. -ορος) possessing full powers (of negotiation)

αὐτός, -ή, -ό (in attributive position) same; (in predicate position) -self, the very; (in oblique cases) him, her, it, them

αὐτόφωρος, -ον caught in the act; ἐπ' αὐτοφώρῳ λαμβάνειν to catch in the act

ἀφαιρέω, ἀφαιρήσω, ἀφεῖλον, ἀφῄρηκα, ἀφῄρημαι, ἀφῃρέθην take away

ἀφανής, -ές unseen, invisible

ἀφανίζω, ἀφανιῶ, ἠφάνισα, ἠφάνικα, ἠφάνισμαι, ἠφανίσθην (pass.) make unseen, hide from sight; disappear

ἀφίημι, ἀφήσω, ἀφῆκα, ἀφεῖκα, ἀφεῖμαι, ἀφείθην neglect, let go

ἀφικνέομαι, ἀφίξομαι, ἀφικόμην, ——, ἀφῖγμαι, —— arrive

ἄχθομαι, ἀχθέσομαι/ἀχθεσθήσομαι, ——, ——, ——, ἠχθέσθην be annoyed; be grieved

βαίνω, -βήσομαι, -ἔβην, βέβηκα, -βέβαμαι, -ἐβάθην go, walk; mount (a chariot)

βαρύς, -εῖα, -ύ burdensome, oppressive

βασανίζω, βασανιῶ, ἐβασάνισα, ——, βεβασάνισμαι, ἐβασανίσθην interrogate under torture, torture

βασανιστής, -οῦ, ὁ questioner, torturer

βάσανος, -ου, ἡ torture, inquiry by torture

βασιλεύς, -έως, ὁ king

βασιλικός, -ή, -όν royal, kingly

βέλτιστος, -η, -ον (sup. adj. of ἀγαθός) best

βελτίων, -ον (gen. -ονος) (comp. adj. of ἀγαθός) better

βίαιος, -ᾱ, -ον violent, forcible

βιαίως (adv.) by force, by violence

βοήθεια, -ᾱς, ἡ help, aid

βοηθέω, βοηθήσω, ἐβοήθησα, βεβοήθηκα, βεβοήθημαι, —— help, aid (+ dat.)

βοηθός, -οῦ, ὁ assistant, helper

βουλείᾱ, -ᾱς, ἡ office of the councillor

βουλευτηρίον, -ου, τό Bouleterion, Council House

βουλευτής, -οῦ, ὁ councillor; member of the Council of the Five Hundred (in Athens)

βουλεύω, βουλεύσω, ἐβούλευσα, βεβούλευκα, βεβούλευμαι, ἐβουλεύθην plan

βουλή, -ῆς, ἡ council; Boulē (Council of the Five Hundred in Athens)

βούλομαι, βουλήσομαι, ——, ——, βεβούλημαι, ἐβουλήθην wish, prefer

βραχύς, -εῖα, -ύ brief

βρέχω, ——, ἔβρεξα, ——, βέβρεγμαι, ἐβρέχθην wet, soak

βρίθω, ——, ἔβρισα, βέβριθα, ——, —— be weighed down with (+ dat.)

Βυζάντιον, -ου, τό Byzantium

βωμός, -οῦ, ὁ altar

γάρ (postpositive particle) for

γαυροόμαι, ——, ——, ——, ——, —— exult, pride oneself in

γε, γ' (postpositive particle) at least, at any rate

γῆ, γῆς, ἡ land, earth

γίγνομαι, γενήσομαι, ἐγενόμην, γέγονα, γεγένημαι, ἐγενήθην happen, occur, arise; become, be

γιγνώσκω, γνώσομαι, ἔγνων, ἔγνωκα, ἔγνωσμαι, ἐγνώσθην judge, form a judgment, think; know

Γλαύκων, -ωνος, ὁ Glaukon (father of Charmides, one of the Thirty)

γλῶσσα, -ᾱς, ἡ tongue, language

γνώμη, -ης, ἡ opinion, belief, frame of mind; intelligence, judgment

γνωστός, -ή, -όν known

γράμμα, -ατος, τό (pl.) letters

γραφή, -ῆς, ἡ indictment

γράφω, γράψω, ἔγραψα, γέγραφα, γέγραμμαι, ἐγράφην write

γυμνός, -ή, -όν naked

γυνή, -αικός, ἡ woman, wife

δάκνω, δήξομαι, ἔδακον, ——, δέδηγμαι, ἐδήχθην bite

δέδοικα (perf. in pres. sense), δείσομαι, ἔδεισα, ——, ——, —— fear

δεῖ, δεήσει, ἐδέησε, ——, ——, —— (impers.) it is necessary (+ acc./inf.)

δείκνυμι, δείξω, ἔδειξα, δέδειχα, δέδειγμαι, ἐδείχθην show

δεινός, -ή, -όν clever; terrible; strange

δειπνέω, δειπνήσω, ἐδείπνησα, δεδείπνηκα, ——, —— dine

δεῖπνον, -ου, τό dinner

δέκα (indecl. num.) ten

δέκατος, -η, -ον tenth

δέομαι, δεήσομαι, ——, ——, ——, ἐδεήθην need (+ gen.); ask (+ gen.)

δεσπότης, -ου, ὁ master, despot

δεύτερον (adv.) second, next

δέχομαι, δέξομαι, ἐδεξάμην, ——, δέδεγμαι,
-εδέχθην receive, accept

δέω, δήσω, ἔδησα, δέδεκα, δέδεμαι, ἐδέθην
bind, put in bonds

δηϊόω, δηώσω, ἐδήωσα, ——, ——, —— lay
waste, ravage

δηλόω, δηλώσω, ἐδήλωσα, δεδήλωκα,
δεδήλωμαι, ἐδηλώθην declare, make clear

δημαγωγός, -οῦ, ὁ leader of the people,
demagogue

δημόκοινος, -ου, ὁ executioner

δημοκρατίᾱ, -ᾱς, ἡ democracy

δῆμος, -ου, ὁ the demos, the people, democracy

δημοτικός, -ή, -όν on the democratic side,
supporting the people

δήπου, δή που (indef. adv.) doubtless,
I suppose, I presume, you will admit

διά (prep. + acc.) on account of

διαβάλλω, διαβαλῶ, διέβαλον, διαβέβληκα,
διαβέβλημαι, διεβλήθην slander

διαγιγνώσκω, διαγνώσομαι, διέγνων,
διέγνωκα, διέγνωσμαι, διεγνώσθην
decide, give judgment, decide a lawsuit

Διαγόρας, -ου, ὁ Diagoras (father of Dorieus)

διαδέχομαι, διαδέξομαι, διεδεξάμην, ——,
——, —— receive one from another

διακονέω, διακονήσω, διηκόνησα, ——,
δεδιακόνημαι, ἐδιακονήθην minister,
serve, follow (+ dat.)

διακόσιοι, -αι, -α two hundred

διακωλύω, διακωλύσω, διεκώλυσα, ——,
——, διεκωλύθην hinder, prevent

διαλέγομαι, διαλέξομαι, ——, ——, ——,
διελέχθην discuss, deliberate, converse

διαλλαγή, -ῆς, ἡ truce

διαμένω, διαμενῶ, διέμεινα, ——, ——, ——
remain, survive

διάνοια, -ᾱς, ἡ thought, intention

διαπέμπω, ——, διέπεμψα, διαπέπομφα,
——, —— send

διαπονέω, ——, διεπόνησα, διαπεπόνηκα,
διαπεπόνημαι, διεπονήθην work hard

διατάττω, διατάξω, διέταξα, ——,
διατέταγμαι, διετάχθην direct, manage

διατελέω, ——, διετέλεσα, διατετέλεκα,
——, —— continue

διατρίβω, διατρίψω, διέτριψα, διατέτριφα,
——, διετρίβην spend time, waste time

διαφθείρω, διαφθερῶ, διέφθειρα/διέφθορα,
διέφθαρκα, διέφθαρμαι, διεφθάρην
destroy utterly

διαφορά, -ᾶς, ἡ disagreement, variance

διαχράομαι, διαχρήσομαι, διεχρησάμην,
——, διακέχρημαι, —— destroy

διαψηφίζομαι, διαψηφιοῦμαι, διεψηφισάμην,
——, διεψήφισμαι, —— vote

διδάσκω, διδάξω, ἐδίδαξα, δεδίδαχα,
δεδίδαγμαι, ἐδιδάχθην teach, teach how
(+ acc./inf.)

δίδωμι, δώσω, ἔδωκα, δέδωκα, δέδομαι,
ἐδόθην give; δίδωμι δίκην suffer
punishment, pay the penalty

διηγέομαι, διηγήσομαι, διηγησάμην, ——,
διήγημαι, —— discuss in detail

διήκω, ——, ——, ——, ——, —— reach,
extend

δίῑημι, διήσω, διῆκα, ——, ——, ——
dismiss

δικάζω, δικάσω, ἐδίκασα, ——, δεδίκασμαι,
ἐδικάσθην judge

δίκαιος, -ᾱ, -ον just

δικαιοσύνη, -ης, ἡ justice

δικαστής, -οῦ, ὁ juror

δίκη, -ης, ἡ justice, penalty

διόμνυμι, διομοῦμαι, διωμοσάμην,
διομώμοκα, διομώμοσμαι, —— swear
solemnly

διώκω, διώξομαι/διώξω, ἐδίωξα, δεδίωχα,
——, ἐδιώχθην pursue

δμωή, -ῆς, ἡ female slave

δοκέω, δόξω, ἔδοξα, ——, δέδογμαι,
-εδόχθην seem, appear; (impers.) seem
best, seem right (+ inf.); (impers.) be
decided (+ inf.)

δόσις, -εως, ἡ a giving, an administering

δοῦλος, -ου, ὁ slave

δραχμή, -ῆς, ἡ drachma

δρόμος, -ου, ὁ run, race, course

δρύφακτος, -ου, ὁ railing

δύναμαι, δυνήσομαι, ——, ——, δεδύνημαι, ἐδυνήθην be able (+ inf.)

δυνατός, -ή, -όν able

δύο, δυοῖν two

δυσμενής, -ές ill-disposed

δυστυχέω, δυστυχήσω, ἐδυστύχησα, δεδυστύχηκα, ——, ἐδυστυχήθην be unfortunate

δώδεκα (indecl. num.) twelve

δῶμα, -ατος, τό house

Δωριεύς, -έως, ὁ Dorieus (a naval lieutenant from Thurii who helped the Spartans)

ἐάν (conj., a contraction of εἰ + ἄν; other forms of the contraction include ἤν, ἄν) if

ἑαυτοῦ, ἑαυτῆς, ἑαυτοῦ (reflex. pron.) himself, herself, itself

ἐάω (imperf. εἴων), ἐάσω, εἴασα, εἴακα, εἴαμαι, εἰάθην allow, permit (+ acc./inf.)

ἑβδομήκοντα (indecl. num.) seventy

ἐγγίγνομαι, ἐγγενήσομαι, ἐνεγενόμην, ἐγγέγονα, ἐγγεγένημαι, —— become

ἐγχειρίδιον, -ου, τό dagger

ἐγχέω, ——, ἐνέχεα, ——, ἐγκέχυμαι, —— pour in

ἐγχωρέω, ἐγχωρήσω, ἐνεχώρησα, ——, ——, —— permit, allow; ἐνεχώρει (3rd person sing. imperf., impers.), be possible

ἐγώ (pers. pron.) I

ἔγωγε = ἐγώ + γε

ἕδρᾱ, -ᾱς, ἡ seat, chair

ἐθέλω, ἐθελήσω, ἠθέλησα, ἠθέληκα, ——, —— wish

εἰ (conj.) if; (in indirect questions) whether
 εἰ γάρ if only (+ optative of wish)
 εἰ δὲ μή otherwise

εἴθε if only, would that (+ optative of wish)

εἴκοσι (indecl. num.) twenty

εἰκοσταῖος, -ᾱ, -ον on the twentieth day

εἰκώς, -υῖα, -ός fitting, reasonable

εἱμαρμένος, -η, -ον ordained, destined (in fem. with μοῖρα supplied, destiny)

εἶμι, ——, ——, ——, ——, —— go

εἰμί, ἔσομαι, ——, ——, ——, —— be

εἶναι περί τι to be occupied with something

εἶπον (used for the aorist of λέγω) said, spoke

εἰρήνη, -ης, ἡ peace

εἰς (ἐς) (prep. + acc.) into, to, toward; for; in regard to; before

εἷς, μία, ἕν one

εἴσειμι (εἶμι), ——, ——, ——, ——, —— enter (present used for future of εἰσέρχομαι)

εἰσέρχομαι, ——, εἰσῆλθον, εἰσελήλυθα, ——, —— enter

εἰσπέμπω, εἰσπέμψω, εἰσέπεμψα, ——, ——, εἰσεπέμφθην send, send in

εἰσπλέω, εἰσπλεύσομαι, εἰσέπλευσα, εἰσπέπλευκα, ——, —— sail into

εἶτα (adv.) then

ἐκ, ἐξ (prep. + gen.) out of, from; because of, in consequence of; ἐκ τούτου thereupon

ἕκαστος, -η, -ον each, every, each one

ἑκατόν (indecl. num.) one hundred

ἐκεῖνος, -η, -ο (demon. pron./adj.) that, that one, the former

ἐκεῖσε (adv.) to that place

ἐκκλησίᾱ, -ᾱς, ἡ assembly

ἐκλείπω, ἐκλείψω, ἐξέλιπον, ἐκλέλοιπα, ἐκλέλειμμαι, —— forsake, abandon

ἐκμοχθέω, ——, ἐξεμόχθησα, ἐκμεμόχθηκα, ἐκμεμόχθημαι, —— work, toil at; weave

ἑκούσιος, -ᾱ, -ον voluntary

ἑκουσίως (adv.) voluntarily

ἐκπηδάω, ——, ἐκεπήδησα, ἐκπεπήδηκα, ——, —— leap up

ἐκπίνω, ἐκπίομαι, ἐξέπιον, ἐκπέπωκα, ——, —— drain a cup dry

ἐκποδὼν ποιεῖσθαι put (something or someone in acc.) out of the way

ἐκπολιορκέω, ἐκπολιορκήσω, ἐκεπολιόρκησα, ——, ἐκπεπολιόρκημαι, ἐκεπολιορκήθην force a besieged town to surrender

ἐκφοιτάω, ——, ——, ——, ——, —— be in the habit of going out, go about

ἔλεγχος, -ου, ὁ cross-examination

ἐλέγχω, ἐλέγξω, ἤλεγξα, ——, ἐλήλεγμαι, ἠλέγχθην prove; (pass.) be convicted

ἐλεέω, ἐλεήσω, ἠλέησα, ——, ——, ἠλεήθην pity, have pity on

ἔλεος, -ου, ὁ pity, compassion

ἐλευθερίᾱ, -ᾱς, ἡ freedom

Ἐλευσίνιος, -ον, ὁ Eleusinian

Ἐλευσίς, -ῖνος, ἡ Eleusis

ἕλκω, -ἕλξω, εἵλκυσα, -εἵλκυκα, -εἵλκυσμαι, -εἱλκύσθην (imperf. εἷλκον) drag about, drag

Ἑλλάς, -άδος, ἡ Greece

Ἕλλην, -ηνος, ὁ a Greek

Ἑλληνίς, -ίδος (fem. adj.) Greek

Ἑλλήσποντος, -ου, ὁ Hellespont

ἐλπίς, -ίδος, ἡ hope

ἐμμένω, ἐμμενῶ, ἐνέμεινα, ἐμμεμένηκα, ——, —— abide by (+ dat.)

ἐμός, -ή, -όν my, mine

ἐμπίμπλημι, ἐμπλήσω, ἐνέπλησα, ἐμπέπληκα, ἐμπέπλησμαι, ἐνεπλήσθην fill

ἐμπίπτω, ἐμπεσοῦμαι, ἐνέπεσον, ἐμπέπτωκα, ——, —— fall in, fall into, fall upon

ἐμποδὼν εἶναι be in the way, be a hindrance

ἔμπροσθεν (adv.) before, in front; (used as noun with τό) the front

ἐν (prep. + dat.) in, among, within

ἐναντίον (prep. + gen.) in the presence of

ἐναντιόομαι, ἐναντιώσομαι, ——, ——, ἠναντίωμαι, ἠναντιώθην oppose, withstand

ἐναντίος, -ᾱ, -ον opposite, opposed to (+ dat.)

ἐναντιώτατος, -η, -ον (sup. adj. of ἐναντίος) most opposite, most opposed to (+ dat.)

ἔνδεια, -ᾱς, ἡ want, need, lack

ἕνδεκα (indecl. num.) eleven

ἕνεκα (prep. + preceding gen.) on account of

ἔνθα (adv.) where

ἐνθάδε (adv.) here

ἔνθεν καὶ ἔνθεν (adv.) here and there

ἐνθρῴσκω, ἐνθοροῦμαι, ἐνέθορον, ——, ——, —— leap upon

ἐνθυμέομαι, ἐνθυμήσομαι, ——, ——, ἐντεθύμημαι, ἐνεθυμήθην lay to heart, consider well, form a plan

ἐννέα (indecl. num.) nine

ἐννοέω, ἐννοήσω, ἐνενόησα, ἐννενόηκα, ——, ἐνενοήθην consider

ἔννομος, -η, -ον lawful

ἔνοχος, -ον liable to, subject to, complicit in (+ dat.)

ἐνταῦθα (adv.) here, there

ἐντεῦθεν (adv.) thereupon

ἐντός (prep. + gen.) within, inside

ἐντρέπω, ——, ——, ——, ——, —— give heed to, pay regard to (+ gen.)

ἕξ (indecl. num.) six

ἐξαιρέω, ἐξαιρήσω, ἐξεῖλον, ἐξῄρηκα, ἐξῄρημαι, ἐξῃρέθην demolish

ἐξαλείφω, ἐξαλείψω, ἐξήλειψα, ——, ἐξαλήλιμμαι, ἐξηλείφθην wipe out, erase

ἐξανδραποδίζω, ——, ἐξηνδραπόδισα, ——, ἐξηνδραπόδισμαι, ἐξηνδραποδίσθην enslave utterly (usually found in middle)

ἐξαπατάω, ἐξαπατήσω, ἐξηπάτησα, ἐξηπάτηκα, ἐξηπάτημαι, ἐξηπατήθην deceive thoroughly

ἐξαρκέω, ἐξαρκέσω, ἐξήρκεσα, ——, ——, —— suffice, be enough

ἔξειμι (εἶμι), ——, ——, ——, ——, —— go out

ἐξελαύνω, ἐξελῶ, ἐξήλασα, ἐξελήλακα, ἐξελήλαμαι, ἐξηλάθην drive out

ἐξέρχομαι, ——, ἐξῆλθον, ἐξελήλυθα, ——, —— go away

ἔξεστι (impers.) it is possible (+ inf.; + dat. or acc./ inf.)

ἐξέτασις, -εως, ἡ review, inspection

ἐξιδιόομαι, ——, ἐξιδιωσάμην, ——, ——, —— appropriate for oneself

ἐξοπλίζω, ——, ἐξώπλισα, ——, ἐξώπλισμαι, ἐξωπλίσθην (mid./ pass.) arm oneself

ἐξορμάω, ——, ἐξώρμησα, ——, ἐξώρμημαι, —— urge

ἐξουσίᾱ, -ᾱς, ἡ power, authority

ἔξω (adv.) outside; (prep. + gen.) outside of

ἑορτή, -ῆς, ἡ feast, festival

ἐπαινέω, ἐπαινέσω/ἐπαινέσομαι, ἐπήνεσα, ἐπήνεκα, ἐπήνημαι, ἐπηνέθην approve

ἐπαναφέρω, ἐπανοίσω, ἐπανήνεγκον, ——, ——, ἐπανηνέχθην bring back, report back

ἐπαναχωρέω, ——, ἐπανεχώρησα, ——, ——, —— retreat, return

ἐπεί (conj.) when, since, after; ἐπεὶ ἤδη when

ἐπειδάν (= ἐπειδή + ἄν) (conj.) whenever

ἐπειδή (conj.) when, since, after; ἐπειδὴ τάχιστα as soon as ἔπειτα (adv.) then, thereupon

ἐπέξειμι (εἶμι), ——, ——, ——, ——, —— prosecute

ἐπεξέρχομαι, ——, ἐπεξῆλθον, ἐπεξελήλυθα, ——, —— examine; prosecute

ἐπέρομαι, ἐπερήσομαι, ἐπηρόμην, ——, ——, —— ask

ἐπί (prep. + gen.) near; (+ dat.) for; (+ acc.) to, toward, in

ἐπιβαίνω, ἐπιβήσομαι, ἐπέβην, ἐπιβέβηκα, ——, —— set foot on

ἐπιβουλεύω, ἐπιβουλεύσω, ἐπεβούλευσα, ἐπιβεβούλευκα, ἐπιβεβούλευμαι, ἐπεβουλεύθην plot against (+ dat.)

ἐπιβουλή, -ῆς, ἡ plot, a plan against (someone)

ἐπιβούλως (adv.) treacherously

ἐπιγίγνομαι, ἐπιγενήσομαι, ἐπεγενόμην, ——, ἐπιγεγένημαι, —— occur, arise

ἐπιδείκνυμι, ἐπιδείξω, ἐπέδειξα, ἐπιδέδειχα, ἐπιδέδειγμαι, ἐπεδείχθην show, exhibit, display

ἐπιθορυβέω, ——, ἐπεθορύβησα, ——, ——, —— shout

ἐπικαλέω, ἐπικαλῶ, ἐπεκάλεσα, ——, ——, ἐπεκλήθην (mid.) call upon, summon, invoke; (pass.) be nicknamed

ἐπιλείπω, ἐπιλείψω, ἐπέλιπον, ἐπιλέλοιπα, ἐπιλέλειμμαι, —— fail, be wanting, give out

ἐπιμελέομαι, ἐπιμελήσομαι, ——, ——, ἐπιμεμέλημαι, ἐπεμελήθην take care of (+ gen.)

ἐπισκευάζω, ἐπισκευάσω, ἐπεσκεύασα, ἐπεσκεύακα, ἐπεσκεύασμαι, ἐπεσκευάσθην repair

ἐπισκήπτω, ἐπισκήψω, ἐπέσκηψα, ——, ἐπέσκημμαι, ἐπεσκήφθην enjoin, lay a strict charge on

ἐπισκοπέω, ἐπισκέψομαι, ἐπεσκεψάμην, ——, ἐπέσκεμμαι, —— look upon, observe, consider

ἐπίσταμαι, ἐπιστήσομαι, ——, ——, ——, ἠπιστήθην know, understand

ἐπιστέλλω, ἐπιστελῶ, ἐπέστειλα, ἐπέσταλκα, ἐπέσταλμαι, ἐπεστάλην enjoin, command

ἐπιτήδεια, -ων, τά provisions, supplies

ἐπιτηρέω, ——, ἐπετέρησα, ——, ——, —— look out for

ἐπιτίθημι, ἐπιθήσω, ἐπέθηκα, ἐπιτέθηκα, ——, ἐπετέθην place on, add; sprinkle; ἐπιτίθημι δίκην impose a penalty, inflict a penalty (+ dat.)

ἐπίτιμος, -ον in possession of the rights of citizenship, enfranchised

ἐπιτρέπω, ἐπιτρέψω, ἐπέτρεψα, ——, ἐπιτέτραμμαι, ἐπετράπην/ἐπετρέφθην permit, allow (+ dat.)

ἐπιχειρέω, ἐπιχειρήσω, ἐπεχείρησα, ἐπικεχείρηκα, ἐπικεχείρημαι, ἐπεχειρήθην try, attempt

ἐπίχειρον, -ου, τό wages, reward; punishment

ἕπομαι, ἕψομαι, ἑσπόμην, ——, ——, —— follow (+ dat.)

ἑπτά (indecl. num.) seven

ἑπτακόσιοι, -αι, -α seven hundred

ἐργάζομαι, ἐργάσομαι, εἰργασάμην/ ἠργασάμην, ——, εἴργασμαι, ἠργάσθην do, perform, accomplish; do something to someone (+ double acc.)

ἔργον, -ου, τό deed, work, task

ἑρμηνεύς, -έως, ὁ messenger, interpreter

ἔρυμα, -ατος, τό defense work, fort

ἔρχομαι, ἐλεύσομαι, ἦλθον, ἐλήλυθα, ——, —— go; come

——, ἐρῶ (ἐρέω), ——, εἴρηκα, εἴρημαι, ἐρρήθην say, speak (of), tell (of)

ἐρωτάω, ἐρωτήσω, ἠρώτησα, ἠρώτηκα, ἠρώτημαι, ἠρωτήθην ask

ἐς old Attic and Ionic form of the preposition εἰς

ἔστι (impers.) it is possible (+ acc./inf.)

ἑστίᾱ, -ᾱς, ἡ hearth

ἑστιάω, ἑστιάσω, εἱστίασα, εἱστίακα, εἱστίαμαι, εἱστιάθην entertain, host

ἐσχατιά, -ᾱς, ἡ border, outlying territory

ἔσχατος, -η, -ον extreme, worst

ἑταίρᾱ, -ᾱς, ἡ female companion, courtesan, concubine

ἑταιρίᾱ, -ᾱς, ἡ political club

ἑταῖρος, -ου, ὁ companion, comrade, associate

Ἐτεόνικος, -ου, ὁ Eteonicus (a Spartan
    commander)
ἕτερος, -ᾱ, -ον other
ἔτι (adv.) still, yet, further
ἔτος, -ους, τό year
εὖ (adv.) well
εὔδηλος, -ον quite clear, manifest
εὐεξάλειπτος, -ον easy to wipe out
εὐήθης, -ες foolish, simpleminded
εὐημερίᾱ, -ᾱς, ἡ good weather
εὐθέως (adv.) at once
εὐθύς (adv.) immediately
εὐθύς, -εῖα, -ύ straight, direct
εὐνή, -ῆς, ἡ bed
εὔξενος, -ον hospitable
εὔορκος, -ον faithful to one's oath
εὕρημα, -ατος, τό discovery, remedy
εὑρίσκω, εὑρήσω, ηὗρον/εὗρον, ηὕρηκα/
    εὕρηκα, ηὕρημαι, εὑρέθην find, discover
εὐσέβεια, -ᾱς, ἡ piety
εὐτρεπίζω, ——, ηὐτρέπισα, ——,
    ηὐτρέπισμαι, —— make ready, get ready;
    restore
εὔφωνος, -ον loud-voiced
εὔχομαι, εὔξομαι, ηὐξάμην, ——, ηὖγμαι,
    —— pray, pray for
ἐφίστημι, ἐπιστήσω, ἐπέστησα/ἐπέστην,
    ἐφέστηκα, ἐφέσταμαι, ἐπεστάθην set up,
    establish; (intrans.) stand
ἐφόδος, -ου, ἡ importation
ἔφοροι, -ων, οἱ Ephors (a board of five
    magistrates in Sparta)
ἐφ' ᾧ on condition that (+ acc./inf.)
ἔχθιστος, -η, -ον (sup. adj. of ἐχθρός) most
    hateful
ἔχθρᾱ, -ᾱς, ἡ hatred
ἐχθρός, -ά, -όν hostile, hated; (as subst.)
    enemy
ἔχω, ἕξω/σχήσω, ἔσχον, ἔσχηκα, -έσχημαι,
    —— (imperf. εἶχον) have, hold, possess;
    be (+ adv. of manner); be able to (+ inf.)
ἕως (conj.) until

ζάω, ζήσω, ——, ——, ——, —— live
ζεύγνυμι, ζεύξω, ἔζευξα, ——, ἔζευγμαι,
    ἐζεύχθην join together, bind

ζητέω, ζητήσω, ἐζήτησα, ἐζήτηκα, ἐζήτημαι,
    ἐζητήθην seek

ἤ (conj.) than, or
ἡγεμών, -όνος, ὁ leader
ἡγέομαι, ἡγήσομαι, ἡγησάμην, ——, ἥγημαι,
    —— lead, lead the way; think, consider
ἡδέως (adv.) gladly
ἤδη (adv.) already
ἥκιστα (sup. adv.) least
ἥκω, ἥξω, ——, ——, ——, —— have come;
    return, arrive
ἡμέρᾱ, -ᾱς, ἡ day
ἡμέτερος, -ᾱ, -ον our
ἥμισυς, -εια, -υ half
ἥρως, -ωος, ὁ hero
ἡσυχίᾱ, -ᾱς, ἡ peace, tranquillity, quiet; ἔχω
    ἡσυχίαν keep quiet
ἧττον (comp. adv.) less
ἥττων, -ον (comp. adj. of κακός) less, worse

θάλαττα, -ης, ἡ sea
θάνατος, -ου, ὁ death
θανατόω, θανατώσω, ἐθανάτωσα, ——, ——,
    ἐθανατώθην put to death
θάπτω, θάψω, ἔθαψα, ——, τέθαμμαι, ἐτάφην
    bury
θαρρέω/θαρσέω, θαρρήσω/θαρσήσω,
    ἐθάρρησα/ἐθάρσησα, τεθάρρηκα/
    τεθάρσηκα, ——, —— have courage
θᾶττον (comp. adv.) more quickly
θάττων, θᾶττον (gen. -ονος) (comp. adj. of
    ταχύς) quicker
θαυμάζω, θαυμάσομαι, ἐθαύμασα, τεθαύμακα,
    τεθαύμασμαι, ἐθαυμάσθην wonder,
    marvel at (+ gen.)
θεά, -ᾶς, ἡ goddess
θέλω shortened form of ἐθέλω
θεός, -οῦ, ὁ god
θεραπεία, -ᾱς, ἡ flattery
θεραπεύω, θεραπεύσω, ἐθεράπευσα,
    τεθεράπευκα, τεθεράπευμαι,
    ἐθεραπεύθην flatter, wheedle
Θετταλίᾱ, -ᾱς, ἡ Thessaly
Θῆβαι, -ῶν, αἱ Thebes

Θηραμένης, -ους, ὁ Theramenes (a moderate oligarch and member of the Thirty)

θνήσκω, -θανοῦμαι, -ἔθανον, τέθνηκα, ——, —— die, be killed

Θράκη, -ης, ἡ Thrace

Θρασύβουλος, -ου, ὁ Thrasybulus (the main leader of the democratic exiles at Phyle)

θρασύνω, ——, ἐθράσυνα, ——, ——, ἐθρασύνθην (mid. and pass.) be bold, take courage

θρασύς, -εῖα, -ύ bold, audacious

θρόνος, -ου, ὁ throne

Θυμοχάρης, -ους, ὁ Thymochares (an Athenian general)

θυσίαι, -ῶν, αἱ offerings, sacrifices, rites

θύω, θύσω, ἔθυσα, τέθυκα, τέθυμαι, ἐτύθην sacrifice (+ dat.)

Ἰδαῖος, -ᾱ, -ον of Mt. Ida (near Troy), Idaean

ἰδίᾳ (adv.) privately

ἴδιος, -ᾱ, -ον private, one's own

ἱερά, -ῶν, τά offerings, sacrifices, rites

ἱκανός, -ή, -όν sufficient, capable, able

ἱκετεύω, ἱκετεύσω, ἱκέτευσα, ——, ——, —— beseech, ask (for something) as a suppliant

ἵνα (conj.) in order that

ἵππαρχος, -ου, ὁ hipparch (general of the cavalry)

ἱππεύς, -έως, ὁ horseman, cavalryman; (pl.) cavalry

ἱπποκόμος, -ου, ὁ groom

Ἱππόμαχος, -ου, ὁ Hippomachus (a member of the Thirty)

ἵππος, -ου, ὁ/ἡ horse, mare

ἵστημι, στήσω, ἔστησα (trans.)/ἔστην (intrans.), ἕστηκα, ἕσταμαι, ἐστάθην set up

Ἱστιαίεας, -ου, ὁ inhabitant of Histiaea (a city in Euboea, which revolted from the Athenian alliance in 447 B.C.E.)

ἰσχυρός, -ά, -όν strong

καθαίρεσις, -εως, ἡ destruction, razing to the ground

καθαιρέω, καθαιρήσω, καθεῖλον, καθῄρηκα, καθῄρημαι, καθῃρέθην destroy, tear down

καθέζομαι, καθεδοῦμαι, ——, ——, ——, —— sit down

κάθημαι, ——, ——, ——, ——, —— be seated, sit

καθίημι, ——, καθῆκα, καθεῖκα, καθεῖμαι, —— allow to return

καθίστημι, καταστήσω, κατέστησα (trans.)/κατέστην (intrans.), καθέστηκα, ——, κατεστάθην establish, place, set (as guards); settle; (intrans.) become, come, arrive, be established

καθοράω, κατόψομαι, κατεῖδον, καθεώρακα, καθῶμμαι, καθώφθην observe

καινός, -ή, -όν new, novel, strange

καίπερ (particle + participle) although

καιρός, -οῦ, ὁ right time, critical time

καίτοι (particle) and indeed, further

κακίων, κάκιον (comp. adj. of κακός) worse

κακός, -ή, -όν bad, evil

κακοτεχνέω, ——, κακετέχνησα, ——, ——, —— act basely

καλέω, καλῶ, ἐκάλεσα, κέκληκα, κέκλημαι, ἐκλήθην call, summon

Καλλίβιος, -ου, ὁ Callibius (commander of the Spartan garrison sent to protect the Thirty)

κάλλιστος, -η, -ον (sup. adj. of καλός) best, most beautiful

καλός, -ή, -όν good, noble, handsome

Καλχηδών, -όνος, ἡ Chalcedon

καλῶς (adv.) well

κάρα, ——, τό head

καρτερέω, καρτερήσω, ἐκαρτέρησα, ——, ——, —— be steadfast, hold out

κατά (prep. + acc.) according to, along, by, down along, throughout

καταβαίνω, καταβήσομαι, κατέβην, καταβέβηκα, ——, —— go down

καταβάλλω, καταβαλῶ, κατέβαλον, καταβέβληκα, καταβέβλημαι, κατεβλήθην strike down

καταγορεύω, ——, ——, ——, ——, —— denounce, charge, accuse (+ gen.)

καταδακρύω, ——, κατεδάκρυσα, ——,
——, —— bewail

καταδιώκω, ——, κατεδίωξα, ——, ——,
κατεδιώχθην pursue closely

καταδύω, καταδύσω, κατέδυσα (trans.)/
κατέδυν (intrans.), καταδέδυκα, ——,
—— cause to sink; (mid. and intrans.)
sink down, be shipwrecked

κατακρίνω, ——, κατέκρινα, ——,
κατακέκριμαι, κατεκρίθην sentence

καταλαμβάνω, καταλήψομαι, κατέλαβον,
κατείληφα, κατείλημμαι, κατελήφθην
seize

καταλέγω, καταλέξω, κατέλεξα, ——,
κατείλεγμαι, κατελέγην enroll

καταλείπω, καταλείψω, κατέλιπον,
καταλέλοιπα, καταλέλειμμαι,
κατελείφθην leave behind

κατάλογος, -ου, ὁ register of citizens

κατάλυσις, -εως, ἡ dissolution, overthrow

κατανοέω, κατανοήσω, κατενόησα,
κατανενόηκα, ——, κατενοήθην
consider

καταπλέω, καταπλεύσομαι, κατέπλευσα,
καταπέπλευκα, ——, —— sail toward
land, put in

κατασιωπάω, ——, κατεσιώπησα, ——,
——, κατεσιωπήθην make silent, silence

κατασκάπτω, ——, κατέσκαψα, κατέσκαφα,
κατέσκαμμαι, κατεσκάφην destroy
utterly, raze to the ground

κατασκευάζω, κατασκευάσω, κατεσκεύασα,
κατεσκεύακα, κατεσκεύασμαι,
κατεσκευάσθην prepare, establish

κατάστασις, -εως, ἡ constitution, system

καταψηφίζομαι, καταψηφιοῦμαι,
κατεψηφισάμην, ——, κατεψήφισμαι,
κατεψηφίσθην vote against, condemn
(+ gen.)

καταψήφισις, -εως, condemnation

καταψηφιστέον (verbal adj.) one must
condemn (+ gen.)

κάτειμι (εἶμι), ——, ——, ——, ——, ——
return

κατέχω, κατασχήσω/καθέξω, κατέσχον,
κατέσχηκα, ——, —— detain

κατηγορέω, κατηγορήσω, κατηγόρησα,
κατηγόρηκα, κατηγόρημαι,
κατηγορήθην speak against, accuse
(+ gen.)

κάτω (adv.) below

κεῖνος, -η, -ον poetic form of ἐκεῖνος

κελεύω, κελεύσω, ἐκέλευσα, κεκέλευκα,
κεκέλευσμαι, ἐκελεύσθην order, urge
(+ acc./inf.)

κέρδος, -ους, τό gain, profit

κηδεστίᾱ, -ᾱς, ἡ connection by marriage

κῆρυξ, -υκος, ὁ herald

κινδυνεύω, κινδυνεύσω, ἐκινδύνευσα,
κεκινδύνευκα, ——, ἐκινδυνεύθην run
a risk

κίνδυνος, -ου, ὁ danger, risk

Κλεόκριτος, -ου, ὁ Cleocritus (herald of the
Eleusinian initiates)

κλοιός, -οῦ, ὁ dog collar

Κλυταιμνήστρᾱ, -ᾱς, ἡ Clytemnestra
(murderous wife of Agamemnon)

κλών, κλωνός, ὁ twig

κόθορνος, -ου, ὁ high boot

κοιμάω, κοιμήσω, ——, ——, ——,
ἐκοιμήθην put to sleep; (mid. and pass.)
go to sleep, sleep

κοινός, -ή, -όν common, shared

κοινωνέω, κοινωνήσω, ἐκοινώνησα,
κεκοινώνηκα, κεκοινώνημαι, —— have
something (+ gen.) in common with
someone (+ dat.)

κοινωνός, -οῦ, ὁ/ἡ partner

Κόνων, -ωνος, ὁ Conon (an Athenian
general)

κρατέω, κρατήσω, ἐκράτησα, κεκράτηκα,
κεκράτημαι, ἐκρατήθην conquer,
overwhelm (+ gen.)

κράτιστος, -η, -ον (sup. adj. of ἀγαθός)
strongest, best

κρίσις, -εως, ἡ judgment, decision

Κριτίας, -ου, ὁ Critias (leader of the extreme
members of the Thirty)

κτάομαι, κτήσομαι, ἐκτησάμην, ——,
κέκτημαι, ἐκτήθην get possession of

κτείνω, κτενῶ, ἔκτεινα/ἔκτανον, -έκτονα,
——, —— kill

κυβερνάω, κυβερνήσω, ἐκυβέρνησα, ——,
  ——, —— guide, be a helmsman
κύριος, -ᾱ, -ον authorized (to negotiate);
  (+ εἶναι) have authority over (+ gen.)
κύων, κυνός, ὁ/ἡ dog
κωλύω, κωλύσω, ἐκώλυσα, κεκώλυκα,
  κεκώλυμαι, ἐκωλύθην prevent
κώνειον, -ου, τό hemlock

Λακεδαιμόνιος, -ου, ὁ Lacedaemonian, an
  inhabitant of Sparta
Λακεδαίμων, -ονος, ἡ Lacedaemon, Sparta
Λακωνική, -ῆς, ἡ Laconia
Λακωνικός, -ή, -όν Laconian
λαμβάνω, λήψομαι, ἔλαβον, εἴληφα, εἴλημμαι,
  ἐλήφθην take, seize, catch
Λάμψακος, -ου, ἡ Lampsacus
λανθάνω, λήσω, ἔλαθον, λέληθα,
  -λέλησμαι, —— escape the notice of
  (+ supplementary part.)
λάσιος, -ᾱ, -ον (and -ος, -ον) bushy
λέγω, λέξω, ἔλεξα (εἶπον preferred), ——,
  λέλεγμαι, ἐλέχθην speak, say
λεηλατέω, λεηλατήσω, ἐλεηλάτησα, ——,
  ——, —— plunder, take booty
λείπω, λείψω, ἔλιπον, λέλοιπα, λέλειμμαι,
  ἐλείφθην leave
Λέσβος, -ου, ἡ Lesbos
λεύω, λεύσω, ἔλευσα, ——, ——, ἐλεύσθην
  pelt, throw stones at
λιβανωτός, -οῦ, ὁ frankincense
λιμήν, -ένος, ὁ harbor
λιμός, -οῦ, ὁ hunger, famine
λόγος, -ου, ὁ word, reason
λοιπός, -ή, -όν remainder, the rest
λυμαίνομαι, λυμαινοῦμαι, ἐλυμηνάμην, ——,
  λελυμάσμαι, —— maltreat, outrage,
  inflict indignities on (+ dat.)
Λύσανδρος, -ου, ὁ Lysander (a Spartan
  general)
Λυσίμαχος, -ου, ὁ Lysimachus (cavalry
  commander supporting the Thirty)

μά (particle) by (+ acc., used in oaths and
  exclamations)
μάθημα, -ατος, τό learning, knowledge

μακρός, -ά, -όν long
μάλα (μάλ᾽) (adv.) very
μάλη, -ης, ἡ armpit
μᾶλλον (comp. adv.) more
  μᾶλλον . . . ἤ more than, rather than
μαρτύρομαι, μαρτυροῦμαι, ἐμαρτυράμην,
  ——, ——, —— call to witness
μάρτυς, -υρος, ὁ/ἡ witness
μέγιστος, -η, -ον (sup. adj. of μέγας) greatest
μεθίστημι, μεταστήσω, μετέστησα (trans.)/
  μετέστην (intrans.), μεθέστηκα, ——,
  μετεστάθην change
Μελάνθιος, -ου, ὁ Melanthius (an Athenian
  general supporting the Thirty)
μέλας, μέλαινα, μέλαν black, dark
μέλλω, μελλήσω, ἐμέλλησα, ——, ——, ——
  be about to (+ fut. inf.); delay (+ pres.
  inf.)
μέλω, μελήσω, ἐμέλησα, μεμέληκα, ——,
  —— be an object of care to (+ dat.)
μέντοι (particle) of course, certainly; μέντοι
  γε of course
μεστός, -ή, -όν full of (+ gen.)
μετά (prep. + gen.) with; (+ acc.) after
μεταβάλλω, μεταβαλῶ, μετέβαλον,
  μεταβέβληκα, μεταβέβλημαι,
  μετεβλήθην change
μεταβολή, -ῆς, ἡ change
μεταπέμπω, μεταπέμψω, μετέπεμψα, ——,
  ——, μετεπέμφθην send for, summon
μεταστρέφω, ——, μετέστρεψα, ——, ——,
  μετεστράφην turn
μεταχειρίζομαι, μεταχειριοῦμαι,
  μετεχειρισάμην, ——, μετακεχείρισμαι,
  μετεχειρίσθην handle
μετέρχομαι, ——, μετῆλθον, ——, ——,
  —— prosecute
μετέχω, μεθέξω, μετέσχον, μετέσχηκα, ——,
  —— share in, share, share in something
  (+ gen.) with someone (+ dat.), take part
  in (+ gen.)
μέτοικος, -ου, ὁ metic, resident alien
μέχρι (prep. + gen.) even to, as far as
μή (adv.) not
μηδείς, μηδεμία, μηδέν no one, nothing
μηδέν (adv.) not at all

Μήλιος, -ον, ὁ Melian, an inhabitant of the island of Melos

μήν, μηνός, ὁ month

μήποτε (adv.) never

μήτε ... μήτε neither ... nor

μήτηρ, -τρός, ἡ mother

μητρυιά, -ᾶς, ἡ stepmother

μητρῴος, -ᾱ, -ον inherited from one's mother, maternal

μηχανάομαι, μηχανήσομαι, ἐμηχανησάμην, ——, μεμηχάνημαι, —— devise, contrive

μιαιφόνος, -ον bloodstained, bloody

μικροπολίτης, -ου, ὁ citizen of a small state

μιμνῄσκω/μιμνήσκω, μνήσω, ἔμνησα, ——, μέμνημαι, ἐμνήσθην remind; call to mind, remember, mention (mid. and pass.)

μισθόω, μισθώσω, ἐμίσθωσα, μεμίσθωκα, μεμίσθωμαι, ἐμισθώθην hire

μνησικακέω, μνησικακήσω, ἐμνησικάκησα, ——, ——, —— remember past injuries

μνηστεύω, μνηστεύσω, ἐμνήστευσα, ——, ——, —— promise in marriage

μοῖρα, -ᾱς, ἡ part, portion, fate, destiny

μόνος, -η, -ον alone, only

μῦθος, -ου, ὁ story, tale

μυρσίνη, -ης, ἡ branch of myrtle, wreath of myrtle

μύστης, -ου, ὁ one who has been initiated, initiate

Μυτιλήνη, -ης, ἡ Mytilene (a city on the island of Lesbos)

ναίω (intrans., only in present and imperfect) dwell

ναός, -οῦ, ὁ temple, inmost part of a temple

ναῦς, νεώς, ἡ ship

νεανίσκος, -ου, ὁ youth

νεκρός, -οῦ, ὁ dead body, corpse

νέος, -ᾱ, -ον new, young

νικάω, νικήσω, ἐνίκησα, νενίκηκα, νενίκημαι, ἐνικήθην conquer, be victorious

Νικόστρατος, -ου, ὁ Nikostratus (an Athenian cavalryman supporting the democrats)

νίφω/νείφω, ——, ἔνιψα, ——, ——, —— snow; (pass.) be snowed on

νομίζω, νομιῶ, ἐνόμισα, νενόμικα, νενόμισμαι, ἐνομίσθην think, consider, believe (+ acc./inf.)

νόμος, -ου, ὁ law

νοσέω, νοσήσω, ἐνόσησα, νενόσηκα, ——, —— be ill, be sick

νόσος, -ου, ἡ illness

νουθετέω, νουθετήσω, ἐνουθέτησα, ——, ——, ἐνουθετήθην warn, advise

νῦν (adv.) now

νύξ, νυκτός, ἡ night

ξένος, -ου, ὁ mercenary; stranger; guest-friend

ξιφίδιον, -ου, τό dagger

ξυρήκης, -ες close-shaven

ὅδε, ἥδε, τόδε (demon. pron./adj.) this, these

ὁδός, -οῦ, ἡ road, path; journey

ὅθεν (rel. adv.) wherefore, whence

οἶδα, εἴσομαι, ——, ——, ——, —— know

οἴκαδε (adv.) home, homeward

οἰκεῖος, -ᾱ, -ον belonging to one's own house

οἰκείως (adv.) in a friendly manner

οἰκέτης, -ου, ὁ house slave, servant

οἰκίᾱ, -ᾱς, ἡ house

οἰκτίρω, ——, ᾤκτιρα, ——, ——, —— pity, have pity on

οἶμαι variant of **οἴομαι**

οἰμωγή, -ῆς, ἡ lament

οἰμώζω, οἰμώξομαι, ᾤμωξα, ——, ——, —— lament, wail aloud

οἴομαι/οἶμαι, οἰήσομαι, ——, ——, ——, ᾠήθην think (+ acc./inf.)

οἷος, -ᾱ, -ον (rel. pron.) such as, as, what sort of, the sort which, of which sort, of such a sort; fit, ready, able (+ inf.); (in comparisons) as, just as

οἷόν τέ ἐστι it is possible (+ inf. or + dat./ inf.)

οἴχομαι, οἰχήσομαι, ——, ——, ——, —— be gone, have gone

ὀκτώ (indecl. num.) eight

ὄλεθρος, -ου, ὁ ruin, destruction

ὀλιγαρχίᾱ, -ᾱς, ἡ oligarchy

ὀλίγος, -η, -ον little, few

ὁμαλός, -ή, -όν level, even

ὄμνυμι, ὀμοῦμαι, ὤμοσα, ὀμώμοκα,
ὀμώμομαι/ὀμώμοσμαι, ὠμόθην/
ὠμόσθην swear, confirm by oath

ὁμογνώμων, -ον (gen. -ονος) like-minded
(+ dat.)

ὅμοιος, -ᾱ, -ον like, resembling, similar
(+ dat.)

ὁμολογέω, ὁμολογήσω, ὡμολόγησα,
ὡμολόγηκα, ὡμολόγημαι, ὡμολογήθην
agree, agree to, admit

ὁμολογουμένως (adv.) by common consent

ὁμοῦ (adv.) together

ὄνομα, -ατος, τό name

ὅπλα, -ων, τά weapons, arms; camp

ὁπλίζω, ὁπλίζομαι, ὥπλισα, ——, ὥπλισμαι,
ὡπλίσθην arm

ὁπλίτης, -ου, ὁ hoplite

ὅποι (indirect interrog. adv.) where, to where,
whither; (indef. rel. adv.) to wherever,
whithersoever

ὁπότε (indirect interrog. adv.) when; (indef.
rel. adv.) whenever

ὅπου (indirect interrog. adv.) where; (indef.
rel. adv.) wherever; (causal adv.) since,
whereas

ὅπως (conj.) how (introduces an indirect
question); in order that (introduces
a purpose clause); how, as (conj. of
manner)

ὁράω, ὄψομαι, εἶδον, ἑώρακα/ἑόρακα,
ἑώραμαι/ὦμμαι, ὤφθην see (+ participial
or ὅτι/ὡς construction)

Ὀρέστης, -ου, ὁ Orestes (son of Clytemnestra
and Agamemnon)

ὅρκος, -ου, ὁ oath

ὁρμάω, ὁρμήσω, ὥρμησα, ὥρμηκα, ὥρμημαι,
ὡρμήθην set in motion, urge on; (intrans.
act. and in mid. and pass.) start from,
hasten from

ὁρμίζω, ὁρμίσω/ὁρμιοῦμαι, ὥρμισα, ——,
——, ὡρμίσθην bring to safe anchor,
anchor; (mid.) lie at anchor

ὅς, ἥ, ὅ (rel. pron.) who, which, that

ὅσιος, -ᾱ, -ον pious, devout

ὅσον (adv.) about, nearly (in reference to
distance)

ὅσος, -η, -ον (rel. adj.) as many as, as much as,
how much

ὅσπερ, ἥπερ, ὅπερ (rel. pron.) the very man
who, the very thing which

ὅστις, ἥτις, ὅ τι (indef. rel. pron./adj.)
whoever, whatever, whichever; (indirect
interrog. pron./adj.) who, what, which

ὅταν (= ὅτε + ἄν) (conj.) whenever

ὅτε (conj.) when

ὅτι (conj.) because; that (introduces indirect
statement)

οὐ, οὐκ, οὐχ (adv.) not

οὐ μόνον . . . ἀλλὰ καί not only . . . but also

οὐδέ (adv.) not even

οὐδείς, οὐδεμία, οὐδέν no one, nothing

οὐδέν (adv.) not at all

οὐκέτι (adv.) no longer

οὐκοῦν (adv.) therefore, accordingly

οὖν (postpositive particle) therefore,
thereupon, so (to continue a narration)

οὔποτε (adv.) never

οὔπω (adv.) not yet, not at all

οὖρος, -ου, ὁ fair wind

οὔτε (adv.) and not

οὔτε . . . οὔτε neither . . . nor

οὗτος, αὕτη, τοῦτο (demon. pron./adj.) this,
this one, the latter; ἐκ τούτου thereupon

οὕτως, οὕτω (adv.) thus, in this way

ὄχλος, -ου, ὁ crowd

πάθημα, -ατος, τό suffering

παῖς, παιδός, ὁ/ἡ child, son

πάλιν (adv.) again, back

παλλακή, -ῆς, ἡ concubine, mistress

παμπληθής, -ές thick, heavy

πανδημεί (adv.) in a mass, as a group

πανταχοῦ (adv.) everywhere

παντελῶς (adv.) completely, entirely

παρά (prep. + gen.) from; (+ dat.) alongside
of, in the presence of, in the house of

παραβαίνω, παραβήσομαι, παρέβην,
παραβέβηκα, παραβέβαμαι, παρεβάθην
transgress

παραγγέλλω, παραγγελῶ, παρήγγειλα,
παρήγγελκα, παρήγγελμαι, παρηγγέλθην

report, transmit a message; order, give
orders (+ dat./ inf.)

παραγίγνομαι, παραγενήσομαι, παρεγενόμην,
παραγέγονα, παραγεγένημαι, ——
stand by, be present at (+ dat.)

παραδίδωμι, παραδώσω, παρέδωκα,
παραδέδωκα, παραδέδομαι, παρεδόθην
hand over, surrender

παραιρέω, παραιρήσω, παρεῖλον, ——,
παρῄρημαι, —— take away

παραιτέομαι, ——, **παρῃτησάμην,** ——,
παρῄτημαι, —— entreat, beg, beseech

παρακαλέω, παρακαλῶ, παρεκάλεσα,
παρακέκληκα, παρακέκλημαι,
παρεκλήθην send for

παραλαμβάνω, παραλήψομαι, παρέλαβον,
παρείληφα, παρείλημμαι, παρελήφθην
receive

Πάραλος, -ου, ἡ the *Paralus* (one of the
Athenian state triremes)

παρασκευάζω, παρασκευάσω, παρεσκεύασα,
παρεσκεύακα, παρεσκεύασμαι,
παρεσκευάσθην prepare

παραχρῆμα (adv.) at once, straightway

πάρειμι (εἰμί), παρέσομαι, ——, ——, ——,
—— be present

παρέχω, παρασχήσω/παρέξω, παρέσχον,
παρέσχηκα, παρέσχημαι, —— furnish,
provide, offer, bring, bring forward

παροράω, παρόψομαι, παρεῖδον, ——,
παρεώραμαι, παρώφθην neglect,
overlook

παρωθέω, ——, **παρέωσα,** ——, **παρέωσμαι,**
—— push aside, reject, slight

πᾶς, πᾶσα, πᾶν all, every, whole, entire

πάσχω, πείσομαι, ἔπαθον, πέπονθα, ——,
—— experience, suffer

πατήρ, -τρός, ὁ father

πάτριος, -ᾱ, -ον ancestral

πατρίς, -ίδος, ἡ native land

πατρῷος, -ᾱ, -ον (and **-ος, -ον**) inherited from
one's father, paternal

Παυσανίας, -ου, ὁ Pausanias (a Spartan king)

παύω, παύσω, ἔπαυσα, πέπαυκα, πέπαυμαι,
ἐπαύθην stop

πείθω, πείσω, ἔπεισα, πέπεικα/πέποιθα,

πέπεισμαι, ἐπείσθην urge, persuade;
(mid.) obey (+ dat.)

Πειραιεύς, -έως, ὁ (Att. gen. **–ῶς**) Piraeus
(the most important Athenian harbor)
(**Πειραιᾶ** = acc.)

πειράομαι, πειράσομαι, ἐπειρασάμην, ——,
πεπείραμαι, ἐπειράθην try, attempt
(+ inf.)

πέλας (adv.) near, nearby

Πελοποννήσιος, -α, -ον Peloponnesian

πέμπω, πέμψω, ἔπεμψα, πέπομφα, πέπεμμαι,
ἐπέμφθην send

πενέστης, -ου, ὁ serf, laborer

πένης, -ητος, ὁ a poor man; (also used as adj.)
poor, of a poor man

πενθέω, ——, **ἐπένθησα,** ——, ——, ——
lament, mourn for

πεντήκοντα (indecl. num.) fifty

πέπλος, -ου, ὁ peplos (a woman's garment)

περαίνω, περανῶ, ἐπέρανα, ——, **πεπέρασμαι,**
ἐπεράνθην accomplish, complete

πέρθω, πέρσω, ἔπερσα/ἔπραθον, ——, ——,
—— ravage, destroy, get by plunder

περί (prep. + gen.) concerning; (+ acc.) about
(with numerals)

περιαιρέω, περιαιρήσω, περιεῖλον, ——,
περιῄρημαι, περιῃρέθην take away, take
down

περιλαμβάνω, περιλήψομαι, περιέλαβον,
περιείληφα, περιείλημμαι, περιελήφθην
surround

περισῴζω, ——, **περιέσωσα,** ——,
περισέσωσμαι, περιεσώθην save from
death

περιχέω, ——, ——, ——, **περικέχυμαι,**
περιεχύθην crowd around, pour around

πηγή, -ῆς, ἡ stream, running water

πιέζω, ——, **ἐπίεσα,** ——, **πεπίεσμαι,**
ἐπιέσθην press

πίνος, -ου, ὁ filth, dirt

πίνω, πίομαι/πιοῦμαι, ἔπιον, πέπωκα,
-πέπομαι, -ἐπόθην drink

πίπτω, πεσοῦμαι, ἔπεσον, πέπτωκα, ——,
—— fall

πιστεύω, πιστεύσω, ἐπίστευσα, πεπίστευκα,
πεπίστευμαι, ἐπιστεύθην trust (+ dat.)

πίστις, -εως, ἡ pledge of good faith, trust

πλεῖστος, -η, -ον (sup. adj. of πολύς) most, in the greatest number

πλείων/πλέων, πλεῖον/πλέον (gen. -ονος) (comp. adj. of πολύς) more

πλεονεκτέω, πλεονεκτήσω, ἐπλεονέκτησα, πεπλεονέκτηκα, ——, —— gain more than one's due, gain an advantage, be greedy

πλέω, πλεύσομαι/πλευσοῦμαι, ἔπλευσα, πέπλευκα, πέπλευσμαι, —— sail

πλῆθος, -ους, τό crowd, number

πλήν (prep. + gen.) except

πλήρης, -ες full of (+ gen.)

πλησίον (adv.) near (+ gen.)

πλούσιος, -ᾱ, -ον wealthy

ποι (enclitic adv.) to some place

ποιέω, ποιήσω, ἐποίησα, πεποίηκα, πεποίημαι, ἐποιήθην do, make; do something (acc.) to someone (acc.); to make (+ direct object = predicate adj. or predicate acc.); to cause (someone to do something) (+ acc./inf.)

πολεμέω, πολεμήσω, ἐπολέμησα, πεπολέμηκα, ——, ἐπολεμήθην be at war, fight, dispute with (+ dat.)

πολέμιος, -ᾱ, -ον hostile; (as subst.) enemy

πόλεμος, -ου, ὁ war

πολιορκέω, πολιορκήσω, ἐπολιόρκησα, ——, ——, ἐπολιορκήθην blockade, besiege

πολιορκίᾱ, -ᾱς, ἡ siege

πόλις, -εως, ἡ city

πολιτείᾱ, -ᾱς, ἡ government, constitution, state, citizenship

πολιτεύω, πολιτεύσω, ἐπολίτευσα, ——, πεπολίτευμαι, ἐπολιτεύθην live as a citizen, govern

πολίτης, -ου, ὁ citizen

πολλάκις (adv.) often

πολυάνθρωπος, -ον populous

πολύς, πολλή, πολύ much, many, great

πονηρός, -ά, -όν wicked, base

πορνεῖον, -ου, τό brothel

πόρπη, -ης, ἡ buckle, brooch

πόσις, -εως, ἡ drink

πόσος, -η, -ον (interr. adj.) how many, how great

ποτάμιος, -ᾱ, -ον (and -ος, -ον) from a river

ποτε (enclitic particle) ever, at any time

πότερον . . . ἤ whether . . . or

που (enclitic adv.) somewhere, anywhere

ποῦ (interrog. adv.) where

πούς, ποδός, ὁ foot

πρᾶγμα, -ατος, τό thing, matter, affair; (pl.) circumstances, affairs, trouble; government, state affairs

πράττω, πράξω, ἔπραξα, πέπραγα/πέπραχα, πέπραγμαι, ἐπράχθην do

πρεσβευτής, -οῦ, ὁ ambassador

πρέσβυς, -εως, ὁ ambassador

πρίν (conj.) until; before (+ acc./inf.)

πρό (prep. + gen.) before

προάγω, προάξω, προήγαγον, προῆχα, προῆγμαι, προήχθην lead, lead forward

προβούλη, -ης, ἡ forethought

πρόγονος, -ου, ὁ ancestor

προδίδωμι, προδώσω, προέδωκα/προὔδωκα, προδέδωκα, προδέδομαι, προὐδόθην betray, hand over

προδότης, -ου, ὁ traitor

προεῖπον (used for aorist of προλέγω) ordered, proclaimed (+ dat./inf.)

προέχω/προὔχω, προέξω, προέσχον, ——, ——, —— excel

προηγορέω, ——, ——, ——, ——, —— act as a spokesman for, speak in defense of (+ gen.)

προθυμέομαι, προθυμήσομαι, ——, ——, ——, προὐθυμήθην be ready, be willing, be eager (+ inf.); desire eagerly

προθυμίᾱ, -ᾱς, ἡ eagerness, zeal

πρόθυμος, -ον well-disposed toward (+ dat.)

προίημι, προήσω, προῆκα, ——, προεῖμαι, προείθην (mid.) suffer, allow

προκαλέω, προκαλέσω, προὐκάλεσα, ——, ——, προὐκλήθην propose

Προμηθεύς, -έως, ὁ Prometheus

πρόνοια, -ᾱς, ἡ foresight, forethought

προπετής, -ές inclined, ready, prone to (+ ἐπί)

πρός (prep. + dat.) near; (+ acc.) near, about,

in respect to, in reference to, in the name
of, by, against, to, toward

**προσβάλλω, προσβαλῶ, προσέβαλον,
προσβέβληκα, ——, ——** strike, dash
against

**προσγίγνομαι, προσγενήσομαι,
προσεγενόμην, προσγέγονα,
προσγεγένημαι, ——** attach oneself to
(+ dat.)

**προσδέομαι, προσδεήσομαι, ——, ——,
——, προσεδεήθην** need, be in want of

πρόσειμι (εἶμι), ——, ——, ——, ——, ——
approach, go toward

**προσέρχομαι, ——, προσῆλθον,
προσελήλυθα, ——, ——** come forward
to speak

προσήκω, ——, προσῆξα, ——, ——, ——
belong to (+ dat.); (impers.) be fitting, it
concerns, it belongs to

πρόσθεν (adv.) before

**προσλαμβάνω, προσλήψομαι, προσέλαβον,
προσείληφα, προσείλημμαι,
προσελήφθην** take as a helper, enlist

**προσμένω, ——, προσέμεινα, ——, ——,
——** wait

**προσπίπτω, προσπεσοῦμαι, προσέπεσον,
προσπέπτωκα, ——, ——** attack

προστάτης, -ου, ὁ leader

**προστάττω, προστάξω, προσέταξα, ——,
προστέταγμαι, προσετάχθην** order

προσφιλῶς (adv.) kindly, in a well-disposed
manner

πρότερον (adv.) previously, before

πρότερος, -ᾱ, -ον (comp. adj. of **πρό**) earlier,
former

**πρωτεύω, πρωτεύσω, ἐπρώτευσα, ——, ——,
——** be the first

πρῶτον (adv.) first

πρῶτος, -η, -ον (sup. adj. of **πρό**) first

πυλίς, -ίδος, ἡ gate

**πυνθάνομαι, πεύσομαι, ἐπυθόμην, ——,
πέπυσμαι, ——** learn by inquiry, learn

πυρά, -ᾶς, ἡ funeral pyre, mound raised on the
place of a funeral pyre, altar

πώποτε (adv.) ever yet

πῶς (interrog. adv.) how

ῥᾳδίως (adv.) easily

ῥῆμα, -ατος, τό word, saying

Ῥόδος, -ου, ἡ Rhodes

Σαλαμίς, -ῖνος, ἡ Salamis

Σάτυρος, -ου, ὁ Satyrus (a member of the
Eleven, the Athenian board of men that
had control over executions)

σαφῶς (adv.) clearly, distinctly

Σελλασίᾱ, -ᾱς, ἡ Sellasia (a city near the
Laconian border)

σεμνός, -ή, -όν holy, sacred

**σήπω, σήψω, ——, σέσηπα, σέσημμαι,
ἐσάπην** make rotten; (perf. used in sense
of pres. pass.) be rotten, become rotten,
rot, molder

σῖτος, -ου, ὁ (pl. **σῖτα, -ων, τά**) food, grain

**σιωπάω, σιωπήσομαι, ἐσιώπησα, σεσιώπηκα,
——, ἐσιωπήθην** be silent

**σκέπτομαι, σκέψομαι, ἐσκεψάμην, ——,
ἔσκεμμαι, ——** examine, consider

σκευοφόρος, -ου, ὁ baggage carrier, camp
follower

σκῆπτρον, -ου, τό scepter, staff

Σκιωναῖος, -ου, ὁ Scionian, an inhabitant of
Scione (a city in the Chalcidice)

σκοπέω, ——, ——, ——, ——, ——
consider

σκύλευμα, -ατος, τό (usually pl.) spoils of war,
arms stripped from an enemy

**σκυλεύω, ——, ἐσκύλευσα, ——, ——,
ἐσκυλεύθην** strip, despoil

**σπένδω, σπείσω, ἔσπεισα, ——, ἔσπεισμαι,
——** make a drink offering; (mid.) make
a treaty, make peace

σπονδή, -ῆς, ἡ libation; (pl.) truce, treaty

σπουδαῖος, -ᾱ, -ον good, earnest

στάδιον, -ου, τό stade (a unit of
measurement)

στατίζω, ——, ——, ——, ——, —— stand

στέγη, -ης, ἡ roof, roofed place, room; (pl.)
house

**στερέω, στερήσω, ἐστέρησα, ἐστέρηκα,
ἐστέρημαι, ἐστερήθην** deprive, rob

στρατεύω, στρατεύσω, ἐστράτευσα, ——,

ἐστράτευμαι, —— march, take to the field

στρατηγέω, στρατηγήσω, ἐστρατήγησα, ἐστρατήγηκα, ἐστρατήγημαι, ἐστρατηγήθην be general

στρατηγός, -οῦ, ὁ general

στρατηλατέω, ——, ——, ——, ——, —— lead an army into the field

στρατοπεδεύω, στρατοπεδεύσω, ἐστραπέδευσα, ——, ἐστραπέδευμαι, —— encamp, take up a position

συγγένεια, -ᾱς, ἡ kinship

συγγράφω, συγγράψω, συνέγραψα, συγγέγραφα, συγγέγραμμαι, συνεγράφην write down

συγχορευτής, -οῦ, ὁ companion in a dance

συκοφάντης, -ου, ὁ sycophant, informer

συκοφαντία, -ας, ἡ blackmail; dishonest prosecution; sycophancy

συλλαμβάνω, συλλήψομαι, συνέλαβον, συνείληφα, συνείλημμαι, συνελήφθην arrest, seize

συλλέγω, συλλέξω, συνέλεξα, συνείλοχα, συνείλεγμαι, συνελέχθην/συνελέγην gather together, summon, call together; (pass.) come together, assemble

συμβουλεύω, συμβουλεύσω, συνεβούλευσα, συμβεβούλευκα, συμβεβούλευμαι, συνεβουλεύθην deliberate, give advice

συμμαχέω, συμμαχήσω, συνεμάχησα, ——, συμμεμάχημαι, —— be allied with (+ dat.)

σύμμαχος, -ον allied; (as subst.) ally

συμπέμπω, συμπέμψω, συνέπεμψα, ——, ——, συνεπέμφθην send together

συμπράττω, συμπράξω, συνέπραξα, ——, ——, —— aid, assist (+ dat.)

συμφοιτητής, -οῦ, ὁ schoolmate

συμφορά, -ᾶς, ἡ misfortune

σύν (prep. + dat.) with

συναλλάττω, συναλλάξω, συνήλλαξα, ——, ——, συνηλλάγην (pass.) be reconciled with

συναρέσκω, ——, ——, ——, ——, —— please, satisfy (+ dat.); (impers.) be pleasing (+ dat.)

συνδέω, συνδήσω, συνέδησα, ——, συνδέδεμαι, συνεδέθην bind together

συνδοκέω, συνδόξω, συνέδοξα, ——, συνδέδογμαι, —— seem good also

σύνειμι (εἰμί), συνέσομαι, ——, ——, ——, —— be with, have dealings with

συνεπαινέω, ——, συνεπήνεσα, ——, —— agree, consent

συνθήκη, -ης, ἡ treaty

συνίστημι, συστήσω, συνέστησα/συνέστην, συνέστηκα, ——, συνεστάθην gather, form

σύνοιδα, συνείσομαι, ——, ——, ——, —— be conscious of, be cognizant of (+ participial construction of indirect statement)

συνόντες, -οντων, οἱ (σύν + ὄντες) associates, comrades

συντίθημι, συσθήσω, συνέθηκα, συντέθηκα, συντέθειμαι, συνετέθην put together, deposit

συρρέω, ——, ——, συνερρύηκα, ——, συνερρύην flow together, gravitate toward

συσκευάζω, ——, συνεσκεύασα, ——, συνεσκεύασμαι, συνεσκευάσθην pack up

συστρατιώτης, -ου, ὁ fellow soldier

συχνός, -ή, -όν many

σφεῖς (σφῶν, σφίσι, σφέας) (3rd person pl. pers. pron.) they

σφέτερος, -ᾱ, -ον their, their own

σῴζω, σώσω, ἔσωσα/ἔσῳσα, σέσωκα, σέσωμαι/σέσῳσμαι, ἐσώθην save

σῶμα, -ατος, τό body

σωτηρίᾱ, -ᾱς, ἡ safety, salvation

σωφρονέω, σωφρονήσω, ἐσωφρόνησα, σεσωφρόνηκα, σεσωφρόνημαι, —— be wise

σώφρων, -ον sensible, discreet, wise

ταλαίπωρος, -ον suffering, miserable

ταράττω, ταράξω, ἐτάραξα, ——, τετάραγμαι, ἐταράχθην stir up, trouble

τάττω, τάξω, ἔταξα, τέταχα, τέταγμαι, ἐτάχθην arrange; appoint, order (+ acc./ inf.)

τάχιστος, -η, -ον (sup. adj. of ταχύς) quickest

ταχύς, -εῖα, -ύ quick

τειχίζω, τειχιῶ, ἐτείχισα, τετείχικα,
    τετείχισμαι, ἐτειχίσθην fortify, build

τεῖχος, -ους, τό wall

τεκμήριον, -ου, τό proof

τελευταῖος, -ᾱ, -ον final

τελέω, τελῶ/τελέσω, ἐτέλεσα, τετέλεκα,
    τετέλεσμαι, ἐτελέσθην complete, finish,
    accomplish

τέταρτος, -η, -ον fourth

τετρακόσιοι, -αι, -α four hundred

τέτταρες, τέτταρα four

τέως (adv.) so long

τητάομαι (present tense only) be in want of,
    be deprived of (+ gen.)

τί (interrog.) why

τίθημι, θήσω, ἔθηκα, τέθηκα, τέθειμαι,
    ἐτέθην put, place

τίκτω, τέξομαι, ἔτεκον, τέτοκα, ——, ——
    give birth, beget, bring forth

τιμάω, τιμήσω, ἐτίμησα, τετίμηκα, τετίμημαι,
    ἐτιμήθην honor

τιμή, -ῆς, ἡ honor, benefit

τιμωρέω, τιμωρήσω, ἐτιμώρησα, τετιμώρηκα,
    τετιμώρημαι, ἐτιμωρήθην avenge, seek
    vengeance for (+ dat.); take vengeance

τιμωρίᾱ, -ᾱς, ἡ vengeance

τιμωρός, -οῦ, ὁ avenger

τίς, τί (interrog. pron./adj.) who? what?

τις, τι (indef. pron./adj.) someone,
    something, a certain one, a certain thing

τιτρώσκω, τρώσω, ἔτρωσα, ——, τέτρωμαι,
    ἐτρώθην wound

τοι (particle) surely

τοιοῦτος, τοιαύτη, τοιοῦτον/τοιοῦτο such as
    this, of such a sort, such

τόλμα, -ης, ἡ boldness, daring

τολμάω, τολμήσω, ἐτόλμησα, τετόλμηκα,
    τετόλμημαι, ἐτολμήθην dare

Τορωναῖος, -ου, ὁ Toronian, an inhabitant of
    Torone (a city in the Chalcidice)

τοσοῦτος, τοσαύτη, τοσοῦτον/τοσοῦτο so
    great, so much, so many

τότε (adv.) at that time, then

τραῦμα, -ατος, τό wound, injury, damage

τρεῖς, τρία three

τρέπω, τρέψω, ἔτρεψα, τέτροφα, τέτραμμαι,
    ἐτρέφθην/ἐτράπην turn, rout

τρέφω, θρέψω, ἔθρεψα, τέτροφα, τέθραμμαι,
    ἐτράφην/ἐθρέφθην maintain, bring up,
    rear, nourish

τριάκοντα (indecl. num.) thirty

τριήρης, -ους, ἡ trireme

τρισχίλιοι, -αι, -α three thousand

τρόπος, -ου, ὁ manner, way

τροχίζω, ——, ——, ——, ——, ἐτροχίσθην
    turn on the wheel, torture

τυγχάνω, τεύξομαι, ἔτυχον, τετύχηκα, ——,
    —— happen to (+ supplementary part.);
    meet, meet upon, obtain (+ gen.)

τύμβος, -ου, ὁ tomb

τυραννέω, τυραννήσω, ἐτυράννησα,
    τετυράννηκα, ——, ἐτυραννήθην be a
    tyrant

τυραννικός, -ή, -όν supporting the tyrant,
    befitting a tyrant, despotic

τυραννίς, -ίδος, ἡ tyranny, absolute power,
    despotic rule

τύχη, -ης, ἡ chance, fortune, misfortune

ὑβρίζω, ὑβριῶ, ὕβρισα, ὕβρικα, ὕβρισμαι,
    ὑβρίσθην outrage, insult; maltreat

ὕβρις, -εως, ἡ hubris, arrogance; violence

ὑμέτερος, -ᾱ, -ον your

ὑπάγω, ——, ὑπήγαγον, ——, ὑπῆγμαι,
    ὑπήχθην bring a person before the
    judgment seat
    ὑπάγω θανάτου bring to trial on a capital
    charge

ὑπέρ (prep. + gen.) on behalf of

ὑπερῷον, -ου, τό upper room of a house

ὑπηρέτημα, -ατος, τό service

ὑπηρέτης, -ου, ὁ attendant, assistant

ὑπισχνέομαι, ὑποσχήσομαι, ὑπεσχόμην, ——,
    ὑπέσχημαι, —— promise (+ fut. inf.)

ὑπό (ὑπ’, ὑφ’) (prep. + gen.) by (with a
    passive verb), to the sound of (musical
    accompaniment); (+ dat.) under one’s
    power

ὑποδέχομαι, ὑποδέξομαι, ὑπεδεξάμην, ——,
    ὑποδέδεγμαι, —— receive hospitably

ὑποθήκη, -ης, ἡ suggestion

ὑπόπτως (adv.) with suspicion

ὑπόσπονδος, -ον under a treaty, under a truce

ὑποτέμνω, ὑποτεμῶ, ὑπέτεμον, ——,
   ὑποτέτμημαι, —— cut off

ὑποχωρέω, ὑποχωρήσομαι, ὑπεχώρησα,
   ὑποκεχώρηκα, ——, —— withdraw,
   retire

ὕστατος, -η, -ον (sup. adj.; no positive form in
   use) last, latest

ὑστεραῖος, -ᾱ, -ον next, following; τῇ δ᾽
   ὑστεραίᾳ (supply ἡμέρᾳ), on the
   following day

ὕστερος, -ᾱ, -ον (comp. adj.; no positive form
   in use) later

φαίνω, φανῶ, ἔφηνα, πέφηνα/πέφαγκα,
   πέφασμαι, ἐφάνην/ἐφάνθην (pass.)
   seem, appear

φανερός, -ά, -όν clear, manifest, evident

φανερῶς (adv.) clearly, openly

φάρμακον, -ου, τό drug

φᾶρος, -ους, τό cloth

φάσκω (only pres. and imperf.) claim, allege,
   say (+ acc./inf.)

φείδομαι, φείσομαι, ἐφεισάμην, ——, ——,
   —— spare (+ gen.)

φέρω, οἴσω, ἤνεγκα/ἤνεγκον, ἐνήνοχα,
   ἐνήνεγμαι, ἠνέχθην bear, carry, cast (a
   vote)

φεύγω, φεύξομαι, ἔφυγον, πέφευγα, ——,
   —— flee; with ὑπό τινος be exiled, be
   banished

φημί, φήσω, ἔφησα, ——, ——, —— speak,
   say; οὐ φημί refuse, deny, say that . . .
   not . . .

φθάνω, φθήσομαι, ἔφθασα/ἔφθην, ——,
   ——, —— anticipate (often with
   supplementary part.)

φιλέω, φιλήσω, ἐφίλησα, πεφίληκα,
   πεφίλημαι, ἐφιλήθην love; love to do, be
   fond of doing (+ inf.) (fut. mid. is used in
   passive sense)

φιλίᾱ, -ᾱς, ἡ friendship

Φιλόνεως, -εω, ὁ Philoneus (murdered friend
   of the speaker's father in Antiphon 1)

φίλος, -η, -ον friendly; dear, beloved; (as
   subst.) friend

φίλτρον, -ου, τό love charm, love potion

φοβέω, φοβήσω, ἐφόβησα, ——, πεφόβημαι,
   ἐφοβήθην frighten; (mid. and pass.) fear,
   be afraid

φονεύς, -έως, ὁ murderer

φόνος, -ου, ὁ murder

φορέω, ——, ἐφόρησα, ——, πεφόρημαι,
   —— carry or bear constantly; (mid.)
   fetch for oneself, fetch regularly

φρήν, φρενός, ὁ heart; mind, seat of thought

φρονέω, φρονήσω, ἐφρόνησα, πεφρόνηκα,
   ——, —— think; μέγα φρονέω be
   presumptuous, be puffed up

φρουρός, -οῦ, ὁ guard, garrison

Φρύγιος, -ᾱ, -ον (and -ος, -ον) Phrygian

Φρύξ, Φρυγός, ὁ Phrygia

φυγαδεύω, φυγαδεύσω, ἐφυγάδευσα, ——,
   ——, ἐφυγαδεύθην banish

φυγάς, -άδος, ὁ/ἡ fugitive, exile

φυλακή, -ῆς, ἡ garrison

φύλαξ, -ακος, ὁ guard

φυλάττω, φυλάξω, ἐφύλαξα, πεφύλακα,
   πεφύλαγμαι, ἐφυλάχθην protect, guard

φυλή, -ῆς, ἡ brigade

Φυλή, -ῆς, ἡ Phyle

φύσις, -εως, ἡ nature

φύω, φύσω, ἔφυσα/ἔφυν, πέφυκα, ——, ——
   bring forth, produce; (pass. and 2nd aor.,
   perf., and pluperf. tenses of the active) be
   born, be begotten

χαλεπός, -ή, -όν difficult

Χαρμίδης, -ου, ὁ Charmides (Plato's uncle
   and a kinsman of Critias)

χειμών, -ῶνος, ὁ storm

χείρ, χειρός, ἡ hand

χειρουργέω, ——, ἐχειρούργησα, ——,
   κεχειρούργημαι, —— execute,
   accomplish

χέρσος, -ον barren of (+ gen.)

χίλιοι, -αι, -α thousand

χιτών, -ῶνος, ὁ tunic, chiton

χιών, -όνος, ἡ storm, snowfall

χοή, -ῆς, ἡ drink offering

χορός, -οῦ, ὁ dance

χράομαι, χρήσομαι, ἐχρησάμην, ——,
κέχρημαι, ἐχρήσθην use, treat (+ dat.)

χρή (imperf. ἐχρῆν), χρῆσται, ——, ——,
——, —— (impers.) it is necessary
(+ inf. or acc./inf.)

χρῆμα, -ατος, τό thing; (pl.) money,
possessions

χρόνος, -ου, ὁ time

χρύσεος, -ᾱ, -ον golden, of gold

χῶμα, -ατος, τό promontory

χώρᾱ, -ᾱς, ἡ land, countryside

χωρέω, χωρήσω, ἐχώρησα, κεχώρηκα, ——,
—— advance

χωρίον, -ου, τό a particular place, spot; land;
fortified post

ψέγω, ψέξω, ἔψεξα, ——, ——, —— blame,
censure

ψεύδομαι, ψεύσομαι, ἐψευσάμην, ——,
ἔψευσμαι, —— lie, speak falsely, speak
in error

ψηφίζω, ψηφιῶ, ἐψήφισα, ——, ἐψήφισμαι,
ἐψηφίσθην vote, vote for

ψῆφος, -ου, ἡ vote

ψήχω, ψήξω, ——, ——, ἔψηγμαι, —— rub
down, curry, comb

ψόφος, -ου, ὁ sound

ψυχή, -ῆς, ἡ soul, spirit

ὧδε (adv.) thus, as follows

Ὠιδεῖον, -ου, τό Odeion (a public building in
Athens)

ὡς (rel. adv.) as; as _____ as possible (with
superlatives); (particle) since, inasmuch
as; on the grounds that (+ part., to
indicate alleged cause); (conj.) in order
that; when; that; (exclamatory adv.) how;
about (+ numeral)

ὥσπερ just as

ὥστε (conj.) so that, so as, that (introduces a
result clause)

ὠφελέω, ὠφελήσω, ὠφέλησα, ὠφέληκα,
ὠφέλημαι, ὠφελήθην aid, help

Index of Grammatical Terms

This index covers grammatical terms only. Page numbers in **boldface** indicate the primary discussion of the term in the Grammar Review or its definition in the notes to the Readings. Page numbers in *italics* indicate where an exercise can be found that focuses on the grammatical construction. For morphologies, students should consult the Table of Contents for the Appendices, pages 295–97.